COMPUTERS AND
INFORMATION SYSTEMS

SECOND EDITION

THE O'LEARY/WILLIAMS INSTRUCTIONAL PACKAGE

Productivity Software. Educational versions of WordPerfect and dBASE III Plus are available from the publisher to supplement the text.

Instructor's Guide by Albert Kagan.

Study Guide by James Adair.

Test Item File by P.S. Associates, Inc.

MicroTest test generator for microcomputers.

Transparencies and Transparency Masters.

University Gradebook by David Herrick. This class recordkeeping software for the IBM PC and compatibles allows you to build a database of class records for up to 300 students.

Related Benjamin/Cummings titles that complement this text include:

Student Edition of Lotus 1-2-3 by T.J. O'Leary.

Hands-On: MS-DOS, WordPerfect, dBASE III Plus and Lotus 1-2-3 by Lawrence Metzelaar and Marianne Fox. This skill-building text is available in two versions, with and without educational versions of WordPerfect and dBASE III Plus.

Computers and Information Systems, Second Edition and these ancillary titles are described in further detail in the section of the preface entitled "To the Instructor." For more information on *Computers and Information Systems, Second Edition,* and all related titles, please call Benjamin/Cummings Publishing at 800-950-BOOK.

A Note on Software

The versions of WordPerfect and dBASE III Plus offered with this text contain all the features of the full-function versions. The only restrictions are as follows.

▶ *WordPerfect Enhanced Version 4.2.* The educational edition saves documents of approximately 50,000 characters (approximately 25-30 pages of text), prints "*WPC" randomly at the ends of paragraphs, does not allow advanced printing features, supports port LPT1 (PRN) for printing, includes a demonstration of the speller and thesaurus but limits the words contained therein, displays a reproduction of the WordPerfect template in lieu of the HELP menus.

▶ *dBASE III Plus.* The educational version will maintain 31 records per data base.

▶ *WordPerfect Purchase Program.* Qualified students and instructors can purchase WordPerfect Corporation software directly from WordPerfect Corporation at a reduced price. See the School Software Direct Order Form at the end of the text for details.

COMPUTERS AND INFORMATION SYSTEMS

SECOND EDITION

T.J. O'LEARY

Arizona State University

BRIAN K. WILLIAMS

THE BENJAMIN/CUMMINGS PUBLISHING COMPANY, INC.

Redwood City, California • Fort Collins, Colorado
Menlo Park, California • Reading, Massachusetts • New York
Don Mills, Ontario • Wokingham, U.K. • Amsterdam • Bonn
Sydney • Singapore • Tokyo • Madrid • San Juan

To my wife, Linda Perley Coats O'Leary,
and my son, Daniel Albert O'Leary

    —T.J. O'L.

To my mother, Gertrude Smoyer Williams

    —B.K.W.

Editor-in-chief: Sally Elliott

Sponsoring Editor: David Jackson

Production Manager: Laura Argento

Production Editor: Mary Shields

Designer: Gary Head

Photo Research: Sarah Bendersky/ InfoEdit

Illustrations: George Samuelson

Part Opening and Cover Photography: David Wakely

Composition: York Graphic Services, Inc.

Color Separations: York Graphic Services, Inc.

Credits and acknowledgments appear at the end of this book. Company names used in parts of the text are fictitious and for educational purposes; any resemblance to actual company names is purely coincidental.

Library of Congress Cataloging in Publication Data
O'Leary, T. J. (Timothy J.)
  Computers and information systems / T.J. O'Leary, Brian K. Williams.
—2nd ed.
  First ed. published as: Computers and information processing. c1985.
  Includes index.
    1. Business—Data processing.   2. Office practice—Automation.
I. Williams, Brian K., 1938– .   II. O'Leary, T. J. (Timothy J.)
Computers and information processing.   III. Title.
HF5548.2.044 1989 658′.054—dc19
ISBN 0-8053-6942-2

  BCDEFGHIJ-DO-89

The Benjamin/Cummings Publishing Company, Inc.
390 Bridge Parkway
Redwood City, California 94065

BRIEF CONTENTS

v

PART 4
COMPUTER-BASED INFORMATION SYSTEMS

PART 5
THE REWARDS AND RISKS OF THE INFORMATION AGE

DETAILED CONTENTS

PART 2
THE USES OF SOFTWARE

3 PERSONAL SOFTWARE YOU CAN
USE: WORD PROCESSING, SPREAD-
SHEETS, DATA BASE, GRAPHICS,
COMMUNICATIONS, INTEGRATED
AND OTHER PACKAGES 58

4 APPLICATIONS SOFTWARE
DEVELOPMENT MAKING THE
COMPUTER WORK FOR YOU 105

5 PROGRAMMING LANGUAGES:
THE DIFFERENT WAYS OF
COMMUNICATING WITH THE
COMPUTER 134

PART 3
THE USES OF HARDWARE AND TECHNOLOGY

7 PROCESSORS AND OPERATING SYSTEMS: REPORT FROM BEHIND THE SCENES 217

8 STORAGE AND FILE ORGANIZATION: FACTS AT YOUR FINGERTIPS 253

14 MANAGEMENT INFORMATION SYSTEMS AND DECISION SUPPORT SYSTEMS—MAKING INFORMATION USEFUL TO MANAGERS 433

15 ARTIFICIAL INTELLIGENCE AND EXPERT SYSTEMS: WISDOM IN A MACHINE 468

PART 5
THE REWARDS AND RISKS OF THE INFORMATION AGE

16 MANAGING INFORMATION RESOURCES: MORE INTEGRATION, MORE EASE, MORE POWER 500

17 PRIVACY, SECURITY, AND ETHICS: KEEPING INFORMATION SAFE 523

18 THE FUTURE: INFORMATION—THE MAIN RESOURCE 544

TO THE INSTRUCTOR: WHY USE THIS BOOK?

We have become used to surprises, but perhaps the real surprises are still to come.

We have become used to startling developments in such separate industries as telephone, overnight delivery, data processing, microcomputers, database, telecommunications, and office technologies. But perhaps the most significant new development is that all these industries have begun to fuse into one—the Information Industry—the product of the 30 year revolution in electronics we have all been living through.

To anyone contemplating or engaged in a career in today's organizations, public sector as well as private, ignoring this monumental change is to concede the advantage before the game has even begun. For the name of the game is not so much courage or luck, or even superior position or intelligence. To prevail in the rest of this century and the next, the name of the game is handling information.

The Promise of This Book: The Student Career Tool

Computers and Information Systems, Second Edition, is designed as a textbook for an introductory college course in computers, information processing, and information systems. No academic prerequisites in mathematics, computer science, programming languages, or business are necessary. We introduce terminology as needed throughout the text.

A question many students ask is: How much does one *really* have to know about computers for most of today's careers? We believe the answer is: Only as much as is useful. This book is intended for people who plan to go into business or the professions—to become managers, administrators, or white-collar professionals—and who therefore will become *users* of the computer. Our aim is to introduce students to the organizational tool they will be using the rest of their working lives.

Accordingly, the book has the following features:

1. The book treats the computer as a tool for end-users. It is possible to learn a great many technical things about computers and information systems. However, most people in business, professional, and nonprofit organizations do not *need* to know all of them. Consequently, we focus only on the technical material that people planning careers in organizational life need to know to do their jobs. Thus, this book presents the computer for what it is: a valuable part of the end-user's tool kit. On the one hand, we show it as a tool for personal professional activities—for word processing, electronic spreadsheets, database management, business graphics, and communications. On the other hand, we show it as a tool for managing corporate information—transaction processing information systems (TPIS), management information systems (MIS), and decision support systems (DSS).

2. Material is arranged to help students with early hands-on use. Many students are impatient to see what computers can do for them right away. Accordingly, after presenting an introductory motivational chapter (Chapter 1, pp. 1–21) and an overview chapter of hardware, software, and systems (Chapter 2, pp. 22–55), we demonstrate (in Chapter 3, pp. 58–104) several uses of popular commercial microcomputer software: word processing, spreadsheets, data base managers, graphics, communications, and integrated packages. Therefore students taking concurrent laboratories involving microcomputer applications programs will have a sense of how such software may be used in an organizational environment. Other aspects of software—structured programming and programming languages (see pp. 134–169)—are described before the main discussion of hardware (Part 3, pp. 172–349), so that students can be better prepared for hands-on manipulation of computers as early in the course as possible.

3. The book has a strong systems orientation.

We believe students should not study hardware and software in a vacuum, but rather within the framework of a total information *system*. Thus, quite early in the book, in Chapter 2 (pp. 22–55), we present an overview of how business systems and computer systems work together. We return to this treatment in great detail in Part 4 (pp. 352–497), when we describe systems analysis and design and the various levels of information systems: transaction processing information systems, management information systems, and decision support systems. *New to this edition:* This part on systems concludes with a new chapter, Chapter 15 (pp. 468–497), which discusses artificial intelligence and expert systems and the impact they have on our ways of using information.

4. We emphasize the integration of microcomputers with mainframes and data bases.

As microcomputers have become more powerful, and as data communications has become more sophisticated, micros have become connected into larger information systems, using mainframes and data bases. This changes the nature of what were formerly more isolated elements. *New to this edition:* A new chapter, Chapter 9 (pp. 285–318), describes data base management systems in considerable detail.

5. The book offers many cases and case problems.

Because we want managers to learn how best to develop and use computer-based in-

formation, we offer three kinds of case examples covering a variety of industries:

▶ **"Curtain raiser" cases begin each chapter**. Drawn from highly readable reports in publications ranging from *Computerworld* to the *Wall Street Journal* to the *Harvard Business Review,* these boxed-off "curtain raiser" case studies, which appear on the second page of each chapter, generally present actual uses of the technology and processes to be discussed. Students thus become engaged in each chapter with a sense of the real-world problems and opportunities associated with the material they are about to read.

▶ **Ongoing "You Are There" cases cover several chapters.** With these in-text cases, we give the student a "hands-on" feeling of participation as the right-hand assistant to a manager or chief executive in four industries: health, films, banking, and clothing. The student thus becomes closely identified with business problem-solving processes.

▶ **Realistic case problems conclude each chapter.** How do you present computer and organizational problems for people without experience in these areas? How do you make case problems meaningful and not silly or superficial? We have tried to present case problems that students will *want* to read—because they provide added information of value and alert them to challenges and opportunities they may actually face. Thus, the case problems introduce topics such as computerized recruitment services, managing cash flow, determining billable time for professionals, and other subjects we hope students will be reluctant to pass up.

6. We have tried to make the material interesting and meaningful.

All of us are dazzled every day by television programs, magazines, and advertising with lively writing and flashy graphics. These are the seductive messages with which education must compete. We believe that, without trivializing the material at hand, we can enhance the educational process by avoiding dullness. Thus, we have tried to write with liveliness and style, using many journalistic devices to hold reader interest. We have also tried to pay attention to the importance of graphics, offering vivid, well-conceived illustrations. And throughout the text and in boxed-off material we have provided historical perspectives, biographical profiles, commentary, how-to tips, and other material that sheds light on the immediacy and pervasiveness of computers in today's organizations.

Finally, we should mention that this book expresses a viewpoint or vision. Facts by themselves are not enough; they are given coherence when expressed with a philosophical viewpoint. Students want to know how to be prepared to deal with computers in business; however, we believe that technology is changing the ways of doing business so rapidly that one cannot possibly be prepared for everything. But one can be prepared with an *attitude*—the attitude that one must be able to cope with all kinds of changes. One must be ready to deal both with old technology and with very new, with a great deal of business information and with very little, with commonplace ways of doing business and with cutting-edge surprises. This is a viewpoint you will find expressed repeatedly throughout this book.

Organization: Options for Using This Book

Computers and Information Systems, Second Edition, is divided into five parts.

Part 1, The Tool for New Careers, introduces the computer as a business tool from a macro point of view. Chapters 1 and 2 provide a general introduction, and then explain how business systems work, how computer systems work, and how the worlds of business and computers fuse together as computer-based information systems.

Part 2, The Uses of Software, starts with material most useful to students in today's for-profit and nonprofit organizations: how to use some prominent commercial software in word processing, spreadsheets, data base management, graphics, communications, and integrated packages. We believe that it is important to have students using computers in a computer lab as early as possible in the course in order to satisfy their desire for hands-on experience and to stimulate their interest in using the computer as an organizational tool. Consequently, we have deliberately organized the book so that practical matters of software precede the issues of hardware (although any instructor who feels that hardware, Part 3, should be taught before software will find the text organization flexible enough to permit this).

Part 2 also covers programming. Although we think it is important that students learn at least some programming logic and problem solving, it is our belief that the ordinary business user of computers in the rest of this century will not be using today's programming languages such as BASIC so much as integrated business software packages and fifth-generation languages. Nevertheless, we believe that structured programming concepts are important—both because of their general applicability to logical thinking and because managers must be able to communicate their needs to programmers—and so we have included a chapter on application software development and a chapter on programming languages.

Part 3, The Uses of Hardware and Technology, covers input and output devices, CPU and operating systems, external storage and file organization, data base management systems, and networks and data communication systems. As we mentioned above, this part can be introduced whenever the instructor desires—or covered in part or skipped altogether. We have written Part 3 from the point of view of executives of the 1990s who will be *using* computers, not designing and installing them, yet who need to have enough familiarity with hardware to communicate their desires to people with more technical backgrounds.

Part 4, Computer-Based Information Systems, covers systems analysis, systems design, transaction processing information systems, management information systems, decision support systems, and artificial intelligence and expert systems—the crucial organization-related disciplines a future manager needs to know. We have illustrated the conceptual information with case studies in order to give students a feel for the problems of the work world and some of the solutions that computers can provide.

Part 5, The Rewards and Risks of the Information Age, addresses some top concerns about the use of computers in our time. Chapter 16 describes the evolution of information systems, the importance of information resource management, and the possible course of computer-based information systems in the future. Chapter 17 covers privacy, security, and legal issues—important and necessary concerns for all of us. The last chapter describes some of the risks in computer technology, including the problems of automation and employment. It also suggests the impact of the technology of the future.

Appendix A presents a history of computers and information processing, and **Appendix B** offers a succinct but complete course in programming in BASIC.

Because teaching a large introductory course can be a rigorous activity, we believe a solid package of supplementary materials is almost as important as a solid textbook. Accordingly, our publisher has produced a supplementary package that provides a complete system of instruction and is sensitive to the needs not only of full-time instructors but also of part-time instructors and teaching assistants. The ancillary items include the following:

1. Instructor's guide. Written by Professor Albert Kagan, of the College of Business, North Dakota State University, the instructor's guide is available on diskette as well as on hard copy. It offers many practical suggestions for using the textbook, and for each chapter in the text it features

▶ Learning objectives
▶ Chapter overview
▶ Lecture outline
▶ Key concepts and key terms
▶ Answers to review questions and case problems.

2. Student study guide. Written by Professor James Adair of the School of Public Health, Harvard University, the study guide is available for students who desire an intensive study of the book's contents. In addition to several "mini-cases," for each chapter in the text the study guide provides

▶ What to look for in the chapter
▶ Key terms
▶ Self-tests in a variety of formats

▶ Comprehensive review tests for each of the five parts of the text
▶ Answers to all self-tests.

3. Test item file. Prepared by P.S. Associates, Inc., the test item file contains approximately 100 items per chapter. *MicroTest*, the Benjamin/Cummings computerized testing program, is available for qualified adopters: contact your local representative or Benjamin/Cummings for information.

4. Transparencies and transparency masters. Approximately 100 illustrations from the text have been collected as transparency masters, and a select number are also available as acetate transparencies.

5. Applications software. To encourage skill in using modern software tools, adopters can obtain educational versions of WordPerfect and dBASE III Plus from Benjamin/Cummings. This software is available alone, or as a package with *Hands-On: MS-DOS, WordPerfect, dBASE III Plus and Lotus 1-2-3* by Lawrence Metzelaar and Marianne Fox. If you plan to use this software in conjunction with the text, please read *A Note on Software.*

6. University Gradebook. Written by David Herrick, of the University of Oregon, *University Gradebook* is class recordkeeping software that allows you to build a database of class records for up to 300 students. Its functions allow you to add or drop students; sort lists alphabetically, by student score, and by student ID number; calculate final grades based on a user-defined weighting system of quizzes, mid-terms, and final exams; calculate class averages; perform "what-if" analyses; and print and display information in a wide variety of formats.

Related Titles. Benjamin/Cummings titles that complement this text include:

▶ *Student Edition of Lotus 1-2-3,* by T.J. O'Leary. This is a special, educational version of the world's leading business productivity software.

▶ *Hands-On: MS-DOS, WordPerfect, dBASE III Plus and Lotus 1-2-3,* by Lawrence Metzelaar and Marianne Fox. This skill-building text is available in two versions, with and without educational versions of WordPerfect and dBASE III Plus.

TO THE STUDENT: WHAT'S IN THIS BOOK FOR YOU?

You are probably a member of a generation that is not afraid of technology. Television has been around as long as you have. You probably use the phone more often than you write letters. An automatic teller machine is a convenience, not an irritation. Personal computers may be unfamiliar, but they are not threats.

But whether you are of this generation that has grown up with three decades of the revolution in electronics or of an older one, you are probably aware that the knowledge of technology will only become more essential to future careers. That indeed is the concern we are addressing in this book: We expect that computers will be the ordinary tools of the future and that most people will be required to use them as a matter of course. Our aim is to help you succeed with these tools.

To assist you we have employed a number of devices:

1. We have tried to make the material both entertaining and meaningful. Organizations and computers are not dull—far from it. Thus, we have tried to convey the fast pace of the Information Revolution that you are living in, the rewards and risks of the workplace, the spirit of enterprise and innovation. What helps some executives and professionals succeed? What makes some organizations outlast others? How does technology help you compete? Such questions suggest stories worth telling, for they are questions that will no doubt be of vital concern to you beyond the classroom.

2. We have included extensive, varied examples and cases. Because this book should above all be practical, we have tried to show in great detail how the Information Revolution is permeating the workplace, as follows:

▶ **Case studies at the beginning of each chapter**: These descriptions of computers and information systems in action are intended to give you a real-world taste of the concepts to come.

▶ **Case examples within chapters**: How does it feel to be using computer technology and concepts in the workplace? We put you in a "hands-on" situation as the valued assistant of a top executive in four enterprises: a health services company, a film production company, an international bank, a stylish clothing manufacturer.

▶ **Case problems at the end of each chapter:** These case problems are not merely repetitions of chapter material, but provide additional valuable information. They are not so much problems as opportunities.

▶ **Boxes:** These include how-to tips, explanations, historical flashbacks, further examples, and other interesting topics that flesh out the text discussion.

3. We have provided many learning aids. The following are designed to help you get a grasp on the material. The **preview** at the beginning of each chapter does just that—preview the important headings in the chapter, to help orient students to the main topics being covered. A **summary** appears at the end of each chapter, which we hope students will find especially helpful when reviewing for tests. The summary also includes important words in boldface (darker) type, the same boldfaced terms that appear throughout the text. **Key terms** sections repeat these terms, and indicate the page in the chapter where the terms are first mentioned. The **review questions** at the end of each chapter consist of questions designed for self-testing before examinations. The **case problems** at the end of each chapter, as mentioned, pose situations that invite you to apply the concepts learned in the chapter. Finally, a **glossary/index** appears in the back of the text, to provide a concise definition of each key term and to refer students to the appropriate discussion within the text.

How you feel about this book is important to us. Any comments, favorable or unfavorable, will be read carefully. Write to us in care of the Computer Information Systems Editor, The Benjamin/Cummings Publishing Company, 390 Bridge Parkway, Redwood City, California, 94065.

T.J. O'Leary
Brian K. Williams

ACKNOWLEDGMENTS

There are only two names on the front of this book, but there are many others who have contributed to it and made us even prouder to have our names on it. At Benjamin/Cummings, we offer particular thanks to the talented production team of Mary Shields, Laura Argento, Sharon Woldy, and Guy Mills. We also appreciate the excellent editorial assistance of David Jackson, Jake Warde, and Devra Lerman, who built on the fine work done by Susan Nelle on the first edition.

Two friends helped in the development of this book, and we are grateful for their efforts: Tom Coffee at Arizona State University and Dr. Charles Paddock at the University of Nevada, Las Vegas. In addition, we are thankful for the assistance of the many publishing professionals who helped in the editing, design, graphics and production of the book: Sarah Bendersky, Carol Dondrea, Liz Ely, Deborah Gale, Gary Head, Brenn Lea Pearson, George Samuelson, Kris Kopping-Sandoe, Steve Sorenson, and York Graphic Services.

Finally, we are grateful to those who reviewed the manuscript of the second edition in its various stages and who provided comments, suggestions and support. Their names appear below.

Reviewers

Gary Armstrong
Shippensburg University

Crosman J. Clark
San Jose State University

Michael L. Davis
Lehigh University

Henry Estrada
Evergreen Valley College

Albert Kagan
North Dakota State University

James E. LaBarre
University of Wisconsin, Eau Claire

Norman Livergood
University of San Francisco

Scott McIntyre
University of Colorado

Richard M. Meyer
Hartnell College

Roger Alan Pick
University of Cincinnati

Matthew Pickard
University of Puget Sound

John Pickett
Georgia Southern University

R. Waldo Roth
Taylor University

David Whitney
San Francisco State University

PROLOGUE:
THE BUSINESS OF CHANGE

Shepherd's Mill is still. Built in the 1730s in Shepherdstown, West Virginia, as one of many rural water mills that converted grain into flour, Shepherd's Mill is now a silent monument to the industrial age that once formed the whole order of society.

In the century and a half of its existence, the mill was modified several times in response to advances in milling and water power technology. In the late 1700s, a conveyor system was introduced that automated the movement of grain through the various stages. In the 1890s, grindstones were replaced by chilled iron rollers, which milled a finer, better flour. The new technique required greater power than before: Other millers went to steam power or water turbines, but the owner of Shepherd's Mill installed the 40-foot-diameter waterwheel shown here. At the same time, he added the wood-frame third floor to the original stone structure.

Today, however, Shepherd's Mill is still, a relic of an economic and technological order long gone by. Though a monument, it has lessons for the present, for it shows how organizations and institutions must adapt to technological change. The mill changed much during it long life. For us living in the Computer Age, however, the changes we will witness in our institutions will be far more dramatic and certainly far more rapid. Indeed, for the rest of our lives, we will need to make it our business to understand the business of change.

THE TOOL FOR NEW CAREERS

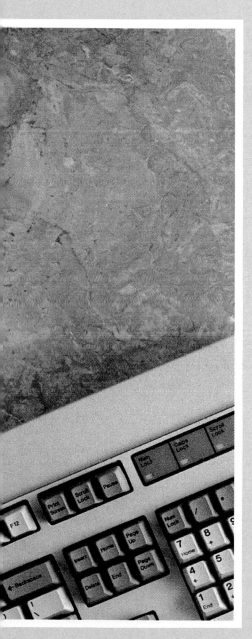

The old ways are changing, and changing fast. Once upon a time, the pace of business enterprise was measured in weeks and days and hours—by the speed of clipper ships or transcontinental trains or the Western Union telegraph. Today it is measured in hours and minutes and seconds—by the speed of the Concorde jetliner or the Telex message or the communications satellite signal. Once, back in 1874, Philo Remington began marketing a curious printing machine, known as a "typewriter," which began the retirement of the quill pen. Today the workplace has been revolutionized by word processing and other office technology, changing the nature of white-collar work more rapidly than at any time in the past hundred years. Once, two decades ago, the Wall Street stock exchanges almost collapsed under the pressure of trading 11 million shares a day. Today they can handle more than twenty-five times that many.

The midwife of these changes is, of course, the computer. The chief characteristic of the computer is that by its speed and its ability to handle enormous amounts of data *it greatly extends our human capabilities.* The result has been the arrival of the Information Age and massive changes in the production, dissemination, and handling of all the information that managers and professional people need to know to bring goods and services to other people. Moreover, in a single human generation, computers have moved beyond churning out payrolls and reports and into marketing, strategic planning, customer service, and many other areas. "The diffusion of technology is changing the way we do business and the way companies relate to customers and suppliers," a Harvard business professor points out. "This is no longer a technological phenomenon but a social one."

In this first part of the book, we begin to examine this phenomenon. First, we give some brief background in computers. Then we show how the computer is being used to benefit those known as end-users—people who are not computer professionals but rather people probably much like yourself: members or soon to be members of business, government, and nonprofit organizations who need information to do their jobs successfully. Finally, we introduce you to systems and systems analysis—business systems, computer systems, and the fusion of the two into business information systems.

Chapter 1

THE COMPUTER SOLUTION: END-USERS AND THE INFORMATION AGE

How do you stay a winner in an era of constant technological change?

Some people seem to know how to do it—and we hope that this book will help you learn to be one of them. Other people lag behind. Listen, for instance, to the phone call that frustrated salesman Fred Coldcall is making to his home office from a roadside pay phone, as described in the box on the following page. Clearly, Fred is not a winner. The fault is not entirely his, however. He is working for a company that is using old technology—technology that may not even seem old because we are all so used to it. As we will see at the end of this chapter, there are several ways that Fred could benefit from new computer-based technology.

What are the hopes people have for computers? In general, there are three: that they will enhance productivity, reduce drudgery, and speed responses to problems. More than this, however, people also expect computers to be used for *strategic* purposes, to help companies compete successfully in the marketplace. Indeed, many of these hopes have been fulfilled on a grand scale, and the benefits still to come promise to be even grander. However, for many people, computers have been a disappointment. They have fostered and will probably continue to foster unrealistic expectations about what they can do. Let us show what we mean.

COMPUTER DREAMS, COMPUTER NIGHTMARES

When the U.S. Supreme Court ruled in the late 1970s that lawyers could run advertisements for themselves—just as restaurants, banks, and most other businesses could—two Oakland, California, attorneys thought they saw a way to take this opportunity, combine it with a novel business strategy and computers, and mass-market legal services to become the "McDonald's of law firms."

The plan involved three strategies:

First, the advertising: "THERE ARE TIMES YOU NEED A LAWYER, AND TIMES YOU DON'T. YANELLO & FLIPPEN HELPS YOU DECIDE," ran one of their ads. They blanketed TV, radio, billboards, newspapers, and mass transit with a $250,000-a-year advertising campaign.

CASE STUDY: WAITING FOR THE OFFICE OF THE FUTURE

The Office of the Present: The Frustrations of Fred

"Darn it, Mary, I was within 20 minutes of Quick Industries this morning."

"Well, Mr. Coldcall, I tried to reach you at the field office. It's lucky that you just phoned in. Anyway, a Mr. Buysome at Quick said that if you still want to bid on their contract, you've got to see him tomorrow at the latest and your proposal has to be in by Friday."

"Which proposal? We've talked about three different jobs."

"He said it was the one with the new specs."

"Oh, no! Peter in sales engineering has those at the district office along with the pricing sheets. Please transfer me to Peter. I'll get back to you."

"Sorry, he's on his line; it's busy."

"I guess I'll have to hold, but I'm in a phone booth."

Some minutes later: "Pete? Fred. Listen. I need the Quick specs and pricing. Can you get them to the field office by noon tomorrow? I'll make a special trip to pick them up."

"Those old things! I suppose I can find them somewhere, but we've changed some of the components and the pricing, so I'll have to update them. I'll try to get them to you by the end of the day."

"Pete, you've got to do better than that."

"Sorry, Fred. I'm already working on three other rush proposals, and I'm expediting two other jobs through some bottlenecks in the factory."

"Pete, for Fred's sake, do your darndest! Now please transfer me back to Mary."

"Mary, two things: arrange the delivery with Peter. Then call Joan at the field office. Tell her we're going to have to work late tomorrow night after I come back from my meeting with Buysome. Tell her also to pull the Quick files and proposal boilerplates. She's the only one there who knows where everything is, how to work the word processor, and the high-quality copier, and. . . ."

"Oh, Fred, Joan just called me from O'Hare. Remember, she's off to Acapulco? Fred . . . Fred . . . are you there?"

—Harvey L. Poppel,
Harvard Business Review

Poor Fred is dead—or is he? In organizations employing modern computer information and communication technology, he could probably pull off a quick sale with Quick Industries. To see how, turn to the box on page 17 at the end of this chapter.

Second, the business strategy: Law has typically been a tradition-bound field, but Yanello & Flippen thought they saw a way to reach clients who had had little contact with lawyers before. Initial consultation fees would be only $20. Other fees would be 20–30% less than those of competing lawyers. They would go after bread-and-butter cases: contracts, wills, divorces, and the like. Clients would pay with credit cards or in installments.

Third, the computer: The computer was as essential to success as any of the other parts, for it would allow Yanello & Flippen to speed up paperwork (the law tends to use a great deal of repetitious material, such as standard "boilerplate" clauses in contracts), decrease the use of high-priced lawyers, and keep track of billings.

The novel strategy appeared to pay off. Over the next four years, Yanello & Flippen Law Offices grew to 20 attorneys in eight Oakland and San Francisco Bay area offices, attracted 16,000 clients, and gathered annual revenues of more than $1 million.

A year later, however, cofounder Ralph Yanello had declared himself personally bankrupt; his partner, Thomas Flippen, had left the business; and the firm itself was down to five attorneys operating on the brink of insolvency.

What went wrong? Part of the answer, according to a *San Francisco Chronicle* article, was that the advertising worked so well that the staff of lawyers, most of them young and inexperienced, was quickly overwhelmed with 100 cases each. Probably equally important, however, were the high expectations for, and misuses of, the computer.

Says the *Chronicle* story:

> The computer system that was supposed to be the firm's ally turned out to be a nemesis. The office went through four different [computers] in as many years. Bills were fouled up, and clients were not billed for as long as a year, attorneys said. Hundreds of thousands of dollars were never collected.
>
> The billing snafu drained endless hours, diverting the firm from creating the legal programming that was supposed to reduce the high cost of legal services.
>
> After the first computer arrived late, with accounting software that Yanello found inadequate, he plunged into developing his own programs, although he had no formal computer training and was advised against it.
>
> Yanello never stopped believing in computers, as if the machines embodied all the rationality that the firm lacked. . . .

In the aftermath, Yanello & Flippen filed a multimillion-dollar lawsuit accusing a local software vendor of failing to provide them with a time-and-billing system, word processing package, and adequate programming and training services, which were deemed "crucial" to their survival.

WINNERS, LOSERS, AND END-USERS

WHO WILL GAIN BY THE INFORMATION REVOLUTION?

There are many such "war stories" about computers, and you will no doubt hear more. We have introduced our book with the sad case of Yanello & Flippen, however, because we feel it is important to go about the study of computers pragmatically. Fortunately, such tales are balanced by a wealth of success stories—as the accompanying box shows. Here also is the place to introduce the distinction between "users" and "end-users." In the past, computer **users** were defined as those with technical training, such as programmers and systems analysts; *end-users* were those who used the benefits of the computers. However, the spread of microcomputers has given many people access to computing power and information never before possible. Today, therefore, **end-users,** because they need to manage information in order to do their jobs, are expected to have more familiarity with computers—particularly microcomputers. Moreover, as computers become more interconnected and able to *share information*, end-users have greater access to more information than ever before.

What is it that we need to understand about computers if we are to make sound judgments? It is that computers and their information are only as good as the people who design them, program them, and—most importantly for readers of this book—use them.

As we stated in the introduction to this part of the book, the computer is a business and professional *tool*. There are two facts about tools: First, tools change. The spade becomes plow becomes tractor. The pen becomes typewriter becomes word processor. Although the tools that evolve may make our lives easier, as the tools change, we must change with them.

Second, tools can do both harm and good. That familiar tool the car causes around 50,000 fatalities a year in the United States, but the car-as-ambulance saves more lives (probably over 30,000 in one month in New York City alone). The computer unquestionably puts some people out of work—but it also brings a good many benefits.

Who will be the winners and losers in the Information Revolution? Let us consider the losers first—since, needless to say, none of us wants to be counted among them.

The Losers

Hardly a job now exists that will not be affected by computer technology. Some, however, have already been affected adversely. Blue-collar manufacturing jobs—the numbing but often well-paying jobs that have existed for unskilled workers in auto plants and the like—have been reduced not only by foreign competition but to some extent by industrial robots, such as the computer-controlled welders and paint-sprayers now found in automobile plants. Many tedious

SUCCESS STORY

System's On-line Timekeeping Aids Law Firm's Billing

MILWAUKEE—The law firm of Frisch, Dudek and Slattery Ltd. here has reportedly improved its billing methods and gained the capacity to generate business trend reports since it installed an integrated word and data processing system.

According to the firm's business manager, John Berres, the system improves the firm's billng of its 1,500 clients by switching the office to an on-line system of timekeeping for its 28 attorneys. Previously, paper time slips made out by attorneys to record their work for a client would be filed by a clerk with other time slips and later retrieved and typed as part of the client's bill.

That path, Berres said, was paved with the potential for errors. Time slips could be lost, or errors could occur in typing. With the on-line system, . . . the time slips are keyed in once; the office's billing secretary can later generate a paper printout for editing. . . .

For technology-skittish attorneys, Berres said, the on-line timekeeping system offers the advantage of allowing the continued use of the paper time slips they've grown used to or, alternatively, the dictation of time slips. The bills themselves can now be gener-ated in greater numbers and with greater speed. "Before, we couldn't bill on a monthly basis," he said, adding that per diem [per day] clients often prefer to be billed in that fashion.

Berres said he especially liked the system's ability to generate reports on the firm's business trends, such as whether the firm is doing more divorce or tax work and what types of work generate most of the firm's income. . . .

While the billing and general ledger features of the [system] did not come on-line until several weeks after the system was installed, the system's word processing capacity was put to use immediately. Five workstations [keyboards and video display terminals] of the system are used for word processing of documents, which range from one paragraph to 100 or more pages.

An average of 50,000 lines is being produced each week by the firm, and turnaround time is reportedly less than one day for most jobs.

—*Computerworld*

Steel-collar worker. Many blue-collar workers fear the prospect of computer-related automation, such as the robot welders used in new-car assembly plants.

but easily learned white-collar jobs—such as those involving filing, sorting, and the typing of lists—are also disappearing. Jobs that consist largely of dispensing information over a telephone—the ones currently occupied by stockbrokers, airline reservations personnel, and the like—may well be endangered species. Some observers even speculate that people serving business travel, such as airline pilots, will find their numbers reduced as business people come to depend more on computerized communications than on travel. Finally, we must count not only those people unwilling to change with the times but, more subtly, those who are unwilling or unable to *capitalize* on the changes.

But the computer will do more than displace jobs. It will also narrow some jobs, make others more complicated, compartmentalize still others, and generally strain previous work styles. Librarians, travel agents, and employment personnel, to name a few occupations, will no doubt find extraordinary changes in their lives. So will administrators and managers. By now, most managers who had hoped to stay safely computer-illiterate have probably changed their minds—if they decided they wanted to continue to be among the winners.

The Winners

The biggest winners will probably be those enterprising "surfers," as they have been called, who, anticipating the wave of technological change, ride the crest of that wave to success. These are the innovators, who can recognize the technological potentials first and implement them before others do. They are the risk-takers who, in the past, were represented, for instance, by the Silicon Valley overnight millionaires behind such names as Hewlett-Packard or Intel or Apple Computer.

But there are a great many other people who are not innovators who clearly will emerge as winners also. Robots may displace some blue-collar workers in industry, but they also are able to rescue others from doing some jobs that humans should not have to do—for instance, working with radioactive materials, handling molten steel, or doing welding in dangerous situations. Computers may remove low-level white-collar clerical jobs, but they also remove a great deal of tedium. Word processing, for example, eliminates the repetitious typing of revised drafts, and computerized filing systems can do away with laborious alphabetizing by hand. Computers may remove the human presence in many business transactions, such as that of the bank teller or the airline reservations clerk, but they also make those transactions faster. Computerized telecommunications not only allows banking or ticket buying to be done via telephone and home computer, it also benefits some single parents, disabled, and others who need to be able to work at home and communicate with co-workers.

Another class of winners consists of those whose careers are directly tied to the computer's existence—people with job titles such as computer repairman or -woman, programmer, systems analyst, and data base manager. Often, having such a job is like riding a tiger, however, because the industry changes so rapidly.

But the winners we are most concerned about in this book are people like you—people who will most likely be working in an office, perhaps in a managerial or professional job, involved in a career that requires knowing something about computers and information processing. Let us show some of the ways white-collar workers will or do benefit. Perhaps nowhere are the benefits more apparent than in that newest of white-collar tools, the microcomputer.

THE MIGHTY

MICROCOMPUTER

EVERY USER'S

PRODUCTIVITY TOOL

An IBM PS/2. Becoming more powerful with each new version, the IBM Personal Computer has been principally responsible for the presence of microcomputers in offices. This version, the IBM PS/2 Model 60, which uses an internal "microchip" known as the 80386 chip, is so powerful that it is blurring the distinction between microcomputers and computers that previously were found only in an organization's data processing department.

Every profession and every trade has its specialized tools, from the hammer of a carpenter to the stethoscope of a physician. White-collar workers, of course, have their own tools—telephones, dictaphones, and photocopiers. In recent years, however, the microcomputer has emerged as an essential instrument for managers, professionals, and others working in offices.

If you have not already put your fingers on the keyboard of a microcomputer, there is virtually no doubt you will. Indeed, much of the rest of this book is predicated on the assumption that you *should* learn to use this machine—that is, it is a necessary skill not just to survive in business but to *prevail*.

As we shall see in Chapter 2, there are presently four different sizes of computers (supercomputers, mainframes, minicomputers, and microcomputers), but it is the microcomputer that has recently had the most dramatic effect—that has in fact redefined the roles of other computers. Also known as *personal computers* and *desktop computers*, **microcomputers** are the smallest and least expensive, costing generally between $200 and $10,000 and being small enough to put on a table top or even hold in your hand. Price, size, and "user-friendliness" are what have made the microcomputer one of the most exciting developments of modern times, for they have made computing power available to many more people than was possible before.

The history of the development of the microcomputer begins with the origin of the microprocessor. Some people confuse the terms microprocessor and microcomputer, but the two are not the same. A **microprocessor**—microscopic processor—is the part of the computer actually responsible for processing information. Microprocessors put the computing power once possible only with room-sized computers into a small electronic machine called a **silicon chip** or **integrated circuit**, which is about the size of a dime and is made out of **silicon** or ocean beach rocks, a **semiconductor** that conducts electric current when it has been "doped" with chemical impurities. Figure 1-1 shows the relationship between a microcomputer and a microprocessor. (A history of the technology of computers is presented in a module following the last chapter of this book.)

Because these machines are becoming so important in our lives, let us look at how they can be used in school, at home, and in your career.

Microcomputers in the Classroom and the Living Room

Perhaps you have encountered personal computers earlier in your education. Apple, Commodore, Tandy–Radio Shack, and IBM in

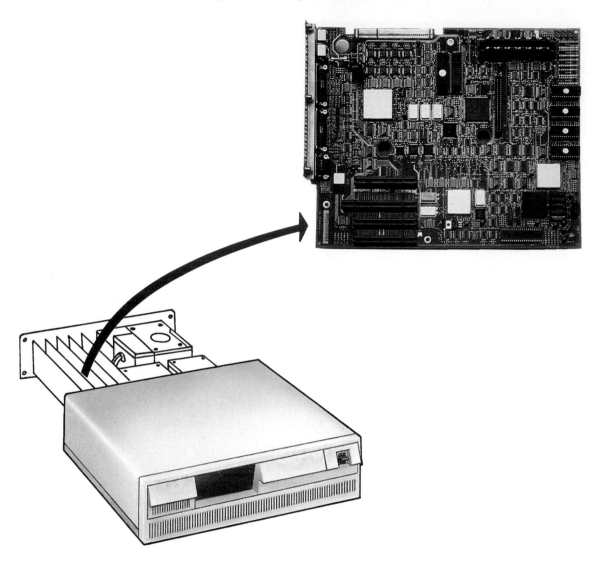

Figure 1-1. Microprocessor and microcomputer. In this IBM PS/2 microcomputer, the system board (system of electrical circuitry) contains several small "silicon chips," otherwise known as microprocessors or integrated circuits.

particular have been active in marketing to schools, and the number of programs being written for educational uses is increasing. Programs are available for everything from vocabulary development to preparation for the College Board exams.

Or perhaps you were first introduced to the microcomputer as a home computer. The extremely volatile market for home computers has been dominated by such names as Apple, Tandy–Radio Shack, Commodore, Atari, and IBM. In one survey, it was found that most people use their personal computer for video games—available games range from Swamp War to (literally!) Kitchen Sink—but the second most common use was for business or office homework, tying with use as a child's learning tool. One of the more interesting services available to home-computer owners is the so-called "information utilities," such as CompuServe or Dow Jones News/Retrieval, which give viewers access via telephone lines to data banks and news and financial services. Many people use their home computers and telephones to exchange messages with others with similar interests and to leave notes on "electronic bulletin boards." Some do home banking and buy and sell stocks through their home computers.

Some people also use home computers to handle personal money matters: checkbook balancing, tax preparation, stock portfolio evaluation, and so on. In addition, they use their computers as word processors to handle report writing and correspondence, as devices for keeping records, and as organizers of personal calendars and schedules.

Microcomputers in the Work World

The reaction to the appearance of microcomputers in the office has been fascinating. Earlier some executives simply ignored their presence, either being afraid of them or feeling it was demeaning to lay hands on a keyboard. Others viewed micros simply as toys or as status symbols in the office power struggles, boasting about the number-crunching abilities of their computers the way car enthusiasts brag about horsepower.

By now, however, most forward-looking managers have found the machine an asset. Small businesses—businesses with less than 100 employees—can use microcomputers to free themselves from the necessity of hiring outside services to handle their computing needs or from having to expend much effort and resources on acquiring larger computers and hiring staffs to run them. Large businesses have also been liberated from being tied exclusively to large computers. In fact, as Figure 1-2 shows, the appearance of microcomputers has enhanced the efficiency of the large ones, the ones known as **mainframe computers.** For example, a microcomputer can be used to communicate with larger computers as if it were a **terminal**—a device with keyboard and video display screen (and possibly a printer) that is used to input data and output information. Yet the micro can also operate by itself, removing the workload from the larger computer. In addition, microcomputers have brought computing power from the guarded mysteries of the data processing department right to users' desks. Let us see what the benefits of microcomputers are for end-users—and how they will help in your career, whatever office you might wind up in.

Some businesses might not seem to require much in the way of office activities. A health club or exercise studio, for example, might seem to consist principally of Nautilus equipment and aerobic-exercise rooms. Let us suppose, however, that your uncle is an executive with a nationwide corporation, TopHealth Inc., that owns a

Figure 1-2. The uses of the microcomputer. In a large business, an office worker may use the desktop microcomputer (1) to retrieve information from (2) a large computer in another location, which in turn has access (3) to various kinds of stored information. The user may (4) display that information on a videoscreen and manipulate it in various ways to suit his or her purposes, then (5) print out the result on a printer.

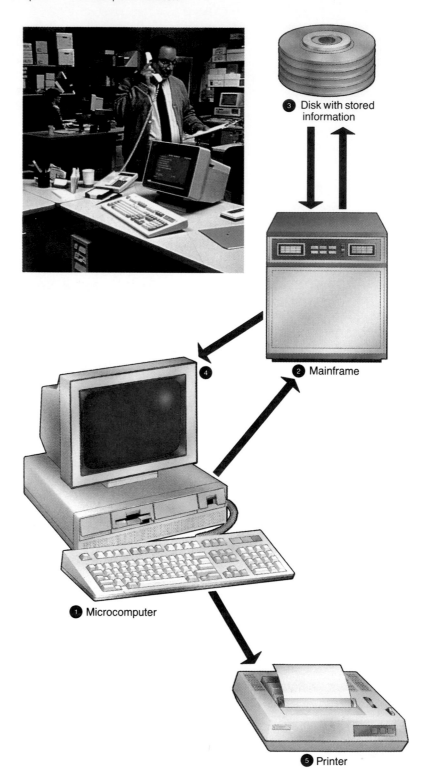

number of health-related businesses, and let us suppose that you have gone to work part time in the office of one of the corporation's chain of exercise studios, Exercise! Unlimited. Here is how the information-handling activities apply.

You receive information generally in number, symbol, or text form—for instance, the names, addresses, and monthly dues of studio members—which is then used to *create* a document, such as a file of members. This document is read, distributed if necessary, and *stored* in a filing cabinet next to your desk. Later you may *retrieve* the membership file, *organize* names in alphabetical order, and at the end of the month *summarize* the dues-paying information to see if the total membership fees coming in are enough to pay expenses, including, of course, your salary. You would then *communicate* this information—to the members behind in their payments and to the studio manager. The manager would then have to *make decisions* about what to do with the profits, if any, or what money to borrow, which late payers to remind, or which expenses to cut in order to improve Exercise! Unlimited's financial picture.

The words we emphasized above—create, store, retrieve, organize, summarize, communicate, and make decisions about information—all describe the principal office activities involved in dealing with information. Figure 1-3 shows how this flow of information might look. Perhaps you and the manager are the only two employ-

Figure 1-3.   Info flow. How information flows in a standard office. This shows how information about new members in a health club is handled.

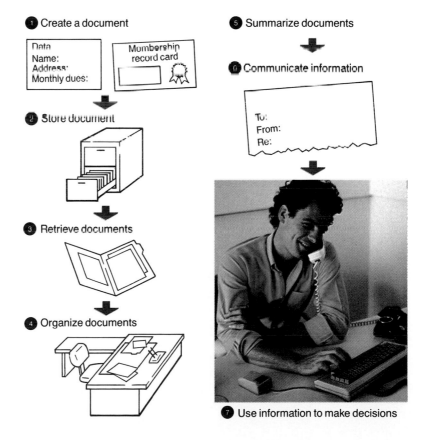

1. Create a document

Data
Name:
Address:
Monthly dues:

Membership record card

2. Store document

3. Retrieve documents

4. Organize documents

5. Summarize documents

6. Communicate information

To:
From:
Re:

7. Use information to make decisions

ees in the office (there are exercise instructors in the studio part). But the purposes and tasks are the same whether an office has one person in it or hundreds—and whether it is a traditional office or one using the latest technology.

How, then, can microcomputer technology help? Let us look at the following:

► Word processors
► Spreadsheets and graphics
► Electronic filing
► Communications and connectivity
► Electronic mail

WORD PROCESSORS

TYPEWRITERS FOR
THE INFORMATION
AGE

The term *word processor* might seem to suggest there is some logical way by which a computer sorts unprocessed words into processed words, but, of course, it does nothing of the kind. A **word processor** is an electronic typewriter with a keyboard linked to a video display screen and a computer—in short, a microcomputer. You do not type immediately onto a piece of paper, however. Rather, the words appear on the video screen and are stored temporarily (either within the computer or on an outside storage device). When you are ready, you can then send these words electronically from the computer to a printer—a typewriterlike device—for printing out on paper.

Unlike the standard office electric typewriter, the word processor can do several marvelous things. Writing becomes more like working with soft clay than like working with hammer and chisel and marble. No more erasing, inserting, or cutting and pasting by hand. With word processing, you can rearrange words and sentences and do deletions and insertions with the punch of a button. As one novelist put it about his word processor, "Once I learned it could do the two essential things a writer really needs—insert and delete—I knew I'd finally moved from the Stone Age to the Space Age."

Word processing is usually considered the first step in bringing an office into the Information Age. You may begin to appreciate this when your uncle announces that the parent company, TopHealth Inc., has decided to put a microcomputer and printer in each of the Exercise! Unlimited offices.

After a few hours spent at the keyboard, you can see why typewriters are no match for word processors—why word processing can boost productivity over typewriters by 50–400%. When you write to studio clients, politely reminding them that their membership fees are past due, you no longer have to send a "Dear Sir or Madam" form letter or type the same letter over and over again with a new name and address at the top. Rather, you can type the text of a letter once and then change the name and address with just a few keystrokes;

the printer will print out a different, typewritten letter each time. The studio manager particularly appreciates the machine because she is a terrible typist, and she can easily correct her typing mistakes electronically instead of using erasers and whiting-out correction fluid.

We will give a more detailed example of how word processing works in Chapter 3.

SPREADSHEETS AND GRAPHICS FASTER COMPUTATIONS AND PRESENTATIONS

In an older office, one not only heard the sound of typewriters but also the mechanical clackety-clack of calculators. But the calculations that are done on microcomputers are not only quieter and faster, they are a whole different category of computations. The **electronic spreadsheet,** first devised in 1979, allows managers to manipulate projected costs much more easily. For instance, if you were a contractor or architect calculating the materials and labor to go into building a house—a house whose selling price was absolutely fixed—you could do all the changing you wanted using your computer (smaller floor plan or larger? redwood lumber or pine? two bathrooms or one?), and the changing figures would automatically change all related figures and totals. The spreadsheet has become absolutely one of the most important and widespread business tools, and we will show you in more detail later how it works.

Spreadsheets have also been linked to the use of **graphics**—visual representations of numerical data—in order to better display results. For instance, a sales manager can compare monthly sales of the top three salespeople during a year by looking at three columns of numbers—but pictures always have far more impact than numbers. Thus, a drawing of the three people's sales histories in chart form will leap off the page. In addition, such drawings can be converted to slides or other forms for visual display to present to outsiders or higher management.

ELECTRONIC FILING AND DATA BASES: REPLACING THE MANILA FOLDER

What does a worker produce? Factory workers can look at the parts or products sitting on the skids at the end of the assembly line. Office workers can look at—paper.

Clerks and secretaries spend 90% of their time handling paperwork, and the results are there for all to see in the four-drawer filing cabinets found in most offices. To fill only *two* of those drawers can cost as much as a new car. At these prices, it makes sense to look for other solutions. For legal documents, insurance forms, patient records, airfreight shipping manifests, and other high-volume records and documents, the solution is electronic filing.

Electronic filing may be defined as technically enhanced storage and retrieval of data or information. For microcomputers, the most popular electronic filing consists of storing computerized information on phonograph-record–like magnetic disks, as we shall describe in the next chapter. These electronic "media," as they are called, allow easy access from one computer to another; for example, files may be stored on a large computer and then **downloaded**— transferred to—a small computer such as a microcomputer.

A notion central to electronic filing—and to a great deal of this book—is that of data base. A **data base** consists of several files, usually stored on magnetic disk, which are *cross-referenced*. That is, each file is like a single file folder in a file cabinet, and you can find that file by looking it up in different indexes—indexes based on last name, social security number, birth date, and so on.

Data bases may be internal or external. An *internal data base* might be Ford Motor Company's list of dealers, which might be stored in the main computer room at company headquarters in Dearborn, Michigan. An *external data base* might be a large public data source called an "information utility" or a specialized data bank, either of which make the information contained in entire encyclopedias available via telephone lines to a subscriber's desktop computer.

Such sophisticated electronic filing may not seem particularly useful, at first, in your two-person office at Exercise! Unlimited. You come to find, however, that having information about studio members on a small magnetic disk that works with your microcomputer is actually quite helpful. Alphabetizing of names is done automatically, address changes are easily updated on the files (no crossing out with ink), and it is easy to have the computer give you birthday reminders so that you can send customers a birthday card.

> ## COMMUNICATIONS
> ## AND CONNECTIVITY:
> ## INTEGRATING
> ## END-USER
> ## COMPUTING

As we mentioned, an important concept of office automation is **connectivity**—that is, the concept that technology *links together* or *integrates* information. When computers are connected—whether by telephone lines, coaxial cable under the floor, or some other means— they can communicate with each other in ways that help users improve their productivity.

Two kinds of computer connections are:

▶ Microcomputer to microcomputer
▶ Microcomputer to mainframe computer

Both of these are illustrated in Figure 1-4.

A microcomputer-to-microcomputer connection enables users to use personal software and exchange information directly. Clearly,

Micro to micro

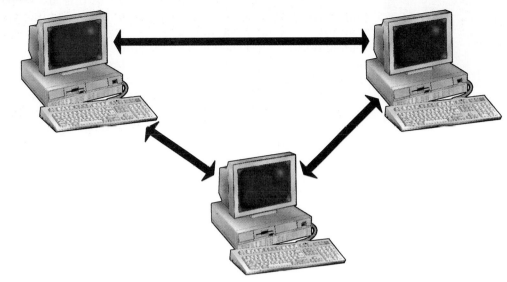

Micro to mainframe

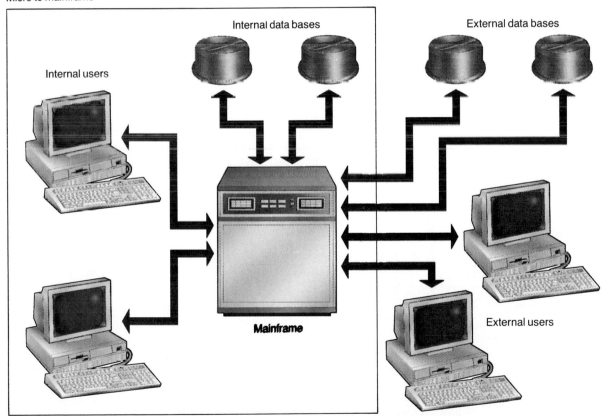

Figure 1-4.   Two kinds of communication connections. *Top*: In the microcomputer-to-microcomputer connection, users—for example, two users within the same office building—can share information directly with each other. *Bottom*: In the microcomputer-to-mainframe connection, users can draw on large data bases of information, both within the same organization and outside of it, and users inside and outside the office may have access to this information.

the exercise studio you're in has no need of this arrangement, but you might find it useful to exchange information with an Exercise! Unlimited studio in another city, linking your microcomputer by telephone line with their microcomputer. You might, for instance, have used your personal data base and spreadsheet software to draw up a profile of the ages, occupations, and so on, of typical members of your studio and want to share it in exchange for information about members of other studios. The result is that each studio can launch effective advertising campaigns for gaining new members.

The microcomputer-to-mainframe connection enables users to gain access to data bases, both inside and outside the company, and use other mainframe tools that we shall discuss later. For instance, your studio manager finds that by hooking up your microcomputer by telephone line to the TopHealth Inc. headquarters, she is able to connect to corporation files, avail herself of new health and marketing knowledge in various data banks, and so on.

ELECTRONIC MAIL:

END OF TELEPHONE

TAG AND MAILROOM

DRAG

WHAT WASTES THE MOST WORKERS' TIME

Meetings	15%
Phone calls	11%
Paperwork	7%
Travel	6%
Office gossip	4%

—Management Recruiters International Survey of American Executives

Electronic mail—sometimes referred to as **electronic mail/message system (EMMS)**—consists of using electronic means to send, store, and deliver messages that you would otherwise deliver verbally by phone or send by mail (either inside or outside the office).

What, you may think, could improve on the telephone for speed in delivering messages? Actually, studies have shown that, for business telephone calls, 70% of the time—repeat: over two-thirds of the time—when a person calls, the other person is not available to take the call. This game, called "telephone tag," is one that we have all played: You call someone, who is not in, and you leave a message for that person to call you back. He or she calls back, and you are not in—and so on.

As for mail, we all know how long it can take to get a document from one far-flung state to another—usually not possible on the same day. Quite often, however, businesspeople find the same lag even within a company's own in-house mail system. This slowness has been dubbed "mailroom drag." Often the drag is so long that it takes a company two days to transmit its mail from one floor to another in the same building.

To appreciate what effect this tag and drag have, consider that the principal activity of middle- and upper-level managers is *transferring information*—either by person-to-person contact or by written documents. Consider also that *half* the conversations executives have are composed of one-way information transfers; that is, no discussions are needed. Clearly, the information could be communicated by written documents—except for the delay of mailroom drag. The alternative is the telephone—except for the delays of telephone tag. Electronic mail, then, is ideal for the one-way communication of

CASE STUDY: RELIEF FOR FRED

Using Computerization to Boost Sales

In 1987, Hewlett-Packard Co., of Palo Alto, Calif., ordered its sales representatives to "do something" to improve sales. When salespeople were given portable computers and cellular mobile telephones, they increased sales 25%. Salespeople found they could eliminate trips back to the office when they used the computers to communicate with colleagues. This gave them the time to make three sales calls a day instead of two, which led to more sales. Consider how computer technology of this sort might help Fred.

A sales professional like Fred Coldcall would be equipped with an easy-to-use, portable intelligent display terminal enabling him to access information and contact people in a variety of timesaving ways. First, Fred would scan publicly available data bases to select his prospect lists. Next, a "traveling salesman" algorithm [logical arrangement] could be used to display a minimum-time travel path among prospects and existing customers. Fred and his office-based assistant, Mary, would use an electronic mail system operating through Fred's terminal to stay in close touch as she scheduled Fred's appointments to match the minimum-travel path. Naturally, the system would reconfigure the path should any appointments be unavailable or canceled. Mary would use her desk-based communicating word processor to send and receive such messages.

Next, Fred would use his terminal while visiting Quick Industries to access the Quick file, as well as the latest specifications and pricing information. Thus he could elicit Mr. Buysome's reaction to the main points of his proposal on the spot and adjust accordingly instead of wasting substantial time and effort preparing a formal proposal. In simpler situations, such as selling personal home insurance, the sales professional could display and print a complete proposal in front of the prospect.

In addition to a portable data terminal, Fred would have a portable telephone that he could use "hands-free" in his automobile and thus convert idle auto travel time to productive time. Not only would this unit enable Fred to place and receive telephone calls while he was on the move but it would also connect him with a central voice message computer. Since this type of system can send and receive messages to and from any telephone, it would enable Fred to communicate with customers and the internal support people who did not have access to a data terminal.

Without having to leave his car, Fred could check the status of an order, coordinate invoice [billing] reconciliation efforts, arrange proposal preparations or sales engineering assistance, and even change his appointment schedule at any hour of the day.

Video technology would also help Fred. Full sound and motion product demonstrations on a videodisc would be accessed, along with standard pricing and availability, through an inexpensive videodisc player attachment to Fred's . . . data terminal. Depending on the type of product, he could view this material with prospects or use it solely to prepare himself. Fred could also keep current with new product and marketing plans by attending videoconferences available periodically at a nearby motel.

—Harvey L. Poppel,
Harvard Business Review

JUST THE FAX, PLEASE: THE FUTURE OF ELECTRONIC MAIL

Right now many businesses such as law firms, banks, and insurance companies communicate by using "fax" or facsimile machines, which translate information such as text and photographs into a dot pattern ("bit-map"), and send it by telephone to receiving facsimile machines that copy the pattern onto paper. By 1990, there are expected to be over a million such machines in the United States.

Another, perhaps even more exciting, breakthrough in electronic mail is the voice store and forward (VSF) system, in which the sender's voice message is electronically stored, then retrieved and reconstructed by the person receiving the message. The technique relies on speech-recognition equipment that analyzes and classifies speech patterns and translates them into electronic impulses that can be accepted by the computer.

information. And, of course, one of its greatest attractions is that it gives the option of providing a permanent copy of the message.

One kind of electronic mail is known as **computer message storing:** The caller sends a message to another person's personal computer terminal, where it is displayed on the screen. If the intended receiver is unavailable, the message is electronically stored in the terminal until the receiver can pick it up. A variation is the **electronic mailbox,** in which the message is stored in a centralized computer "post office," which users must check periodically.

The Exercise! Unlimited studio you work at already has a telephone answering machine. Why, you wonder, do you need electronic mail? Actually, in an exercise studio run by two people, you certainly do not. But when you visit your uncle in his office in the Public Relations Department at TopHealth Inc., headquartered in St. Louis, you begin to see the benefits. Your uncle does not deal only with short memos from other executives. He also deals with long documents relating to health legislation, which are sent to him by the corporation's government-watcher in Washington, D.C. He must keep abreast of new health administrative rulings from the Department of Health and Human Resources and from the health bureaucracies in all 50 state capitals. He also has people around the country watching for articles in local newspapers that affect TopHealth's business. Although much of this information could be sent by overnight package delivery, your uncle needs to have it quickly enough to formulate a corporate response. And nearly all of it is too long to be left as a message on a telephone answering machine.

THE NEW FRONTIER OF THE INFORMATION REVOLUTION

"Can there really be anything new under the sun?" asks organizational psychologist Evan Peelle. "It may seem somewhat paradoxical, but at the close of the 20th century there still appears to be an ever-growing number of uncharted areas to explore. The enigma of our modern world is that the more we advance, the more of the unknown we discover."

Because the human mind has a unique curiosity and drive to grow, says Peelle, we continue to create new frontiers to challenge ourselves and new ideas for meeting those challenges—the latest frontier being high technology.

Information technology, from microcomputers to data banks, will change everything about future career paths. It will change the nature of competition, as we will continue to show throughout this book. It will change the products and services that are provided, speeding up production and distribution. It will change the markets, erasing geographic and other boundaries. It will change production economics, so that in some cases it will be just as inexpensive to make products singly as to make them in quantity. And it will change the relationships between people in the professions and business—suppliers and buyers, producers and customers, employers and employed. To you, the reader of this book, there is only one question:

Will you be ready for these changes?

SUMMARY

► The hopes people have for computers are three: to enhance productivity, reduce drudgery, and speed responses to problems. Computers are also used for business strategic purposes, to help companies compete successfully in their marketplaces.

► Computer **users** are people with technical training, such as programmers and systems analysts. **End-users** use the benefits of computers, but nowadays are expected to have more familiarity with computers—particularly microcomputers—than they used to, because they need to manage information in order to do their jobs. Moreover, as computers become more interconnected and able to *share information*, end-users have more access to information than ever before.

► The computer is a business *tool*, which means it is only as good as the people who design it, program it, and use it. There are two facts about tools. First, tools change; to utilize tools effectively, we must change with them. Second, tools can do both harm and good; the computer will put some people out of work while bringing benefits to others.

► The computer is changing the nature of work. Some jobs are adversely affected: Some are being displaced by computers, while others are made more complicated, narrower, or compartmentalized. Blue-collar jobs such as unskilled workers in auto plants and white-collar jobs such as filing, giving information over a telephone, and serving business travel are particularly vulnerable.

► Some jobs are enhanced and made more productive by the computer, and the computer will continue to create new jobs and business opportunities. People who will benefit will be those who are technological innovators, blue-collar workers delivered from doing dangerous work, white-collar workers doing tedious work, and those who gain by doing business via telephone and home computer, such as single parents and the disabled.

► Businesspeople will benefit by having electronic message systems with which to transmit memos and reports, desktop computers to help do "what-if" calculations and turn numbers into colorful graphs, large data banks with which to put together studies in rapid time, and integrated communications between different computers that leads to improved productivity.

► There are four sizes of computers, but the smallest and least expensive, the microcomputer, is the one that readers of this book are apt to be familiar with. The **microcomputer** is also known as a personal or desktop computer.

► The microcomputer owes its existence to the **microprocessor**—microscopic processor—which is the part of the computer responsible for processing information. Also called a **silicon chip** or **integrated circuit**, a microprocessor is made of **silicon,** a nonmetallic substance found in beach rocks, which is a **semiconductor**; that is, it will conduct electric current when doped with chemical impurities. Integrated circuits are extremely reliable, compact, and inexpensive to operate because the travel time for electricity is reduced, leading to low power use.

► As to personal uses of microcomputers, it has been found that most people use their home computers principally for video games. The second most common use is a tie between business and office homework and child's learning tool. The home computer is also used for personal finances, for word processing, and for access to "information utilities," which give viewers access via telephone lines to data banks and news and financial services.

► Some executives have ignored or been intimidated by microcomputers and others view them as toys or status symbols. However, people in small business find that the microcomputer frees them from the necessity of hiring outside services for computing needs or from having to expend effort and resources on acquiring large computers and staffs to use them. People in large businesses find that microcomputers can be used to communicate with **mainframe computers** or larger computers. That is, the microcomputer can be used as a **terminal**—a device with keyboard and video display screen used to input and output information—or as a computer by itself, removing the workload from larger computers.

▶ Offices vary greatly, and the ways of handling business information are changing; however, the principal office activities in dealing with information are to create, store, retrieve, organize, summarize, communicate, and make decisions about information.

▶ Microcomputer technology can handle office information in the areas of word processors, spreadsheets and graphics, electronic filing, communications and connectivity, and electronic mail.

▶ A **word processor** is an electronic typewriter with a keyboard linked to a video display screen and a computer; the typed words appear on the screen and are stored for later printing. Word processing allows the user to rearrange words and sentences, delete, and insert, by punching a button. Word processing is the first step in office automation and can significantly boost productivity over that possible with typewriters.

▶ **Electronic spreadsheets** allow managers to manipulate projected costs more easily. Spreadsheets have been linked to the use of **graphics**—visual representations of numerical data—in order to better display results.

▶ **Electronic filing** is the technically enhanced storage and retrieval of data or information. It cuts the time needed for handling paperwork, eliminates the need for filing cabinets, and enables office information systems to link electronically with other systems, so that, for instance, files stored on a large computer can be **downloaded** or transferred to a smaller computer.

▶ A notion central to electronic filing is that of **data base.** A data base consists of several files that are cross-referenced so that an item of information can be found by looking it up in several indexes. Data bases may be internal—within a company—or external, which means they can be large public data sources called "information utilities" or specialized data banks; both make information available over the telephone to subscribers with microcomputers.

▶ A concept of office automation is **connectivity**— that technology links together or *integrates* information. When computers are connected, they can be used to communicate with each other in ways that help users improve their productivity. Two kinds of computer connections are (1) microcomputer to microcomputer, which enables users to use personal software and exchange information directly, and (2) microcomputer to mainframe computer, which enables users to gain access to data bases both inside and outside the company.

▶ **Electronic mail,** also called **electronic mail/message system (EMMS),** uses electronic means to send, store, and deliver messages. One kind is **computer message storing,** in which the message is sent to be displayed on or stored in a computer. Another kind is an **electronic mailbox,** in which the message is stored in a centralized computer "post office," which users must check periodically.

KEY TERMS

REVIEW QUESTIONS

1. What went wrong with Yanello & Flippen's strategy for success?

2. What effects, both good and bad, will the computer have on the nature of work in the near future?

3. Name various personal, business, and educational uses for the microcomputer.

4. Describe the benefits of the microcomputer to business.

5. Name the seven office activities concerned with handling business information.

6. What are the benefits of word processors? Of electronic spreadsheets? Of electronic filing and data bases?

7. What are the two types of electronic mail discussed?

CASE PROBLEMS

Case 1-1: Survival of the Yellow Pad

Suppose you have some money to invest, and you are considering buying stock in companies involved in office supplies. You have been reading about offices using less paper because of the switch to electronic equipment. You then read in the *New York Times* (itself made of paper, of course!) that despite predictions of paperless electronic offices, more yellow legal pads are being manufactured in the United States than ever before. As one writer asks, "Can a word processor draw squiggles?" You also learn that technology is generating more paper than ever: Electronic data storage makes more information available on paper for those who need it or think they need it, photocopiers make it easier to generate multiple copies, fear of power blackouts makes office workers generate backup copies of printouts. Thus, there seems to be more paper being produced. On the other hand, offices have only begun to phase in the electronic gear that could reduce traditional ways of using paper.

Your assignment: The company that makes the most legal pads is Ampad, based in Holyoke, Massachusetts. Assuming their stock is available to the public, do you think you should put your money into this company for a long-term investment? Why or why not?

Case 1-2: Tractors of the Future

Looking at electronic office technologies today, says a work and technology specialist at the Massachusetts Institute of Technology, is like having an opportunity over a century ago to say, "What do we want to do about the factory assembly line?" That is, there is an opportunity now to address issues of the effects of technology while their installation and use is in an early stage. Indeed, as others have pointed out, there have been few examples to show that people have thought through the impact of new technologies such as the automobile, the tractor, the elevator, or the superhighway, even though these have had profound effects on workers and on how the nation operates and functions.

Your assignment: What do you think microcomputers and new information technology will mean for shifting office work from cities to rural or suburban areas or even out of the country? What will such technology do for the "social office"—make work more lonely and tedious or bring people together more? Already some computers can understand simple voice commands. How would all the technologies so far discussed be changed if voice technology is expanded so that less input by keyboard is required?

Chapter 2

OVERVIEW OF BUSINESS INFORMATION SYSTEMS AND COMPUTER SYSTEMS: HOW THE TWO CAN WORK TOGETHER

How often do we operate by principles of rationality when making decisions?

Suppose you arrive at a theater where you are planning to see a play. You discover you have lost the ticket, worth $10, to see the play. Would you simply buy another ticket? No, says a Stanford University psychologist, Amos Tversky.

Now let's start over. Suppose you have not previously bought a ticket, and plan to spend $10 for one when you get to the theater. You arrive at the box office and find you have lost a $10 *bill*. Would you go ahead and spend another $10 for the ticket. Yes, says the psychologist.

There is really no monetary difference here—either way you have already lost $10. Clearly, then, psychological factors greatly influence people's decisions. Yet it is crucial that we bring some sort of rationality to decision making—in a word, we must impose some sort of *system*.

Take the matter of constructing houses and buildings. Most of us think of buildings as more or less "custom-made." But is there any reason why a building such as a post office, because of its standardized function, cannot be reduced to some standard designs? As the case on the next page shows, coupling computer systems and information systems can lead to the solution of important organizational problems.

SOME SYSTEMATIC DEFINITIONS

In this chapter we will see how information—specifically business information—as a system works. We will also see how a computer system works. We will then put the two together to see how information is enhanced with computer-based systems.

System is a common but loosely used word. Is a freeway system the same as a nervous system? Is a grading system the same as a betting system? (Some might say so.) Let us give some definitions: A

CASE STUDY: NEW WAVE IN ARCHITECTURE

Two Architects Deliver Computer-Designed Post Offices

Mᴇᴍᴘʜɪꜱ, Tenn.—All new post offices built in the United States will be based on the designs of two architects who have developed a computerized design system described as a "new wave in architecture."

Francis Mah and Martin E. Gorman Jr., both of Memphis, have developed a computerized design system that Mah says is unprecedented.

"This is revolutionary," he said. "I think it's a new wave in architecture."

U.S. Postal Service officials say the system will save $5 million during its first year and cut in half the time needed to complete each of the 200 post offices the service builds annually.

The design system, dubbed the "Kit of Parts," breaks the traditional post office building into six basic components, including the service lobby, the work room where the mail is sorted, and so on. Using a computer instead of traditional architectural drawings, Mah and Gorman designed multiple variations of each of these six parts.

"It's like basic building blocks, really," Gorman said.

These "blocks" can be manipulated and multiplied on a computer screen until a new post office has been designed that meets the needs of a specific site.

"They can develop a complete building just by using a computer," said Phil Ferrari, contracting officer with the Southern Region of the U.S. Postal Service. "We expect to be using this system as far into the future as we can see."

Mah said the basic design components allow 16,000 arrangements—and these can be expanded upon indefinitely by adding parts. "It's almost infinite. It's more than you could ever use."

Ferrari said the reasons the post office was adopting the "Kit of Parts" were very basic: "Time and money."

He said about 200 post offices are built in the country each year. Previously, each one had taken about 2½ years to complete, from design to occupation.

With the "Kit of Parts," each post office will take about a year to finish, he said. "Instead of having working drawings, we're issuing computer tapes," Mah said. Local architects simply will plug the tapes into their computers and manipulate the program until it meets their needs. . . .

Mah said the "Kit of Parts" was a "distillation of the design and building process into its simplest components.

"Birds, people, we all spin from the same building blocks. If life can be so varied and different and wonderful, and all of that grows out of a DNA block—just four amino acids—making a building should be a lot easier than that."

—John Beifuss, *The Commercial Appeal*, Memphis, TN. 9/84. Reprinted by permission.

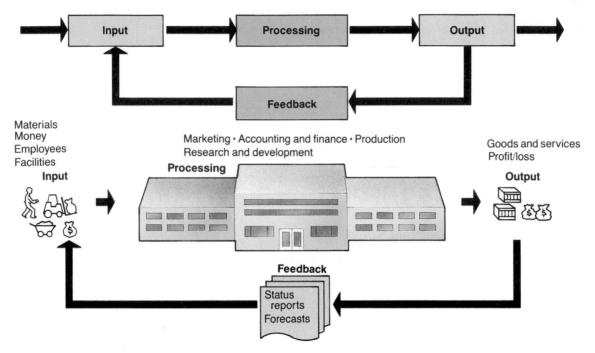

Figure 2-1.   The basis of a system.
Top: This chart, called an IPO chart
(*IPO* stands for input, processing, and
output), shows the four parts of a system as it will be understood in this
book. *Bottom:* Macro view of a firm.
The organization chart is explained
further in Figure 2-2.

system is *a collection of interrelated parts that work together for a
common purpose.* For our uses, we will consider a system with four
parts:

▶ **Inputs**—things that enter the system from the environment.
▶ The **processor**—the part that operates on the inputs to transform
them into something.
▶ **Outputs**—the products of the processing.
▶ **Feedback**—communication back to the system, either from the
environment or from within the system itself.

These four parts are shown in the upper part of Figure 2-1,
which is called an **IPO chart.** IPO stands for input, processing, and
output. (Incidentally, the term *IPO chart* is also the name given to a
particular program design form produced by IBM.)
We can see how these parts can be used to describe a number of
systems—the circulatory system of the human body, the electrical
power system of New York City, some of the ecosystems of nature—
but let us apply them here to information and computers.

WHAT A BUSINESS
INFORMATION
SYSTEM IS

All businesses have information systems of some type. In fact, *business* information systems are perhaps the single most important type of information system. Let us look at this type in more detail.

What is the purpose of a business firm? Beyond simple survival, there are two purposes: to make goods and services, and to make a profit. To achieve these purposes, of course, requires a certain amount of effort—the funds of investors, the labors of employees, and so on. As the lower part of Figure 2-1 shows, the purposes and activities of a business can be described as a system with the same four parts mentioned in the top half of the figure:

▶ *Input* is the investment in materials, money, employees, and facilities.

▶ *Processing* is the activity of converting the input—the investment and materials—into a finished product or service and selling it.

▶ *Output* consists of the goods and services that are produced and the profit or perhaps, unfortunately, the loss.

▶ *Feedback* consists of market forecasts and status reports about the products and profitability, which may suggest there should be more investment if profits are up and less investment if profits are down.

The Four Subsystems of Business

The overview of the business shown in the lower part of Figure 2-1 is a *macro* or overall view of a business system. But there is also a *micro* view, a closer examination of the business in which the system is broken down into smaller parts or *subsystems*. The important subsystems of a business—and the ones that you will see referred to throughout this book—are its four *functional* areas—namely:

▶ **Marketing**—the area concerned with sales forecasting, advertising, pricing, selling, and logistics (the movement of goods to market).

▶ **Accounting and Finance**—the area concerned with generating and investing capital (money) and with accounting operations.

▶ **Production**—the area concerned with purchasing raw materials, inventory control (**inventory** consists of physical goods on hand), and production scheduling.

▶ **Research and Development**—the area concerned with developing new products and improving existing products.

The four functional subsystems (which may be expanded—for instance, to include human resources) of a business are frequently

Systems Theory

There are all kinds of systems: biological, political, theological, mechanical, and so on. There is a system to nearly everything—to the relationship of the 52 bones in the foot, to the irrigation of a farmer's field, to the exchange of currency between nations. A system is defined as a collection of interrelated parts that work together for a common purpose. The fact that a system does not seem to be working very well does not change the fact that it is nevertheless a system.

The Makings of a System

In systems theory there are six important concepts:

1. *Inputs* are the elements that enter the system from outside it.
2. The *processor* is the part that operates on the inputs to transform them into something else.
3. *Outputs* are the products of the processing.

4. *Feedback* is communication back to the system, either from within the system or from outside it.
5. The **environment** is the world outside the system.
6. The **boundary** is the separation line between the system and the environment.

The figures on these facing pages illustrate these six concepts. Note that the input and output act as the connections—the interfaces—between the system and the environment.

Feedback is used to modify the system's operations; feedback is communication concerning the effects of the output. Depending on the kind of feedback, a system can be closed or open. Closed systems are those in which the feedback is only from within the system. Open systems are those in which feedback is from outside the system. Systems that have both internal and external feedback are classified as open systems, such as the one shown in the figure.

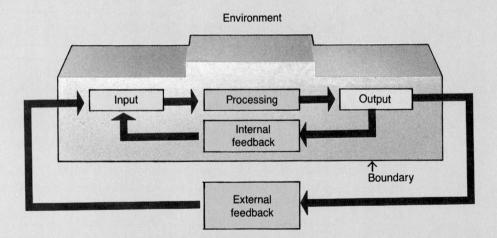

The elements of a system. *Above:* The concepts illustrated here make up the principal elements of a system: *input, processing, output, environment, boundary,* and *feedback.* A system situated in an environment can be compared to an office building in a city. Note that there are two feedback loops. The one contained within the system is an internal feedback loop. The one going through the environment outside the system is an external feedback loop. *Upper right:* System concepts can be applied to a computer system consisting of a terminal, CPU, and printer. *Lower right:* A business firm exists as a *system* in an environment of suppliers, customers, government regulators, and competitors. From the environment it draws inputs of employees, materials, facilities, and money. It produces outputs of finished goods and services for customers and, if successful, profits for itself. The processing part of the firm consists of four *subsystems* or functional departments: Marketing, Accounting and Finance, Production, and Research and Development.

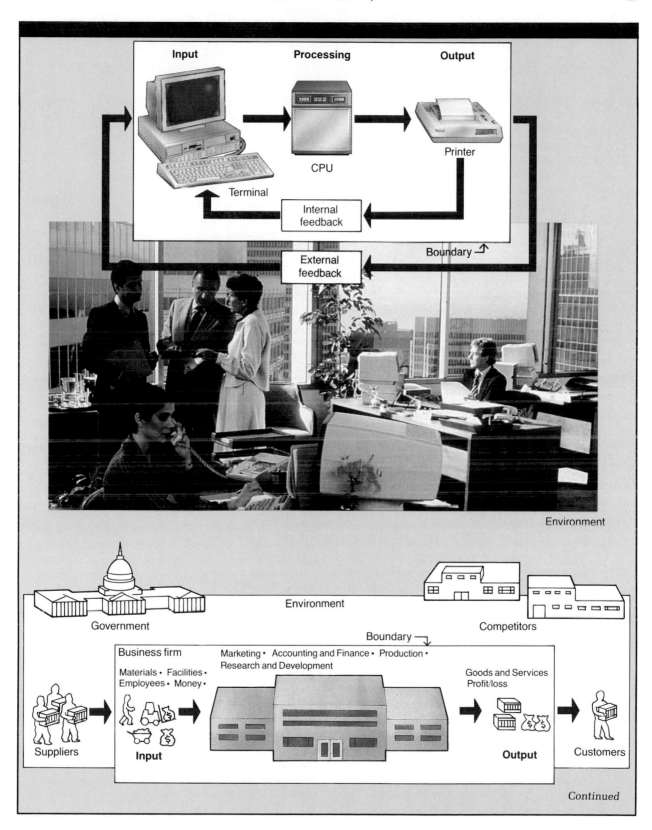

Input   Processing   Output

Terminal

CPU

Printer

Internal feedback

External feedback

Boundary

Environment

Environment

Government

Competitors

Boundary

Business firm   Marketing • Accounting and Finance • Production •
Research and Development

Materials • Facilities
Employees • Money •

Goods and Services
Profit/loss

Suppliers   **Input**

Output   Customers

Continued

Systems Theory, *Continued*

Computer Systems and Subsystems

By themselves, these abstract concepts we just described may not seem to mean much. Since we will spend a great deal of time studying computers, let us show how the concepts of a system relate to a computer.

Consider the simple computer system shown in the top of the figure on the previous page. The *input* device is a terminal. Instructions, in the form of data and programs, come from a person in the *environment* (in an office, say), outside the computer system's *boundaries.* The input unit accepts data and programs and transmits them to the central processing unit, the CPU. *Processing* of the program and data is done by the CPU to produce information. This information is transmitted to the printer, an *output* unit.

This system represents an open system because it has two feedback loops. The *external feedback* loop consists of someone looking at the information produced by the printer and, if necessary, using the terminal to make modifications in the data or the program. The *internal feedback* loop consists of the part of the software in the computer known as the operating system, which "orchestrates" the activities of the computer. For instance, after one data processing job has been completed, the operating system instructs the input device to begin handling the next job.

This computer system can also be viewed as a collection of *subsystems.* For instance, the printer is a subsystem consisting of input (information from the CPU), processing (the actual printing), output (the completed computer printout), and feedback. The feedback devices tell the printer's input unit when a report has been completely printed out. They also signal when the printer is out of paper so a human operator can refill it.

Let us extend the concept of system further. The computer system we have just described can be part of a much larger and more complex business information system. That is, the computer can be considered a *subsystem* that facilitates the flow of information throughout the *system* of the business organization.

An Organization's Information Systems

An organization, whether profit or nonprofit, does not exist by itself, of course. It, too, is part of a larger economic system, as shown in the figure on page 27. For instance, as part of the larger system, a for-profit company draws the inputs of employees, materials, facilities, and money from the outside environment. The company processes these items into outputs of goods and services to sell to customers, and it is hoped that profits are one of the outputs also. The environment in which the firm must operate includes not only suppliers and customers but also government regulators and competitors, among other things.

We can also look at the firm as being made up of several subsystems. Each subsystem consists of a *functional area,* which can be a department of a company—namely, Marketing, Accounting and Finance, Production, and Research and Development. In turn, each functional area has its own input, processing, and output.

All the subsystems or functional departments of a profit-oriented organization make up a system with two common goals: (1) to produce goods and services and (2) to produce a profit. Information from various subsystems are input to other subsystems, so that there exists an information system that ties together and coordinates the departments. Although each department has specific goals, the information system interrelates them and focuses them on the two main goals of the organization as a whole—to produce goods and services and to make a profit.

Marketing · Accounting and finance · Production · Research and development

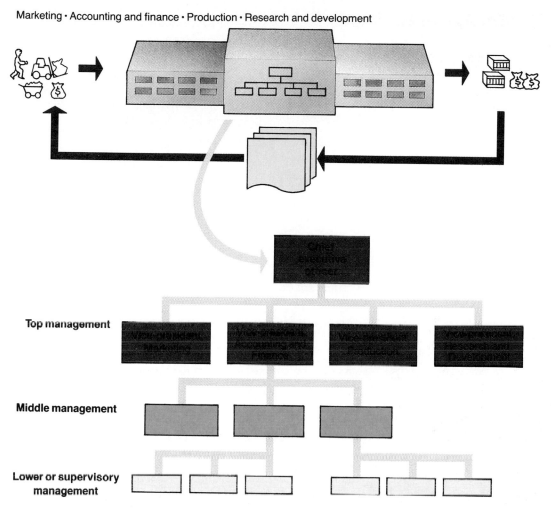

Figure 2-2. One view of a business information system. *Top:* The macro view of a firm has a functional organization chart *(bottom)* with four departments: Marketing, Accounting and Finance, Production, and Research and Development.

reflected in the firm's **organization chart,** a schematic drawing showing the hierarchy of formal relationships among employees. Figure 2-2 repeats the macro view of the firm and shows an example of its organization chart. The role of managers, of course, is to coordinate these subsystems for the common goal of producing company products and profits.

Note that there are three levels of management within each functional area: *top, middle,* and *lower* (or *supervisory*). Picture the chief executive officer (CEO, or president) of TopHealth Inc. standing in his or her office looking at the company's organization chart, which shows the CEO at the top. Now let us, in essence, take that chart down off the wall, lay it flat, and spread it out into a wheel (see the pie-shaped drawing in Figure 2-3). The CEO is now sitting at the hub of the wheel, surrounded by the four departments.

Figure 2-3. Functional area management responsibilities. Note the four departments of Marketing, Accounting and Finance, Production, and Research and Development.

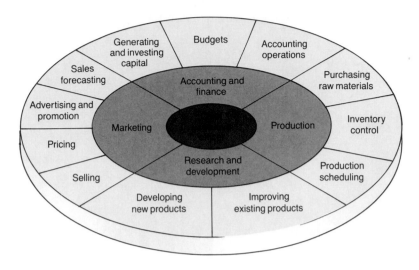

The Responsibilities of Managers

The wheel in Figure 2-3 demonstrates how the four functions of Marketing, Accounting and Finance, Production, and Research and Development must be coordinated in order for an organization to achieve its purposes.

For this coordination to happen, managers must perform their primary activity—decision making. The decision making must occur in five areas:

▶ Planning
▶ Organizing
▶ Controlling
▶ Communicating
▶ Staffing

Let's examine these five areas, considered the classic tasks of management, in greater detail.

Planning Planning, of course, is what you do to try to get yourself or your organization from your present position to an even better position. **Planning** requires that you set objectives and develop strategies and policies for achieving them. Whatever you do in planning lays the foundation for the other four management tasks.

Organizing To achieve company goals, you must organize all parts of the company in a coordinated and integrated effort. **Organizing** is the act of making orderly arrangements and structures to best use company resources.

Controlling There you are, planned and organized, but how do you accomplish the results? By **controlling,** the process by which you establish standards of performance, measure employee results, correct mistakes, and minimize deviations from the objectives. The key to control is *feedback.* Feedback enables you as a manager to head off problems before they become too severe.

Communicating **Communicating** is sharing information with other people, whether face to face or over the phone, via memo or by closed-circuit television. Communicating may be more important than any of the other four tasks: After all, if you cannot explain what you are planning and organizing for, how can you expect to accomplish results? Once again, of course, feedback is important.

Staffing **Staffing** has to do with people, of course—selecting them, training them, developing them.

With all this, we see that a business organization is a complex enterprise. It consists of four functional areas, with three levels of managers, performing five management tasks—all of which must be coordinated for the success of the whole endeavor.

How can computers assist in this effort? Before we answer that question, let us consider what a computer system is.

WHAT A COMPUTER SYSTEM IS

A computer needs four components in order to operate: hardware, software, data, and people.

▶ **Hardware** consists of the machines and electronic equipment in the system—the keyboard, the video display screen, the computer itself, and so on.

▶ **Software** consists of the programs available to run the system. A **program** is a set of step-by-step instructions that directs the computer to perform specific tasks.

▶ **Data** consists of the raw facts that have not yet been processed into information. When raw facts have been turned into *useful* facts, they are called **information.**

▶ *People* need no definition, of course, but it is people that make the other three components work. Whatever one's fears about the takeover of a machine society, the machines cannot run by themselves.

Some writers point out that *procedures* are also needed to make a computer system work, but for the moment we will limit our concern to these four components.

Input, Processing, and Output

As Figure 2-4 shows, a computer system closely resembles the system we showed in the IPO chart in Figure 2-1. That is, a computer system consists of:

▶ Input
▶ Processing (to which we add Storage)
▶ Output

Figure 2-4 shows the arrangement for a microcomputer system, but the principle is the same for larger systems. The hardware responsible for this process works as follows:

▶ **Input units** take data (such as dates, hours worked, pay rates) in machine-readable form and send it to the processing unit.
▶ **Processing** is performed by the central processing unit, or **processor,** a machine with electronic circuitry that converts input data into information. It executes the computer instructions called for by the program. The processor contains **primary storage,** which holds the data and instructions while they are being worked on by the processor. **Secondary storage** consists of devices *outside of* the processor that can store additional data. This storage *supplements* the primary storage in the processor.
▶ **Output units** make the processed data, now called information, available for use in the form of printed reports, columns of figures, pie charts or bar graphs, and so on.

Let us now get into the all-important discussion of how a computer system works. This discussion is principally about hardware; we will begin to describe software in the next several chapters. In order to understand how software is supposed to work, however, you need to understand the arrangement of hardware in a computer system. Some of the different kinds of hardware are shown in the system illustrated in Figure 2-5. We will repeat parts of this figure in the discussion that follows.

Input: Taking It All In

As Figure 2-6 shows, there are several different kinds of input devices and input **media**—the materials, such as magnetic tape, on which data are recorded. The following devices represent some of the most common ways of inputting—putting in—data to the computer system for processing.

Keyboard   Probably the most common input device, a **keyboard** consists of a typewriterlike keyboard of letters, numbers, and special

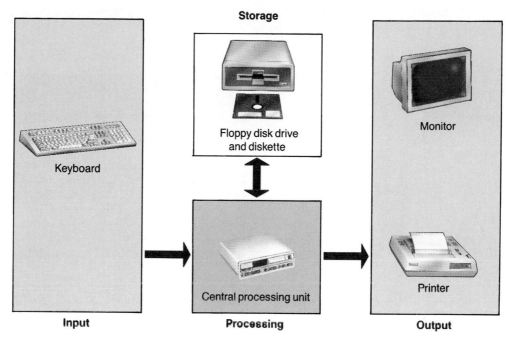

Figure 2-4. A computer system. All computer systems essentially follow the same arrangement: input, processing (including storage), and output. Shown here is the arrangement for a microcomputer system, but larger computer systems operate on the same principle.

characters; it may also have special keys peculiar to computer or word processing usage. The keyboard usually appears along with a video screen called a **display screen,** and together they are called a **terminal** or **display terminal.** Often you see these referred to as a **VDT** for **video display terminal.**

Magnetic Tape **Magnetic tape** looks like audiocassette tape, but it comes on a reel. As we shall see, magnetic tape nowadays is primarily used for making back-up (duplicate) copies of information stored on disks.

Magnetic Disk A **magnetic disk** is a round platter with a magnetized surface that stores data as electronic impulses. There are two kinds of magnetic disks: hard and flexible.

▶ **Hard disks:** A **hard disk** is made of rigid metal and coated with ferrous oxide, and it looks something like a long-playing stereo record. Hard disks may come in stacks known as **disk packs,** with space between the disks. Both top and bottom surfaces are used for recording data (except for the disks on the very top and bottom of the stack). Hard disks require **disk drives** (see Figure 2-6)— mechanical machines with a spindle in the middle on which a disk pack can be mounted and which can be rotated at very fast

Input

Processing

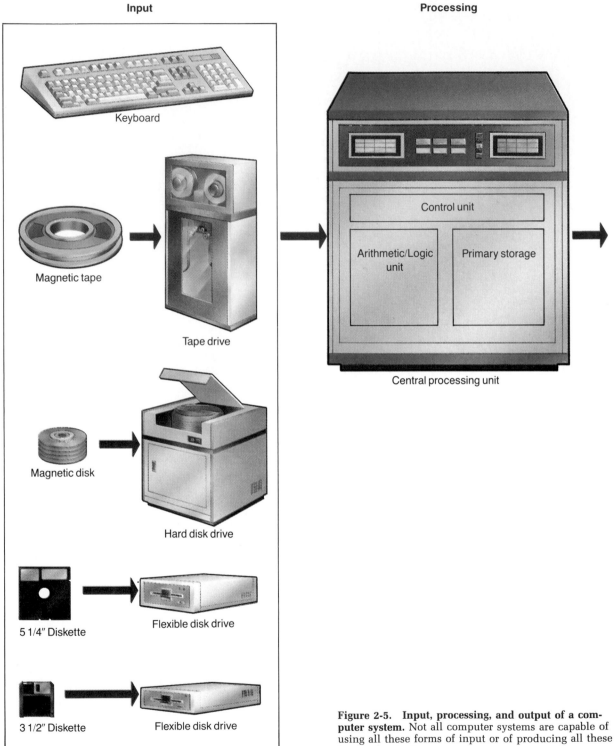

Figure 2-5. Input, processing, and output of a computer system. Not all computer systems are capable of using all these forms of input or of producing all these forms of output.

Output

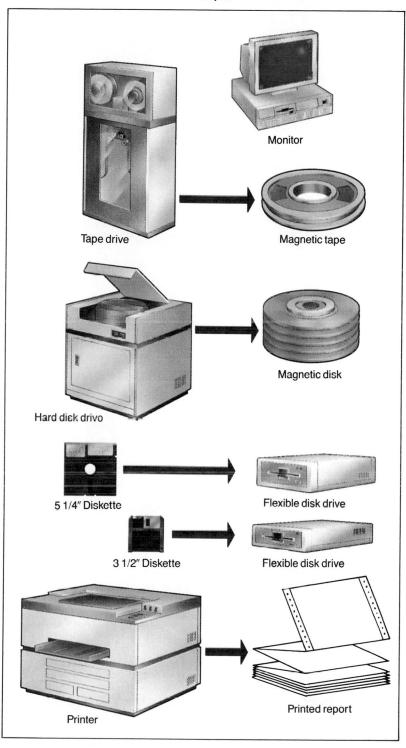

Monitor

Tape drive

Magnetic tape

Hard disk drive

Magnetic disk

5 1/4" Diskette

Flexible disk drive

3 1/2" Diskette

Flexible disk drive

Printer

Printed report

Figure 2-5, *continued.*

Figure 2-6. Input media and devices.

Input

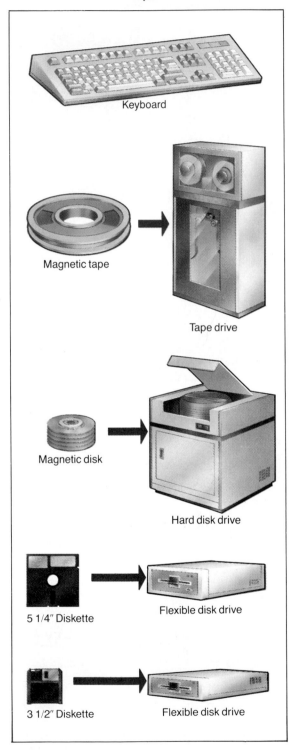

Keyboard

Magnetic tape

Tape drive

Magnetic disk

Hard disk drive

5 1/4″ Diskette

Flexible disk drive

3 1/2″ Diskette

Flexible disk drive

Figure 2-7. The central processing unit.

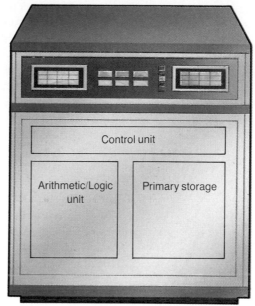

Central processing unit

speeds—to record or input data. The disk drive translates the data on the disk into electronic impulses, which are sent to the part of the computer called the central processing unit.

► **Diskettes:** A **diskette**—also known as a **flexible disk** or **floppy disk** or simply **"disk"**—is made of oxide-coated plastic material and is usually of two kinds. (1) a 5¼-inch disk that looks something like a 45 rpm phonograph record encased in a paper envelope and that is actually somewhat flexible ("floppy"), and (2) a 3½-inch disk (called a "micro-floppy") that is encased in plastic and that is not flexible. Used with microcomputers, the diskette requires a **flexible disk drive** (shown in Figure 2-6) to translate data on the disk into electronic impulses.

We will describe this array of input devices in more detail in Chapter 6.

Processing and Storage: Brains and Backup

The processor itself—the **central processing unit,** or **CPU,** which is often called the computer's "brain"—consists of three parts. As Figure 2-7 shows, these are:

► The control unit
► The arithmetic/logic unit
► Primary storage

The Control Unit   The **control unit** contains circuitry that directs the entire computer system to carry out or execute the program instructions; that is, it coordinates the other parts of the computer.

The Arithmetic/Logic Unit   The **arithmetic/logic unit** contains the electronic circuitry that performs all arithmetic operations and logical operations. **Arithmetic operations** are the four standard math operations: addition, subtraction, multiplication, and division. **Logical operations** consist of the six basic comparison operations: equal to (=), less than (<), greater than (>), not equal to (< >), less than or equal to (<=), and greater than or equal to (>=).

Primary Storage   Primary storage is referred to by a variety of names: **main memory, main storage, internal storage,** and simply **memory.** The main memory is the part of the computer that holds data and instructions for processing—at least temporarily, until you turn the computer off or someone else wants to use it for his or her programs. The capacity or size of primary storage is often expressed by the letter **K** for **kilobyte,** which represents 1,024 bytes. A **byte** represents one character (letter, number, symbol) of data. You may hear a salesperson in a computer store say that a computer has "640 K" of memory, which translates into 640 times 1,024 bytes, or 655,360 characters of memory.

Secondary Storage   Secondary storage (also called **auxiliary storage**) is found physically *outside* the processor. Secondary storage can take many forms, but three of the most common are:

▶ Magnetic tape
▶ Hard disk
▶ Diskette

The processor and secondary storage are explained in more detail in Chapters 7 and 8, respectively.

Output: The Uses of Computing

As Figure 2-8 shows, many input media and devices can be used for output:

▶ Magnetic tape
▶ Hard disk
▶ Diskette

And let us add two other common ones:

▶ The monitor
▶ The printer

Figure 2-8. Output media and devices.

Output

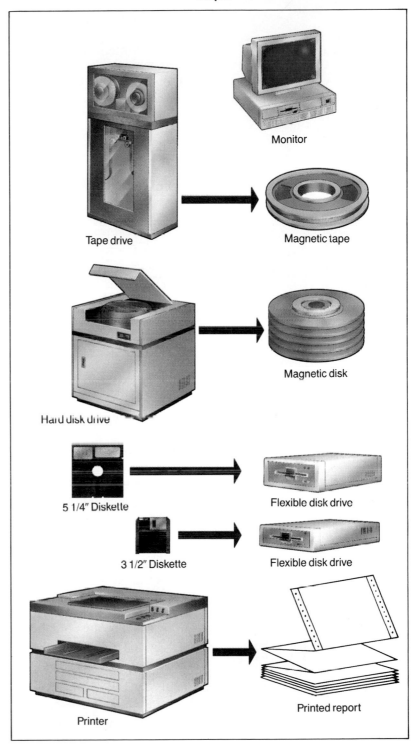

Figure 2-9.   Computer world. The four types of computers are shown on these pages: supercomputer, mainframe, minicomputer, and microcomputer.

The device that gets the most use, perhaps, is the display screen. However, the printer is a close second. **Printers** are machines that produce printed documents under the control of the program in the computer. Printers can be **impact printers,** which form images as typewriters do, striking characters against a ribbon and forming an image on paper. Or they can be **nonimpact printers,** which form images using laser beams or using specially coated papers that respond to electrostatic impulses. Some printers print a character at a time, others a line and even a page at a time.

We shall have more to say about output devices in Chapter 6.

Those Marvelous Machines: Supercomputers, Mainframes, Minis, and Micros

Usually computers are sorted into four categories, from large to small (although some people classify the first two in one category):

▶ Supercomputers
▶ Mainframes
▶ Minicomputers
▶ Microcomputers

Actually, there are also other categories: ''mini-supercomputers,'' ''super-minicomputers,'' and even ''super-microcomputers.'' However, for clarity, we will stay with the four classes above. Examples of each of the categories are shown in Figure 2-9.

These categories are traditionally based on the criteria of cost and performance. However, the classifications become fuzzier all the time as technology makes smaller machines more powerful. The IBM PS/2, for example, may be considered a microcomputer by most people, but some models in that line often outperform some older computers that are larger and more expensive.

Supercomputers   Sometimes referred to as ''monsters'' or maxicomputers, **supercomputers** are the fastest and most powerful computers. These huge machines, such as the Cray Y-MP, built by Cray Research, Inc., are used principally for very special applications—such as worldwide weather forecasting or weapons research—requiring an enormous number of calculations in a very short period of time.

Mainframes   Before the other sizes of computers were built, all data processing was done on mainframes, and thousands are in use today in large and medium-sized companies as well as in universities and government agencies. A **mainframe** is the largest, fastest, and most expensive category of general-use computers. The cost of a mainframe and supporting equipment and services can range from $250,000 to $10 million or more, and primary storage is capable of holding several million characters of information and is able to process around 5 million instructions per second. Because of their size and speed, mainframes usually must be placed on special raised floors that allow cool air to circulate up through the hardware devices.

Mainframes are useful not only because they can store an enormous amount of data—all the information on students in a university, for example, or on policy holders for a large nationwide insurance company—but also because they can support several terminals. Some hospital systems, for instance, have over 200 terminals, which are used to enter medical records into the computer as well as for other tasks.

Minicomputers The **minicomputer** resembles the mainframe but is of medium size and speed and costs considerably less—$10,000 to about $250,000. Developed in the late 1960s for special purposes, minicomputers were adopted as general-purpose machines by small businesses in much the same way that large businesses have used mainframes. Businesspeople like them because they can support several terminals and can handle most accounting functions efficiently. Some minicomputers do not require special wiring and air conditioning or an extensive support staff.

Prior to the 1970s, most organizations put their computer facilities and all related activities in one location. In other words, there was **centralized data processing.** However, in the seventies the trend was toward **decentralized** or **distributed data processing.** As business needs and computer applications increased and central computer departments became overloaded, users began to supplement their large, central mainframe computers with a number of minicomputers located in whatever branch office or area the processing was required. In the distributed data processing system, however, the minicomputers located at the remote sites are connected to the mainframe—known in this usage as the **host** computer—by communications lines such as telephone lines.

Microcomputers We covered microcomputers in Chapter 1. As we mentioned there, **microcomputers** are desktop or personal computers costing between about $200 and $10,000, depending on their size (pocket size, laptop, or desktop), the type of processor they use, and what kind of **peripheral devices** are used—that is, the kind of input and output and secondary storage devices.

Like minicomputers, micros help take the load off mainframes. Indeed, as they have become more powerful, they have shouldered more jobs previously done by minis. As an end-user, you will probably find yourself using microcomputers to gain access to the data in a mainframe (through telephone lines perhaps), then **"downloading"** it—that is, capturing it on your microcomputer's secondary storage— and finally manipulating that data any way you see fit at your own desk. With ordinary white-collar users tapping into mainframes like

---

WHAT CAN A SUPERCOMPUTER DO?

Carrying exactitude to a staggering extreme, a Japanese computer scientist has calculated the value of pi to more than 134 million decimal places. . . .

The new pi was calculated by Yasumasa Kanada of the University of Tokyo using a new Nippon Electric Corporation SX-2 supercomputer with extra memory banks. He printed out the digits, enough to paper a gymnasium, and indeed, the Japanese papered a gymnasium.

The calculation will stand as a monument of scientific trivia. The most fastidious engineer will never need more than the first few handfuls of these digits. Still, pi, the ratio of a circle's circumferance to its diameter, is the longest known and most revered of all constants of nature, and lately there has been a surprising revival of interest in the act of computing it. . . .

In the latest record-setting calculations, which take a day or so, supercomputers must manipulate gigantic numbers in their memories, multiplying 100 million digits at a time. Advances in computer science have led to much more efficient ways of handling basic multiplication than the traditional methods.

—James Gleick, *New York Times*

this, you can see why the role of the mainframe—previously accessible only through data processing specialists and experts—is being redefined in many organizations.

Computer Choices

The appearance of microcomputers in mainframe organizations has created some interesting problems. Some data processing department directors worry that chaos will result if individual managers are allowed to order any kind of micros they wish, so they have attempted to prohibit the purchase of micros altogether—a futile gesture, since microcomputers are so inexpensive that some managers have purchased them out of their own pockets. Other data processing directors have simply ignored the appearance of company-wide micros—also a mistake, since too many different makes of microcomputers may be incompatible with the company mainframe and may be difficult to maintain.

Probably the best approach is that taken by firms such as Mobil Oil, which encouraged the purchase of microcomputers, gave support and direction to employee acquisitions, and provided training programs. Other organizations have created **information centers** to help end-users become familiar with the computing and information resources available to help them. Usually staffed by computer professionals, information centers help users select equipment, learn software packages, develop custom applications, and retrieve information from the organization's mainframe.

This concludes our overview of how a business information system operates and how a computer system operates. Let us now try to put the two systems together as a *computer-based information system.*

THE COMPUTER-BASED INFORMATION SYSTEM

As we saw in Figure 2-2, the flow of information within the organization can be quite complex. Information flows across the functional areas. Sales forecasts by the Marketing department, for instance, are essential to production schedules for the Production department if people in that group are to know what kinds of priorities to assign. The flow of information must also work vertically within a functional area. For example, middle managers need status reports from supervisory personnel below them in order to coordinate their own work.

The study of how information flows and the creation of better systems of information is called **systems analysis and design.** Computer-based information systems can enhance the flow of information.

Information flows in several ways:

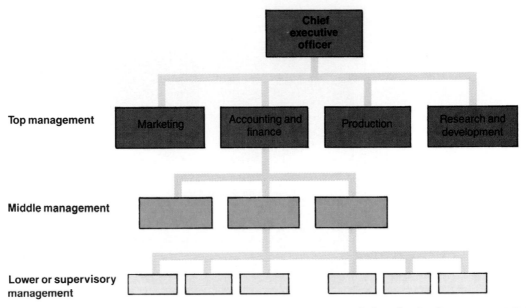

Figure 2-10. Four functional areas with three levels of management. Information flows up and down the ranks of managers as well as among the four functional areas.

▶ Information follows the IPO model, as was shown in Figure 2-1. It comes into the organization as *input* in the form of employees, materials, facilities, and money. It is *processed and stored* in the four functional areas of Marketing, Accounting and Finance, Production, and Research and Development. It is *output* as goods and services and as profit or loss.

▶ Within each of the four functional areas—Marketing, Accounting and Finance, Production, and Research and Development information flows up and down through three levels of managements: top, middle, and lower. This is shown in Figure 2-10.

▶ The managers within these three levels and four areas do the things managers are paid to do—namely, make decisions about planning, organizing, controlling, communicating, and staffing.

Now let us introduce a new concept: Within each of the three levels of management there is—or should be—some sort of *centralized business information system,* shared by managers in the four functional areas, as shown in Figure 2-11. This information system may be a collection of filing cabinets, but what we are talking about is a computerized information system. If you are a manager, what this means is that you most likely have a computer terminal on your desk so that you can make inputs to the information system and draw outputs from it in order to help you make your decisions.

There are three levels or subsystems of information systems. These correspond to the three levels of management:

Figure 2-11.   The centralized business information system. Such an information system exists for each of the three levels of management: top, middle, and lower.

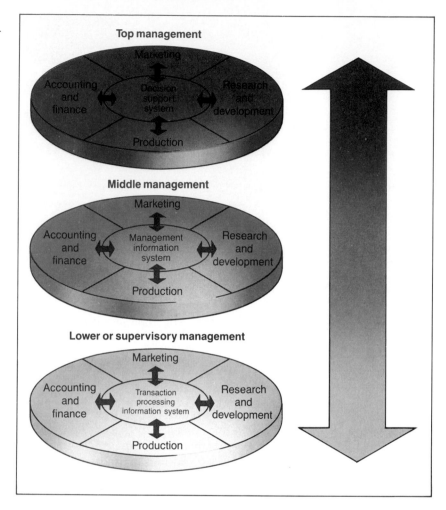

▶ For lower-level or supervisory management: transaction processing information systems

▶ For middle management: management information systems

▶ For top management: decision support systems

Some overlaps occur, but each system is intended for a particular level of manager, as Figure 2-11 shows. Moreover, each type of information system is truly different from the others, as we shall see.

The three systems are described in considerable detail later in the book; here we describe them only briefly.

Transaction Processing Information Systems

A **transaction processing information system (TPIS)**—also known as an **electronic data processing system**—is defined as a computer-based means of capturing or storing transactions so that they can be reproduced when necessary. A **transaction** is an event that is to be recorded—for example, the hiring or termination of an employee, the sale of a product, the receipt of materials for inventory, or records of client complaints.

The outputs of a transaction processing information system are:

▶ Documents needed to do business—bills (invoices), shipping orders, paychecks, mailing lists, and the like.

▶ Listings of transactions that have occurred, for confirmation or reference—such as a listing of all past due customer accounts.

▶ Electronic records for a corporate data base for later use in making decisions about a variety of applications.

A transaction processing information system is the first information system that a company develops. As mentioned, it is usually oriented toward assisting the lower-level or supervisory manager. It is concerned with the actual operation of the company, with the performance of standard operations and procedures, particularly accounting operations.

Management Information Systems

Transaction processing information systems first became popular during the 1950s. In the sixties, managers became aware of another use for the information systems concept. Not only could low-level managers avail themselves of computer-produced information to help with day-to-day problems, middle-level managers also could use the same information in summarized form as standardized reports to help them make decisions.

Management information systems (MISs) are concerned with creating standard reports that summarize transaction processing data. Typically developed by companies as the next step after they have developed transaction processing information systems, MISs are characterized by the following features:

▶ Their information is aimed at middle managers.
▶ The information is intended to generate reports.
▶ Reports are predetermined and inflexible.

Decision Support Systems

MIS reports were found to be appropriate for middle managers, but not flexible enough to support many decision-making tasks, particularly those of top-level managers, who required information in less structured form. In the 1970s, interest began to shift toward providing better information assistance to top-level managers. The result has been **decision support systems (DSSs).**

Unlike an MIS, which tends to produce standard, predetermined reports, a DSS is designed to have greater flexibility and be capable of helping managers analyze unstructured kinds of problems. Whereas transaction processing information systems are oriented toward lower-level managers and MISs toward middle-level managers, DSSs are oriented toward top-level managers. (For the record, we should mention that some people consider DSSs part of MISs.)

Some characteristics of DSSs are as follows:

▶ Information is oriented toward top managers and executive decision makers.

▶ DSSs are **interactive**—that is, they are initiated and controlled by the user.

▶ The systems emphasize flexibility, adaptability, and quick response.

Growth in software that is easy to use has greatly facilitated the use of DSSs by top-level managers.

EXPERT SYSTEMS

PICKING AN

EXPERIENCED BRAIN

One of the most exciting developments in computer-based information systems has been the new discoveries arising out of the field of **artificial intelligence (AI),** a field of study concerned with ways in which computers can simulate human intelligence, imagination, and intuition. One very promising area of AI is known as expert systems.

Expert systems are computer programs that have been developed by processing and distilling the knowledge of an expert or many experts in a particular field—for instance, geologists or bank loan officers. The expert systems themselves then become expert consultants to users. However, they can apply the experience without bias, telling us on demand what assumptions are being made and what their line of reasoning is—and can do so without becoming tired and cranky and without trying to bluff us with their opinions; indeed, they can tell us the limit of their knowledge and estimate the uncertainty of their conclusions.

Where do expert systems fit into the computer-based information systems—TPISs, MISs, and DSSs—that we just described? Whereas these are *general* information systems, expert systems are *specific approaches* or tools for solving specific problems, such as loan approval. When artificial intelligence and expert system technologies are merged into so-called **expert decision support systems,** they provide tools that assist decision makers by recommending specific actions.

THE SYSTEMS
ANALYSIS AND
DESIGN PROCESS
AN OVERVIEW

To get back to basics for a minute, we defined a system as a collection of interrelated parts that work together for a common purpose. In a computer-based information system, we said, the purpose of the system is to enhance the flow of information within the organization. As we saw, the information flow can be complex: input (as employees, materials, facilities, and money) into the organization, processed through four departments and three levels of management, and output from the organization as goods and services and profit and loss.

Now, let us ask: How are these computer-based information systems developed? And what happens if you need to change something? What if something arises either inside or outside of the organization that dictates a change in the system? Many changes have only isolated effects on a few people in an organization and will not affect the organization's computer-based information system. Other changes, however, can affect more people and will require changes in the organization's information systems. Consider the following:

▶ Consumer demands lead to new product lines—which, in turn, lead to changes in computer systems for ordering materials. For instance, a long-time maker of wheelchairs found itself playing catch-up in making lighter, more mobile chairs, which were popular with disabled young people who wanted to play tennis and basketball.

▶ New government regulations alter the business environment. Long distance networks such as Telenet and Tymnet, for instance, which rent private telephone lines and were able to provide cut-rate networking costs to computer users, had to consider the problem of what would happen if the government decided to regulate them the way it does the regional Bell telephone companies.

▶ A new data processing manager decides to introduce a new kind of word processing software within a large organization, thus making obsolete all the files that were produced on the old word processing software.

Because changes like these may affect an organization's computer-based information system, then, they must be studied with care. Fortunately, there are specific, well-defined procedures for developing information systems, evaluating the need for changes, and implementing these changes. One of the best known set of procedures is a five-step problem-solving process called the **systems life cycle,** shown in Figure 2-12, which consists of the following steps:

1. **System investigation: "What is not working right?"**—in which information needs are identified and the feasibility of meeting those needs is determined.

Figure 2-12.   The systems life cycle.
The five steps of investigation, analysis, design, implementation, and maintenance, along with their feedback loops, make up the activity of systems analysis and design.

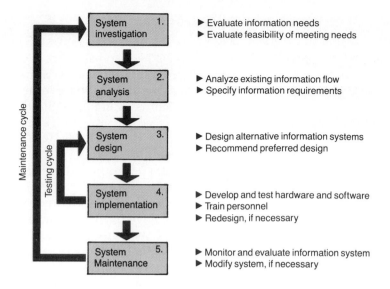

System investigation 1.	▶ Evaluate information needs ▶ Evaluate feasibility of meeting needs
System analysis 2.	▶ Analyze existing information flow ▶ Specify information requirements
System design 3.	▶ Design alternative information systems ▶ Recommend preferred design
System implementation 4.	▶ Develop and test hardware and software ▶ Train personnel ▶ Redesign, if necessary
System Maintenance 5.	▶ Monitor and evaluate information system ▶ Modify system, if necessary

Maintenance cycle

Testing cycle

The gifted amateur. An end-user, a non–computer professional, and a systems analyst, a computer professional, work together to design a computer system that will serve the user's particular needs.

2. **System analysis: "What needs to be done?"**—in which the effectiveness of the company's existing information flow is evaluated and the new information requirements are specified in detail.

3. **System design: "How should a new system work?"**—in which alternative information systems are designed and a preferred design is recommended.

4. **System implementation: "How do you get it running?"**—in which new hardware and software are developed and tested, personnel are trained, and any necessary redesign is accomplished.

5. **System maintenance: "How do you take care of it?"**—in which the information system is monitored and evaluated and, if necessary, modified.

   "All pretty abstract stuff," you may be thinking, "and how is it going to help me?" What we have presented here, however, is only the start. As we shall see, the concepts of systems and systems design and analysis are extremely valuable—and not just for computer professionals but for people like you: ordinary computer users. It is highly likely during the course of your career, in fact, that you may be called upon to work with a computer professional to help design a computer system that will do what *you* want it to do—to make your job easier.

GOING FORWARD

"Forward spin" is not a term you need to know or even one that is encountered often. An idea, product, or even information is said to have "forward spin" if it isn't useful yet but will be very soon. Perhaps "forward spin" characterizes the information you have learned in this chapter—it is not yet useful but soon will be.

Useful very soon, in fact: In the next chapter we will begin to put the computer to work for you as a serious tool.

SUMMARY

▶ In business management, as well as public administration, some sort of rationality—a system—must be imposed on the process of decision making.

▶ A system is a collection of interrelated parts that work together for a common purpose. Business systems may be enhanced by computer-based information systems.

▶ A system, for our purposes, has four parts: (1) inputs—things that enter the system from the environment; (2) a processor—the part that operates on the inputs to transform them into something; (3) outputs—the products of the processing; (4) feedback—communication back to the system. An IPO chart (input, processing, output) shows how these parts are related.

▶ Businesses have two purposes: to make goods and services and to make a profit. These purposes are served by activities that correspond to the four parts of a system: (1) Input is the investment in employees, materials, facilities, and money. (2) Processing converts the input into a finished product or service and sells it. (3) Output is the goods and services produced plus the profit or loss. (4) Feedback consists of market forecasts and status reports.

▶ The four parts of the system constitute the macro view. The micro view reveals smaller parts, or subsystems. The important subsystems of a business are its four functional areas: (1) Accounting and Finance—concerned with generating and investing capital (money) and with accounting operations; (2) Marketing—concerned with sales forecasting, advertising, pricing, selling, and logistics; (3) Production—concerned with purchasing raw materials, inventory control, and production scheduling; (4) Research and Development—concerned with improving products and developing new ones.

▶ The four functional subsystems of a business are frequently reflected in an organization chart—a drawing depicting the formal lines of authority within an organization.

▶ The three levels of management within each functional area are (1) top, (2) middle, and (3) lower, or supervisory.

▶ The role of managers is to coordinate the subsystems to produce company products and profits. Decision making is the primary activity of managers, and it occurs in five areas: (1) planning, (2) organizing, (3) controlling, (4) communication, and (5) staffing.

▶ Planning attempts to get the organization from its present position to a better one; it requires setting objectives and developing strategies and policies for achieving them. Planning lays the foundation for the other four management tasks.

▶ Organizing coordinates and integrates all the parts and efforts of the company; it is the act of making orderly arrangements and structures to best use company resources.

▶ Controlling establishes standards of performance, measures employee results, corrects mistakes, and minimizes deviations from the objectives. The key to control is feedback, which enables managers to head off problems before they become severe.

▶ Communicating is sharing information with other people by any means. Communicating may be more important than any of the other four management tasks.

▶ Staffing involves selecting people and training and developing them for their jobs.

▶ The four parts of a computer system are (1) hardware—the machines in the system, such as the keyboard, the video screen, and so on; (2) **software**—the **programs** (step-by-step instructions that direct the computer to perform specific tasks) that run the system; (3) **data**—the raw facts that have not yet been processed into information (raw facts turned into useful facts are called **information**); and (4) people, to make the system work.

▶ A computer system resembles the IPO chart in that it also involves input, processing, and output. The hardware components of this system are (1) **input units,** which take data in machine-readable form and send it for **processing** to the (2) processor, the central processing unit, a machine with electronic circuitry that converts input data into information and then sends it to (3) **output units,** which make the information available for use.

▶ Processors contain **primary storage,** which holds data and instructions while they are being worked on by the processor, and **secondary storage,** which consists of devices outside the processor that can store additional data. This storage supplements the primary storage.

▶ Some of the common input devices and input **media** are the keyboard, magnetic tape, and magnetic disks, both hard disk and flexible disk.

▶ The **keyboard,** probably the most common input device, is a typewriterlike keyboard of letters, numbers, special characters, and usually some specialized keys. The keyboard usually is connected to a **display screen,** and together they are called a **terminal** or **display terminal.** Often these are called a **video display terminal (VDT).**

▶ **Magnetic tape** looks like audiocassette tape, but it comes on a reel.

▶ **Magnetic disk** is a round platter with a magnetized surface. It may be hard or flexible.

▶ A **hard disk** is made of rigid metal and coated with ferrous oxide. Hard disks generally come in stacks called **disk packs,** with space between the disks. Hard disks require **disk drives**—machines with a spindle in the middle on which a disk pack can be mounted and rotated at very high speed—are required to record or input data to the central processing unit.

▶ **Flexible disks,** which are also known as **diskettes, floppy disks,** or just **disks** are made of oxide-coated plastic and are used with microcomputers. They require a **flexible disk drive** to translate data on the disk into electronic impulses, which are sent to the central processing unit.

▶ The processor—the **central processing unit,** or **CPU,** often called the computer's "brain"—has three parts: (1) the control unit, (2) the arithmetic/logic unit, and (3) primary storage.

▶ The **control unit** contains circuitry that directs the entire computer system to carry out, or execute, the program instructions.

▶ The **arithmetic/logic unit** contains the electronic circuitry that controls all **arithmetic operations** (addition, subtraction, multiplication, division) and **logical operations** (the six basic comparison operations of =, <, >, <>, <=, and >=).

▶ Primary storage is referred to by a variety of names: **main memory, main storage, internal storage,** and simply **memory.** The main memory holds data and instructions for processing. Its capacity is often expressed by the letter **K** for **kilobyte,** which represents 1,024 bytes. A **byte** represents one character of data.

▶ Secondary storage, or **auxiliary storage,** is outside the processor. The three most common forms of secondary storage are (1) magnetic tape, (2) hard disk, and (3) flexible disk.

▶ For output, one can use magnetic tape, hard disks, flexible disks, display screens, and printers. **Printers** produce printed documents under the control of the computer program. Printers can be **impact printers,** which form images as typewriters do, or they can be **nonimpact printers,** which form images using specially coated papers that respond to electrostatic impulses. Some printers print a character at a time, others a line at a time.

▶ There are four categories of computers, in order from large to small: (1) supercomputers, (2) mainframes, (3) minicomputers, and (4) microcomputers.

▶ **Supercomputers,** also called "monsters" or "maxicomputers," are the fastest and most powerful computers. They are principally used for worldwide weather forecasting, weapons research, and other very special applications requiring an enormous number of calculations in a short time.

▶ **Mainframes,** built before the other computers, are the largest, fastest, and most expensive general-purpose computers. Primary storage can hold several million characters of information and process around 5 million instructions per second. Mainframes are useful because they can store an enormous amount of data and because they have numerous terminals.

▶ **Minicomputers** resemble mainframes but are of medium size and speed and cost less. Minicomputers were developed in the late 1960s for special purposes but were later adopted as general-purpose machines by small businesses. They can support several terminals and handle most accounting functions.

▶ Before the 1970s, most organizations put their computer facilities and related activities in one location for **centralized data processing.** In the 1970s, the trend was toward **decentralized** or **distributed data processing:** Users began to supplement their large, central mainframe computers with a number of minicomputers located in branch offices or other data processing areas. The minicomputers link up to the mainframe, or the **host** computer, by communications lines such as telephone lines.

▶ **Microcomputers** are desktop or personal computers. Their cost varies depending in part on the kind of **peripheral devices** used—the input–output and secondary storage devices.

▶ Microcomputers can be used to **download** data from mainframes; that is, microcomputers can use telephone lines to capture data in their secondary storage.

▶ Although the mainframe continues to be the mainstay of computing power for large businesses, the microcomputer is having a significant effect on business and is presenting various problems that require well-planned purchasing and training programs to solve. Some organizations have created **information centers** to help end users become familiar with the computing and information resources available to them; these information centers are staffed by computer professionals.

▶ The study of how information flows and the creation of better systems of information flow is called **systems analysis and design.** Information flows in several ways: (1) It follows the IPO model in that it comes into the organization as *input* in the form of employees, materials, facilities, and money; it is *processed and stored* in the four functional areas— Marketing, Accounting and Finance, Production, and Research and Development. It is *output* as goods and services and as profit or loss. (2) Within each of the four functional areas, it flows up and down through three levels of managements: top, middle, and lower. (3) People within the three management levels and four functional areas make decisions about planning, organizing, controlling, communicating, and staffing.

▶ Each of the three management levels should have a centralized business information system, shared by managers in the four functional areas. Three levels of information systems correspond to the three levels of management: (1) for lower-level or supervisory management, transaction processing information systems (TPISs); (2) for middle management, management information systems (MISs); (3) for top management, decision support systems (DSSs).

▶ **Transaction processing information systems (TPISs)**—which are also known as **electronic data processing systems** and which became popular during the 1950s—are computer-based means of capturing **transactions** (events to be recorded) to be reproduced when necessary. The outputs of a transaction processing information system are (1) documents needed to do business, (2) listings of transactions that have occurred, and (3) electronic records for a corporate data base for later decision making.

▶ A transaction processing information system is the first information system that a company develops. It concerns the actual operation of the company— standard operations and procedures, particularly accounting operations.

▶ **Management information systems (MISs),** which were developed during the 1960s, create standard reports that summarize transaction processing data. They are typically developed after transaction processing information systems and have the following characteristics: (1) Their information is aimed at middle managers. (2) The information is intended to generate reports. (3) Reports are predetermined and inflexible.

▶ **Decision support systems (DSSs)** were developed in the 1970s to assist top-level managers. These systems have greater flexibility and can help analyze unstructured kinds of problems. Some DSS characteristics are as follows: (1) Information is oriented toward top managers and executive decision makers. (2) They are **interactive** (initiated and controlled by the user). (3) They emphasize flexibility, adaptability, and quick response. (4) They accommodate the personal decision-making styles of individual managers.

▶ **Artificial intelligence (AI)** is a field of study concerned with ways in which computers can simulate human intelligence, imagination, and intuition. An offshoot of AI is known as expert systems.

▶ **Expert systems** consist of computer-based information systems that have been developed by processing and distilling the knowledge of experts in a field. Expert systems are specific approaches or tools for solving problems, unlike the general information systems of TPIS, MIS, and DSS.

▶ **Expert decision support systems** use expert system technologies to assist decision makers by recommending specific actions.

▶ Computer-based information systems are developed or are modified by a five-step problem-solving process called the **systems life cycle.** The five steps are: (1) system investigation, in which information needs are identified and the feasibility of meeting those needs is determined; (2) system analysis, in which the effectiveness of the company's existing information flow is evaluated and new information requirements are specified; (3) system design, in which alternative information systems are designed and a preferred design is recommended; (4) system implementation, in which new hardware and software are developed and tested and personnel are trained; (5) system maintenance, in which the information system is monitored and evaluated and if necessary modified.

KEY TERMS

Accounting and Finance, p. 25

Arithmetic/logic unit, p. 38

Arithmetic operations, p. 38

Artificial intelligence (AI), p. 46

Auxiliary storage, p. 38

Byte, p. 38

Central processing unit (CPU), p. 37

Centralized data processing, p. 41

Communicating, p. 31

Controlling, p. 31

Control unit, p. 38

Data, p. 31

Decentralized data processing, p. 41

Decision support system (DSS), p. 45

Disk, p. 37

Disk drive, p. 32

Disk pack, p. 32

Diskette, p. 37

Display screen, p. 32

Display terminal, p. 32

Distributed data processing, p. 41

Download, p. 41

Electronic data processing system, p. 44

Expert system, p. 46

Expert decision support system, p. 46

Feedback, p. 24

Flexible disk, p. 37

Flexible disk drive, p. 37

Floppy disk , p. 37

Hard disk, p. 32

Hardware, p. 31

Host, p. 41

Impact printer, p. 40

Information, p. 31

Information center, p. 42

Inputs, p. 24

Input unit, p. 32

Interactive, p. 46

Internal storage, p. 38

IPO chart, p. 24

Keyboard, p. 32

Kilobyte (K), p. 38

Logical operations, p. 38

Magnetic disk, p. 32

Magnetic tape, p. 32

Main memory, p. 38

Main storage, p. 38

Mainframe, p. 40

Management information system (MIS), p. 45

Marketing, p. 25

Media, p. 32

Memory, p. 38

Microcomputer, p. 41

Minicomputer, p. 41

Nonimpact printer, p. 40

Organization chart, p. 29

Organizing, p. 30

Output unit, p. 32

Outputs, p. 24

Peripheral device, p. 41

Planning, p. 30

Primary storage, p. 32

Printer, p. 40

Processing, p. 32

REVIEW QUESTIONS

1. Define *system*. Describe the parts of a system. How can a business be described as a system?

2. What are the four subsystems of business?

3. Name the five areas of decision making that are the concern of managers.

4. Discuss the four components that a computer needs in order to operate.

5. What are the four categories of computers? Compare them.

6. Describe the flow of information within a computer-based information system. What are the three kinds of computer-based information systems and to which levels of management do they correspond?

7. Describe the five steps of systems analysis and design—the systems life cycle.

CASE PROBLEMS

Case 2-1: Careers in the Information Industry

As Chapters 1 and 2 make clear, organizations are undergoing a great deal of transition. This is sure to be reflected in the jobs of the future. Washington, D.C. psychologist S. Norman Feingold points out, for example, that 28% of the work force in the United States was in manufacturing in 1980, but in the year 2000 it will probably be only 11% and in the year 2030 only 3%. Today, he says, 55% of the workers in the United States are in the information industries, and by the end of the century it will probably be 80%. Some of the emerging career areas in the information industry are: operation of information systems—abstractors, indexers, biographic searchers, information brokers; management of information systems—supervisors of facilities that organize knowledge of a specific subject area; design of information systems—programmers who write or modify programs to solve information problems; research and teaching—computational linguists, information scientists, teachers of information science; and consulting or selling of information. "Information is a limitless resource," says Feingold. "Unlike finite industrial resources such as oil, ore, and iron, there is an inexhaustible supply of knowledge, concepts, and ideas as people gain further education."

Your assignment: Based on your reading so far, what possible emerging career areas in the information industry or business information processing can you determine that might be of interest to you? Your opinion may be guided by what Feingold has called the following characteristics of an emerging career. An emerging career is one that:

▶ Has become increasingly visible as a separate career area in recent years.

▶ Has developed from preexisting career areas, such as medical care and personal or business services.

▶ Has become possible because of advances in technology or actual physical changes in our environment.

▶ Shows growth in numbers of people employed or attending emerging education and training programs.

▶ Requires skills and training.

▶ Does not appear and then disappear in a short period of time.

Case 2-2: What If Computers Are *Not* Productive?

After the buildup we have made for the case that computers are terrific in raising productivity, what if you then came across an article (true) in *Fortune* magazine headed "The Puny Payoff from Office Computers"? And then suppose a bit later you saw another article, this time in *Computerworld*, titled "Study Finds PCs [Personal Computers] Not Fully Utilized." What's going on here? According to the first story, U.S. businesses have spent billions of dollars on computers, but a study by an economist in the investment banking house of Morgan Stanley found that "white-collar productivity—output per worker hour—stands just about where it was in the late 1960s." In the second article, you read that a study by the firm Touche Ross & Co. surveyed 526 companies and found that "Small business has heartily embraced microcomputers but may not be using them effectively."

Your assignment: Do a study yourself (or pretend you will) of an office with which you are familiar that has one or more microcomputers. Determine if microcomputers are being used effectively or not—and if not, why not. Below are some of the reasons computers have not been as productive as hoped. Rephrase these as questions for your survey and then add some possibilities of your own.

▶ People try to teach themselves on microcomputers because the machines are so inexpensive that companies do not want to pay consultants' fees or tuition for courses.

▶ New users are so elated at the few tasks they are able to teach themselves that they do not explore beyond the functions that they can learn without formal instruction.

▶ Computers are underused; many personal computers bought during the "PC boom" of earlier years sit idle much of the time.

▶ Computers are used in ways that partly wipe out their efficiencies. For instance, electronic mail produces a lot of "electronic junk mail," such as trivial messages to people who do not need to receive them.

▶ Word processing, because of the ease of revision, brings out perfectionism, such as additional drafts being made even when they are not really necessary.

▶ Computers are used for applications with low payoffs—that is, for trying to make people's present jobs more efficient rather than changing the way work is done.

PART 2

THE USES OF SOFTWARE

Where are you now? Where do you want to be? How do you want to get there? These are the questions managers and professionals continually ask.

As we stated earlier, the principal business of your career will be managing change—and when dealing with computerized information systems, software is the principal means of handling the problems of change. Want to put out a report in a hurry, get comments on it from several departments, and rewrite it in time to get it out by overnight express tomorrow? Word processing can cut the time by hours or even days. Want to figure out different possibilities for pricing a product, opening a store, or hiring new staff? You can easily project different alternatives using so-called electronic spreadsheets, as we shall describe. We are rapidly reaching the era of the "easy computer," with software that makes computing truly, in that hackneyed term of the computer industry, "user-friendly."

It is in your interest to get up and running on computers as soon as possible. In the next three chapters, we show you how, beginning with ready made software we think you'll find of particular value in the job market, then describing application software development, and the programming uses you will probably need to know about in your future career. Although the chances are you will not become a computer professional, knowing how software works and is developed will help you make intelligent buying decisions and be a more effective user of computers.

Chapter 3

PERSONAL SOFTWARE YOU CAN USE: WORD PROCESSING, SPREADSHEETS, DATA BASE, GRAPHICS, COMMUNICATIONS, INTEGRATED AND OTHER PACKAGES

Ultimately, probably, there is no completely escaping boredom. A certain amount of tedium is simply built in to the process of being alive. No doubt this partly explains why people take risks in mountain climbing and sky diving. It—and the quest for profits—also partly explains why the entrepreneurial spirit is alive and well: People not only seek fortune and fame, they seek adventure, stimulation, and relief from boredom.

But what is more boring than doing work over or doing work that is not useful because of management inefficiencies? Computers may not necessarily make work more interesting—although in many cases they can indeed do that. However, as the case study on the next page makes clear, computers and software can take a lot of the waste and inefficiency out of work—and thus some of the boredom.

THE SOFTWARE EXPLOSION

Computers have been around for over 30 years, becoming more powerful on the one hand and smaller and more accessible on the other. Yet for most of their history, computers have remained the province of specialists in corporate data processing departments. Why is it that only in recent years have we begun to see computers on general managers' desks? The answer is *software*. The software that makes computers genuinely useful and accessible to nearly everyone has

CASE STUDY: KEEPING HUMAN-SERVICE ORGANIZATIONS RUNNING

The Business of Helping Others

Government agencies are under great pressure to reduce costs for human services, whether health care, rehabilitation programs for juvenile offenders, job training, or whatever. Many nonprofits are also struggling with diminished sources of philanthropy. Thus, it is critical that human-service organizations, whether nonprofit or for-profit, operate on sound business principles. Consider the following hypothetical organization.

The Children's Place of Duluth, Minnesota, is a nonprofit institution that counsels juvenile runaways and places children in foster homes. Feeling the squeeze between rising costs and declining donations, the director and staff realize they must change their way of operating.

As a first step, the chief bookkeeper, Joan Holland, recommends that The Children's Place stop using an outside computer firm for handling the accounting services and other recordkeeping. Instead, she advises they buy a microcomputer—perhaps an IBM PS/2 model 50—and some popular software. "That outside firm is costing us more than they're worth," she says. "We can do the work more cheaply ourselves. Also, we'll have a computer available for other purposes."

There is some discussion as to which software to get. The director, Jim Winthrop, is in favor of acquiring three well-known applications programs: a word processing program, WordPerfect; a spreadsheet-and-graphing program, Lotus 1-2-3; and a data base manager, dBase III Plus. "These are the most popular programs in their fields," Winthrop says. "We can't go wrong getting those."

Holland argues otherwise. "We do a lot of crossover work," she says. "We write letters to people soliciting donations, for example, but then we keep track of who donates, how much, and when for follow-up and tax purposes. We need programs that will work together to exchange information back and forth."

Finally, therefore, The Children's Place purchases an integrated software package, Symphony, which combines not only word processing, spreadsheet, and database programs, but also graphics and communications capabilities—all of which easily trade information with each other. However, because most staff members have had little direct contact with microcomputers, and some are somewhat intimidated by the machines, an outside expert is brought in to run a two-day training program.

In the next few weeks, the data base program is used like an electronic index-card filing system. Different files are set up to record the names and addresses of donors, prospective donors, members of the board of trustees, foster families, and others. The word processing program is used to write letters soliciting contributions—actually, it is an identically worded letter, but with different names and salutations. When contributions are received, the word processor is used to send a note of thanks.

The electronic spreadsheet, a worksheet that allows one to express and project financial data, is used to record sources of contributions and types of expenditures. These records may also be expressed in graph or pictorial form, so that members of the board can instantly grasp the financial picture.

The communications program is used, along with the microcomputer and a special telephone hookup, to gain access to large databanks that list organizations and foundations that contribute money to nonprofit human-services programs.

"In the beginning, the staff was quite nervous about using the microcomputer system," director Winthrop reports to board members six months later. "Now, however, they are completely comfortable with it and are so productive they wonder how they ever got along without it."

Figure 3-1. Ten top-selling software programs. The Top 10 may vary from year to year, although some oldies such as dBase III and 1-2-3 seem to appear on most lists. This list is based on units shipped. (*Source:* IMS America, Ltd.)

10 Top-Selling Software Programs

1. 1-2-3—Lotus Development Corp.
2. PageMaker—Aldus Corp.
3. dBase III Plus—Ashton-Tate
4. Symphony—Lotus Development Corp.
5. DisplayWrite IV—IBM
6. Word—Microsoft Corp.
7. WordPerfect—WordPerfect Corp.
8. AppleWorks—Apple Computer, Inc.
9. Excel—Microsoft Corp.
10. Works—Microsoft Corp.

been a fairly recent development, having made its appearance soon after that of the personal computer.

But what a development! There has been a veritable explosion in software use. Some microcomputer trade magazines now and then list the business software blockbusters—somewhat like the top 40 hits in the record industry. The best sellers are intended for general business applications: word processing, filing and manipulating data, financial modeling, and accounting. Among some of the best known are the word processing programs WordPerfect, Microsoft Word, and WordStar; the spreadsheets Lotus 1-2-3 and SuperCalc 4; the database managers dBase III Plus and R:base 5000; and the integrated packages Symphony and Framework. A list of the top business programs for a recent year is shown in Figure 3-1.

Software is developed by three different sources:

▶ **Internal programmers,** people employed by companies to do such tasks as developing payroll programs. The demand for experienced programmers is high and is expected to continue—especially for maintaining existing large programs.

▶ **Software consultants,** also known as third-party suppliers—freelancers or employees of consulting firms who can bring a corporate client certain types of expertise or offer temporary personnel who can bring solutions to the client's programming problems (and who do not cost the client in fringe benefits).

▶ **Packaged software manufacturers,** companies that develop programs in accounting, payroll, inventory management, and the like, that are not tailored to the requirements of any particular client but are available "off the shelf" for anyone to use. Examples of such developers—often called "publishers"—of software for microcomputers are Lotus, publisher of 1-2-3; Ashton-Tate, developer of dBase; and Microsoft, which produced Word and Windows.

Figure 3-2. Major applications of business software. Word processing is the leading application used in business. (*Source:* Future Computing/Data Pro.)

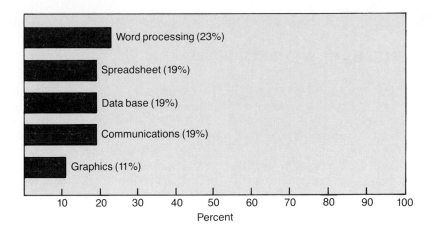

The software packages are the ones making up the best-seller lists mentioned above. Their advantage over internally developed and third-party developed software is that they are generally widely tested and are mass-produced; thus, they are relatively inexpensive. However, their flexibility is limited, and modifications can be costly if not impossible.

For the manager, however, packaged software is not merely the wave of the future; indeed, the wave has already washed well up on the beach. As Figure 3-2 demonstrates, sales have jumped several-fold in recent years. The most important applications in business are word processing and spreadsheets—about 2 million packages of each were sold in 1986, according to Dataquest. **Integrated packages**—a collection of programs that work together to accomplish specific objectives, such as Lotus 1-2-3—went from 34,000 packages shipped in 1984 to more than 750,000 in 1986. Clearly, packaged software is being used increasingly in a variety of businesses. This means that it will be more important for you to learn how to use packaged software than even how to do programming.

Let us, then, take a look at those software packages you will probably find useful in your college and professional careers to create documents, analyze data, and file information. You may also find some of these useful for your personal needs on a home computer. We will examine six kinds of software:

▶ Word processing
▶ Spreadsheet
▶ File management/data base
▶ Graphics
▶ Communications
▶ Integrated

END-USER GETS SUPPORT

The customer *is* always right, right? Too often, however, a customer gets lip service rather than true service.

To manufacturers of microcomputer software, customers are known as "end-users," or simply "users," and many such users have been highly dissatisfied with the kind of support—that is, service—they have received from software and hardware makers. However, it is not just the manufacturers' fault; quite often it is the client company's fault.

J. Daniel Couger, professor of computer and management science at the University of Colorado in Colorado Springs, reports in *Computerworld* (May 25, 1987) that a study of 17 software-buying companies found that some realized only a 2-to-1 return on their investment in micro hardware and software whereas others realized returns of 6-to-1—millions of dollars difference.

"In the 11 problematic firms," he writes, "there was a proliferation of micros and micro software, which were installed by inexperienced people—the users. The principal problem was lack of adequate planning for end-user computing. Had the firms standardized on micro hardware and software, train-

ing could have been more consistent, the learning curve simplified and downtime reduced."

Progressive firms have learned that internal support for end-users is important. Examples of such support, according to Couger, are:

▶ Providing maintenance for only certain types of microcomputers, which thus encourages end-users to acquire only those types.

▶ Providing centralized purchasing in order to obtain quantity discounts for micros and micro software, and limiting the number of micros available, in order to ensure that they are compatible.

▶ Providing training on only certain types of software, motivating users to confine their activities to just those types.

▶ Providing software that shares files so that when users develop data it can be shared with others.

▶ Providing a central agency to obtain new versions or releases of software, then implementing them for all interested users, thus reducing problems of incompatibility and inconsistency.

WORD PROCESSING

CREATING, STORING,

AND RETRIEVING TEXT

Without a word processor, you cannot imagine that you need one. With one, you cannot imagine doing without it. A word processor is so much better than a typewriter because:

▶ It is far, far easier to make corrections: deleting, inserting, and replacing—the principal correcting activities—can be done electronically, just by pressing keys on the keyboard.

▶ Spelling can be checked automatically, by running your text through a "spelling-checker" program.

▶ "Thesaurus" programs enable you to quickly find the right word or alternative word.

▶ A variety of type styles (fonts) enables you to put out better-looking documents.

▶ A feature known as "mail-merge" allows you to send out form letters with ease—the same letter to different people.

DESKTOP PUBLISHING

Be Your own Publisher

What if you are an unpublished writer with something to say, but you have been unable (or unwilling to take the time) to interest a book publisher in your manuscript? The answer is: Use a microcomputer such as an IBM microcomputer or Macintosh, some "desktop publishing" software such as PageMaker or Ventura Publisher, and a laser printer to put together your own publication, then market and distribute it yourself.

Desktop publishing—also known as *electronic publishing* and sometimes *corporate electronic publishing*—is essentially a marriage of the microcomputer and printing. How does it differ from word processing? It differs mainly in that it enables you to incorporate text *and* graphics on the same page in creative fashion: You can take graphics from a separate file and, in effect, "pour" them onto a page of text.

Professional phototypesetting systems or graphic workstations can also do this, but there are some important differences:

Desktop publishing. Example of PageMaker screen.

► Professional systems can cost up to a million dollars, depending on their capabilities, compared to around $10,000 for a desktop publishing system (including computer, printer, and software). Desktop publishing software ranges up to about $1,000.

► The quality is not at all the same—a phototypesetter may have a resolution (number of dots per inch used to reproduce the image) of 2,500 dots per inch, whereas a laser printer has 300 dots per inch.

► Desktop publishing software does not mix graphics and text as easily—they are usually on two different files. As Lloyd Rieber in *Printing Journal* (September 1987) put it, "You cannot change words that exist on the graphics without going back to the graphics file, fixing the words, then re-pouring the entire graphic back into the page."

Still, there are many uses that do not require expensive, high-quality equipment. Desktop publishing is suitable for such applications as brochures, catalogs, newsletters, menus, posters, letterheads, advertisements, and forms and graphs—and some people are, as we mentioned, using it for books, at least those that do not require high-quality artwork.

Besides a microcomputer with keyboard and (preferably) a laser printer, a desktop publishing setup requires: software for formatting and laying out text and graphics, a graphics terminal, and a mouse.

► It is easier to change the format of the document—margins, headings, spacing, and so on—since it is done electronically.

As we saw in Chapter 1, a **word processor** includes the following basic components: a computer, a keyboard, a display screen, a printer, and a word processing program. Some word processors also have a **mouse,** a device that you roll on a table top to move a **cursor,**

THE MOUSE THAT ROLLED

In using a computer, it helps to know how to type, since most *data*—the words in your report or numbers in your spreadsheet, for example—are entered through the keys on a keyboard. In addition, most *commands* are entered through the keyboard. However, with the right kind of computer, a great many commands can be entered using a marvelous device called a mouse.

    We are not talking about biotechnology here. The mouse is not a rodent but a small, movable, hand-held device that can be rolled on a table or desk top and in turn will manipulate a graphic pointer on the display screen. The pointer can be used to activate commands such as "Delete" or "Save" without one's having to use the keyboard. The mouse can also be used to go directly to the place on the screen where you wish to insert a word or other data.

    Why do people call it a mouse? When it was first

A mouse.

invented in the 1960s, it had three protruding control buttons that looked like mouse ears and a connecting cable to the computer that looked like a mouse tail. Now, with Apple's Macintosh personal computer, for example, the mouse has one button.

    The main benefit of a mouse is that it frees users from the constraints of the keyboard; they need not memorize or look up a lot of keyboard command codes in order to do their work. This allows them to concentrate on what's happening on the screen.

or pointer, on the display screen. A word processor can be a machine that does nothing else (a dedicated word processor). Or it can be a computer—typically a microcomputer—that can do word processing in addition to other tasks.

    Word processing software is designed to allow the creation, editing, formatting, storing, and printing of text. In the beginning, there were numerous commercial word processing systems in which computer hardware and software were bundled together as a unit, such as the IBM DisplayWriter, the Wang Wangwriter, and the DEC Decmate. Many of these are still in use, although IBM's discontinuation of the DisplayWriter in 1986 may mark the end of an era in office equipment, with personal computers replacing these specialized ("dedicated") machines. For personal or microcomputers, word processing software packages are sold separately, usually recorded on a floppy disk. Some of the best known of these are WordPerfect, Microsoft Word, WordStar, MacWrite, MultiMate, and PFS:Write.

Writing with Word Processing: Getting a Job in the Film Industry

Let us pretend you are about to finish school and are seeking that first career job. This is no summer job search. You are going to take some risks and try to find the job you want. Indeed, you are going to

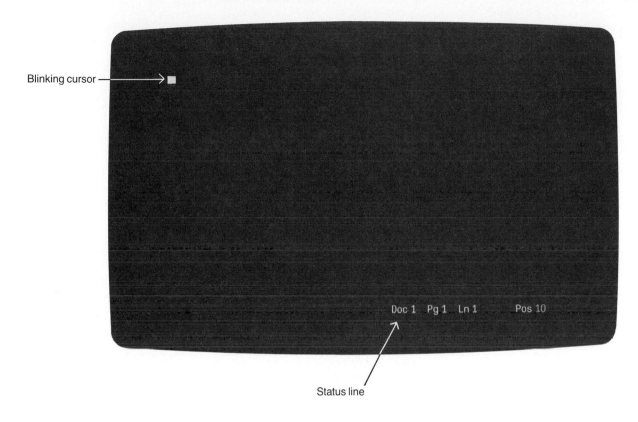

Blinking cursor

Doc 1 Pg 1 Ln 1   Pos 10

Status line

Figure 3-3. WordPerfect. This is the opening screen for this word processing program. The status line shows that the cursor is located in document 1, page 1, line 1, position (or column) 10.

try to find a job in one of the most competitive, highly paid industries there is—the movie industry.

This is not going to be a job in front of the camera, however. You are looking for something on the business side. You have read that over 75% of the feature films made in the industry today never turn a profit, so it is crucial for film companies to keep track of costs and expenses on individual pictures. Maybe, you think, with your business background the industry could use your help. You decide to compose a job-inquiry letter to the head of a film production company, using your WordPerfect word processing program on your microcomputer.

Loading and Screen Format You load the program—that is, make it operable within the computer—by inserting the WordPerfect diskette into one of the two disk drives (drive A, which is often on the left side of the computer) and a blank diskette into the other (drive B). You turn on the computer, which puts the program into the computer's main memory. You are now ready to create a document or file. A **file** is defined as anything you store as a unit—it is like a manila folder in a filing cabinet.

A clear screen will appear on your monitor, as shown in Figure 3-3. Notice at the far left side of the illustration the *cursor,* an always

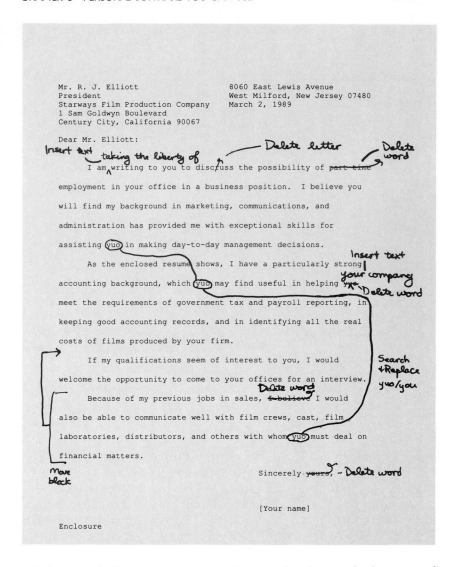

blinking underline that acts as a pointer and indicates the location of the next character to be typed. Using a combination of keys on the keyboard (such as arrow keys) or a mouse, you can move the cursor anywhere on the screen.

At the bottom of the screen (see Figure 3-3) on the *status line* are certain notations that indicate the exact position of the cursor (which document—WordPerfect allows you to work on two documents at the same time, by pressing keys to switch back and forth from one screen to another—and which page, line, and position or column). Note that the cursor is listed as being in position 10 (Pos 10) instead of position 1. This is because WordPerfect automatically sets margins of 1 inch—an inch equals 10 positions—on each side of the page; these margins are standard for a letter or document typed on 8½ by 11 inch paper. It is easy to vary the margins if you wish.

Text Formatting in word processing allows you to do the following:

Figure 3-4. Writing a letter on a word processor. *Left page:* This is how the first draft of a letter might look using a WordPerfect word processing program. Note that corrections and changes are easily made. In the first line, the word *discruss* can be changed to *discuss* by repositioning the cursor under the r and pressing the DELETE key. Similarly, the words *part-time* can be deleted from the first line with little effort. To insert the phrase *taking the liberty of* in the first sentence, you simply move the cursor to that position and type in the phrase. If you have a tendency to transpose letters, as in "yuo" for "you," you can use the search and replace function to make the correction and replacement throughout the entire document. If you decide that the next-to-last paragraph makes a better conclusion to the letter, you can use the "cut-and-paste" or block move to accomplish this. *Right:* This is the final draft, after editing and reformatting. Note the changes in format: Double spacing is now single spacing, the right side of the text is justified (evened up) instead of "ragged right," paragraphs are no longer indented, and the sizes of the margins have been changed.

```
                                         8060 East Lewis Avenue
                               West Milford, New Jersey 07480

                                         March 2, 1989


Mr. R. J. Elliott
President
Starways Film Production Company
1 Sam Goldwyn Boulevard
Century City, California 90067

Dear Mr. Elliott:

I am taking the liberty of writing to you to discuss the
possibility of employment in your office in a business
position.  I believe you will find my background in
marketing, communications, and administration has provided
me with exceptional skills for assisting you in making day-
to-day management decisions.

As the enclosed resume shows, I have a particularly strong
accounting background, which you may find useful in helping
your company meet the requirements of government tax and
payroll reporting, in keeping good accounting records, and
in identifying all the real costs of films produced by your
firm.

Because of my previous jobs in sales, I would also be able
to  communicate  well  with  film  crews,  cast,  film
laboratories, distributors, and others with whom you must
deal on financial matters.

If my qualifications seem of interest to you, I would
welcome the opportunity to come to your offices for an
interview.

                                         Sincerely,

                                         [Your name]


Enclosure
```

▶ Set line spacing—single-spaced, double-spaced, and so on. This spacing can be changed even after you have typed the whole document.

▶ Set the right, left, top, and, bottom margins—the space bordering the text. This, too, can be changed later.

▶ Text may be **justified**—evened up in the margin, as appears in typeset materials (like this book)—or **unjustified,** with a "ragged" appearance.

▶ All or part of the text may be typed ALL CAPITALS, **boldface,** underlined, or positioned to the left or right or in the center of the page.

Note the different formats of the two drafts of the same letter in Figure 3-4: double-spaced versus single-spaced, unjustified right margin versus justified, different size margins around the text.

ON-LINE OUTLINERS

You know what an outline is.

I. It has a main topic.
   A. It has a subtopic.
      1. It has specific aspects of the subtopic.
      2. You can even break it down further. . .
         a. . . . Like this

Outliners are software tools that help people get their ideas "down on paper" (or disk) and then easily organize them. As one professional writer put it, "What I have been looking for is the ability to approach my writing with an outline that will stay with me as I write. I want to be able to see its parts and its entire form when I need it. The outline must be amendable and it must assist in getting new ideas down as fast as my mind can fly. It must then help me with subsequent reorganization."

The one he found helpful was an "outline processor" that came with the word processing program Microsoft Word. However, other versions are available with Framework, ThinkTank, Streamline, and WordPerfect. A person running a financial management business said she found Framework's word processing outlining capability "a wonderful thinking tool. It lets me juggle concepts around, then flesh out my framework with words or plug-in notes or data from another file."

Outliners differ from word processors in that they make reorganizing and presenting ideas very easy. You enter a "headline," and the computer links all indented information that follows with that headline.

```
I.    Big Game Reserve

      A.   Permits
           1. Animals
           2. Hunting Hours
           3. Tags
           4. Annual Totals

      B.   Big Game Hunts and Conservation
           1. Permit Reduction
           2. Legal Age
           3. Deer and Elk Exceptions

      C.   Hunter Education Program
           1. Hours of Instruction
           2. Blue Card
           3. Goals and Improvements

II.   Campgrounds

III.  Wilderness Mountain Area

IV.   Lone Pine Reservoir
```

Outlining in WordPerfect.

Thus, you can move large blocks of text by simply identifying that headline. You can also print out different versions of an outline—for instance, just the Roman numeral headings as an outline for a talk, or a more complete version as the basis for drafting a manuscript. (The headlines are then removed, and the manuscript magically appears.)

Outliners can be purchased independently or as an integrated tool with some word processors.

Creating Text Let us now begin the process of writing the letter. As with a typewriter, you can create a rough draft of your letter by simply typing it on a keyboard and watching the text appear on the screen. However, you will notice some real benefits:

▶ Typing is faster than it is on a typewriter, since you don't need to hit a carriage return key (there is no carriage); any word that crosses the right-hand margin is automatically moved to the left on the next line down—a feature called **automatic carriage return** or **word wrap.**

▶ You will also find that you don't need to be concerned about making a few typing errors: You can easily back up and *erase* an error, *insert* a new word between two existing words, or switch into **overtype** or type-over mode and replace old material with new words.

The first draft of your letter is shown in double-spaced form in Figure 3-4.

Editing Text Word processing is not magic, but it almost feels that way when it comes to correcting typographical errors. Here are some of the things you can do:

▶ The cursor can easily be moved anywhere on the screen, using certain pointer keys on the keyboard or perhaps a mouse, if you have one.
▶ As mentioned, an editing change is easily made—by inserting, deleting, or overtyping. Once it is made, the text will **reformat**— automatically adjust all the lines that follow so that (for justified text) the text is all even.
▶ You can edit using the **search and replace** function, in which you indicate to the program that you want to search out a certain word (for example, "mankind") and replace it with another word (for example, "humankind"). The cursor will pause at each instance throughout the document and give you a choice as to whether or not you want to replace it.

"Cutting and Pasting" or Block Move In the old days, if you decided to shift blocks of lines or paragraphs around in a document, you had to use scissors and a paste pot. Now such **cutting and pasting** is known as a **block move** function. It allows you to do the following:

▶ You can *copy* from one place in the document to another, as if you were typing out the words to a song and wanted to repeat the chorus after each verse. The copy function leaves the original material where it was, but repeats it in the new location you specify.
▶ You can *move* a block of material from one place to another. This deletes the material in the old location.
▶ You can *read and write* from other files, which allows you to combine different documents (files), as when you are copying different addresses for a form letter. For example, you **read** (obtain) the name and address from one file (a list of names and addresses) and **write** it to (copy it on) the file with your standard job-seeking letter—and you do this every time you want to send a new "individualized" letter.

An example of cutting and pasting appears in Figure 3-4.

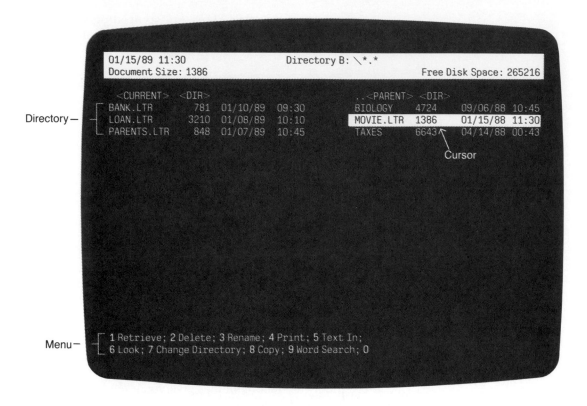

Figure 3-5.   Directory and menu.
The cursor is positioned over the file MOVIE.LTR in the directory. The menu at the bottom of the screen offers several commands—for example, pressing the 1 key for Retrieve will retrieve the text of this letter from the data disk and bring it to the screen so that you can then edit it.

Storing and Printing Text   It is a good idea to store or **save** your text on the disk while you are typing it—say, every 10 minutes or so—in case of power failure, for example. Every time you execute the Save command, it will update the file on the disk with your most recent version. Needless to say, you would probably want to save the final version—especially if it is a document you might use again some time, such as a résumé. You might save your present letter under a particular **filename**—just like the name you might put on a cardboard file folder—such as MOVIE.LTR (short for "movie letter"). However, you may also find that after you print out the document there are still some changes or corrections you want to make.

You print out your document simply by turning on the printer attached to the computer and pressing a couple of keys. Suppose a day or so later, however, you decide the printed letter (which you have not yet sent) still does not seem right. In that case, you load the program and data disks into the disk drives again and turn on the computer. By pressing a few keys, you can then call up a **directory** on your screen, as illustrated in Figure 3-5, which lists all the filenames on your data disk. Moving the highlighted cursor over the right filename, you can then follow the **menu** or list of commands available and press a 1 key to retrieve your letter to the screen. You can then reformat the letter, re-edit it, and print it out again.

Perhaps you can begin to see how word processing can make you a *better* writer: The inclination you might feel working at a typewriter to let small flaws go by because you cannot bear the thought of retyping an entire page is not such an issue here because the flaws are so easily and quickly corrected.

What to Look for in Word Processing Programs

As mentioned, there are numerous word processing programs and the costs vary dramatically. Some of the desirable features are as follows:

▶ **Screen-oriented.** Whenever you enter or edit text, you can see the changes directly on the screen. This is known as "What You See Is What You Get"—WYSIWYG (pronounced "wissiwig").

▶ **Live screen.** Corrections can be made to the text immediately as you see it on the screen. You do not have to shift the word processor into a special editing mode.

▶ **Menus and "Help" options.** A menu is a list of commands that you can type in through the keyboard to make editing, formatting, and other changes. There may be few commands on a simple word processing program such as those intended for children (for example, The Bank Street Writer), but there may be many on a program like WordPerfect, in which case a menu that appears on the screen is useful. A **Help option** is also useful when you do not know how to do a particular operation on the system.

▶ **Restoring text.** Some word processors allow you to recover pieces of text that you may have accidentally deleted. WordPerfect, for example, saves the last three chunks of deleted text for recovery if needed.

▶ **Backup capability.** Some word processing systems have a "fail-safe" capability, so that if you erase part of a file by mistake there is a backup file you can use. WordStar has this feature.

▶ **Form letter generator or "mail-merge."** This feature allows you to merge files, such as names and addresses from mailing lists along with a letter, so that you can produce letters that appear to be individually typed.

▶ **Spelling checker.** Some word processing programs can be linked to a proofreading program consisting of a dictionary of correctly spelled words. The Spelling Checker of WordPerfect contains three dictionaries: a common word list, a main word list, and a supplemental list (which you can custom-tailor to your special spelling needs). The 4.2 version of WordPerfect contains 115,000 words in its Spelling Checker. You still have to know when a correctly spelled word is being *used* incorrectly, however—for example, "there" and "their" or "hair" and "hare."

> ▶ **Thesaurus.** Some word processing programs have a thesaurus to help clarify the exact meaning of a word by producing a list of synonyms. WordPerfect's Thesaurus contains more than 10,000 words.

> ▶ **Memory-based versus disk-based.** Some word processing systems will only be able to type documents that are less than a certain length because most of the program is in the computer memory. Others hold most of the program (as well as the document you are typing) on a disk. The first method is faster, because all the information is in the computer's memory, but disk-based systems allow storage of longer documents.

> ▶ **Windows.** Some word processing programs offer a feature that allows you to divide the screen into two parts or **windows** and view two documents or files or different parts of the same document at the same time.

SPREADSHEETS

NIMBLE NUMBER

MANIPULATION

What is a **spreadsheet?** Traditionally, it was simply a blank sheet of paper divided into rows and columns that accountants and financial analysts used to produce a wide range of reports, from income and balance sheets to cash budget plans. Preparing these sheets took enormous quantities of time.

All that began to change in October 1979, however, when a program known as VisiCalc, an electronic spreadsheet, was shipped to customers *(see box)*. Since then, there have emerged perhaps five dozen such electronic financial programs. Among the most popular are Lotus 1-2-3, Multiplan, Excel, VP-Planner, SuperCalc 4, and PFS:Plan.

The reason for the popularity of electronic spreadsheets is their simplicity, flexibility, and, most important, their "what-if" capability. The "what-if" part can be demonstrated by assuming that, for example, you are thinking about buying a new car and are wondering whether you can afford the monthly payments. With an electronic spreadsheet you can vary the number of possibilities: the total price of the car (what if it is $15,000? what if $10,000?), the size of the down payment ($2,000? or $3,000?), the number of months you have to pay off the loan covering the balance (36 months? or 48?), and the interest rates on the loan (9%? 10%?). By holding three of these factors constant and varying the fourth (the down payment, say), you can figure out the different possible monthly payments you could make.

This is the kind of financial analysis that businesspeople do all the time—not only accountants, but others as well. Spreadsheets are used for sales projections, expense reports, income and balance sheet preparation, and nearly any other numerical problem that used to be attacked with pencil and paper.

Let us demonstrate how a spreadsheet works.

FLASHBACK

The Invention of the Spreadsheet

VisiCalc alone is credited with selling thousands of microcomputers for business use. Indeed, it has been observed that the electronic spreadsheet was the first legitimate business application of what until then had been a machine for hobbyists and game players. Because VisiCalc was originally programmed to operate on an Apple II computer, this one piece of software alone had an enormous impact in altering the Apple image from that of a game computer to that of a business computer.

VisiCalc came into public consciousness when, in 1978, Dan Fylstra and a friend, on an initial investment of $500, cofounded a firm to market the electronic spreadsheet as a project for a marketing course while graduate students at the Harvard Business School. However, Fylstra did not invent VisiCalc. The idea for the spreadsheet occurred to another student, Daniel Bricklin, while staring at columns of numbers on a blackboard during classes at Harvard Business School. In those days, when a figure in one column of such a spreadsheet was changed, all the rest had to be recomputed and changed by hand. "Just one mistake on my calculator," Bricklin recalled for *Time* magazine, "and I would end up moaning, 'My God, I got the whole series of numbers wrong!'" During the winter of 1978 he and another student, Robert Frankston, both M.I.T. graduates, worked long hours developing their VisiCalc (visible calculator) spreadsheet for small computers.

However, when the pair attempted to market the new software, it received a lukewarm reception. It was then that Fylstra entered the picture and began an energetic marketing campaign, eventually turning it into the most popular small business program around. The company, called Personal Software, moved to California's Silicon Valley in 1979 and later changed its name to VisiCorp. Despite the introduction of other Visi- products, such as VisiSchedule, VisiPlot, and an integrated program called Visi On, the company's fortunes soured. Perhaps a good part of their undoing was the appearance of a more sophisticated invention—Lotus Corporation's 1-2-3, which combined the spreadsheet with a data base program and the ability to do graphics, all in one integrated package.

Dan Bricklin.

Dan Fylstra.

"What If . . .?": Calculating the Affordable Apartment

You got the job, and you are moving to southern California to work for Starways Film Production Company! Based on this offer, you decide to see what you can afford in the way of an apartment. You also decide to continue your schooling, probably at night, and so you need to allow for tuition and other school expenses. Thus, you need to figure out your projected income versus your projected expenses. What better instrument to use than a spreadsheet, such as the spreadsheet part of Lotus 1-2-3? This software package, incidentally, is called 1-2-3 because it combines (1) a spreadsheet program, (2) a data base program, and (3) a graphics program, as we shall describe later.

Loading and Screen Format   You load the Lotus 1-2-3 program much as you did the word processing program—the program disk in drive A, the data disk (if you need it because you want to save your work for later use) in drive B—then turn on the computer.

The monitor screen will resemble that shown in Figure 3-6. Notice the following:

▶ Most of the screen consists of a *worksheet area* made up of *column headings* across the top (identified by letters) and *row headings* down the left-hand side (numerals). The invisible place on the screen where a particular column and row intersect is called a *cell,* and its position is referred to as a *cell address*—for example, *A1* refers to the very first (top and left) position.

▶ One screen shows only 20 rows and 8 columns. But that is only a small part of the spreadsheet available to you. In actuality, as the second part of Figure 3-6 shows, the screen can be expanded out to several rows and columns. Lotus 1-2-3 (release 2) can be expanded out to 256 rows and 8192 columns.

▶ Above or below the worksheet area is the *control panel.* This section consists of an *entry contents line,* which will display information about the format of the cell and what the cell contains, and the *main menu/edit line,* which has two purposes: (1) to list command choices and (2) to edit cell contents. The *submenu line* displays additional commands and presents brief descriptions of the commands.

▶ There are two basic "modes" of operation: The *Menu* mode allows you to exercise the commands on the menu, such as "Copy" or "Print." The *Ready* mode allows you to enter data—in the form of labels, numbers, and formulas—into the cells in the worksheet.

▶ You can move around the worksheet to various cells using pointer keys on the keyboard.

▶ A single screen full of data is known as a **page** or a **window.** You can move from screen to screen—page by page, like viewing a roll of microfilm on a microfilm reader, by **scrolling**—moving right or

---

THE TYRANNY OF THE OLD-FASHIONED SPREADSHEET

In the old days . . . a financial spreadsheet was manufactured out of actual paper and ink. It often measured two feet across and was unlikely to remain long on top of a desk without having coffee spilled on it. Against its typically dull-green Eye-Ease background were crosshatched some 7,500 spaces into which accountants, bookkeepers, treasurers, and business planners squeezed their numbers, tiny oblong by tiny oblong, pencil by resharpened pencil. It was white-collar sweatshop work; a manager performing a five-year projection involving even a handful of products could count on many weekends in the office and wastebaskets full of jettisoned calculations.

—Robert A. Mamis, *Inc.*

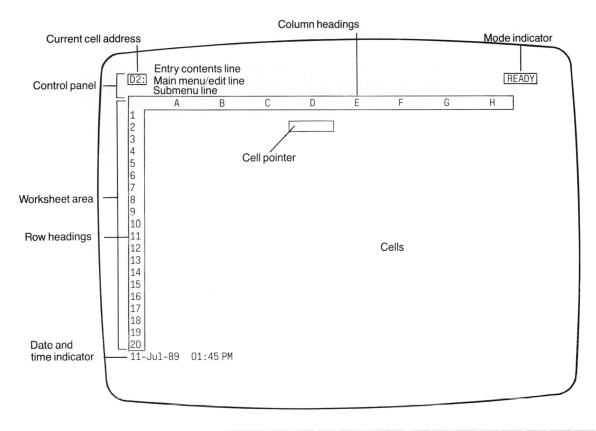

Current cell address

Column headings

Mode indicator

Control panel

Entry contents line
Main menu/edit line
Submenu line

D2:

READY

Cell pointer

Worksheet area

Row headings

Cells

Date and
time indicator

11-Jul-89   01:45 PM

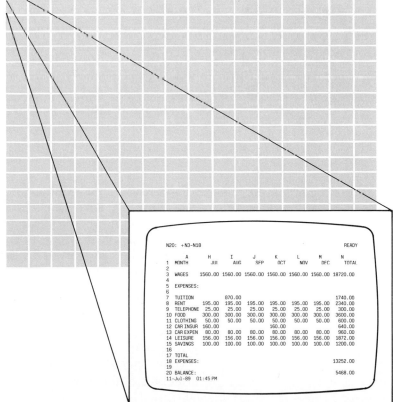

Figure 3-6. A spreadsheet screen.
Top: Screen format for Lotus 1-2-3
spreadsheet before any data has been
entered. *Bottom:* Example of how an
electronic spreadsheet can be expanded to several screens, thus giving
the user more rows and columns,
even if not all of them can be viewed
at one time.

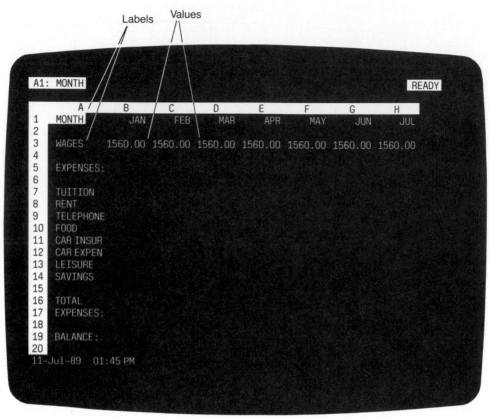

Figure 3-7.   Spreadsheet screen with labels and values. The labels consist of months at the head of the columns and the wages, types of expenses, and totals to the left of the rows. The values are numbers entered on the spreadsheet—in this case, the values for wages.

left, up or down, a line or page at a time. The column headings and row headings will stay in place or shift as necessary so that you can always tell what cell address any particular cell of data has.

Labels and Values   Column and row headings are known as **labels.** Labels are usually words—for example, in Figure 3-7, *WAGES* or *MAY*—but can also be numbers (such as a social security number). In your case, you want to project your income and expenses over a 12-month period. Thus, as Figure 3-7 shows, you type months for labels as column headings and types of expenses and income for row headings. To enter labels (or any other information) on the spreadsheet, you use the keyboard to move the cursor to the appropriate place and type in whatever you need to type. Correcting information is done the same way; it is like erasing and rewriting with pencil and eraser on paper.

A **value** is a number contained in a cell. As Figure 3-7 shows, line 3, *WAGES*, expresses the values for the various months of what you will earn in January through December. (Although at this point the screen you are viewing does not extend past July, the values from August through December are still there.) You also insert values for your expenses; Figure 3-8 shows the expenses for the last seven months of the year.

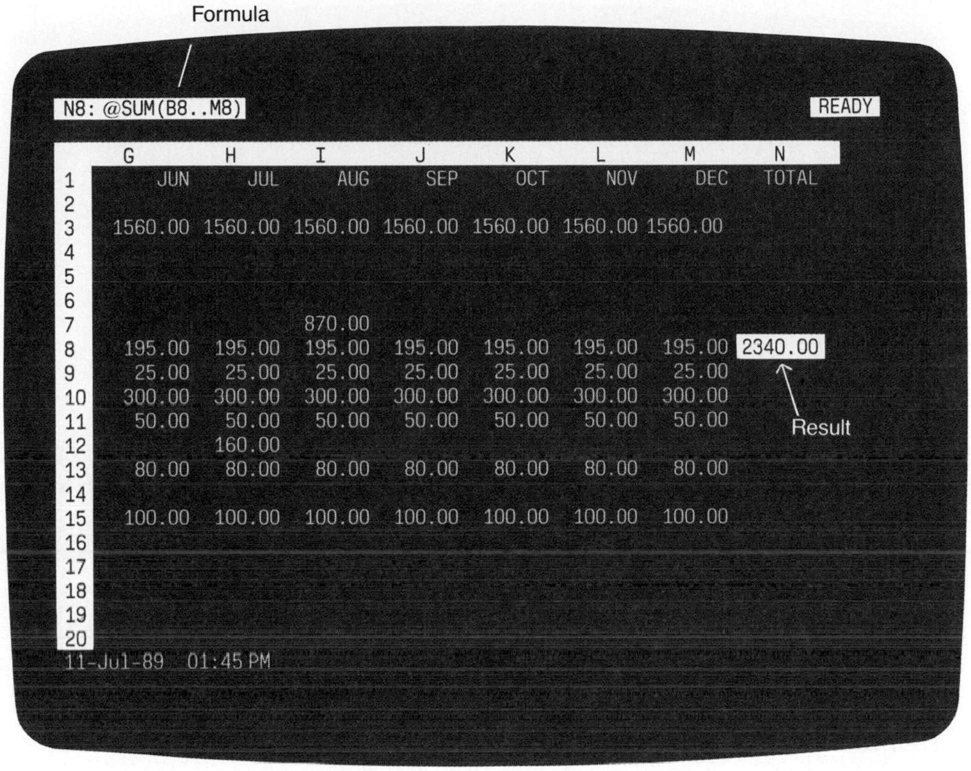

Formula

Figure 3-8. Calculating formulas.
The formula, given on the top line, can be read as: "In cell N8 give the sum of cells B8 through M8." The result is indicated at the far right, column N, row 8.

Formatting Data You can make a number of changes depending on how you want to display data:

▶ You can change the position or **justification** of a label—centered, flush left, or flush right within its cell.

▶ You can change the width of the column—for example, from one space up to (in Lotus 1-2-3) 240 spaces.

▶ You can change how you wish numbers to be displayed. How many decimal positions, if any, do you want? Do you want a dollar sign ($) or percentage sign (%) to appear? Do you want long numbers separated by commas (for example, 1000000 or 1,000,000)?

Depending on the spreadsheet, these formatting options can be applied to only one cell, column, or row; to groups of cells, columns, or rows; or to an entire spreadsheet.

Formulas **Formulas** are instructions for calculations; they create relationships between numbers in particular cells. Formulas are what spreadsheets are really all about because they are the things that make "what-if" analysis easier. That is, as we suggested with the car purchase information earlier, you can leave all the data the same

```
 Set Up  Create  Update  Position  Retrieve  Organize  Modify  Tools  01:34:05 pm


   Record#  CITY         ZIP    AD_DATE   DEPOSIT  FIRST_MON LAST_MON
         3  Burbank      91504  12/14/88     500       500        0
         4  Inglewood    90302  12/19/88     400       450        0
         7  Northridge   91326  12/23/88     550       550        0
         6  Pasadena     91108  12/02/88     350       450      450
         8  Pasadena     91108  12/14/88     400       650      650
        11  Pasadena     91108  12/18/88     575       625      625
         2  Santa Monica 90403  12/20/88     500       525      525
         9  Santa Monica 90403  12/15/88     450       600      600
         1  Torrance     90501  12/27/88     395       395      395
         5  Westwood     90024  12/14/88     525       525      525
        10  Westwood     90024  12/12/88     575       575      575
 ASSIST           //<B:>//APARTMEN            //Rec: 3/11        //        //
                Press any key to continue work in ASSIST.
```

Figure 3-9. Calculating another formula. This shows the formula for computing leisure-time expenses in January.

and change the formula, or you can do the reverse—change parts of the data but leave the formula the same. Formulas are defined in the status area of the spreadsheet and may take a form something like "A3 = A1 + A2," which means "the total of the contents of the cell in row A, column 3 is equal to the contents of cell A1 plus the contents of cell A2."

Applying the formulas to your living expenses and looking at line 8, *RENT*, we see that you have budgeted $195 a month for rent each month for a 12-month period. To calculate the total for the entire year—as shown in cell N8 in Figure 3-8—we use the formula expressed on the top line: N8: @SUM(B8 . . M8). This translates as: "In cell N8 give us the sum of all the values in cells B8 through M8." The result, indicated by the cursor in cell N8, is $2,340. The totals of other expenses are computed in a similar manner.

Another example: Let us say you have arbitrarily decided to budget 10% of each month's wages for leisure-time expenses. (You want to go see a few of those films whose business aspects you will be handling for Starways.) You place the cursor in cell B14, as shown in Figure 3-9, after having typed the formula expressed above on the entry contents line: B14: + B3*0.1. This translates as: "In cell B14 give us the value that is the total of the value in cell B3 multiplied by 10%." (The sign "*" means "multiplied by." The number "0.1" is

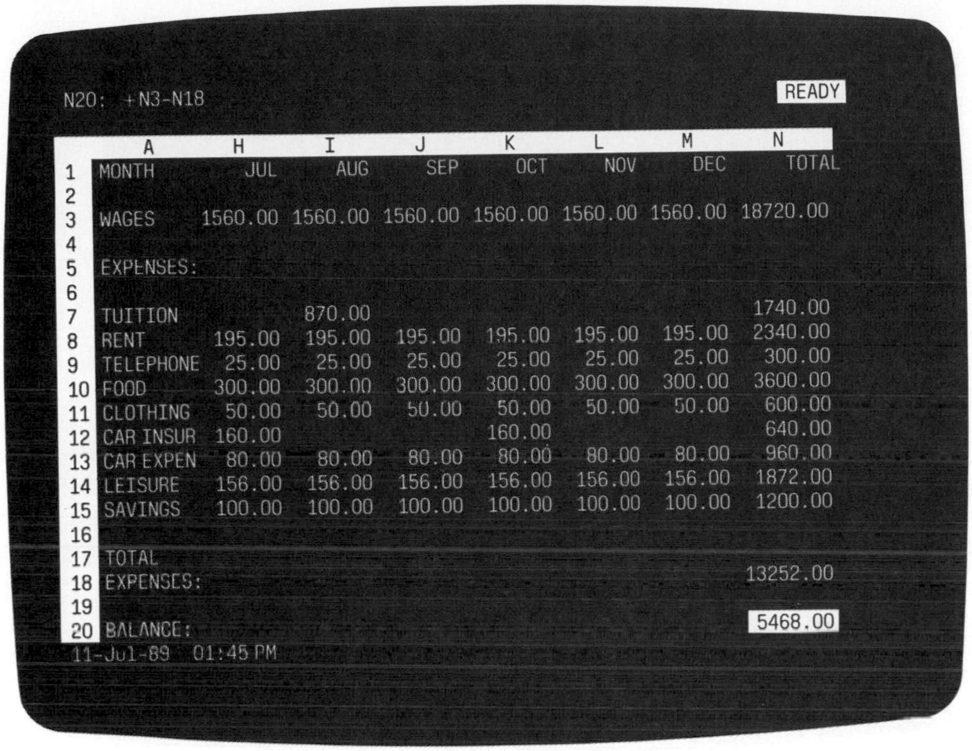

```
N20:  +N3-N18                                                    READY

         A       H       I       J       K       L       M       N
1  MONTH          JUL     AUG     SEP     OCT     NOV     DEC     TOTAL
2
3  WAGES        1560.00 1560.00 1560.00 1560.00 1560.00 1560.00 18720.00
4
5  EXPENSES:
6
7  TUITION              870.00                                  1740.00
8  RENT          195.00  195.00  195.00  195.00  195.00  195.00 2340.00
9  TELEPHONE      25.00   25.00   25.00   25.00   25.00   25.00  300.00
10 FOOD          300.00  300.00  300.00  300.00  300.00  300.00 3600.00
11 CLOTHING       50.00   50.00   50.00   50.00   50.00   50.00  600.00
12 CAR INSUR     160.00                  160.00                  640.00
13 CAR EXPEN      80.00   80.00   80.00   80.00   80.00   80.00  960.00
14 LEISURE       156.00  156.00  156.00  156.00  156.00  156.00 1872.00
15 SAVINGS       100.00  100.00  100.00  100.00  100.00  100.00 1200.00
16
17 TOTAL
18 EXPENSES:                                                   13252.00
19
20 BALANCE:                                                     5468.00
11-Jul-89  01:45 PM
```

Figure 3-10. Ahead or behind? This screen shows how you might come out ahead if your rent is $195 a month.

the same as ".10" or 10%; the zero has been omitted.) So $156.00 is the amount that you have allowed yourself to spend on leisure-time activities in January. The leisure budgets for the other 11 months are calculated by the same formula, with different results depending on the monthly wage level.

Of course, you are also interested in how you are going to come out at the end of the year—whether you are ahead or behind financially. You can do this by calculating your balance, as shown in Figure 3-10, which means subtracting your total expenses from your total wages. The formula for this, given on the entry contents line, is N20: + N3 − N18, which means: "For the value in cell N20, calculate the value of N3 (which is total wages) minus the value of N18 (which is total expenses)." You are pleased to see, of course, that you are coming out ahead, with $5,468.00 at the end of the year—a nice cushion in case things fall through at Starways.

Recalculation   As mentioned, this "what-if" aspect is what makes electronic spreadsheets so much better than paper spreadsheets: You can change one number (or more) in the spreadsheet, and the results will **recalculate** automatically. You can do this for all the values on the spreadsheet or for *ranges*—that is, for the data contained within whatever beginning and ending rows and columns you specify.

N3: @SUM(B3..M3)   READY

	H	I	J	K	L	M		A	N
	JUL	AUG	SEP	OCT	NOV	DEC		MONTH	TOTAL
1							1		
2							2		
3	1560.00	1560.00	1560.00	1560.00	1560.00	1560.00	3	WAGES	18720.00
4							4		
5							5	EXPENSES:	
6							6		
7		870.00					7	TUITION	1740.00
8	195.00	195.00	195.00	195.00	195.00	195.00	8	RENT	2340.00
9	25.00	25.00	25.00	25.00	25.00	25.00	9	TELEPHONE	300.00
10	300.00	300.00	300.00	300.00	300.00	300.00	10	FOOD	3600.00
11	50.00	50.00	50.00	50.00	50.00	50.00	11	CLOTHING	600.00
12	160.00				160.00		12	CAR INSUR	640.00
13	80.00	80.00	80.00	80.00	80.00	80.00	13	CAR EXPEN	960.00
14	156.00	156.00	156.00	156.00	156.00	156.00	14	LEISURE	1872.00
15	100.00	100.00	100.00	100.00	100.00	100.00	15	SAVINGS	1200.00
16							16		
17							17	TOTAL	
18							18	EXPENSES:	13352.00
19							19		
20							20	BALANCE	5468.00

11-Jul-89   01:45 PM

Figure 3-11.   Alternative rents. These three screens show how you might come out (*above*) ahead at the end of the year in income over expenses; (*opposite, top*) behind, if your rent is too high; (*opposite, bottom*) still ahead if your rent is a more moderate $500 a month. Note the split screens: Column A, containing the row labels, has been positioned next to column N, the totals column, for ease in identifying final results.

After talking to your friend John, who comes from Los Angeles, you are convinced that your original estimate of $195 per month for rent is much too low. You want to revise your estimate to $750 per month. Now, you ask, "Can I afford it?"

Look at the first screen in Figure 3-11 (above). This shows your original computations, based on $195 a month. Your total balance for the year is ahead: You have $5,468.00 left over after expenses.

Next look at the second screen in Figure 3-11 (opposite, top). You have changed all the values on line 8, *RENT*, to $750 each month. The spreadsheet recalculates your entire financial picture almost immediately. Unfortunately, as cell N20 shows, this kind of rent is too much: it puts you in the hole $1,192.00 for the year.

Now look at the last screen in Figure 3-11 (opposite, bottom). You try a monthly rent of $500 instead. This works out much better: You come out with $1,808.00 left over for the year.

What to Look for in Spreadsheets

As mentioned, there are numerous spreadsheet programs and they differ greatly in cost and performance. Some guidelines as to what to look for are:

N8: @SUM(B8..M8)   READY

	H	I	J	K	L	M		A	N
	JUL	AUG	SEP	OCT	NOV	DEC	1	MONTH	TOTAL
2							2		
3	1560.00	1560.00	1560.00	1560.00	1560.00	1560.00	3	WAGES	18720.00
4							4		
5							5	EXPENSES:	
6							6		
7		870.00					7	TUITION	1740.00
8	750.00	750.00	750.00	750.00	750.00	750.00	8	RENT	9000.00
9	25.00	25.00	25.00	25.00	25.00	25.00	9	TELEPHONE	300.00
10	300.00	300.00	300.00	300.00	300.00	300.00	10	FOOD	3600.00
11	50.00	50.00	50.00	50.00	50.00	50.00	11	CLOTHING	600.00
12	160.00			160.00			12	CAR INSUR	640.00
13	80.00	80.00	80.00	80.00	80.00	80.00	13	CAR EXPEN	960.00
14	156.00	156.00	156.00	156.00	156.00	156.00	14	LEISURE	1872.00
15	100.00	100.00	100.00	100.00	100.00	100.00	15	SAVINGS	1200.00
16							16		
17							17	TOTAL	
18							18	EXPENSES:	19912.00
19							19		
20							20	BALANCE	-1192.00

11-Jul-89   01:45 PM

N8: @SUM(B8..M8)   READY

	H	I	J	K	L	M		A	N
	JUL	AUG	SEP	OCT	NOV	DEC	1	MONTH	TOTAL
2							2		
3	1560.00	1560.00	1560.00	1560.00	1560.00	1560.00	3	WAGES	18720.00
4							4		
5							5	EXPENSES:	
6							6		
7		870.00					7	TUITION	1740.00
8	500.00	500.00	500.00	500.00	500.00	500.00	8	RENT	6000.00
9	25.00	25.00	25.00	25.00	25.00	25.00	9	TELEPHONE	300.00
10	300.00	300.00	300.00	300.00	300.00	300.00	10	FOOD	3600.00
11	50.00	50.00	50.00	50.00	50.00	50.00	11	CLOTHING	600.00
12	160.00			160.00			12	CAR INSUR	640.00
13	80.00	80.00	80.00	80.00	80.00	80.00	13	CAR EXPEN	960.00
14	156.00	156.00	156.00	156.00	156.00	156.00	14	LEISURE	1872.00
15	100.00	100.00	100.00	100.00	100.00	100.00	15	SAVINGS	1200.00
16							16		
17							17	TOTAL	
18							18	EXPENSES:	16912.00
19							19		
20							20	BALANCE	1808.00

11-Jul-89   01:45 PM

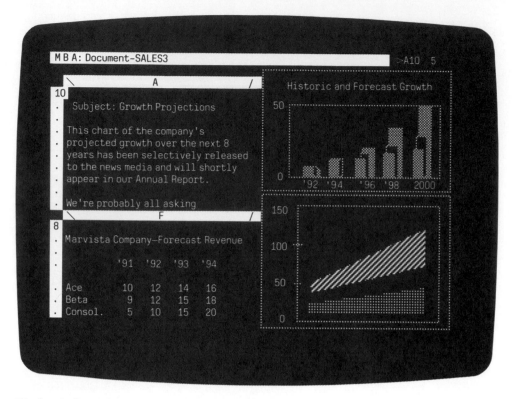

Figure 3-12.   We do windows. Some software, such as the Context MBA, allows for "windows," or sectors from different programs, to be visible at the same time.

▶ **Screen format:** The spreadsheet must allow for clear presentation and insertion of labels for rows and columns and must allow information appearing on the screen to be edited easily.

▶ **Size of spreadsheet:** As mentioned, some spreadsheets are larger than others. However, some spreadsheets cannot be used all at once because of the limitations of the computer's memory. Some have more cells, but, on the other hand, some have cells that can hold more characters. (Context MBA holds 502 characters in each cell, as opposed to 240 for Lotus 1-2-3.)

▶ **Multiple windows:** Some spreadsheets allow for multiple windows. The MBA spreadsheet, for example, can show graphs in three windows with values changing as data is changed in a table in the fourth window. Figure 3-12 shows windows.

▶ **Calculation flexibility:** A spreadsheet should be able to work for both an engineer and a financial analyst or other specialist. That is, the equations used to define cell relationships should include not only the basic arithmetic operations but also any specialized formulas.

▶ **File access:** The spreadsheet should be able to interact with files from other programs. Often you may wish to display an entire spreadsheet in a report, but this is best accomplished if the spreadsheet and word processing files can be combined.

▶ **Good documentation: Documentation** is computer industry jargon for instruction manuals. The bane of the industry is that, in the past, documentation has been badly written or otherwise inadequate. Although spreadsheets are easy to use, clear and complete documentation helps. Valuable parts of the documentation are tutorials, sample problems, discussion of various applications, and reference sections.

FILE MANAGEMENT
AND DATA BASE
MANAGEMENT

We have considered two of the most common business activities—creating documents (word processing) and analyzing and summarizing data (spreadsheets). Now let us consider the third: filing information.

Many people seem to be able to get along for years with their important records—birth certificates, tax records, and so on—simply thrown in a box in the back of a closet, although, of course, it is somewhat time-consuming to dig the records up when they are needed. Organizations, however, cannot operate this way. Imagine the number of irate customers, employees, suppliers, and tax collectors there would be if such things as customer accounts, payroll records, supplier invoices, and past income tax statements were left in disarray. The success of an organization is quite often linked to its having orderly and accessible files, as we saw in the case of the Yanello & Flippen law firm in Chapter 1.

File folders and cabinets might help you organize that material in your closet, but manual filing systems are often inefficient for an institution's files because they occupy too much space, are difficult to organize, and not always easily accessible (a file may be located in the marketing department, for instance, but the sales and engineering departments may need it also). Instead, files are often computerized. Programs designed to assist in this filing task are called **data base managers** or **data base management systems,** which you will often see expressed in management literature and software ads by the common abbreviation **DBMS.**

The concept of a data base has become a key one in business and will become even more so in the years ahead. A **data base** may be simply a collection of information, such as an encyclopedia or telephone book, but the data base we are concerned with is a *computerized* collection of information. Specifically, a data base is a collection of *integrated* data that can be used for a variety of applications.

At one point, data bases were pretty much the province of the data processing departments of large corporations. Large data bases are still located on mainframes, as we shall discuss in Chapter 9, but data base management systems are also available for microcomputers. Indeed, with the appearance of desktop computers and the success of the dBase and PFS:File software programs, data bases and files have become available to everyone, end-users as well as data processing experts. Among the most popular data base programs

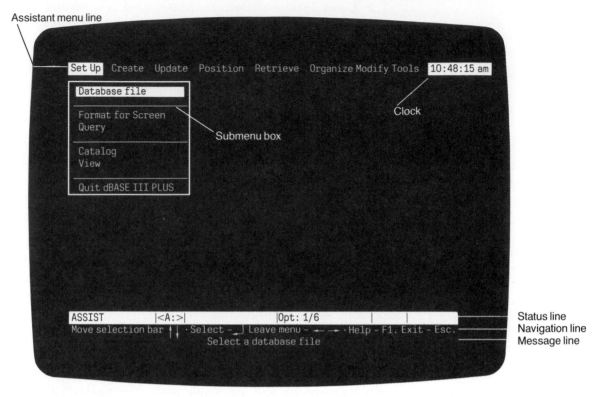

Figure 3-13. The dBase III Plus main screen. Called "the Assistant," this main screen enables users to call a command on the menu line ("Set Up") that will call up a submenu, the box headed "Database file," which offers further commands.

have been dBase II and III (and dBase III Plus), PFS:File, PFS:Report, R:base 5000, and R:base System V.

Where to Find It: The Right Apartment

It has been said that a microcomputer data base management system is to text what an electronic spreadsheet is to numbers. With some types of computerized filing systems, you can put in whatever information you need to file and update—say, all customer orders, with amounts and dates—and later pull it out in different ways. Some filing software allows you just to feed in data in whatever way you wish, then retrieve it and combine it for display on the screen, and finally print it out according to how you want it.

For instance, suppose you decide to look into your friend's warnings about apartment rental expenses in the Los Angeles area. You could make a list of apartment possibilities, based on a reading of the for-rent ads in several editions of the *Los Angeles Times* in your college library. To record your findings, you use dBase III Plus, a data base management system.

Loading and Screen Format   You load the data base management program much as you did the word processor and spreadsheet programs: the program disk in drive A and the data disk in drive B. (Actually, dBase III Plus requires you load *two* program disks into

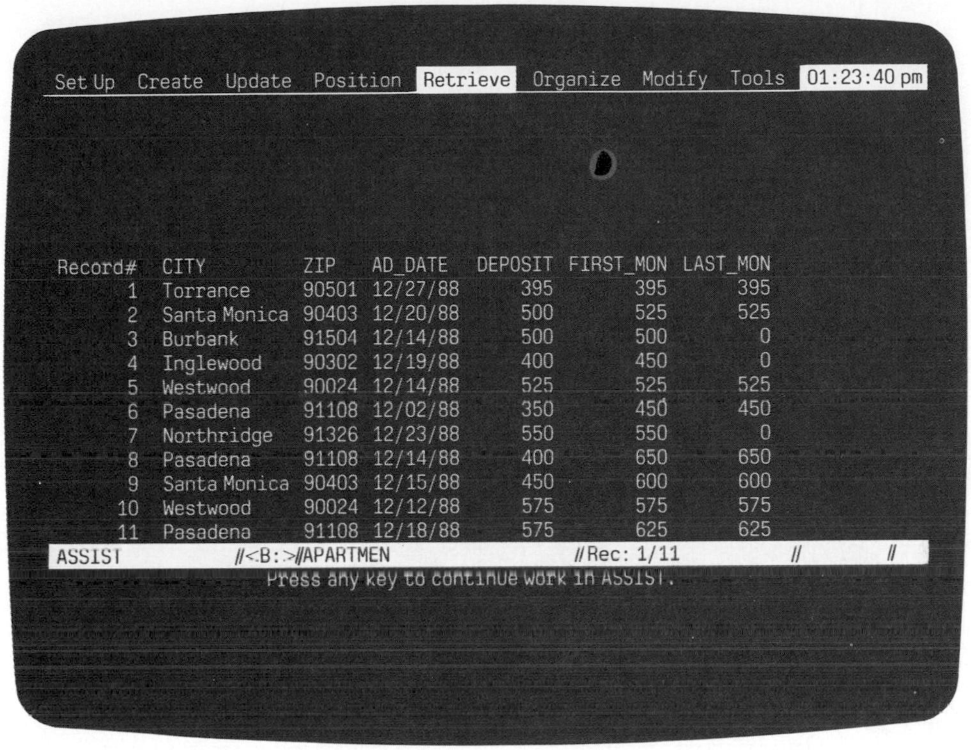

```
Set Up  Create  Update  Position  Retrieve  Organize  Modify  Tools  01:23:40 pm




                                              🖰

Record#  CITY          ZIP    AD_DATE   DEPOSIT  FIRST_MON  LAST_MON
      1  Torrance      90501  12/27/88   395       395        395
      2  Santa Monica  90403  12/20/88   500       525        525
      3  Burbank       91504  12/14/88   500       500          0
      4  Inglewood     90302  12/19/88   400       450          0
      5  Westwood      90024  12/14/88   525       525        525
      6  Pasadena      91108  12/02/88   350       450        450
      7  Northridge    91326  12/23/88   550       550          0
      8  Pasadena      91108  12/14/88   400       650        650
      9  Santa Monica  90403  12/15/88   450       600        600
     10  Westwood      90024  12/12/88   575       575        575
     11  Pasadena      91108  12/18/88   575       625        625
ASSIST           //<B:>//APARTMEN                //Rec: 1/11      //          //
                 Press any key to continue work in ASSIST.
```

Figure 3-14. Data input for a filing system. This screen shows several southern California–area apartments listed according to city and zip code, date apartment appeared in the for-rent ads, and whether landlord requires up-front payment of security deposit and first and last months' rent.

drive A—first system disk 1, which is then removed and replaced with system disk 2.)

The opening screen appears as shown in Figure 3-13. Called "the Assistant" in dBase, this main screen displays on the top line an *assistant menu line*, which lists eight menu options (such as "Update" and "Retrieve") and the time of day. Pressing keys that exercise one of these menu options will produce a *submenu box*; in Figure 3-13, the command "Set Up" produces a submenu box with three options.

At the bottom of the screen are three lines of information. The *status line* indicates the state of various optional settings. The *navigation line* provides instructions on how to use the menu. The *message line* provides information about the highlighted menu choice.

For each apartment listing, you want to include the location (city) of the apartment, the zip code, the date the ad appeared, and whether the landlord requires up-front payment of security deposits and first and last months' rent. Your first step, then, is to design the structure of your data base files. A data base consists of *fields* of information—in this case, the fields labeled CITY, ZIP, AD_DATE, DEPOSIT, FIRST_MON, LAST_MON. Once you have this structure of fields set up, you can then insert the data for each apartment (a complete apartment listing would be considered a *record* here). The data, listed just as you came across it, in no particular order, is shown in Figure 3-14.

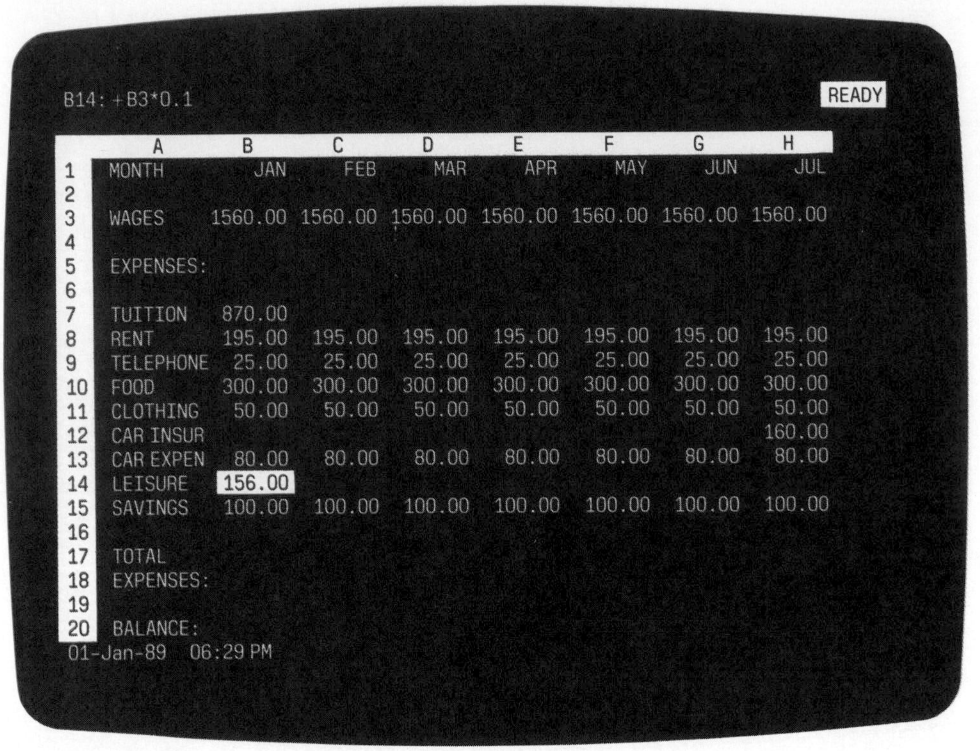

```
B14: +B3*0.1                                                    READY

            A         B        C        D        E        F        G        H
 1   MONTH        JAN      FEB      MAR      APR      MAY      JUN      JUL
 2
 3   WAGES     1560.00  1560.00  1560.00  1560.00  1560.00  1560.00  1560.00
 4
 5   EXPENSES:
 6
 7   TUITION    870.00
 8   RENT       195.00   195.00   195.00   195.00   195.00   195.00   195.00
 9   TELEPHONE   25.00    25.00    25.00    25.00    25.00    25.00    25.00
10   FOOD       300.00   300.00   300.00   300.00   300.00   300.00   300.00
11   CLOTHING    50.00    50.00    50.00    50.00    50.00    50.00    50.00
12   CAR INSUR                                                        160.00
13   CAR EXPEN   80.00    80.00    80.00    80.00    80.00    80.00    80.00
14   LEISURE    156.00
15   SAVINGS    100.00   100.00   100.00   100.00   100.00   100.00   100.00
16
17   TOTAL
18   EXPENSES:
19
20   BALANCE:
     01-Jan-89   06:29 PM
```

Figure 3-15.   Data resorted. This screen shows the apartments reordered alphabetically by city.

What now can you do with these records? Now we can begin to see the uses of a data base management system: You can *organize* the information. In Figure 3-15, for instance, the records are sorted out alphabetically by city. Or you can compare all the apartment listings you have found in Pasadena (see Figure 3-16). This is known as sorting on a *key field*—the field in this case being the city, although you can also sort according to other fields you previously indicated were key, such as ranking security deposits in order from least to most expensive.

You can also use this program to produce professional-looking reports, such as that shown in Figure 3-17, on page 88, with a report title ("Southern California Apartments"), more English-like column headings, and new columns of calculated data derived from other fields of data. In Figure 3-17, for example, a new column has been created under the heading "Up-Front Total," which combines all three deposits—security, first month, and last month—so that you can see which apartments will require the biggest cash outlay before you can move in.

A salesperson could find another use for such an electronic filing system. For example, the representative could put all customer orders in with amounts and dates and then, right before the next trip to New Orleans, say, get a printout that listed all customers in that city who had made purchases within the last year, spent more than

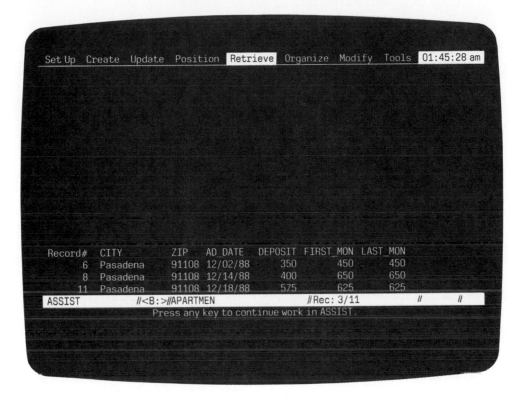

```
Set Up  Create  Update  Position  Retrieve  Organize  Modify  Tools  01:45:28 am

Record#   CITY          ZIP    AD_DATE   DEPOSIT  FIRST_MON  LAST_MON
      6   Pasadena      91108  12/02/88   350       450        450
      8   Pasadena      91108  12/14/88   400       650        650
     11   Pasadena      91108  12/18/88   575       625        625
ASSIST              //<B:>//APARTMEN              //Rec: 3/11        //          //
                   Press any key to continue work in ASSIST.
```

Figure 3-16. Sorting on a key field.
By asking the program to sort out particular fields—in this case, a particular city, *Pasadena*—you can group
information together in a useful way.

$1,000 in a single order, and ranked by total orders. This way he or
she could organize the New Orleans trip according to which customers were worth spending the most time seeing.

What to Look for in Data Base Programs

A complex DBMS system can take several hours to learn, so the main
thing you need to figure out is what you will use the software *for*.
You also need to consider how much memory you have in your computer. If the entire program will not fit in main memory, you may
have to bring parts of it in from the disk on a regular basis—a slower
process.

Here are some other points to consider in a data base program:

▶ **Ease of use.** As mentioned, many such programs take a long time
to learn. In particular, look for how *key fields* or *keywords* are
used. These are the names such as social security number, gender,
or name by which you can access the same file. Some programs
limit the keywords to only one or two. Some programs allow you
to type in the keyword separately; others require that you move
the cursor to the keyword and press a key.

```
                        Southern California Apartments

         City          Security     First Month    Last Month      Up-Front
                        Deposit        Deposit       Deposits        Totals
       ==========      ========     ==========    ==========      =======

       Burbank            500           500            0            1000
       Inglewood          400           450            0             850
       Northridge         550           550            0            1100
       Pasadena           350           450          450            1250
       Pasadena           400           650          650            1700
       Pasadena           575           625          625            1825
       Santa Monica       500           525          525            1550
       Santa Monica       450           600          600            1650
       Torrance           395           395          395            1185
       Westwood           525           525          525            1575
       Westwood           575           575          575            1725
```

Figure 3-17. Professional-looking report. Modifying the headings and format can make information produced from a data base useful for ordinary readers.

▶ **Size of data base.** How much data will you need to put in a record? Only 20 characters? Several pages worth? Whether you plan to store only names and addresses or several pages of data, your use determines your need. Some data base management systems are limited only by the physical capacity of the disk in use.

▶ **Formulas for computations.** Simple programs include no formulas. Sophisticated programs include a variety of formulas that can handle technical data.

▶ **Flexibility.** Simple programs freeze the format of a record; others allow you to add more data and change the format later.

▶ **Printing.** Plain-looking reports may be suitable if you are using a DBMS for your own research, but if reports are going to outsiders you may want a sophisticated system that can print both all or part of a record.

▶ **Interaction with other programs.** This is becoming essential so that you can manipulate the data on your data base efficiently. Some DBMS programs allow you to use word processing files as input to the data base programs. Others allow you to use the program to generate mailing lists and labels. Others allow you to produce graphic presentations.

Integrated End-User Computing

In an earlier box, we pointed out ways that companies can better support the end-user in microcomputer hardware and software. In general, says the University of Colorado's professor Couger (*Computerworld,* May 25, 1987), companies have followed four strategies:

1. **Interactive terminal access.** In this strategy, one of the earlier ones, companies provided employees with the ability to interact with a computer, but in a limited way. Technical support came from computer professionals, but mostly in the form of helping the users learn such basic tasks as order processing rather than in helping them solve their personal computing needs.

2. **Information centers.** The next step in assistance, *information centers* consisted of physical locations within an organization to which users could go for training, technical assistance, and help in retrieving information from data bases, such as a data base containing information on customers. Now the information center is not located in just one place, but is supposed to provide service to users wherever they are.

3. **Microcomputing.** The third strategy was for users to acquire their own personal computers and software, which meant they got their support from outside the organization. Simultaneously, however, the low cost and user-friendliness of these systems put users outside the control of their firms' data processing setup, which meant they did not have access to corporate data bases.

4. **Integrated end-user computing.** This strategy provides the best of the other three and enhances them. Microcomputers can be made compatible with a firm's mainframe computers so that users can access data bases and use sophisticated mainframe tools, yet they can also use the microcomputers as "stand-alone" tools. In addition, in this strategy, microcomputers fully communicate with each other and have access to data bases outside the organization.

COMPUTER
GRAPHICS

PICTURE THIS!

What is the most effective way to communicate information and ideas for decision making? Graphics, says a study made back in 1981 by the Wharton Applied Research Center at the University of Pennsylvania. According to this survey, we retain only 10% of information we hear but 50% of information presented with visual aids—quite a difference.

Maybe you already sense this intuitively just because you know what it's like to live in the television age. But imagine being a manager grappling with a computer printout of numbers late at night, trying to make sense out of them, and you can probably understand why businesspeople appreciate having business graphics. As the illustrations in Figure 3-18 show, charts and graphs can convey meaning far more quickly than numbers can. For special presentations, you can also use animation to communicate your ideas. And, as we will see, some integrated software packages allow you to take statistical information you have generated from spreadsheets and present them in visual form.

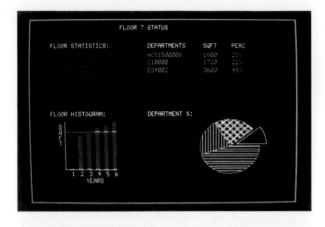

Figure 3-18. Business graphics. Analytical graphics, such as pie charts and bar graphs, help users analyze business data. Presentation graphics are more sophisticated and are designed to help communicate ideas to others.

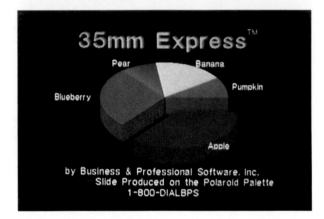

Business computer graphics can be divided into two types:

▶ Analytical
▶ Presentation

Analytical graphics help you analyze data you have compiled. Most analytical graphics are part of larger integrated graphics packages, which means they may be fast and convenient to use but you have less control over what they look like. For instance, you may be confined to drawing pie charts and bar graphs. However, formatting, scaling, and labeling are automatic, so that the program is easy to use. Examples of analytical graphics software are Lotus 1-2-3, PFS:Graph, and ChartMaster.

Presentation graphics are designed to help you communicate a message to other people. It is one thing to determine the solutions to some problems, it is quite another to convince someone else. Presentation graphics help you sell your ideas to your boss or client. Thus, the requirements become different; you need something to *impress* people—something on the order of what a graphics artist would do for you. A presentation-quality graphics program usually will produce a variety of pie, bar, line, organizational, and other charts and will display them in color or black and white on the video screen or printed out on a printer or **plotter,** a printerlike device that produces charts, maps, and drawings in two or three dimensions.

User-friendliness is particularly important because most managers do not have the time to learn how to use complicated graphics software. More than this, however, good graphics programs help a person present *effective* graphics. As one specialist in business graphics points out, "The average person is not trained in the graphic arts. If you pick up a blank piece of paper and ask them to create something themselves—forgetting about their drawing skills—they will do a terrible job. They will lay things out badly, the proportions will be bad, they'll select colors that are just outrageous." Good software includes instructions on how to best select and present graphs and charts. And, of course, the more you use business graphics, the better they are apt to become.

COMMUNICATIONS

BRINGING IT

TOGETHER

Everything you have done so far with software can be sent to another computer—provided you have the right equipment and right communications software. Besides your microcomputer, the equipment consists of a telephone and a device called a **modem**—short for "modulator/demodulator"—which takes the signals from your computer (known as modulated signals) and turns them into signals that can be transmitted over a telephone line (demodulated). We will describe this process in more detail in Chapter 10.

Communications software consists of diskettes that you insert in your micro and that enable you to send or receive information over the telephone lines. Some popular brands of communications software are Smartcom II, Crosstalk XVI, Apple Access II, IBM PC Net, PFS:Access, and MacTerminal. An example of a menu from one communications program is shown in Figure 3-19.

What can you do with a communications program? The possibilities are almost endless—and very exciting. You can:

▶ Gain access to current information—news, weather reports, airline schedules, stock quotations

▶ Perform tasks over the phone—buy airline and concert tickets, do "teleshopping" (order discount appliances, and so on), do home banking and bill paying

▶ Communicate with other microcomputer users—exchange messages, share software, play games

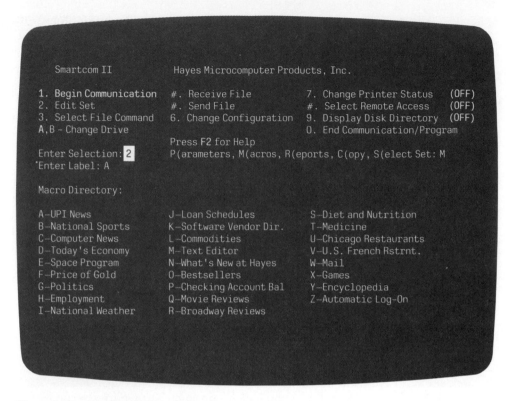

Figure 3-19.   Communications software. Smartcom II offers a menu to help users begin a communications session.

▶ Access on-line data bases

Accessing on-line data bases, some of which are known as "information utilities" (such as CompuServe, The Source, Dow Jones News/Retrieval), is an activity that can be extremely useful. There are now perhaps 3,000 on-line data bases and they cover virtually any topic you might be interested in. With the right equipment and software, therefore, you can do library-type research without having to leave your desk. For students, academic and scientific data bases such as Bibliographic Retrieval Service (BRS) and Dialog are particularly helpful.

As you might imagine, with so many data bases available, *searching* for information can be a problem, particularly since the telephone company and each data base charge you for your time on-line and even for each reference you access. However, so-called *software search aids* are available that help select an on-line service and develop a search strategy while you are "off-line," when no costs are incurred. Examples of software search aids are Sci-Mate Searcher, Pro-Search, and Search Helper.

PICKING PACKAGES

How to Buy Business Software for a Personal Computer

Choosing software packages for a microcomputer is complicated by the fact that there are hundreds of programs offered. Indeed, there are perhaps over 12,000 programs available just for microcomputers alone. Although many programs are for educational and personal uses, a great many business programs are available in the areas of accounting, business graphics, data processing management, decision support, end-user communications, inventory control, file and mail list management, finance and planning, office administration, personnel, preventive maintenance, product procurement, project management, sales and marketing, small business administration, shipping, and word processing. In addition, there is industry specific software, such as for advertising, banking and finance, medicine and health care, and retail.

Key questions you should ask the seller about each software package before you buy are the following:

1. How much does it cost?
2. What specific problems does it solve?
3. What are its key features?
4. What kind of hardware, operating system, and internal storage is required?
5. What kind of documentation and self-paced training, if any, is available?
6. If problems arise, what kind of field or store support and telephone support is available?
7. What kind of warranty is offered, if any?
8. Can you give me the names of users with problems like mine who are using this software?

INTEGRATED PACKAGES

SOFTWARE FOR MULTIPLE USE

The five kinds of business software we have discussed will unquestionably make your professional work life easier. But there can still be a hassle associated with going from one application to another. Integrated software eliminates this trouble.

Integrated software programs are a collection of programs that work together to accomplish specific objectives. Such software is of two types:

▶ **Integrated applications,** which are designed to perform specific related business tasks such as accounts payable and accounts receivable.

▶ **Integrated tools,** which are designed to perform a variety of business tasks such as word processing and filing.

Integrated Applications

Integrated applications are packages consisting of several programs, each designed to perform a specific business function and each of which can be used alone, but all sharing a common format.

Integrated applications software programs share data and work together by accessing the same files and using one program's output as the input for another program. A typical package might include programs for accounts payable, accounts receivable, inventory control, payroll records, and sales analysis.

Integrated Tools: Multitask Business Packages

The software package that we call the integrated tool is the kind that puts together several programs such as those we have discussed—word processing, spreadsheets, data base management, and/or business graphics—in such a way that they can share data with each other. Some offer another capability—communications—so that, with the proper hardware, you can use telephone lines to receive or transmit data.

Lotus 1-2-3 offers spreadsheets, data base management, and business graphics. Symphony is an expanded version of 1-2-3 that also offers word processing and communications programs and that can be run on the IBM PC. Another program, called Framework, likewise offers all five. Thus, you can do a variety of business tasks without having to have three computers. For instance, Symphony includes programs for word processing, spreadsheet analysis, file management, graphics, and communications. Other well-known integrated packages are AppleWorks, Context MBA, ENABLE, Open Access, Electronic Desk, and the Smart Software Series.

An integrated tool allows separate programs to work together by sharing data and information and allows the transfer of data from one program to another. For example, data could be collected by a file management system to create a data base, then analyzed by using a spreadsheet, summarized in graph form using the graphics program, and finally summarized in a final document created with a word processing program. In addition, any part of this project might be sent to someone at another microcomputer, using the communications program.

Figure 3-20; (facing page). An integrated package: Symphony. *Top:* Example of use of pie chart graphics based on spreadsheet analysis. *Bottom:* Use of windows to split screen so that a memo can be written while the writer is looking at the spreadsheet analysis.

An example of an integrated program appears in Figure 3-20. This shows what you might do with the program Symphony after you have created the structure of a data base and entered and sorted all records, then summarized the records in spreadsheet form. At this point, you can graph the results and use word processing to write a summary memo about the results, splitting the screen with windows so that you can analyze the tabulations as you write your memo.

You may find that none of the specific programs in an integrated package is as good by itself as a "stand-alone" program—you can do far more with the WordPerfect word processing program, for instance, than you can with the documentary ("Doc") or word processing part of Symphony. Nevertheless, the fact that all the programs are tied together and are easily shared with each other is what makes integrated software so valuable.

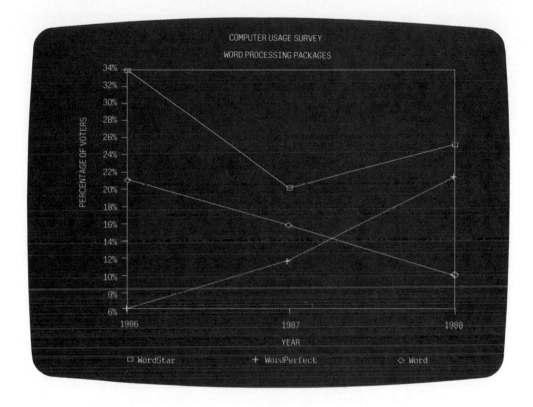

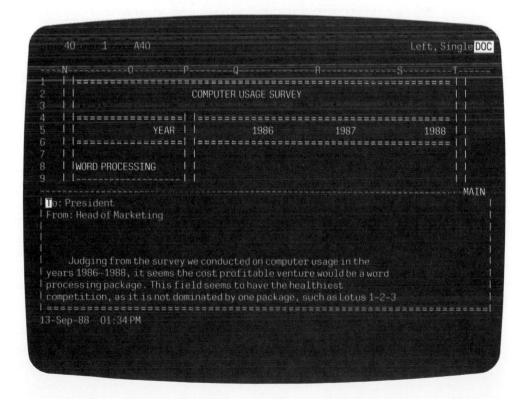

SOME OTHER
USEFUL SOFTWARE

The personal software business has boomed into an industry with perhaps 27,000 different products. Who can keep track of all the programs available, let alone become skilled at more than a few of them? It takes 20 to 40 hours, for instance, to learn Lotus 1-2-3 alone.

Nevertheless, let us describe a couple of programs that may become important to you.

Desktop Management or Memory-Resident Software

How about a program that you can run along with a word processing, spreadsheet, or data base management program that gives you immediate access to such "desktop accessories" as a your personal phone directory, your appointment calendar, a calculator, a notepad, and an automatic telephone dialer (useful for continuing to dial a number when you encounter a busy signal)? Programs like Sidekick, The Desk Organizer, and Memory Mate are **desktop managers** that are called **memory-resident programs**—they stay in your computer's memory all the time (until the power is turned off)—and, no matter what other program you are using, can be activated by pressing a key, without disturbing the other program. This software can enable you to keep your desk free of notepads, pencils, phone directories, and hand calculators. An example of this kind of software is shown in Figure 3-21.

Project Management

What do you do when you create a major business project—for example, produce a motion picture? You do cost estimates, time estimates, and perhaps feasibility studies. Once the project is under way, you track the work's progress and reschedule when things don't go as planned. All this is pretty tedious stuff when done by hand, but **project management software** is available that enables you to automate the process. Indeed, Blue Cross/Blue Shield of Detroit was able to plan a project in two hours with this software that by hand would have taken eight to ten days. As Figure 3-22 shows, with an Apple Macintosh computer and software known as MacProject, you can design, draw, and calculate the interacting elements of a project and show the results in presentation form. Other software is available under the names of Time Line, Harvard Total Project Manager, Microsoft Project, and Super-Project Plus.

Like spreadsheets, project management software also enables you to perform "what-if" analyses—that is, to try out different work plans and schedules and let you see how slippage in one area will affect another area. In addition, this software assists people in re-

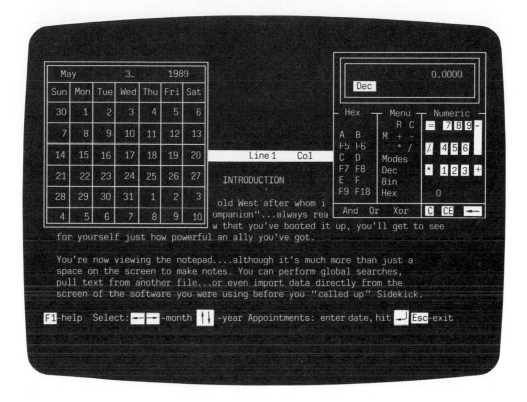

Figure 3-21. Memory-resident software: Sidekick. In this desktop manager, you can, for instance, work on a word processing program, but bring up a window of an appointment calendar or calculator (shown here) or other desktop aids. The calculator can be manipulated through keys on the keyboard.

porting their work progress to each other—an important factor on large projects, where it is difficult to know what everyone else is doing.

Most project management software packages allow at least the following basic activities: planning the project, creating activities, assigning resources (money, materials, people, and so on) to activities, estimating the costs of those resources, deciding which activities to schedule first, and determining critical points that must be attained for the project to stay on schedule. However, we must point out that such programs primarily reflect time, cost, and resource management. That is, they do not consider the very human and important elements of, for instance, employee motivation and assurance of quality work. Moreover, such programs are not easy to handle, and the user needs to understand subjects typically covered in advanced courses on management and operations/production management (such as CPM, PERT, and Gantt charts).

Windowing or "Multitasking" Software

As personal computers have been developed with larger memories—in the IBM Personal System/2 line of computers, for example, the

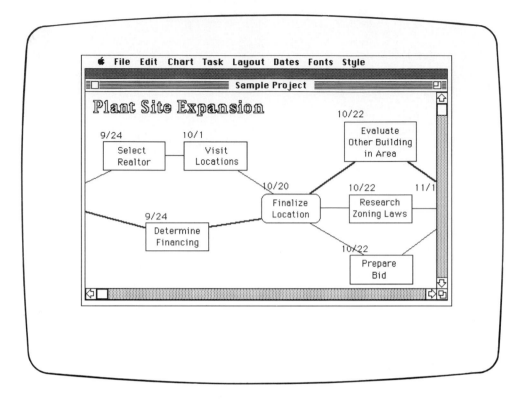

**Figure 3-22.   Project management
software.** In this example using
MacProject, which works on the Macintosh computer, a schedule chart has
been created that shows which tasks
must be accomplished and when, in
order for a project to be completed.

directly accessible memory is 30 times greater than in the older PC
models—they permit what is known as multitasking. Desktop managers merely enable *task switching*—shuttling back and forth between, say, a word processing program and a notepad or calculator—
but this only places one application program on hold while allowing
you to work on another. With **multitasking,** a personal computer can
run a number of applications programs simultaneously.

Among the **windowing** or multitasking programs (also known as
applications integrator programs) are Windows, Desqview, and Top
View. An example of a Windows screen is shown in Figure 3-23.

ONWARD TO

APPLICATIONS

SOFTWARE

DEVELOPMENT

As you journey to southern California to begin your job with Starways Film Production Co., think how prepared you will be with all
the business tools at hand. A decade ago none of these tools was
available. That is an indication of how fast technology has revolutionized our lives—and it will give you some sense of the changes to
come during the rest of your working life.

Why, you might think after reading this, is there any reason for a
manager to learn anything more about how software is created—

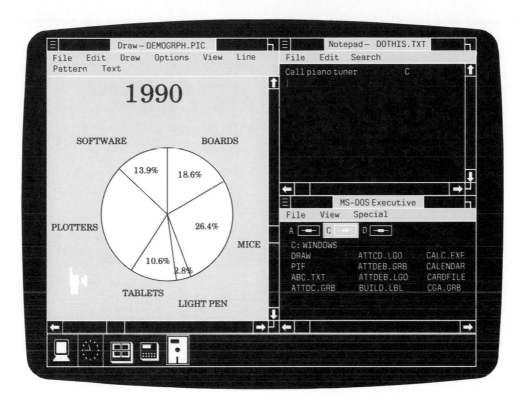

Figure 3-23. Multitasking. Example of Microsoft's Windows program.

what is called "applications software development"? Why, with all the packaged, off-the-shelf software available, does one need to know anything about the intricacies of telling a computer step by step what to do?

The answer is: Applications software development covers a lot more than you probably think. Packaged software will not cover all business applications and there will probably be times when you will want custom-made programs. In addition, you need to be able to understand what programmers do—if you are going to be able to deal with them from a management perspective. Finally, applications software development programming is more than just inputting data to a machine; it is a series of *problem-solving techniques* applicable to other facets of your career.

We show what we mean in the next chapter.

SUMMARY

▶ Computers and software can take much of the waste and inefficiency, and some of the boredom, out of work.

▶ Although computers have been around for over 30 years and have become more powerful at the same time they have become smaller and more accessible, it is recent software that has made them truly useful and accessible to nearly everyone.

▶ Software development has been explosive. The bestsellers, such as WordPerfect, WordStar, Lotus 1-2-3, PFS:File, and dBase, are intended for general business applications—that is, word processing, filing and manipulating data, financial modeling, and accounting.

▶ Software is developed by three different sources: (1) *internal programmers*—people employed by companies to do such tasks as developing payroll programs; (2) *software consultants*—also known as third-party suppliers, who are freelancers or employees of consulting firms offering certain types of expertise or temporary personnel solutions to programming problems; (3) *packaged software manufacturers*—companies, often called "publishers," that develop programs that are available "off the shelf" to anyone.

▶ Software packages are the best sellers and have the advantage of being widely tested and mass-produced; thus, they are relatively inexpensive. However, their flexibility is limited and modifications may be impossible.

▶ Packaged software is being used increasingly in many businesses, thus making it important for people in business to learn how to use it.

▶ Six of the most important software packages involve (1) word processing, (2) financial spreadsheets, (3) file management/data base management, (4) graphics, (5) communications, and (6) **integrated packages**—a collection of programs that work together to accomplish specific objectives.

▶ A **word processor** includes (1) a computer, (2) a keyboard, (3) a display screen, (4) a printer, and (5) a word processing program. Some word processors also have a **mouse,** a device that can be rolled on a table top to move a cursor on the screen. The **cursor** is a blinking mark that acts as a pointer and indicates the location of the next character to be typed. It can be moved anywhere on the screen.

▶ Word processing is designed to allow the creation, editing, formatting, storing, and printing of text.

▶ A **file** is anything stored as a unit.

▶ **Text formatting** concerns the look of the document. Formatting allows the user to set line spacing within the text and size of margins around the text. Text may be **justified,** or evened up in the margin, or **unjustified,** uneven in the margin. Text may be typed all capital letters, underlined, and boldface.

▶ In word processing, one creates text by typing it on the keyboard; the text appears on the screen. Any word that crosses the right-hand margin is automatically moved to the left on the next line down, which is called **word wrap** or **automatic carriage return.**

▶ Word processing makes editing, inserting, and deleting text easy using the cursor. Once changes are made, the text will **reformat** automatically. Some programs have an **overtyping** feature, whereby you can simply type over what you have written.

▶ The **search and replace** function instructs the computer to automatically search for and replace, in the entire document, any words the user wants to change.

▶ The **cut and paste** or **block move** feature allows the user to easily move words, phrases, and other material within the text. This feature allows the user to **read** (obtain) data from other files and **write** (copy it on) the file then in use.

▶ A single keystroke can **save** or store a document on a diskette for later use. The document is stored under a particular **filename,** like the name on a file folder. To retrieve the file, you might look at a **directory,** which lists all filenames on a disk. You could then use a **menu,** or list of commands available, to retrieve the file from the disk and move it into the computer, so it will appear on the display screen. You could then print it out again.

▶ Some of the desirable features of word processing programs are as follows: (1) They are screen oriented—editing changes can be seen directly on the screen. (2) The screen is live—text corrections are seen immediately on the screen. (3) They have menus and Help options. A **Help option** assists the user who does not know what to do next. (4) They allow one to to restore text that has been accidentally deleted. (5) They have backup capability—a second file is available if the first one is accidentally erased. (6) They have a form letter generator or "mail-merge" feature—the user can merge files. (7) They have a spelling checker—a proofreading program that automatically checks spelling. (8) They have a thesaurus that presents synonyms.

▶ Memory-based word processing systems are able to type only documents that are less than a certain length because most of the program is in computer memory; disk-based systems allow storage of longer documents, but they are slower than memory-based systems.

▶ **Windows**—split screens—allow the user to look at one file while working on another.

▶ A **spreadsheet** traditionally was a large sheet of paper divided into rows and columns that accountants and financial analysts used to produce reports. VisiCalc introduced the first electronic spreadsheet in 1979; since then it has been followed by Lotus 1-2-3 and other spreadsheets.

▶ Electronic spreadsheets are popular because they are simple, flexible, and they have "what-if" capability—a feature that allows the user working with numbers to easily recalculate the results as different variables are changed. They are used for sales projections, expense reports, income and balance sheet preparation, and other numerical problems. Figures can be easily changed, and rows and columns can be inserted and deleted.

▶ An electronic spreadsheet (such as Lotus 1-2-3) consists of a *worksheet area* made up of *column headings* across the top and *row headings* down the left-hand side. The place where a particular column and row intersect is called a *cell*, and its position, designated by the coordinates of column letter and row number, is referred to as the *cell address*.

▶ The *control panel*, which is above or below the worksheet area, consists of: (1) the *entry contents line*, which displays information about the format of the cell and what it contains, and (2) the *main menu/edit line*, which lists command choices and allows the user to edit the cell contents. A *submenu line* displays additional commands.

▶ A single screen full of data is known as a **page** or a **window.** The user can move from screen to screen by **scrolling,** moving up or down or from side to side.

▶ Column and row headings are called **labels,** and they must begin with a letter or a word. To enter labels, one can use the keyboard to move the cursor to the appropriate place and type in the information.

▶ A **value** is a number contained in a cell. Calculations are done by formulas.

▶ **Formulas** are instructions for calculations; they create relationships between numbers in particular cells. Formulas are defined in the status area of the spreadsheet. When a number is changed in a cell, the results of the formula in which that cell is involved will **recalculate** automatically.

▶ When working with electronic spreadsheets, the user sees only a part of the sheet; to see both the first column and the last column, one must split the screen.

▶ There are a number of spreadsheet programs. Following are guidelines for choosing one: (1) Screen format—clear presentation and insertion of labels; screen information must be easily edited. (2) Size of spreadsheet—is it large enough? Can the spreadsheet be used all at once? (3) Multiple windows—allowing the user to see more than one screen at once. (4) Calculation flexibility—cell relationships should include not only basic arithmetic operations but any specialized formulas. (5) File access—the spreadsheet should be able to interact with files from other programs. (6) Good **documentation**—the instruction manuals should be easy to use, clear, and complete.

▶ Information filing systems and filing management are important to businesses; the success of a business is often linked to its having orderly and accessible files. Manual filing systems are inefficient, difficult to organize, and not always easily available. However, computerized filing programs—called **data base managers** or **data base management systems (DBMSs)**—can facilitate filing and filing management.

▶ A **data base** is a computerized collection of information, or *integrated* data, that can be used for a variety of applications.

▶ Data consists of *records*, such as various names and addresses; each part of a record (such as a name) is called a *field*. Records may be entered into a data base in any order and then organized in various ways by sorting them according to *key field*—for example, alphabetically by the field of people's last names.

▶ Points to consider in choosing a data base management program are as follows: (1) Ease of use—are key fields easy to use? (2) Size of data base—is the amount of data that can be stored limited? (3) Formulas for computations—are formulas sophisticated enough for one's needs? (4) Flexibility—can formats of records be changed? (5) Printing—is the format sophisticated enough to print out reports for outsiders? (6) Interaction with other programs—can other programs provide input to the data base?

▶ Graphics is the most effective way to communicate information and ideas for decision making. Charts and graphs can convey meaning far more quickly than numbers can. Some integrated software packages allow the user to take statistical information and present it in visual form. There are two types of business computer graphics: (1) analytical and (2) presentation.

▶ **Analytical graphics** help the user analyze compiled data. They are usually part of larger integrated graphics packages, which are fast and convenient to use but which offer less control over visual form.

▶ **Presentation graphics** are designed to help the user communicate a message to other people; they usually will produce a variety of visual forms and display them in color or black and white on the video screen or printed out to a printer or **plotter,** a printerlike device that produces charts, maps, and drawings in two or three dimensions.

▶ Good business graphics programs are "user-friendly" and *effective*, and they include instructions on how to best select and present graphs and charts.

▶ **Communications software** consists of diskettes that enable a microcomputer to send and receive information over telephone lines. Such software requires a **modem** to turn the modulated signals produced by the microcomputer into the demodulated signals that can be transmitted over a telephone line.

▶ With communications software, users can communicate with other microcomputer users, order merchandise via computer, do home banking, and other tasks. They can also gain access to on-line data bases known as "information utilities." Because so many such data bases are available, software search aids are useful in helping develop a search strategy.

▶ The functions of the five kinds of business software discussed (word processing, electronic spreadsheets, data base management, graphics, and communications) can be combined into **integrated software programs,** which are a collection of programs that work together to accomplish specific objectives. There are two types of integrated software: (1) *integrated tools*, which combine programs in one package, and (2) *integrated applications*, which combine programs to focus on a particular business activity.

▶ An integrated tool, which runs on a microcomputer, allows one package of separate programs to work together by sharing data and information and allows the transfer of data from one program to another. An example of integrated tool software packages is Symphony, which includes programs for word processing, spreadsheet analysis, file management, and graphics.

▶ Integrated applications refer to packages consisting of several programs, each designed to perform a specific business function and each of which can be used alone, but all sharing a common format. Integrated applications software programs work together by accessing the same files and using one program's output as the input for another program.

▶ **Desktop managers,** or **memory-resident programs,** remain in the microcomputer's main memory and enable the user to get immediate access to an appointment calendar, calculator, or other "desktop accessory" without disturbing other programs currently being worked on, such as a spreadsheet program.

▶ **Project management software** allows the user to track work in progress on a major business project and reschedule when necessary. Most such software allows people to plan a project, create activities, assign resources, estimate costs, and determine critical scheduling points.

▶ With **multitasking software** or **windowing software,** also known as *applications integrator programs*, the user can run a number of applications programs simultaneously.

KEY TERMS

Integrated package, p. 61

Integrated software program, p. 93

Justified, p. 67

Label, p. 76

Memory-resident program, p. 96

Menu, p. 70

Modem, p. 91

Mouse, p. 63

Multitasking software, p. 98

Overtyping, p. 69

Page, p. 74

Plotter, p. 91

Presentation graphics, p. 90

Project management software, p. 96

Read, p. 69

Recalculate, p. 79

Reformat, p. 69

Save, p. 70

Scrolling, p. 74

Search and replace, p. 69

Spreadsheet, p. 72

Text formatting, p. 66

Unjustified, p. 67

Value, p. 76

Window, p. 72

Windowing software, p. 98

Word processor, p. 63

Word wrap, p. 68

Write, p. 69

REVIEW QUESTIONS

1. Name the three sources of software development.
2. How does word processing make the creation and editing of documents easy?
3. Describe some of the desirable features of a word processing program.
4. What is Lotus 1-2-3? How is it used?
5. Describe the "what-if" capability and its application.
6. What are some of the desirable features to look for in electronic spreadsheets?
7. How would you use a data base management system?

CASE PROBLEMS

Case 3-1: The Electronic Spreadsheet and Managing Cash Flow

One of the most important concepts of business is *cash flow*. Most of us as individuals know what it feels like to be waiting for money to come in while the expenses are piling up; companies have the same problem. Cash flows into a firm at different times than it flows out, so the firm may have to borrow money for the short term while it waits for cash from sales, rents, or whatever to come in.

For example, a farmer may have to borrow money in the spring for seed and fertilizer and make payments for equipment and land throughout the year, but get no income until crops are harvested and sold in the late summer. It is important, therefore, that the farmer figure out *total* expenses and *total* income in order to know how much to borrow and whether the farm will be profitable that year.

Your assignment: Suppose it is January and you are a farmer with access to an electronic spreadsheet. How would you set up the following categories in order to determine cash flow and profitability? (You can write these categories down on paper also.) The point of this exercise is that theoretically you should be able to go to a banker with your spreadsheet and show how much money you need to borrow. This is the kind of activity that many businesspeople such as farmers need to do all the time.

The categories are: Current cash on hand, $125,000. Projected expenses of $20,000 a month for labor for 12 months, February payment of $40,000 for seed and fertilizer, April payment of $40,000 for equipment, and land payments of $5,000 a month for 12 months. In September, you project you will receive $365,000 in sales, and you will have to set aside $45,000 for taxes. Now, in January, you currently have $125,000 cash on hand. How much money will you have to borrow between now and September per month? If you pay 15% interest for the total amount that you borrow for the year, how much money will you have left as net income?

Case 3-2: Training Firms for Computers

A survey by one temporary-help service organization found that 56% of the 511 executives polled felt that inadequately trained staff or a lack of staff altogether prevented them from using modern word processing machines effectively. This is the reason, therefore, why there has been such growth in companies that specialize in training people in how to operate microcomputers and software.

Your assignment: This is a growth area in which those who have experience can help others who have not had experience. Now that you have read about word processing, explain some of the specific time-saving activities to someone who has not read this chapter.

Chapter 4

APPLICATIONS SOFTWARE DEVELOPMENT: MAKING THE COMPUTER WORK FOR YOU

The software packages we described in Chapter 3 are intended for *general* applications. However, organizations often require custom-tailored software that will instruct a computer—micro, mini, or mainframe—how to perform a *specific* data processing or computational task. Such software is called **applications software** or **applications programs.** A **program** is a series of detailed steps to be completed in order to solve a problem. These may be thought of as a logical sequence of instructions that direct the computer to perform whatever operations we wish.

The importance of understanding programming—and the consequences of good and bad programming—may be appreciated by a reading of the case study on the next page.

WHAT IS APPLICATIONS SOFTWARE DEVELOPMENT?

Applications software development is, of course, the process of creating applications software. There are two ways by which you, as an end-user, might accomplish this:

▶ **Work with a systems analyst.** If you are interested in creating applications software that will fit in with your organization's information system, you would enlist the help of a **systems analyst,** an information specialist who has expertise in systems analysis, design, and implementation. You would go about your task using the steps in the five-step *systems life cycle* we described in Chap-

CASE STUDY: PROGRAMMING ERROR AND HUMAN LIVES

Is There a Better Way to Write Programs?

The countdown was coming to an end. Lying on their backs in the cockpit of the space shuttle *Columbia,* astronauts John Young and Robert Crippen could see pelicans flying along the beach at Cape Canaveral. Straight ahead the stars had given way to the deep blue of early morning. Within less than an hour they would be the first people to fly the space shuttle into orbit, the first Americans in space in more than five years.

Then, 20 minutes before launch time, warning lights at Mission Control began to flash. Something was wrong with the computer system. The countdown was halted; the computer analysts went to work. They had three hours before the flight would have to be scrubbed.

It became apparent that nothing was physically wrong with the computers. All of the circuits were working. The communication lines were intact. The problem seemed to lie instead in the programs, in the software, that told the computers what to do.

Technicians immediately realized they faced a serious problem. The software on board the space shuttle consists of nearly 500,000 elaborately inter-woven instructions. Finding a programming error, a bug, in that web would be like trying to find a single misspelled word in an encyclopedia. Soon the news began to circulate: The maiden flight of the space shuttle would have to be delayed.

"It was precisely the type of error that one would expect," says the Dutch computer scientist Edsger W. Dijkstra (pronounced DIKE-stra). He inhales on his cigarette, then continues. "You see, most of NASA's software is full of bugs."

His eyebrows arch with pleasure, a sure sign that a story follows. "I saw the first moon shot in 1969, when Armstrong, Aldrin, and Collins went to the moon, and shortly thereafter I met Joel Aron of IBM's Federal Systems Division, who I knew had been responsible for a large part of the software. So when I saw Joel at the swimming pool of our hotel in Rome, I said, 'Joel, how did you do it?' 'Do what?' he said. I said, 'Get that software to work okay.' 'Okay?' he said. 'It was full of bugs. In one of the trajectory computations, we had the moon's gravity repulsive rather

than attractive, and this was discovered by accident five days before count zero.'"

Dijkstra draws back in his chair, the picture of astonished outrage. "When I had regained my composure, I said, 'Those three guys, they have been lucky.' 'Oh yes,' Joel said."

For more than 20 years, Dijkstra has been fighting against the kind of programming that inevitably leads to bugs in computer software. To him, the way organizations like NASA program computers is foolhardy at best, perilous at worst. He believes there is another way, a better way. It involves structuring how a person thinks about programming so that programs themselves acquire a firm mathematical basis. The discipline his work has spawned, called structured programming, has been one of the most important advances in computer software of the past two decades.

—Steve Olson, *Science 84*

ter 2 (system investigation, analysis, design, implementation, and maintenance). You would use this sophisticated approach, for example, if you were trying to create accounts receivable software (to tell you what money is owed to or has been received by your company) to fit into your organization's accounting information system. As we shall see in Chapters 11 and 12, working with a systems analyst and applying the systems life cycle is a process that is important for complicated undertakings.

▶ **Work with a programmer—or do it yourself.** If you are interested in creating applications software only to achieve a specific task for a specific end-user, such as yourself, you may not need to seek out such sophisticated advice or go through such a complicated process. You can work with a programmer or perhaps even do it yourself. In this chapter we show you how.

Whether the applications software that is being produced is supposed to be integrated with the computerized information systems of a large organization or need only work within the microcomputer of one user, the process of developing it is the same: it is a six-step process known as the **program development cycle** or the **program life cycle**—namely:

1. Define the problem.
2. Design a solution.
3. Write—that is, code—the program.
4. Test—that is, debug—the program.
5. Document the program
6. Maintain the program.

It is important to note that the program life cycle is not the same as the systems life cycle. Rather, the program life cycle is only one step—step 4, Systems Implementation—in the systems life cycle. Figure 4-1 shows how the program life cycle and the systems life cycle differ and how they work together.

To help you put these concepts to some use, let us say that by now you have joined Starways Film Production Company in Century City, California, and are working on the business side of their operation. Mr. Elliott, the president, has the show business habit of referring to everyone by first name or endearment, but he can be of the bare-knuckles school of business when it comes to cost overruns on pictures. As he explains to you, only about 2 out of 500 films are sold by their independent producers, such as Starways, to a major studio distributor for an immediate profit. Usually, the studio gets the picture on a releasing deal and pays the producer back out of money earned, which means the investors in the picture take a long time to get their money back. The upshot is that it is imperative that costs be controlled on a film while it is in production.

The first step in the programming life cycle is to *define the problem.* Known as *program analysis,* this means specifying program objectives, outputs, input requirements, and processing requirements; evaluating feasibility; and documenting the program analysis.

The second step is to *design a solution.* Called the *program design,* this stage may use structured program design tools: top-down program design, structure charts, flowcharts, and pseudocode.

The third step is to *write the program.* Writing is called *coding.* A good program should be readable, efficient, reliable, and detect error conditions. This is helped with structured coding which uses the three structures *sequence, selection,* and *loop.*

The fourth step is to *test the program.* Testing is also called *debugging.* The program is tested for syntax errors and logic errors.

The fifth step is to *document the program.* This helps programmers update and maintain the program.

The sixth step is to *maintain the program.*

Figure 4-1.   The program life cycle. These six steps of the programming cycle may be used by an individual end-user or programmer to solve a specific task or, when more complicated applications software is developed, as the implementation step in the systems life cycle.

Elliott is irate about the way payroll in particular has been handled on some recent Starways-backed films. There has been a good deal of sloppiness, with overpayments going to several of the cast and crew and late payments to a good many others. One of your initial assignments is to be his personal financial watchdog, as it were, on a new film going into production whose working title is *Dynamite Bay*. The film crew is going on location shooting in Australia, and planning is critical. There will be over 100 cast and crew members traveling, ranging from major players to a wind-machine operator.

In the past, the payroll system for films on location was maintained by an accountant who operated with a manual system. Sometimes, if the accountant was ill or if there were cast changes, there was difficulty in keeping the payroll system straight. You decide to see if you can set up a payroll procedure using a portable computer that can be used on location. The main thing is to get the paychecks out on time so that morale on the picture will not suffer, which could lead to costly production delays.

You meet with a computer programmer and the *Dynamite Bay* accountant to see what can be worked out. You begin with the first of the six steps: defining the problem.

1. DEFINING THE PROBLEM

Defining the problem, also known as **program analysis,** involves the following six tasks:

▶ Specify the objectives of the program.
▶ Specify the outputs.
▶ Specify the input requirements.
▶ Specify the processing requirements.
▶ Evaluate the feasibility of the program.
▶ Document the program analysis.

These tasks are shown in Figure 4-2. In this stage you not only want to determine the input and output requirements but also to get a sense of how much everything will cost.

Specifying the Objectives of the Program

In order to avoid having the right solution to the wrong problem, we need to be sure we know what the problem actually is. Making a clear statement of the problem depends, of course, on its size and complexity. If the problem is small and does not involve other sys-

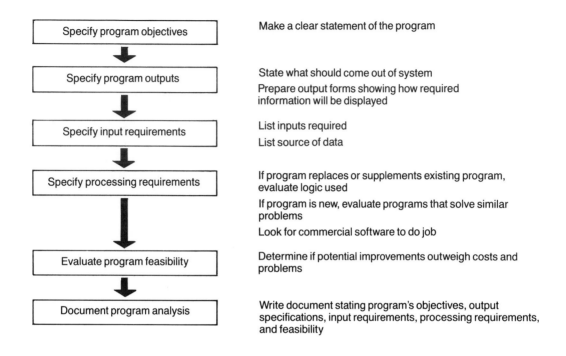

Specify program objectives	Make a clear statement of the program
Specify program outputs	State what should come out of system Prepare output forms showing how required information will be displayed
Specify input requirements	List inputs required List source of data
Specify processing requirements	If program replaces or supplements existing program, evaluate logic used If program is new, evaluate programs that solve similar problems Look for commercial software to do job
Evaluate program feasibility	Determine if potential improvements outweigh costs and problems
Document program analysis	Write document stating program's objectives, output specifications, input requirements, processing requirements, and feasibility

Figure 4-2.   The first task of applications development. Six tasks of defining the problem.

tems of instructions, then we can probably state the problem easily and proceed immediately to the second step, "Design a solution." However, many problems interact with an already existing information system (such as the manual system of processing paychecks) or will require a series of programs and so require very complete analysis, meaning careful coordination of people, procedures, and programs. We will discuss such systems analysis and design in detail in Chapters 10 and 11.

In your meeting with the *Dynamite Bay* accountant and programmer, you agree on the program objective:

Figure 4-3. Weekly paycheck for
***Dynamite Bay* film crew and cast.**
This sketch shows the output format
you wish to produce. In this case, the
check is for one of the staff members
in the sound department on the picture, Amy Gardner, a cableperson, but
the format can be used for other staff
members also.

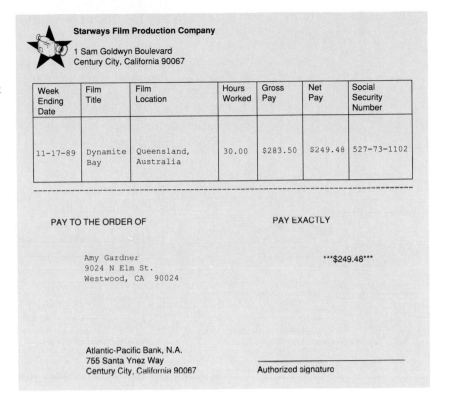

*Program objective: To develop a computerized payroll
system that will print payroll checks on location, replacing the manual system.*

Specifying the Outputs

Before you know what should go into a system, you need to say what
should come out. The best way to specify the outputs is to prepare
some output forms that show how the required information will be
displayed. The best person to design the output forms is the ultimate
user of the information, although forms can also be designed by the
programmer (or by a systems analyst). The forms should be examined to see that they are useful and have neither too much nor too
little detail.

In your *Dynamite Bay* meeting, you, the programmer, and the
accountant agree on the output specifications:

Output specifications: Weekly paycheck.

You then specify the basic format of the paycheck, as shown in Figure 4-3. For this pass, the details are not critical.

Specifying the Input Requirements

Now that you have determined the outputs, you need to define the input and data. To do this, you list the inputs required and the source of the data. For example, in a payroll program, the *inputs* could be employee time sheets and the *source* of the input could be either the employees themselves or their supervisors. You need to be sure that the source of the data is constant—that data will be available in the future when you need it.

At the *Dynamite Bay* meeting, you agree on the input requirements as follows:

> *Input requirements: There are two sources of input.*
> 1. *INPUT: Time sheet, with week ending date and hours worked that week*
>   *SOURCE: Employee's supervisor*
>   *FORMAT: Example shown in Figure 4-4, top*
> 2. *INPUT: Employee data, including pay rate*
>   *SOURCE: Personnel file*
>   *FORMAT: Example shown in Figure 4-4, bottom*

Specifying the Processing Requirements

Now you have to determine the processing requirements for converting the input data to output. If the proposed program is to replace or to supplement an existing one, you will want to make a particularly careful evaluation and identification of present processing procedures, noting the logic used and any improvements that could be made. If the proposed system is not designed to replace an existing system, you would be well advised to look over another system in use that addresses a similar problem.

In either case, you will want to look for commercially available software that can do the job, so that you will not have to write your own programs. You may not find anything that meets your needs, but if you do, it will greatly reduce the time, cost, and uncertainty of program development.

The programmer advises you and the *Dynamite Bay* accountant that the processing procedures are uncomplicated. There are a number of commercial software packages available that will fit the bill, but they are more complex than you require and you might as well save the expense. You agree on processing requirements thus:

> *Processing requirements: Paychecks may be produced by multiplying the number of hours an employee works by his or her rate of pay per hour, then calculating deductions to determine net pay, and then printing the payroll check.*

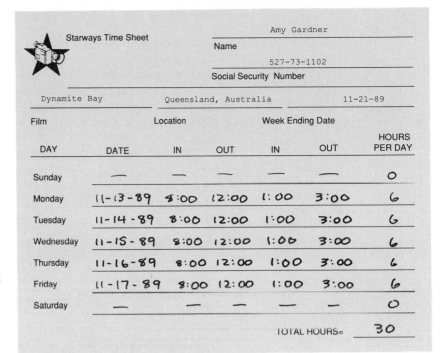

Figure 4-4. *Dynamite Bay* **payroll input.** *Top:* sketch of employee time sheet—in this case, a hypothetical one for Amy Gardner. This time sheet would be completed by her supervisor, the Production Manager. *Bottom:* Format for personnel file, source of second input, which includes employee pay rate; specific example of Amy Gardner's personnel file.

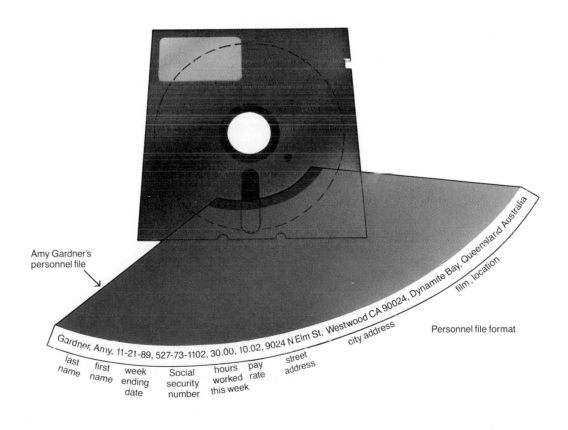

Evaluating the Feasibility of the Program

Now you need to see if what you have accomplished so far is enough to make a new program feasible. If the program is intended to replace an existing system, you need to determine if the potential improvements outweigh the costs and possible problems. A new computer program, after all, has to be judged like any other new business investment. Thus, evaluating program feasibility is the "Go/No go" stage.

The *Dynamite Bay* accountant does not think the computer system for producing paychecks is worth all the bother. The programmer, however, thinks it would not be that difficult to implement since the film crew is already packing along a portable computer for other purposes. You break the tie by voting to go ahead:

> *Feasibility: The film crew's portable computer, plus a simplified payroll program, will be an adequate on-site payroll system. Costs to develop the program will be less than purchasing a packaged program.*

Documenting the Program Analysis

Before concluding the program analysis stage, it is best to write up a document stating the results of this first phase. This document should contain statements on the program's

- ▶ Objectives
- ▶ Output specifications
- ▶ Input requirements
- ▶ Processing requirements
- ▶ Feasibility

In other words, the document should describe everything you have done so far. In view of Mr. Elliott's intense interest in *Dynamite Bay*'s profitability, you decide this is an especially good idea.

2. DESIGNING A SOLUTION

You know you have a problem and have identified it in the "Define the problem" or program analysis stage. Now you need to plan a solution to meet the objectives you specified there. This second stage is called the **program design** stage; it consists of designing a solution.

Structured program design is a method of designing a computer program in such a way as to minimize complexity. Among the tools used in this stage are:

Figure 4-5. Top-down design. This example for the *Dynamite Bay* movie payroll shows the three principal program modules and their functions. Notice how the control module transfers to the module A entry point, reads the data, then exits and transfers back to the control module. It then transfers to the module B entry point, makes all the calculations and prints the paycheck, then exits and transfers back to the control module. The sequence is then repeated for another employee's wage data and paycheck.

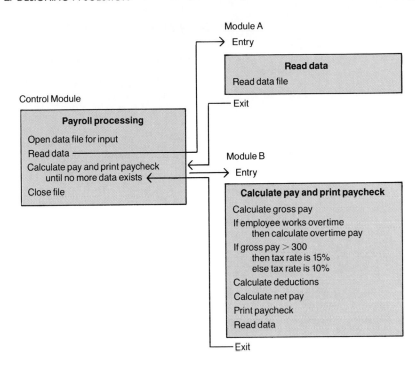

Control Module

Payroll processing

Open data file for input
Read data
Calculate pay and print paycheck
  until no more data exists
Close file

Module A
> Entry

Read data
Read data file

— Exit

Module B
> Entry

Calculate pay and print paycheck

Calculate gross pay
If employee works overtime
  then calculate overtime pay
If gross pay > 300
  then tax rate is 15%
  else tax rate is 10%
Calculate deductions
Calculate net pay
Print paycheck
Read data

— Exit

▶ Top-down program design
▶ Flowcharts
▶ Pseudocode

Whether to use all or only some of these tools is up to the programmer.

Top-Down Program Design

Top-down program design is a structured design technique in which the programmer, having determined the outputs to be produced and the inputs required, identifies the major processing steps that the program must perform. These major processing steps are called program **modules.** A module is a set of logically related program statements.

The modules for the *Dynamite Bay* payroll problem are shown in Figure 4-5. Notice that there are three modules in this example:

▶ **Control Module:** The module labeled *PAYROLL PROCESSING* is called the *control module*; this main module controls the operation of the other two, *READ DATA* and *CALCULATE PAY AND PRINT PAYCHECK.*

▶ **Module A:** The *READ DATA* module is concerned with the inputs—the word *data* represents several items of data, including number of hours worked and wage rate per hour.

▶ **Module B:** The module called *CALCULATE PAY AND PRINT PAYCHECK* specifies the processing requirements and the output required—that is, the paycheck.

Top-down design has some rigid rules:

▶ Each module can have only *one entry point and one exit point,* so that the logic flow of the program is easy to follow.

▶ When the program is **executed**—programmer talk for "run through the computer"—it must be able *to move from one module to the next in sequence until the last module has been executed.* Thus, in Figure 4-5, program control moves from Control Module to Module A, back to Control Module, then to Module B, then back to Control Module, then to Module A again—and so on.

▶ Each module should be *independent and should have a single function.* For example, a module that is used to compute withholding tax should not also be used to compute pension benefits. If a module is independent, it can be easily changed later without having to change other modules.

▶ Each module should be of *manageable size*—have no more than 50 program instructions—*in order to make the design and testing of the program easier.* Module B in Figure 4-5, for instance, has only seven program instructions.

Flowcharts

One of the most widely used devices for designing programs is the **flowchart,** which graphically presents the logic needed to solve a programming problem. A **program flowchart** presents the detailed sequence of steps needed to solve the problem. Program flowcharts are frequently used to visualize the logic and steps in processing. Figure 4-6 presents a program flowchart for the *Dynamite Bay* payroll problem.

There are only a few standard flowchart symbols necessary to solve almost any programming problem. These are explained in Figure 4-7.

Pseudocode

An alternative or supplement to flowcharts, **pseudocode** is a narrative rather than graphical form of describing structured program logic. It allows the program designer to focus on the *logic* of the program and not on the details of programming or flowcharting.

Computer Programming: Why Bother to Learn It?

With all the off-the-shelf applications software available, why should you—or any ordinary manager or administrator—learn how to write programs? Apart from pure curiosity, perhaps there are two reasons:

▶ Despite the numerous ready-made programs available, you might not find one that does the job exactly the way you want it. Knowing programming allows you to modify commercial programs or even write your own.

▶ Knowing how to program may give you a competitive edge in your company because it shows you understand more about computers than most general managers.

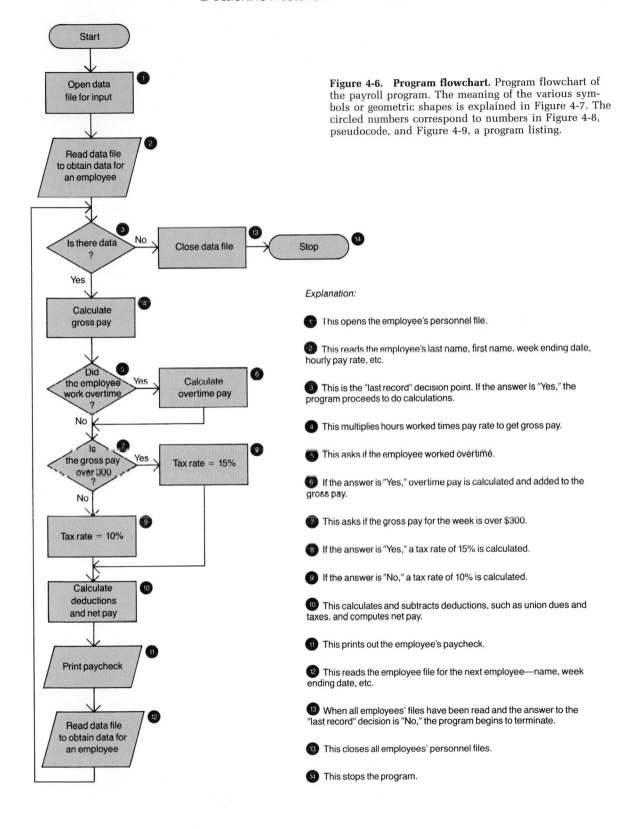

Figure 4-6.   Program flowchart. Program flowchart of the payroll program. The meaning of the various symbols or geometric shapes is explained in Figure 4-7. The circled numbers correspond to numbers in Figure 4-8, pseudocode, and Figure 4-9, a program listing.

Explanation:

1. This opens the employee's personnel file.

2. This reads the employee's last name, first name, week ending date, hourly pay rate, etc.

3. This is the "last record" decision point. If the answer is "Yes," the program proceeds to do calculations.

4. This multiplies hours worked times pay rate to get gross pay.

5. This asks if the employee worked overtime.

6. If the answer is "Yes," overtime pay is calculated and added to the gross pay.

7. This asks if the gross pay for the week is over $300.

8. If the answer is "Yes," a tax rate of 15% is calculated.

9. If the answer is "No," a tax rate of 10% is calculated.

10. This calculates and subtracts deductions, such as union dues and taxes, and computes net pay.

11. This prints out the employee's paycheck.

12. This reads the employee file for the next employee—name, week ending date, etc.

13. When all employees' files have been read and the answer to the "last record" decision is "No," the program begins to terminate.

13. This closes all employees' personnel files.

14. This stops the program.

Figure 4-7. Symbols used in program flowcharting.

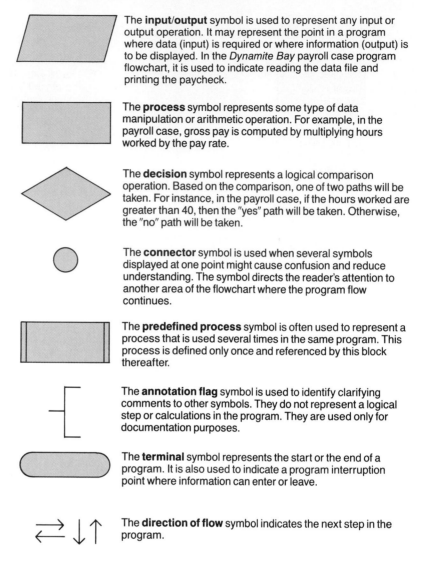

The **input/output** symbol is used to represent any input or output operation. It may represent the point in a program where data (input) is required or where information (output) is to be displayed. In the *Dynamite Bay* payroll case program flowchart, it is used to indicate reading the data file and printing the paycheck.

The **process** symbol represents some type of data manipulation or arithmetic operation. For example, in the payroll case, gross pay is computed by multiplying hours worked by the pay rate.

The **decision** symbol represents a logical comparison operation. Based on the comparison, one of two paths will be taken. For instance, in the payroll case, if the hours worked are greater than 40, then the "yes" path will be taken. Otherwise, the "no" path will be taken.

The **connector** symbol is used when several symbols displayed at one point might cause confusion and reduce understanding. The symbol directs the reader's attention to another area of the flowchart where the program flow continues.

The **predefined process** symbol is often used to represent a process that is used several times in the same program. This process is defined only once and referenced by this block thereafter.

The **annotation flag** symbol is used to identify clarifying comments to other symbols. They do not represent a logical step or calculations in the program. They are used only for documentation purposes.

The **terminal** symbol represents the start or the end of a program. It is also used to indicate a program interruption point where information can enter or leave.

The **direction of flow** symbol indicates the next step in the program.

A pseudocode to a program, says one writer, "is as beneficial as a sentence outline is to a research paper." Just as an outline contains enough specifics to ensure that you will not overlook any pertinent details when you are drafting your research paper, so a pseudocode will contain enough specifics as to what information or calculations are needed to be performed within the major "outline" areas—the modules—that no major points will be missed.

As a manager, you may find pseudocode helpful because it allows you to get a preview of the program before the programmer actually starts putting it into flowchart or code form.

Figure 4-8. Pseudocode. This example shows how the *Dynamite Bay* payroll could be expressed in narrative rather than graphical form. DO WHILE means the computer should continue to *do* the processing *while*— that is, so long as—the conditions apply, namely, that "more employees exist" for whom paychecks must be made up. When that condition no longer exists, the program is instructed to END DO—that is, stop processing. Note that IF a certain condition exists, THEN certain steps must follow (or ELSE certain other steps must follow), until the condition no longer exists, at which point the computer is instructed to END IF. The IF and THEN would be expressed in a flowchart as the diamond-shaped decision symbol. The circled numbers correspond to the relevant portions of the program flowchart in Figure 4-6 and the actually coded program shown in Figure 4-10.

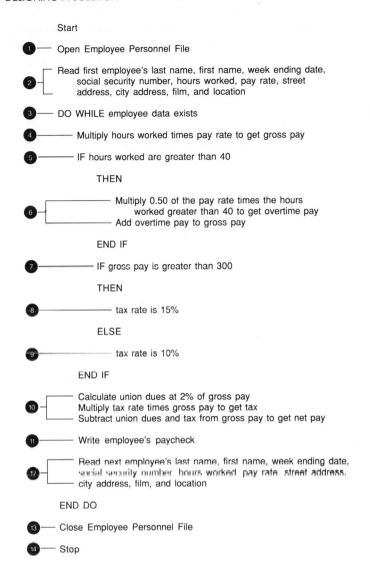

Figure 4-8 presents some pseudocode for the *Dynamite Bay* problem; parts of it are based on the structured coding discussed in another few pages.

Document Program Design

At the end of the program design stage, a formal document should be prepared to guide future users. How long and detailed the document is depends on the size and complexity of the program. How important the document is also varies. If the program is so specialized that it will be used only once, it will deserve a different kind of document than that of a typical business program that is to be used over and over.

3. WRITING THE PROGRAM

Writing the program is called **coding**. In this step, you use the logic you developed in the program design stage to actually write the program. This coding stage is, as we mentioned, what many people mean when they say "programming," but it really is only one of the six steps.

What programming language should you use for a program? Pascal? BASIC? COBOL? FORTRAN? Other? We will defer this question to the next chapter, when we discuss several programming languages. Here we will discuss what makes a good program regardless of the language used.

What Makes a Good Program?

As in other areas of life, there are many ways to get to the same place. Traditional styles of programming *can* yield correct results just as structured programming can. But why take extra time, make extra mistakes, and produce a program that your successors may or may not be able to figure out after you have moved on?

Here are some of the qualities of a good program:

▶ It should be easily readable and understandable by people other than the original programmer. This is accomplished by including comments within the program.

▶ It should be efficient, increasing the programmer's productivity.

▶ It should not take excessive time to process, or occupy any more computer memory than necessary.

▶ It should be reliable, able to work under all reasonable conditions, and always get the correct output.

▶ It should be able to detect unreasonable or error conditions and indicate them to the programmer or operator without stopping all operations—that is, "crashing" the system.

Three factors that help make programs efficient are: (1) the statements can be arranged into patterns that enhance readability, (2) the variables—**variables** are symbolically named entities to which may be assigned a value or values—used are carefully and descriptively named, and (3) comments can be inserted into the program to document the logic patterns used.

As Mr. Elliott's right-hand person on the *Dynamite Bay* payroll project, you are particularly interested in anything that holds costs down. Thus, for instance, you would probably want the program to screen out any obvious errors in input data. For example, except for the salaries of the top stars, you would not want the wage rate per hour incorrectly input at $300 per hour. The program should catch obvious and common errors of this sort, although, of course, it cannot catch everything. You also want the program to be easily maintained and updated by other programmers, since you hope the same program can be used on other Starways productions.

Structured Coding: Avoiding "Spaghetti Code"

This is a very important discussion, for it has to do with the very nature of the logic of writing programs. *Structured coding* has been developed to take much of the guesswork out of programming, to assist programmers to produce programs of quality on a regular basis. It calls for rigid programming standards in which only three basic logic structures can be used.

Once you have done your top-down design, breaking down the principal modules into lower-level functional modules, you can then proceed to write *any* program using a combination of three—and just these three—basic logic structures:

▶ Sequence
▶ Selection
▶ Loop

These three structures, shown in Figure 4-9, work as described in the following sections.

Sequence Structure The **sequence structure**—also known as *simple sequence*—is easily defined: It is simply *one program statement followed by another*. An example for the payroll program, where the sequence structure is used to calculate deductions, is shown in the top part of Figure 4-9.

Selection Structure The **selection structure** occurs when a decision has to be made. It may be defined as: *A test must be made, and the outcome determines the choice of one of two paths to follow*. The selection structure was used in the payroll example to decide whether an employee's tax rate was 15% OR 28%, as shown in the middle part of Figure 4-9.

The selection structure is also known as an **IF-THEN-ELSE structure,** because that is how you would formulate the problem when making the decision or test. For example, in our program, you could say, "IF gross pay is over $300, THEN tax rate is 28%, ELSE tax rate is only 15%."

Figure 4-9. Sequence, selection, and loop logic structures. The examples at right are taken from the *Dynamite Bay* payroll flowchart in Figure 4-6.

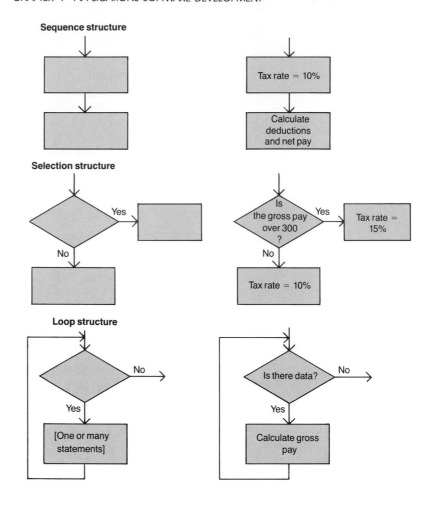

Loop Sequence The **loop structure**—also known as an *iteration structure*—may be defined as: *A process may be repeated as long as a certain condition remains true.* The structure is called a "loop" because the program loops around again and again. We see this in the *Dynamite Bay* program example in which the loop structure is used to process the payroll (see Figure 4-6). The program will continue to loop repeatedly until the answer to the question in the first selection structure ("Is there more data?") is *no*, not *yes*—in other words, until there are no more employees to figure weekly wages for. Then the program will close the data file and stop.

The loop structure is also known as a **DO UNTIL structure** in the principal form in which the loop is used. This is a handy way of thinking about the loop structure while you are writing a program. For example, in our payroll case, you could express the loop as: "DO process the payroll program UNTIL there is no more data to process." A variation is the **DO WHILE structure.** For example, in our payroll case, you could express the loop as: "DO process the payroll program WHILE there are employees whose time cards need processing."

FLASHBACK: BEFORE STRUCTURED PROGRAM DESIGN

A Bowl of Spaghetti

The best way to show why structured coding is important is to go back to the "Sage of Software," as he has been called, Edsger Dijkstra. In 1968, Dijkstra published a letter in the *Communications of the ACM* (Association for Computing Machinery), which appeared under the heading, "Go To Statements Considered Harmful." The GO TO (often expressed as GOTO) is a transfer of control within a program: The program is told to go to another line in the program. In his letter, Dijkstra contended that the GOTO statements were overused to the point where a program could be compared to a bowl of spaghetti. That is, if you drew a line from each GOTO statement in a program to the statement to which it transferred, the result would be a picture that looked like a bowl of spaghetti. Since then, people have referred to a program that uses a lot of GOTOs as "spaghetti code."

Two years before Dijkstra's letter, the *Communications of the ACM* had also published a paper by C. Bohm and G. Jacopini that proved mathematically that any problem solution could be constructed using only three basic logic structures—the ones referred to in the text under the names *sequence, selection,* and *loop.* It is noteworthy that these three structures have remained unchanged since they were proposed in 1966.

The first major project using structured programming was a large undertaking done for the *New York Times*, the results of which were published in 1972.

Edsger Dijkstra.

The task was to automate the newspaper's vast clipping file in such a way that a user could browse through summaries of the paper's articles, using a list of index terms, and automatically retrieve the text of the article, which was stored on microfiche, and display it on a terminal. The project involved 83,000 lines of code, took 22 calendar months, and involved 11 person-years, yet it came in ahead of schedule and under budget—and with only 21 errors during the five weeks of acceptance testing. Only 25 additional errors appeared during the first year of the system's operation—an unheard-of record in the days of spaghetti code. Since then, structured programming has gained wide acceptance.

Although other logic sequences exist, it has been proven mathematically that any program can be written with just these three.

Having worked through the logic of the program in structured form, you are now in a position to actually write it or code it—assuming you know what programming language to write it in. Since the *Dynamite Bay* film crew is taking a portable computer with them, one that will run the language known as Pascal, you ask the programmer to code it in Pascal. This program is shown in Figure 4-10. We will describe Pascal in more detail in Chapter 5, along with a discussion of other programming languages.

The program has been written, so you are now ready to run it and test it on the computer.

```pascal
Program Payroll(input,output);

{Program Description:

{This program will read in information from the employee data file about an
individual, and then calculate his net pay for the week, subtracting taxes as
well as union dues automatically. The program will output a check in the
correct amount to the individual in question.}
}

Type

    Name = Packed array[1..25] of char;
    Employee_Info = record
        Last_name : name;
        First_name : name;
        Week_date : name;
        Social_Security : name;
        Hours_worked : real;
        Pay_rate : real;
        Street_address : name;
        City_address : name;
        Film_name : name;
        Film_location : name;
    End;
    data_file = file of employee_info;

Var
    Empdat : data_file;
    Employee : employee_info;


(********************************************************************)

Procedure READ_FILE( Var Employee : Employee_info;
                     Var Empdat    : Data_file);

{This procedure reads in the employee information from the file EMPDAT into
the employee record}
}

Begin
    Read(EMPDAT, Employee);
End;


(********************************************************************)

(Procedure COMPUTE_PAYROLL( Employee : Employee_info);

{This procedure will compute the employee's payroll, deduction both taxes
and union dues, outputing a check to the employee in question.}
}
```

Figure 4-10.   Pascal program for
Dynamite Bay **payroll program.**
The circled numbers correspond
to the pertinent portions of the
flowchart in Figure 4-6 and pseudocode in Figure 4-8.

```
    Var

 ─ Gross_pay : real;
 ─ overtime_pay : real;
   union_dues : real;
   tax_rate : real;
   tax : real;
   Net_pay : real;

   Begin
④── gross_pay : = employee.hours_worked * employee.pay_rate;
⑤ ─ If employee.hours_worked > 40.00 then
        Begin
⑥──────── overtime_pay : = ((employee.pay_rate * 0.5) *
                            (employee.hours_worked_40.00));
        End;
⑦─ If gross_pay > 300 then
⑧ ─    tax_rate : = 0.15
     Else
⑨──    tax_rate : = 0.10
     Union_dues : = 0.02 * gross_pay;
⑩─  Tax : = tax_rate * gross_pay;
     net_pay : = gross_pay─union_dues─tax;
     writeln;
     writeln;
     writeln;
     writeln;
     writeln;
     writeln;
     writeln(employee.week_date:9,employee.film_name:17,
             employee.film_location:26,employee.hours_worked:3:2,'$',
             gross_pay:3:2,'$',net_pay:3:2,' ',
             employee.social_security:12);
⑪   writeln;
     writeln;
     writeln(employee.first_name:31,' ',employee.last_name:11);
     writeln(employee.street_address:39, $',
             net_pay:3:2);
     writeln(employee.city_address:40);
   end;


   (**************************************************************)

   Begin (* Main program *)
①   Assign(empdat,'b:e.dat');
    Reset(empdat);
③─ While not eof(empdat) do
        Begin
②────────  Read_file(employee,empdat);
           compute_payroll(employee);
⑫──   End;
⑬─ Close(empdat);
⑭─ End.
```

4. TESTING THE PROGRAM

Testing means running the program and fixing it if it does not work, or **debugging** it (getting the errors or bugs out), as programmers call it. Let us consider two types of bugs or errors: syntax errors and logic errors.

A **syntax error** is a violation of the rules of whatever programming language the programmer is writing in. For example, if the programmer is trying to print a line and is writing in the Pascal language, he or she needs to use the output statement *WRITE*. If the statement *WWRITE* is used, it is a syntax error.

A **logic error** is when the programmer has used an incorrect calculation or left out a programming procedure. If the programmer forgot to write in a procedure for computing overtime pay in the *Dynamite Bay* example, that would be a logic error. The program would still produce paychecks, but some would be wrong.

There are a number of ways by which syntax and logic errors are weeded out.

Structured Walkthroughs

A **structured walkthrough** is a formal review process designed not only to verify computer code but also to evaluate the documentation and the design of the program. In this process, a coded program is submitted to a review team of three or four programmers, including the one who produced the code. After the review, the program's overall completeness, accuracy, and quality of design are discussed.

Typically, the program is put through **desk-checking,** a phase similar to proofreading, in which the entire program is reviewed—that is, programmers check the printout while sitting at their desks—statement by statement, for syntax and logic errors. Following this, the program is further checked by manually tracing the program—that is, by running sample data (both correct and incorrect data) manually through the program.

Structured walkthroughs are more than just attempts to check a particular coded program. Their purpose also is to help standardize the design and coding process and produce error-free coding. It has been found to be an effective technique for identifying programming errors and increasing programmer productivity.

Checking for Syntax Errors

In the next stage, the program is sent to the computer. Using a translator program, the computer attempts to convert each coded program statement from the programming language in which it was written—Pascal, COBOL, or whatever—into a form it will accept, a form known as *machine language,* the lowest level of computer language. (This process is discussed further in Chapter 5.) Before the program can be executed, the entire program must be free of any syntax errors. Typically, these syntax errors are readily identified by the computer when it attempts to translate the program.

Checking for Logic Errors

After all syntax errors have been corrected and the program code has been successfully translated into machine language, the program can be tested for logic errors, usually using sets of test data designed to thoroughly test all aspects of the program. The test data should cause each program statement to execute at least once. Both the tested output and the sequence of operations are compared against a manual desk check.

It is important to catch these errors, both syntax and logic, as early in the programming process as possible. The costs associated with correcting these errors increases dramatically the later they are discovered.

Document Program Verification

When the program has been tested and corrected, it is now a production program and ready for use. A **program verification document** should be prepared that lists the final program, discusses the checking and testing procedures used, and presents the test data and test results.

Note that *testing the program* is not the same as proving the program completely error-free. Even well-tested programs have errors pop up months and even years later.

5. DOCUMENTING

THE PROGRAM

Although program documentation is presented here as the fifth stage in the programming process, actually it has been an ongoing practice from the beginning. The importance of program documentation is sometimes minimized; it cannot be overstated, however, for programs intended for frequent use in business applications. Without proper documentation, it is very difficult for a programmer, even the original programmer, to update and maintain a program.

The final document should contain the following information:

▶ **Program analysis document,** with a concise statement of the program's objectives, outputs, inputs, and processing procedures.

▶ **Program design document,** with detailed flowcharts and other appropriate diagrams.

▶ **Program verification document,** outlining the checking, testing, and correction procedures along with a list of test data and solutions.

▶ **Log** used to document future program revision and maintenance activity.

6. MAINTAINING THE PROGRAM

After the program has been fully tested and has become operational, it typically will require maintenance to modify or update it. This activity is so commonplace that many organizations have specialists called maintenance programmers.

Maintenance is particularly important in the payroll application since tax-related computations must have the tax percentages and the like changed annually or whenever a government changes the tax basis.

Once software is supposedly working, it is commonly believed, maintenance is minimal and can be handled by programmers on a catch-as-catch-can basis. As a consequence, says Roger Pressman, in *Software Engineering: A Practitioner's Approach,* organizations budget only 10–15% of their total programming budgets for maintenance. In reality, however, the effort and cost actually expended on maintenance is 55–70%—a highly significant difference.

END-USER APPLICATIONS DEVELOPMENT

We have seen in the *Dynamite Bay* example that you needed the help of a programmer to create this payroll program. Could you have done it by yourself?

The answer is: yes—and you may be required to do this kind of project in the future. Indeed, a whole new field has sprung up called *end-user applications development*—meaning that you the user (the end-user) can create business application programs without the assistance of a programmer.

Why would you even want to bother? The reasons are that:

▶ Programming is extremely labor-intensive and expensive.

▶ Software takes a long time to develop.

Software costs are high—even greater than hardware costs—because programmers (and systems analysts) are very well paid. In many companies, end-users may wait three years before programmers can get around to their requests for applications development projects. Moreover, the time required to develop applications is sometimes so long that the resulting software is obsolete by the time it is completed. As a result, the productivity of software development has become such a key issue that it is estimated that by 1990 three-quarters of all applications software development will be performed by end-users—people like you.

There are, then, some alternative ways you could develop the *Dynamite Bay* payroll program:

▶ You can use some of the software packages we mentioned in the last chapter, such as spreadsheets or database managers, to create your own applications software. Technically these kinds of packages are called *fourth-generation software.*

▶ You can hire an expert, such as a systems analyst, to work directly with you, using sophisticated fourth-generation software packages that are too technical for you, to create the applications software.

▶ You can buy, from an outside source, a software package already preprogrammed with your application—for example, a payroll program tailored to movie companies shooting on location. (After all, two-thirds of the American movies being filmed are made outside Los Angeles.)

▶ You can use special applications software development tools— for example, CASE (for computer-aided software engineering) and CAP (for computer-assisted programming).

MOVING ON TO
LANGUAGES

Languages are described as occurring in "generations," from first through fifth. You have already had an introduction to the fourth generation, but programmers mainly use third generation—and what do you suppose is meant by that?

This concludes the six steps of application programming development. In the next chapter, we will discuss the languages of principal interest to managers and business users.

SUMMARY

▶ Software written to perform a specific task is called **applications software** or **applications programs.** A **program** is a series of detailed steps to be completed in order to solve a problem.

▶ **Applications software development** is the process of creating software. End-users may do this either by working with a systems analyst or by doing it themselves (perhaps with the help of a programmer). A **systems analyst** is an information specialist who has expertise in systems analysis, design, and implementation.

▶ All programming processes follow the **program development cycle** or **program life cycle,** consisting of six steps: (1) Define the problem. (2) Design a solution. (3) Write—that is, code—the program. (4) Test—that is, debug—the program. (5) Document it.

(6) Maintain it. The program life cycle is not the same as the systems life cycle; rather, it is step 4 in the systems life cycle—Systems implementation.

▶ Defining the problem—**program analysis**—involves six tasks: (1) Specify the objectives of the program. (2) Specify the outputs. (3) Specify the input requirements. (4) Specify the processing requirements. (5) Evaluate the feasibility of the program. (6) Document the program analysis (provide statements on the preceding five tasks).

▶ The second step of the programming process is the **program design** stage, during which a solution to the problem is designed. **Structured program design** minimizes complexity; it uses one or more of the following tools: (1) top-down program design, (2) flowcharts, and (3) pseudocode.

▶ **Top-down program design** is a structured design technique in which the programmer, having determined the outputs to be produced and the inputs required, identifies the major processing steps, called **modules** (logically related program statements). This type of design has some rigid rules: (1) Each module can have only one entry point and one exit point. (2) When the program is **executed** (run through the computer), it must be able to move from one module to the next in sequence until the last module has been executed. (3) Each module should be independent and have a single function. (4) Each module should be of manageable size to make the design and testing of the program easier.

▶ **Flowcharts,** which are widely used for designing programs, graphically present the logic needed to solve a programming problem. A **program flowchart** presents the detailed sequence of steps needed to solve the problem.

▶ **Pseudocode** is a narrative rather than a graphical form of describing structured program logic. It focuses on the logic of the program rather than on the details of programming or flowcharting.

▶ A formal document should be prepared at the end of the program design stage to guide future users.

▶ The third step of the programming process—writing the program, or **coding**—uses the logic developed in the design stage.

▶ A good program should (1) be easily readable and understandable by people other than the original programmer; (2) be efficient, increasing the programmer's productivity; (3) not take excessive time to process, or occupy more computer memory than necessary; (4) be reliable, able to work under all reasonable conditions; and (5) be able to detect unrea-

sonable or erroneous conditions and indicate them to the programmer or operator.

▶ In an efficient program, (1) the statements can be arranged into patterns that enhance readability; (2) the **variables** (symbolically named entities to which may be assigned a value or values) used are carefully and descriptively named; and (3) comments can be inserted into the program to document the logic patterns used.

▶ Structured coding—developed to take much of the guesswork out of programming—can be used to write *any* program using a combination of three basic logic structures: (1) sequence, (2) selection, and (3) loop.

▶ The **sequence structure,** also known as *simple sequence*, is simply one program statement followed by another.

▶ The **selection structure,** or **IF-THEN-ELSE structure,** occurs when a decision has to be made, and the outcome determines the choice of one of two paths to follow—IF this is true, THEN do this command; IF not true, do ELSE.

▶ The **loop structure,** or iteration structure, refers to a process that may be repeated as long as a certain condition remains true. This is also known as a **DO UNTIL structure**—DO command UNTIL there is no more data to process. A variation of this is the **DO WHILE structure**—DO command WHILE there is data to process.

▶ The fourth step of the programming process is testing the program, or **debugging** it, which means running the program and fixing it if it does not work. Debugging involves two types of errors. A **syntax error** is a violation of the rules of whatever programming language is being used. A **logic error** is the use of an incorrect calculation or the omission of a programming procedure.

▶ A **structured walkthrough,** used to weed out syntax and logic errors, is a formal review process designed not only to verify computer code but also to evaluate documentation and the design of the program. In this process, a review team checks the program's completeness, accuracy, and quality of design. The program is put through **desk-checking,** during which it is reviewed statement by statement for syntax and logic errors. Following this, the program is traced manually, with both correct and incorrect sample data being run through it. Structured walkthroughs also help to standardize the design and coding process.

▶ To eliminate additional syntax errors, the program is sent to the computer, which attempts to convert (translate) each coded program statement from the programming language in which it was written into a form the computer will accept—known as *machine language,* the lowest level of computer language.

▶ To eliminate additional logic errors, a set of test data will be run that has been designed to test thoroughly all aspects of the program.

▶ The fifth step in the programming process, documenting the program, actually has been ongoing from the beginning of the process. It is very important for programs intended for frequent use in business applications. Without a proper **program verification document,** it is difficult for a programmer to update and maintain a program.

▶ The final document should contain the following information: (1) Program analysis document, with a concise statement of the program's objectives, outputs, inputs, and processing procedures; (2) program design document, with detailed flowcharts and other appropriate diagrams; (3) program verification document, outlining the checking, testing, and correction procedures along with a list of test data and solutions; (4) a log used to document future program revision and maintenance activity.

▶ The sixth step in the programming process, maintaining the program, is required to modify or update the program. This is usually done by maintenance programmers.

▶ In the field of end-user applications development, end-users can create business application programs without the assistance of a programmer. Alternatives available to end-users are as follows: (1) Use spreadsheets, data base managers, or similar "fourth-generation software" to create programs; (2) hire systems analysts to use their own technical software to create programs; (3) buy software packages already preprogrammed for their specific applications; (4) use special applications software development tools, such as CASE (for computer-aided software engineering) and CAP (for computer-assisted programming).

KEY TERMS

Applications program, p. 105

Applications software, p. 105

Applications software development, p. 105

Coding, p. 120

Debugging, p. 126

Desk-checking, p. 126

DO UNTIL structure, p. 122

DO WHILE structure, p. 122

Executed, p. 116

Flowchart, p. 116

IF-THEN-ELSE structure, p. 121

Logic error, p. 126

Loop structure, p. 122

Module, p. 115

Program, p. 105

Program analysis, p. 109

Program design, p. 114

Program development cycle, p. 107

Program flowchart, p. 116

Program life cycle, p. 107

Program verification document, p. 127

Pseudocode, p. 116

Selection structure, p. 121

Sequence structure, p. 121

Structured program design, p. 114

Structured walkthrough, p. 126

Syntax error, p. 120

Systems analyst, p. 105

Top-down program design, p. 115

Variable, p. 120

REVIEW QUESTIONS

1. Why should someone planning a business management career learn about computer programming?

2. What are the six steps of the programming process?

3. Describe the process of program analysis.

4. What makes a good program?

5. Describe how a program is debugged and checked for errors.

6. Why is program documentation important, and what information should it contain?

CASE PROBLEMS

Case 4-1: A Program for Billable Time

Professionals such as lawyers, accountants, and advertising executives must keep a careful accounting of their time so they can charge clients correctly. Sometimes this can be done with paper and pencil or time cards and calculators, but as an enterprise gets larger and clients multiply, keeping track of time can get to be a real hassle.

An advertising agency, for instance, will bill clients on an hourly basis, which means that agency employees must keep track of which hours on which jobs to bill to which clients, then summarize the results at the end of the month. Moreover, higher-level employees will charge more per hour than lower-level employees. All this must be carefully recorded so that the agency can substantiate its billing in case the client questions it.

Your assignment: Suppose you are running an advertising agency, with different clients with different products and with two levels of employees within your agency—"creative" (such as copywriters and artists) and "account managers," the latter of whom charge half again as much as the former for their hourly work. When you look at this, you can see it is not greatly different from the *Dynamite Bay* payroll application. You can identify your clients as Client A, Client B, and so on; the products whose ad campaigns you are working on as A-1, A-2, and so on; and the employees in your shop as Creative-1, Creative-2, Account Manager-1, Account Manager-2, and so on. Using the programming steps outlined in this chapter, see if you can solve the problem of writing a general program with which to keep track of billable time.

Case 4-2: Saving for College

Sometimes when you are learning a new method of problem solving, it helps to try it out on a problem for which you already know the answer. We will do this here.

Let us suppose you are a banker who is trying to interest parents in beginning a savings plan to help put their children through college. On average, a single year of room, board, and fees or tuition costs about $5,800 at a state university and about $12,000 a year at some private colleges and universities. If inflation continues, it will, of course, cost even more in the future.

Table 4-1 (which assumes college expenses will rise 7% a year and that savings will earn 10% a year) shows how much a family must save every month, depending on the age of the child.

Your assignment: See if you can construct a flowchart, much like a simple version of the flowchart shown in Figure 4-7, in which the program reads the file for children of the different ages shown in the table and the program shows the alternative monthly amounts to be saved for state institution versus private institution.

Table 4-1 Saving for College

Child's Age	Estimated Total College Cost		Savings Needed per Month through College	
	State	Private	State	Private
3	$73,080	$94,500	$108.10	$139.79
6	59,950	77,400	127.24	164.53
9	48,720	63,000	153.24	198.14
12	39,440	51,000	192.53	248.97
15	32,480	42,000	268.54	347.25

PROGRAMMING LANGUAGES: THE DIFFERENT WAYS OF COMMUNICATING WITH THE COMPUTER

English has become one of the important international languages of business. But a North American traveling on business in, say, the Far East quickly discovers that English is not enough outside the hotels and executive suites. If, on your way to Australia for the *Dynamite Bay* location shoot, you find yourself with a couple of days' layover in Tokyo, you will soon discover that to get around the city and make yourself understood in local shops and restaurants, you will need a translator.

Computers are the same way: You speak English, but their local dialect is machine language, which in printed form is apt to be an incomprehensible page after page of ones and zeros. How can you communicate with the computer?

LEVELS OF LANGUAGE

The solution to communicating with the computer is to develop a third language—a language that can be understood by both you and the computer. This is what a **programming language** is—a set of rules that provides a way of instructing the computer to perform certain operations.

The choice of programming language—step 3 of the programming process in Chapter 4—is, however, an important one. There are perhaps 150 programming languages in existence—and these are just the ones that are still being used; we are not counting the ones that, for one reason or another, are considered obsolete. How do you know whether to use JOVIAL instead of HEARSAY, DOCTOR instead of STUDENT, COBOL instead of SNOBOL? Actually, it is not as difficult as it looks because certain languages are used for certain disciplines. In this chapter, we will deal with those of primary interest to prospective managers: BASIC, COBOL, PL/I, and RPG. We will also describe some languages that have scientific applications—FORTRAN, Ada, and Pascal—and one that is in between, called simply "C."

First, however, we need to discuss the notion of levels of language. Programming languages are said to be lower or higher, depending on whether they are closer to the language the computer itself uses (lower, which means 0s and 1s, as we shall explain) or to the language that people use (higher, which means more English-like). In this chapter we shall consider five levels of language:

1. Machine languages
2. Assembly languages
3. Procedural languages
4. Problem-oriented languages
5. Natural languages

The high-level languages—such as Pascal, BASIC, and COBOL—are the ones used to code applications programs, so we shall emphasize them. The closer the level is to human speech, the more it is described as a "user-friendly" language. The term *user-friendly*, incidentally, is one that is used (or was) a great deal throughout the computer industry. While it describes an ideal—that a piece of equipment or software should be easy for an untrained person to use—it also appears frequently in manufacturers' ads—and what ad is not trying to be friendly?

MACHINE LANGUAGE
BINARY SPOKEN HERE

We think of computers as being quite complicated, but actually their basis is very simple: They rest on the concept of electricity being turned "on" and "off." From this on/off, yes/no, two-state system, sophisticated ways of representing data have been constructed using the binary system of numbers. The **binary system** is based on two digits: 0 and 1. By contrast, the decimal system that we all use is based on ten digits: 0 through 9. The numbers 1, 2, and 3 in the decimal system are represented in the binary system as 1, 10, and 11, respectively. Letters of the alphabet are also represented as numbers: In one system, the letter A is represented as 1000001. Commas, semi-

CASE STUDY: PROGRAMMERS AT WORK

The User's Place in Programming

"Programming begins," writes Susan Lammers, *"when a technologist enters into a private dialogue with a machine and ends when a thousand, or a million, users accomplish a task that is perhaps impossible to perform in any other way."* Lammers interviewed several well-known programmers. The following are responses from John Page, cofounder of Software Publishing and creator of PFS:File, and Dan Bricklin, codeveloper (with Bob Frankston) of VisiCalc—*"two men,"* Lammers points out, *"who helped bring computing to the masses and gave the rest of us the opportunity to be programmers."*

*L*ammers: What were your major design considerations in making *PFS:File* different from other programs on the market at the time?

John Page: What I thought was an application that ordinary people could use, much as they do a telephone or a car. The goal was a program as easy to learn as an appliance. It was an interesting design trade-off because it meant pursuing maximum intelligibility rather than maximum performance and functionality. That's a bit like the phone system, which isn't very sophisticated on the outside. You dial the number, the phone rings, and you talk to people. But to make that happen, a great deal of complex technology must be marshalled behind the scenes. Designing *PFS:File* worked in the same way: simple on the outside, backed by sophisticated technology.

In designing *PFS:File*, I stumbled over an odd software design principle: Complicated programs are far easier to write than straightforward programs—the exact opposite of what you'd expect. It's easy to write complicated programs because you reflect the complexity back onto the user; you force the user to make all the hard decisions. With a very simple program, however, the designer has to figure out the answers alone. . . .

Lammers: Do you think small software operations will survive? Or will the software industry be dominated by a handful of huge companies?

Dan Bricklin: Today, people are writing their own programs. Any spreadsheet user is; it's just that the language is different now. Bob Frankston likes to tell a story about the telephone company. Back in the 1920s, people said telephone usage was growing so fast that by 1950 everybody in the country would have to be an operator. By 1950 people said that prediction had been wrong. Actually, it was right, because everybody *was* an operator—they just had dial

colons, and other special characters are also represented as bunches of 0s and 1s.

In the early days of computers, with machines such as the ENIAC, which used vacuum tubes, one could actually see the tubes lit up or unlit, corresponding to the 1/0 binary state—the switch was either on or off. In addition, in those early days there was no such thing as software. There was only hardware with electrical on/off switches. Whenever a program was to be run, all the switches had to be set—sometimes as many as 6000 switches for a single program. Then for the next program the switches had to be reset, a process that might take weeks. Were we to try the same thing today with the *Dynamite Bay* payroll program, it might require three to four times as many switches.

Since those days, machine switches have been replaced by machine programming—programs with statements consisting of 0s and 1s that electrically set the switches, with 0 representing off and 1

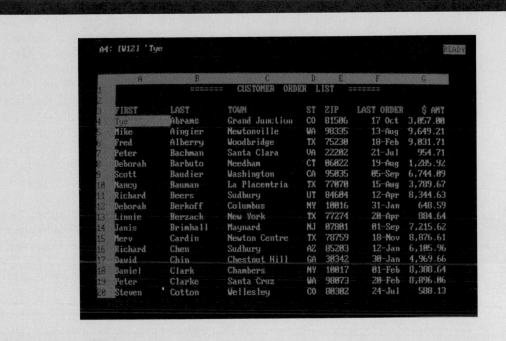

telephones. The technology had made it easy enough to be an operator.

It's the same with programming. We're just making the users do more of the programming themselves, but they don't know it. Using style sheets with *Microsoft Word* is doing programming, as is using spreadsheets. There's an inherent cottage-industry component to programming. We constantly improve the available tools—the operating systems, the environments, the languages. Consequently, the user can always do more than was previously possible.

—Excerpt from Susan Lammers, "Programmers at Work," *PC World*. Reprinted by permission of Microsoft Press. © 1986 by Microsoft Press.

representing on. This has made changing from one program to another considerably easier.

Still, programming directly in **machine language**—the lowest level of programming language, in which information is represented as 0s and 1s—is very tedious and time-consuming. A programmer must keep track of a tremendous amount of detail. Moreover, he or she must understand the technical operations of the computer.

In the *Dynamite Bay* payroll program, the gross pay was calculated by multiplying the number of hours worked by the pay rate. Six lines of machine code are required to perform this multiplication, one line of which looks like this:

11110010 01110011 11010010 00010000 01110000 00101011

Clearly, working with this kind of code is not for everybody.

Programming in machine code has one advantage over programming at other language levels—namely, its execution is very fast and efficient because the computer can accept the machine code as is (higher-level languages must be converted to machine code before they are usable). However, in addition to the complexity and sheer tedium involved in working at this level, there is a severe disadvantage to machine language: There is no one standard machine language. Rather, there are machine *languages*. The languages are machine-dependent, and programs written in machine language for one computer model will not, in all likelihood, run on a different model computer. Although the machine language for a particular computer is supplied by the manufacturer, few applications programs are written in machine languages.

Let us be grateful then, as you worry about getting your payroll program up and running for Mr. Elliott, that you do not live at a time when your programmer has to do all the coding and debugging in 0s and 1s.

ASSEMBLY LANGUAGES

PROGRAMMING WITH ABBREVIATIONS

It became clear early on that working with 0s and 1s could turn people themselves into ciphers. In the 1950s, to reduce programming complexity and provide some standardization, assembly languages were developed. **Assembly languages,** also known as **symbolic languages,** use abbreviations or mnemonic codes—codes more easily memorized—to replace the 0s and 1s of machine languages.

Actually, assembly languages do not replace machine languages. In fact, for an assembly language program to be executed, it must be converted to machine code. The assembly language program is referred to as a **source program;** the machine language program is an **object program.**

What does assembly language look like? The machine language statement presented above—

11110010 01110011 1101001000010000111000000101011

—could be expressed in an assembly language statement as:

PACK 210(8,13),02B(4,7)

However, for this assembly statement to be executed, it must be translated into the machine statement, because the computer can recognize only 0s and 1s.

Assembly language code is very similar in form to machine language code. In fact, the first assembly languages had a one-to-one correspondence—15 assembly statements, for example, would be translated into 15 machine statements. This one-to-one correspondence was still so laborious, however, that assembly language instructions called **macro instructions** were devised, which executed batches of one-to-one instructions. That is, one line of assembly language code would correspond to many lines of machine language code.

Assembly languages offer several advantages:

▶ They are more standardized and easier to use than machine languages.

▶ They operate very efficiently, although not as efficiently as machine languages.

▶ They are easier to debug because programs locate and identify syntax errors.

However, there are still some disadvantages:

▶ The programs frequently are quite long.

▶ Though less abstract than machine languages, assembly language programs are still complex.

▶ Though more standardized than machine languages, assembly languages are still machine-dependent.

Contemplating the fact that someone else is going to have to be able to use your *Dynamite Bay* payroll program, your programmer decides not to work in assembly language. The two of you agree on a program written in a language that is a little more user-friendly. Let us step up to high-level languages.

HIGH-LEVEL
LANGUAGES

MORE USER-
FRIENDLINESS

High-level languages assisted programmers by reducing still further the number of computer operation details they had to specify, so they could concentrate more on the logic needed to solve the problem. To see this, you need only look at Figure 5-1, in which the same instruction—"Calculate gross pay"—is expressed in three different ways: in machine language, in assembly language, and in the high-level language known as COBOL. Here we see that the six lines of 0s and 1s of machine language can be expressed in COBOL in a single line of English (or almost English): MULTIPLY HOURS-WORKED BY PAY-RATE GIVING GROSS-PAY ROUNDED (that is, "rounded off").

Figure 5-1. Why people like high-level languages. In this comparison, a single line of an English-like high-level language, COBOL, is expressed by its equivalent in an assembly language and a machine language.

COBOL

MULTIPLY HOURS-WORKED BY PAY-RATE
GIVING GROSS-PAY ROUNDED

Assembly

PACK   210(8,13),02B(4,7)

PACK   218(8,13),02F(4,7)

MP   212(G,13),21D(3,13)

SRP   213(5,13),03E(0),5

UNPK 050(5,7),214(4,13)

OI   054(7),X'FO'

Machine

```
11110010 01110011 1101 001000010000 0111 000000101011
11110010 01110011 1101 001000011000 0111 000000101111
11111100 01010010 1101 001000010010 1101 001000011101
11110000 01000101 1101 001000010011 0000 000000111110
11110011 01000011 0111 000001010000 1101 001000010100
10010110 11110000 0111 000001010100
```

A high-level language, then, is an English-like programming language (at least in English-speaking countries; elsewhere in the world they are written in other human languages).

The Kinds of High-Level Languages

Languages are often referred to by generations, the idea being that machine languages were **first-generation** and assembly languages were **second-generation. High-level languages** are sometimes used to refer to all languages above the assembly level. Here we will subdivide high-level languages into three kinds or generations:

▶ Procedural-oriented—or third-generation
▶ Problem-oriented—or fourth-generation
▶ Natural—or fifth-generation

Eight important high-level languages you may come across in the course of your career are shown in Table 5-1. We will describe these in the next few sections.

Table 5-1. Eight Important Programming Languages. The languages, the meaning of their abbreviations, the year in which they were developed, and their principal application are given below.

Language	Application
FORTRAN—FORmula TRANslator (1954)	Scientific
COBOL—COmmon Business-Oriented Language (1959)	Business
PL/I—Programming Language One (1964)	Scientific, business
RPG—Report Program Generator (1964)	Business reports
BASIC—Beginners' All-purpose Symbolic Instruction Code (1965)	Education, business
C—developed for UNIX operating system (about 1970)	Systems, scientific programming
Pascal—after French inventor Blaise Pascal (1971)	Education, scientific, systems programming
Ada—after Ada, the Countess of Lovelace (1980)	Military, general

Compilers and Interpreters: Translating from High to Low

For a high-level language to work on the computer, it must be translated into machine language. There are two kinds of translators—*compilers* and *interpreters*—and high-level languages are called either *compiled languages* or *interpreted languages.*

In a **compiled language,** a translation program is run to convert the programmer's entire high-level language program, which is called the **source code,** into a machine language code. This translation process is called a **compiling run.** The machine language code is called the **object code** and can be saved and either run (executed) immediately or later. The execution of the object code is called a **production run.** The most widely used compiled languages are COBOL and FORTRAN.

In an **interpreted language,** a translation program converts each program statement to machine code just before the program statement is to be executed. Translation and execution occur immediately, one after another, one statement at a time. Unlike the compiled languages, no object code is stored and there is no compiling run, only a production run. This means that in a program where one statement is executed several times (such as reading an employee's payroll record), that statement is converted to machine language each time it is executed. The most frequently used interpreted language is BASIC.

Compiler languages are better than interpreter languages in that they can be executed faster and more efficiently once the object code has been obtained. On the other hand, interpreter languages do not need to create object code and so are usually easier to develop—that is, to code and test. Interpreter languages are frequently used for **interactive programming,** the kind of programming in which the user and the computer carry on a dialogue—that is, interact—with each other.

Let us now describe the first of the high-level languages, procedural languages.

PROCEDURAL LANGUAGES

FAVORED BY PROGRAMMERS

High-level languages are often classified according to whether they solve general problems or specific problems. General-purpose programming languages are called **procedural languages,** or **third-generation languages.** They are languages such as Pascal, BASIC, COBOL, and FORTRAN, which are designed to express the logic—the *procedure*—of a problem. Because of their flexibility, procedural languages are able to solve a variety of problems. (Languages designed to solve specific programs, called problem-oriented languages, are described in the next major section.)

Procedural languages have many advantages over machine and assembly languages:

▶ The program statements resemble English and hence are easier to work with.

▶ Because of their English-like nature, less time is required to program a problem.

▶ Once coded, programs are easier to understand and to modify.

▶ The programming languages are machine-independent.

However, procedure-oriented languages still have some disadvantages compared to machine and assembly languages:

▶ Programs execute more slowly.

▶ The languages use computer resources less efficiently.

Let us now consider the following procedure-oriented languages:

▶ BASIC

▶ COBOL

▶ PL/I

These are often used in business. In addition, there are some procedure-oriented languages that are intended for nonbusiness use:

▶ FORTRAN
▶ Pascal
▶ Ada
▶ C

BASIC: For Beginners and Microcomputerists

If you are already involved in programming a microcomputer, you may well be working in BASIC. Developed in 1964 at Dartmouth College with college students specifically in mind, **BASIC**—short for *B*eginner's *A*ll-purpose *S*ymbolic *I*nstruction *C*ode—is by far the most popular computer language and is well suited to the beginning as well as the experienced programmer. It is also an *interactive* language, which means that it permits user and computer to communicate with each other directly during the writing and running of programs.

Because most microcomputers use BASIC, you can be pretty sure that the one being used by the film crew on location for *Dynamite Bay* will run a program written in this language. Hence, you could have instructed your programmer to write the payroll program in BASIC, as shown in Figure 5-3. The circled reference numbers in the program part of the figure refer to the flowchart and pseudocode shown in Figure 5-2 on the opposite page.

BASIC is easy to learn, even for a person who has never programmed before, which is why it has had such commercial success. Entering data is easy, as are inserting changes and additions. The original BASIC had a specific syntax, but since 1964 there have been numerous extensions so that there now exist several versions. Like English itself, BASIC has developed into a number of dialects with similar features.

One reasonably standard version of BASIC is presented in an appendix at the end of this book for those interested in doing hands-on programming.

COBOL: The Old-Time Favorite

Developed in 1959, **COBOL**—which stands for *CO*mmon *B*usiness-*O*riented *L*anguage—is the most frequently used programming language in business. Now this general-purpose compiler language has been developed for nearly all large computers used in business information processing. Indeed, it has been estimated that between 60% and 80% of application programs written for business purposes are written in COBOL.

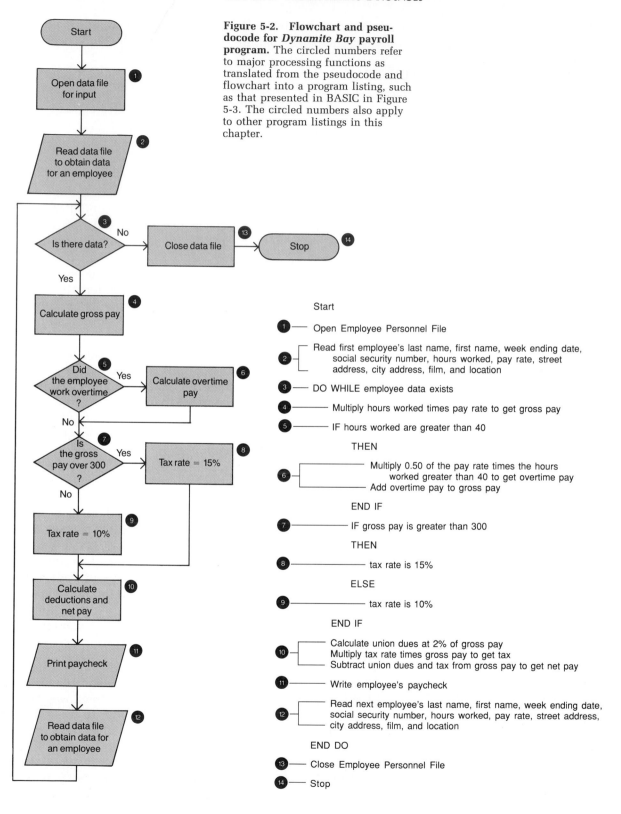

Figure 5-2.   Flowchart and pseudocode for *Dynamite Bay* payroll program. The circled numbers refer to major processing functions as translated from the pseudocode and flowchart into a program listing, such as that presented in BASIC in Figure 5-3. The circled numbers also apply to other program listings in this chapter.

Start

① — Open Employee Personnel File

② ⎡ Read first employee's last name, first name, week ending date,
     │   social security number, hours worked, pay rate, street
     ⎣   address, city address, film, and location

③ — DO WHILE employee data exists

④ — Multiply hours worked times pay rate to get gross pay

⑤ — IF hours worked are greater than 40

     THEN

⑥ ⎡ Multiply 0.50 of the pay rate times the hours
     │   worked greater than 40 to get overtime pay
     ⎣ Add overtime pay to gross pay

     END IF

⑦ — IF gross pay is greater than 300

     THEN

⑧ — tax rate is 15%

     ELSE

⑨ — tax rate is 10%

     END IF

⑩ ⎡ Calculate union dues at 2% of gross pay
     │ Multiply tax rate times gross pay to get tax
     ⎣ Subtract union dues and tax from gross pay to get net pay

⑪ — Write employee's paycheck

⑫ ⎡ Read next employee's last name, first name, week ending date,
     │   social security number, hours worked, pay rate, street address,
     ⎣   city address, film, and location

     END DO

⑬ — Close Employee Personnel File

⑭ — Stop

Figure 5-3. BASIC. Program for *Dynamite Bay* payroll problem. BASIC uses short, cryptic variable names and is very unstructured because of an overabundance of the use of GOTOs.

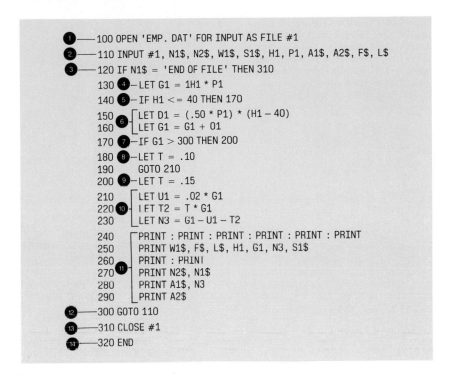

```
① ── 100 OPEN 'EMP. DAT' FOR INPUT AS FILE #1
② ── 110 INPUT #1, N1$, N2$, W1$, S1$, H1, P1, A1$, A2$, F$, L$
③ ── 120 IF N1$ = 'END OF FILE' THEN 310
       130 ④ ─ LET G1 = 1H1 * P1
       140 ⑤ ─ IF H1 <= 40 THEN 170
       150 ⑥ ┌ LET D1 = (.50 * P1) * (H1 − 40)
       160   └ LET G1 = G1 + 01
       170 ⑦ ─ IF G1 > 300 THEN 200
       180 ⑧ ─ LET T = .10
       190      GOTO 210
       200 ⑨ ─ LET T = .15
       210   ┌ LET U1 = .02 * G1
       220 ⑩ ┤ LFT T2 = T * G1
       230   └ LET N3 = G1 − U1 − T2
       240   ┌ PRINT : PRINT : PRINT : PRINT : PRINT : PRINT
       250   │ PRINT W1$, F$, L$, H1, G1, N3, S1$
       260   │ PRINT : PRINT
       270 ⑪ ┤ PRINT N2$, N1$
       280   │ PRINT A1$, N3
       290   └ PRINT A2$
⑫ ── 300 GOTO 110
⑬ ── 310 CLOSE #1
⑭ ── 320 END
```

Thus, for the *Dynamite Bay* payroll program, you could have had the programmer write it in COBOL, assuming the personal computer being used by the film crew had a COBOL compiler. The result would look like the program shown in Figure 5-4, and the output—the paycheck for cableperson Amy Gardner—would look like that shown in Figure 5-5.

Writing in COBOL is much like writing a paper. You write sentences, which tell the computer which operations to perform. Several sentences dealing with the same operation are grouped into paragraphs, similar paragraphs are grouped in sections, and sections are grouped into a division. As Figure 5-4 shows, there are four divisions, organized in a structural hierarchy:

▶ The *Identification Division* presents the name of the program and the programmer. There may be other paragraphs for documentation purposes.

▶ The *Environment Division* indicates the computer to be used (in our example, it is a minicomputer called a PDP-1170). The input–output section matches the logical variable names used in the program (such as PRINT-FILE) with the physical input or output devices (in this case, PRINTER).

▶ The *Data Division* consists of a file section and a working-storage section. This division lists all the data items to be input (including employee names, hours worked, deductions, and the like),

Figure 5-4. COBOL. Program for *Dynamiteay* payroll problem. Circled numbers correspond to the numbers in the flowchart and pseudocode in Figure 5-2. Notice the four divisions (separated by rows of asterisks) and the sections within divisions.

```
IDENTIFICATION DIVISION.
  PROGRAM-ID. PAYROLL.
  AUTHOR. [YOUR NAME]
****************************************************************
ENVIRONMENT DIVISION.
  CONFIGURATION SECTION.
    SOURCE-COMPUTER. PDP-1170.
    OBJECT-COMPUTER. PDP-1170.
  INPUT-OUTPUT SECTION.
    FILE-CONTROL.
       SELECT DATA-FILE ASSIGN TO ''EMPL.DAT''.
       SELECT PRINT-FILE ASSIGN TO PRINTER.
****************************************************************
DATA DIVISION.
  FILE SECTION.
    FD DATA-FILE
       LABEL RECORDS ARE STANDARD
       DATA RECORD IS DATA-RECORD.
    01 DATA-RECORD              PICTURE X(115).
    FD PRINT-FILE
       LABEL RECORDS ARE OMITTED
       DATA RECORD IS PRINT-REC.
    01 PRINT-REC               PICTURE X(133).
  WORKING-STORAGE SECTION.
    01 PROGRAM-FLAG.
       05 MORE-DATA-EXISTS     PICTURE XXX VALUE 'YES'.
    01 WS-DATA-RECORD.
       05 LAST-NAME            PICTURE X(10)    VALUE SPACES.
       05 FIRST-NAME           PICTURE X(6)     VALUE SPACES.
       05 WEEK-DATE            PICTURE X(8)     VALUE SPACES.
       05 SOCIAL-SECURITY      PICTURE X(11)    VALUE SPACES.
       05 HOURS-WORKED         PICTURE 99V99    VALUE ZEROES.
       05 PAY-RATE             PICTURE 99V99    VALUE ZEROES.
       05 STREET-ADDRESS       PICTURE X(14)    VALUE SPACES.
       05 CITY-ADDRESS         PICTURE X(18)    VALUE SPACES.
       05 FILM-NAME            PICTURE X(15)    VALUE SPACES.
       05 LOCATION-OF-FILM     PICTURE X(25)    VALUE SPACES.
    01 VARIABLES NEEDED.
       05 GROSS-PAY            PICTURE 999V99    VALUE ZEROES.
       05 OVERTIME-PAY         PICTURE 999V99    VALUE ZEROES.
       05 UNION-DUES           PICTURE 999V99    VALUE ZEROES.
       05 TAX-RATE             PICTURE 999V99    VALUE ZEROES.
       05 TAX                  PICTURE 999V99    VALUE ZEROES.
       05 NET-PAY              PICTURE 999V99    VALUE ZEROES.
       05 OT-PREMIUM           PICTURE 999V99    VALUE ZEROES.
       05 OT-HOURS             PICTURE 999V99    VALUE ZEROES.
       05 DEDUCTIONS           PICTURE 999V99    VALUE ZEROES.
    01 DETAIL-LINE-ONE.
       05 FILLER                 PICTURE X         VALUE SPACE.
       05 WEEK-DATE-OUT          PICTURE X(8)      VALUE SPACES.
       05 FILLER                 PICTURE X         VALUE SPACE.
       05 FILM-NAME-OUT          PICTURE X(15)     VALUE SPACES.
       05 FILLER                 PICTURE X         VALUE SPACE.
       05 LOCATION-OF-FILM-OUT   PICTURE X(25)     VALUE SPACES.
       05 FILLER                 PICTURE X         VALUE SPACE.
       05 HOURS-WORKED-OUT       PICTURE Z9.99     VALUE ZEROES.
       05 FILLER                 PICTURE X(3)      VALUE SPACES.
       05 GROSS-PAY-OUT          PICTURE $$$$.99   VALUE ZEROES.
       05 FILLER                 PICTURE X         VALUE SPACE.
       05 NET-PAY-OUT1           PICTURE $$$$.99   VALUE ZEROES.
       05 FILLER                 PICTURE X         VALUE SPACE.
       05 SOCIAL-SECURITY-OUT    PICTURE X(11)     VALUE SPACES.
```

```
01 DETAIL-LINE-TWO.
    05 FILLER                 PICTURE X(25)    VALUE SPACES.
    05 FIRST-NAME-OUT         PICTURE X(6)     VALUE SPACES.
    05 FILLER                 PICTURE X        VALUE SPACES.
    05 LAST-NAME-OUT          PICTURE X(10)    VALUE SPACES.
01 DETAIL-LINE-THREE.
    05 FILLER                 PICTURE X(25)    VALUE SPACES.
    05 STREET-ADDRESS-OUT     PICTURE X(14)    VALUE SPACES.
    05 FILLER                 PICTURE X(20)    VALUE SPACES.
    05 NET-PAY-OUT2           PICTURE $$$$.99  VALUE ZEROES.
01 DETAIL-LINE-FOUR
    05 FILLER                 PICTURE X(25)    VALUE SPACES.
    05 CITY-ADDRESS-OUT       PICTURE X(18)    VALUE SPACES.
********************************************************************
```

```
PROCEDURE DIVISION
    MAIN-PARA.
①   ┌ OPEN-INPUT DATA-FILE
    └        OUTPUT PRINT-FILE
②   ─ PERFORM READ-DATA-PARA.
      PERFORM PAYROLL-PROCESSING-PARA
③   ──────UNTIL MORE-DATA-EXISTS = "NO"
⑬   ┌ CLOSE DATA-FILE
    └        PRINT-FILE.
⑭  ─ STOP-RUN.
    READ DATA PARA.
      READ DATA-FILE INTO WS-DATA-RECORD
          AT END MOVE "NO" TO MORE-DATA-EXISTS.
    PAYROLL-PROCESSING-PARA.
④  ─ MULTIPLY HOURS-WORKED BY PAY-RATE GIVING GROSS-PAY ROUNDED
⑤  ─ IF HOURS-WORKED GREATER THAN 40
        THEN
    ┌        MULTIPLY .50 BY PAY-RATE GIVING OT-PREMIUM ROUNDED
    │        SUBTRACT 40 FROM HOURS-WORKED GIVING OT-HOURS ROUNDED
⑥  │        COMPUTE OVERTIME-PAY ROUNDED = OT-PREMIUM * OT-HOURS
    └        ADD OVERTIME-PAY TO GROSS-PAY
        ELSE
            NEXT SENTENCE.
⑦  ─ IF GROSS-PAY GREATER THAN 300
        THEN
⑧  ────── MOVE .15 TO TAX-RATE
        ELSE
⑨  ────── MOVE .10 TO TAX-RATE.
    ┌ MULTIPLY GROSS-PAY BY .02 GIVING UNION-DUES ROUNDED.
⑩  │ MULTIPLY GROSS-PAY BY TAX-RATE GIVING TAX ROUNDED.
    │ ADD UNION-DUES, TAX GIVING DEDUCTIONS ROUNDED.
    └ COMPUTE NET-PAY ROUNDED = GROSS PAY P DEDUCTIONS.
    ┌ MOVE WEEK-DATE TO WEEK-DATE-OUT.
    │ MOVE FILM-NAME TO FILM-NAME-OUT.
    │ MOVE LOCATION-OF-FILM TO LOCATION-OF-FILM-OUT.
    │ MOVE HOURS-WORKED TO HOURS-WORKED-OUT.
    │ MOVE GROSS-PAY TO GROSS-PAY-OUT.
    │ MOVE NET-PAY TO NET-PAY-OUT1.
    │ MOVE SOCIAL-SECURITY TO SOCIAL-SECURITY-OUT.
    │ WRITE PRINT-REC FROM DETAIL-LINE-ONE AFTER ADVANCING 7 LINES.
⑪  │ MOVE FIRST-NAME TO FIRST-NAME-OUT.
    │ MOVE LAST-NAME TO LAST-NAME-OUT.
    │ WRITE PRINT-REC FROM DETAIL-LINE-TWO AFTER ADVANCING 3 LINES.
    │ MOVE STREET-ADDRESS TO STREET-ADDRESS-OUT.
    │ MOVE NET-PAY TO NET-PAY-OUT2.
    │ WRITE PRINT-REC FROM DETAIL-LINE-THREE.
    │ MOVE CITY-ADDRESS TO CITY-ADDRESS-OUT.
    └ WRITE PRINT-REC FROM DETAIL-LINE-FOUR.
⑫ ─ PERFORM READ-DATA-PARA.
```

```
11-21-89 DYNAMITE BAY. QUEENSLAND: AUSTRALIA. 30.00 $283.50-249.48. 527-73-1102


                AMY     GARDNER
                9024 N ELM ST.                        $249.48
                WESTWOOD CA 90024
```

Figure 5-5.   COBOL output. Example of payroll output produced by
COBOL program.

describes where the data will be stored within the computer, and
gives the format to be used for the output results.

▶ The *Procedure Division* contains the actual processing instructions, mirroring the steps mapped out in the flowchart.

Because it has been absorbed so well into the business environment, COBOL clearly must have a number of advantages, and indeed
it does:

▶ It is easier to understand—more so than BASIC, as a comparison
of the two programs shows—because of its English-like statements. In business, this is a real advantage since it allows
nonprogrammers to get into a program and follow its logic.

▶ It is self-documenting, which means that few ongoing comments
in the program are needed. This also makes COBOL easy for programmers to learn.

▶ It can be used for almost any business programming task, and is
especially designed to handle business data, such as addresses,
dollar amounts, and purchased items.

However, there are also a number of disadvantages:

▶ It is wordy—precisely because it is so readable—and so you cannot write a compact COBOL program, even for a simple task.

▶ It is not as suited for mathematics, as are other languages such as
FORTRAN.

▶ It slows programmer productivity.

The American National Standards Institute (ANSI) first standardized COBOL in 1968 and again in 1974, producing a version
known as **ANSI-COBOL.** The advantage of standardization is that
COBOL is reasonably machine-independent, so that a COBOL program developed for one computer can be run with only slight modifications on another machine for which a COBOL compiler has been
developed.

2 + 2:

The BASIC Way, the COBOL Way, the PL/I WAY

The long programs shown in the *Dynamite Bay* payroll examples may seem a bit complicated at this point. How would it seem if we used BASIC, COBOL, and PL/I to perform one of the first arithmetic operations probably any of us ever learned—adding 2 + 2? The following shows how.

In BASIC:

```
10 REM THIS IS A PROGRAM TO ADD TWO
   NUMBERS
20 READ A, B
30 LET X = A + B
40 PRINT X
50 DATA 2, 2
60 END
```

The REM instruction (REM stands for "Remark") tells you what the program is. READ instructs the computer to assign variables A and B the values shown in line 50, the DATA statement; that is, A is 2 and B is 2. Line 30 indicates that X will become the value of the math computation A + B, which is 2 +2, or 4. When line 40, PRINT, is reached, the value of X, or 4, is shown. Line 50 has already been dealt with by the statement READ in line 20. Finally, line 60 marks the end of the program.

In COBOL:

```
IDENTIFICATION DIVISION.
    PROGRAM-ID. ADDITION EXAMPLE.
    AUTHOR. [YOUR NAME].
****************************************************
ENVIRONMENT DIVISION.
  CONFIGURATION SECTION.
    SOURCE-COMPUTER. PDP—1170.
    OBJECT-COMPUTER. PDP—1170.
****************************************************
```

```
DATA DIVISION.
  WORKING-STORAGE SECTION.
    01 NUMBER-ONE PICTURE 9 VALUE 2.
    01 NUMBER-TWO PICTURE 9 VALUE 2.
    01 ADD-TOTAL PICTURE 9.
****************************************************
PROCEDURE DIVISION.
    COMPUTE ADD-TOTAL =
    NUMBER ONE + NUMBER TWO.
  DISPLAY ADD-TOTAL.
  STOP RUN.
```

The COBOL version of this exercise is much wordier than the BASIC version—a drawback of even the simplest COBOL programs.

In PL/I:

Intended as a "universal language," useful for both science and business, PL/I would handle the 2 + 2 problem this way:

```
SAMPLE: PROCEDURE OPTIONS (MAIN);
  DECLARE (NUMBER_ONE, NUMBER_TWO,
  ADD_TOTAL) FIXED DECIMAL(3);
  NUMBER_ONE = 2;
  NUMBER_TWO = 2;
  ADD_TOTAL = NUMBER_ONE +
  NUMBER_TWO;
  PUT PAGE LIST(ADD = ,TOTAL);
END;
```

In recent years, ANSI has been promoting **COBOL-85,** a 1980s updating of the 1974 version. The purpose of the new version is to remove "dead wood," such as making several lines in the Identification Division optional instead of mandatory. In addition, the new version offers structured programming facilities and, in general, tries to make the language more flexible.

The problem is that older COBOL programs will not always run on it; parts of them must be revised. For instance, all COBOL languages have **reserved words**—words with exact meanings, such as PROGRAM-ID (see the second line in Figure 5-4). A programmer may not use these words for variable names; **variable names** are names that can be whatever the user or programmer wants, such as PAYROLL. However, COBOL-85 adds some *new* reserved words, which means that if old programs had used them as variable names, they now must be changed—possibly an expensive proposition for a business that has all along been using these names as variable names.

PL/I: For General Purposes

PL/I, which stands for Programming Language One, was introduced by IBM in 1964 and promoted as a "universal language"—a compromise between COBOL, which is not especially useful for science and mathematics, and FORTRAN, which (as we shall see) is. PL/I was to be general purpose: neither for business nor science alone but for both. An ANSI committee produced a PL/I standard language in 1976. A version is available for use with small computers.

PL/I has a modular structure. A module can stand alone as a program or become part of a more complex program. This makes the language useful for both novice programmers, who need to learn only a certain part of the language in order to do applications of interest to them, and for expert programmers, who can use all the many options available.

There are several advantages to PL/I:

▶ The modular structure allows the use of structured programming concepts.

▶ It has built-in features that can identify and correct common programming errors.

▶ The language is very flexible, with few coding restrictions: Statements can appear in any column, for instance, which is not true of other languages.

Needless to say, however, PL/I has its drawbacks:

▶ It requires a lot of main storage in the computer, which means it is not usually found in use with minicomputers and microcomputers.

LANGUAGES OVERHEARD IN HOTEL LOBBIES

If you were to go to business conventions, depending on which you went to, you might hear one of the following languages discussed.

ALGOL. Introduced in 1960, ALGOL (for *ALGO*rithmic *L*anguage) has been popular in Europe but has never really caught on in the United States. Intended for scientific and mathematical projects, its programs tend to be easy to read, but it has limited input–output capability. It is the forerunner of PL/I, Pascal, and Ada.

APL. Introduced by IBM in 1968, APL (for *A Pro*gramming *L*anguage) is especially useful for processing tables and arrays—that is, groups of related numbers. However, there are many special characters in this language and so a special keyboard is required. The many special symbols for a large group of operators means that the language is only apt to be available on machines with large memories.

LOGO. If you are at a convention of school teachers, you may well hear reference to "turtle graphics." This means they are talking about LOGO, a language developed at M.I.T. as a dialect of LISP, which is used to command a triangular pointer on a video screen which is called a "turtle" and which is used to plot various graphic designs. This variant of LOGO, with its simple commands, is useful for teaching some fundamentals of programming to young children.

Modula-2. Defined in 1978, this language grew out of Pascal. The most outstanding improvement is its modular structure, which allows a program to be partitioned into units with well-defined connections.

Smalltalk. This language, which was invented at the Palo Alto (California) Research Center, created by Xerox Corporation, is designed to support an especially visual computer system. A keyboard is used to enter text into the computer, but all other commands are accomplished with the use of a mouse, a gadget moved around on the table top which directs the cursor on the video screen. The principles of Smalltalk were successfully adapted by Apple Computer in their Lisa and Macintosh microcomputers.

SNOBOL. Invented by Bell Telephone Laboratories in the early 1960s, SNOBOL is widely used for manipulating alphanumeric or special characters and has found use in text editors and language processors.

▶ It has so many options that some people feel it loses its usefulness.

▶ It is more difficult to learn all parts of it than is the case with COBOL.

Because for many years PL/I was available only on IBM computers, companies worried about finding themselves locked into IBM equipment, with no choice of alternatives. Because, in addition, PL/I did not seem to have tremendous advantages over COBOL for business uses, it did not seem to many people worth the effort of changing languages and risking becoming totally dependent on IBM.

FORTRAN: The Language of Science

Maybe you will never write a line of code of FORTRAN, but knowing something about it—or about any of the other principal languages used by scientists and engineers *(see box)*—might be just what will give you a competitive edge. After all, you would hate to find yourself in the company of engineers and scientists and confusing

COBOL, SNOBOL, ALGOL, and LOGO (the names do sound somewhat alike).

FORTRAN—short for *FORmula TRANslator*—was developed by IBM and introduced in 1954. The first high-level language, **FORTRAN** is a scientific-mathematical language and is still the most widely used language among scientists, mathematicians, and engineers.

By now you would probably have settled on Pascal, BASIC, or COBOL as the language in which to write the *Dynamite Bay* payroll program, but, if you had asked the programmer to express it in FORTRAN, the result would be as shown in Figure 5-6.

The benefits of FORTRAN are several:

▶ It is more compact than COBOL. Indeed, its brevity and simplicity are the reasons it is so popular.

▶ It is very useful for processing complex formulas, such as those used in science, engineering, and economics. It is even useful for business, if there are not extensive data files.

▶ Many application programs for scientists and engineers have been written in FORTRAN, and programs written for one computer are usually easily modified for other makes of computers.

And then there are the disadvantages:

▶ FORTRAN is not as structured as COBOL.

▶ It is not as able as COBOL to handle large amounts of input and output data.

▶ It is more difficult to read and understand a FORTRAN program, which makes it more difficult to change.

Pascal: The Simple Language

Pascal was named after the 17th-century French mathematician and philosopher Blaise Pascal and was developed in the mid-1970s. It has become quite popular in computer science educational programs in the universities of Europe and now the United States. One version of Pascal called TURBO Pascal has become very popular for microcomputer applications. Its principal significance is that it was developed to take advantage of structured programming concepts.

You and the programmer agree that the Pascal version of the *Dynamite Bay* payroll program is the best way to go, and this version is shown in Figure 5-7. Although it looks more like a COBOL program than either the BASIC or FORTRAN variations, it actually is more closely related to the BASIC version, for it is relatively easy to learn and is frequently available on microcomputer systems.

The benefits of Pascal are:

Knowing What the Tool Should Achieve

It is precisely the ability to think in terms of proper abstractions that is the hallmark of a competent programmer. Even more, he or she is expected to be able to jump from one level to another without mixing them up. A structured language is enormously helpful in this endeavor, but it does not do it for you. It is like with a horse: you may guide it to the water, but it has to do the drinking itself. I am afraid that this simple truth is in stark contrast to the numerous lulling advertisements being published in such abundance. They cleverly reinforce themselves with slogans like *Switching to Pascal solves all your (programming) problems* and *Our Computer speaks Pascal*, and, in fact, represent nothing more than an extremely aggressive sales campaign. . . .

Let me emphasize the point: neither owning a computer nor programming in a modern language will itself solve any problems, not even yours. But it may be instrumental. Predominantly, I have noticed, more effort is spent on obtaining those instrumental tools than on mastering them. And this is a grave mistake. Perhaps the most effective precaution against it is this rule: Know what the tool is to achieve and what you are going to use it for before you acquire it. This holds for language as well as computers.

—Niklaus Werth, *Byte*

Figure 5-6. FORTRAN. There would probably be no reason to write the *Dynamite Bay* program in FORTRAN, but if the programmer did so, it would look like this. The circled numbers correspond to the flowchart and pseudocode shown in Figure 5-2. FORTRAN is even more cryptic than BASIC. For example, the formatting and printing in FORTRAN (number 11) is far more difficult to understand than the corresponding code in BASIC, COBOL, and Pascal.

```
        INTEGER LNAME(10)
        INTEGER FNAME(6)
        INTEGER WKDATE(8)
        INTEGER SOCSEC(11)
        REAL HOURS
        REAL PAY
        INTEGER STREET(14)
        INTEGER CITY(18)
        INTEGER FILM(15)
        INTEGER LOCAT(25)
        REAL GROPAY
        REAL OTPAY
        REAL UNION
        REAL TAXRT
        REAL TAX
        REAL NETPAY
      C
 (1)    CALL ASSIGN (99, 'EMPLOY.DAT')
 (2)    READ(99,10) LNAME,FNAME,WKDATE,SOCSEC,
        &               HOURS,PAY,STREET,CITY,FILM,LOCAT
     10 FORMAT(10A1,6A1,8A1,11A1,F5.0,F5.0,14A1,18A1,15A1,25A1)
      C
 (3) 20 IF (LNAME(1) .EQ. '#') GO TO 110
 (4)    GROPAY = HOURS * PAY
 (5)    IF (HOURS .LE. 40) GO TO 30
 (6)    OTPAY = (.50 * PAY) * (HOURS - 40)
        GROPAY = GROPAY + OTPAY
     30 (7) IF (GROPAY .GT. 300) GO TO 40
 (9)    TAXRT = .10
        GO TO 50
     40 (8) TAXRT = .15
     50    UNION = .02 * GROPAY
 (10)   TAX = TAXRT * GROPAY
        NETPAY = GROPAY - UNION - TAX
        WRITE (7,60)
     60 FORMAT (1H,///////)
        WRITE (7,70) WKDATE, FILM, LOCAT, HOURS, GROPAY, NETPAY, SOCSEC
     70 FORMAT (1H,1X,8A1,1X,15A1,1X,25A1,1X,F5.2,3X,
        &          '$',F6.2,1X,'$',F6.2,1X,11A1,///)
 (11)   WRITE (7,80) FNAME, LNAME
     80 FORMAT (1H,25X,8A1,1X,10A1,/)
        WRITE (7,90) STREET, NETPAY
     90 FORMAT (IH,25X,14A1,20X,'$',F6.2,/)
        WRITE (7,100) CITY
    100 FORMAT (1H,25X,18A1)
 (12)   READ(99,10) LNAME,FNAME,WKDATE,SOCSEC,
        &               HOURS,PAY,STREET,CITY,FILM,LOCAT
        GO TO 20
 (14) 110 END
```

Figure 5-7.   Pascal. The *Dynamite Bay* program written in Pascal looks like this. Circled numbers correspond to those in Figure 5-2. Pascal is structured and easy to understand. Pascal procedures are modules of the program and are independent of each other, leading to good structured techniques.

```
Program Payroll(input,output);

{Program Description:

{This program will read in information from the employee data file about an
individual, and then calculate his net pay for the week, subtracting taxes as
well as union dues automatically. The program will output a check in the
correct amount to the individual in question.}
}

Type

   Name = Packed array[1..25] of char;
   Employee_Info = record
      Last_name : name;
      First_name : name;
      Week_date : name;
      Social_Security : name;
      Hours_worked : real;
      Pay_rate : real;
      Street_address : name;
      City_address : name;
      Film_name : name;
      Film_location : name;
   End;
   data_file = file of employee_info;

Var
   Empdat : data_file;
   Employee : employee_info;


(*******************************************************************)

Procedure READ_FILE( Var Employee : Employee_info;
                     Var Empdat   : Data_file);

{This procedure reads in the employee information from the file EMPDAT into
the employee record}
}

Begin
   Read(EMPDAT, Employee);
End;


(*******************************************************************)

(Procedure COMPUTE_PAYROLL( Employee : Employee_info);

{This procedure will compute the employee's payroll, deduction both taxes
and union dues, outputing a check to the employee in question.}
}
```

```
    Var

—  Gross_pay : real;
—  overtime_pay : real;
   union_dues : real;
   tax_rate : real;
   tax : real;
   Net_pay : real;

   Begin
④ ——  gross_pay : = employee.hours_worked * employee.pay_rate;
⑤ — If employee.hours_worked > 40.00 then
        Begin
⑥ ———— overtime_pay : = ((employee.pay_rate * 0.5) *
                          (employee.hours_worked_40.00));
        End;
⑦ — If gross_pay > 300 then
⑧ —    tax_rate : = 0.15
     Else
⑨ ——   tax_rate : = 0.10
   ⎡ Union_dues : = 0.02 * gross_pay;
⑩ —⎢ Tax : = tax_rate * gross_pay;
   ⎣ net_pay : = gross_pay—union_dues—tax;
     writeln;
     writeln;
     writeln;
     writeln;
     writeln;
     writeln;
   ⎡ writeln(employee.week_date:9,employee.film_name:17,
   ⎢       employee.film_location:26,employee.hours_worked:3:2,'$',
   ⎢       gross_pay:3:2,'$',net_pay:3:2,'',
   ⎢       employee.social_security:12);
⑪ ⎢ writeln;
   ⎢ writeln;
   ⎢ writeln(employee.first_name:31,'',employee.last_name:11);
   ⎢ writeln(employee.street_address:39,$',
   ⎢       net_pay:3:2);
   ⎣ writeln(employee.city_address:40);
   end;


   (********************************************************************)

   Begin (* Main program *)
  ⎡ Assign(empdat,'b:e.dat');
① ⎣ Reset(empdat);
③ — While not eof(empdat) do
       Begin
② ———— Read_file(employee,empdat);
         compute_payroll(employee);
⑫ ——  End;
⑬ — Close(empdat);
⑭ — End.
```

▶ It is simpler to learn than other languages because you need to know only a few rules of coding to write some simple programs.

▶ It is excellent for scientific applications use.

▶ It has excellent graphics capabilities.

Until recently a drawback was that Pascal had limited input and output capabilities, and so was thought not to have serious business uses. However, several accounting systems are now in Pascal.

Ada: New Try at a National Standard

Presented late in 1980, **Ada** is named for Lady Ada Augusta, a 19th-century Englishwoman known as the Countess of Lovelace in England, who earned the title of "the first programmer." (See Appendix A at the end of this book for more about her contributions.) Ada was developed under the sponsorship of the U.S. Department of Defense and was originally intended to be a standard language for weapons systems. However, it not only has military applications but commercial ones as well.

The advantages of Ada are:

▶ It has more general input and output capability than Pascal, which might make it more favorable to industry.

▶ It is a structured language, with a modular design that allows pieces or modules of a large program to be written, compiled, and tested separately before the entire program is put together.

▶ It has features that permit the compiler to check for errors before the entire program is run, so that it is easier to write error-free programs.

The drawbacks of Ada are as follows:

▶ Although some experts believe Ada is easy to use, others think it is too complex.

▶ Ada has also been called too unwieldy and inefficient.

▶ Its size may hinder its use on microcomputers, although the development of more powerful microcomputer chips may obviate this concern.

At present, it is probably too early to tell what its acceptance will be, although since Ada is required by the Department of Defense on military computers, we will no doubt be hearing more about it.

C: For Systems and Scientific Use

C—that's the entire name for it, and it does not "stand" for anything— is a general-purpose language particularly suited to systems programming, such as writing operating systems, but also for major numerical, text processing, and data base programs, which makes it useful for scientific applications.

C was developed at Bell Laboratories for the first UNIX operating system. Indeed, about 12,000 of the 13,000 lines of code for the original UNIX were written in C (the rest were written in assembler language). Thus, C is more of a *low-level* than high-level language, although it can be used either way.

The advantages of C are that:

▶ It works well with microcomputers.

▶ It has a high degree of "portability" or "mobility"—that is, it can be run without change on a variety of different computers.

▶ It has excellent speed, and so is very efficient.

▶ It is easy to write compilers for.

However, it also has some blemishes:

▶ It is not a good language for checking *types* of data—whether integers, characters, and so on.

▶ It has no input/output routines built directly into the language, which means these aspects must be provided by outside programs.

Programmers' Problem—Their Artistic Soul

Jim Johnson, president of Human Edge Software, likes to categorize programmers. "First of all, there is the craftsman who does journeyman work without complaint. That's the [person] we look for," he said. "You can measure their productivity. Then there's the prima donna, who does something good once in a while, but would rather spend time pontificating. There's the artist/hacker type who can do beautiful work over a short period of time. Their personalities are such that they tend to be beaten down by their [spouses]. They are also a flighty group and may quit a project without finishing it. A 'relief' pitcher type of programmer is necessary to bail them out sometimes."

Johnson says programmers tend to be optimists and cannot accurately estimate completion times.

—John C. Dvorak, *San Francisco Examiner*

What's Wrong with Third-Generation Languages?

Valuable as third-generation languages are, they have several drawbacks for ordinary users like yourself:

▶ **They typically require the services of a programmer—and programmers may not be available.** Applications programmers have been in short supply for several years—often because so much programmer time is required simply to keep existing applications software in operation—and so there is not a lot of talent left to spare to develop new applications.

▶ **New programming applications may take too long—both to develop and to implement.** Especially in today's organizations, conditions often change fast. A project that might take months to develop and put into place—such as a job classification and pay system for all of Starways's employees—simply takes too much time. If you're trying to get a movie like *Dynamite Bay* out in a few weeks, you don't have time for that.

▶ **They may cost too much.** Systems analysts and programmers are expensive people to employ, and so is sophisticated hardware. Might it not be better if you could do it yourself on a microcomputer?

▶ **Users often don't know exactly what they want.** Some applications can be specified in detail in advance—for example, air traffic control or airline reservations. With other applications, users

dBASE III PLUS

For Reports

Some fourth-generation languages have grown out of packaged software, such as the package we described in Chapter 3, dBase III Plus. The example below shows a relatively simple program that, when run, will allow the end-user to edit a record. The user will never have to worry about the upkeep of the database; the program itself will take care of it.

```
          Begin program and initialize variables

erase
Set Exact ON
Store 'Y' to answer
*
**** Determine field to edit on
*
Accept 'Which field do you wish to edit from (COMPANY, LNAME, CODE)? --> ' to FLd
*
**** Prompt user for names to edit
*
Do While !(Answer) — 'Y'
   Erase
   Accept ' Edit Whom? ' to Whom
   If !(Fld) = 'CODE'
      Count for Code = Val(Whom) to Whoms
      Count for !(&fld) = !(whom)
   Endif
   If !(Fld) # 'CODE'
      Count for !(&fld) = !(Whom) to Whoms
   Endif
*
**** Check for names existence
*
   If Whoms = 0
      ?
      ? '&Whom does not exist in the database'
   Endif
*
```

continued, top of page 159

may not know what they want until they've tried out a version of it and then know what they need to modify.

What do all these drawbacks suggest? The answer: Do it yourself.

Let us therefore step up to fourth-generation languages and so-called application generators.

PROBLEM-ORIENTED
LANGUAGES AND
APPLICATION
GENERATORS

Third-generation languages, such as BASIC or Pascal, require you to instruct the computer in step-by-step fashion. **Fourth-generation languages,** also known as **problem-oriented languages,** are high-level languages designed to solve specific problems or develop specific applications by enabling you to describe what you *want* rather than step-by-step procedures for getting there.

```
**** Edit for one person
*
    If Whoms = 1
        If !(Fld) = 'CODE'
            Locate for code = Val(Whom)
        Endif
        If !(Fld) # 'CODE'
            Locate for !(&Fld) = !(Whom)
        Endif
        Store # to Recno
        Edit Recno
    Endif
*
**** Edit for more than one name
*
    If Whoms > 1
        ?
        If !(Fld) = 'CODE'
            List for Fld = Val(Whom) Company,Address,Lname,Code
        Endif
        ?
        If !(Fld) # 'CODE'
            List for !(&Fld) = !(Whom) Company,Address,Lname,Code
        Endif
        ?
        Accept 'Which one to edit (by record number) -->' to Recno
        Edit &Recno
    Endif
*
**** Ask user for more data to edit
*
?
    Accept 'Edit more data (Y/N)? -->' to Answer
Enddo
Set Exact OFF
```

Fourth-generation languages may be categorized into several kinds of applications development tools:

▶ Personal computer applications software
▶ Query languages and report generators
▶ Decision support systems and financial planning languages
▶ Application generators

Let us explore these helpful problem-solvers.

Personal Computer Applications Software

You have already, of course, been introduced to applications software for personal computers, but the ones we are particularly concerned with here are spreadsheets, database managers, business graphics, and integrated packages. Learning to use Lotus 1-2-3 or Symphony, Ashton-Tate's Framework, or dBase III Plus can help you develop your own applications for administrative procedures, paperwork-avoidance systems, and other solutions to organizational problems. For example, by using an integrated package with spreadsheet and word processing programs, you might be able to develop your own payroll program for the *Dynamite Bay* project.

Query Languages and Report Generators

Query languages allow people who are not programmers to search a data bank (data base), using certain selection commands. Query languages, for example, are used by airline reservations personnel needing flight and ticket information. People in the business department at Starways might use query languages to find which movie distributors are overdue on their accounts.

Report generators are designed for people needing to prepare reports easily, although ordinary users like yourself may require the help of systems analysts or other computer professionals in order to learn these kinds of languages. People using report generators need not be concerned with solution procedures so much as with the input and output. One example of a report generator is RPG. Developed at IBM and introduced in 1964, **RPG** stands for Report Program Generator, and that is what it is designed to do: generate business reports. The latest version is RPG III. With minimal training, users can learn to fill out specifications in very detailed coding forms (see Figure 5-8) for such common business applications as accounts receivable and accounts payable, and a report will then be produced with little effort. The language can also be used for some file updating.

Decision Support Systems and
Financial Planning Languages

We spend quite a bit of time on decision support systems later. For now, let us simply identify a **decision support system** as interactive software designed to help managers make decisions.

Financial planning languages are particular kinds of decision support systems that are employed for mathematical, statistical, and forecasting procedures, among other uses.

Both types of languages find applications in developing complicated business models—hypothetical representations of management problems.

Application Generators

As we described in the last chapter, modules are major processing steps in a program; that is, each module is a set of logically related program statements, an example being the module headed "CALCULATE PAY AND PRINT PAYCHECK" back in Figure 4-5 in Chapter

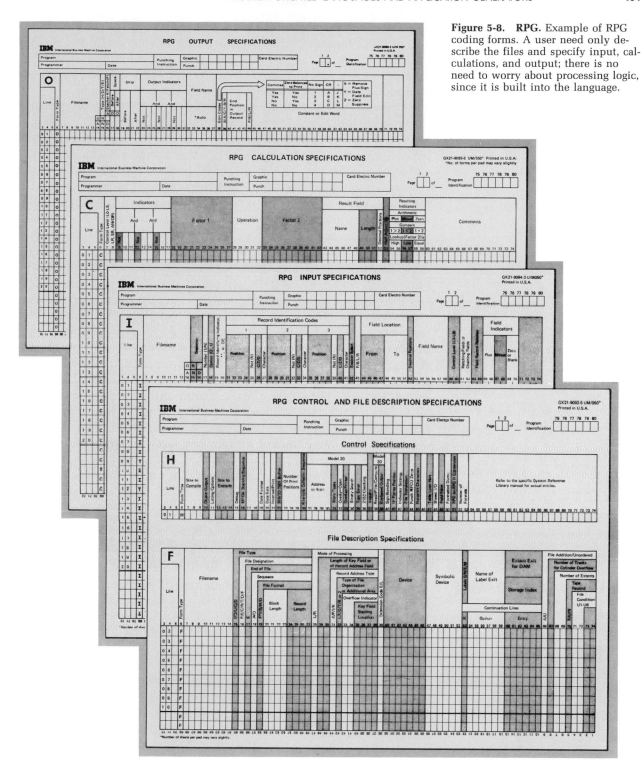

Figure 5-8. RPG. Example of RPG coding forms. A user need only describe the files and specify input, calculations, and output; there is no need to worry about processing logic, since it is built into the language.

4. An **application generator** consists of a software system with numbers of these modules, preprogrammed for various functions, so that the programmer or user can simply state which function is needed for a particular application, and the system will select the appropriate modules and run a program to meet the user's needs.

How is this marvelous shortcut possible? The answer is that many applications tend to be performed in the same way. A module to calculate pay and print a paycheck clearly will work in many different industries. Producing reports—that is, information output— and updating files are also routine data processing operations. Thus, an application generator will select the precoded modules and alter them for your particular application. Where your application is unique, the application generator will provide a module that permits you to enter program code (in BASIC or COBOL, for example) that will attend to those unique parts.

Several kinds of applications development tools are shown in Figure 5-9. Some application generators are reserved for data processing professionals, and are designed to run on minicomputers and mainframes. Others are designed to run on microcomputers, and some are suitable for users like yourself. At Starways, for instance, you might use an application generator such as Nomad 2, in which you sit before a terminal and respond to questions from the applications generator that enable you to define the inputs, processes, and output formats. The application generator will then produce code in accordance with your answers that will produce a **prototype,** or experimental version, of the program you want, which you can then modify as necessary until it perfectly fulfills the applications.

Fourth-generation languages may seem to be a breeze once you get used to them. However, the best is yet to come: fifth-generation or natural languages.

NATURAL LANGUAGES

"NATURAL" TO

HUMANS

Keep an eye on these. There are many **fifth-generation** or **natural languages,** and although they are mainly in the developmental stage, they promise to have a profound effect—particularly in artificial intelligence and expert systems, as we shall see in later chapters. Natural languages have two characteristics:

▶ They are designed to make the connection humans have with computers more natural—more humanlike.

▶ They are designed to allow the computer to become "smarter"— to actually simulate the learning process by remembering and improving upon earlier information.

The basis for natural languages is the concept of **recursion.** This term, borrowed from mathematics, describes the effect you have

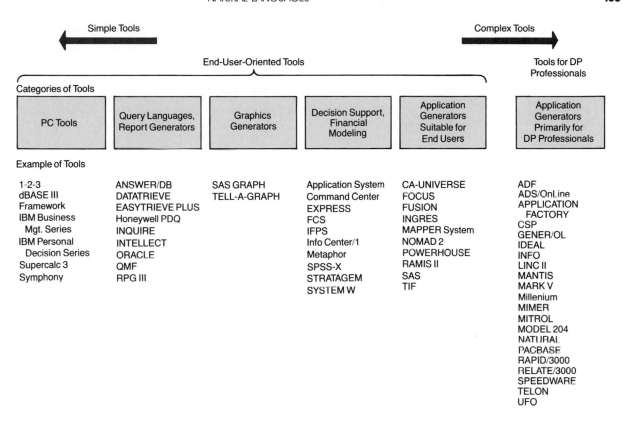

when standing between two parallel mirrors, in which the images repeat themselves into infinity. Another example would be the picture of a man on a book cover who is shown holding the book with the picture of himself holding the book, and so on. In programming, recursion means a procedure or function that calls itself. Examples are shown in the two natural languages described below, LISP and PROLOG, which we will describe in more detail in a later chapter.

Figure 5-9. Types of development tools. Note the wide variety of end-user tools —five different categories. The simpler tools, such as Lotus 1-2-3 and dBase III, run on personal computers. More complex tools, such as the application generators suitable for end-users, run on mainframes.

LISP

"To call LISP a programming *language*," says one writer, "is not merely a bit of wishful thinking, because—in the same way that some things that can be said in French do not translate into English and vice versa—LISP expressions can be sufficiently rich or complex in content that a description of their purposes in English becomes a very long-winded affair indeed."

Developed at the Massachusetts Institute of Technology in 1958 and used extensively in the United States, **LISP** is an artificial intelligence programming language that mimics a sort of human thinking ability. It is used interactively at a terminal to process mainly characters and words rather than numbers. These mainly alphanumeric symbols are combined into sentencelike shapes and are then manipulated to produce paragraphlike and even chapterlike shapes. LISP contains a fairly small dictionary, whose terms have fairly short definitions, but you can then modify or add to those definitions as you see fit. For example, the word *capitalism* could represent a long string of ideas.

PROLOG

Used a great deal outside the United States, and particularly popular in Europe and Japan, **PROLOG** was invented in 1970 in France and is a form of logic programming used to solve problems that require symbolic representations of objects and the relationships between them. Among the many applications of PROLOG, according to one writer, are relational data bases and expert systems, mathematical logic, semantics, plan formation, architectural design, symbolic equation solving, and biochemical analysis and drug design.

FROM SOFTWARE
TO HARDWARE

We turn now from a discussion of software to a discussion of hardware. Why study software *before* hardware? The first piece of advice most experts give about buying a microcomputer is: Choose software before hardware. This kind of advice could apply to the selection of larger computer systems as well. The computer is valueless to us unless it can use the *right kind* of software for our needs.

Now we have some sense of how we can tell the computer what we want to do, using the right kind of software package or programming approach and programming language. In Part 3, we look at the machines at our disposal.

SUMMARY

▶ To communicate with the computer, one uses a **programming language,** which can be understood by both the user and the computer. A programming language is a set of rules that provides a way of instructing the computer to perform certain operations.

▶ There are more than 150 programming languages, not counting obsolete ones. Those of primary interest to prospective managers are BASIC, COBOL, PL/I, and RPG. We also describe FORTRAN, Ada, Pascal, and C.

▶ Programming languages are said to be lower or higher, depending on whether they are closer to the language of the computer (machine language) or the language of the user (in this case, more English-like).

▶ The **binary system** is a sophisticated way of representing data; it is based on two digits—0 and 1—that represent the turning off and on of electricity. All programming is based on the binary system.

▶ There are five levels of programming language: (1) machine languages, (2) assembly languages, (3) procedural languages, (4) problem-oriented languages, and (5) natural languages.

▶ **Machine language** is the lowest form of programming language; information is represented as 0s and 1s, and it is very tedious and time-consuming to use. There is no single machine language, which means that such a language is machine-dependent. However, its execution is fast and efficient because the computer can accept the machine code as is.

▶ **Assembly languages,** also known as **symbolic languages,** were developed to reduce programming complexity and provide some standardization. These languages use abbreviations or mnemonic codes to replace the 0s and 1s of machine languages. Assembly language must be converted to machine code to be executed. The assembly language program is called a **source program;** the machine language program is an **object program.**

▶ **Macro instructions** are assembly language instructions devised to offer a one-to-many correspondence to machine code, meaning that one assembly statement can be translated into many machine statements.

▶ Assembly languages have several advantages: (1) They are more standardized and easier to use than machine languages. (2) They operate efficiently. (3) They are easy to debug because programs locate and identify syntax errors. They also have some disadvantages: (1) The programs are often long. (2) They are still complex. (3) They are still machine-dependent.

▶ **High-level languages,** which are English-like programming languages, are used to code applications programs. High-level languages are sometimes used to refer to all languages above the assembly level (machine languages are thought of as **first-generation** and assembly languages as **second-generation**). They may be subdivided into three kinds or generations: (1) procedural-oriented—or third-generation; (2) problem-oriented—or fourth-generation; and (3) natural—or fifth-generation.

▶ A high-level language must be translated into machine language to work on the computer. There are two kinds of translators—compilers and interpreters. High-level languages are called either compiled languages or interpreted languages.

▶ In a **compiled language,** a translation program is run to convert the programmer's high-level language program, called the **source code,** into a machine language code, called the **object code.** The translation process is called a **compiling run;** the execution of the object code is a **production run.** The most widely used compiled languages are COBOL and FORTRAN.

▶ In an **interpreted languages,** a translation program converts each program statement to machine code just before the program statement is to be executed. Translation and execution occur immediately. In this case, there is no compiling run, only a production run. The most frequently used interpreter languages are BASIC and Pascal. Interpreter languages are frequently used for **interactive programming,** the kind of programming in which the user and the computer carry on a dialogue, or interact, with each other.

▶ High-level languages are often classified according to whether they solve general problems (procedural languages) or specific problems (problem-oriented languages).

▶ **Procedural languages,** or **third-generation languages,** are general-purpose programming languages such as BASIC and COBOL, which are designed to express the logic—the procedure—of a problem. The advantages of procedural languages over machine and assembly languages are that: (1) they resemble English and so are easier to work with, (2) they take less time to program a problem, (3) the coded programs are easier to understand and modify, and (4) the programming languages are machine-independent. The disadvantages are that: (1) they execute more slowly, and (2) they use computer resources less efficiently.

▶ The procedural languages of interest in business are BASIC, COBOL, and PL/I. Others intended for non-business use are FORTRAN, Pascal, Ada, and C.

▶ **BASIC**—*Beginner's All-purpose Symbolic Instruction Code*—was developed in 1964 at Dartmouth College with the intent to provide every educated person with computer experience. It is the most popular computer language and can be used by beginners as well as experienced people. BASIC is an *interactive*, procedure-oriented language that permits user and computer to communicate with each other directly. Most microcomputers use BASIC.

▶ **COBOL**—*COmmon Business-Oriented Language*—is a general-purpose, procedure-oriented compiler language developed in 1959; it is the most frequently used programming language in business. Writing in COBOL is like writing a paper: One writes sentences that tell the computer which operations to perform. Sentences are grouped into paragraphs, paragraphs into sections, and sections into one of four divisions: (1) the Identification Division presents the name of the program and the programmer (other paragraphs may be used for documentation purposes). (2) The Environment Division indicates the computer to be used. (3) The Data Division comprises a File Section and a Working-Storage Section; it lists all the data items to be input, describes where the data will be stored, and gives the format to be used for the output results. (4) The Procedure Division contains the actual processing instructions, mirroring the steps mapped out in the flowchart.

▶ COBOL has several advantages: (1) It is easy to understand—even more so than BASIC. (2) It is self-documenting. (3) It can be used for almost any business programming task. COBOL also has some disadvantages: (1) It is wordy. (2) It is not well suited for mathematics. (3) It is not as speedy as other languages. COBOL uses **reserved words**—words with exact meanings that cannot be used for **variable names,** which can stand for whatever the programmer (or user) wants.

▶ **ANSI-COBOL,** a standardized version of COBOL produced by the American National Standards Institute, is reasonably machine-independent. The newest ANSI-COBOL, called **COBOL-85,** will not always run older programs because of the addition of new reserved words.

▶ **PL/I**—*Programming Language One*—was introduced by IBM in 1964 as a "universal language"—a compromise between COBOL and FORTRAN to apply to both scientific-mathematical problems and general purposes. ANSI produced a PL/I standard language in 1976. PL/I is a procedure-oriented language with a modular structure in which a module can stand alone as a program or become part of a more complex program. It is useful for both novice and expert programmers. PL/I has several advantages: (1) Its modular structure allows the use of structured programming concepts. (2) It has built-in features that can identify and correct common programming errors. (3) It is very flexible, with few coding restrictions. It also has some disadvantages: (1) It requires a lot of main storage in the computer. (2) It has so many options that some people think it loses its usefulness. (3) It is more difficult to learn than COBOL.

▶ **FORTRAN**—*FORmula TRANslator*—was introduced by IBM in 1954 as the first high-level language. It is the most widely used scientific-mathematical language. FORTRAN has several advantages: (1) It is more compact than COBOL. (2) It is very useful for processing complex formulas. (3) Many applications programs for scientists and engineers have been written in it. It also has some disadvantages: (1) It is not as structured as COBOL. (2) It is not as able to handle large amounts of input and output data. (3) It is more difficult to read and understand, and thus harder to change.

▶ **Pascal**—developed in the mid-1970s and named after the 17th-century French mathematician and philosopher Blaise Pascal—takes advantage of structured programming concepts. It is relatively easy to learn and is frequently available on microcomputer systems. Pascal has several advantages: (1) It is simpler to learn than other languages. (2) It is excellent for scientific applications use. (3) It has excellent graphics capabilities.

▶ **Ada**—developed under the sponsorship of the U.S. Department of Defense and named for Lady Ada Augusta ("the first programmer")—was originally intended to be a standard language for weapons systems, although it also has commercial applications. Ada has several advantages: (1) It has more general input and output capability than Pascal. (2) It is a structured language, with a modular design that allows pieces or modules of a large program to be written and tested separately before the entire program is put together. (3) It permits the compiler to check for errors before the entire program is run. It also has some disadvantages: (1) Some people think it is too complex. (2) It has been called unwieldy and inefficient. (3) Its size may hinder its use on microcomputers, although the development of more powerful microcomputer chips may obviate this concern.

▶ **C** is used for systems programming, such as writing operating systems, and also for major numerical, text processing, and data base programs, which makes it useful for scientific applications. Its advantages are: (1) It works well with microcomputers. (2) It can be run without change on a variety of different computers. (3) It has excellent speed. (4) It is easy to write compilers for. Its drawbacks are: (1) It is not good for checking types of data. (2) It has no input–output routines built directly into the language.

▶ Third-generation languages have several drawbacks for end-users: (1) They require the services of a programmer. (2) New programming applications may take too long to develop and implement. (3) They may cost too much. (4) Users don't always know exactly what they want.

▶ **Fourth-generation languages,** also called **problem-oriented languages,** are high-level languages designed to allow end-users (not just programmers) to solve specific problems or develop specific applications. They may be categorized into four kinds of applications development tools: (1) personal computer applications software, (2) query languages and report generators, (3) decision support systems and financial planning languages, and (4) application generators.

▶ Personal computers applications software consists of spreadsheets, data base managers, business graphics, integrated packages, and similar programs.

▶ **Query languages** allow people who are not programmers to search a data base—such as an airlines reservation system—using selection commands. **Report generators** are designed to help people prepare reports easily. An example is **RPG**—for Report Program Generator—introduced in 1964, which is used to generate business reports; the latest version is RPG III, which is used for common business applications such as accounts receivable.

▶ **Decision support systems** are interactive programs designed to help managers make decisions. **Financial planning languages** are particular kinds of decision support systems used for mathematical, statistical, and forecasting procedures.

▶ An **application generator** consists of a software system with numbers of modules, preprogrammed for various functions, so that the user can simply state which function is needed for a particular application. Some applications generators will produce a **prototype** or experimental version of an applications program, which can then be modified until it perfectly fulfills the applications.

▶ **Fifth-generation languages,** or **natural languages,** have two characteristics: (1) They are designed to make the connections humans have with computers more humanlike. (2) They are designed to enable the computer to remember and improve upon earlier information—that is, simulate learning. The basis for natural languages is **recursion**—a procedure or function that calls itself. Two examples of natural languages are LISP and PROLOG.

▶ Developed at M.I.T. in 1958, **LISP** is an artificial intelligence programming language that mimics a sort of human thinking ability, combining alphanumeric symbols into sentencelike shapes. **PROLOG,** which was invented in France in 1970, is used to solve problems requiring symbolic representations of objects and the relationships between them.

KEY TERMS

REVIEW QUESTIONS

1. Describe the different levels of programming language.
2. What system does machine language use to represent data?
3. What are some of the advantages of assembly language?
4. Why are high-level languages easier than machine or assembly languages?
5. How are assembly and high-level languages translated into machine language?
6. Name the five generations of computer language.
7. Name some languages that would perform well for scientific and mathematical applications. Why?
8. Name some languages that would perform well for business applications. Why?
9. What are the advantages of natural languages?

CASE PROBLEMS

Case 5-1: COBOL or Ada?

COBOL became the dominant programming language for business largely because the Department of Defense (DOD) made a great effort not only to develop the language in order to standardize computer languages but also because it specified the use of COBOL in many contracts it awarded. Today it is perhaps the most widespread programming language in the world.

In the early 1970s, DOD developed Ada as a uniform, all-purpose programming language in order to control runaway software costs and to simplify the use of hardware. Will it become the language of the future? An article in *High Technology Business* (September 1987) says, "The growing use of the Ada programming language in military computers is less a tribute to its appeal than to the diligence of the Department of Defense, which now demands the language. But interest in Ada is building in nondefense markets as well, partly because business managers are becoming sold on Ada's ability to cut costs and boost software quality."

Your assignment: Let us say you are already working in a management trainee position for a defense contractor. Most of the present programming is still done in COBOL, and it is part of your job to communicate with programmers. Since you are already working full time, it is difficult for you to take more than one night course, but you are determined to take at least one in programming. Let us assume you have taken BASIC. Now you can take either COBOL or Ada. Which one would you take and why?

Case 5-2: A Turn Toward Turing?

There is one programming language we did not mention in the text: Turing. Named in honor of Alan Turing, a brilliant British mathematician and computer theorist, **Turing** is a general-purpose language developed in 1983 at the University of Toronto by Jim Cordy, Richard Holt, and J.N.P. Hume. Turing is said by its developers to be simpler than BASIC and more powerful and elegant than Pascal or PL/I. Moreover, they claim, Turing offers superior debugging, portability (can be used on different makes of computers), and modular programming capabilities. Most important, neither Pascal nor PL/I use modular programming techniques, which allow a building-block approach to system design and maintenance and ensure accuracy and flexibility. As a general-purpose language, Turing is useful for basic data processing, microcomputer, and scientific applications. However, its developers admit that at present Turing is not as good as COBOL for large file processing applications such as are used for business data processing.

Your assignment: One of the decisions you may well face in the future is whether a business or installation you are working for should convert to a more efficient programming language than the one it has been using for some time. Consider the following: Would you use Turing if you were working for a scientific research and development laboratory? If not Turing, then what? Would you use Turing for a payroll program for a microcomputer to be carried on location by a movie company? If not Turing and not Pascal or BASIC, then what? Would you consider converting to Turing if you were working for a large insurance company that already had thousands of records written in COBOL?

PART 3

THE USES OF HARDWARE AND TECHNOLOGY

"We are in the midst of a major structural change, as information rapidly replaces energy as society's main resource," says futurist Leon Martel, author of *Mastering Change: The Key to Business Success*. Unlike energy, he says, information does not disappear—it is infinite.

In the Computer Age, Martel states, information already has added to the value of goods and services by increasing labor's efficiency and shortening the time it takes to develop products. The future promises more effiency as automation and robots transform the assembly line, which produces millions of identical products, into a system that can turn out small batches to suit diverse needs and tastes.

Martel differs with another famous futurist, John Naisbitt, who believes that the most reliable way to anticipate the future is by understanding the present. "The present will be different tomorrow," says Martel. "It's not going to be the same as it is today. My argument is that the best way to prepare for the future is to understand change."

For companies to be successful, he believes, they must become actively involved in recognizing that change is occurring and identifying developments that will affect their businesses. Some companies have prospered because they accepted change, others have gone under because they ignored it. An example is a scientific instrument maker that in 1967 commissioned a study of what life would be like 100 years in the future but failed to foresee that within 5 years inexpensive pocket calculators would replace the company's main product, the slide rule.

If today is an insufficient guide to tomorrow, does this mean that the types of hardware and technology we are about to study in this part—input and output, central processing unit and operating systems, storage, data bases, and networks—will be be obsolete? The answer is both yes and no. To see why, turn the page.

INPUT AND OUTPUT: PROBLEMS IN, SOLUTIONS OUT

"Being educated is what is left over when everything else is forgotten," writes the famous psychologist B. F. Skinner. Being educated in this sense is what we hope you will be after you have finished reading this chapter. The hardware you are starting to read about here may someday be forgotten because it may well change dramatically during your lifetime. Indeed, some of the equipment is changing even as you read this.

But there are at least two good reasons for reading this chapter anyway, reasons that will have an important bearing on your career:

▶ Many of the *concepts* that we describe will remain true even as the equipment changes. This means both hardware concepts and business concepts, as the case study on the next page shows.

▶ Many executives—particularly data processing managers—are working with older hardware, such as 10- and even 20-year-old IBM mainframes.

This, then, is what we mean by being educated: You will need to come away from this part of the book prepared for anything—for dealing with the cutting edge of technology sooner than you think and for muddling through with equipment that industry watchers wrote off years ago.

CASE STUDY: NEW INNOVATIONS IN INPUT AND OUTPUT

The Talking Machine: The Communications Idea of the Future Is at Work Right Now

In 1976, when he was seventeen years old, Robert Marince of Aliquippa, Pennsylvania, severed his spine in an automobile accident. Three years later, a mathematician named Stephen Gill co-founded the Votan company in Fremont, California, and the company's products have since given Robert Marince an independence and control he never believed possible. He is still flat on his back. His breath still comes from a sighing mechanical respirator. But when he wants the lights off, or a different TV channel, or the temperature turned up in the fish tank beside his bed, all he has to do is ask and his personal computer blinks on to do his bidding. This requires no keyboard, no complicated codes. When Robert wants something done, he simply says so. "Dial a call," he'll tell the computer. "What call would you like me to dial, Master?" the computer replies, and like an efficient secretary, it soon has the party on the line. . . .

Using a Votan program called VoiceKey and a microphone, Robert first taught the computer to associate the sound of his voice speaking a word with a particular stroke on the keyboard. This is called a "training run." The computer digitized his voice, building an electronic profile of each word. Then it extracted key vocal features and compressed them into a "template," which was stored for later comparison. Now when Robert says, "Dial a call," the computer matches what it "hears" with its library of templates, identifies the command and asks for the number. . . .

Votan is the country's leading supplier of voice recognition and voice output products. Founded in 1979, the company introduced its first products in 1981 and has been continually refining them since. The products by now are capable of continuous voice recognition, which means that users can speak at a normal, conversational pace. The technology also recognizes voices in a noisy environment, a feature that makes it handy for use on a factory floor. (Product inspectors, for example, can wear headsets and dictate information to the computer without ever taking their hands off the products being inspected.)

—William Poole, *Image*

INPUT AND OUTPUT

DATA INTO

INFORMATION

"Satisfaction guaranteed or your garbage back," says the slogan on the scavenger truck. Input and output operate in essentially the same way. Programmers use the acronym **GIGO**—short for "Garbage In, Garbage Out"—to mean that the quality of the information that comes out is no better than the quality of the data put in.

Data consists of letters, numbers, symbols, shapes, colors, temperatures, sounds, or other raw material. For the computer to convert these to information, the data must be made available in *machine-readable* form. That is the purpose of the input devices to be described here: to convert the stuff of life into forms the computer can handle.

The computer processes the raw data into information, but that information is still only in machine-readable format until output devices convert it to a form people can use. Actually, the forms of output are practically limitless. Although some of the output devices that we will describe in this chapter may at some time become obsolete, it is an important principle that the computer can operate *any* machine that can be made to run by electricity. As Ted Nelson wrote a few years ago in *The Home Computer Revolution*, giving free rein to the possibilities:

> Computers can activate printers, picture screens, lawn sprinklers, musical instruments, juke boxes, music synthesizers, rocket launchers, atomic weapons, electric trains, cameras, water pistols, puppets, exhibits, theater lights, fish feeders, cattle gates, movie projectors, bells, whistles, klaxons, foghorns and chimes.

In this book, however, we are less concerned with rocket launchers and puppets than we are with more familiar output devices such as video terminals and printers.

We shall now describe the most important input devices. In the second half of the chapter we shall describe output devices. Of course, no single computer system has all the possible different types of input and output devices. Some of the devices are designed for special applications and are ineffective in other applications.

To show you how useful this equipment will probably be in your future career, let us imagine that you have left Starways Film Production Company for a career in international banking. (You found that the business side of movie making was as crazy as the creative side.) You have moved to Atlantic-Pacific Bank NA (the NA stands for North America), headquartered in Boston. You begin with a job in the Boston office that is essentially an internship; it allows you to move around and get familiar with different parts of the bank's operation. As you are about to discover, input and output are a great deal of what banking is all about.

INPUT BATCH VERSUS TRANSACTION PROCESSING

There are two basic methods of handling data:

▶ Batch processing—in which data is saved up and input at one time, as a batch

▶ Transaction processing—in which data is not saved up but is input as it is created, as transactions happen

Let us see how these work.

Batch Processing

In **batch processing,** the data is originally recorded on a source document such as a payroll time sheet, as in the *Dynamite Bay* payroll example in the last chapter. The data from the source documents are then accumulated and input to the computer in a batch all at one time, as would be the case at the end of the week for everyone working on the *Dynamite Bay* film.

Transaction Processing

With **transaction processing,** data is input to the computer as soon as it is created—that is, at the time of a transaction. For example, many retail stores use cash registers that are directly connected to the store's computer. When you buy a sweater on credit at a department store, for example, the sales clerk records the sale on the cash register, which immediately notifies the store's central computer to post the purchase against your charge account for later billing, updates the clothing department's sales figures, and advises higher management of decreasing inventory (by one unit, at least) in sweaters. Transaction processing is also called **real-time processing,** because a transaction is processed fast enough that the results can come back and be of use immediately. It is also called **on-line processing,** because it works by having the user's terminal directly connected to—"on line" with—the computer.

Batch and Transaction Processing at the Bank

In your new job with Atlantic-Pacific Bank, you find both batch and transaction processing in operation. *Batch processing* is used to service those customers in a branch bank who hate to stand in line at a teller window to make deposits to their checking accounts. Instead, they put their cash, checks, and deposit slips in an envelope and drop them into the convenient No-Wait Deposit box in the bank's lobby. Late that afternoon, bank personnel open all the envelopes and key the deposits into the bank's computer, all in one batch—that is, in one session.

Transaction processing takes place when customers make withdrawals at the automatic teller machines. When they punch in the numbers to withdraw cash from their checking or savings account, the machine provides them with a slip of paper telling them the amount withdrawn and their new account balance—an instant process.

Some kinds of input equipment work only for batch and some only for transaction processing, but many will work for both. Let us consider the various categories.

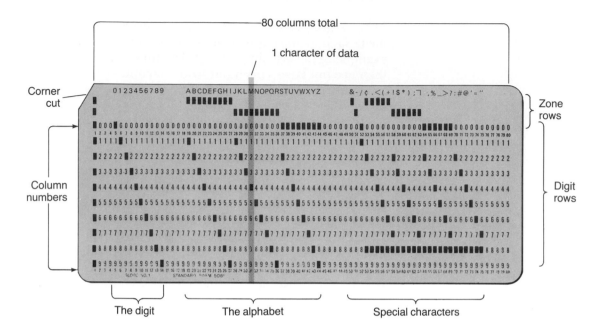

Figure 6-1.   Punched card. A punched 80-column card. Each digit, letter, or special character is represented by a unique combination of punched holes. One character of data—the letter M is highlighted here—is represented by two punched holes in particular rows. Keypunched cards are placed in a card reader; light passing through the punched holes causes electronic signals representing data to be sent to the computer.

TAKING IT ALL IN

KEYBOARD VERSUS

DIRECT ENTRY

In general, data is entered in one of two ways:

▶ By keyboard entry
▶ By direct entry

In *keyboard entry*, data is input to the computer *after* the transaction that produced the data has taken place. Also, using the keyboard, someone copies the data from its original source document. This is the case with the no-wait deposits; someone at the bank scoops up all the checks, cash, and deposit slips from the No-Wait Deposit box at the end of the day and keys them into the computer to record them in people's checking or savings accounts.

In *direct entry*, data is made into machine-processable form at the time the transaction is being made. No one has to enter the data manually through a keyboard later. You see this with oil company credit cards. When you paid for your gas while traveling for Starways, you charged it on a Shell, Texaco, or similar credit card. A service station attendant would run your credit card through an imprinting device, which would imprint your credit card number on an invoice slip. Although the attendant wrote up the transaction with a pen on the slip, he or she also recorded the date, dollar amount, and dealer with the imprinting device, which produced machine-readable numbers. You kept the invoice slip, but the dealer sent a carbon copy to the oil company's accounting department. At the end of the month, someone in the accounting department collected all the imprinted copies of all your transactions and put them directly into a machine that automatically read the machine-readable numbers on the slips and computed the total amount you owed; no retyping or keying was required.

If you have ever tried to haggle with a store about a "computer error" in your bill, you know what true frustration is. Most mistakes, however, are not computer errors but *people* errors: Someone probably keyed in the wrong data. Thus, you can already see why there is a trend toward less keying of data and more use of direct entry: It not only saves on labor, because data has to go through fewer hands, but for the same reason it also saves on errors.

Let us consider the input devices and recording material used for keyboard entry and direct entry.

KEYBOARD ENTRY

In **keyboard entry,** data is recorded on either of two kinds of *media* or *materials:*

▶ *Paper* media, such as punched cards
▶ *Magnetic* media, such as cassette, diskette, tape, or hard disk

Except for the keyboards used for paper media, the keyboard entry device most commonly used is the computer terminal. Let us look at the paper and magnetic media first and then the types of computer terminals.

Punched Cards

Punched cards, an example of which is shown in Figure 6-1, were the first form of input used for computers, and they are still used in a number of places, principally because they are there—the equipment for using them was bought and paid for years ago.

Punched cards are stiff paper cards punched with holes that represent data. The holes are punched using a **keypunch machine,** which has a typewriterlike keyboard. After a stack of cards has been punched, it is taken to a **card reader,** which translates the card holes into electrical impulses, which in turn are input to the computer.

Magnetic Media

Data on paper cards is represented by punched holes. Data on magnetic media, such as tape or disk, is represented by magnetized spots. Probably the most familiar kind of device for magnetic keyboard entry is a **key-to-diskette device** such as a microcomputer or word processor, a machine by which you key in data through the keyboard onto a floppy disk or diskette. A **key-to-tape device** uses recording tape—in cassette, cartridge, or reel form—similar to the audio tape used in stereo tape players. A **key-to-disk device** uses a magnetic recording disk that is somewhat like a long-playing record that has concentric grooves rather than continuous grooves. We talk about both tape and disk in more detail in Chapter 8.

Magnetic media have several advantages over punched cards:

▶ They can be used over and over again, by recording over previous data. (Punched cards can be used only once.)

▶ They are easier to correct, for the same reason.

▶ The input devices are quieter. The machines in a keypunch room make an incredible racket—so much so that many keypunch operators wear earplugs.

▶ The input devices are also more reliable since they are electronic rather than mechanical—hence they have fewer moving parts to break down.

▶ Of great importance, magnetic media take less storage space. A closetful of punched cards can be stored on a few reels of tape.

▶ Most important, the data can be accessed faster by the computer.

Computer Terminals

The most popular keyboard entry device bar none is the computer terminal. For starters, terminals may be either video display terminals (VDTs) or hard-copy terminals, depending on whether the words and numbers you type appear on a screen or on paper (Figure 6-2). Let us examine these characteristics of terminals further.

Video Display Terminals   A **video display terminal,** which everyone calls a **VDT,** is a terminal with a keyboard and a cathode-ray tube or televisionlike screen. This terminal may also be called a **cathode-ray tube terminal** or **CRT.** In computer jargon, **hard copy** is paper output—that is, a computer printout; **soft copy** is output on a computer screen. A VDT is thus sometimes called a soft-copy terminal.

Figure 6-2.   Terminal. A CRT terminal and keyboard.

A walk through the airport en route to your new Atlantic-Pacific Bank job shows VDTs galore. They are at the airline counters so that ticket sellers can check on your reservation. They are in the corridors and lounges in the form of arcade video games. They are at the car rental desks so agents can determine what cars in the fleet are on hand for you to take out. And at the bank itself, display screens are everywhere: They are the windows through which the bank watches the ebb and flow of money.

As an input device, the display screen has several advantages:

▶ It is compact and inexpensive.

▶ It allows erroneous data to be easily corrected.

▶ It allows files to be updated on the spot and allows access to these files.

And it has some disadvantages:

▶ It does not make a permanent record of any transaction (unless a printer is added).

▶ Some people have difficulty adjusting to reading and editing on a screen instead of paper—although this problem usually disappears with use.

Hard-Copy Terminals   A keyboard with printer attached is called a **hard-copy terminal** or **teleprinter.** Now, at whatever location the terminal happens to be, you can make a permanent paper record of the data input or the information output. The convenience is akin to that of your adding up numbers on a calculator that produces a paper tape: If you make a mistake, you can look back at the tape to see what it was—mistakes can easily get by you if you are just using a regular pocket calculator (as you may have noticed when balancing your checkbook).

The hard-copy terminal has the advantage of producing a permanent record. However, it also has two disadvantages:

▶ The printing process makes it slower than the CRT terminal.

▶ It can be quite noisy, although recently developed printers are quieter.

Intelligent Terminals   As we have seen, microcomputers can be used as "stand-alone" computers—many microcomputers in homes are used this way—or they can be used simply as terminals to gain access to information in other computers. At minimum, an **intelligent terminal** includes a keyboard, electronics to convert data to machine-readable code, communication equipment such as a telephone line and modem, an output device such as a display screen, a processing unit, internal storage to do some data processing, software consisting of a programming language and editing programs, and secondary storage such as magnetic disk.

If you have a microcomputer, such as an IBM PC or PS/2, Apple IIe, or Macintosh, it can become an intelligent terminal for a mainframe just by the addition of a telephone or other communication link that connects it to the larger computer. At Atlantic-Pacific Bank, you discover, you can gain information on exchange rates for foreign currencies by using your micro to access the bank's main computer. You can then use your own microcomputer spreadsheet to analyze the data at your desk in any way you want. In addition, you find Atlantic-Pacific has launched a program of home banking, whereby bank customers can use their home computers as intelligent terminals to connect with the bank's mainframe. This allows users to pay bills, move funds from one checking account to another, and otherwise do a limited amount of over-the-phone banking.

DIRECT ENTRY

There are certain basic skills without which one can be somewhat handicapped in living in the 20th century—reading, for instance (although one out of five adults in the United States cannot read this sentence), and elementary mathematics. Learning to drive a car may give you more freedom. And so may learning to type. The keyboard probably will always be with us, and it will become more important as computers become more commonplace instruments.

However, because keyboard entry depends on human skills and because to err is human, direct data entry has become more and more attractive. **Direct entry** is a form of input that does not require data to be keyed by someone reading from a source document. Direct entry creates machine-processable data right on paper or magnetic media or feeds it directly into the computer's CPU, thus eliminating the possibility of errors being introduced, as might happen in the keying process. Clearly, then, direct entry represents the wave of the future.

The most popular direct-entry devices are:

▶ Magnetic-ink character recognition.
▶ Optical-character recognition
▶ Optical-mark recognition
▶ Digitizers
▶ Image scanners
▶ Point-of-sale terminals
▶ Touch-tone devices
▶ Light pens
▶ Mice
▶ Speech-recognition devices

We will describe these below. No doubt you already are aware of many of them.

Magnetic-Ink Character Recognition

Abbreviated **MICR,** which is pronounced "miker" to rhyme with "biker," **magnetic-ink character recognition** is a method of machine-reading characters made of ink containing magnetized particles. Developed by the banking industry in the 1950s to make it easier to process checks, the system uses the futuristic-looking kind of numbers you see printed at the bottom of your check, as shown in Figure 6-3.

"What do the MICR check numbers mean?" you ask on the first day of your new job at Atlantic-Pacific. Although it is not the only application, check processing is by far the most common use of MICR, you are told. Examine the check and machines shown in Figure 6-3. All blank checks have a check-routing symbol so that the checks can be routed back to a particular bank. The routing code consists of both the transit number and the account number printed on the checks. After a check is cashed, the amount of the check is keyed (inscribed) by the bank in the lower right-hand area of the check. The check is then cleared through the Federal Reserve System by using a MICR reader/sorter, which reads and verifies the magnetic-ink characters. The data is then sent directly to a computer for processing or to an external storage device at one of the Federal Reserve Banks. The checks are next sorted by bank number, routed to the appropriate home bank via the transit number, and then to the customer's account via the account number.

The advantages of the MICR system over other systems are that:

▶ The codes can be read by both machines and people.

▶ It is fast, accurate, and automatic.

▶ The amount of human involvement—and hence human error   is reduced.

However, there are still two disadvantages:

▶ The MICR system is limited to only 14 characters.

▶ Some manual keyboarding is still required—namely, at the point where the amount must be inscribed in MICR characters on the bottom right-hand corner of each check.

Optical-Character Recognition

Developed by the U.S. Postal Service in hopes it would assist in mail sorting, the direct-entry technology known as **optical-character recognition,** abbreviated **OCR,** consists of special characters—letters,

ELECTRONIC FUNDS TRANSFER

If banks could have their way, there would be no paper checks. The steps involved in handling checks are a hassle that banks are trying to get out of. This is the reason why, for instance, when you open up a new checking account at a bank you may have to ask that your cancelled checks be returned to you; otherwise, the bank will just store images of the front and back of the cancelled checks on microfilm.

Actually, banks would like to have everyone transfer funds electronically. You can do this in a very limited way on automatic teller machines now (mainly between your own checking accounts and some credit cards). For people who own personal computers and the necessary telephone links, some banks offer home banking services. Thus, sitting at home in front of your video display terminal, you can use special passwords known only to you and the bank in order to move funds from one account to another and pay bills to utilities and certain large stores.

If electronic funds transfer systems are ever implemented on anything like the scale of some forecasts, turning us into a virtually "cashless" society, MICR systems will be much less significant than they are now.

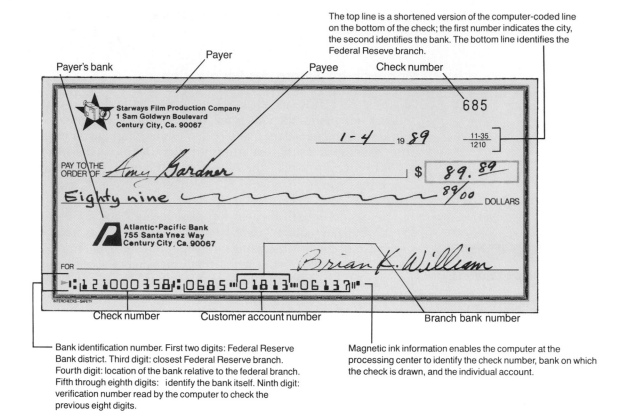

The top line is a shortened version of the computer-coded line on the bottom of the check; the first number indicates the city, the second identifies the bank. The bottom line identifies the Federal Reseve branch.

Payer's bank

Payer

Payee

Check number

Starways Film Production Company
1 Sam Goldwyn Boulevard
Century City, Ca. 90067

685

1-4   19 89

11-35
1210

PAY TO THE
ORDER OF   Amy Gardner $ 89.89

Eighty nine   89/00   DOLLARS

Atlantic·Pacific Bank
755 Santa Ynez Way
Century City, Ca. 90067

FOR

Brian K. William

⑆121000358⑆ 0685 ⑈01813⑈ 06137⑇

INTERCHECKS—SAFETY

Check number

Customer account number

Branch bank number

Bank identification number. First two digits: Federal Reserve Bank district. Third digit: closest Federal Reserve branch. Fourth digit: location of the bank relative to the federal branch. Fifth through eighth digits: identify the bank itself. Ninth digit: verification number read by the computer to check the previous eight digits.

Magnetic ink information enables the computer at the processing center to identify the check number, bank on which the check is drawn, and the individual account.

Figure 6-3.   Magnetic-ink character recognition. *Top:* The meaning of the symbols on your check. Note that the MICR characters in the lower right-hand corner of the check are put there by the bank after the check is cashed; hence, the numbers *should* correspond to the amount for which you wrote the check. *Bottom, fore-ground:* A magnetic-character in-scriber. This machine is used to in-scribe magnetic numbers in the lower right-hand corner of each check after it comes to the bank for processing. *Bottom, background:* A MICR reader/sorter. This machine processes checks with MICR numbers, reading them at the rate of 750–1500 characters per minute, and sorting the checks into different compartments.

Figure 6-4. Optical-character recognition. *Left:* A standard OCR typeface. *Right:* A wand reader, a hand-held photoelectric scanning device that can read OCR characters.

numbers, and special symbols—that can be read by a light source that converts them into electrical signals that can be sent to the computer for processing. OCR that uses *preprinted* characters has found many uses. This means that *someone* must key the characters to begin with, but once they are on the document—most commonly retail price tags, cash register receipts, utility bills, and phone bills—they need not be keyed again for entry into the computer. Most OCR devices read a standard typeface, the most common of which is shown in Figure 6-4.

The most popular OCR input device is the hand-held **wand reader,** as shown in Figure 6-4. The wand reflects light on the printed characters, and the reflection is converted by photoelectric cells to machine-readable code. You often see sales clerks in department stores use the wand to read retail tags and send data to the store's computer for billing and merchandise-reordering purposes.

The advantages of OCR are:

▶ It has all of the benefits of MICR plus it has a larger set of characters: 42 instead of 14.

▶ Using a wand reader does not require *any* manual keying of data.

▶ Data is electronically transferred from source document to computer.

The drawbacks, however, are that:

▶ OCR wand readers can recognize only a special set of characters.

▶ They are still somewhat temperamental, often requiring several passes of the wand over the characters.

Figure 6-5. Digitizer. This device can be moved over drawings or photographs, converting them to data that can be stored in a computer or presented on a CRT screen or paper.

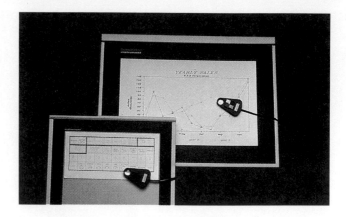

Optical-Mark Recognition

Abbreviated **OMR, optical-mark recognition** is also known as mark-sensing; an OMR device senses the presence or absence of a mark. You see this form of direct entry used in tests such as the College Board's Scholastic Aptitude Test and the Graduate Record Examination, in which the test taker answers multiple-choice questions by filling in little boxes on a form with a special pencil. The answer sheet is then graded by an OMR machine that uses a light beam to recognize the marks and convert them to electric signals that can be processed by the computer. Advantages of OMR are:

▶ No manual keying of data
▶ Low cost

The disadvantages are:

▶ Strict format specifications—special forms and pencils must be used
▶ Limited applications for business purposes because of lack of flexibility, since all potential responses must be anticipated

Digitizers

One of the more interesting forms of direct entry, a **digitizer** is a device that, as Figure 6-5 shows, can be moved over a drawing or photograph and convert it to digital data. The digital data can then be stored in a computer, represented on a display screen, or printed out on paper. The principle behind the device is that each part of the drawing represents a point on a set of horizontal and vertical axes (that is, a pair of X–Y coordinates), so that any given point can be identified. Indeed, there may be 1,000 points per square inch. Digitizers are useful for mapmaking.

Figure 6-6. Scanner. This scanner from Palantir Corp. can read printed pages, distinguishing type from images, and store the result as electronic signals in a computer.

Image Scanners

Image scanners are devices that can identify typewritten characters or images automatically and convert them to electronic signals that can be stored in a computer. The process of image scanning, sometimes known as **bit-mapping**, can identify different type fonts by scanning each character with light and breaking it into light and dark dots, which are then converted into digital code. These devices are valuable for law, accounting, or other firms that need to store thousands of documents. Figure 6-6 shows an example of a scanner that can convert typed text to electronic codes without assistance from a human operator.

Point-of-Sale Terminals

Abbreviated **POS, point-of-sale terminals** (see Figure 6-7) are the latest model in the evolution of cash registers. Seen often in grocery and department stores, a POS terminal consists of a keyboard for entering data, a display screen or digital display area for displaying dollar amounts, and a printer for printing out the list of items and prices for the customer.

Some POS terminals are also **bar-code readers**—photoelectric scanners that read the **bar codes** or vertical zebra-striped marks or bars printed on most products (see Figure 6-8). Supermarkets and other retail stores use a bar-code system called the Universal Product Code (UPC). The bar code identifies the product to the store's computer, which stores the latest price on the product. The computer

Figure 6-7.   Point-of-sale terminal.
A standard POS terminal, used to
enter sales data.

automatically tells the cash register or POS terminal what the price
is and prints the price and the product name on the customer's receipt.

POS terminals offer several advantages:

▶ The skill level of sales clerks and supermarket checkers need not
be as high as for those working in stores without POS systems.
▶ Checkout is faster.
▶ Current sales and inventory information is maintained automatically.

But, of course, there are some disadvantages:

▶ Back-up systems are required, because if there is computer failure, the POS devices fail, too.
▶ The equipment is expensive.
▶ Some states require that prices be stamped on the merchandise,
since bar codes cannot be read by customers. This means stores
must do double duty on price marking: putting prices in the
store's computer that correspond to the bar codes, and stamping
prices or putting price stickers on the cans and boxes.
▶ Shopper's note: A store may advertise an item as being on sale or
mark a sale price on an item, but someone may forget to put the
reduced price in the computer. Thus, keep your eye on the digital
readout display when the sale merchandise goes past the bar-code
scanner.

Figure 6-8. Bar-code reader. *Top:* Example of bar-code—the Universal Product Code used on retail products. *Bottom:* What bar-code readers do in a department store. The clerk moves the product's bar code (1) past the bar-code reader, which reads it with a light beam and sensor. The price and description of the item, which is stored in (2) the computer system, is sent to (3) the POS terminal, where it is (4) printed out as a receipt for the customer. The information from the POS terminal is also used by the store, on the one hand, (5) for accounting purposes and, on the other hand, (6) for restocking store inventory and (7) for analyzing which products sell better than others.

Double-check code

General product category I.D.

Begin/end code

Begin/end code

Manufacturer I.D. number and binary code

Product I.D. number and binary code

76956 14151

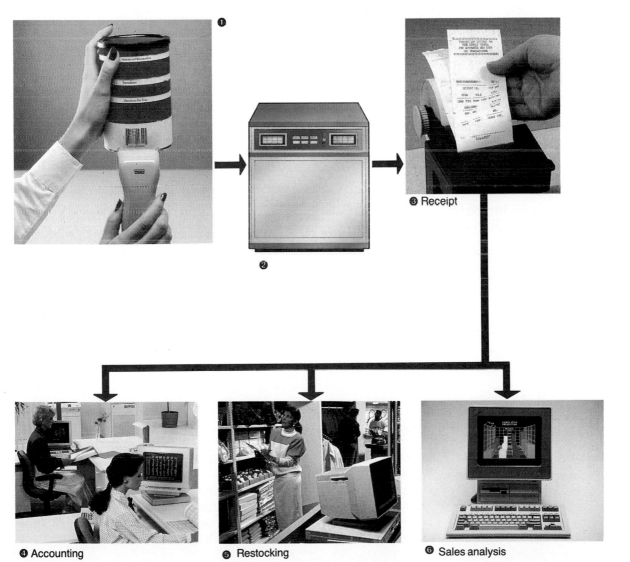

❶

❷

❸ Receipt

❹ Accounting

❺ Restocking

❻ Sales analysis

Figure 6-9. A card dialer. A credit card check is being performed over telephone lines.

Figure 6-10. Light pen. When a pen with a light-sensitive cell at the end is placed against the screen of this graphic display terminal, it closes a photoelectric circuit, enabling the terminal to identify the point on the screen.

Touch-Tone Devices

One of the things you discover about working for Atlantic-Pacific Bank is that credit is a subject bankers care a lot about. There are many occasions when merchants need to check credit instantaneously, and a touch-tone device is a way to help them do it. A **touch-tone device** is an instrument that sends data over ordinary telephone lines to a central computer. An example (see Figure 6-9) is a **card dialer,** which reads a customer's credit card, checks the customer's creditworthiness over the phone with a computer, and reports the results to the local merchant.

Light Pens

Used in designing products from blue jeans to airplanes, a **light pen** consists of a light-sensitive penlike device that, when placed against the display screen of a particular kind of terminal, closes a photoelectric circuit that identifies the $X–Y$ coordinates to the computer. This allows the user to create a drawing right on the screen. Figure 6-10 shows an example of a light pen developed for personal computers.

Mice

We described the mouse briefly in an earlier chapter, but to repeat: A **mouse** is a direct-entry input device that has a ball on the bottom and is attached by a cord to a computer terminal (see Figure 6-11). When rolled on the table top, the mouse directs the location of the cursor or pointer on the screen. The pointer can then be used to draw pictures on the screen or point to a particular instruction.

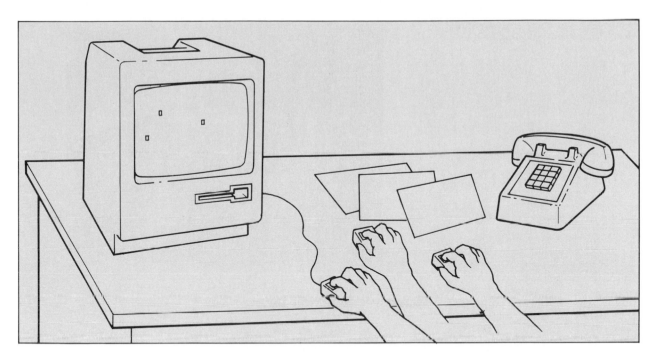

Figure 6-11.   Mouse. *Top:* Movement of the mouse on the desk top makes a corresponding movement of the cursor on the CRT screen. *Bottom:* The screen of a Macintosh computer. Note the symbols (called *icons*) along the left side, which represent various "brush strokes" and artist's options. The mouse's cursor may be used to select one of these options and then to create drawings or different type styles on the screen.

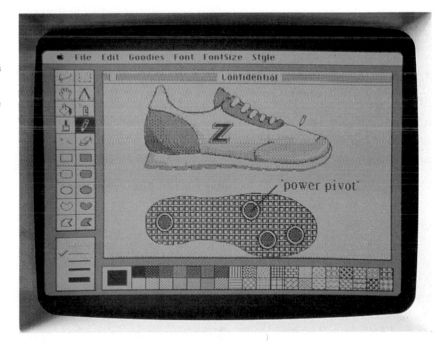

Figure 6-12. Speech-recognition device. The system frees an operator's hands for other activities.

Speech-Recognition Devices

This is the voice of the future, the ultimate data entry device. **Speech-recognition devices** or **voice-recognition systems** (Figure 6-12) convert the spoken word into a numeric code, which is matched against a code stored in a computer. You speak a word into the microphone, the word is displayed on the screen for your visual verification, and you confirm that the input is correct. Speech-recognition devices are presently being used by quality-control inspectors in factories and baggage handlers in airports. Some video games can respond to shouted commands. Some microcomputers can be made to understand such spoken orders as "store" and "copy."

Most speech-recognition systems operate by being previously "trained" to the user's voice. That is, they match the operator's spoken word to patterns previously stored in the computer. Systems that are "speaker-independent"—that can recognize the same word spoken by many different people—can be built by sampling how several people say the same word and storing several patterns for each word, but the vocabularies must be restricted. Moreover, it is difficult to build systems to recognize continuous speech, since people normally run their words together.

The advantages of voice-recognition devices are as follows:

▶ Input is very controlled, with great accuracy.

▶ Input is readily verified and corrected.

▶ The user's hands are free to perform tasks other than keying data.

▶ There are numerous potential applications.

▶ They open the doors to use by computer illiterates or by business-people with little previous computer experience.

The disadvantages are:

Figure 6-13. **Automatic teller machine.** An ATM mounted on the wall of a bank.

▶ Such systems are expensive.

▶ Vocabulary is limited.

▶ Speed of entry is slow.

Ultimately, however, their technologies are the cornerstones of natural language processing, as we have described.

AUTOMATIC TELLER
MACHINES

Automatic teller machines or **ATMs,** those wonderful devices you see on the outside of bank walls and in shopping malls (see Figure 6-13), are actually specialized forms of input devices for transaction processing. ATMs allow you to withdraw funds even in the middle of the night, assuming you meet three criteria: (1) You have a credit card–like ATM card, which you insert into a slot in the machine; (2) you have a secret code number, which you punch in on the ATM keys; and (3) you have enough funds in your checking account to cover the withdrawal. The ATM also allows you to make deposits, loan payments, and charge card payments and to borrow money against a bank credit card. ATMs can be installed at numerous locations, since all are connected to the bank's main computer.

At Atlantic-Pacific Bank, you discover that many people actually *prefer* doing bank business with an ATM rather than a human teller. It is less embarrassing to learn from an ATM than from a person, after all, that you have insufficient funds. There are other advantages also:

▶ As mentioned, service is available to customers 24 hours a day without increased bank employee costs.

▶ A lot of routine banking tasks can be accomplished with fewer manual errors.

But inevitably there are some disadvantages:

▶ The system may fail—and there may be no backup in the form of humans who can help process transactions using paper.

▶ There are security problems—ATMs have been broken into, stolen cards have been used, and people have been mugged near ATMs.

This concludes our discussion of input. Now let us consider the other side of the story—output.

OUTPUT THE RESULTS OF PROCESSING

Output is what we are all impatient to receive, of course. It is, we hope, the solution to the problems we have input to the computer. The solutions are now inside the computer in machine-readable form; the purpose of output devices is to make them people-readable.

As we mentioned, output devices represent an ever-growing list, but we shall describe only a few. The two most popular are:

▶ Terminals
▶ Printers

However, there are several others that we shall also examine:

▶ Plotters
▶ Computer output microfilm
▶ Audio-response devices
▶ Robots

TERMINALS

Terminals, particularly video diplay terminals (VDTs), are the real windows on the computing process. To the usual clutter on an executive's desk—telephone, calendar, pen-and-pencil set, family photographs—must now in many cases be added the green or amber luminescence of the VDT screen.

There are three principal types of terminals:

▶ Alphanumeric
▶ Graphics
▶ Flat panel display

Alphanumeric Terminals

Alphanumeric terminals are so called because they display alpha-numeric output—that is, letters, numbers, and special characters such as $, ?, and *. These are the kinds of terminals you frequently see on secretaries' desks for word processing, on travel agents' desks for making plane and hotel reservations, and on stockbrokers' desks for reading stock prices. They look like television screens (9- or 12-inch, as measured diagonally corner to corner) and most offer 80 characters per line, with 24 lines visible at one time. We showed an example of an alphanumeric terminal back in the top part of Figure 6-2.

As you are finding out at Atlantic-Pacific, banks are full of these terminals, and they have many advantages:

▶ They are relatively inexpensive.
▶ They are quite reliable.
▶ The format of the output on the screen can be varied widely.
▶ Training cost for users is small.
▶ Information can be rapidly transferred to the screen via telephone lines (at up to 960 characters per second) or by direct lines (at up to 55,000 characters per second).

They also have a few disadvantages:

▶ No hard copy is available, although the addition of a printer can eliminate this problem.
▶ The screen size limits the amount of information that can be displayed at any one time.

Graphics Terminals

Computer output in graphics form can be spectacular, and this method of presenting information has come into its own in a major way. One might be tempted to scoff at the notion of businesspeople spending their time drawing "pretty pictures," but the research is pretty hard-headed on this point: In one famous study, Hewlett-Packard found that whereas people could absorb words and numbers at up to 1,200 words per minute, they could absorb numeric information displayed in graphic form at the equivalent of up to 40

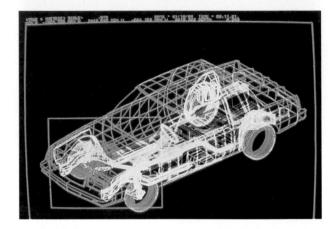

Figure 6-14. Three levels of graphics. Graphics terminals have three levels of complexity in graphics. *Left:* Two-dimensional graphics such as pie charts and line graphs. *Right:* Two-dimensional angle forms. *Bottom:* Three-dimensional graphics, such as might be used in product design; the airplane fuselage shown here can be rotated on the screen, allowing aircraft designers to see all sides.

million words per minute. This statistic makes it graphically clear, as it were, why **graphics terminals**—terminals that can display both alphanumeric and graphic data, such as charts and maps—are no longer used just by scientists and engineers but have been embraced by businesspeople as well. They simply make it easier to do business.

As Figure 6-14 shows, there are three levels of complexity in graphics produced:

▶ *Two-dimensional graphics,* the simplest level, consist of pie, line, and bar graphs, the kind of graphics discussed with personal computer software back in Chapter 3.

▶ *Two-dimensional angle forms* are the kind of graphics found in such uses as topographic maps.

▶ *Three-dimensional graphics* are used in product design, since they allow designers to turn the object on the screen to look at it from different perspectives.

Two particular uses of computer graphics that you are apt to come across in business go under the abbreviations of CAI and CAD/CAM. **CAI** stands for **computer-assisted instruction,** whereby the computer is used to help teach instructional materials. CAI may take the form of simulation, demonstration, tutorial, or drill and practice. Although more often found in schools, it is a method of instruction also found in company training programs. Railroads, for instance, have found it is cheaper—and certainly safer—to teach prospective locomotive engineers using simulation than to send them out on an actual diesel.

CAD/CAM stands for **computer-aided design/computer-aided manufacturing.** CAD is used by engineers, architects, and others to design products, buildings, and manufacturing processes. Two- and three-dimensional pictures can be shown on the screen, combined with other drawings, rotated, enlarged, reduced, and otherwise manipulated. CAM is used to physically manufacture products; for example, a CAD-developed program for a particular piece of clothing or apparel may be fed to a garment-cutting machine, which will cut cloth to the exact fit—and then make thousands of copies of the same thing. A variant on CAD/CAM is **computer-assisted engineering (CAE),** in which graphics are used to assist in developing such complicated products as airplanes.

The advantages of graphics terminals are:

▶ They can present information in easily grasped form.

▶ They can present it quickly and reliably.

Flat Panel Displays

Most terminals use the same technology as TV sets—a long cathode-ray tube—to project images on a screen. As a result, they are quite bulky, which makes them not very portable. However, **flat panel displays** are alphanumeric or graphics terminals that, so far, use one of two technologies: **liquid crystal display (LCD),** which emits no light of its own but which consists of liquid crystal molecules lined up by an electric field in ways that alter their optical properties, and the **electroluminescent (EL) panel,** which, when electrically charged, actively emits light rather than passively reflecting it and which can be viewed under almost any lighting conditions. Figure 6-15 shows an example of flat panel displays. An example of a microcomputer using the LCD flat panel is the laptop Toshiba 1100. A version of the EL display was produced by Hewlett-Packard in its Integral computer.

The advantages of flat panel displays over VDTs are considerable:

▶ They are more compact—hence more portable.

▶ They have lower power consumption.

COLORS YOUR THINKING: MONOCHROME VERSUS RGB MONITORS

A display screen can show one color or several colors, depending on what kind of monitor you buy.

A monochrome screen is one color (on a dark background). The colors usually favored are amber, green, or white, in about that order of preference. The original Apple Macintosh featured black on a white background—actually probably the best arrangement because it resembles the black ink on paper that most people are usually also reading (for instance, when copying from a source document) at the same time they are using their computer, and so it is not as "contrasty" to the eyes.

An *RGB* screen is color; the RGB stands for "red-green-blue," which are not the so-called primary colors (red-*yellow*-blue) out of which other colors are made on a television set, for example. However, an RGB monitor allows you to view the products of graphics software, such as pie charts and bar graphs, in various color designs.

Figure 6-15. Flat panel display. Example of liquid crystal display.

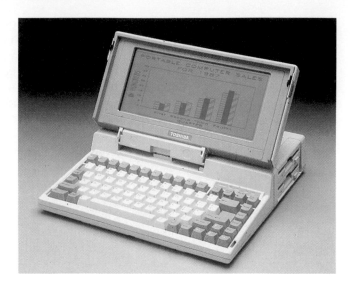

▶ They have greater daylight visibility.

▶ They have longer expected life.

▶ They can be linked with touch-sensitive panels.

However, they do have their disadvantages:

▶ They cost more than conventional terminals.

▶ They are somewhat fragile.

▶ They cannot show color.

Despite their drawbacks, the outlook for flat panel displays—especially for special applications—is positive.

PRINTERS PUTTING
IT ON PAPER

Terminals and the "soft copy" they produce are fine as far as they go. But what if you want hard copy?

There are many reasons why you might want paper output. In word processing, of course, paper output is quite often *the* result you want. Presentation graphics are another reason for needing printed output. And, of course, you cannot cash a paycheck that only appears on a display screen; to get hard currency, you need that check as hard copy. Finally, there are many legal reasons why you might want a record on paper. As movie mogul Sam Goldwyn is supposed to have said, "A verbal contract isn't worth the paper it's printed on."

Classifying Printers

Hard copy is produced by printers and plotters, but here we will deal with **printers,** those machines that produce printing or graphics on paper. Printers are classified according to:

▶ Speed
▶ Print quality
▶ Printing method

Speed Printers may print a *character at a time*—such printers are called **serial printers**—or a *line at a time*. Printers may be as slow as 600 characters per minute for some home computer printers or as fast as 21,000 lines per minute for some laser printers. There are also machines that are **page printers**—they print a page at a time—but they may be low-speed or high-speed. Low-speed page printers are often laser printers, and are very common in offices. High-speed page printers use xerographic, photographic, or laser technologies; are very expensive, costing many thousands of dollars; and are used in large businesses for very specialized applications.

Print Quality Printers may be *draft quality* or *letter quality*. **Dot matrix printers** construct a character by using a matrix of pins (see Figure 6-16). This, you notice, follows the principle of those time-and-temperature signs you see hanging in front of some of Atlantic-Pacific's branch banks: The same matrix or grid may be used to construct a variety of numbers. Although some dot matrix printers can print letter quality images, others produce images with a somewhat fuzzy appearance—acceptable for certain kinds of work, such as writing internal memos to your boss, but not for impressing customers of the bank.

Letter-quality printers produce printed characters that resemble those produced by an office typewriter. The "letter quality," in fact, means they are able to produce print that *is* of good enough quality to write letters to, for instance, bank customers. Letter-quality printers are generally more expensive than dot matrix printers.

Printing Method Printers can be either *impact printers* or *nonimpact printers*. An **impact printer** forms characters by physically striking a type device—a hammer—against inked ribbon to form characters on paper; in other words, it is like a typewriter. **Nonimpact printers** form characters by using heat, lasers, photography, or ink spray, often on a special kind of electrostatic or sensitized paper. Because there is no physical contact between printer and paper, nonimpact printers are quieter than impact printers.

The types of impact and nonimpact printers are described below.

Figure 6-16.　Dot matrix printing.
The letter A is printed on a dot matrix printer by the print head's repeatedly activating a vertical row of pins as it moves along the ribbon. Dot matrix printers often produce an image with a somewhat fuzzy appearance, although some can produce as many as 10,000 dots per square inch, thus making their image nearly the same as that of letter-quality printers.

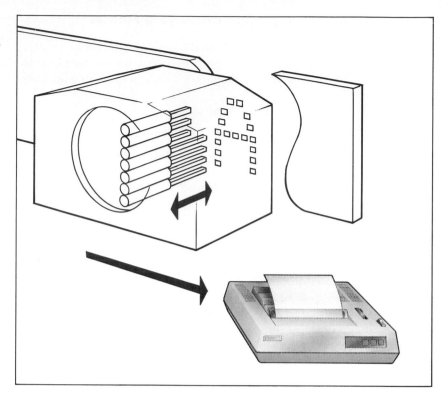

Impact Printers

There are five basic designs for impact printers: chain, band, drum, matrix, and daisy wheel. The differences between these designs is the manner in which the characters are transferred from the type elements to the paper.

Chain　A **chain printer** consists of several sets of characters connected together on a printing chain that, like a bicycle chain (see Figure 6-17), revolves in front of the paper. Hammers are aligned with each position, and when the appropriate character passes by, the hammer in that position strikes the paper and ribbon against it. An advantage of chain printers is that the chains can be changed for different type fonts or styles.

Band　A **band printer** (Figure 6-17) operates somewhat like a chain printer. Also called a "belt printer," a band printer uses a horizontally rotating band. The characters on the band are struck by hammers through the paper and ribbon. Band printers too have a variety of type fonts available.

Drum　The **drum printer** is a line printer in which embossed characters are wrapped around a cylinder or drum, as shown in Figure 6-17. Each band around the drum consists of one each of the 64

Figure 6-17. Three kinds of printer mechanisms. *Top:* Chain printer, which can reach speeds of up to 3,000 lines per minute. *Middle:* Drum printer, which can print up to 3,000 lines per minute. Type styles cannot be interchanged. *Bottom:* Belt or band printer, which can print up to 2,000 lines per minutes. The belt or band can be changed easily to make different styles of type available.

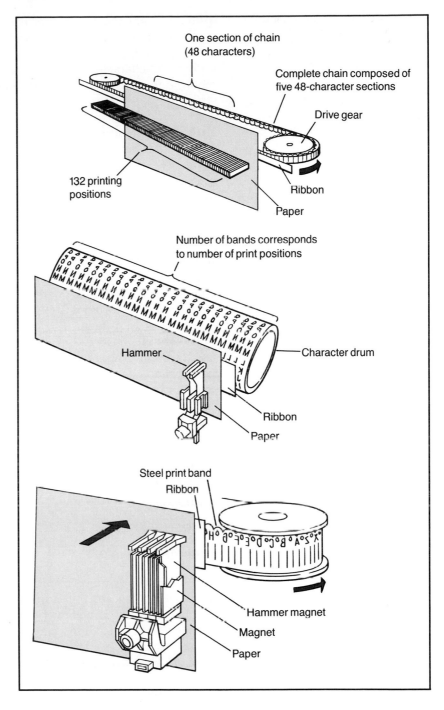

different characters the printer is able to print. The number of bands on the drum equals the number of characters the printer is able to print on one line. For example, a drum with 132 bands will be used with a 132-character printer. One entire revolution of the drum is required to print each line. Print hammers opposite each print band strike the paper against the proper character as it goes by.

Matrix   As mentioned, in the **matrix printer** or the dot matrix printer, the characters are formed by arranging dots closely together. Typically, such printers are character-at-a-time devices. Often, matrix printers are **bi-directional**; that is, the print head first moves to the right, printing out the line, then moves to the left, printing out the line. It is not like a typewriter, which always prints every line starting at the left.

The great advantage of dot matrix printers is that they can print any shape instructed by the software—not just letters and numbers. The quality of dot matrix printers has increased dramatically and is now very close to letter quality; indeed, for most people, the better dot matrix printers are indistinguishable from letter-quality printers.

Daisy-wheel   In the **daisy-wheel printer,** the print mechanism consists of a removable wheel with a set of spokes, each containing a raised character (see Figure 6-18). The wheel rotates to align the correct character, which is then struck with a hammer. Although noisier and slower than dot matrix, daisy-wheel printers are used for professional correspondence because they produce letter-quality type.

Variations of the daisy-wheel printer are the *ball printer,* which has the characters on a ball that rotates to the appropriate letter, and the *thimble printer,* which has a pivoting head to locate the appropriate letter.

Nonimpact Printers

As mentioned, nonimpact printers do not strike the paper to form characters. They are therefore much quieter than impact printers and, because they have fewer moving parts, they are generally more reliable. We will examine six types of nonimpact printers: electrostatic, magnetic, ink jet, xerographic, laser, and thermal. Some of these are shown in Figure 6-19.

Electrostatic   The **electrostatic printer** operates by depositing invisible charges on the paper's surface in the shape of characters. The paper is then passed through a toner containing ink particles of the opposite charge. The ink adheres to the paper only at the charged locations. Electrostatic printers are very reliable because they have few moving parts; however, toner and special electrostatic paper are an extra cost.

Figure 6-18. Daisy wheel. *Top:* Photo of daisy-wheel print mechanism, with *(top left)* close-up of one a pair of the spokes. *Bottom:* How a daisy wheel works. The daisy wheel spins to bring the desired spoke into position. A hammer then hits the wedge, which strikes the spoke against the ribbon.

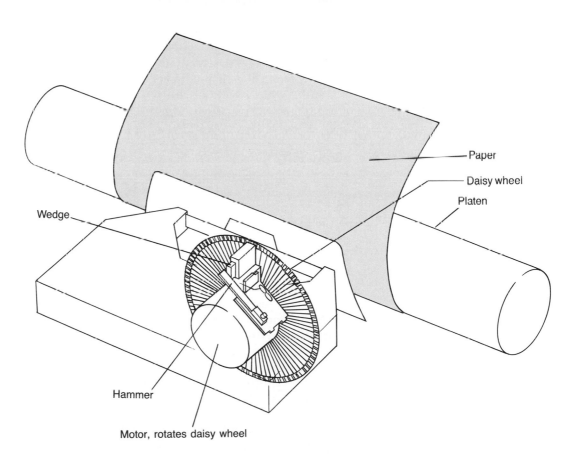

Paper

Daisy wheel

Platen

Wedge

Hammer

Motor, rotates daisy wheel

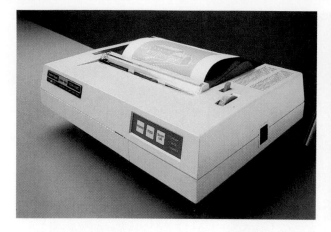

Figure 6-19. Nonimpact printers.
Left: Photo of ink-jet printer. *Right:*
Photo of laser printer.

Magnetic   The **magnetic printer** is like the electrostatic in that characters are formed by electric charges. However, the charges are not deposited directly onto the paper; they go to a moving belt that passes through the toner, picks up the ink, and then transfers the ink to paper. The advantage of this process is that special paper is not required; however, magnetic printing is slower than electrostatic printing because of the extra processing step.

Ink-Jet   An **ink-jet printer** actually sprays small droplets of ink onto the surface of the paper at a very rapid rate. The print is letter quality, and a wide variety of colors are available. This printer has become popular because it is able to duplicate color directly from the CRT for color graphics.

Xerographic   Developed by Xerox Corporation, the **xerographic printer** combines computer and Xerox office copier technology. Characters are formed on a drum as in a Xerox photocopying machine, the drum is treated with a toner, and characters are then transferred to paper. The printer can be operated not only directly from a computer but also off-line from magnetic tape or disk storage. Although very fast and producing very high quality print, the printer is quite expensive.

Laser   The **laser electrographic printer** creates characters on a drum, utilizing a laser beam light source. The characters are then treated with a toner and transferred to paper. Laser printers produce very high quality images and in the past were very expensive; however, in recent years prices have dropped dramatically.

Laser printing has given rise to the industry known as **desktop publishing.** As we mentioned in a box in Chapter 3, desktop publishing is a form of do-it-yourself publishing of brochures, forms, manuals, newsletters, and the like, which is practiced by quick-print shops and by departments within organizations. For an investment of about $10,000–$15,000, you can buy a sophisticated laser printer, a microcomputer, and appropriate software that permits you to do

DESKTOP PUBLISHING: DO IT YOURSELF

Two years ago, neither Victoria nor Glen Reed knew anything about the publishing field, and neither possessed the raw materials to start a business. Now, not only have they authored their own book, *Best Buys in San Francisco*, they have produced and published it through their own company, Morning Star Press. Such a feat has required something more than the frisky enthusiasm of entrepreneurs. The Reeds have discovered a cheap, highly efficient and powerful force known as desktop publishing, or DTP.

True to its name, DTP takes the expensive, complicated technology of publishing—typesetting, design, pasteup, printing—simplifies the process, reduces costs and literally puts the capability on the desk top. Now, with a personal computer, such as an Apple Macintosh, the appropriate software and a laser printer, anyone can put out almost any kind of publication in just about any format. With a few punches on their PC keyboard, would-be publishers can set type in a variety of sizes and styles, create interesting graphics and design pages. The final product need only be sent to an offset printer to generate multiple copies.

When was the last time you created a résumé, a business report, a church newsletter or even a business card? DTP can make any of these products professional-looking and visually interesting. Even the ubiquitous company memo can become enticing enough to read. Publishing has never been so easy.

Or so cheap. A complete package, including laser printer, costs about $10,000 (a traditional typesetting system can cost $70,000). If this is too much for poverty-line publishers, they need not even make this initial investment. Copy/computer centers are now springing up, where customers can rent a computer for around $6 an hour plus other high-tech helpers for an additional low fee. The Krishna Copy centers in Berkeley and San Francisco are part of this new breed of service center. There, users can rent computer publishing equipment by the hour or work on a PC at home, take the finished product—in the form of a diskette—and print it out on the establishment's laser printer (for 30 cents a page).

—Eric Pfeiffer, *Image*

---

typesetting, page layouts, and even illustrations right on your own desk.

Thermal The **thermal printer** creates characters by converting electrical impulses to heat energy, which is then transferred to special heat-sensitive paper using a dot matrix print head. Thermal printers are inexpensive and reliable; though they require no ribbon, they do require special paper.

PLOTTERS DRAWING

MACHINES

Plotters are special-purpose output devices used to reproduce hardcopy drawings—bar charts, engineering drawings, maps, even three-dimensional illustrations. There are two types of plotters—flatbed and drum, as shown in Figure 6-20.

The **flatbed plotter,** also called a **table plotter,** is one in which paper is held stable and a pen or pens of different colors, controlled

Figure 6-20.   Plotters. *Left:* Flatbed plotter. Note four pens of different colors which inscribe image on paper. *Right:* Drum plotters.

by a computer program, move about on the surface. Some flatbed plotters are quite large.

In the **drum plotter,** the pen or pens are held stationary and the paper is rolled on a drum.

The primary advantage of these devices is their ability to produce consistently accurate drawings very quickly—at least compared to human artist counterparts. (Actually, they operate quite slowly, at least when they are attached to microcomputers.) Past disadvantages have been the limited availability of software and the development costs associated with creating appropriate software, although this is changing.

COMPUTER OUTPUT
MICROFILM

Banking is an industry that depends on records, but imagine if all the records had to be on paper. How many warehouses would be required to store all the loan applications and check records? Paper may be the easiest form for people to use, but it takes a lot of space. What produces output that costs less than paper, can store the equivalent of a 210-page report on a 4-by-6-inch sheet, and is perhaps 20 times faster than a high-speed printer? The answer is computer output microfilm, as shown in Figure 6-21.

A **computer output microfilm** or **COM** system consists of a computer to produce original documents or images and a recording machine to prepare the microfilm, miniature photographic images. If the microfilm is produced directly from the computer, it is called "on-line." If it is produced from magnetic tape and is not directly linked to the computer, it is called "off-line."

Microfilm may be produced on a roll of film (16, 35, or 105 millimeter) or on a 4-by-6-inch sheet called **microfiche,** often called "fish." To read microfilm requires a microfilm reader, such as the

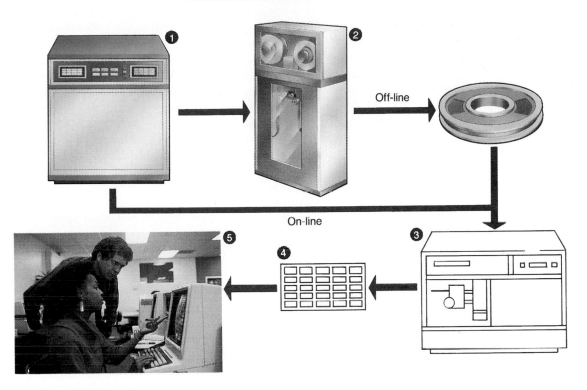

Figure 6-21. Computer output microfilm. This illustration shows COM off line and on line. In the *off line* version, the data comes directly off (1) the computer and onto (2) magnetic tape on a tape drive. The data on the tape is then run through (3) a microfilm recorder. In the *on-line* version, the data goes directly from (1) to (3). The microfilm recorder converts the data to images stored on microfiche. After the microfiche is (4) developed, it may be viewed on (5) a microfilm viewer or CRT.

kind you see in libraries. Banks use COM to record checks that have been deposited, since the original checks, of course, are returned to the payers (although many banks are trying to get out of the business of returning cancelled checks).

Although microfilm has many advantages—storage capability, fast retrieval, and ability to store graphics and figures—it also has disadvantages in that it requires special equipment for viewing and for producing hard-copy documents. In addition, it cannot be updated on the same sheet or roll. Nonetheless, it has been found to be economical in situations requiring that a very high volume of documents be reproduced or a large number of documents be stored and maintained.

AUDIO-RESPONSE

DEVICES

Audio-response or **voice-output devices** make sounds that seem like human voices but actually are prerecorded vocalized sounds that may be synthesized. Voice output is not nearly as difficult to engineer as voice input, and indeed by now you are no doubt aware of several situations in which such "voices" are used—in cars, in soft drink machines, in airports, in supermarkets, and for some of those voices that sound like telephone operators when you misdial and are told "Please hang up, and dial your call again." Voice output is, in fact, being heard all over.

Audio machines can verbalize instructions while one is simultaneously performing another task. For instance, a microcomputer might repeat numbers aloud as they are being entered into a spreadsheet, to help the user double-check for accuracy. Or it might verbally coach users through complicated programs, help students learn foreign languages by pronouncing sentences as they are typed in, and speak what children write to help them make an instant connection between text and meaning.

ROBOTS COMPUTER AUTOMATION IN THE FACTORY

Want a robot built to order? A Colorado company will make you one in the shape of a milk carton that can talk and move. Or, if you prefer, you may have a furry robot that can ride a tricycle.

Are these the kinds of robots that are going to be important in the future? Actually, these are purely for entertainment and are only one variety. **Robotics**—the study of the design, construction, and use of robots—is a serious engineering field.

Unlike standard assembly-line machines, which are designed to perform one function, **robots** have two qualities that make them flexible. They are *multifunctional,* which means they are able to do more than one task, and they are *reprogrammable,* which means they can be reprogrammed to carry out many kinds of tasks. These two characteristics mean that, unlike traditional kinds of machinery, robots are not as apt to become obsolete.

There are four areas of robotics (see Figure 6-22), as explained below.

▶ **Large industrial robots:** These are computer-controlled tools used on factory assembly lines to perform skills previously performed by human beings, such as welding or paint spraying. Although automatic machinery in the form of stand-alone machine tools has been in use for years on production lines, industrial robots—also known as **flexible manufacturing systems (FMSs)**—are far more versatile. Most robots operate by electronic impulses through a claw, but others use hydraulic pressure for heavy work.

▶ **Small industrial robots:** These highly reprogrammable systems generally handle objects up to 20 pounds. These include machine vision systems—robots that "see" with television-camera vision systems—that can be used for parts inspection, production identification, and robot guidance. Other robot systems operate by touch, measuring sizes and shapes, temperature, hardness, and so on.

▶ **Mobile robots:** These are the kind that people think of when they hear the word *robot*—namely, peoplelike machines that can roll

Figure 6-22. Three areas of robotics. *Top left:* A machine vision system; laser beams and electronic cameras check door fits and alignments of body components. *Top right:* Industrial robots used for welding chassis in an auto plant. *Bottom:* A mobile robot used to deliver interoffice mail.

around and talk. Some can also serve drinks at cocktail parties and do vacuuming (up to a point), and there is a great deal of discussion about building robots for household tasks. Some have called these machines "showbots"; they are not true robots since they are not multifunctional and reprogrammable. These robots have some use in offices as mailmobiles.

▶ **Artificial intelligence or expert systems:** This is the most promising and awesome area of all. **Artificial intelligence (AI)** is the field of study concerned with exploring tasks for computers to do that previously were reserved for human intelligence, imagination, and intuition. A National Research Council report has predicted that AI will affect the circumstances of human life profoundly. AI will "surely create a new economics, a new sociology and a new history. If artificial intelligences can be created at all, there is little reason to believe that they could not lead swiftly to the construction of superintelligences able to explore significant mathematical, scientific or engineering alternatives at a rate far exceeding human ability.'' Artificial intelligence already has created **expert systems,** computer programs that essentially copy the knowledge—both textbook knowledge and tricks of the trade—of human experts in a particular field. We devote an entire chapter to artificial intelligence and expert systems later in the book.

THE THINKING THAT GOES INTO IT

In between input and output is a great deal of ''thinking''—the calculations that the computer must make to turn problems into solutions, data into information. In the next chapter, we will show how this is done in detail.

SUMMARY

▶ Although hardware may change radically, the concepts it embodies may not, and the old hardware may not be rapidly replaced with the new; therefore, managers must be prepared to work with both old equipment and new technology.

▶ **GIGO** is an acronym for ''Garbage In, Garbage Out,'' which means that the quality of information that comes out of a computer is no better than the quality of the data put in.

▶ *Data* is the raw material (letters, numbers, symbols, shapes, colors, sounds, etc.) that must be converted into *machine-readable* form for the computer to process into information.

▶ Input devices convert data into machine-readable information.

▶ Output devices convert the information to a form people can use. The types of these devices are almost limitless because a computer can operate any machine (output device) that can run on electricity.

▶ No one computer system has all the possible different types of input and output devices.

▶ The two basic methods of handling data (input) are (1) **batch processing,** in which data is collected on source documents and then accumulated and input all at one time (as a batch), and (2) **transaction processing,** in which data is input as it is created (as transactions happen).

▶ Transaction processing is also called **real-time processing** because a transaction is processed so fast

that the results can be used immediately, and **on-line processing** because the user's terminal is directly to connected to (''on-line'' with) the computer.

▶ Some input equipment works only for batch processing, some only for transaction processing, and some for both.

▶ Input devices receive data either by keyboard entry or by direct entry.

▶ In **keyboard entry,** data is input to the computer *after* the transaction that produced the data has taken place; someone, using the keyboard, copies the data from its source document. In **direct entry,** data is made into machine-processable form at the time the transaction is made. Because people do the keying, errors may occur during keyboard entry; thus the trend is toward greater use of direct-entry input devices.

▶ Keyboard entry records data on two kinds of *media,* or materials: (1) paper media, such as punched cards, and (2) magnetic media, such as cassette, diskette, tape, or hard disk. Except for paper media, the computer terminal is the most commonly used keyboard entry device.

▶ **Punched cards**—the first form of input used for computers—are stiff paper cards punched with holes that represent data. The holes are punched using a **keypunch machine.** A **card reader** translates the card holes into electrical impulses, which are then input to the computer.

► Data on magnetic media, such as tape or disk, is represented by magnetized spots. A familiar kind of device for magnetic keyboard entry is a **key-to-diskette device** such as a microcomputer or word processor—a machine by which you key in data through the keyboard onto a floppy disk or diskette. A **key-to-tape device** uses recording tape—in cassette, cartridge, or reel form—similar to the audio tape used in stereo tape players. A **key-to-disk device** uses a magnetic recording disk that is somewhat like a long-playing record that has concentric grooves rather than continuous grooves.

► Magnetic media have several advantages over punched cards: (1) They can be reused. (2) They are easier to correct. (3) The input devices are quieter. (4) The devices are also more reliable (they are electronic rather than mechanical, so there are fewer moving parts to break down). (5) They take less storage space. (6) The data can be accessed faster by the computer.

► The computer terminal is the most popular keyboard entry device. It can be a video display terminal or a hard-copy terminal; it can also be an intelligent terminal.

► **Hard copy** is a paper output (computer printout); **soft copy** is output on a computer screen.

► A **video display terminal (VDT),** or **cathode-ray tube terminal (CRT),** is a terminal with a keyboard and a CRT, or televisionlike, screen; it is also called a soft-copy terminal. As an input device, the VDT has several advantages: (1) It is compact and inexpensive. (2) It allows erroneous data to be corrected easily. (3) It allows files to be updated on the spot and allows access to these files. Its disadvantages include: (1) It makes no permanent record of transactions. (2) The screen is difficult for some people to read.

► A **hard-copy terminal,** or **teleprinter,** is a keyboard with a printer attached. The hard-copy terminal has the advantage of producing a permanent record; however, it also has two disadvantages: (1) The printing process makes it slower than the display terminal. (2) It can be noisy.

► **Intelligent terminals** include a microcomputer that allows users to do programming as well as to input and to receive data from a larger computer. An intelligent terminal includes at least a keyboard, electronics to convert data to machine-readable code, communications equipment, an output device, a processing unit, internal storage for data processing, software consisting of a programming language and editing programs, and secondary storage.

► The most popular direct-entry devices are (1) magnetic-ink character recognition, (2) optical-character recognition, (3) optical-mark recognition, (4) digitizers, (5) point-of-sale terminals, (6) touch-tone devices, (7) light pens, (8) mice, and (9) speech-recognition devices.

► **Magnetic-ink character recognition (MICR)** is a method of machine-reading characters made of ink containing magnetized particles. It was developed in the 1950s by the banking industry to make check processing easier. MICR has several advantages: (1) The codes can be read by both machines and people. (2) It is fast, accurate, and automatic. (3) Human involvement—and thus human error—is minimized. Its disadvantages are (1) it is limited to only 14 characters and (2) some manual keying is required (for example, when the MICR characters are inscribed on a check).

► **Optical-character recognition (OCR)** was developed by the U.S. Postal Service to assist in mail sorting. It consists of special characters (letters, numbers, and symbols) that can be read by a light source that converts them into electric signals that can be sent to the computer for processing. The special characters are preprinted; thus, someone must initially key the characters. However, they are not keyed again for data entry into the computer. The most common OCR input device is the hand-held **wand reader,** which reflects light on the printed characters, whose reflection is converted by photoelectric cells to machine-readable code. OCR has several advantages: (1) It has all the benefits of MICR plus a larger set of characters (42). (2) Using a wand reader does not require any manual keying of data. (3) Data is electronically transferred from source document to computer. Its main disadvantage is that OCR wand readers can recognize only a special set of characters.

► **Optical-mark recognition (OMR),** also known as *mark-sensing,* senses the presence or absence of a mark, such as those made by a pencil on a special preprinted examination form. The advantages of OMR are (1) that it requires no manual keying of data and (2) that it is inexpensive. Its disadvantages are (1) that strict format specifications (for example, special forms and pencils) must be used and (2) that it has limited business applications.

► A **digitizer** is a device that can be moved over a drawing or photograph to convert the picture to digital data, which can then be stored in a computer, displayed on a display screen, or printed out on paper.

▶ **Image scanners** are devices that can identify type-written characters or images automatically and convert them to electronic signals that can be stored in a computer. The process of image scanning, sometimes known as **bit-mapping,** can identify different type fonts by scanning each character with light and breaking it into light and dark dots, which are then converted into digital code.

▶ **Point-of-sale (POS) terminals** are the latest model in the evolution of cash registers. They consist of a keyboard for entering data, a display screen or digital display area for displaying dollar amounts, and a printer for providing a list of items and prices for the customer. Some POS terminals are **bar-code readers**—photoelectric scanners that read the **bar codes** (zebra-striped vertical marks or bars) printed on many products. POS terminals have several advantages: (1) Their use enables stores to hire less skilled sales clerks and checkers. (2) Checkout is faster. (3) There is better credit control. (4) Current sales and inventory information is maintained automatically. The disadvantages include: (1) Back-up systems are required in case the computer, and thus the POS devices, fails. (2) The equipment is expensive. (3) Stores may have to do double duty on price marking, because some states require that prices be stamped on the merchandise for customers to read.

▶ A **touch-tone device** is an instrument that sends data over ordinary telephone lines to a central computer (for example, a **card dialer** reads a customer's credit card, checks the customers's credit status, and reports the results to the local merchant).

▶ A **light pen** consists of a light-sensitive penlike device that, when placed against the display screen of a particular kind of terminal, closes a photoelectric circuit that identifies the X–Y coordinates to the computer. This allows the user to create a drawing right on the screen.

▶ A **mouse** is a direct-entry device with a ball on the bottom and attached with a cord to a computer terminal. When rolled on the table top, the mouse directs the location of the cursor or the pointer on the screen to draw pictures or give commands.

▶ **Speech-recognition devices,** or **voice-recognition systems,** convert the spoken word into a numeric code, which is matched against a code stored in a minicomputer. Then when one speaks into the microphone, the word is displayed on the screen for verification. Speech-recognition devices are the ultimate data entry devices. Already machines are being produced that recognize voices, but they are

primitive. They usually operate by being "trained" previously to the user's voice. Systems that are "speaker-independent"—that can recognize the same word spoken by many different people—can be built, but it is difficult to do so and the vocabularies are limited. Voice-recognition devices have several advantages: (1) Input is accurately controlled. (2) Input is readily verified and corrected. (3) The user's hands are free to perform tasks other than keying. (4) There are numerous potential applications. The disadvantages are that (1) such systems are expensive, (2) their vocabulary is limited, and (3) the speed of entry is slow.

▶ A specialized form of input device for transaction processing that is neither purely keyboard nor purely direct entry is the **automatic teller machine (ATM).** The ATM has the advantages of (1) making banking services available to customers 24 hours a day without increased bank employee costs and (2) completing many routine banking tasks without many manual errors. However, if the system fails there may be no backup to help process transactions using paper. Other disadvantages are that the ATM can run out of money at night or on weekends, that it introduces several types of security problems, and that it reduces human interaction, which may have a negative effect on customer relations.

▶ The purpose of output devices is to make the solutions to computer input people-readable. The two most popular output devices are *terminals* and *printers.* Others are plotters, computer output microfilm, audio-response devices, and robots.

▶ Terminals—mainly video display terminals (VDTs)—are the windows on the computing process. There are three principal types of terminals: *alphanumeric, graphics,* and *flat panel display.*

▶ **Alphanumeric terminals** display alphanumeric output (letters, numbers, and special characters). They look like 9- or 12-inch television screens. These terminals have many advantages: (1) They are relatively inexpensive. (2) They are reliable. (3) The format on the screen can be varied widely. (4) The training cost for users is small. (5) Information can be transferred rapidly to the screen via telephone lines or by direct lines. However, with alphanumeric terminals, no hard copy is available (unless a printer is added) and the screen size limits the amount of information that can be displayed at one time.

▶ **Graphics terminals** can display both alphanumeric *and* graphic data, which is significant because research has shown that people can absorb numeric information displayed in graphic form much faster than in nongraphic form. There are three levels of complexity in graphics produced: (1) *two-dimensional graphics,* the simplest level, which consist of pie, line, and bar graphs; (2) *two-dimensional angle forms,* such as those found in topographic maps; and (3) *three-dimensional graphics,* which are used in product design because they allow designers to turn the object to be viewed from different perspectives.

▶ Two common business uses of computer graphics are **computer-assisted instruction (CAI)** and **computer-aided design** or **manufacturing (CAD/CAM) (computer-assisted engineering,** or **CAE,** is a variant). In CAI the computer is used to present instructional materials. It may take the form of simulation, demonstration, tutorial, or drill and practice. CAD is used by engineers, architects, and others to design products, buildings, and manufacturing processes. With CAD, two- and three-dimensional pictures can be shown on the screen, combined with other drawings, rotated, enlarged, reduced, and otherwise manipulated. CAM is used to physically manufacture products. The advantages of graphics terminals include: (1) They can present information in easily grasped form. (2) They can present information quickly and reliably. Their disadvantages are (1) that graphics software is expensive and (2) that no hard copy is available unless a printer or plotter is added.

▶ **Flat panel displays** are alphanumeric or graphics terminals that do not use a cathode-ray tube to project images on the screen; instead they use a **liquid crystal display (LCD)** or an **electroluminescent (EL) panel** that glows when electrically charged. The advantages of flat panel displays over VDTs are that (1) they are more compact and portable, (2) they consume less power, (3) they have greater daylight visibility, and (4) they have greater expected longevity. Their disadvantages are that (1) they cost more than conventional terminals, (2) they are somewhat fragile, and (3) their reliability is currently uncertain.

▶ **Printers** produce hard copy. They are classified according to *speed, print quality,* and *printing method.*

▶ Printers may print a character at a time **(serial printers)** or a line at a time; they may be as slow as 600 characters per minute (some home computer printers) or as fast as 21,000 lines per minute (laser printers).

▶ **Page printers** print a page at a time, and may be low speed or high speed. Low-speed page printers are often laser printers, and are very common in offices. High-speed page printers use xerographic, photographic, or laser technologies; are very expensive; and are used in large businesses for very specialized applications.

▶ Printers may be *draft quality* or *letter quality.* **Dot matrix printers** construct characters by using a matrix of pins; these characters usually appear a bit fuzzy, although some dot matrix printers can print letter-quality images.

▶ **Letter-quality printers** produce printed characters that resemble those produced by an office typewriter. They are generally more expensive than dot matrix printers.

▶ Printers can be either *impact printers* or *nonimpact printers.* An **impact printer** forms characters by physically striking a type device (a hammer) against inked ribbon to form characters on paper (like a typewriter). **Nonimpact printers** do not strike paper to form images; instead they form characters by using heat, lasers, photography, or ink spray, often on electrostatic or sensitized paper. Because there is no physical contact between printer and paper, nonimpact printers are quieter than impact printers. Also, because they have fewer moving parts, nonimpact printers are generally more reliable.

▶ There are five basic designs for impact printers. (1) *chain,* (2) *band,* (3) *drum,* (4) *matrix,* and (5) *daisy wheel.*

▶ A **chain printer** consists of several sets of characters connected on a printing chain that revolves in front of the hammer. When the appropriate character passes by, the hammer strikes the paper and ribbon against it. The chains can be changed for different type fonts or styles.

▶ A **band printer** ("belt printer") operates similarly to a chain printer in that it uses a horizontally rotating band; the characters on the band are struck by hammers through the paper and ribbon.

▶ A **drum printer** is a line printer in which embossed characters are wrapped around a cylinder or drum. Each band around the drum consists of one each of the 64 different characters the printer is able to print; the number of bands on the drum equals the number of characters the printer is able to print on one line. One entire revolution of the drum is required to print each line.

► A **matrix** or dot matrix printer forms characters by arranging dots closely together. Matrix printers are often **bi-directional;** that is, the print head first moves to the right, printing out a line, then moves to the left, printing out the next line. Dot matrix printers can print any shape instructed by the software—not just letters and numbers.

► In the **daisy-wheel printer,** the print mechanism consists of a removable wheel with a set of spokes, each containing a raised character. The wheel rotates to align the correct character, which is then struck with a hammer. These printers are noisier and slower than dot matrix printers, but they do produce letter-quality type. Variations of the daisy-wheel printer are the *ball printer* and the *thimble printer.*

► Among the types of nonimpact printers are *electrostatic, magnetic, ink jet, xerographic, laser,* and *thermal.*

► The **electrostatic printer** operates by depositing invisible charges on the paper's surface in the shape of characters. The paper is passed through a toner containing ink particles of the opposite charge, and the ink adheres to the paper only at the charged locations. These printers are very reliable; however, they require special paper.

► The **magnetic printer** also form characters by using electrical charges; however, the charges go to a moving belt that passes through the toner, picks up the ink, and transfers the ink to the paper. Magnetic printing is slower than electrostatic printing, but it does not require special paper.

► An **ink-jet printer** sprays small droplets of ink rapidly onto the surface of the paper. The print is letter quality, and many colors are available.

► The **xerographic printer** was developed by the Xerox Corporation. It combines computer and Xerox office copier technology. Characters are formed on a drum, the drum is treated with a toner, and characters are transferred to paper. This printer can be operated either from a computer or from magnetic tape or disk storage. It is very fast and produces high-quality print; however, it is very expensive.

► The **laser electrographic printer** creates characters on a drum using a laser beam light source. The characters are then treated with toner and transferred to paper. These printers produce very high quality images but are very expensive. Laser printing has given rise to **desktop publishing,** a form of do-it-yourself publishing of brochures, forms, manuals, and newsletters, using a laser printer, microcomputer, and appropriate software that permits typesetting and page layouts.

► The **thermal printer** creates characters by converting electrical impulses to heat energy, which is transferred to special heat-sensitive paper using a dot matrix print head. Although these printers require special paper, they are inexpensive and reliable.

► **Plotters** are special-purpose output devices used to reproduce hard-copy drawings. The two types of plotters are *flatbed* and *drum.* The **flatbed plotter**—also called a **table plotter**—holds the paper still and allows a pen or pens of different colors, controlled by computer, to move about on the surface. The **drum plotter** holds the pens stationary and the paper rolls on a drum. These devices' main advantage is their ability to produce consistently accurate drawings very quickly. Their disadvantages are the limited availability of software and the high costs associated with developing it.

► A **computer output microfilm (COM)** system consists of a computer to produce original documents or images and a recording machine to prepare microfilm (miniature photographic images). The microfilm is called "on-line" if it is produced directly from the computer; it is called "off-line" if it is produced from magnetic tape. Microfilm can be in roll form or sheet form (called **microfiche**). To read microfilm requires a microfilm reader. Microfilm has several advantages: (1) It increases storage capability. (2) The information on it can be quickly retrieved. (3) It can store graphics and figures. (4) It is economical when used to process a large number of documents. Its disadvantages are (1) that it requires special equipment for viewing and for producing hard-copy documents and (2) that it cannot be updated on the same sheet or roll.

► **Audio-response** or **voice-output devices** make sounds that seem like human voices but are prerecorded vocalized sounds. They are much easier to engineer than voice-input devices.

► **Robotics** is the study of the design, construction, and use of robots. It is a serious engineering field that is becoming increasingly important. **Robots** have two qualities that make them flexible: (1) they are *multifunctional,* which means that they can do more than one task, and (2) they are *reprogrammable,* which means that they can be reprogrammed to carry out many kinds of tasks.

► There are four areas of robotics: (1) **Large industrial robots:** computer-controlled tools, or **flexible manufacturing systems (FMSs),** used on factory assembly lines to perform tasks previously performed by human beings. (2) **Small industrial robots:** reprogrammable robots that handle objects up to 20 pounds and that can "see" using television-camera vision systems so they can be used for inspection, identification, and guidance functions. (3) **Mobile robots:** peoplelike machines that can roll around and talk and perhaps perform a few functions. These are not true robots because they are not multifunctional and reprogrammable. (4) **Artificial intelligence (AI):** the field of study concerned with exploring tasks computers do that previously were reserved for human intelligence, imagination, and intuition. This is the most promising and awesome area of robotics. Artificial intelligence has already created **expert systems,** which are computer programs that essentially copy the knowledge of human experts in a particular field.

KEY TERMS

REVIEW QUESTIONS

1. Describe how the computer transforms raw data into usable information using input and output devices.
2. What are some of the most commonly used input and output devices?
3. What is the difference between batch processing and transaction processing?
4. Direct entry is more reliable than keyboard entry. Why?
5. How are printers classified, and what are some of the kinds of printers available?
6. How can color graphics be reproduced on hard copy by computer?
7. Describe some of the ways robotics can affect industry.
8. What is artificial intelligence?

CASE PROBLEMS

Case 6-1: Popularity Contest: Dvorak versus QWERTY

In moving from typewriter to word processor, perhaps the time has come to get rid of old QWERTY. What is QWERTY, you query? They are the top-left letter keys on any ordinary typewriter keyboard—and have been ever since Christopher Sholes designed the modern typewriter in 1867. The reason for laying out the letters in that particular way is that Sholes was afraid that fast typists would jam the works on his primitive machine. Thus, he deliberately removed the most useful keys from the middle row—the home row—to slow down their flying fingers. Even after the technology improved, the arrangement of keys persisted, particularly after the touch-typing system became popular.

In 1930, August Dvorak, of the University of Washington, invented his own keyboard. All vowels and punctuation marks were placed on the left side. The most common consonants were placed on the right. The arrangement allowed 70% of the keys to be hit in the home row, whereas QWERTY typists use the home row less than a third of the time. Tests have shown Dvorak to be the more efficient system. Speeds can be improved by 5–25%, with roughly half the number of errors.

Of course, QWERTY lingers on, because—with 30 million keyboards in the United States alone—no one has wanted to be retrained. In 1983, however, the American National Standards Institute (ANSI) officially adopted Dvorak as an alternative to QWERTY. This is important news because ANSI is the organization that sets so many industrial standards for American products.

Your assignment: Let us say you are in charge of long-range planning for an organization that does not do a great deal of word processing but wants to have executives communicate with each other by terminals. More than half the executives do not know how to type, and so in-house training will be required. Which kind of keyboards would you order, QWERTY or Dvorak, and why? In weighing your decision, consider that there have been cases in which entire countries have changed important standards or ways of doing things overnight. (Sweden switched from driving on the left-hand side of the road to driving on the right; Great Britain switched to a decimal system for its currency.) Do you think this could be accomplished with Dvorak?

Case 6-2: Rules for Small Business Survival

Almost the opposite of *Fortune* magazine, which is aimed in great part at readers in big business, *Whole Earth Review* (formerly *CoEvolution Quarterly*) is published by *Whole Earth Catalog* and, like the catalog, emphasizes tools and skills for living. One early issue (Spring 1984) presented an article—since expanded into a book, *Growing a Business*—by entrepreneur Paul Hawken on how to survive in small business. Among the pieces of advice offered by Hawken:

▶ Start at the beginning: Usually when people start a business, they have an image of where they want to end up and too often they "associate a successful business with the trappings: a carpet, computer, car, secretary." Instead, Hawken says, "If you haven't had experience in starting a business before, start small, very small, and use your minuteness and obscurity as an opportunity to learn. This means low overhead, frugal means, hands-on."

▶ Entrepreneurs are risk-avoiders: Most people think an entrepreneur is "a gung-ho, three-sheets-to-the-wind risk-taker." Hawken disagrees. Entrepreneurs see a market, idea, or product that others do not or discount, but to the entrepreneurs the need is obvious. "There is no risk because they are totally identified with the end result. They are not studying the market, they *are* the market. . . . What an entrepreneur will then do is try to identify every possible risk and obstacle that could prevent him or her from achieving that goal, and eliminate as many as possible."

▶ If it is a good idea, it is probably too late: If you have a new idea, you should talk it up with your friends, eliminating responses from people who always say nice things and listening to those who speak their mind. If the latter say it is a wonderful idea, you are in big trouble, says Hawken. "If you have an idea for a business and it is so good that everyone recognizes that it is great, you are too late. . . . In most cases, somebody is already there." Thus, if your friends look confused when you mention your idea or if they laugh at it, you may be on to something.

Your assignment: "Don't try to figure out the market—be it," says Hawken. Large companies may spend great sums trying to launch thousands of new food products each year, but only a fraction succeed, so what do they know? Your best bet is not to look for a business to go into but to do something that satisfies a personal passion, that is close to home. Look back over this chapter and determine which of the input and output devices interest you. Then see how they might be linked to a possible business of interest to you. The business that will satisfy you, says Hawken, "is probably sitting around the house someplace. If not there, it is around the yard, in the garage, or on your desk."

Chapter 7

PROCESSORS AND OPERATING SYSTEMS: *REPORT FROM BEHIND THE SCENES*

Perhaps one of the strongest quests in life is for power. You seek power, in the personal sense, not necessarily to dominate other people but to enhance your ability to control events, to have more flexibility to do things, to gain a wider range of skills and choices. The computer gives us power, for it expands our ability to do all these things. "What the lever was to the body," says Charles P. Lecht, author of *The Waves of Change*, "the computer system is to the mind."

Power is a word often used to describe how well computers provide the leverage Lecht talks about. When people speak of the power of computer *hardware*, they usually mean power in a specific sense—namely, how much data can its internal memory hold and how quickly can data be processed? When they speak of the power of computer *software*, they usually mean, how flexible is it? How much can it do?

COMPUTER POWER

TO THE PEOPLE

In this chapter, we describe the two critical things you need to know about most computers that give them—and therefore you—their power. The first is the *central processing unit*, which is part of the hardware; the second is the *operating system*, which is critical system software. Whereas in Chapter 6 we described how application programs and data could be converted into machine-readable form by input devices, here we need to show how hardware and software actually process them.

217

PROCESSOR

AND MEMORY

THE CENTRAL

PROCESSING UNIT

How much data does a computer actually hold in its internal memory? (This is the memory inside the machine itself, not that on external disk or tape.) Peter Laurie, in *The Joy of Computers*, points out that an 8-bit microcomputer, which is what the original Apple II was, has 65,536 memory locations inside it. If each memory location stores one number, letter, or special character, and the contents of each of these memory locations were written out on an ordinary index card, the cards laid end to end would stretch for about six miles. This would reach from the southern tip of Manhattan Island, New York, to the middle of Central Park. For 16-bit machines, the cards would cover more than 100 miles. Says Laurie:

> Imagine having to run up and down such an array, picking up a card here, reading it, rushing off over the horizon to read the one it referred to, tear back, pick up two more and doing the sums they commanded on the trot. This is not an unreasonable analogy because no computer ever does anything that you could not do with pencil and paper. It just does it a lot faster and more accurately—so much so, in fact, that it can give a quantum jump in work possibilities.

That describes the 16-bit memory. The 32-bit memory—as in the Apple Macintosh and the Compaq 386—is ten times faster.

As Figure 7-1 shows, the memory is considered part of the central processing unit (at least in large computers; on a microcomputer it is not). The **central processing unit,** which you will nearly always hear referred to as the **CPU,** is hardware that interprets and executes program instructions and communicates with the input, output, and external storage devices. The CPU has been compared to the human brain; however, the brain is superior in that it can hold up to 3 billion pieces of information at one time compared to only millions for a computer. It also consumes very little energy, whereas a mainframe computer may produce enough energy to heat a house. On the other hand, the computer can send information at speeds of 654,000 feet per second (compared to the brain's 350 feet per second) and is certainly easier to repair when something goes wrong!

In your new job with Atlantic-Pacific Bank, you are in a position to appreciate how important computer processing speeds are. In banking, more than in most businesses, time literally means money—and the time lost in processing checks and credit card transactions because of slow computers is not time a bank willingly gives up.

The Three Parts of the CPU

The CPU consists of three components, which are shown in Figure 7-1 and which are described below:

CASE STUDY: COMPUTER POWER

For Some Users, One Computer Just Isn't Enough

When it comes to computing power, Mark Lutton feels he has the best of both worlds—the deskbound and the transportable. The senior software specialist with Data Resources, of Lexington, Mass., uses a Compaq Deskpro 286 at work, an IBM XT-compatible, which he built himself, at home, and a Radio Shack Model 100 at home and when he travels.

Mr. Lutton uses the Model 100 mainly for taking notes, as well as for doing taxes and performing other bookkeeping tasks. At a three-day conference sponsored by Microsoft for OS/2 developers [programmers writing applications for Microsoft's operating system], for example, he had his Model 100 handy for taking notes on every session he attended.

"I can carry it easily with me," he said, "and there's no way I could set up a desktop PC at the conference."

When he came home, he transferred data between his lap-top and desktop machines, using a [connecting] modem cable and software. . . . When it was all transferred, he had 120 pages of notes—information that he otherwise would not have had.

While Mr. Lutton normally uses the powerful Compaq '286 machine, he has no ax to grind about always needing the most powerful computer available. Rather, he carefully decides which computer is best suited to certain tasks. "The lap-top is suited very well for when I need to have a small computer and only need to take notes; otherwise, I'll use a desk PC," he said.

Aside from using it to take notes, he finds use for the Model 100 as a diagnostic tool in maintaining a telecommunications program at work. He also uses it to do his taxes, since he had the Model 100 first, and his program is on that.

While the desktop PC certainly has more power, Mr. Lutton appreciates the speed with which his small lap-top can power up. "It can take two minutes for my desktop to warm up and boot, where with the lap-top, it's ready to go as soon as I hit the button," he said.

Normally, Mr. Lutton loads information from the Model 100 into his desktop computers, but at times he sends data in the other direction. He will, at times, use his desktop PC to log onto [the information utility] CompuServe, download programs for the Model 100 to his desktop machine and transfer the programs to the Model 100.

If he were buying from scratch today, he said he would still want a lap-top PC and a deskbound one. He is not sure whether the lap-top would be the Model 100, however. While he likes its small size and low weight, he would like more power as well.

Preston Gralla, *PC Week*

Figure 7-1.   The central processor.
The central processing unit (CPU) has
two parts: the control unit and the
arithmetic/logic unit. Primary storage
is temporary storage for data instructions at the time the program is being
executed. Note that the three components are joined by a bus.

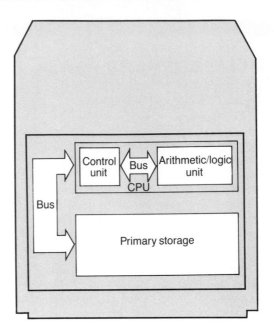

▶ The controller
▶ The arithmetic/logic unit
▶ Primary storage

Note, in Figure 7-1, that the communications among these three
units are made through physical connections known as a **bus.**

The Controller   Like a traffic cop, the **controller**—also known as the
control unit—directs and coordinates the rest of the system in carrying out program instructions. It also tells input devices when additional input is needed and notifies output devices that information is
available for output.

The controller does not store data or programs—that is done by
the primary storage unit, as we shall see. But the control unit assigns
and records the locations within primary storage, where data and
programs are stored. As each statement in the computer program is
input, the control unit also interprets that statement and directs the
other two CPU components.

The Arithmetic/Logic Unit   The **arithmetic/logic unit,** abbreviated
ALU, is the part of the CPU that calculates and compares data, based
on instructions from the controller. Because the ALU controls the
speed of calculations and because speed is a very important concern
of computer users, it receives a great deal of attention from computer-design engineers.

The two operations performed by the ALU are arithmetic operations and logical operations. *Arithmetic operations* consist of the four standard mathematical calculations—addition, subtraction, multiplication, division. *Logical operations* consist of the three common comparison operations; in comparing numbers the ALU will find that one is equal to (=), less than (<), or greater than (>) the other.

Primary Storage Unit   As we mentioned earlier in the book, the **primary storage unit** is also called **memory, main storage,** or **internal storage,** and it is that part of the CPU that holds (1) data for processing, (2) instructions for processing (the program), and (3) processed data waiting to be output. (Secondary or auxiliary storage—which we shall describe in the next chapter—consists of external storage such as magnetic disk or magnetic tape.)

Computer Processing Speeds

If a computer has two reasons for being, it is that it works extremely quickly and is able to process great quantities of data. On older microcomputers, an instruction may be executed in less than a **millisecond,** which is one-thousandth of a second. Most new microcomputers can execute an instruction in microseconds—a **microsecond** is one-millionth of a second. Supercomputers operate in the **nanosecond** range—one-billionth of a second. To give you a sense of how fast a nanosecond is. If a nanosecond were equal to one minute, then a minute would be equal to 1,900 years.

How Data Is Stored

Primary storage consists of thousands of memory locations. Each such location has an *address*—a number—just like the box numbers on mailboxes in the post office. Unlike P.O. boxes, however, each memory location stores only one instruction or piece of data. The controller manipulates the data and instructions by referring to the locations (addresses)—for example, "Multiply the contents of location 1 times the contents of location 2 and put the results in location 3." The locations always remain the same, but new data and new instructions may be placed into them. Just as when new letters are put into a mailbox, the address does not change, only the contents. An important point: Obviously, there must be *enough* locations in primary storage to hold both data and instructions; otherwise the program will not work—which explains why some microcomputers have memories that are too small (have too little capacity) to handle complicated programs and data.

An example of how data and instructions are manipulated is given in the box on the following page.

NANOSECOND AS A PIECE OF STRING

What's a nanosecond? It's a billionth of a second (10^{-9}), and it's the basic time interval of a supercomputer's internal clock. Navy Commander Grace Hopper has to explain the meaning of a nanosecond to some nontechnical computer users. She wonders, "How can I get them to understand the brevity of a nanosecond? Why not look at it as a space problem rather than a time problem? I'll just use the distance light can travel in one billionth of a second." She pulls out a piece of string 11.8 inches (30 cm) long and tells her visitors, "Here is one nanosecond."

—Roger von Oech, *A Kick in the Seat of the Pants*

HOW PRIMARY STORAGE WORKS

A Problem of Interest

Of considerable interest to bankers is interest, the profit on money loaned. If you sit down with your Lotus 1-2-3 or other spreadsheet on your computer at Atlantic-Pacific and compute alternative interest rates for alternative amounts of money loaned for alternative lengths of time, all such data and instructions must be manipulated by the central processing unit. This suggests, by the way, why you need a computer with a fairly large capacity in memory: It must have room to hold not only the program, such as 1-2-3, but also all the data or numbers you are working with.

Let us suppose you are not using packaged software but are writing the program yourself to compute the interest rate. As an inducement to get people to borrow more, Atlantic-Pacific Bank offers a lower interest rate on larger loan amounts. Thus, let us say for the sake of this exercise that the bank charges a regular interest rate for loans up to $1,000 and half that interest rate as a special interest for any amounts beyond $1,000. (Actually, if you can find a deal like this, grab it! No bank would really do this.) Let us say you already have a program written for calculating interest on loans up to $1,000. If you wrote a program in pseudocode for calculating interest on loans over $1,000, it would look like this:

IF loan is greater than 1000

THEN

   multiply 0.50 of the regular loan interest rate times the amount greater than 1000 to get special interest

   add special interest to regular interest

END IF

We will say that the regular interest rate is 10%. With the bank's special deal, the borrower of $1,500 will have to pay 10% of $1,000, or $100, in interest on the first $1,000 borrowed. On the additional $500, the borrower will have to pay interest at half the regular interest rate, or 5%. Thus, interest on the additional $500 will be $25 (the result of .05 × $500). In all, the borrower will have to repay $125 in interest plus the $1,500 the bank loaned, for a total of $1,625. (Actually, computations of interest are usually more complicated than this.)

How do these numbers get handled inside the computer? Take a look at the illustration. The computer goes through the following steps:

1 Money loaned 1500	2	3	4 Special interest amount
5	6 Regular interest rate .10 (10%)	7	8 Regular interest amount 100

1. The controller reads the statement, "IF loan is greater than 1000" from the program in primary storage—actually, this would be expressed as "IF data in address 1 is greater than 1000"—and the controller would then tell the ALU to make the logical comparison (that is, see if the loan is greater than 1000). The ALU answers yes. The controller then moves to the THEN statement.

1 Money loaned 1500	2	3	4 Special interest amount 25
5	6 Regular interest rate .10 (10%)	7	8 Regular interest amount 100

2. The controller reads the statement, "multiply 0.50 of the regular loan interest rate times the amount greater than 1000 to get special interest" from primary storage. (The computer would actually express this as "multiply 0.50 times the data in address 6 times the data over 1000 in address 1 to provide data for address 4.") The controller contacts the ALU to make the calculation, which it does, first determining "0.50 times regular interest rate" and storing the answer, 5, in the ALU, then determining "money loaned minus 1000" and storing that answer, 500, in the ALU. The controller then contacts the ALU to calculate ".05 times 500," which the ALU does and returns the answer of 25 to the controller. The controller then stores this answer in primary storage in address 4, Special Interest Amount.

1 Money loaned 1500	2	3	4 Special interest amount 25
5 Total interest 125	6 Regular interest rate .10 (10%)	7	8 Regular interest amount 100

3. The controller reads the next statement, "add special interest to regular interest" from primary storage. (This can be expressed as "add data from address 4 to data in address 8, to provide data in address 5.") The ALU calculates this and returns the answer, 125, to the controller, which stores it in address 5.

This example is greatly simplified because each memory address would actually contain only one instruction. Moreover, the data and instructions would not be readable in English but in machine language—that is, in 0s and 1s.

BINARY BUSINESS

HOW ELECTRICITY

REPRESENTS DATA

To the standard measures by which we live—of currency, weather, distance, and so on—we must now add another for the Information Age: that of computer storage capacity. As mentioned, if the microcomputer you are using does not have enough storage, for example, it may not be able to do everything you want. Storage capacity is principally expressed using the letter K, which can be thought of as representing 1,024 characters. (We will describe this in more detail in a moment.) When you buy software, you may see listed on the package—as on Lotus 1-2-3, for example—"System Hardware Requirements: . . . 256K bytes of memory," which means the program is designed to run on an IBM Personal Computer with at least 256K of storage capacity. That is, the computer must be able to hold at least 256 × 1,024, or 262,144 characters of data.

On and Off

But how, you may wonder, does such data get represented in the computer? You can think of a computer as consisting of a long series of switches, each turned either on or off. This on/off corresponds to electricity being turned on or off or to a magnetic field being positive or negative. Indeed, in the early days of computers, one could actually see the light in vacuum tubes go on and off.

These two states of on and off can be represented by the **binary system** of numbers—that is, a number system using only the two digits 0 and 1. (The decimal system that we are all accustomed to, by contrast, uses 10 digits—0, 1, 2, 3, 4, 5, 6, 7, 8, 9.) In the binary system, the 0 is represented in the computer by the off state and the 1 by the on state

When applied to computers, each 0 or 1 in the binary system is called a **bit** (which stands for binary digit). Because bits alone cannot represent numbers, letters, and special characters, they are combined into groups of eight bits called **bytes** (pronounced "bites"). Each byte, or group of zeros and ones, represents one character of data; that is, a letter, digit, or special character (such as ? or $).

The letter **K,** the unit of capacity of primary storage, stands for **kilobytes,** which is 1,024 bytes. On newer-model personal computers, primary storage may be expressed as one **megabyte**—one million bytes ("mega" means million). Some manufacturers of large computers even speak of **gigabytes**—billions of bytes. Microcomputers were limited to 640K of memory for a long time because of the restrictions of the microprocessor, but the Intel 80386 chip, which became available in 1987, permits as much as 16 megabytes, and even more under certain forms of "memory stretching." Mainframe computers may be 16 megabytes or more.

Two by Two: Binary Numbers

Presumably because our ancestors had ten fingers, our numbering system is decimal, or base ten. Our counting system, then, is based on some obvious physical characteristics. But the world is full of other characteristics for which we often use such names as "couple," "pair," "duet," and "twins." Counting by twos is called the binary numbering system. Since computers use electricity, which has two states—"on" and "off"—they must use the binary system. In order for us to do business, we must convert decimal numbers to binary on input to the computer.

Binary numbers are manipulated the same way as decimal numbers. The difference is that binary has only 0 and 1, whereas decimal has ten numbers, 0 through 9. However, when adding the 1s in binary, you carry them to the top of the left column—a maneuver familiar to you in adding columns of decimal numbers. In binary, then, 1 + 1 equals 10 (this is 2 in decimal); 1 + 1 + 1 equals 11 (3 in decimal) and 1 + 1 + 1 + 1 equals 100 (4 in decimal), as the following shows:

$$
\begin{array}{r}
1 \\
+ 1 \\
\hline
10 \\
+ 1 \\
\hline
11 \\
+ 1 \\
\hline
100 \\
\end{array}
$$

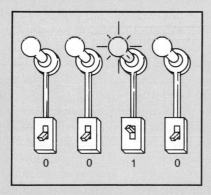

Here are the numbers 0 through 9 in base 10 as written in base two:

Base 10	Base two	Base two with preceding zeros added
0	0	0000
1	1	0001
2	10	0010
3	11	0011
4	100	0100
5	101	0101
6	110	0110
7	111	0111
8	1000	1000
9	1001	1001

The zeros added in front of each base two number do not change the meaning of the number (just as, in decimal, 0015 is the same as 15). When working with computers, every column must be filled in with something, because electricity is either off (0) or on (1).

Continuing, we see that decimal numbers 10 through 16 are as follows in binary:

Base 10	Base two
10	1010
11	1011
12	1100
13	1101
14	1110
15	1111
16	10000

Clearly, numbers in the binary system can get long very quickly. For instance, the decimal number 5,000 is the binary number 10011100010000.

Binary bulbs. The decimal number 2, which is 0010 in binary, could be expressed with on and off light bulbs, with "on" for 1 and "off" for 0.

Bytes into Codes

Combinations of bytes—that is, of 0s and 1s—can be used to represent the complete alphabet, the decimal numbers 0 through 9, and special characters. There are different sets of combinations or coding schemes, the most common being:

▶ 4-bit binary coded decimal (BCD)
▶ 8-bit Extended Binary Coded Decimal Interchange Code (EBCDIC)
▶ 7-bit American Standard Code for Information Interchange (ASCII)

The three are compared in Figure 7-2. Let us take a look at these.

Binary Coded Decimal   Popular with the first computers, **binary coded decimal (BCD)** is used to code numeric data. It consists of 0s and 1s grouped into units of four bits each (some BCD code is six bits). For example, the decimal number 4,196 is represented by the four digits 4, 1, 9, and 6, each written in binary (base two):

$$0100 \quad 0001 \quad 1001 \quad 0110$$
$$= \quad 4 \qquad\;\; 1 \qquad\;\; 9 \qquad\;\; 6$$

The problem with this code is that it runs out of new combinations in each 4-bit sequence very quickly, since there are only 16 possible combinations of 0s and 1s in each 4-bit unit. Ten combinations are needed to represent the decimal digits 0 through 9, leaving only six combinations—clearly not enough to represent the 26 upper- and lowercase characters of the alphabet and the special characters needed.

Extended Binary Coded Decimal Interchange Code   By expanding the byte from four bits to eight, it is possible to represent alphabetic and special characters as well as numeric. The **Extended Binary Coded Decimal Interchange Code,** abbreviated **EBCDIC** (pronounced "*eb*-see-dick") not only allows alphabetic characters but also allows them in uppercase and lowercase. One of the two most popular 8-bit codes used, EBCDIC was developed by IBM and is used in most IBM computers, as well as in machines produced by other manufacturers.

    The eight bits—which, as mentioned, are usually referred to as a *byte*—are divided into two parts, the first four bits being called **zone bits** and the second four bits being called **numeric** or **digit bits.** The combination of zone bits with numeric bits allows for 256 possible arrangements. (If six bits are used, only 64 arrangements are possible—not enough to cover numbers, special characters, and the upper- and lowercase alphabets.) Note, for instance, that the follow-

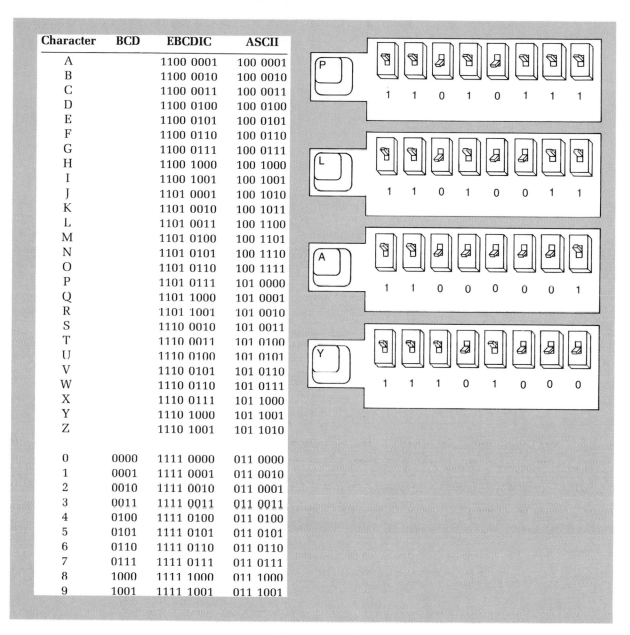

Character	BCD	EBCDIC	ASCII
A		1100 0001	100 0001
B		1100 0010	100 0010
C		1100 0011	100 0011
D		1100 0100	100 0100
E		1100 0101	100 0101
F		1100 0110	100 0110
G		1100 0111	100 0111
H		1100 1000	100 1000
I		1100 1001	100 1001
J		1101 0001	100 1010
K		1101 0010	100 1011
L		1101 0011	100 1100
M		1101 0100	100 1101
N		1101 0101	100 1110
O		1101 0110	100 1111
P		1101 0111	101 0000
Q		1101 1000	101 0001
R		1101 1001	101 0010
S		1110 0010	101 0011
T		1110 0011	101 0100
U		1110 0100	101 0101
V		1110 0101	101 0110
W		1110 0110	101 0111
X		1110 0111	101 1000
Y		1110 1000	101 1001
Z		1110 1001	101 1010
0	0000	1111 0000	011 0000
1	0001	1111 0001	011 0010
2	0010	1111 0010	011 0001
3	0011	1111 0011	011 0011
4	0100	1111 0100	011 0100
5	0101	1111 0101	011 0101
6	0110	1111 0110	011 0110
7	0111	1111 0111	011 0111
8	1000	1111 1000	011 1000
9	1001	1111 1001	011 1001

Figure 7-2.   Three computer coding schemes: BCD, EBCDIC, ASCII. These are binary representations for letters and numbers; special characters are also included (not shown). The bits—0s and 1s—may be thought of as "off" and "on" switches, as in the word "PLAY" shown above expressed in EBCDIC.

ing both have the same numeric bits but different zone bits, so that one byte can represent a letter and the other a number:

	Byte	
Zone bits	Numeric bits	
1100	0010	= B
1111	0010	= 2

American Standard Code for Information Interchange   The second most popular code, the 7-bit **American Standard Code for Information Interchange** is usually referred to by its abbreviation, **ASCII** (pronounced "*as*-key"). ASCII is frequently used in data communications, nearly always in microcomputers, and in several large computers.

Note in Figure 7-2 that a byte consists of seven bits (rather than eight, as in EBCDIC), allowing for 128 possible arrangements—fewer than the 256 possible combinations of EBCDIC. Because some computers are designed for 8-bit rather than 7-bit codes, an 8-bit version of ASCII has been developed called **ASCII-8.**

The Parity Bit: Tip-off to Errors

To err is not just human, although too often the expression "computer error" is simply a coverup for human mistakes. Dust, static electricity, high humidity, and other factors can affect the sending of data to and through a computer. Obviously, at Atlantic-Pacific Bank, which transmits a lot of financial information through communications lines, errors in transit can mean substantial losses. Although the computer typically cannot tell you the exact error, frequently it can tell you that there is one. One of the ways the computer detects errors is through the use of a parity bit, which is used in transmitting data.

A **parity bit,** also called a **check bit,** is simply an additional bit attached to the byte. That is, in EBCDIC, it would be a ninth bit, as shown in Figure 7-3. (In ASCII, the extra bit would be the eighth bit.) The addition of this extra bit allows the computer to detect errors in character representation.

Notice that if you add up the number of 1s in a byte, the total will be either odd or even (1100 0001 has three 1s and therefore is odd, 1100 0011 has four 1s and so is even). In an *even parity* format, the extra parity bit is set to either 0 or 1 in order to make the number of 1s an even number. Thus, for the EBCDIC letter A, which is 1100 0001 and which is odd, a parity bit of 1 is added so that the 9-bit sequence is 1 1100 0001, making the number of 1s even. Any time a 9-bit sequence shows up in the computer as odd, the computer

Figure 7-3. **The parity bit.** This an example of an even parity format. The parity bit is always such that the 9-bit sequence is even. If any one of the 1 bits is missing, the computer will display an error message to the computer operator.

	Parity bit			
EBCDIC letter A	1	1100	0001	Even—four 1s
EBCDIC letter C	0	1100	0011	Even—four 1s
Error in EBCDIC letter C	0	1100	0010	Odd—three 1s (last 1 dropped)

(when using an even-parity format) will display an error message so the computer operator can take corrective action.

An *odd parity* format is the reverse of even parity—the parity bit is set to make the number of 1s odd. Odd parity is used on some systems. Either way, the parity bit is not infallible in catching errors—after all, suppose *two* 1s were missing from 1 1100 0001 in an even-parity system. But it has been shown to be very effective in detecting the majority of coding errors.

Storage Designs

The storage capacity of a computer is part of its design. There are three types of designs:

▶ Word-addressable
▶ Character-addressable
▶ Byte-addressable

These describe what will fit into each storage location or address.

Word-Addressable In a **word-addressable** design, each address stores a fixed number of characters—for example, a single data item such as BAKER or a single program instruction such as ADD, as expressed in binary numbers. A computer **word** consists of the number of bits that constitute a common unit of information, as defined by the computer system. The length of the word depends on the computer system. The earliest microcomputers had 8-bit word sizes, but minicomputers and most new microcomputers have 16-bit words. Mainframes and some minicomputers have 32, supercomputers have 64, and some very large machines have 128-bit words. In general, the larger the word size, the more powerful the computer because the computer can transfer more information at a time. Word-addressable design is common in large, powerful computers used for scientific calculations. Although this kind of design makes for efficient computation, it is not efficient in allocating storage.

Character-Addressable In a **character-addressable** design, each address stores a single character. This means that an item of data or a program instruction could require several storage locations. Character-addressable storage is common in microcomputers. It is characterized by lower efficiency for calculations but higher efficiency in storage allocations.

Byte-Addressable   The third design type, **byte-addressable** storage can store data in either manner—by character or by word—according to instructions written in the computer program. There are two versions of byte-addressable storage. A *fixed version* design is commonly used for scientific applications; a *variable version* design is used for business applications. Byte-addressable design is most frequently used with large computers that service both scientific and business applications.

THE UPWARD CURVE
OF STORAGE
TECHNOLOGY

We stand on the verge of some technological breakthroughs in storage technology. Some of the machines with which you will no doubt be working in the next couple of years will use "state-of-the art" technology, but some will not. Let us consider, therefore, some old and new:

▶ Magnetic core
▶ Semiconductor
▶ Superconductor

Magnetic Core Storage

A technology that is fading away but is still present in some of today's mainframe computers, **magnetic core storage** consists of pinhead-sized rings strung like beads on intersecting wires, as shown in Figure 7-4. Electricity runs through the wires and magnetizes the cores to represent bits. Many cores are strung together, creating a screen 6 by 11 inches called a core plane; such planes are stacked one above the other to create the computer memory.

The biggest advantage of magnetic core memory is that it is **nonvolatile.** That is, the magnetized cores will retain their charge even when the power supply to the computer is shut off. Magnetic core storage is also fairly fast and safe. However, as the cost of other forms of storage, such as semiconductor, goes down, magnetic core storage becomes less attractive.

Semiconductor Storage

Semiconductors—also known as **integrated circuits** and **silicon chips**—are complete electronic circuits made out of silicon, the second most common element in the earth's crust. The chip may be less than one-eighth inch square and have hundreds of electronic compo-

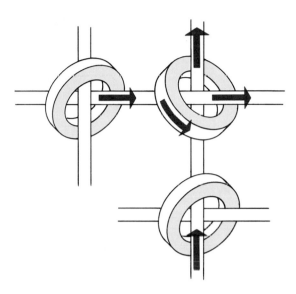

Figure 7-4. Magnetic core memory. *Left:* A woman holds up a magnetic core memory, which measures 6 by 11 inches. Such magnetic core memories are now being supplanted by quarter-inch-square silicon chips, shown being held by tweezers. *Right:* Magnetic cores, each a few hundredths of an inch in diameter, are mounted on wires. When electricity is passed through the wire on which a core is strung, it can be magnetized as "on" to represent 1 or "off" to represent 0 in the binary system.

nents on it. Although semiconductors have the disadvantage of losing data once the power to them is turned off—they are **volatile**—they have spectacular advantages:

▶ *They are small.* A semiconductor is half the size of your thumbnail, yet contains the power of an old room-sized ENIAC computer (one of the first computers built) and can hold a thousand times more data than a single magnetic core. Despite the size of a microcomputer, if you open it up you will find there is only a single chip for a CPU, and you will have to look hard to find it since it is less than one-half inch square. Nevertheless, a 64K chip can store 65,536 bytes or characters of data.

▶ *They are economical.* Because of mass production methods, a semiconductor can be bought for a few dollars—an incredible buy, considering its power. Semiconductors also have extremely low power requirements.

▶ *They are reliable.* Producers put them through a rigorous "burning in"—testing—so that chips rarely fail, perhaps once in 33 million hours of operation.

Figure 7-5.   The Intel 386 "super-chip." This is magnified several times. One such chip, the size of half a thumbnail, may power the calculations in a microcomputer.

An example of a chip is shown in Figure 7-5. Several different sized chips are available. A 16-megabit chip—meaning a chip that can hold 16 million bits on a piece of silicon smaller than a postage stamp—can contain the equivalent of 1,600 pages of double-spaced typed text.

RAM and ROM, PROM and EPROM

There are several different types of chips, which are referred to by their initials: RAM, ROM, PROM, EPROM. These represent different types of semiconductor storage.

RAM   Standing for **random-access memory,** the letters **RAM** are very common in conversations about microcomputers. RAM refers to storage in which data and programs can not only be obtained from primary storage but also can be put into it. When you hear of a 64K RAM microcomputer, then, it means that you can put 65,536 bytes or characters of data and programs into it. RAM is volatile—the contents of the memory disappear once the current is turned off.

ROM   An abbreviation for **read-only memory**—the word *read* means you can retrieve data—**ROM** describes chips in which programs are built into the primary storage at the factory and cannot be changed by you, the user. You can read them, but not alter them. You find these particularly, for instance, in calculators that have a square root function. ROMs are often also called **firmware** because they contain programs that are "firm"—they cannot be altered. ROM is nonvolatile; the contents do not disappear when the current is turned off.

PROM   Short for **programmable read-only memory, PROM** chips are another kind of firmware that can be programmed once and only once. They are like ROM in that the contents cannot be altered. However, they are custom-made by the manufacturer to meet particular customer needs and have the advantage of being able to operate faster than typical application programs written in a high-level language.

EPROM   EPROM chips are simply erasable PROM firmware; **EPROM** stands for **erasable, programmable read-only memory.** The erasure requires a special process involving ultraviolet light; thus, accidental erasing is impossible.

More Bang for the Byte: Increasing CPU Efficiency

Computer efficiency has been increased by improvements in the way data is moved, both within the CPU and to and from it. This has been accomplished in three ways:

▶ Registers
▶ Control units
▶ Channels

Registers   The CPU has primary storage, of course, but it also has some special purpose storage devices called registers. **Registers** act as temporary holding locations for instructions and data, but they are not part of primary storage. There are different types of registers, among them:

▶ An **accumulator,** located in the ALU, which holds accumulated data.
▶ A **storage register,** which holds data that is to be sent to or taken from primary storage and which is also in the ALU.
▶ An **instruction register,** which is located in the controller and which is used to decode instructions.
▶ An **address register,** also located in the controller, which holds the address of a location containing data called for by an instruction.
▶ A **general register,** which has varied uses such as for arithmetic and addressing.

   Not all computers have registers, but most do, though perhaps not all those just listed. The main advantage of registers, as we mentioned, is speed. They can operate very quickly in manipulating instructions or data or in performing computations, as directed by the CPU.

Control Units   The control units we are talking about are not the same as the controller in the CPU. These are part of an input or output device or are located between the CPU and such devices. The purpose of these **control units** is to reduce the CPU time spent waiting to receive input data or output information. The device is important because the typical CPU operates 10,000 times faster than its accompanying input and output devices. A control unit enhances the efficiency of the CPU by supplying a temporary storage or **buffer** area for data waiting to be input to the CPU or information awaiting output. The control unit gathers data from an input device and sends it to the CPU at speeds much faster than the input devices. It outputs information the same way. Control units are typically part of an input terminal where input is done a character at a time. A buffer collects the data one character at a time until it reaches capacity; then, as soon as the CPU is ready for the data, it empties its contents at a rapid rate.

Channels   Also designed to reduce CPU time spent waiting for inputting of data and outputting of information, **channels** may be part of the CPU or outside it as a small, separate computer located near the CPU. Channels are of two types, selector and multiplexor. A **selector** services only one input or output device, a **multiplexor** services several. Selectors are used with high-speed devices such as tape drives and disk drives; multiplexors are used with lower-speed devices, such as terminals.

Superconductors

Is there any point in having *more* powerful CPUs when we already have such powerful supercomputers? Indeed there is: Information technologies are what advanced countries have to sell, and there is worldwide competition not just between companies but between entire nations. The Japanese are well aware of this, as are many European countries. As we will see later in this book, the fields of artificial intelligence and expert systems require more computer power.

Computer and semiconductor makers have been exploring new ways of making internal memory speedier. Some companies are building computers using an approach known as parallel processing *(see box page 236–237)*. A number of scientists are inquiring into the possibility of building so-called **biochips**—chips made, through genetic engineering, of organic materials *(see box)* that replace today's inorganic silicon chips.

Of particular interest are new developments in superconductors. **Superconductivity** means that electricity is conducted with practically no loss of energy. The activity was first observed in 1911, when Dutch scientist Heike Onnes observed that some metals become superconductive when cooled to almost zero Kelvin (zero on the Kelvin scale is equivalent to −459 degrees Fahrenheit). However, the only material that would get near that temperature was

BIOCHIPS

Growing Computer Power

No prototypes have yet been built, but scientists and engineers have proposed that *biochips*—organic molecules or genetically engineered proteins—could conceivably be produced. Their advantage is they would allow entirely new styles of data processing, suitable for such complex tasks as pattern recognition. Two types of biochips have been contemplated— *digital* biochips in which organic molecules would turn the flow of electrons on and off, like today's sili-con chips, and *analog* biochips, in which protein enzymes would be capable of graded responses and so provide other forms of computation presumably not based on a binary system of representing data.

Will such biological circuitry indeed come about? There are many research steps to take, none of which have yet been taken.

Stay tuned to the 21st century.

expensive liquid helium; consequently, ever since then, scientists have been looking for materials that will show superconductivity at warmer temperatures. A superconductor operating at room temperature would be an incredible technological breakthrough, offering the promise of desktop supercomputers. Liquid nitrogen offers superconductivity at a temperature of 77 Kelvin, which is fine for some large applications, such as refrigeration, but not for consumer uses. Scientists at the University of California, Berkeley, have achieved superconductivity at 292 Kelvin (66 Fahrenheit), but only for a short period of time.

If and when consistent superconductivity at room temperature is achieved, the applications in electronics are limitless. Electromagnets would be far more powerful than today's conventional electromagnets and require far less energy. Computers built using superconductive materials would be far faster, and the electronic systems of the future would pack 100 or more times the processing power in the space they have now.

Let us now turn from hardware and the processor/memory to software and the operating system.

OPERATING SYSTEMS

ORCHESTRA

CONDUCTORS

FOR SOFTWARE

A lot of housekeeping goes on during the operation of a computer, housekeeping that would be a nuisance if you, the user or programmer, had to do it all yourself. What takes it out of your hands is the **operating system,** a set of programs that allows the computer system to direct its own resources and operations, much as an orchestra conductor directs an orchestra (see Figure 7-6, page 238).

Among the tasks the operating system will take care of are: coordinating the flow of data to and from the CPU and from input and

SPEEDING UP THE COMPUTER

Avoiding the "von Neumann bottleneck" with Parallel Processing

*For many years, computers have been **serial machines**, capable of working on only one instruction at a time. As the following shows, with parallel processing several instructions may be performed simultaneously, using several processors or CPUs—in the same time that it used to take one instruction.*

Faster and cheaper computers will allow users to do things they can't today—operate a typewriter by voice, for example. Companies and nations alike will face the opportunities and dangers that always accompany a major innovation. The stakes are high: the new technology will affect all information-age businesses, ranging from electronic mail networks to computer manufacturing. . . .

The transformation will be based on one fundamental idea: that the way to speed up computers is to divide the labor among many inexpensive data-processing devices rather than continue the present quest for ever faster single processors made with ever more exotic materials and techniques. Called parallel processing, the new approach is analogous to mass-producing shoes with unskilled labor on assembly lines instead of handcrafting them with skilled workmen. . . .

Today's supercomputers are too slow for many potential tasks. Some jobs now take weeks or months—for example, simulating the airflow around an entire airplane in flight. Users have identified additional applications that would take hundreds or thousands of times longer; one would create a minutely detailed three-dimensional model of a fusion reactor's interior at work.

Unfortunately, performing these tasks will be impractical as long as computer makers stick with the present dominant design—the "von Neumann architecture," named for the Hungarian-American genius John von Neumann, who helped develop it near the end of World War II. In the von Neumann approach a single main processing unit calls forth programmed instructions and data from memory in sequence, manipulates the data as instructed, and either returns the results to memory or performs other operations (see illustrations). With only one processor at work, the pace of computation is set by the speed of the processor's electronic circuits. . . .

A formidable barrier is what IBM's eminent computer scientist John Backus . . . has identified as the "von Neumann bottleneck." That is the single channel along which data and instructions must flow between a conventional computer's central processor and its memory. Like a constriction in a pipe feeding raw material to a factory, the von Neumann bottleneck can limit the pace of production.

The faster, smarter, cheaper alternative to von Neumann's architecture, many designers agree, is parallel processing. The latent advantages of parallelism have long been recognized; even von Neumann was impressed by discoveries in the 1940s about how animal brains process information in a parallel manner. Had electronic hardware not been so costly in his day, he might have designed a machine more like a brain.

That economic constraint no longer applies. A technology called VLSI (for "very large-scale integration") makes it possible to reproduce computer circuits with hundreds of thousands of transistors on a single tiny silicon chip almost as easily and cheaply

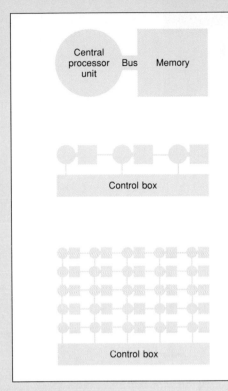

Oldest: The ultimate coarse-grained architecture is the von Neumann machine, with one main processor and memory bank. Instructions from the processor and data from memory flow back and forth through the bus, which limits processing speed.

Newer: Intermediate-grain computer architectures have few powerful processor-memory units under the control of a central computer (the control box). Each processor can work alone on a job or with other processors.

Newest: Fine-grained architectures use many processors. The latticelike arrangement resembles that of the Connection Machine under development at Thinking Machines Corp. Columbia University has mounted a "Non Von" project—that is, not von Neumann—and proposes an architecture with a million processors arranged in a branching, treelike structure.

as printing pages of a book. This capability affords designers a tantalizing way around the von Neumann bottleneck: put many processors on a single chip. Processors could operate simultaneously on different parts of a problem and even specialize in performing particular operations at great speed. Another type of parallelism, called active or associative memory, can immensely speed up certain computing tasks, such as retrieving information from data bases, by eliminating the role of the central processor in searching through memory. In essence, each piece of data would be stored with its own tiny processor, smart enough to respond when a centralized computer calls for that item. . . .

Some proponents of parallelism hope that it will make possible machines that learn things on their own—computers able to do jobs no programmer knows how to tell them to do.

—Tom Alexander, *Fortune*

Figure 7-6.   The operating system as orchestra conductor. A collection of programs within the computer, the operating system for a microcomputer controls the system's operations: input from the keyboard, recording of data on or retrieving of data from the disk in the disk drive, output to a terminal, or printing to a printer.

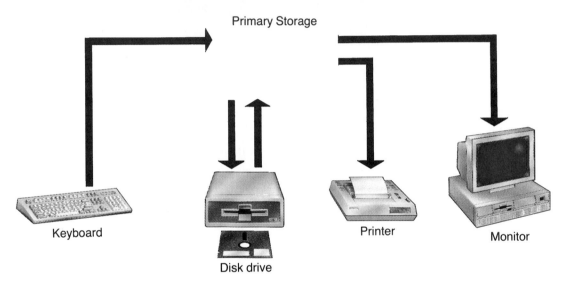

Primary Storage

Keyboard

Disk drive

Printer

Monitor

output devices, assigning and recalling memory addresses, reporting on the sizes of files, preventing multiple users from getting into each other's files, preventing one person from writing data into a file at the same time another person is reading data from it, and allowing one user to send a message to another.

In general, then, an operating system has three purposes:

▶ It controls computer system resources.
▶ It executes computer programs.
▶ It manages data.

Why is it important for you, as a computer user rather than computer professional, to know anything about something as seemingly technical as operating systems? After all, it is not as though you will

Figure 7-7. Control-oriented and processing-oriented programs. Two uses of the operating system.

Supervisor program in primary storage

Control-oriented programs	Processing-oriented programs
▶ Batch processing	▶ Language translators
▶ Multiprogramming	▶ Utility programs
▶ Multiprocessing	▶ Library programs
▶ Virtual storage	

be called upon to create or modify anything with them. There are, however, some good reasons for becoming familiar with this subject—the principal one being that the kind of operating system you choose has a lot to do with the kind of computers, and the kinds of software—particularly in microcomputers—available to you.

An operating system can contain two types of programs, as Figure 7-7 shows:

▶ Control-oriented programs
▶ Processing-oriented programs

Control-Oriented Programs: The Uses of the Operating System

Control-oriented programs are concerned with the overall management of the computer system. The master program, known as the **supervisor program,** is located principally in primary storage (see Figure 7-7). Like an orchestra conductor, it controls the entire operating system and calls upon other operating system programs located in secondary storage when they are needed.

Among the functions of the control-oriented programs are to allow:

▶ Batch processing

▶ Multiprogramming—scheduling of multiple-user programs

▶ Multiprocessing—concurrent execution of multiple programs, when the hardware will support it

▶ Virtual storage—storage of a very large program in both primary storage and disk storage

Batch Processing   A major control function of the operating system is to schedule one job to follow another automatically without human intervention. The running of **jobs**—user programs—one after another is **batch processing.** An applications programmer prepares identifiers, which are interpreted by the operating system, marking the beginning and end of each job.

Multiprogramming   In the old days, computers would read a single program into primary storage and operate on that program exclusively until it was done—a type of processing known as **serial processing.** However, because a computer's CPU operates faster than its input and output units, this meant the CPU was not being used a good deal of the time. In **multiprogramming,** more than one program is executed concurrently (see Figure 7-8). "Concurrently" is not the same as "simultaneously," because the first means that one program will be operated on by the CPU while the other is held in primary storage, then programs are switched. However, because they are both processed during the same period of time (the same 15 minutes, for instance), the CPU is not idle, and different users get their programs run in ample time. Multiprogramming is often used for batch programs such as payroll, accounts receivable, financial planning, sales and marketing analyses, and quality control.

Multiprocessing   Whereas in multiprogramming only one program can be executed at any one time in the CPU, with **multiprocessing** more than one program can be executed simultaneously in computers that consist of two or more independent CPUs linked together for coordinated operation. Indeed, the CPUs can work together on the same program as well as on different programs.

Figure 7-8. Multiprogramming. Programs are executed concurrently, with one printing out while others handle tasks of secondary storage from tape drive and disk drive; a fourth is being processed by the CPU. The purpose of multiprogramming is to keep the CPU from being idle.

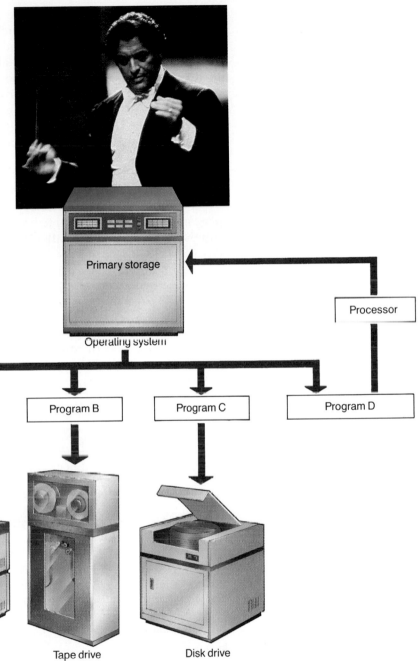

Because the job of scheduling and mediating the tasks of the input and output units and the independent CPUs is so complex, some multiprocessing systems combine a large CPU called the *host computer* with a small CPU called a *front-end processor*. The job of the front-end processor is to handle the tasks of inputting data from different input devices, which allows the host computer to concentrate on processing complicated applications programs.

Sometimes two large CPUs are combined to work independently on small jobs and work together on large, complex jobs.

Virtual Storage　For many years, if you were a programmer you had to limit the size of your applications programs to the size that would fit into the CPU and its primary storage. If you had a very large program, you were required to break it up into smaller programs and run them one at a time. To alleviate this problem, virtual storage was developed. With **virtual storage,** you can store part of the program on a secondary storage device—specifically disk storage—and bring the operating system into primary storage for execution as needed. Since only part of the program is in storage at any one time, the amount of primary storage needed for a program is minimal.

Virtual storage can be implemented by *paging, segmentation,* or a combination of both. **Paging** means that a program is broken up into blocks each of the same size—generally 2K or 4K blocks—that fit into spaces of corresponding size in primary storage. In **segmentation,** a program is broken up into different size blocks—which could be 30K, 20K, and 10K—that are then distributed throughout primary storage in locations not necessarily next to each other; the operating system keeps track of the locations of the segments throughout the primary storage.

Processing-Oriented Programs

Processing programs are operating system programs designed to simplify processing operations and reduce the time and cost of program preparation. Three of the most widely used types of processing programs are (refer back to Figure 7-7):

▶ Language translators
▶ Utility programs
▶ Library programs

Language Translators　A program written in COBOL, BASIC, or other high-level language needs to be translated into machine language; this is the task of a **language translator,** or **translator program.** If you are using a high-level language, the translator program is called a **compiler** or, sometimes, an **interpreter.** If you are using an assembly language, the translator is called an **assembler.**

Utility Programs Sorting, merging, updating, and transferring data from an input device to an output device are repetitive tasks that are easily handled by prewritten, standard programs. These programs are called **utility programs,** and they are used for converting files from one form to another (such as from tape to disk) and for sort/merge operations (such as sorting out data on files and merging it with other files).

Library Programs Supplied by the computer manufacturer or a software firm, or written by the user, **library programs** contain frequently used programs or subroutines. They are written in machine language for faster execution time.

OPERATING WITH

OPERATING SYSTEMS

MS-DOS AND UNIX

Atlantic-Pacific Bank is having to face the same problems as many other large corporations. What kinds of microcomputers should they buy? Should they tie into the bank's mainframes? And—since the bank wants users of microcomputers to be able to trade data and software back and forth directly—what kind of operating system should it favor?

In the old days, when a company bought or leased a computer, the operating system came with it. Unfortunately, if you bought an IBM machine, the chances were very good that its operating system was not compatible with one that would run on a Hewlett-Packard or Honeywell or other computer. Now, however, computer users are interested in **generic operating systems** operating systems that work with more than one manufacturer's computer system.

One early version, written by Gary Kildall in 1973 and produced by Digital Research, Inc., of Pacific Grove, California, was **CP/M,** which stands for Control Program/Microcomputers and was designed for 8-bit microcomputers. At one time this was the best-known operating system, with hundreds of microcomputer applications programs written to go with it, but it has since waned in popularity.

There are several operating systems available, including many for mainframes (see Figure 7-9), but let us consider the following, which run on microcomputers:

▶ MS-DOS
▶ UNIX

Early in the 1980s, the leading business operating systems for microcomputers were CP/M and MS-DOS. However, these two operating systems were mainly designed for single users of 8-bit and 16-bit microcomputers. With the growing power of microcomputers,

Figure 7-9.   Operating systems for IBM mainframes.

**Mainframe
system
software**

CICS	Customer Information Control System. Connects user terminals to computer.
CMS	Conversational Monitor System. Connects user terminals to computer.
DOS	Disk Operating System.
MVS	Multiprogramming with Virtual Storage. Operating system.
OS	Operating System.
TSO	Time-Sharing Option. Connects user terminals to computer.
VM/370	Virtual Machine. Operating system for IBM model 370 computers.
VM/XA	Virtual Machine/Extended Architecture. Operating system.

some of which are capable of running mainframe applications, and with 32-bit microcomputers coming into use, there is a good chance that UNIX may become more of an industry standard.

MS-DOS

By a stroke of bad luck, Gary Kildall of Digital Research was away when IBM executives came calling in 1980 to discuss buying an operating system for their soon-to-be-announced IBM Personal Computer. IBM thereupon went back to the person who had recommended Kildall, a young man named William Gates of Microsoft Corp. of Bellevue, Washington. Gates and Microsoft then proceeded to help IBM create its **MS-DOS,** which stands for Microsoft Disk Operating System. With a great many companies licensed to use it, MS-DOS has become the standard operating system for 16-bit microcomputers. Microsoft has also developed its own version of UNIX, which it calls XENIX.

UNIX: The AT&T Standard

Developed in 1971 by Bell Laboratories and available under license from Western Electric (part of American Telephone & Telegraph), **UNIX** is a very sophisticated multiprogramming, time-sharing operating system that was originally designed for minicomputers but now runs on mainframes and is being pushed for microcomputers.

THE ADVANTAGES OF OS/2

In early 1987, International Business Machines announced a new line of personal computers, named Personal Systems/2. At the same time, Microsoft Corp., maker of MS-DOS, stated it was working on OS/2—there did not seem to be an OS/1—as an operating system, to be released a year or so later.

OS/2 has two distinct advantages over [MS-DOS]. First of all, it breaks the 640K memory barrier of previous operating systems, increasing tremendously the amount of RAM, or directly accessible memory, at the disposal of the computer. The new machines can utilize up to 16 megabytes of RAM, which is about 30 times as much as the present PC line has to work with. . . .

The high-powered Models 50, 60 and 80 are machines of a different color entirely—quite literally, their cases being of a lighter hue than those of I.B.M.'s older machines. With their high-powered operating system, not only do these machines eliminate the constraints of the 640K barrier, but they permit true multi-tasking, the second significant advantage they have over the present generation of personal computers.

A true multi-tasking makes it possible for a single personal computer to run a number of applications programs simultaneously. It is one of those concepts bandied about by computer cognoscenti but rarely contemplated by the rest of us, because until now, no true multi-tasking system has been available.

Multi-tasking might at first appear to be an underwhelming idea because most people are accustomed to using their computers primarily for one task—say word processing or spreadsheeting. However, this lack of interest will probably turn out to be a case of not knowing what we have been missing.

The growth of memory-resident programs over the past couple of years provides a parallel example. Software like Sidekick and Graph in the Box allow one to switch quickly and effortlessly back and forth between a main program such as a word processor and a utility such as an outliner or a notepad.

This shuttling back and forth, however, is not true multi-tasking, it is merely task switching, which places one application on hold while another is brought into play. The Sidekick-style programs are a software Band-Aid, developed to compensate for the inherent limitations of the hardware and operating systems available.

In its wholly developed form, OS/2 will allow true multi-tasking.

—Erik Sandberg-Diment, *New York Times*

UNIX has become popular principally because AT&T for many years licensed the system to universities for a nominal fee, as a result of which many computer science students became accustomed to it. As they became professional programmers, they urged the acceptance of UNIX in industry.

EVEN MORE STORAGE

We have described primary storage at length in this chapter, as well as the mechanisms of the operating system that make primary storage operate at peak efficiency. However, with the enormous amounts of information that must be dealt with in the business world, it is clear that more than primary storage is needed. In the next chapter we will explore computer storage external to the CPU.

SUMMARY

▶ The **central processing unit (CPU)** is hardware that interprets and executes program instructions and communicates with the input, output, and external storage devices. The CPU has three parts: (1) the controller, (2) the arithmetic/logic unit, and (3) primary storage. The communications among these three units are made through a **bus.**

▶ **The controller,** or **control unit,** directs and coordinates the other units in carrying out program instructions. It also tells input devices when additional input is needed and notifies output devices that information is available for output. The controller does not store data but assigns and records the locations within the storage unit where data and programs are stored.

▶ The **arithmetic/logic unit (ALU)** calculates and compares data, based on instructions from the controller. The ALU controls the speed of calculations and thus is extremely important to computer users and computer-design engineers. The ALU performs two operations: *arithmetic operations,* which consist of the four standard mathematical calculations—addition, subtraction, multiplication, and division—and *logical operations,* which consist of the three common comparison operations—equal to (=), less than (<), and greater than (>).

▶ The **primary storage unit**—also called **memory, main storage,** or **internal storage**—holds (1) data for processing, (2) instructions for processing, and (3) processed data waiting to be output.

▶ Small computers may execute an instruction in less than a **millisecond** (one-thousandth of a second). Many computers can execute an instruction in a **microsecond** (one-millionth of a second). Supercomputers work in the **nanosecond** range (one-billionth of a second).

▶ Primary storage consists of thousands of memory locations. Each location has an *address*—a number like a post office box number. Each memory location stores only one instruction or piece of data. The controller manipulates the data and instructions by referring to the locations. The locations always stay the same, but new data and new instructions may be placed in them—the address does not change, only the contents.

▶ All computers start with the notion of two states: on and off. On/off corresponds to electricity being turned on and off or a magnetic field being positive

or negative. These two states are represented by the **binary system** of numbers, which uses only the digits 0 ("off") and 1 ("on"). Each 0 and 1 in the binary system is called a **bit** (binary digi*t*). Bits alone cannot represent letters, numbers, and special characters, so they are combined into groups of four to eight bits called **bytes.** Each byte represents one character of data.

▶ The letter **K,** the unit of capacity of primary storage, stands for **kilobyte,** which is 1,024 bytes. On large computers, primary storage may be expressed as **megabytes** (millions of bytes) or even **gigabytes** (billions of bytes).

▶ To represent the alphabet, the decimal numbers 0 through 9, and special characters, bytes are commonly combined in three different ways (coding schemes): (1) binary coded decimal (BCD), (2) Extended Binary Coded Decimal Interchange Code (EBCDIC), and (3) American Standard Code for Information Interchange (ASCII).

▶ **Binary coded decimal (BCD),** popular with the first computers, is sometimes used to code numeric data. It consists of 0s and 1s grouped into units of four (or six) bits each. This code runs out of new combinations in each 4-bit sequence very quickly, since there are only 16 possible combinations of 0s and 1s in each 4-bit unit. Thus, it does not provide enough combinations to represent numeric digits, the alphabet, and special characters.

▶ **Extended Binary Coded Decimal Interchange Code (EBCDIC),** developed by IBM, consists of units of eight bits each, which enable it to represent both alphabetic and numeric, as well as special characters—and the alphabetic characters in both uppercase and lowercase. The eight bits (one byte) are divided into four parts: the first four are **zone bits** and the second four are **numeric,** or **digit, bits.** The combination of zone bits with numeric bits allows for 256 possible arrangements.

▶ The **American Standard Code for Information Interchange (ASCII),** the second most popular code after EBCDIC, is frequently used in data communications, nearly always in microcomputers, and in several large computers. In this code, a byte consists of seven bits, allowing for 128 possible arrangements (an 8-bit version, called **ASCII-8,** has been developed).

▶ Computer errors are detected through the use of a **parity bit,** also called a **check bit,** which is an additional bit attached to the byte that allows the computers to tell whether a 1 bit in the byte has been lost. If a bit has been lost, the computer will signal a data error to the operator. In an *even parity* format, the extra parity bit is set to either 0 or 1 to make the number of 1s an even number. Any time a 9-bit sequence shows up in the computer as odd, the computer will display an error message. An *odd parity* format is the reverse of even parity—the parity bit is set to make the number of 1s odd. Although it is not infallible, the parity system is very effective in detecting the majority of coding errors.

▶ There are three types of computer storage-capacity designs: (1) word-addressable, (2) character-addressable, and (3) byte-addressable.

▶ In a **word-addressable** design, each address stores a fixed number of characters called a computer **word,** which consists of the number of bits that constitute a common unit of information, as defined by the computer system. The length of the word depends on the system. In general, the larger the word size, the more powerful the computer. Word-addressable design is common in large, powerful computers used for scientific calculations. Although it makes for efficient computation, it is not efficient allocation of storage.

▶ In a **character-addressable** design, each address stores a single character, which means that an item of data or a program instruction could require several storage locations. Commonly used in microcomputers, this design is characterized by lower calculation efficiency but greater storage-allocation efficiency.

▶ In **byte-addressable** design, data can be stored in either manner by character or by word—according to instructions written in the computer program. There are two versions of byte-addressable storage: *fixed version,* which is commonly used for scientific applications, and *variable version,* which is used for business applications. Byte-addressable design is used most frequently with large computers that serve both scientific and business applications.

▶ Two storage devices used today use the technologies of (1) magnetic core and (2) semiconductor.

▶ **Magnetic core storage,** which is becoming obsolete, consists of pinhead-size rings strung like beads on intersecting wires with electricity running through them that magnetizes the cores to represent bits. Many cores are strung together, creating a 6-by-11-inch screen called a *core plane.* Such planes are stacked one above the other to create the computer

memory. The biggest advantage of magentic core memory is that it is **nonvolatile,** which means that the magnetized cores will retain their charge even when the computer's power supply is shut off. This form of storage is also fairly fast and safe but is becoming more expensive than other forms of storage.

▶ **Semiconductors**—also called **integrated circuits** and **silicon chips**—are complete electronic circuits made of silicon. These chips are very small (several sizes are available) and have hundreds of electronic components on them. Although they are **volatile** (they will lose data when the power to them is turned off), they have some important advantages: (1) They are small—about half the size of a thumbnail—but very powerful and can hold a thousand or more times more data than a single magnetic core. (2) They are economical and have low power requirements. (3) They are reliable.

▶ There are several types of chips, representing different types of semiconductor storage: RAM, ROM, PROM, and EPROM.

▶ **RAM—random-access memory**—refers to storage in which data and programs can not only be obtained from primary storage but also can be put into it.

▶ **ROM—read-only memory**—describes chips in which programs are built into the primary storage at the factory and cannot be changed by the user; they can be "read" meaning that data can be retrieved—but they cannot be altered. ROM is also called **firmware.**

▶ **PROM—programmable read-only memory**—is a kind of firmware that can be programmed only once; then the contents cannot be altered. It is custom-made by the manufacturer and can operate faster than typical programs written in a high-level language.

▶ **EPROM—erasable, programmable read-only memory**—is erasable PROM firmware. The erasure requires a special process involving ultraviolet light that makes accidental erasure impossible.

▶ **Registers** act as temporary, special-purpose holding locations for instructions and data; they are not part of primary storage. There are different types of registers: (1) **accumulators,** located in the ALU, which hold accumulated data; (2) **storage registers,** which hold data that is to be sent to or taken from primary storage, also located in the ALU; (3) **instruction registers,** which are located in the controller and which are used to decode instructions; (4) **address registers,** also located in the controller, which hold the address of a location containing data called for by an instruction; and (5) **general registers,** which have varied uses. Most computers have registers, whose main advantage is speed.

▶ **Control units** (not the same as the *controller* in the CPU) are part of an input or output device and are located between the CPU and the device. Their purpose is to increase CPU efficiency by supplying it with a temporary storage or **buffer** area for data waiting to be input or information awaiting output, thus reducing the wait time. Control units gather data from an input device and send it to the CPU much faster than the input device could. They output information the same way. These units are typically part of an input terminal.

▶ **Channels** also reduce CPU waiting time for inputting of data and outputting of information. They may be part of the CPU or outside of it. There are only two types of channels: selector and multiplexor. **Selectors** service only one input or output device and are used with high-speed devices such as tape drives and disk drives; **multiplexors** service several input or output devices and are used with lower-speed devices, such as terminals.

▶ Although no prototypes have been built, **biochips**— organic molecules or genetically engineered proteins—could conceivably be produced. Two types of biochips have been contemplated: *digital,* in which organic molecules would turn the flow of electrons on and off, and *analog,* in which protein enzymes would be capable of graded responses and so provide other forms of computation not based on a binary system of data representation.

▶ With **superconductivity,** a possible future storage technology, electricity is conducted with practically no loss of energy. A superconductor metal operating at room temperature would offer the promise of desktop supercomputers.

▶ The **operating system** is the set of programs that allows the computer system to direct its own resources and operations. It (1) coordinates the flow of data to and from the CPU and from input and output devices, (2) assigns and recalls memory addresses, (3) reports on the size of the files, (4) prevents multiple users from getting into one another's files, (5) prevents one person from writing data into a file at the same time another person is reading data from it, and (6) allows one user to send a message to another. An operating system has three purposes: (1) controlling computer system resources, (2) executing computer programs, and (3) managing data. The two types of operating systems are (1) control-

oriented programs and (2) processing-oriented programs.

▶ **Control-oriented programs** are concerned with the overall management of the computer system. The master program—also called the **supervisor program**—is located principally in primary storage. Control-oriented programs allow several functions: (1) batch processing, (2) multiprogramming, (3) multiprocessing, and (4) virtual storage.

▶ **Batch processing** refers to the running of **jobs**—user programs—one after another without human intervention.

▶ **Multiprogramming** is the opposite of **serial processing,** the old type of processing in which a computer would read a single program into primary storage and operate on that program exclusively until it was done (the CPU was not being used much of the time). In multiprogramming, more than one program is executed concurrently (not simultaneously, however). In this case, the CPU is not idle. Multiprogramming is often used for batch processing.

▶ In **multiprocessing** more than one program can be executed simultaneously in computers that consist of two or more independent CPUs linked together for coordinated operation. The CPUs can work together on the same program or independently on different programs. Some complex multiprocessing units combine a large CPU called the *host computer* with a small CPU called a *front-end processor.* The front-end processor handles the tasks of inputting data from different input devices, which allows the host computer to concentrate on processing complicated applications programs.

▶ **Virtual storage** was developed to allow programmers to run very large programs at one time. With virtual storage, one can store part of the program on a secondary storage device (disk storage) and bring it into primary storage execution as needed. Virtual storage can be implemented by (1) **paging,** meaning that a program is broken up into same-size blocks that fit into spaces of corresponding size in primary storage, (2) **segmentation,** in which a program is broken up into different-size blocks that are distributed throughout primary storage in locations not necessarily next to each other and that are tracked by the operating system, or (3) a combination of both.

▶ **Processing programs** are operating system programs designed to simplify processing operations and to reduce the time and cost of program operation. The three most widely used types of processing programs are (1) language translators, (2) utility programs, and (3) library programs.

► **Language translators** are **translator programs** that translate high-level languages and assembly languages into machine language. A **compiler,** or **interpreter,** translates high-level languages; an **assembler** translates assembly language.

► **Utility programs** are prewritten, standard programs that convert files from one form to another and perform sort/merge operations. They handle many repetitive tasks such as sorting, merging, updating, and transferring of data from an input device to an output device.

► **Library programs** contain frequently used programs or subroutines; they are written in machine language for fast execution.

► **Generic operating systems** are operating systems that work with more than one manufacturer's computer system. Two of the most popular generic systems are MS-DOS and UNIX. An early version, **CP/M** (Control Program/Microcomputers), designed for 8-bit microcomputers, is no longer popular.

► **MS-DOS,** which stands for Microsoft Disk Operating System, was developed for IBM and became the standard operating system for 16-bit microcomputers.

► **UNIX,** developed in 1971 by Bell Laboratory researchers, is a very sophisticated multiprogramming, time-sharing operating system originally designed for minicomputers but now used with mainframes and, increasingly, with microcomputers. For years AT&T licensed this system to universities.

KEY TERMS

Accumulator, p. 233

Address register, p. 233

American Standard Code for Information Interchange (ASCII), p. 228

Arithmetic/logic unit (ALU), p. 220

ASCII-8, p. 249

Assembler, p. 242

Batch processing, p. 240

Binary coded decimal (BCD), p. 226

Binary system, p. 224

Biochip, p. 234

Bit, p. 224

Buffer, p. 234

Bus, p. 220

Byte, p. 224

Byte-addressable, p. 230

Central processing unit (CPU), p. 218

Channel, p. 234

Character-addressable, p. 229

Check bit, p. 228

Compiler, p. 242

Controller, p. 220

Control-oriented program, p. 240

Control unit, p. 234

CP/M, p. 243

Digit bit, p. 226

Erasable, programmable read-only memory (EPROM), p. 233

Extended Binary Coded Decimal Interchange Code (EBCDIC), p. 249

Firmware, p. 232

General register, p. 233

Generic operating system, p. 243

Gigabyte, p. 224

Instruction register, p. 233

Integrated circuit, p. 230

Internal storage, p. 221

Interpreter, p. 242

Jobs, p. 240

Kilobyte (K), p. 224

Language translator, p. 242

Library program, p. 243

Magnetic core storage, p. 230

Main storage, p. 221

Megabyte, p. 224

Memory, p. 221

Microsecond, p. 249

Millisecond, p. 249

MS-DOS, p. 249

Multiplexor, p. 234

Multiprocessing, p. 240

Multiprogramming, p. 240

Nanosecond, p. 249

Nonvolatile, p. 230

Case 7-2: Choosing Operating Systems: UNIX or MS-DOS?

Users choosing an operating system frequently consider only applications and costs, but there is more to it than that. More and more, it is important that systems integrate with each other. Microcomputers need to exchange information with minicomputers, mainframes, and other microcomputers. Computers, word processors, and other devices may share common facilities, such as electronic filing, laser printing, or communications processors.

At one time, UNIX had only 700 applications programs at a time when an estimated 10,000 would run on CP/M. Then came the rapid rise of the personal computer running MS-DOS, and buyers flocked to the microcomputer, avoiding UNIX because of its lack of software and difficulty for ordinary users (as opposed to programmers) to learn to use. Now, however, UNIX looks more acceptable because it can handle multiple tasks simultaneously and run on machines ranging from personal computers to mainframes. It is also becoming important in key areas such as supercomputers, electronic publishing, and departmental computing. In 1988, IBM and Microsoft introduced OS/2 as a new standard operating system for the latest generation of IBM computers, the PS/2 line.

Your assignment: Let us suppose that you are running a construction company that handles several construction jobs for the U.S. government, and you are having to use an outside computer firm to meet government requirements. You could make considerable immediate savings if you bought the government-required computing activities in-house, but the programs you want only run with MS-DOS at present. You also want to be able to do all those other activities mentioned above, for which UNIX is best suited. OS/2 has yet to establish a track record, though it could be important. What should you do?

Chapter 8

STORAGE AND FILE ORGANIZATION: FACTS AT YOUR FINGERTIPS

Empty out your wallet, desk, and bank safe-deposit box, if any. How many personal paper documents do you have in your possession? About 40?

This may not sound like much. But if you consider that this is the number for each man, woman, and child in the United States, it works out to 887 billion paper documents stored in various personal, business, and archival files—the number estimated by Strategic, Inc., a San Jose, California, research firm.

The soaring cost of managing paper documents is obviously one of the reasons for going electronic—for storing files in a computer system. Indeed, says Strategic, Inc., although microcomputers tend not to employ major innovations in storage technology—at least they haven't in the past—they are nevertheless having a profound effect on data storage, for they are allowing relatively inexperienced computer users to set up their own electronic files, often replacing paper filing systems.

The storage capabilities of microcomputers are creating a revolution on the personal level.

SECONDARY STORAGE
THE ELECTRONIC LIBRARY

Figure 8-1 shows the four basic hardware components of a microcomputer system—input, CPU, output, and secondary storage. The first three could convert data into machine-readable form, process it, and output information in people-readable form, and do it all without the fourth component, secondary storage. However, as you can quickly appreciate just from having used a personal computer, this very much limits what you can do. Indeed, for business uses, secondary storage is indispensable. Until the technology is drastically changed, it seems unlikely that a computer could be built that was large enough to hold all the customer records of Atlantic-Pacific Bank, say, inside the computer itself.

CASE STUDY: THE STORAGE REVOLUTION

The Light Touch: Storage and the Compact Disk

Light is about to become tremendously important for storing data. No doubt you are already familiar with audio compact disks (CDs), which were introduced commercially in 1983 and since then have sent LP record sales into decline. When a CD is played, a laser scans the microscopic pits in the disk's aluminum surface and beams the information to a computer chip, which converts it into sound. Now CDs are being talked up as important storage devices. These disks are also called "write-once" or "read-only memory" (ROM) because the information is prerecorded at the factory and cannot be modified by the user.

We've seen it coming for a long time, but now the CD-ROM is here. CD-ROM is the name agreed on for using compact disks as read-only storage for computer information. The CD-ROM disk drive is about the size and price of a good floppy-disk drive. Each CD-ROM disk can hold hundreds of megabytes of information: programs, data, text files, music and speech, animation and motion pictures—all can be put onto the disk and accessed.

Phillips has CD-ROM drives for sale, and there are already a number of commercially available CD-ROM disks, along with software to access the data. Activenture, Gary Kildall's new company, has Grolier's *Academic American Encyclopedia* with a really neat indexing system; in a few seconds to tens of seconds, you can search through the whole encyclopedia. It took less than a minute to find all the references to science fiction. . . .

The Phillips people tell me there are about 40 data bases on CD-ROMs. These include back issues of newspapers, stock-market histories, all kinds of financial data, technical manuals, math handbooks, you name it. . . .

CD-ROM disks can be manufactured for about $5 each in quantity and contain all the text information in the *Encyclopaedia Britannica*. A single CD-ROM disk can contain more text than the best *industrial-quality* line printer will print over its useful lifetime. A set of 20 of these disks would make an encyclopedia like nothing that ever existed: illustrations could include motion pictures and stereo. The article on space could include shots of *Apollo* 11 taking off, and so forth. . . .

CD-ROMs will change the whole nature of scholarship. Even all these years, only a handful of scholars have had access to the original text of the Dead Sea Scrolls; now, everything known about them, including video copies of not only the scrolls themselves but every word of commentary ever written about them, can be put onto a single CD-ROM disk and still have room for everything known about, say, the archaeology of Jericho. . . .

A few years ago, I said that by the year 2000, anyone in a Western nation who seriously wanted to would be able to get the answer to any answerable question. I'm now more than confident I was right—except that it may happen much sooner than I thought.

—Jerry Pournelle, *Byte*

Storage

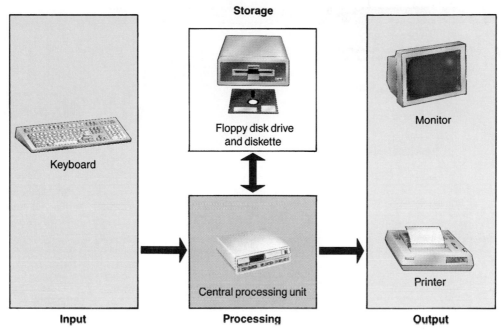

Keyboard

Floppy disk drive and diskette

Monitor

Central processing unit

Printer

Input　　　　　　　**Processing**　　　　　　　**Output**

Figure 8-1. The four hardware components of a computer system. Although the system needs only input, CPU, and output in order to operate, the fourth component—secondary storage—is the one that expands its usefulness, particularly for businesspeople, who must sort through numerous files.

The Advantages of Secondary Storage

Although primary storage can process data faster, secondary storage has a number of advantages:

▶ **Economy:** It is more economical to store data on magnetic media than in a filing cabinet, or most certainly in primary storage.

▶ **Capacity:** There is much more capacity in secondary storage than in primary storage—indeed, "off-line" storage is practically unlimited.

▶ **Security:** Data is usually stored in secondary storage so that it is safe from tampering by unauthorized people or from natural hazards and degradation.

As we have seen, **primary storage,** also known as **internal storage,** is the storage within the CPU. **Secondary storage**—also called **external storage** or **auxiliary storage**—consists of storage outside the computer itself. There are two types of secondary storage: *direct access* and *sequential access.*

These three alternative forms of storage—primary, direct access, and sequential access—may be arranged in a continuum, as shown

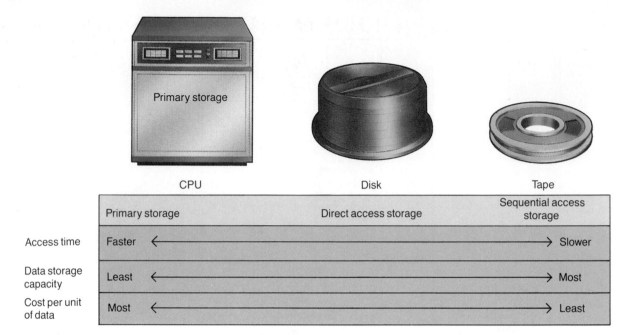

		CPU		Disk		Tape

	Primary storage	Direct access storage	Sequential access storage
Access time	Faster ⟵⟶		Slower
Data storage capacity	Least ⟵⟶		Most
Cost per unit of data	Most ⟵⟶		Least

Figure 8-2. The storage continuum.
As one moves from left to right on this scale, access time becomes slower, data storage capacity greater, and cost per unit of storage less.

in Figure 8-2, with faster speed of access at the left and larger capacity at the right:

▶ **Primary storage:** This storage within the CPU is the fastest in terms of the computer accessing stored data; however, the capacity for storing data is the most limited. The cost per unit of data stored is also the most expensive of the three categories.

▶ **Direct access storage:** This form of secondary storage is slower than primary storage but faster than sequential access storage, as we shall explain. However, it is also more expensive than sequential access storage.

▶ **Sequential access storage:** The bottom of the hierarchy, this form of secondary storage is quite slow, but it has almost unlimited storage capacity and is the least expensive.

We described primary storage in Chapter 7. Let us now consider the two types of secondary storage: direct access and sequential access.

Direct Access Storage

Direct access storage requires an input/output device that is directly connected to the CPU; that is, it is said to be **on-line,** making the stored data available to the CPU at all times. Such storage devices are called **direct access storage devices (DASDs).**

An example of direct access media is a magnetic disk, such as the diskettes used with a personal computer. Here, as we will explain, it is far easier to go directly to the file you want; it is as though you move the record arm on your stereo directly to the song on the the LP record you want to play instead of having to listen to all the songs preceding the one you really want to hear. As mentioned, direct access storage is less expensive and has greater capacity than primary storage; however, it is not nearly as fast.

Sequential Access Storage

Sequential access storage is **off-line;** the data in this kind of storage is not accessible to the CPU until it has been loaded onto an input device. An example of sequential access media is a reel of tape: Records are stored in sequence—alphabetically, say—one after the other. A stack of punched cards is another example of sequential media.

A reel of tape can hold a great deal of data, which is perfect for many of a bank's purposes. The problem, however, is that if you are looking for a customer name far into the alphabet—O'Leary or Williams, say—you have to run the tape past all the earlier files first, a relatively slow process.

Being outside the CPU and not directly connected to it, sequential access storage is much slower than either primary storage or direct access storage. However, it has much greater—indeed, unlimited—capacity and is considered to be more secure because it is stored off-line and not directly accessible to anyone who has gained access to a computer's CPU.

The two forms of secondary storage are described in more detail below. In general, direct access uses magnetic disk and sequential access uses magnetic tape.

SEQUENTIAL ACCESS
STORAGE THE USES
OF MAGNETIC TAPE

As mentioned, in sequential processing, files of data are stored one after the other, and users gain access to the files in the same way—by examining the files one after the other, starting with the first file and going through all successive ones until they find the right one.

The two principal sequential access storage devices are magnetic tape devices and magnetic disk devices; we will concentrate on the first one here.

Magnetic Tape Devices

The most common medium for sequential access storage, **magnetic tape** consists of plastic tape of the sort found on reel-to-reel stereo tape recorders. Indeed, in the past a pitch made by some home computer manufacturers was that you could save money on your com-

Figure 8-3. Magnetic tape storage.
Near right: A magnetic tape drive, with parts labeled. Tapes are always protected by glass from outside dust and dirt. *Opposite page, top:* Magnetic tape reel and tape, with read/write head. There may be up to 2,400 feet of tape on a reel of this size. When a tape is being read, magnetized spots on the tape cause current in the read coil, which is then sent to the CPU. When a tape is being written, the CPU sends electric current through the write coil, which causes spots to be magnetized on the iron oxide coating the tape. *Lower left:* Examples of tapes used in mainframe computers. *Lower right:* Magnetic tape cartridge used in minicomputers.

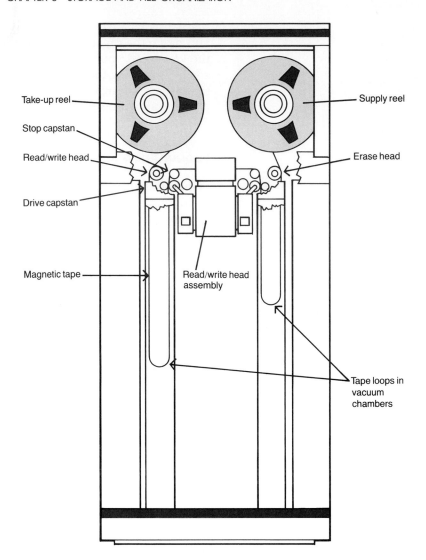

puter system by using an audio tape recorder, if you already had one, as a storage device. Such cassette tapes are usually 200 feet long and can record 200 characters to the inch.

The reels used with minicomputers and mainframes, on the other hand, take tape that is a half inch wide, nearly half a mile long (2,400 feet), and capable of storing 6,250 characters to the inch. This entire book could be stored on only the first 25 feet of one of these tapes. The devices on which such tapes are run are called **magnetic tape drives** or **magnetic tape units** (see Figure 8-3). Often about the size and shape of a refrigerator, these machines consist of two reels—a **supply reel** and a **take-up reel,** as shown in the illustration—along with a read/write head and an erase head. In computer parlance, **read** means to retrieve data from, **write** means to record data on.

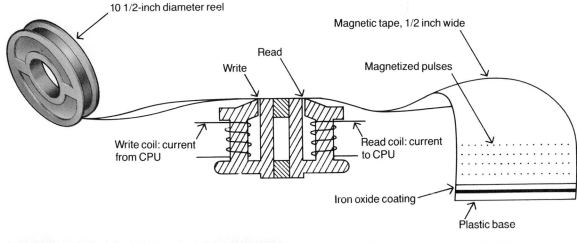

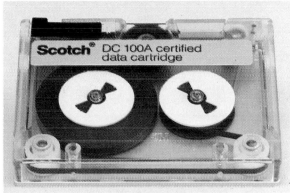

(Read is like playing a tape recorder, write is like recording on it.) The **read/write head,** then, is an electromagnet that *reads* magnetized areas on the tape (which represent data), converts them into electrical signals, and sends them to the CPU. It *writes*—that is, records—data on the tape from the CPU. If there is previous data on the tape, it also erases that data, using the **erase head,** as it writes the new data.

What Do You Call Data?

We defined the terms of raw data in the margin in Chapter 2, but let us repeat the definitions here:

▶ A **character,** also called a *byte*, is a letter, number, or special character (such as $ or #). Characters (bytes) are typically made up of eight bits (0s and 1s).

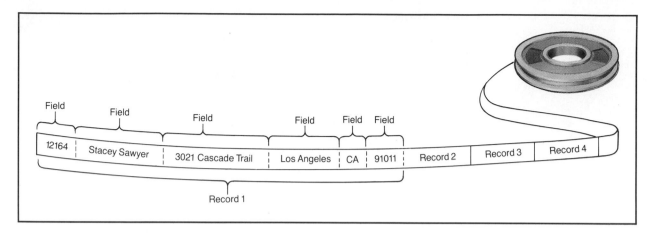

Field   Field   Field   Field   Field Field

| 12164 | Stacey Sawyer | 3021 Cascade Trail | Los Angeles | CA | 91011 | Record 2 | Record 3 | Record 4 |

Record 1

Figure 8-4.   How data is organized.   Whether on a reel of tape (as shown here) or a magnetic disk, data is organized into characters, fields, records, and files. A *character* is an individual letter, number, or special character; a *file* is a group of related records.

▶ A **field,** which is made up of one or more characters, contains an item of data. For example, an Atlantic-Pacific Bank customer would have a name field (last and first names), a street address field, a city field, a state field, a zip code field, and an account number field.

▶ A **record** is a collection of related fields. Thus, one bank customer's name, address, city, state, zip code, and account number would comprise a record.

▶ A **file** is a collection of related records. Thus, all the data about customers on the Christmas Savings Plan list would be a file.

▶ A **data base** is a collection of interrelated data, a systematic or structured organization of files available for central access and retrieval. A data base allows specific data items to be retrieved for specific applications—for instance, all bank customers living in a particular zip code area for notification that an automatic teller machine has just been installed in the branch bank in their neighborhood.

The terms *field* and *record* are illustrated in Figure 8-4. We will describe data base, which is a fairly complex concept, in a later chapter.

How Data Is Represented on Tape

As mentioned, data is represented on tape by invisible magnetized spots, the presence or absence of a spot corresponding to a 1 bit or a 0 bit. Perhaps the most common way of organizing data, as Figure

Figure 8-5. How data is represented on magnetic tape. This shows how the numbers 1 through 5 are represented in EBCDIC code, using a combination of 1 bits (magnetized spots) and 0 bits (no magnetization). The parity bit—shown here in the middle of the tape, which is where it usually appears—is used to represent an odd-parity system. If a 1 bit were missing, it would signal the computer that it was even—and that something was wrong. (Incidentally, if you look in the EBCDIC table in Figure 7-2, you will see that the number 1 is represented as 1111 0001. However, the bits do not appear in that order on the tape here, as the bit reference numbers show (starting with 0 and ending with 7). The letter P stands for parity bit.

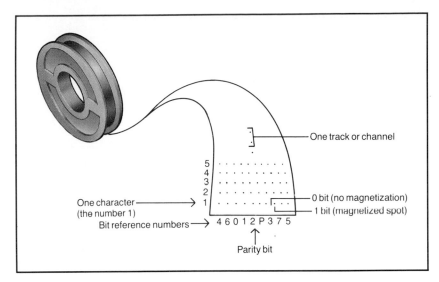

8-5 shows, is a 9-track code. That is, the tape is divided into nine tracks or channels that run the length of the tape. Each row across the nine tracks represents a single EBCDIC or ASCII character plus a parity bit, as shown in Figure 8-5.

Blocking

When data is written onto a tape, it is usually divided into logical records—for example, checking account records. However, some room is usually left between records for stopping space, since you cannot stop a tape exactly where you want; like a car when slowing down, the tape needs some allowance for deceleration. The space also allows time for the tape to accelerate as it starts. These spaces, shown in Figure 8-6, are called **interrecord gaps (IRGs).** A typical space is three-fifths of an inch long.

If each record is short, then a large number of interrecord gaps will be required, which means that much of the tape—indeed, as much as 90%—will be blank. In such cases, some of the records will be pulled together and the interrecord gaps will be eliminated and replaced by **interblock gaps (IBGs),** gaps between blocks of records (see Figure 8-6). **Blocking** is the activity of putting records together into blocks of records.

Getting It on Tape: Benefits and Drawbacks

As Figure 8-7 shows, reels of magnetic tape are often maintained in **tape libraries**—special rooms made safe from forces that might dis-

STREAMERS

In the past, the simplicity and lower cost of magnetic tape processing made it a better alternative to magnetic disk processing. This is no longer true, and today, for the most part, magnetic tape is used to make back-up (duplicate) copies of files on magnetic disk. Because there is no need to start and stop tapes during the process of making a backup, so-called *streamer* tape drives are used. Streamer tape drives store IBGs "on the fly," and thus the IBG occupies only 1/100 inch, compared to 1/2 inch for start/stop drives. Consequently, streamer tape drives use a much larger percentage of the tape for data storage—about 97%.

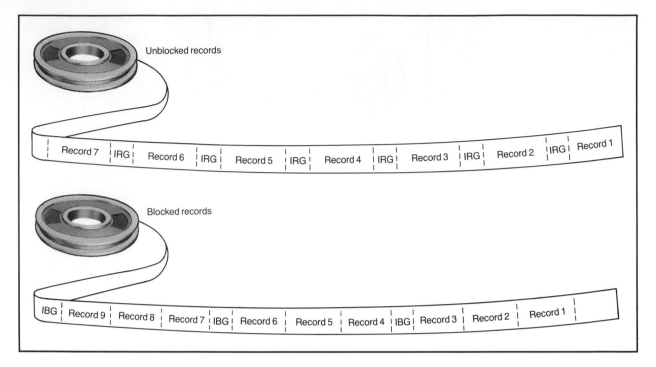

Figure 8-6.   Blocking. *Top:* Spaces between records on this tape are called interrecord gaps; these spaces are about three-fifths of an inch long. *Bottom:* When short records are grouped together into blocks of several records in order to minimize blank spaces on the tape, the spaces between blocks are called interblock gaps.

turb the magnetization and therefore data, such as static electricity, heat, and dust. The existence of such libraries suggests the first two of six advantages of tape:

▶ It can hold a lot of data in a compact space.
▶ It is portable. It is easily mailable. (Try mailing 240 boxes of punched cards, at 2,000 cards per box—the equivalent of one 2,400-foot reel of tape.)
▶ It is not expensive, costing less than $15 per reel.
▶ It can hold records of different lengths.
▶ Tape can be erased and reused.
▶ A tape reel requires use of a **write ring**—a device that fits around the hub—before it can be used, thus ensuring it will not be written on accidentally. This explains the expression "No ring, no write."

The fact that tape is an off-line storage medium, however, poses some drawbacks:

▶ It does not give fast access to data, since the tape must be manually mounted on a tape drive by an operator.

Figure 8-7. Keeping track of tapes. A tape library. This special room keeps tapes safe from dust, heat, static electricity, and other forces that might disturb the magnetization on the tapes. Tape librarians keep track of the locations of magnetic tapes.

▶ It is relatively slow. It can only access data sequentially, which means, as previously stated, that you must go through all preceding records before you come to the record you want.

▶ It can be physically damaged by dust, heat, and tearing and, of course, by people touching it or dropping it.

DIRECT ACCESS
STORAGE THE
USES OF MAGNETIC
AND OPTICAL DISK

Magnetic disk is another form of sequential access storage, but it is far better for direct access storage—which magnetic tape cannot be. A **magnetic disk** can be of two forms:

▶ Flexible or "floppy" disk
▶ Solid or hard disk

Flexible Disk

You may already be familiar with flexible disks from working with personal computers. Made of a thin film of plastic with metal oxide and encased within a sleeve of nonremovable paper or plastic (see Figure 8-8), **flexible disks,** more often spoken of as **diskettes, floppy disks,** or **"floppies,"** are used principally with microcomputers. Originally manufactured at 8 inches in diameter, they are now generally 5¼ inches in size (called **minifloppies**). Even more advanced are 3½-inch disks (**microfloppies**), which began to be widely accepted

Figure 8-8. Disks and disk drives.
Near left: The parts of a 5¼-inch
minifloppy or floppy disk. *Middle:* A
5¼-inch minifloppy shown with part
of protective jacket removed. *Bottom:*
A rigid 3½-inch microdisk, which
can fit into a shirt pocket. *Opposite
page, top:* Disk drive for 5¼-inch
floppy disk. The read/write head is
able to move across the disk, giving it
access to information anywhere on
the disk. This is known as "random
access." *Bottom:* A 5¼-inch floppy
disk drive, with cover removed to
show interior.

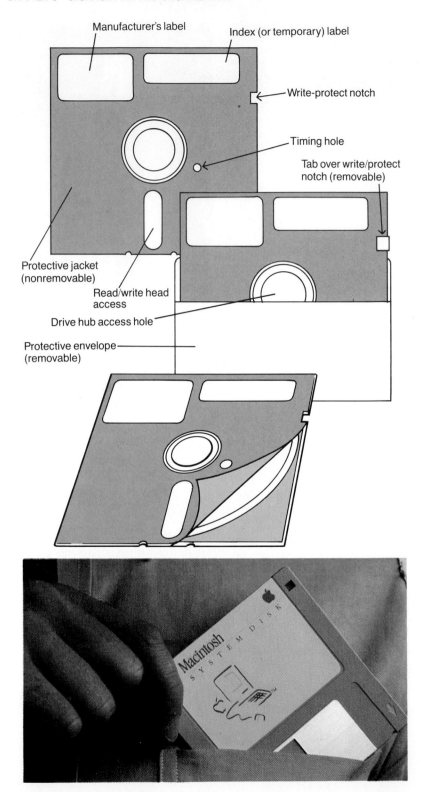

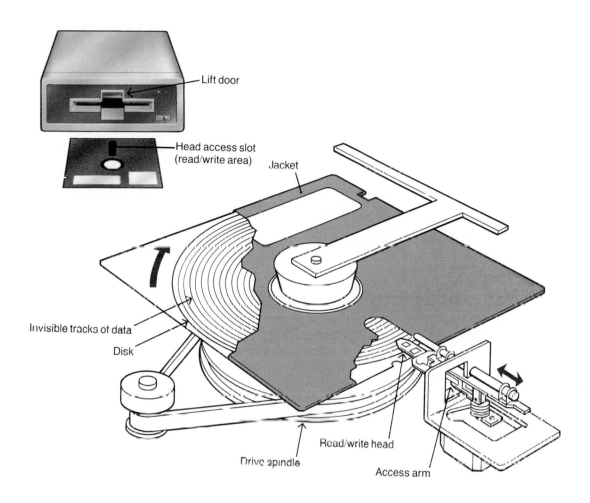

Lift door

Head access slot
(read/write area)

Jacket

Invisible tracks of data

Disk

Read/write head

Drive spindle

Access arm

with the appearance of Apple's Macintosh computer and which appear also in the IBM Personal System/2 microcomputers. Because of the hard plastic jacket—as opposed to flexible plastic liner and paper jacket—the sliding metal shutter to cover the access slot, the metal hub, and the plastic disk, microfloppies are preferable to minifloppies: They are more durable, hold more data, last longer, and operate better in the disk drive. On the horizon are even smaller diskettes such as 1.8 inch and 2.5 inch.

Flexible disks are inserted into a **disk drive** (see Figure 8-8), a mechanical machine with a spindle in it. A read/write head within the disk drive retrieves data from and records data on the disk. In a flexible disk system, the read/write head actually makes contact with the rotating disk.

Solid Disk

Made of rigid metal coated with a metal oxide, **solid disks** are seen in the following forms, as shown in Figure 8-9:

▶ As an 8- or 5¼-inch disk permanently mounted for use with a microcomputer.

▶ As a 14-inch disk also permanently mounted in a disk drive unit for use with a larger computer system. The entire unit may be removable.

▶ As stacks of 14-inch disks in a disk pack. Some disk packs are removable; others are not.

Let us first describe the hard disks that are used with microcomputers, since these have become popular and you may find yourself using them also. Then we will consider how hard disks work, for they are not simply the same as your stereo and LP record.

Hard Disk for Microcomputers

Hard disk drives use a disk formed from aluminum and coated with a magnetic recording medium. Unlike floppy disks, the hard disk drive is a **sealed data module**—it has disk, access arms, and read/write head sealed inside it, and the read/write heads, instead of riding directly on the disk, float on a cushion of air over the disk surface. The technology for the data module is commonly called **Winchester technology.** A hard disk drive for a microcomputer is shown in Figure 8-9.

Although hard disk drives may be five times more expensive than floppy disk drives, they can store far more information. Some hard disk drives can hold 100 megabytes of information—equivalent to about 2,000 pages—as opposed to half a megabyte on one 5¼-inch floppy disk. Moreover, a hard disk drive can transfer information up to ten times faster than floppy disk drives can—a fact you can appreciate if you are trying to load a lot of text into your computer for word processing or data for your electronic spreadsheet.

Disk, Disk Pack, and Disk Drive

Unlike a phonograph record, the tracks on a disk (whether flexible or hard) are not a single spiral that moves the arm from the outside to the center. Rather, as Figure 8-10 shows, they are a series of closed (concentric) circles. A typical hard disk has 200 to 800 of these tracks, which, incidentally, are invisible to the naked eye.

Data is read from or written on the disk by a disk drive unit containing an **access arm** (see Figure 8-10), which moves a read/write head over a particular track. With solid disk, the access arm

Figure 8-9. Three types of solid disks. *Top left:* Made for microcomputers, this is an example of hard disk, a 5¼-inch Seagate Technology hard disk drive. *Top right:* A sealed data module, which has disk, access arm, and read/write head sealed within it. Used with minicomputers, the entire unit is removable. *Bottom:* A disk pack being removed from a disk drive. This disk pack contains more than one disk.

HARDCARD

Adding a hard disk to a microcomputer could mean losing one of the two floppy disk drives or taking up room on one's desk with an external hard disk. One alternative is a hard disk on a 1-inch-thick card that plugs into an expansion slot in the computer. An example is the Hardcard 40 from Plus Development Corporation, which is a 42.3-megabyte hard disk on a single card that fits into an IBM PS/2 model 30, IBM PC or compatible.

does not actually touch the disk; rather, it floats above the surface, just close enough to detect the magnetized data. Sometimes this close tolerance can cause serious problems: A piece of dust, for instance, can stick to the read/write head and scratch the disk—an event known as a **head crash.** When this happens, the data can be lost and the disk is no longer usable.

Although many disk drives have only one access arm, some are constructed to accept **disk packs,** which consist of several disks assembled together, like a stack of phonograph records but with space between the disks. The space allows the access arms to move in and out, each with two read/write heads—one to read the disk surface above it, one to read the disk surface below it (see Figure 8-10). The disk pack has 11 disks with 20 recording surfaces; the top and bottom are not used because they are more apt to be damaged when the disk pack is being mounted on the disk drive. All access arms move at the same time; however, only one of the 20 read/write heads will be activated at any one time.

Access time to locate data on hard disks is 10 to 100 milliseconds (a millisecond is one-thousandth of a second), compared to 100

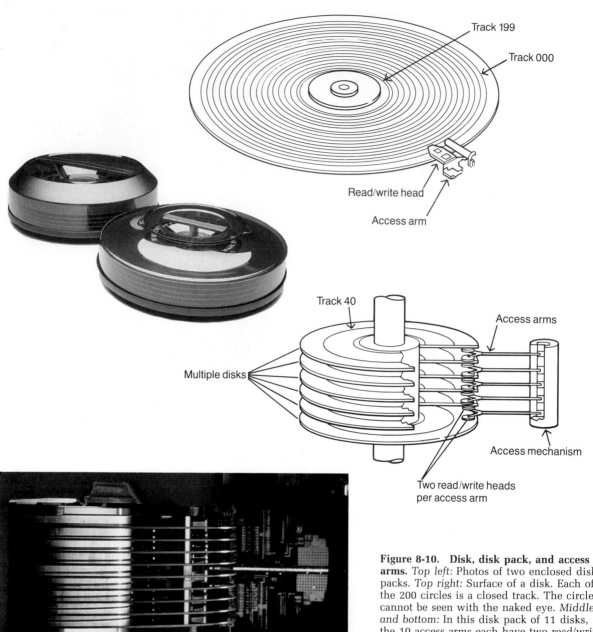

Figure 8-10.   Disk, disk pack, and access arms. *Top left:* Photos of two enclosed disk packs. *Top right:* Surface of a disk. Each of the 200 circles is a closed track. The circles cannot be seen with the naked eye. *Middle and bottom:* In this disk pack of 11 disks, the 10 access arms each have two read/write heads. The 10 access arms move simultaneously, slipping between the disks, but only one read/write head operates at one time. The top disk has data only on its bottom side, and the bottom disk has data only on its top side.

to 600 milliseconds on flexible disks. **Access time**—the time between when the computer requests data from a secondary storage device and when the transfer of data is completed—consists of four factors: seek time, head switching, rotational delay time, and data transfer.

Seek time is the time it takes an access arm to get into position over a particular track. **Head switching** is the activation of a particular read/write head over a particular track and surface. **Rotational delay time** is the time it takes for the particular record to be positioned under the read/write head. **Data transfer** is the time it takes for the transfer of data from disk track to primary storage. The average access time for most disk drives is less than 25 milliseconds—fast, but not nearly as fast as the actual processing speeds of computers, which are measured in microseconds or nanoseconds.

Disk Addressing: Two Approaches

In order for access arms to find data on a disk, the exact address of the data must be known. (This is not something you have to worry about personally; it is handled by the operating system.) There are two approaches to disk addressing:

▶ Cylinder method
▶ Sector method

Cylinder Method Used with solid disk packs, the **cylinder method** uses a vertical method of addressing, as shown in Figure 8-11. Because all access arms move simultaneously, they therefore all move to the same track (called a cylinder here) on all 20 surfaces at once. Thus, data can be addressed by the track (or cylinder) number, the disk surface, and the record number on that track on that disk surface. This is shown in Figure 8-11 (top).

Sector Method Used with flexible disks and single disks (and sometimes with multiple disks), the **sector method** divides the surface of a disk into pie-wedge-shaped sectors, as shown in Figure 8-11 (bottom). Data addresses then consist of the track number, a surface number, and a sector number of the record.

Putting Data on Disks: Benefits and Drawbacks

It might seem from the foregoing that magnetic disk has it all over magnetic tape, and indeed there are a number of advantages:

▶ Disks can be used for both sequential and direct processing.

Figure 8-11.   Methods of disk addressing. *Top:* Cylinder method of data organization. If there are 200 tracks on a single surface, there are 200 cylinders in the disk pack. *Bottom:* Sector method of data organization.

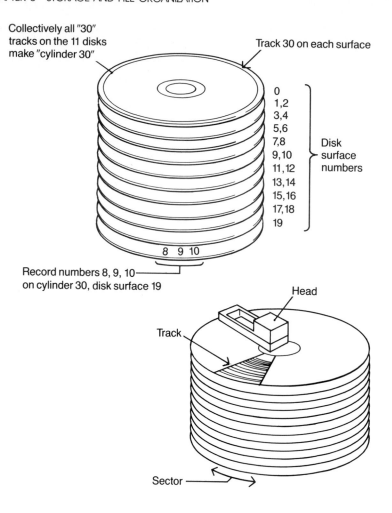

Disks can be on-line—connected directly to the CPU at all times, thereby greatly reducing access time and allowing data files to be updated immediately.

► People using disk storage can interact with stored information immediately and get rapid responses to their inquiries.

► Files stored on disk can be linked by software so that several files can be updated at once from a single transaction.

Nevertheless, there are still some disadvantages:

► Sequential processing with disk is actually slower than it is with tape for many applications.

► Disks are 25 times more expensive than tape.

Figure 8-12. A mass storage device. This IBM Mass Storage System consists of honeycomblike cells, each of which holds a cartridge 2 inches in diameter by 4 inches long and with a 771-inch long strip of magnetic tape. A single cartridge can store 50 million bytes.

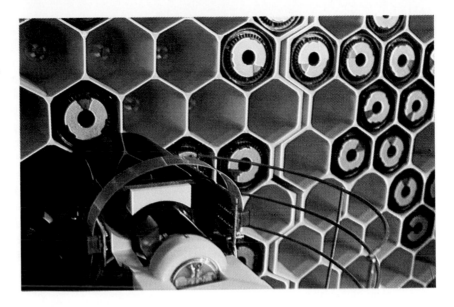

▶ When files are updated on disks, the original files are destroyed—which is not the case with tape. (A tape and new updates will be merged to create a new tape, but the old tape is kept unchanged.)

▶ Tapes are more secure than disks from access by unauthorized persons because they are off-line storage.

MASS STORAGE

Mass storage devices combine the low-cost, high-capacity advantages of magnetic tape with the on-line advantages of magnetic disk, yet the technology resembles neither. As Figure 8-12 shows, one type of **mass storage device** consists of honeycombed storage compartments containing data cartridges.

Storage is relatively slow—retrieval takes seconds rather than milliseconds—because it takes a few seconds for the device to find the particular cartridge called for by the CPU and another few seconds to transfer data from the mass storage device to magnetic disk and thence to the CPU. However, mass storage is still faster than the time required to mount a tape reel on a tape drive. Moreover, storage capacity is tremendous: The IBM 3850, for instance, can store the equivalent of a library of 400,000 volumes. This kind of storage is only required, however, for applications such as those that might be conceived by the Census Bureau or the Internal Revenue Service, organizations that deal with millions of files.

Another, faster kind of storage consists of optical disks, as explained below.

OPTICAL DISKS

REVOLUTION

IN STORAGE

Figure 8-13.   Optical disk storage.
This 4¾-inch compact disk can store
the equivalent of 250,000 pages of
typewritten information.

THE USES OF OPTICAL DISK: LOCATING THE "NIGHT STALKER"

One of the most interesting [optical disk] applications is at the California Department of Justice in Sacramento, where a large fingerprint identification system was installed early [in 1985]. In the massive effort to locate the serial killer dubbed the "Night Stalker," fingerprints from 390,000 people were on optical disk. It took only 3½ minutes to locate the alleged murderer's prints and he was arrested a few hours later.

When the Night Stalker case was run on the system, only 28 of a planned 114 optical disk drives had been installed. Nevertheless, the system performed so well that similar systems costing $50 million each have been ordered by the counties of Los Angeles and San Bernardino in California, and the city of Calgary in Canada. A smaller system has been in operation by the Alaska State Police for almost two years.

—Edward S. Rothchild, *Datamation*

Perhaps the most exciting development in external storage, as we suggested in the case study at the beginning of the chapter, is **optical disk** technology, which was inspired by the videodisk recordings of audiovisual performances for playback on television—that is, laser recording systems. In this technology, a light beam burns tiny pits or holes into the surface of an aluminum disk; the presence of a hole represents a 1 bit, the absence of a hole represents a 0 bit. To read the data, a laser scans these areas and sends the data to a computer chip for conversion. At present, optical disks appear in six diameters: 3½, 4¾, 5¼, 8, 12, and 14 inches. An optical disk offers far more storage capacity than a floppy—500 megabytes on a single disk.

The two principal kinds of optical disks are read-only and write-once disks. They are used in the same way, but they are manufactured differently. The leading kind of read-only disks, which are manufactured by pressing, like long-playing records, are **CD-ROMs,** which stands for "compact disk—read-only memory"; these consist of molded plastic disks on which data is stored in microscopic pits, which are later read or accessed by a laser scanner. CD-ROMs cannot be written on or changed by the user. Write-once disks consist of metal-film disks that are marked or "burned in" by lasers in such a way that they are difficult or impossible to undo. Once written, however, although data cannot be erased, it can be read many times without deterioration. Thus, the drives are known as **WORM drives** for "write once, read many."

The advantages of optical disks are enormous:

▶ They can store an awesome amount of data—gigabytes and even terabytes (one trillion bytes) of data can be stored in a single optical drive. Indeed, a 4¾-inch disk (Figure 8-13) can store the equivalent of 250,000 *pages* of typewritten information. One 14-inch disk can replace 50 reels of standard magnetic tape.

▶ Costs are relatively low: Gigabytes of data on a CD-ROM can be made accessible on a personal computer for less than $1,000.

▶ The error rate is lower than that for magnetic disks.

▶ Not only data, but text, music, speech, animation, and even moving pictures can be stored on a disk.

With such advantages, small wonder that both the Internal Revenue Service and the Library of Congress are taking a hard look at optical disk technology. By 1991, according to one report, optical disks are expected to capture 20% of the $40 billion market for computer storage devices.

Yet there are disadvantages:

▶ Optical disks have not been accepted yet—partly because no standard size has been developed.

▶ Read-only disks, such as CD-ROMs, can only be read from; they cannot be written on. Thus, the user has access only to data that was imprinted at the factory.

▶ Write-once disks by definition can be written to only once—again, the data is often imprinted at the factory, although users may also write their own data—and thus such disks are not reusable, the way magnetic disk and tape are.

FUTURE STORAGE

ALTERABLE OPTICAL

DISKS AND

OTHER MARVELS

Write-once optical disks have the advantages of capacity, low cost, ruggedness, and transportability. However, once information has been laser-burned as a hole on the disk, it is present forever. Such permanence is often desirable, but many times you might want to alter the data. Fortunately, **erasable** or **alterable** optical disks have become available, both for mainframes and for personal computers. Such disks have the advantages we just cited, yet are easily alterable.

Disks may also continue to shrink in size. Eastman Kodak, for instance, has developed a 1.85-inch floppy disk for storing electronic still images. The 800K disk can store up to 50 images.

Research is also proceeding on developing chip-mounted devices—that is, devices made of solid-state electronic chips—for secondary storage. One of these is the charged couple device, which, it is hoped, will be fast, compact, and cheap to produce. A disadvantage, however, is that it is volatile—it loses data when the power is turned off.

FILE ORGANIZATION

Whatever kind of machines or media are used to store data, there must be some way of putting that data in order. Let us consider how this is done.

Three Ways to Organize Files

There are two basic types of files: master and transaction.

▶ A **master file** is a complete file containing all records current up to the last update.

▶ A **transaction file** is a file containing *recent* changes to records that will be used to update the master file.

There are three ways in which these types of files may be organized:

► Sequential files

► Direct files

► Index sequential files

There is also a fourth way of organizing files—by data base filing system—but, as mentioned, we shall describe this later. Here we will look at the first three.

Sequential File Organization

In **sequential file organization,** files are stored one after another in ascending or descending order, as determined by their record keys. A **key** is a particular field of a record that is usually chosen as an identifier of that record. The key may be a number, such as your social security number—this is a very common identifier—or it may be alphabetic, such as your last name. To find a record in a sequential file, the computer starts at the beginning of the file and checks each record's key until it finds the one you want.

The most commonly used media for sequential files is magnetic tape, although magnetic disk and punched cards are also used. Sequential files are often used for applications that require periodic updates of a large number of records—that is, where updates are *batched* together for processing—such as payroll, billing, and preparation of customer accounts. At Atlantic-Pacific Bank, for instance, it is used to update customer loans.

To update a sequential file, the old master file and the transaction file are input together as data, along with an update program. The result, as Figure 8-14 shows, is a new master file. The old master file and transaction file are kept as backups in case the system fails and the new master file has to be recreated.

The advantages of sequential file processing are several:

► It is well suited to a number of business applications, such as payroll and billing.

Figure 8-14. Sequential file organization. Sequential updating of a magazine subscription list. Each key here represents an entire subscriber's magazine label—name, address, zip code, and date of expiration. The old master file consists of records of all the subscribers until last month, when subscription changes came in. The changes are reflected in the transaction file and consist of additions (new subscribers), deletions (cancellations or expirations), and revisions (changes of address, usually). Records for both transaction file and master file must be in order by key, perhaps arranged from low numbers to high, before the updating can be done. (This means the numbers on the transaction tape actually have to be presorted.) During processing, the computer reads records from the transaction and master files and takes action on whichever of the two keys is lower in number. If the master file record key is lower, there is no change. If the master file record key is higher, the transaction is added to the master file. If the keys are the same, the record in the master file should be revised or deleted. As the processing proceeds, a new master file is produced that incorporates all the changes from the transaction file. An error report is also produced that calls attention to deletions and revisions of names that do not exist or additions that were already in the master file—perhaps because of mistakes by magazine subscription agencies. The updated master file is used to produce new subscription labels every month, in time for the magazine's latest mailing.

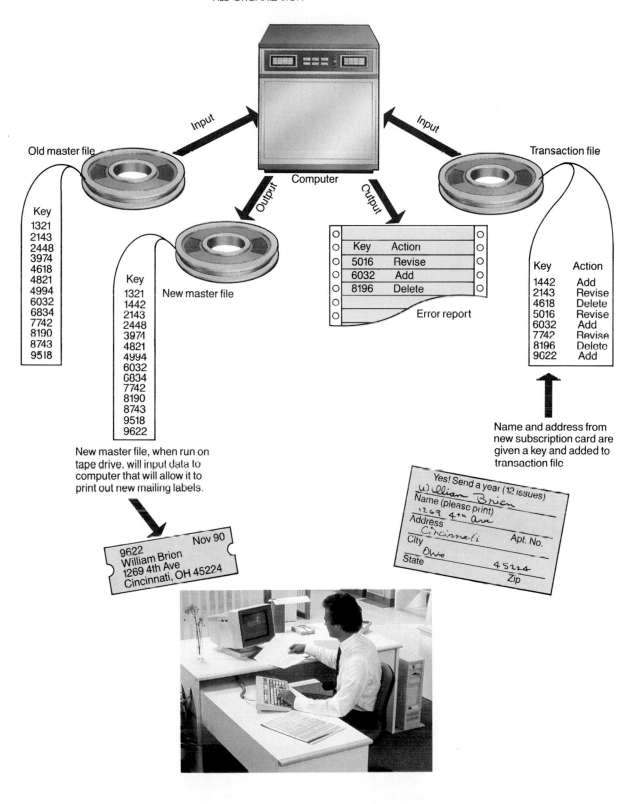

Input

Old master file

Transaction file

Computer

Input

Output

Output

Key	
1321	
2143	
2448	
3974	
4618	
4821	
4994	
6032	
6834	
7742	
8190	
8743	
9518	

New master file

Key	
1321	
1442	
2143	
2448	
3974	
4821	
4994	
6032	
6834	
7742	
8190	
8743	
9518	
9622	

Key	Action
5016	Revise
6032	Add
8196	Delete

Error report

Key	Action
1442	Add
2143	Revise
4618	Delete
5016	Revise
6032	Add
7742	Revise
8196	Delete
9622	Add

Name and address from
new subscription card are
given a key and added to
transaction file

New master file, when run on
tape drive, will input data to
computer that will allow it to
print out new mailing labels.

9622   Nov 90
William Brien
1269 4th Ave
Cincinnati, OH 45224

Yes! Send a year (12 issues)
William Brien
Name (please print)
1269 4th Ave
Address
Cincinnati   Apt. No.
City
Ohio
State   45224
Zip

► It is the best kind of file organization for uses in which there are frequent and large updates.

► It can use magnetic tape, which is inexpensive and has large storage capacity.

But there are some disadvantages:

► The entire master file must be read to update it—even if only the very last record on the file needs to be changed.

► If there is an unanticipated inquiry, it is difficult to locate a particular record.

Direct File Organization

If the number of records to be updated is small and if updated transactions arrive irregularly, direct access processing is better than sequential processing, for this method allows you to update your files whenever you want and get a status report whenever you want that will be as up to date as your last transaction.

With **direct file organization,** you can go directly to the record you want. You do not have to sequence files by key nor do the records need to be stored one after the other; they can be distributed in seemingly random fashion. Direct file organization requires, however, that the data be stored on a direct access storage device such as a magnetic disk. In addition, you must, of course, have a way of finding the records, which means that there must be a scheme for maintaining the addresses of all the records.

There are two ways of maintaining addresses for direct file organization:

► Directory approach
► Transformation approach

The Directory Approach In the **directory approach** to addressing, every time data is stored on the direct access storage device an entry is made automatically into a table called the **directory.** The directory is located on the storage medium and records reference numbers—which are keys for the records stored on the disk—and their corresponding storage addresses, which are the locations of the complete record for each key. When you want to find a particular record, the computer finds that record's key in the directory and then the address corresponding to that key.

The Transformation Approach In the **transformation approach** (also called *indirect addressing*) to direct file organization, some arithmetic calculation is used with the key field, which produces the address of the desired record. For example, suppose the direct access storage device has a three-digit storage address and suppose the key to the record you want is a particular year. One transformation process would be to take the year, divide it by the closest prime number, and save only the remainder. The record corresponding to that year will be stored in an address equal to this remainder plus 1.

Although these methods of finding a record sound complicated, they have some important benefits. The advantages of direct file organization are:

▶ Transactions can be used to update master files directly from terminals. There is no need to batch transactions, as in sequential file processing.

▶ Several files can be updated simultaneously.

But there are some drawbacks:

▶ Because the updating is done on the original file, the previous master file is lost. Therefore, there is no back-up master file available in case something goes wrong.

▶ More users have access to the master file through their terminals. Consequently, there is a greater chance of data being deliberately or accidentally altered—so information security is reduced.

Index Sequential File Organization

The above two kinds of file organization—sequential and direct—clearly have their place. As we mentioned, sequential is better when a master file needs periodic updates with a relatively large volume of alterations. Direct is better if there are irregular updates and the volume of updates is small.

In some cases, however, file updates can be batched, but there is an ongoing need to get to records rapidly for data inquiries. At Atlantic-Pacific Bank, for instance, the daily deposits are batched to create a transaction file, which is then used at the end of the banking day to update the master file of checking-account balances. However, throughout the day, customers occasionally want to know what their account balances are. Although a sequential file organization would be suitable for updating account balances, it would be too inefficient to allow tellers to search for an individual depositor's account balance. The answer: index sequential file organization.

A compromise between sequential and direct, **index sequential file organization** stores records in a file in sequential order, but the file also contains an index. The index lists the key to each record stored and the corresponding disk address for that record. The index works somewhat like the index in the back of a book. For instance, to find the word *COBOL*, you could start at page 1 and read until you came to the word *COBOL*—that would be sequential processing. Or you could go to the back of the book to the index and look up *COBOL*

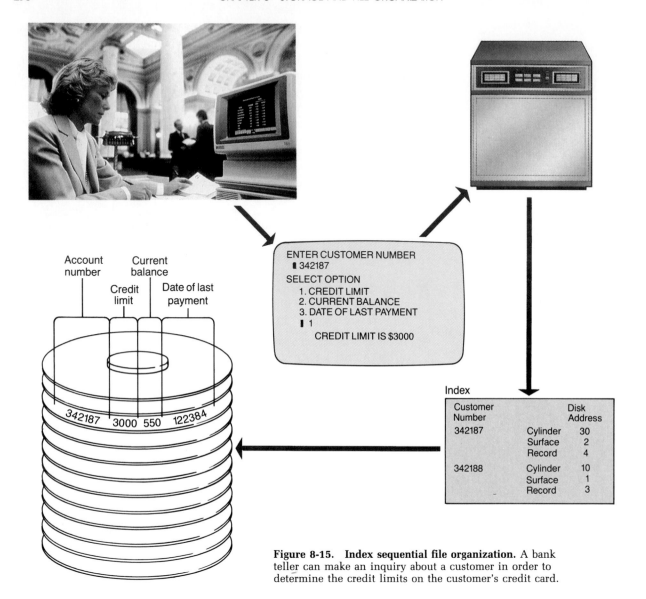

Figure 8-15.   Index sequential file organization. A bank
teller can make an inquiry about a customer in order to
determine the credit limits on the customer's credit card.

and the page number given and then go to the right place. In much
the same way, the computer can use an index sequential file organization to locate records in an index sequential file. A further example of how this works is given in Figure 8-15.

The advantages of index sequential file organization are as follows:

▶ It allows efficient processing of large batch updates.

▶ It permits you to retrieve data quickly and efficiently.

The disadvantages are:

► The method makes less efficient use of storage than other methods.

► Access to particular records is slower than it is with direct file organization.

► The hardware and software required to carry out this method are more expensive than that required for other methods.

ON TO THE INFORMATION WAREHOUSE

This discussion of secondary storage may seem unduly technical for what might be useful in your career. However, as we will see in the next chapter, it is the development of computer storage that has permitted one of the most fascinating information resources available to you—huge data bases, the equivalent of warehouses of information that can be manipulated for many different uses.

SUMMARY

► The soaring cost of managing paper documents is an important reason for using electronic storage. The availability of such storage can also create huge data bases that can be manipulated for many purposes.

► **Secondary storage,** also known as **external storage** or **auxiliary storage,** is storage outside the computer itself. It is indispensable because it is unlikely that all the records of a large corporation, for example, could be stored inside the computer itself (called **primary storage** or **internal storage**).

► Although primary storage can process data faster, secondary storage has several advantages: (1) It is more economical. (2) It has greater storage capacity. (3) The data it stores is generally safe from tampering and natural hazards.

► There are two types of secondary storage: *direct access* and *sequential access.* In order of speed and cost of use, after primary storage—which is fastest, most limited, and most expensive of the three types of storage—is **direct access storage. Sequential access storage** is the slowest form of storage, but it has unlimited capacity and is the least expensive.

► Direct access storage requires an input/output device. A **direct access storage device (DASD)** is directly connected to the CPU, thereby keeping the stored data **on-line** (available to the CPU at all times). A magnetic disk is an example of direct access storage media.

► Sequential access storage is **off-line** (the data is not accessible to the CPU until it has been loaded onto an input device). Examples of sequential access storage media are a reel of magnetic tape and a stack of punched cards.

► **Magnetic tape,** the most common medium for sequential access storage, consists of plastic tape such as that on reel-to-reel tape recorders. The devices that run the tapes are called **magnetic tape drives** or **magnetic tape units.** These machines consist of two reels—a **supply reel** and a **take-up reel**—plus a **read/write head** and an **erase head. Read** means to retrieve data from and **write** means to record data on. The read/write head reads magnetized areas on the tape—which represent data—converts them into electrical signals, and sends them to the CPU. Read/write heads also write, or record, data on the tape from the CPU. Old data on the tape may be erased using the erase head.

► In referring to data, certain terms are used: A **character** is a letter, number, or special symbol. A **field** is made up of one or more characters and contains an item of data. A **record** is a collection of related fields. A **file** is a collection of related records. A **data base** is a collection of interrelated data, a systematic or structured organization of files available for central access and retrieval.

▶ Data is represented on tape by invisible magnetized spots, the presence or absence of a spot corresponding to a 1 or 0 bit. The most common way of organizing data is a by a 9-track code.

▶ When data is written onto a tape, it is usually divided into logical records. Spaces are usually left between records, and these are called **interrecord gaps (IRGs).** A typical space is three-fifths of an inch long. If each record is short, there will be many interrecord gaps, which means that much of the tape will be blank. To save space, the records can be pulled together and the interrecord gaps can be replaced by **interblock gaps (IBGs),** which are gaps between blocks of records. **Blocking** is the activity of putting records together into blocks.

▶ Reels of magnetic tape are often maintained in **tape libraries,** which are special rooms designed to protect tapes from forces that might disturb the magnetization, such as static electricity, heat, and dust.

▶ Magnetic tape has five advantages: (1) It can hold a lot of data in a compact space. (2) It is portable and easily mailable. (3) It is inexpensive. (4) It can hold records of different lengths. (5) It can be erased and reused. Because tape is an off-line storage medium, it poses some drawbacks: (1) It does not provide fast access to data because the reel must be manually mounted. (2) It is relatively slow because it can only access data sequentially. (3) It can be physically damaged by dust, heat, tearing, and by people touching or dropping it.

▶ A tape reel requires use of a **write ring**—a device that fits around the hub—before it can be used, thus ensuring it will not be written on accidentally. This explains the expression ''No ring, no write.''

▶ **Magnetic disk** is generally used for direct access storage, and it can be either flexible (''floppy'') or solid (hard).

▶ **Flexible disks**—also called **diskettes, floppy disks,** or **''floppies''**—are made of plastic and encased within a nonremovable plastic jacket. They are used principally with microcomputers. They are usually 5¼ inches in size **(minifloppies)** or 3¼ inches **(microfloppies).** Flexible disks are inserted into a **disk drive,** where a read/write head contacts the rotating disk and retrieves data from and also records data on the disk.

▶ **Solid disks** are made of rigid metal and can be (1) an 8- or 5¼-inch disk permanently mounted for use with a microcomputer, (2) a 14-inch disk permanently mounted in a disk drive for use with a larger computer system, or (3) a stack of 14-inch disks in a disk pack.

▶ A hard disk drive is a **sealed data module**—it has disk, access arms, and read/write head sealed inside it, and the read/write head floats on a cushion of air over the disk surface. The technology for the data module is commonly called **Winchester technology.** Hard disk drives are more expensive than floppy disk drives and are more sensitive to environmental conditions, but they can store more information and transfer information faster.

▶ Data is read from or written on the disk by a drive unit containing an **access arm,** which moves a read/write head over, not on, a particular track (one of a number of concentric circles) on the disk. If something sticks to the read/write head—dust, for example—it may scratch the disk and cause a **head crash,** ruining the disk and losing the data.

▶ Many disk drives have only one access arm, but some can accept **disk packs,** which consist of several disks assembled together with space between them. The spaces accommodate a series of access arms, each with two read/write heads—one to read the disk surface above it and one to read the surface below it.

▶ **Access time** is the time between when the computer requests data from a secondary storage device and when the transfer of data is completed. It consists of four factors: (1) seek time, (2) head switching, (3) rotational delay, and (4) data transfer.

▶ **Seek time** is the time it takes an access arm to get into position over a particular track. **Head switching** is the activation of a particular read/write head over a particular track and surface. **Rotational delay time** is the time it takes for the particular record to be positioned under the read/write head. **Data transfer** is the time it takes for transfer of data from disk track to primary storage.

▶ For access arms to find data on a disk, the exact address of the data must be known. The two approaches to disk addressing are (1) the cylinder method and (2) the sector method. The **cylinder method** is used with solid disk packs; it employs a vertical method of addressing. The **sector method** is used with flexible disks and, generally, with single disks; it divides the surface of a disk into pie-wedge-shaped sectors.

▶ Magnetic disks have several advantages: (1) They can be used for both sequential and direct processing. (2) They can be on-line, thereby reducing access time and allowing immediate file updating. (3) People using disk storage can interact with stored information immediately and get rapid responses. (4) Files stored on disk can be linked by software. The disadvantages include: (1) Sequential processing with disk is usually slower than it is with tape. (2) Disks are more expensive than tape. (3) When files are updated on disks, the original files are destroyed, which is not the case with tape. (4) Tapes are more secure than disks from unauthorized access because they are off-line storage.

▶ **Mass storage devices** use their own technology to combine the low-cost, high-capacity advantages of magnetic tape with the on-line advantages of magnetic disk. They consist of honeycombed storage compartments containing data cartridges. These devices are slower than disk but faster than tape, and they have tremendous storage capacity.

▶ **Optical disk** technology was inspired by the videodisk recordings of audiovisual performances for playback on television. A light beam burns tiny holes into the surface of an aluminum disk; the presence of a hole represents a 1 bit, the absence of a hole represents a 0 bit. To read the data, a laser scans these areas and sends the data to a computer chip for conversion. At present, optical disks appear in six diameters: 3½, 4¾, 5¼, 8, 12, and 14 inches.

▶ The two principal kinds of optical disks are readonly and write-once disks. The leading kind of readonly disks, which are manufactured by pressing, like long-playing records, are **CD-ROMs,** which stands for "compact disk—read-only memory." These consist of molded plastic disks on which data is stored in microscopic pits, which are later read or accessed by a laser scanner. CD-ROMs cannot be written on or changed by the user. Write-once disks consist of metal-film disks that are marked or "burned in" by lasers in such a way that they are difficult or impossible to undo. Once written, however, although data cannot be erased, it can be read many times without deterioration. Thus, the drives are known as **WORM drives** for "write once, read many."

▶ The advantages of optical disks are as follows: (1) They can store gigabytes and even terabytes (one trillion bytes) of data in a single optical drive. (2) Costs are relatively low. (3) The error rate is lower than that for magnetic disks. (4) Not only data, but text, music, speech, animation, and even moving pictures can be stored on a disk. The disadvantages are: (1) Optical disks have not been accepted yet—

partly because no standard size has been developed. (2) Read-only disks, such as CD-ROMs, can only be read from; they cannot be written on. Thus, the user has access only to data that was imprinted at the factory. (3) Write-once disks by definition can be written to only once and thus such disks are not reusable, the way magnetic disk and tape are.

▶ It is expected that **erasable** or **alterable** optical disks will soon be available, which would have the advantages cited yet be easily alterable.

▶ One solid-state electronic chip-mounted device being developed for secondary storage is the charged couple device.

▶ Files are usually organized. There are two types of files and three ways of organizing them. A **master file** is a complete file containing all current records. A **transaction file** contains recent changes to records that will be used to update the master file. These files can be organized sequentially, directly, or sequentially with an index.

▶ With **sequential file organization,** files are stored one after another in ascending or descending order, as determined by their record keys. A **key** is a particular field of a record that is usually chosen as an identifier of that record. It can be numeric or alphabetic, and it allows the computer to find the file you want. Magnetic tape is generally used for sequential files. This type of file is commonly used for applications that require periodic updates of a large number of records. Sequential files have several advantages: (1) They are well suited to many business applications. (2) They are the best kind of file organization where frequent and large updates are necessary. (3) They can use magnetic tape, which is inexpensive and has large storage capacity. Their disadvantages include: (1) The entire master file must be read to update a sequential file. (2) Records must be carefully sequenced according to their keys, which is time-consuming. (3) When there is an unanticipated inquiry, it is difficult to locate a particular record.

▶ **Direct file organization** is used when the number of records needing to be updated is small and when updated transactions arrive irregularly. In direct file organization, files are not sequenced by key or stored one after the other; distribution can be random, and one can go directly to the record one wants. However, data must be stored on a direct access storage device such as a magnetic disk pack, and there must be some system for maintaining the address of all the records. This can be done in two ways: by directory approach or by transformation approach.

▶ The **directory approach** uses a table called a **directory** to record entries that are automatically made in the table every time data is stored on the direct access storage device. The directory is on the storage medium, and it records reference numbers (keys) and corresponding storage addresses. The computer uses the record's key in the directory to find the stored file you want.

▶ The **transformation approach** to direct file organization uses some arithmetic calculation with the key field to produce the address of the desired record.

▶ Direct file organization has some advantages: (1) Transactions can be used to update master files directly from terminals. (2) Several files can be updated simultaneously. The disadvantages include: (1) Because the updating is done on the original file, the previous master file is lost. (2) Because more users have access to the master file through their terminals, there is a greater chance that data might be altered.

▶ **Index sequential file organization** is a compromise between sequential and direct file organization. It stores files in sequential order, but the file also contains an index that lists the key to each record stored and the corresponding disk address for that record. Its advantages include: (1) It allows efficient processing of large batch updates. (2) It can retrieve data quickly and efficiently. This system also has several disadvantages: (1) It makes less efficient use of storage than other methods because the index must also be stored. (2) Access to particular records is slower than it is with direct file organization. (3) The necessary hardware and software are more expensive than those required for other methods.

KEY TERMS

REVIEW QUESTIONS

1. How does secondary storage differ from primary storage? What advantages does it offer?
2. Compare sequential access storage to direct access storage. What types of technology does each type of storage use? What are the advantages and disadvantages of each?
3. How is data represented on tape?
4. What is meant by the term *blocking*?
5. Describe how a disk pack operates.
6. What is mass storage?
7. Describe one of the three methods of file organization.
8. Describe how a CD-ROM disk operates.

CASE PROBLEMS

Case 8-1: Bits and Bites—Computers in Restaurants

Because people like to eat—and to eat out, when they can afford it—the food service industry is expanding. McDonald's opens 500 new restaurants every year, and Kentucky Fried Chicken and Burger King continue to expand throughout the world. Adults eat out on the average of three times a week and would like to eat out more, and so thousands of small-business people are encouraged to start up new eateries. The reasons are that starting a restaurant does not take a lot of capital, running one does not require an advanced degree, and the market potential is enormous. Still, the restaurant business is a perilous one, and the failure rate is extremely high.

One restaurant owner who has done well is former Washington Redskins' football star Joe Theismann, who uses a computer to help in managing his restaurant in Bailey's Crossroads, Virginia. The multi-user microcomputer is used by five employees, including the restaurant manager, the kitchen manager, and the office manager. Besides recording several thousand transactions, averaging about $20 each, in the general ledger each week, the management has found the computer useful for keeping track of which areas of sales—food and beverage—are most profitable, what method of payment customers are using (cash or credit card), and variables such as the cost of goods to help establish pricing. The restaurant seats 200 patrons.

Your assignment: Suppose you are installing a computer system for a chain of 20 restaurants. For this you may need something larger than a microcomputer, although you could have a microcomputer in each restaurant as a terminal connected via telephone lines to the central computer. As is the case with Joe Theismann, you will be recording thousands of transactions and will be analyzing them for different purposes. Consider the pros and cons of the different storage systems discussed in this chapter as applied to your needs.

Case 8-2: A Little Insurance—Hard Disk versus Floppy Disk

Many microcomputer users who convert to hard disk do not want to go back to floppies. Hard disk is many times faster, makes much more data available, and in other ways is much more convenient (no more searching through file boxes for floppy disks, for example). There are some disadvantages, however. Some software cannot be put on hard disk by any legal means. In addition, you have to consider backing up the information that is on hard disk, since even hard disk drives can fail. The backup might consist of a floppy disk or reel-to-reel tape, the kind that, once you get them running, just keep on going; they do not start and stop like regular magnetic tape drives.

Your assignment: As an independent insurance agent, you would find a microcomputer a definite asset—and not just to remind you of clients' birthdays. You could use it to store data on clients, policy changes, payment dates, and so on. You could also use a spreadsheet to show prospective clients the various kinds of policy options. Once you build your business to a certain level, you may find it a headache to have to keep track of a lot of floppy disks. On the other hand, even with a hard disk, you may find yourself using floppies for back-up purposes, because risking failure of your hard disk is risking loss of your business. Discuss whether or not you ought to buy a hard disk system for your business.

Chapter 9

DATA BASE MANAGEMENT SYSTEMS: FACTS EVERY WHICH WAY

You are going through your wallet, sorting out pieces of paper, when you come across a telephone number with no name attached to it. Another slip of paper has an address with no name. Whose are these? Of course, you could call or write, but perhaps you are too embarrassed to.

Maybe, however, you could find out by visiting a telephone company office and looking through a so-called reverse telephone directory, which lists telephone numbers in numerical order, followed by the subscribers' names. Or you could go by the local registrar of voters and look at some precinct voting lists, which list addresses first, followed by the residents' names.

These notions suggest what makes data bases valuable: they make it possible for you to find and sort information in different ways. When you step up to an automatic teller machine at Atlantic Pacific Bank, for instance, you find that you can look up how much money you have in your checking account just by pushing a few buttons; a teller in any branch of the bank can find out the same thing just by keying in your checking-account number. A much more sophisticated kind of model is described in the box on the next page.

DATA BASES

WHAT THEY ARE,

WHY WE NEED THEM

You were introduced to microcomputer data bases back in Chapter 3, with dBase III Plus. In this chapter, we will describe data bases not only for microcomputers but also for minicomputers and mainframes, and describe both in considerably more detail.

Even if you were born years before computers became common, you have been using data bases for years: telephone books, cookbooks, directories, encyclopedias. The difference is that these data bases have not been *computerized*. When we use the term **data base**, then, we mean a collection of related data that can be structured or organized in various ways to support the wide variety of processing and retrieval needs of organizations and individuals.

285

CASE STUDY: DATA BASE

Physician Offers Preview of Computers in Office Practice

Computerized data bases are helpful not only in business, but also in many other professions. The following shows a model being used by a Palo Alto, California, physician in conjunction with Stanford University Hospital.

Dr. Andrew Newman doesn't pretend to be clairvoyant, but he has a pretty good idea of what the practice of medicine will be like in the year 2000—he's already practicing medicine this way in his office at 1101 Welch Rd., Palo Alto.

Newman can do his part in admitting patients to the hospital or having them discharged without leaving his office. He can also find out the precise status of all of his patients in the hospital, including the types and amounts of medication they have received in the past few hours and whether they've been moved to a different bed during the night. Soon, he'll be able to get the results of laboratory tests just as easily.

The secret is Newman's computer, and the fact that he's hooked up to the [Stanford University Hospital] medical information system. That gives him instant access to all of the hospital records on his patients. That information could take hours, or even days, to track down through the usual methods of leafing through written records. . . .

"My office is a prototype," Newman said. "Once the system is up and running we're going to try to have every single physician in town get some type of computer and hook into the system."

Those who do will enormously simplify their own record-keeping and their dealings with hospital records, Newman said. A physician will have all the medical information on a patient, plus all the necessary insurance information and data on Medicare or MediCal, all available within seconds on the computer screen.

When the patient is discharged from the hospital, all the information on medication that was administered in the hospital and given to the patient on discharge will be readily available to the physician. . . .

Besides all the advantages of instant information, Newman said, "there are other tremendous benefits" provided by computers.

One such benefit will be the ability to tap into the National Library of Medicine and get information in minutes that would require hours of painstaking research in a printed library.

To show how that service works, Newman decided to check on all references in the national library to hyperbaric oxygen therapy that have been published since 1980. He found 1,354 references to hyperbaric, 33,748 to oxygen and 306,393 to therapy—but only 355 to all three words, hyperbaric oxygen therapy.

It's easy to break those references down even further, he noted, by searching through titles. Then a magazine article or professional document can be called up on the computer screen to provide detailed and specific information.

Another spinoff benefit of computerized medicine is what Newman calls the "business aspect." Instead of having someone spend half an hour on the telephone trying to track down insurance information on a patient for billing, as happens frequently now, physicians will be able to look at the hospital data base and find all the relevant information in about one minute. . . .

Stanford considers the system as a model that it hopes will be in widespread use at other medical institutions in the future.

The system will also make it possible for people to carry small cards with all their basic medical information. Those cards can be put into computers at hospitals around the country and will provide major medical diagnoses, pictures of chest X-rays, electrocardiograms, etc. . . .

—Ron Goben, *Stanford University Campus Report*

If you are contemplating a career in organizational life, consider what, in fact, an organization *is*: In addition to people, equipment, and buildings, it is a specialized collection of information—of production and marketing secrets, contacts, money owed, and so on. Small wonder, therefore, that a hurricane or fire wiping out a bank's files could put that company out of business in a matter of days, even hours. And, conversely, perhaps we can see why it is important to understand how to get access to this information: Knowledge is power, and a person who can lay hands on information in an organization's files is in a more competitive position.

These, then, are the reasons for learning about data base management: Learning how to manage data is part of what being a manager or professional is. Knowing how a data base is designed will enable you to understand who gets access to what information and how that information is collected. It will also allow you to converse with data processing people so that you can convey exactly what you want.

Let us begin to examine what data bases are all about.

From Files to Data Bases

At one university, it was determined that there were 75 separate collections of files containing data on students: data on admissions, scholarships, registration, residence halls, fraternities, and so on. It was possible, in other words, for information on one student to be in 75 different places, and the data was stored in different arrangements or formats.

This suggests why there was a need for data bases: Whenever a specific requirement arose, a file was created. Each new application required a new file, but none of them were integrated or linked together. This points up the drawback of what has been called *file processing* as opposed to data base management.

The disadvantages of traditional file processing are as follows:

▶ **Data redundancy:** The same data elements appeared in many different files and often in different formats, which made updating files time-consuming.

▶ **No data integrity:** Because it was difficult to update data, frequently some files were not updated, so the data lacked "integrity" or accuracy. For instance, a person's address might be up to date in one file but not in another.

▶ **Unintegrated data:** With data spread around in different files and not linked together, the data was not as useful. One file would have only the data for which the file was created—and no other kind of data. For instance, a person's credit rating might be terrific in one file but awful in another. Updating, then, would have to be done in more than one file.

▶ **Program and file dependence:** Different programs might be written, each with its own files. With different files already established in different arrangements or formats (for example, some with a student's school address first, some with home address first), programmers were unable to develop new programs because the file formats already dictated the kind of programming required—and different programs for different files. It might seem better to tear all the files and programs down and start over with one file format for all files and one program—a highly expensive task in the short run, though probably desirable in the long run.

Because of all these drawbacks, traditional file processing was a hindrance both to users and programmers. As information became a more valued commodity, so also became the arrangements for gaining access to it and manipulating it. Enter the concept of data base.

Creating Data Bases: The Early Difficulties

Creating a *data base*—which we may briefly define as a computerized, nonredundant collection of logically related records or files—allowed records that were previously stored in independent files throughout an organization to be consolidated as a common pool of data, to which access could be gained by many different application programs. In the early 1960s, however, when data base concepts were first developed to replace file processing, creating integrated files was a difficult problem, for two reasons:

▶ **Organizational problems:** Information is power, and no one likes to give up power. However, the concept of data base meant that data that was previously the exclusive property of one department had to be shared with other departments. This requirement demanded cooperation by all users, as well as care on the part of the people designing the data base, who had to define input data in a way that was useful to people in all departments.

▶ **Technical problems:** As the organizational problems suggest, converting and integrating several old files into one single integrated file posed some technical problems—not the least of which was that this one file was much, much larger than the previous collection of files. As a result, it took longer to find and retrieve information, which led to the installation of expensive hardware and software to reduce this time.

Despite these early problems—the expense of additional equipment and the inefficiency of early systems—the developers persevered, and by the late 1970s data base systems were widely used. The key to this widespread use was the development of specialized data base management systems.

DATA BASE MANAGEMENT SYSTEMS

INTEGRATION OF SOFTWARE, HARDWARE, AND PEOPLE

How do you integrate collections of data effectively and efficiently into a data base within an organization? The answer is:

▶ **Software:** Complex, specialized software known as *DBMS*, which we discuss below, to integrate the data.
▶ **Hardware:** Sophisticated computers and storage devices to provide quick access to data in a large data base system.
▶ **People:** *Data base administrators*, discussed below, whose job it is to get the system to cooperate with the people in the organization and the people to cooperate with the system.

Let us look at these.

The Software: The Data Base Management System

It's important to understand that the term **data base management system**—which you see abbreviated everywhere as **DBMS**—refers to software. It is defined as a system of software packages for creating, storing, updating, and accessing data stored in a data base, a set of computer programs that create a link between users and a computerized data base. A DBMS works in conjunction with control programs in the computer's operating system, whose primary functions are to input, process, and store data during processing. As Figure 9-1 shows, a DBMS is supposed to help users—that is, an organization's managers and application programmers—manage items stored in a data base and gain access to those items.

The objectives of a DBMS are to:

▶ Make data easy to access and change, by making data independent of the programs used.
▶ Reduce duplication of data.
▶ Define the logical and physical characteristics of data.
▶ Provide ways of managing file directories to access and respond to requests for data.
▶ Protect data integrity (accuracy).
▶ Provide for data security.

Let us now see how a data base management system actually works.

The Organization of a Data Base   As we stated in Chapter 8, data consists of *characters* or *bytes* (such as letters and numbers), which in turn are grouped as *fields* (such as name, street address, city),

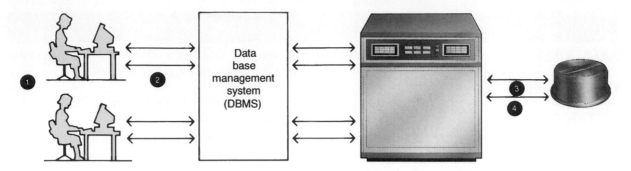

Figure 9-1.   How a data base management system works. (1) Managers need special information. (2) Managers use DBMS to query data base. (3) The data base is stored on a direct access storage device, such as a disk drive. (4) Information is received in seconds or minutes.

which in turn are grouped as *records* (a customer's complete name and address is a record), which finally are grouped as *files* (collections of related records). As Figure 9-2 shows, a data base is made up of all of these.

The Data Dictionary   How do you keep track of all the words that exist in English? With a dictionary. A DBMS operates the same way: A **data dictionary** is an automated way of keeping track of the names of all the data in the system. We say "names" because data must be identified by consistent names so that all application programs can have access to them. The data dictionary is a sort of a central depository for information about the data base; it contains data definitions and structure of the data and sets the standards for creating and using data.

The person who decides what the data dictionary is supposed to do is the data base administrator. Some of the characteristics of the data dictionary he or she has to determine are shown in the box.

Data Languages   Also called **sublanguages, data languages** consist of software that links the data base and the application program (such as dBase III Plus) that users will use to gain access to the data base. Data languages—what might be called "software interfaces"—are of two kinds, as shown in Figure 9-3 on page 293:

▶ **The data definition language:** This language consists of commands used in a DBMS to define the characteristics and structure of the data at a high enough level so that a common programming language, such as COBOL, or a query language, such as dBase III (see below), can be employed to gain access to the data.
▶ **The data manipulation language:** This language allows a programming language, such as COBOL, to gain access to and manipulate the data definition language in the data base.

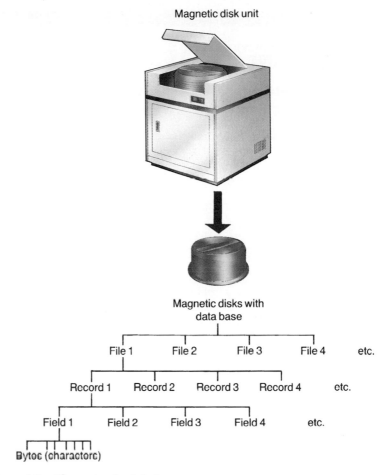

Figure 9-2. The parts of a data base.

Batch Processing or On-line Processing As a user, you can gain access to the DBMS during both kinds of processing—batch or on-line. *Batch processing*, as we mentioned earlier, is when all transactions are processed at one time, as is often the case with payroll or accounts payable. In this case, a traditional programming language, such as the business language COBOL, is supplied with special commands by the DBMS in order to give it access to the data base. The command FIND, for example, is a typical DBMS command but not a COBOL command; however, it can be used in a COBOL program once it has been precompiled and translated.

On-line processing takes place when data is available to the user at all times. On-line processing uses programs that are part of the DBMS and that do not require precompiling in order to use them. These programs are not like specific applications programs such as accounts payable programs, but rather are more general data manip-

The DD Doctor

The Data Base Administrator Takes Care of the Data Dictionary

The major responsibility of the data base administrator is to take care of the data dictionary, a sample page of which is shown below. The circled numbers explain what the various parts mean.

①*Name of Data Element*: Unique, unambiguous, easy to use and remember; it is named in a logical and meaningful way.

②*Definition:* Meaning of the data element.

③*Derivation Rules:* If data element has been calculated from other values (e.g., sum, average, ratio), then the exact equation is specified, along with the number of decimal places and rounding-off procedures.

④*Units:* Units of measure (e.g., dollars, inches, pounds).

⑤*Format:* How data is stored—letters, numbers, order, etc. (e.g., 012595 represents the date 01/25/95).

⑥*Width of Field:* Number of spaces to allow maximum value of data element.

⑦*Validity Rules:* Checking or verification procedures, if necessary (e.g., to check that the value is within a reasonable range).

⑧*Status:* Indicates whether the data element is operational, under consideration for adoption, or to be adopted on a certain date.

⑨*Comments:* Any remarks to clarify the description of this data element.

DATA ELEMENT DICTIONARY

① Name of Data Element :	Marital status
Variable :	MARITALSTAT
② Definition :	Shows if employee legally married
Classification & Coding :	1. Unmarried 2. Married 3. Other
Uses :	For determining tax deductions and employee profile
③ Derivation Rules (if any)	Source is Form 301B completed by employee.
④ Units (if any) :	None
⑤ Format :	Numeric · Justification :
⑥ Width of Field :	One digit

⑦ Validity Rules :	Required [x] Definite Error	Range 1-3	Content	Other
	Optional [ ] Possible Error			

PERSON PROCESSING FORM :	Sally Lerman
Date Issued :	01/11/89
⑧ Status :	Ready for entry
⑨ Comments :	If "Other" category more than 2%, then additional subclassifications should be specified.

Figure 9-3. Data languages: "software interfaces."
Data languages, which link the data base (through the operating system) and the user's application program (such as dBase III Plus), consist of two types: the data definition language and the data manipulation language.

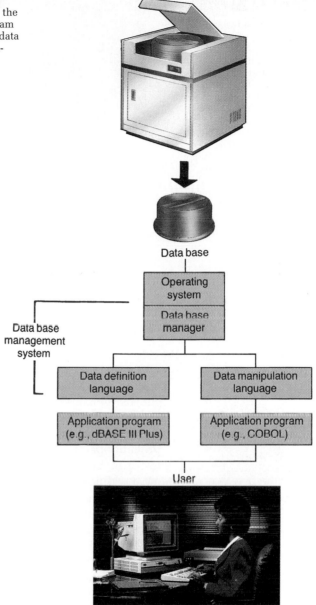

Figure 9-4. How a query language works. The user (1) queries the data base management system through the keyboard, using commands such as LIST or SELECT. For example, if you wished to look at certain records, you might use the command VIEW or DISPLAY or SEARCH. If the program does not understand the query, it interrupts. If it does understand it, it passes the query to (2) the access routines, which check (3) the data definitions and (4) the data dictionary to determine the location of data. When (5) the data is located with access routines, it is sent to (6) a display routine, which (7) displays the result on the screen.

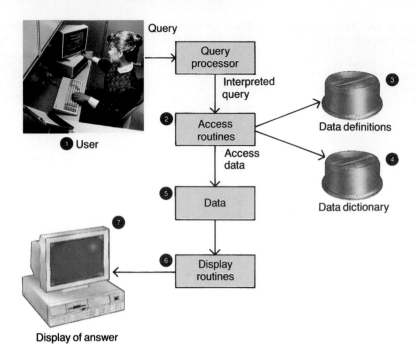

ulation and sorting programs that use what are called *query languages*, discussed next.

Query Languages   Query languages are the languages that will probably be of particular interest to you. **Query languages** are easy-to-learn, high-level retrieval languages that are understandable to most ordinary users, such as managers, and do not require programming experience. Examples of microcomputer query languages that you may well become involved with are dBase III Plus and R:base System V. Query languages have commands such as ADD, COMPARE, DELETE, ENTER, INDEX, PRINT, REPORT, SAVE, SORT, and UPDATE. They allow you to ask questions of a data base on the order of "How many of a certain item are needed by a given date?"

Figure 9-4 shows how a query language works.

Lest we have left the impression that query languages are *too* easy to use, we must point out that users are apt to be disappointed when they ask questions of the data base that cannot be answered—simply because the data is not there or the means of accessing it has not been established. Thus, we recommend that when you begin to use data bases, you take a little time to learn something about the data and the kinds of questions the data base will allow.

Sharing Resources   Suppose you and another person at Atlantic-Pacific Bank, using separate terminals and unbeknownst to each other, are simultaneously accessing a customer's record in the bank's

data base. You are about to report that the customer is a top candidate for a loan, but meanwhile your co-worker is revising the record to show that, in fact, the customer is a terrible credit risk.

To avoid such embarrassments, a DBMS must be able to control concurrent processing of shared data. Special commands are needed to lock in or freeze records that might be modified or deleted.

Security and Flexibility As we shall see in the next chapter, one of the major reasons for an organization's having a data base is that people can tap into it from all over—not just from all over the building but from all over the country, and beyond. Clearly, this means the information in the data base must be kept secure. A DBMS, then, must allow for special codes or *passwords* that allow authorized users to get into certain portions of the system but keep unauthorized users out.

Yet the DBMS must also be flexible: When an employee quits, the system must allow a password to be easily changed. Unloading, altering, and reloading of the data base, as well as cleaning up files and other "housekeeping" matters are details the DBMS must attend to.

The Hardware: Equipment to Support the DBMS

Is any *special* equipment needed to support a DBMS? Actually, no—although frequently *more* hardware may be needed. Because files must be direct access files in a data base, storage media such as punched cards or magnetic tape clearly cannot be used; magnetic disks are required.

Yet often an organization will find it has to buy more disk drives and disk packs than it had before simply because an increase in direct access storage space is required. Moreover, the demand for more and faster data, plus the space occupied by the DBMS software itself, puts increased demands on the computer's CPU; thus, some organizations may purchase a second CPU, known as a **data base machine,** whose sole function is to manage the data base and store the DBMS program. This specialized unit for performing data base operations is often called a **back-end processor.**

The People: Whose Data Base Is It, Anyway?

We stated that one of the great benefits of having a DBMS is that it takes access to a data base out of the hands of the programmers and allows average managers to do this themselves. Yet the data base is not *controlled* by the managers, nor by the programmers, systems developers, or operations personnel who are involved in it. Then, who does control it? The answer is a person whose job did not even exist a few years ago: the data base administrator.

THE DATA BASE ADMINISTRATOR

THE PERSON

IN CHARGE

We live in the age of the specialist. In a university, who keeps campus heating and air conditioning systems going, who invests the university's endowment funds, who evaluates home country transcripts of foreign students? In each case, a different specialist—and your university or college also may well have a data base administrator.

Certainly Atlantic-Pacific Bank has such a person. The **data base administrator**, abbreviated **DBA**, is spicificially assigned to data base management activities. This person's job is to work with systems analysts on issues relating to the data base. He or she must resolve conflicts among users and among technical people working on the data base and DBMS and protect the data base so it can be used effectively. Clearly, this role requires good negotiation and arbitration skills.

The DBA has three tasks:

▶ Manage data activity
▶ Manage the structure of the data base
▶ Evaluate the performance of the DBMS

Let's say you have an eye on possibly working into this job at Atlantic-Pacific. What will you have to learn to do?

Managing Data Activity

Users perform data activity on a DBMS, but the data base administrator manages this activity—and an important job it is, since the data base is only as valuable as the data is accurate and accessible. Managing consists of determining what are called "processing rights" and being responsible for updating, backup, and recovery of data.

Processing Rights   Who has access to what kind of data? Whereas in a file processing system, users have direct control over their own files and data bases, but not over those of their co-workers, in an organization using a data base everyone could have access to the data. However, with a DBMS, all data entry must be standardized and coordinated; you cannot just put facts into a file haphazardly. **Processing rights** specify who is allowed to enter data and in what format, and who has access to that data. Processing rights, then, must be negotiated among users, with the DBA acting as arbitrator or traffic cop. Once these rights have been determined, the DBA documents them, and afterward investigates any violations and forces compliance (by limiting access to the data base). The DBA also must provide training for data base users.

Update, Backup, Recovery Whenever problems arise with the data base requiring updating, back-up files, or recovery of data that somehow has been lost, the DBA has to step in, investigate, and develop solutions:

▶ **Updating:** This is an ongoing and critical activity. It's the DBA's job to control and monitor *who* has the authority to update and alter the contents of a data base.

▶ **Backup:** This task is also critical—particularly for a transaction-oriented data base, which contains day-to-day current business operations (orders received, billing data, inventory status, and the like).

▶ **Recovery:** As we describe in a later chapter, fire, flood, sabotage, and other disasters can damage a data base. The DBA must institute preventive measures, such as install fire extinguishers or TV surveillance cameras, or store back-up copies of software in a different location.

Managing Data Base Structures

As we will see later in this chapter, there are different types of organizations or structures under which a data base may be set up. Some structures are more appropriate than others for certain purposes, and the DBA needs to help users figure out which is best, then develop procedures for gaining access, updating, and managing changes.

The DBA also has to help manage changes in the structure and other aspects of the data base system. Users will want new capabilities or changes in procedures. Operations people will want new equipment. Systems development people will want to try better ways of doing things. The DBA must deal with them all.

Evaluating DBMS Performance

If managing processing rights and managing data base structure entail dealing with people, the DBA's third task, evaluating the performance of a DBMS, has to do with software and equipment. Because the DBMS can require huge amounts of computer memory in order to operate, the data base administrator must monitor the CPU to see that it is not being overtaxed by demands on the system. The DBA also must keep an eye on how the housekeeping software is doing in making the DBMS run smoothly. If things are not going well, it is up to the DBA to begin investigating larger CPU allocations—that is, proposing the purchase of computers with bigger processing units.

The box on the following page offers more information on the data base administrator.

DBA a DBA

Doing Business as a Data Base Administrator

DBA also stands for *doing business as*, as you might see in the fictitious-name legal notices in the newspaper ("The following persons are doing business as The Hi-N-R-G Company . . ."), which are known as "DBA ads." Let us see what it takes to do business as a data base administrator.

What kind of training does a DBA need? Surprisingly, not a great deal of computer science background is required, although of course a certain amount of data processing experience is needed. Actually, it helps to have a pleasant personality and to be people-sensitive—to be a good diplomat with excellent interpersonal skills and political savvy, able to deal both with senior managers in departments using the data base and with subordinate data processing personnel.

What is the DBA's level in the organization? As the following organization charts show, the DBA may a *line* manager, reporting to the vice-president of data processing just as the other managers do, or a *staff* person, which removes the DBA from the daily problems of the other managers. Note, however, that the DBA works mainly with departmental users; he or she does not usually have much direct control over the data processing people, who actually operate the data base.

What are the actual tasks of a data base administrator? These are best summarized in table form, as shown on the following page.

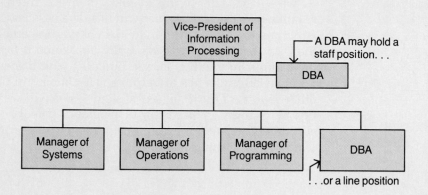

DBA in the hierarchy. The DBA may be placed in two different locations within a business organization.

Data base design
Content
  Creation
  Reconciling differences
Dictionary/Directory
  Create
  Maintain
Data compression
Data classification/coding
Data integrity
  Backup
  Restart/recovery

Data base operation
DED custodian/authority
  Maintain
  Add
  Purge
Data base maintenance
  Integrity
    Detect losses
    Repair losses
  Recovery
  Access for testing
  Dumping
Software for DED/DD
  Utility programs
  Tables/indexes for
    end user
  Storage
  Physical record structure
  Logical-physical mapping
  Physical storage device
    assignments
Security/access
  Assign passwords
  Assign lock/key
  Modifying passwords/keys
  Logging
  Cryptography
  Modification

Retrieval
  Search strategies
Statistics
  Access
  Frequency of processing
  Space use
  User utilization
  Response time
Design operational
  procedures
  Access to data base
  Access for testing
  Interfaces
  Testing system

Monitoring
Quality of data
  validity
Performance
Efficiency
Cost
Use/utilization
Security/privacy
Audit
Compliance
  Standards
  Procedures

Other functions
Liaison/communications with:
  End users
  Analysts/programmers
Training on data base
Consultant on file design
Design operational
  procedures
  Access to data base
  Access for testing
  Interfaces

The functions of a data base administrator.

DATA BASE STRUCTURES LIST, HIERARCHICAL, NETWORK, RELATIONAL

There are two types of structures to consider in a data base. As Figure 9-5 shows, the **physical structures** are the location of records on storage devices, such as a disk; these structures are behind the scenes and are completely invisible to users. **Logical structures** are the way records are related together for the user's purpose. Records may not actually be stored together, in the same physical location on a disk, but may be pulled together from many locations in order to be useful to the user in a particular application; thus, they are *logically* but not *physically* related.

Also, a data base may be viewed by data base administrators and systems analysts from three perspectives:

▶ The **schema** of a data base: Pronounced "skee-muh," this is the logical view—how records in the data base are logically or conceptually linked in ways that are useful to all users. (However, only the DBA may actually understand the schema.)

▶ The **subschema** of a data base: This is part of the schema and is also a logical view, but of a particular application—how records in the data base are linked in ways useful to a particular user. (Not all people in an organization may need to, or should, have access to all the data in a data base. A particular programmer may need access only to a list of the company products, say, and the DBA provides that user with the limited information or subschema to access that data.)

▶ The **internal view** of a data base: This is the same as the physical view—how and where the data is actually arranged when stored on disk.

Unless you go into the technical side of computing—as a programmer, systems analyst, or data base administrator—you will not need to worry about the physical arrangement of data. However, because data bases will be very much a part of your future, you should be aware of the different kinds and their advantages and limitations—that is, the different logical relationships of data.

There are four different types of logical data structures:

▶ List
▶ Hierarchical
▶ Network
▶ Relational

These four types are represented in Figure 9-6. Different data base management systems use these different designs. Let us take a look at them.

Figure 9-5. Logical versus physical records. *Logical records* in a data base are those the user sees. *Physical records* are the actual arrangement of records on the disk.

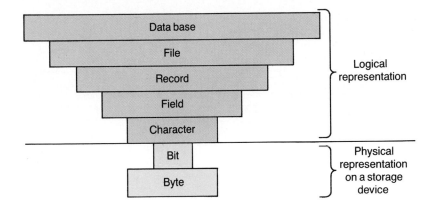

| Data base |
| File |
| Record |
| Field |
| Character |

} Logical representation

| Bit |
| Byte |

} Physical representation on a storage device

The List Structure: Pointers and Chains

In the **list structure,** records are linked together through the use of pointers. As Figure 9-7 shows, a **pointer** is a number or other field in a record that points out—identifies—the storage location of another record that is logically related, then links it and other pointed-to records so that they form a list or chain through the data base.

For example, a freelance artist may perform a number of different tasks (ads, brochures, etc.) for the advertising department of Atlantic-Pacific Bank throughout the year, and is paid each time she bills. At the end of the year, the bank will send her a summary (for tax purposes) of the total dollars she earned. In each case, as Figure 9-7 shows, the list structure is used to link each of her bills (invoices), using a pointer—a number   to connect the list of transactions. Of course, each transaction is stored in many physically separated locations in the data base disk storage.

Although the list structure has the advantage of simplicity, it has the disadvantage of pointers becoming too numerous and lists too long, thereby requiring more storage space and increasing the time it takes to gain access to data.

Hierarchical Structures: Parent and Children

In the **hierarchical structure,** fields or records are structured in **nodes** or multiple levels, like the roots of an upside-down tree, as shown in Figure 9-8. The units farther down the system are subordinate to the ones above, like the hierarchy of employees in a corporation or soldiers in the military. Finding a record usually requires that you start at the top of the hierarchy—you have to go through the general, as it were, before you can get to the foot soldiers. The nodes below are called *children*, and the nodes above are called *parents*;

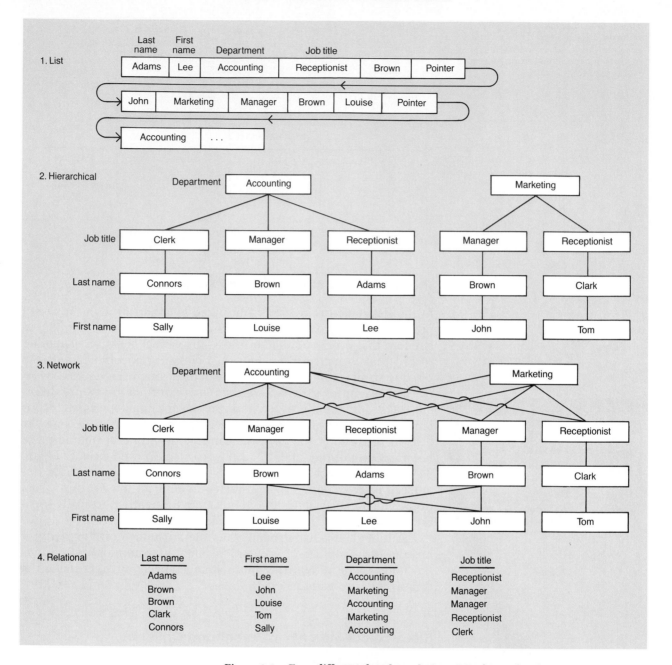

Figure 9-6.   Four different data base designs. List, hierarchical, network, and relational are the four most common models used in data base management systems. These are explained further in Figures 9-7 through 9-10.

Figure 9-7. List structure and pointers. Each pointer links a related record in the file and strings all such records together in listlike form.

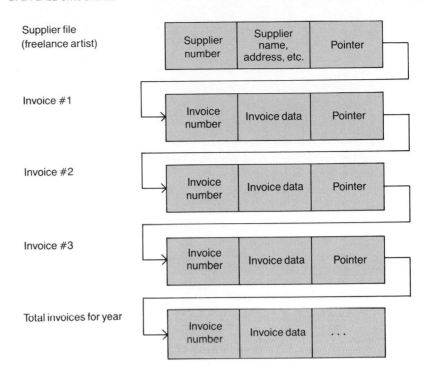

note, however, that a parent may have several children, but a child will have only one parent. The very top node is called the *root*. Hierarchical structures are referred to as *one-to-many relationships*.

One drawback of the hierarchical data base system is that if you delete one node, all the subordinate units are deleted, and a subordinate unit cannot be added without a node. Thus, suppose that when you were considering moving from the West Coast to Atlantic-Pacific Bank in Boston you had a data base composed of a log of apartment addresses. Each address would have subordinate nodes of the number of rooms, the owner's name and phone, the rent, and the distance from work. If you deleted an apartment address (say it was too expensive), you would also delete all subordinate units—but suppose you wanted to stay in touch with the owner because he or she had other apartments? Or suppose you had the same owner listed under several different root addresses, and his or her telephone number was changed? You would have to search the entire data base to change the telephone number in all places.

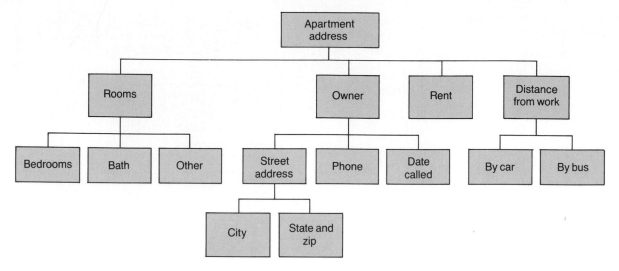

Figure 9-8.   Hierarchical data base. Each subordinate has one superior, but superiors may have more than one subordinate. The top unit is called the root.

Network Structures: One Child, Many Parents

A **network** data base has records in hierarchical arrangements, but the record can participate in several relationships. That is, there are additional links besides the root system of the hierarchy, as Figure 9-9 illustrates. Whereas in the hierarchical arrangement, each child has only one parent, in the network data base each child may have more than one parent. Such a data base is said to have a *many-to-many relationship*. Thus, there is more than one way to reach a particular node—down through more than one root and even sideways from one node to another on the same level. Any data element can be related to any other data element.

Relational Structures: Tables in the "Natural Manner"

The structure most widely implemented at present, a **relational data base** is made up of many tables. Data elements are stored in those tables according to their relationships to one another. Unlike hierarchical and network data structures, relational structures do not have records. The tables in relational data bases are like files and are called **relations.**

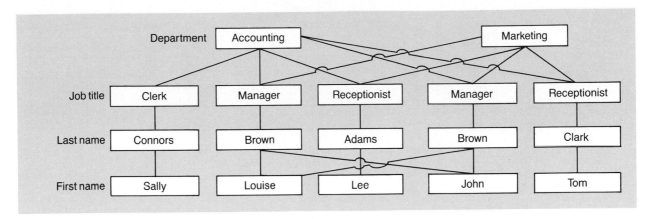

Figure 9-9. Network data base. Note that there are multiple superiors for each subordinate. Thus, there are many ways to locate a particular data item.

Figure 9-10 shows how a relational data base works. Note that the tables are made up of rows and columns. The rows in the tables, called **tuples,** are like records. The columns, called **attributes,** are like fields. When considering moving to Atlantic-Pacific in Boston from Los Angeles, you could have had a data base composed of a log of telephone calls that you made to Boston inquiring about apartments. On that data base, you could have entered the address of the apartment, the phone number, the date you called, the apartment owner's name, the rent, the number of rooms, the distance in miles to work, and anything else of interest. As the illustration shows, these items can be linked in relations or pairs in several tables—address/phone, address/distance, distance/rent, and so on. You could then have retrieved data about any of these apartments simply by referring to the particular fields of data—rent, number of rooms, or whatever.

Clearly, a relational data base management system can be useful because of its ability to cross-reference data and retrieve data automatically. Indeed, the special aspect of the relational structure is that it allows people to view data and relationships in a natural manner—users need not be aware of such things as "structures" and "linked lists."

Address/phone pairs	
Address	Phone
1269 4th Ave.	750-3606
19 Encline Ct.	282-3430
160 Manchester	326-1951
etc.	

Address/distance pairs	
Address	Distance
1269 4th Ave.	3 miles
19 Encline Ct.	7 miles
160 Manchester	30 miles

Distance/rent pair	
Distance	Rent
3 miles	$650
7 miles	$350
30 miles	$400

Figure 9-10.   Relational data base.
Items in a data base are linked in relations or pairs.

If you get involved with data base management systems for microcomputers, you may well become involved in relational structures, since some micro software, such as the R:base series, use this
form.

The major advantages of the relational structure are as follows:

▶ You do not need to know a programming language. Some network
and hierarchical structures, by contrast, require that you know a
language, such as COBOL or a particular query language, in order
to install and use them.

▶ It is flexible. You do not have to consider all possible fields before
setting up a data base. Rather, you can put the basic files you need
in one table and then set up additional fields as needed that relate
to the main table. Moreover, you can add, delete, or modify existing structures without difficulty. Other data base structures are
much more rigid.

▶ It is easy to understand. The table format is a convenient form to
understand and use. Moreover, data is accessed by content,
whereas in the hierarchical and network form it is accessed by
address.

The disadvantage of the relational structure is that searching the
data base can be time-consuming. Hence, the structure is primarily
used on smaller data bases, such as those useful with microcomputers; hierarchical and network structures are used on minicomputers
and mainframes. Relational DBMSs usually require more computer
memory, processing time, and on-line storage—what is called in the
trade "high overhead."

MICRO VERSUS MINICOMPUTER AND MAINFRAME DATA BASES

It is possible, even likely, that you will learn to deal with data base management systems for microcomputers before you deal with those for minicomputers and mainframes. Sooner or later, however, you will probably find yourself having to get information from the only place that has it: the company's large computer.

Only a mainframe can handle the large amounts of data that concern an organization's complete day-to-day operations and that cover a variety of different users with different needs. As you might expect, therefore, the people charged with establishing this organizationwide data base—the DBA and other computer professionals—have to give a lot of thought as to how it should be done because the cost can run into hundreds of thousands of dollars. Indeed, as we shall describe, it requires the problem-solving skills known as systems analysis and design to set up an enterprise of this scope.

Microcomputer DBMSs are used either by individuals or organizations that do not require or cannot afford the mainframe version or by larger organizations to supplement the existing mainframe DBMSs. In large companies, a microcomputer may be used to download parts of the mainframe data base (sometimes called "taking a slice" of the data base) so that users can manipulate the information on their own desktop machines. This procedure gives users more control over the data, while, at the same time, freeing up the larger computer's resources.

Some Mainframe DBMSs

- Burroughs: DMS II
- CINCOM Systems: TOTAL
- Cullinet: IDMS
- IBM: DB2, IMS
- Intel: SYSTEM 2000
- ORACLE
- Software AG: ADABAS

THE FIVE TYPES OF DATA BASES

In the beginning, data bases were developed that were intended to cross over the division lines of an organization, so that, say, the Research and Development department could use the same data as the Marketing department. This idea, however, turned out to be too ambitious, and most such data bases—they were largely tried in the 1970s—were unsuccessful.

Later the people who designed data bases began to think about creating specialized data bases. Now an organization usually has more than one type of data base. Some data bases are limited to particular regions. Others are limited to particular departments or purposes—marketing, production, or human resources, for example. One of the reasons data bases have multiplied is the growth in the number of personal computers or executive workstations within organizations. As Figure 9-11 shows, we may now identify five kinds of data bases:

Does End-User Computing *Really* Benefit Organizations?

Problems are not diminishing with the widespread growth of end-user computing. On the contrary, they are expanding.

Surface issues include excessive equipment cost, inefficient users, inefficient applications and friction between the end-user computing technical staff and the rest of the MIS [Management Information Systems] department. Below-surface issues include the proliferation of data bases, software products and PC machine types and the problem of interfaces between tools and developing systems that are difficult to maintain. . . .

The data proliferation problem is perhaps the most insidious and costly. Data base security procedures prevent user access to on-line data bases, ex-

cept in retrieval mode, so they cannot alter the data. Users who want to manipulate data to perform analyses must be provided with copies of a data base. The resultant problem is inconsistency of reports when users are using data bases that are not as up-to-date as the reports produced by the transaction-processing applications.

The solution that has been used is to give everyone current data. In this mode, a "shadow" data base copy is provided daily from the corporate mainframe. While the currency problem is resolved, a significant increase in data base cost occurs.

—J. Daniel Couger, *Computerworld*

▶ Common operational
▶ Common user
▶ Distributed
▶ Personal user
▶ External

Let's take a look at these.

Common Operational Data Base

A **common operational data base,** also referred to as a **transaction data base** or **production data base,** contains detailed data generated by the operations of the organization—sales, production, inventory levels, and accounting, for example.

Common User Data Base

Also called an **information data base** or a **management data base,** the **common user data base** contains selected and summarized data and information from common operational data bases and also from external data bases (described below). Such a data base is called "common" because it is commonly shared by many managers using

Figure 9-11. The five types of data bases. The appearance of microcomputers and executive workstations in offices has led to the development of the five different kinds of data bases shown here.

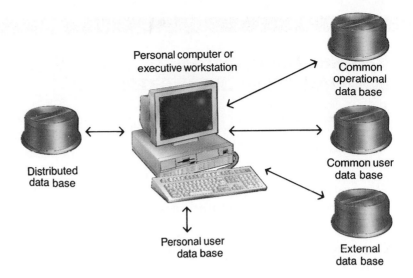

Personal computer or executive workstation

Common operational data base

Distributed data base

Common user data base

Personal user data base

External data base

personal computers or executive workstations. As we will see later in the book, it is used to help support management information systems and decision support systems—programs that help managers make decisions.

Distributed Data Base

One of the things that makes data bases so useful is that they can be linked by communication networks—by a cable to a room down the hall or by a satellite to another continent, for example. In other words, data bases can be *distributed*—located in another place from where the users are located. A **distributed data base** is one in which the logical location of the data is not the same as that of the user; use and updating can be done from remote locations. In addition, the data may be located in more than one physical location.

Deciding on the physical location of a distributed data base can be quite important. Should it be in central headquarters? Or should it be in local workplaces—branch or regional offices and manufacturing plants? Note that data, as in a branch bank, is by and large created, processed, and used at the local site. Yet that same data is also needed at the regional level and at central headquarters, as well as being needed occasionally at other branches. At Atlantic-Pacific Bank, for instance, the powers that be have a choice as to where to put the data base or data bases:

▶ **Completely centralized data base:** A single, centralized data base—known as a **global data base**—may be the simplest design, but it may not be efficient because regional or local banks may perform more reliably with greater autonomous control and authority.

GETTING COMPUTERIZED INFORMATION OVER THE TELEPHONE

Computerized Data Banks

As we described earlier, if you have a computer, telephone, and a communications device called a modem, plus appropriate software, you can use your micro to obtain information about almost any subject. Some of the principal data banks and their specialties are the following:

▶ **After Dark and Brkthru**: After Dark is available only at night and offers less information than Brkthru. The data banks emphasize arts and humanities, medical, education, and science and technology.

▶ **Bibliographic Retrieval Services**: Business information; over 60 different on-line data bases.

▶ **CompuServe**: Consumer and business services; electronic mail.

▶ **Dialog Information Services**: Business, technical, scientific; over 170 data bases in many fields.

▶ **Dow Jones News/Retrieval**: Business, investments, stocks, world news.

▶ **Knowledge Index**: Many of the Dialog services offered at reduced rates after business hours.

▶ **Mead Data Central**: News, business, law; distributor of NEXIS, carrying information from over 100 publications and news services, and LEXIS, library of legal information.

▶ **Newsnet**: Business, consumer information; newsletters.

▶ **SDC Information Services**: Business, science, technology; the SDC Orbit Search Service has over 70 on-line data bases.

▶ **The Source**: Consumer services.

Specialized data banks are also available for investors and money managers to track companies and finances; these include CompuStat, Value Line, Chase Econometric Associates, and Data Resources, Inc. (DRI).

▶ **Local data bases:** Completely consistent with the idea of distributed data processing are **local data bases,** which are based in each branch and/or regional office. However, with this approach it is difficult for the organization as a whole to collect organizationwide information and statistics.

▶ **Local and global data bases:** This approach offers the best of both worlds—and also, to some extent, the worst of both. Although local data bases allow branch offices to work efficiently with their local data and the global data base allows headquarters to summarize local along with organizationwide data, the combination still creates problems in data reliability. Updating, for instance, can be a constant irritant on both local and central levels.

Whichever of these three methods is chosen, the result will be a trade-off: in number of processing and communication costs, in amount of service to provide users, in degree of processing performance and control desired.

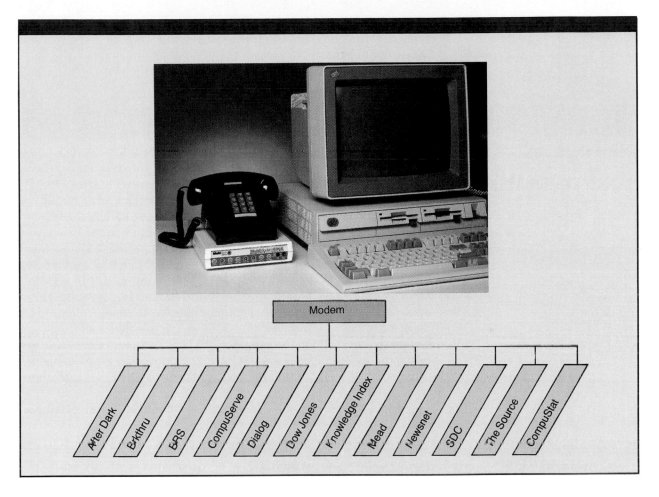

Personal User Data Bases

Whatever your future career, a personal user data base may very well be of interest to you. A **personal user data base** is a collection of records that are integrated but of use mainly to one individual, like your personal file in the bottom drawer of your desk. Usually stored on a personal computer, a personal data base is used, for example, for document report files, spreadsheet files, and personal data files. A salesperson, for instance, would find this kind of data base useful in keeping track of customers and prospective customers.

External Data Base

An **external data base** is generally an enormous data base that exists outside one's own organization but that sells or makes available its contents to many users. Although some such data bases are government-owned, most of the well-known ones are private. Also known as **information utilities** or **data banks** *(see box)*, some private external data bases you may well use at some time are CompuServe, The Source, Dow Jones News/Retrieval, Dialog Information Services, and Mead Data Central.

THE PROS AND CONS OF DBMSs

Now that you have had a look at data base management systems, you can see what a terrific idea they are. Imagine how it must have been in the old days trying to put together a companywide study for Atlantic-Pacific Bank of, say, the kind of depositors who would be good credit card risks. How many letters, phone calls, and trips to branch banks would it take to cull these kinds of records? How up to date would the information be by the time you pulled it all together?

Note, however, that a data base is an inefficient use of a computer—at least from the standpoint of the computer, for a DBMS takes an enormous amount of storage and processing capacity. However, it is an efficient use of *people's* time, for it enables them to be more productive. And, because people costs—their salaries—are becoming more expensive whereas hardware and software costs are becoming less, data base processing makes more and more economic sense. For this reason, data base processing will become more widely used in the future.

Let us, however, consider both the advantages and disadvantages.

The Advantages of DBMS

By now you can appreciate the advantages of data base management systems compared to the old file processing systems:

▶ They offer superior service and performance.
▶ They allow better control over data.
▶ They reduce data duplication and increase data integration.
▶ They give managers access to information without their having to get the assistance of programmers.
▶ They provide better control and security of data.
▶ They increase productivity by providing information more efficiently and effectively.

The Disadvantages of DBMS

For all that, however, there are still some disadvantages:

▶ A DBMS is expensive and difficult to install.
▶ It uses more hardware than is typically required.

▶ It requires a great deal of planning and agreement, not to mention sophistication, in order to implement it.

▶ It requires an enormous amount of time to create a data base. Data entry time is typically underestimated.

▶ Because all data is located in one place, it is more vulnerable to errors or failures.

▶ The concept of the data base is becoming increasingly more complex.

ON TO THE
WIRED WORLD

Even in this present day and age, there are still many data bases—the old-fashioned collections of data that are *not* computerized—that are not readily accessible. Professors writing books on specialized topics, for example, journey to libraries all over the world in order to gain the information they need. Even many computerized data bases are inaccessible because they are limited to one organization or one geographical place.

Thus, having large *amounts of information* available is only one part of the picture. It is also important to make the information *accessible*. This is where networking and data communications come in—the subject of the next chapter.

SUMMARY

▶ A **data base** is a computerized, nonredundant collection of logically related records or files that can be structured or organized in various ways to support the wide variety of processing and retrieval needs of organizations and individuals.

▶ Traditional file processing has four disadvantages: (1) Data redundancy—the same data elements appear in many different files and often in different formats, which makes updating files time-consuming. (2) No data integrity, because frequently some files are not updated. (3) Unintegrated data, because data is spread around in different files and so is not as useful. (4) Program and file dependence, because programmers have to work with whatever formats and programs individual files are written in.

▶ Creating a data base allows records that were previously stored in independent files throughout an organization to be consolidated as a common pool of data, to which access could be gained by many different application programs.

▶ When data base concepts were first developed, creating integrated files was difficult, for two reasons:

(1) There were organizational problems—cooperation in sharing information was required of all users, and the people designing the data base had to define input data in a way that was useful to people in all departments. (2) There were technical problems—integrating several files into one very large integrated file led to installation of expensive hardware and software to reduce access time.

▶ Integrating collections of data effectively and efficiently into a data base within an organization requires three things: (1) Complex, specialized software (a DBMS) to integrate the data, (2) sophisticated computers and storage devices to provide quick access to data, and (3) people known as data base administrators, whose job it is to get the system to cooperate with the people in the organization and the people to cooperate with the system.

▶ A **data base management system (DBMS)** is a system of software packages for creating, storing, updating, and accessing data stored in a data base, a set of computer programs that create a link between users and a computerized data base. A DBMS works in conjunction with control programs in the computer's operating system, whose primary functions are to input, process, and store data during processing.

▶ The objectives of a DBMS are to: (1) make data easy to access and change, by making data independent of the programs used; (2) reduce duplication of data; (3) define the logical and physical characteristics of data; (4) provide ways of managing file directories to access and respond to requests for data; (5) protect data integrity (accuracy); and (6) provide for data security.

▶ Data in a data base consists of *characters* or *bytes* (such as letters and numbers), which in turn are grouped as *fields* (such as name, street address, city), which in turn are grouped as *records* (a customer's complete name and address is a record), which finally are grouped as *files* (collections of related records).

▶ A **data dictionary** is an automated way of keeping track of the names—which must be consistent—of all the data in the system. The data dictionary is a sort of a central depository for information about the data base; it contains data definitions and structure of the data and sets the standards for creating and using data.

▶ Also called **sublanguages, data languages** consist of software that links the data base and the applications programs users will use to gain access to the data base. Data languages are of two kinds: (1) the **data definition language,** which consists of commands used in a DBMS to define characteristics and structure of the data at a high enough level so that a common programming language or query language can be employed to gain access to the data; (2) the **data manipulation language,** which allows a programming language to gain access to and manipulate the data definition language in the data base.

▶ Users can gain access to the DBMS during both batch processing and on-line processing.

▶ *Batch processing* is when all transactions are processed at one time. In this case, a traditional programming language is supplied with special commands by the DBMS to give it access to the data base. The command FIND, for example, is a typical DBMS command but not a COBOL command; however, it can be used in a COBOL program once it has been precompiled and translated.

▶ *On-line processing* takes place when data is available to the user at all times. On-line processing uses programs that are part of the DBMS and that do not require precompiling in order to use them. These programs are not like specific applications programs but rather are more general data manipulation and sorting programs that use *query languages.*

▶ **Query languages** are easy-to-learn, high-level retrieval languages that are understandable to most ordinary users and do not require programming experience. Query languages have commands such as ADD, COMPARE, DELETE, ENTER, INDEX, PRINT, REPORT, SAVE, SORT, and UPDATE.

▶ Information in a data base must be kept secure. A DBMS, then, must allow for special codes or *passwords* that allow authorized users to get into certain portions of the system but keep unauthorized users out. Yet the DBMS must also be flexible, allowing passwords to be easily changed and handling "housekeeping" matters.

▶ No special equipment is needed to support a DBMS, although frequently more hardware may be needed. Because data base files must be direct access, the storage medium must be magnetic disks. Also, since the demand for more and faster data, plus the space occupied by the DBMS software itself, puts increased demands on the computer's CPU, some organizations may purchase a second CPU, known as a **data base machine,** or **back-end processor,** whose sole function is to manage the data base and store the DBMS program.

▶ The data base is controlled by the **data base administrator (DBA)** who is specifically assigned to data base management activities. This person works with systems analysts on issues relating to the data base, resolves conflicts among users and among technical people working on the data base and DBMS, and protects the data base so it can be used effectively.

▶ The DBA has three tasks: (1) Manage data activity, (2) manage the structure of the data base, and (3) evaluate the performance of the DBMS.

▶ Managing consists of determining "processing rights" and being responsible for updating, backup, and recovery of data.

▶ **Processing rights** specify who is allowed to enter data and in what format, and who has access to that data. Processing rights are negotiated among users, with the DBA acting as arbitrator. Once they have been determined, the DBA documents them and afterward investigates any violations and forces compliance (by limiting access to the data base). The DBA also must provide training for data base users.

▶ Updating is an ongoing and critical activity. The DBA controls and monitors *who* has the authority to update and alter the contents of a data base.

▶ Backup is also a critical task—particularly for a transaction-oriented data base, which contains day-to-day current business operations (orders received, billing data, inventory status, and the like).

▶ Helping in recovery from disasters that damage a data base by storing back-up copies of software in a different location, and preventing damage through such measures as installing fire extinguishers or TV surveillance cameras, are all part of a DBA's job.

▶ In the DBA's third task, evaluating the performance of a DBMS, he or she monitors the CPU to see that it is not being overtaxed by demands on the system. The DBA also monitors housekeeping software. If things are not going well, the DBA must begin investigating larger CPU allocations—that is, proposing the purchase of computers with bigger processing units.

▶ There are two types of structures to consider in a data base. The **physical structures** are the location of stored records on storage devices; they are behind the scenes and completely invisible to users. **Logical structures** are the way records are related together for the user's purpose. Records may not actually be stored together, in the same physical location on a disk, but may be pulled together to be useful to the user in a particular application; thus, they are *logically* but not *physically* related.

▶ A data base may be viewed from three perspectives. (1) The **schema** is the logical view—how records in the data base are logically or conceptually linked in ways that are useful to all users. (2) The **subschema** is a part of the schema and is also a logical view, but of a particular application—how records in the data base are linked in ways useful to a particular user. (3) The **internal view** of a data base is the same as the physical view—how and where the data is actually arranged when stored on disk.

▶ There are four different types of logical data structures: list, hierarchical, network, and relational.

▶ In the **list structure,** records are linked together through the use of pointers. A **pointer** is a number or other field in a record that points out—identifies—the storage location of another record that is logically related, then links it and other pointed-to records so that they form a list or chain through the data base. The list structure is simple, but pointers often become too numerous and lists too long, thereby requiring more storage space and increasing the time it takes to gain access to data.

▶ In the **hierarchical structure,** fields or records are structured in **nodes** or multiple levels, like the roots of an upside-down tree. The units farther down the system are subordinate to the ones above. The nodes below are called *children*, and the nodes above are called *parents*. A parent may have several children, but a child will have only one parent. The very top node is called the *root*. Hierarchical structures are referred to as *one-to-many relationships*. One drawback of the hierarchical data base system is that if one node is deleted, it deletes all the subordinate units, and a subordinate unit cannot be added without a node.

▶ A **network** data base has records in hierarchical arrangements, but the record can participate in several relationships. That is, there are additional links besides the root system. In the network data base each child may have more than one parent. Such a data base is said to have a *many-to-many relationship*. Thus, there is more than one way to reach a particular node—down through more than one root and even sideways from one node to another on the same level. Any data element can be related to any other data element.

▶ The structure most widely implemented at present, a **relational data base** is made up of many tables, and data elements are stored on those tables according to relationships that the parts have to the whole. The tables are like files and are called **relations.** The rows in the tables, called **tuples,** are like records. The columns, called **attributes,** are like fields. A relational DBMS can cross-reference data and retrieve data automatically. It allows people to view data and relationships in a natural manner—they need not be aware of such things as "structures" and "linked lists."

▶ The major advantages of the relational structure are: (1) Unlike some network and hierarchical structures, no knowledge of a programming language is required in order to install and use it. (2) It is flexible. You can put the basic files you need in one table and then set up additional fields as needed that relate to the main table. Moreover, you can add, delete, or modify existing structures without difficulty. (3) It is easy to understand. The table format is a convenient form to understand and use. Moreover, data is accessed by content, and not by address.

▶ However, with the relational structure, searching the data base can be time-consuming—hence, the structure is primarily used on smaller data bases, such as those useful with microcomputers. Relational DBMSs usually require more computer memory, processing time, and on-line storage.

▶ Only a mainframe can handle the large amounts of data that concern an organization's complete day-today operations and that cover a variety of different users with different needs. Microcomputer DBMSs are used either by individuals or organizations that do not require or cannot afford the mainframe version or by larger organizations to supplement the existing mainframe DBMSs. In large companies, a microcomputer may be used to download parts of the mainframe data base so users can manipulate the information on their own desktop machines; this gives them more control over the data, while at the same time freeing up the larger computer's resources.

▶ There are five kinds of data bases: common operational, common user, distributed, personal user, and external.

▶ A **common operational data base,** also referred to as a **transaction data base** or **production data base,** contains detailed data generated by the operations of the organization—sales, production, inventory levels, and accounting, for example.

▶ Also called an **information data base** or a **management data base,** the **common user data base** contains selected and summarized data and information from common operational data bases and also from external data bases. It is commonly shared by many managers using personal computers or executive workstations.

▶ A **distributed data base** is one in which the logical location of the data is not the same as that of the user; use and updating can be done from remote locations. In·addition, the data may be located in more than one physical location.

▶ There are three possibilities for placement of this kind of data base: (1) The **global data base** is a completely centralized data base. Although it may be the simplest design, it may not be efficient because regional or local offices may perform more reliably with greater autonomous control and authority. (2) **Local data bases** are based in each branch and/or regional office. With this approach it is difficult for the organization as a whole to collect organization-wide information and statistics. (3) Local and global data bases together offer the best of both worlds— and also, to some extent, the worst of both. The combination still creates problems in data reliability. Updating, for instance, can be a constant irritant on both local and central levels.

▶ Each method represents a trade-off: in number of processing and communication costs, in amount of service to provide users, in degree of processing performance and control desired.

▶ A **personal user data base** is a collection of records that are integrated but of use mainly to one individual. Usually stored on a personal computer, a personal data base is used, for example, for document report files, spreadsheet files, and personal data files.

▶ An **external data base** is generally an enormous data base that exists outside one's own organization but that sells or makes available its contents to many users. Some such data bases are government-owned, but most of the well-known ones are private. Also known as **information utilities** or **data banks,** some private external data bases are CompuServe, The Source, Dow Jones Information Service, Lockheed Information Systems, and Mead Data Central.

▶ There are several advantages to DBMSs compared to the old file processing systems: (1) They offer superior service and performance. (2) They allow better control over data. (3) They reduce data duplication and increase data integration. (4) They give managers access to information without their having to get the assistance of programmers. (5) They provide better control and security of data. (6) They increase productivity by providing information more efficiently and effectively.

▶ The disadvantages of DBMSs are as follows: (1) A DBMS is expensive and difficult to install. (2) It uses more hardware than is typically required. (3) A great deal of planning, agreement, and sophistication is required in order to implement it. (4) An enormous amount of time is required to create a data base. (5) It is more vulnerable to errors or failures. (6) The concept of the data base is becoming increasingly more complex.

KEY TERMS

Attribute, p. 305

Back-end processor, p. 295

Common operational data base, p. 308

Common user data base, p. 308

Data bank, p. 311

Data base, p. 285

Data base administrator (DBA), p. 296

Data base machine, p. 295

Data base management system (DBMS), p. 289

Data definition language, p. 290

REVIEW QUESTIONS

1. List four disadvantages of traditional file processing.
2. What are the objectives of a data base management system?
3. Explain data dictionary, data languages, and query languages.
4. Describe the functions of the data base administrator.
5. Explain how a list structure type of data base works.
6. Explain how a hierarchical structure works.
7. Explain the network structure.
8. Explain the relational structure.
9. Distinguish among the five kinds of data bases: common operational, common user, distributed, personal user, and external.

CASE PROBLEMS

Case 9-1: Data Base Proliferation: A Data Base for Data Bases?

The number of records on publicly available data bases—data banks to which one might have access via a computer terminal linked to a telephone line—stood at 1.68 *billion* in 1985: ten times more than in 1976, according to an information scientist at the University of Illinois at Urbana-Champaign, as reported in *The Futurist* (July–August 1986). About 57% of all data bases are located in the United States, says Professor Martha E. Williams, who compiled and wrote the world's first directory of data bases. "Some 36% of the data bases contain numeric data, such as farm production statistics or U.S. census data," she says. "Another 36% contain bibliographic information, such as references to articles in scholarly journals." It is possible to call up electronic facsimiles of entire articles, such as the full text of legal cases, or an edition of a newspaper such as the *New York Times.*

Your assignment: This assignment may well turn out to be eminently useful to you, although it requires a bit of library work. Your goal is to get familiar with data bases that could help you in the future. You do not need to know precisely what is *in* the data bases, only that they exist—so that later, if you wish, you can use them to research an area, do a report, launch a business, or whatever. Feel free to choose any area of interest to you—a specific kind of business, social cause, financial information, law, and so on. As a starter, you might try to find Martha E. Williams's book, *Computer-Readable Data-Bases: A Directory and Data Source Book*.

Case 9-2: Making a List and Checking It Twice—and Three Times and . . .

Martin Lerner, president of American List Corp. in Great Neck, N.Y., has become a wealthy man by compiling computerized lists of names of high school and college students and then renting them out for 3 to 5 cents per name. Clients eager to reach 2.5 million high school seniors, for instance, include the armed forces, American Express, *Time,* Columbia Records, Chase Manhattan Bank, and some 700 colleges and trade schools. (If you have received a mailing from any of these, now you know how they may have gotten your name.)

How Lerner and his staff compile these names is interesting. In the beginning, according to *Business Week* (September 8, 1986), Lerner approached Long Island high schools, and if they did not cooperate, he bought yearbooks from students and lists from photographers who took pictures for schools. In acquiring the names of some 3.5 million university students, he has learned some tricks to the trade. "My staff can call up a dormitory blind, get a student on the line, and do a deal with him for his directory," he explains. "They want the money first, but they send the directory. Kids are honest."

Your assignment: It is possible you could become a list maker yourself, selling names to American List Corp. or its important rival, Metromail Corp., of Lincoln, Neb. Because of the constant turnover of high school seniors and college students, such lists will always be in demand. However, if you were to enter the names of, say, your college class into a microcomputer data base, using a program such as dBase III Plus or R:base System V, you might be able to organize it in ways that could make it available for more than one purpose. Look through college directories and see the different possible ways students' names could be organized (home town, major, etc.). Perhaps you have the basis for a business. What kinds of companies might be interested in buying these different kinds of lists?

Chapter 10

NETWORKS AND DATA COMMUNICATIONS: BRINGING US TOGETHER

Inventions often come about because of attempts to get an edge on the competition. The direct dial telephone—in which calls are placed directly, without the assistance of an operator—was invented by an Indiana undertaker in 1889 who had the strongest of reasons for eliminating reliance on operators: One of the local telephone operators was the wife of his main rival, and he was convinced she was deliberately diverting calls for undertakers to her husband's funeral parlor.

Without the direct dial telephone there could probably be no long-distance computer communications. But for a long time, computer systems and communications systems were separate industries. The industry that developed COBOL had little to do with the industry that developed cable. Then, somewhere in the late fifties and early sixties, the two industries began to fuse.

The merger became particularly evident in 1984, when American Telephone & Telegraph—forced by the U.S. Department of Justice to divest itself of regional telephone companies in return for being allowed to enter the computer business—announced a line of several computer products. A few weeks earlier, IBM announced it had joined forces with broadcasting network CBS and nationwide retailer Sears, Roebuck & Co. in the formation of Trintex, a joint venture in the videotex business. **Videotex** is the sending and receiving of words and pictures to at-home video screens so that people can do shopping, banking, and other tasks from their living rooms. Thus, AT&T, the communications giant, and IBM, the computer giant, seemed pitted to do battle in the two-way electronic services field. Although none of these endeavors has yet turned into a spectacular business success, there seems no clearer example of what people anticipate the new world of the Information Age will be like.

CASE STUDY: MOBILE MODEMS

On-line on the Road

Imagine a paperless society where time is never wasted and information is quite literally at your fingertips anywhere you go. That's the vision of the future the folks at Spectrum Cellular have.

Through the use of its cellular modem products, and a laptop computer and mobile phone, the diminutive Dallas company is promoting portable transmission of data. This means that anyone who uses an office computer can continue to work and to send and receive data even while away from the workplace—on a call with a client, at a construction site, or on the way to a police or fire department emergency. . . .

Spectrum Cellular modems—working in conjunction with a laptop computer and a mobile phone—can allow:

▶ A salesperson working with a customer in the field to get information on the availability or specifications of a particular product from the home office and to expedite the ordering process.

▶ A real estate agent whose client's eye is caught by a certain property while the two are traveling around a community to tap into the Multiple Listing Service on-line for the facts (and perhaps even to call the owner to arrange a showing).

▶ An insurance adjustor to relay a damage estimate immediately to his office and get a response in minutes for the waiting client, skipping a step or two and a delay of several days.

▶ Firemen speeding to a fire in a large building to get crucial statistics on that building from the department computer (for instance, that there's 5,000 gallons of oil stored in the west wing) so that they can react to what *could* happen.

▶ A journalist working on a rapidly breaking story to type notes and send the story as it develops, without leaving the room to make a call to her publication or station and thereby missing valuable information.

▶ A police officer to spend more time on enforcing the law than on waiting for air time with the dispatcher or on filling out paper forms. . . .

The word *cellular* is a key: it refers to the honeycomb-like framework of overlapping cells by which locations of low-powered transmitters are planned in a city. . . . When a mobile caller passes from one "cell" to another in moving through the city or when a particular channel is overloaded, a cell-to-cell "hand-off" can occur.

—*Link-Up* magazine

TELECOMMUNICATIONS AND COMPUTERS

Videotex is only one of the services possible within the field of **data communications,** an all-encompassing term that refers to the way in which data is transmitted from one location to another, whether it is a letter borne by Pony Express or a telephone call beamed by satellite. Data communications includes anything that has the four elements of sender, transmission line, message, and receiver. This, of course, would describe you and a caller having a conversation over a

telephone line, but it also describes the communications between parts of a computer system when input and output units, processor, and storage devices are spread out in dispersed locations. Working for Atlantic-Pacific Bank, you are in a position to see how important data communications is to banking. From ATMs to credit checking to keeping up with changing foreign-exchange rates, banking today depends on data communications.

Telecommunications is a form of data communications—specifically, communicating at a distance using either electromagnetic signals, such as those in telephone, radio, or television, or light energy, such as that in optical fiber lines. **Teleprocessing** combines "telecommunications" and "data processing" and means data processing at a distance; a teleprocessing system consists of terminals connected to a central computer by communication lines. Quite often telecommunications and teleprocessing are in the form of a network, an interconnected system of computers and/or peripheral devices at different locations. There are various kinds of networks, and, as we shall see, the whole idea of networks is one of the most exciting things to come along in recent years, for it expands the uses of computers considerably.

Whether telephone or computer system, a telecommunications system has three basic parts:

▶ Communications interface—the sending and receiving instruments
▶ Transmission—the communications channel
▶ Communications processing—devices to enhance communications

Let us show how these work.

SENDING A MESSAGE

COMMUNICATIONS

INTERFACES

Before you can send a message as voice, video, data, or whatever, you need some sort of device at your end of the communications line that will convert your ideas into the signal to be transmitted. A telegraph key is one example of such a **communications interface,** a telephone handset is another, a microphone is still another.

Here we are principally concerned with sending computer data. Because of the extensive telephone network already in place throughout North America and the world, a great deal of computer communications is over telephone lines. The telephone was built for voice transmission, which requires an **analog signal**—an electronic signal that will represent a range of frequencies. However, most input and output devices and most CPUs will only send and receive **digital signals,** which are merely the presence or absence of an electronic pulse.

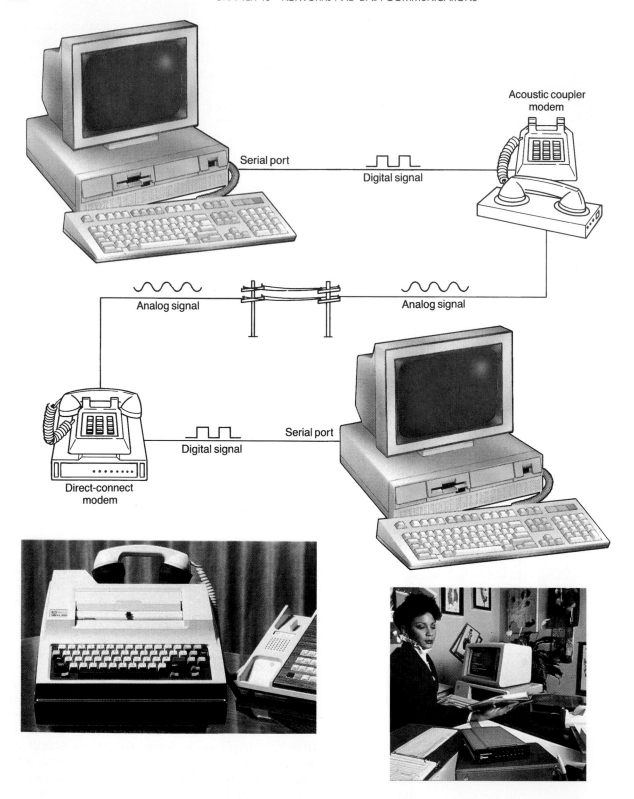

Serial port

Digital signal

Acoustic coupler modem

Analog signal

Analog signal

Direct-connect modem

Serial port

Digital signal

Figure 10-1. Digital to analog and back. *Opposite page, top:* A modem converts the digital signal's pulse and absence of a pulse—the binary 1s and 0s—into the analog signal of the telephone, which has a wider range of frequencies in order to accommodate the human voice. A modem at the receiving end converts the analog signal back into the digital signal for use by the second computer. *Lower left:* An acoustic coupler. This style of modem allows a standard telephone handset to be placed in the cradle. *Lower right:* A modem. When a modem is housed in a box separate from the computer, it is called a *stand-alone.* Some modems are housed within the computer housing (*onboard*) and are not visible to the user.

The device that converts digital signals to analog and the reverse is a **modem,** the tool for communications interfacing. *Modem* is short for "modulate/demodulate; **modulation** is the name of the process of converting from digital to analog and **demodulation** from analog to digital.

As Figure 10-1 shows, a modem may be an acoustic coupler modem or a direct-connect modem. An **acoustic coupler** is a modem with a cradle of rubber cups that will accept a standard telephone handset; this kind of modem is not used as much now, primarily because it is slow at transmitting and receiving data. A **direct-connect modem** connects directly to a telephone line. For microcomputers, direct-connect modems are of two types: stand-alone and internal. The **stand-alone modem** stands apart from the computer and is connected by a cable to the computer's serial port (a term we will explain in a moment). The **internal modem** is usually a plug-in circuit board that you may have installed at a computer store, but in some portable computers it is built in at the factory. Both types have modular telephone jacks in their rear panels. With one you connect the modem to the telephone wall jack; with the other you plug in your telephone so that you can do both voice communication and data communication over the same telephone line.

Data travels in two ways—serially and in parallel. With **serial data transmission,** bits flow in a continuous stream, like cars crossing a one-lane bridge; the bits flow in a series. With **parallel data transmission,** each bit making up a character flows through a separate line at the same time as the others, like cars moving together at the same speed on a freeway with several lanes. Serial transmission is the way most data is sent over telephone lines, and the plug-in board making up the serial connector in a microcomputer's modem is usually called a **serial port,** although it may also be called an **RS-232C connector** or an **asynchronous communications port.** Parallel transmission is not used for communications over telephone lines, although it is a standard method of sending data from a computer to a printer.

The speed with which information is sent is expressed in **baud rates** or **bits per second (bps).** Because of industry standardization, only a few different bps speeds are used for personal computers. They include 300, 1,200, 2,400, 4,800, and 9,600 baud rates. In most computer systems, a baud is equivalent to one bit, and baud rates can be converted to bps directly. That is, 300 baud equals 300 bps, and so on.

Not all computer communications must be converted from digital to analog and back. In computer systems where input, output, CPU, and secondary storage are all reasonably close together—within the same building, say—data can be transmitted digitally through special cables. Also, Sprint has installed a nationwide fiber-optic network in which essentially the process will be reversed from that of the present telephone system: Digital data will be converted to analog signals for transmission.

THE COMMUNICATION CHANNEL: TRANSMISSION

The communication channel, like a freeway or turnpike for cars, is the route along which data is transmitted. Telecommunications **transmission** is described by four characteristics:

▶ Direction of flow of data
▶ Communication lines or data roadways
▶ Speed of data transmission
▶ Sequencing, or modes of transmission

Direction of the Flow of Data

There are three directions or modes of data flow in a telecommunications system, as shown in Figure 10-2:

▶ Simplex
▶ Half-duplex
▶ Full-duplex

Simplex　Like a one-way street, **simplex transmission** allows data to travel in one direction only. Some terminals or processors are send-only or receive-only. Some POS terminals, for example, are send-only; some printers are receive-only devices.

Simplex transmission is not frequently used in telecommunications systems today, and it is generally used only when the terminal or processor requires it.

Half-Duplex　**Half-duplex transmission** is in both directions, but not simultaneously. Sometimes called "one way at a time" transmission, in half-duplex communications, data flows only in one direction at any one time, like traffic on a one-lane bridge or two people having a very polite conversation. For example, a POS terminal may transmit sales data to a distant CPU, and then the CPU may respond by acknowledging the receipt of that data.

Half-duplex transmission requires terminals or processors that can both send and receive messages. In addition, the transmission lines must be able to operate in either direction. The process of reversing the direction of transmission is called **overhead** and requires a certain amount of **turnaround time,** such as 20 to 200 milliseconds—time that can be significant if a large number of direction reversals occur.

Full-Duplex　Sometimes called "two-way operation," **full-duplex transmission** is just that; like cars on a two-lane, two-way street, data can be transmitted back and forth simultaneously. It is clearly the fastest of the three forms of transmission because not only is data

Figure 10-2. Three kinds of transmission lines. *Top:* Simplex—one-way flow of data. *Middle:* Half-duplex—one-way-at-a-time flow of data in either direction. *Bottom:* Full-duplex—simultaneous two-way flow of data.

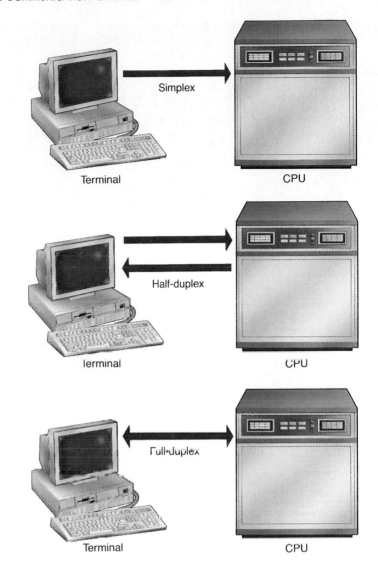

moving both ways at the same time but the turnaround time is eliminated. Almost all teleprocessing is now full duplex.

Important Connections: Data Roadways

There are three major roadways or transmission media through which data can be made to flow:

▶ Wire cable
▶ Microwave
▶ Fiber optics

These are shown in Figure 10-3.

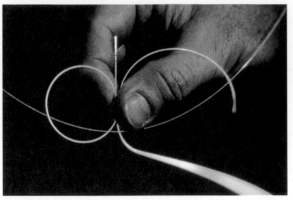

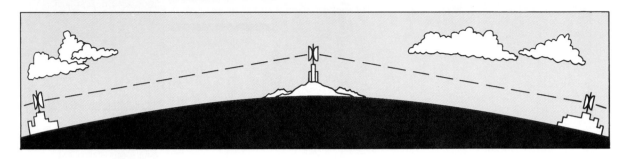

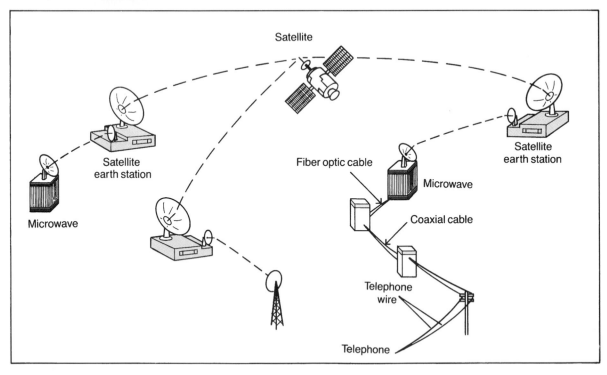

Wire Cable The oldest and still most common transmission line, **wire cable** is a major part of the nation's telephone system. Originally, telephone lines were simply pairs of copper wires strung between poles. Later these wire pairs were improved upon by the development of cables in which several hundred pairs of wires were bundled together to form a single cable. A more recent improvement is **coaxial cable,** in which multiple wires are replaced by a single solid core. You are apt to see coaxial cable used to link parts of a computer system located on one site.

Microwave A more recent development, **microwave transmission** consists of high-frequency waves that travel in straight lines through the air rather than through wires. Because the waves cannot bend with the curvature of the earth, they are relayed via antennas placed on the tops of buildings—including those of banks—and mountains and located usually every 25 to 35 miles. More than half of the telephone system is now made up of microwave technology.

Figure 10-3. **Four kinds of communication lines.** *Opposite page, top left:* Bundled copper wire telephone lines, originally designed for voice communication, are still the most popular means of carrying remote data communications, although the system is being updated with fiber-optic *(lower left in photo)* and other technology in order to better handle data communications. *Top right:* Fiber-optic cables consist of hairlike glass fibers, which carry voice, television, and data signals using lightwave communication. Honeycombs of crystal within the cable hold fibers in precise alignment. *Middle:* Microwave transmission requires that microwave repeater stations be located every few miles because the signal travels by line of sight and hence cannot bend around the curvature of the earth. *Bottom:* Satellites collect data from several sources and relay the messages to microwave earth stations.

Communications satellites in space, orbiting 22,000 miles above the earth, are also used as microwave relay stations because they rotate at the precise point and speed above the equator that makes them appear stationary to microwave transmitters on the ground. Among the dozens of satellites now orbiting the globe and handling voice, video, and data communications are those launched by **INTELSAT,** short for *International Telecommunications Satellite Consortium.* INTELSAT began with the Early Bird satellite in 1965 and now forms a worldwide communications system of over 100 countries. It accounts for most long-distance international communications. The United States's representative to the consortium is **COMSAT** (Communications Satellite Corporation).

Other satellite systems include those owned by RCA, the Americom system, which was the first to offer domestic communications service via satellite; Western Union, which launched its Westar system in 1974; AT&T, which leases satellites from COMSAT; Satellite Business Systems, put together by IBM, Aetna Life and Casualty Insurance Company, and COMSAT and which began operating in 1981; and American Satellite Company, developed by Fairchild Industries and Continental Telephone Company, which leases satellite usage from Western Union. Because of increasing telephone costs and decreasing satellite costs, satellite transmission is becoming a more popular form of data communications.

Fiber Optics One of the most exciting new communication technologies is **fiber optics,** in which data is transmitted as pulses of light through tubes of glass half the diameter of a human hair. Among the many advantages of fiber optics are that the materials are lighter and less expensive than wire cables, more flexible than microwave and not limited to line-of-sight transmission, and faster and more reliable at transmitting data than the other communications materials. However, with fiber optics the distance with which information may be transmitted is limited.

Speed of Data Transmission

Nearly any kind of message can be converted into analog form for transmission, but different messages require different numbers of bits. A burglar alarm signal may take 40 bits, a typical interoffice memo 3,000 bits, a newspaper-quality photograph 100,000 bits, a high-quality photograph 2 million bits. Obviously, then, the *speed* with which a communications line can transmit data becomes important for certain kinds of purposes.

As mentioned, data transmission rates are measured in bits per second (bps). Each kind of communication line has a certain speed or capacity for transmitting that information; this is called the **bandwidth** of that medium. Some of the bandwidths are as follows:

▶ *110–9600 bps:* Called **voiceband,** this includes the bandwidth of the standard telephone line.
▶ *9600–256,000 bps:* Called **medium band,** this includes the bandwidth of special leased lines frequently used to support high-speed terminals connected to CPUs.
▶ *256,000–1 million bps:* Called **broadband** or **wideband,** this is the highest-quality channel and is used to support CPU-to-CPU communications.

Two factors determine how fast data can be transmitted:

▶ Capabilities for sending and receiving CPUs
▶ The kind of transmission line or medium

Capabilities of CPUs   Data cannot be transmitted faster than it can be produced or received faster than it can be processed. Thus, the processing speeds of sending and receiving CPUs are important. Today microcomputer CPUs are in the voiceband range; the most common transmission rates are 300, 1,200, and 2,400 bps. Minis and mainframes, of course, operate much faster and commonly transmit and receive in medium band and broadband speeds.

Transmission Media   As you might expect, the older forms of transmission lines are not as speedy as, say, fiber optics. Thus, wire cable, such as coaxial cable, can send data at 50 million bps; however, common telephone lines are restricted to voiceband rates (up to 9,600 bps). Newer transmission technologies are faster: microwave—up to 45 million bps, satellites—up to 50 million, fiber optics—up to 275 million.

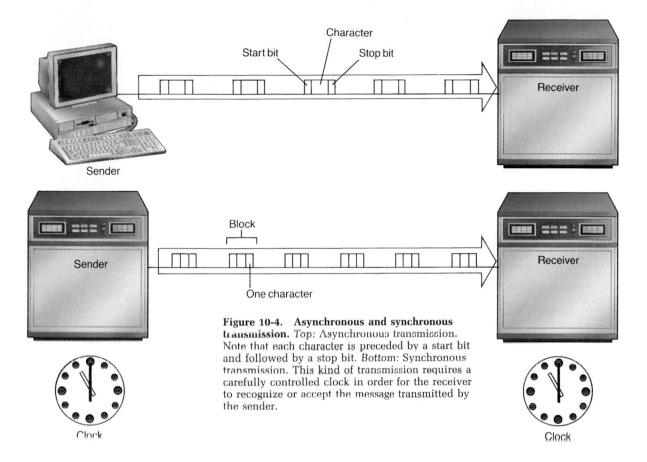

Figure 10-4. Asynchronous and synchronous transmission. *Top:* Asynchronous transmission. Note that each character is preceded by a start bit and followed by a stop bit. *Bottom:* Synchronous transmission. This kind of transmission requires a carefully controlled clock in order for the receiver to recognize or accept the message transmitted by the sender.

Mode of Transmission: Asynchronous and Synchronous

Data can be transmitted in two modes or sequences:

▶ Asynchronous—one character at a time
▶ Synchronous—groups of characters at a time

Asynchronous Transmission Data travels down the transmission line the way people travel down the highway in a bus—in a group. In **asynchronous transmission,** data is sent and received one character at a time, and each character, which is composed of seven or eight bits, is preceded by a "start" bit and followed by a "stop" bit. This is illustrated in Figure 10-4. The advantage of asynchronous transmission is that the data can be transmitted at any time that is convenient for the sender.

In order for a transmission to be successful, there must be a line **protocol,** a set of rules for the exchange of information between sender and receiver. The protocol in asynchronous transmission is that the start and stop bits indicate to the receiver the arrival of data. This type of protocol is often used for terminals with slow speeds.

Synchronous Transmission　In **synchronous transmission** data is sent without start and stop bits. For the data transmission to be meaningful to the receiver, however, sender and receiver must be synchronized by a carefully controlled clock. That is, the blocks of characters are sent and received in a timed sequence. This type of transmission requires more expensive equipment than does the first kind, but data is transmitted faster.

COMMUNICATIONS
PROCESSORS

Communications processors resemble computer CPUs in that they have similar circuitry, have memories, and can be programmed, but their purpose is limited: to enhance data communications between two points. Communications processors fall into three broad categories (although there is some overlap):

▶ Message switchers
▶ Multiplexers and concentrators
▶ Front-end processors

Message Switchers

Atlantic-Pacific Bank's mainframe is in the Boston headquarters, but it is connected to three terminals in another branch bank across the state in Pittsfield. This is not an unusual arrangement; it makes sense for a single CPU to serve several terminals since the CPU operates at much greater speeds than the terminals do. As Figure 10-5 shows, there are two ways to connect the terminals to the CPU:

▶ Use three long-distance lines for the three terminals.
▶ Use a *single* long-distance line to connect all three terminals and have a switching device called a message switcher at the Pittsfield branch bank.

A **message switcher** is a processor that receives data messages from terminals, determines their destination, and routes them one at a time to the CPU. It distributes messages coming from the CPU to the appropriate terminal.

The advantage of a message switcher, of course, is that it reduces long-distance transmission costs, since only a single line is needed. Although only one terminal at a time can communicate with the CPU, message switchers are efficient, with low-speed terminals that are intermittently used at remote sites.

Figure 10-5. With and without a message switcher. *Top:* Each terminal has its own long-distance line connecting it to the CPU in Boston. *Bottom:* A single long-distance line connects the CPU to the three terminals in Pittsfield, but a message switcher in Pittsfield is used to distribute incoming messages from the CPU and pick up outgoing messages.

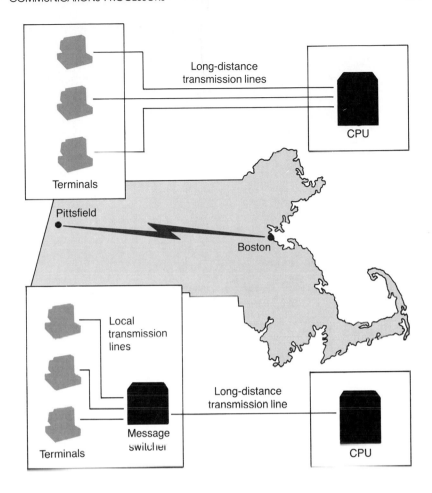

Multiplexers and Concentrators

Like a message switcher, a multiplexer allows several terminals to use one line to communicate with a CPU; however, it allows the terminals to send their messages *simultaneously.* A **multiplexer,** in other words, collects messages from various senders, puts them in order, and transmits them along a broadband channel at very high speeds to the receiver.

A **concentrator** is essentially a smart multiplexer: It can be programmed, has more processing capability, and is more flexible than a multiplexer.

Multiplexers and concentrators are frequently used at terminal sites having heavy input and output requirements.

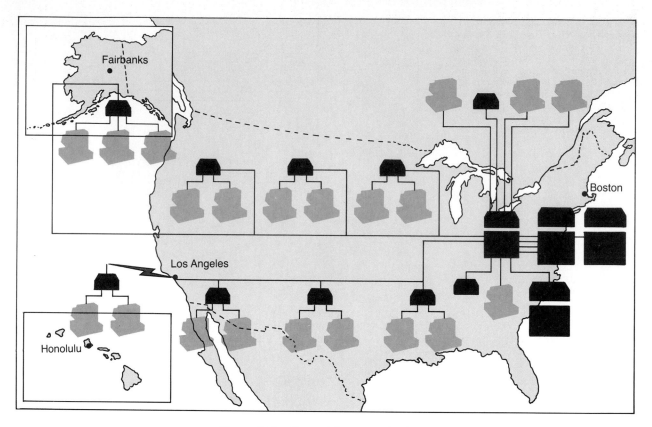

Figure 10-6.   How a telecommunications system works. Terminals are linked to concentrators, which are microcomputers or minicomputers used for communications purposes. The computer's digital signal is changed to an analog signal by the sending modem, then changed back to digital by the receiving modem. The front-end processor is a micro- or minicomputer that relieves the central computer of some of its communications tasks.

Front-End Processors

A **front-end processor** is located at the site of the CPU or the host computer and its purpose is to relieve the central computer of some of the communications tasks, leaving the larger computer free for processing applications programs.

Here we can see that communication processing and data processing equipment are nearly alike. Indeed, front-end processors *are* computers: They have some identical circuitry and perform many of the operations that data processing equipment performs. The only difference between the two kinds of equipment is their purpose.

An example of how these several communications devices work is shown in Figure 10-6.

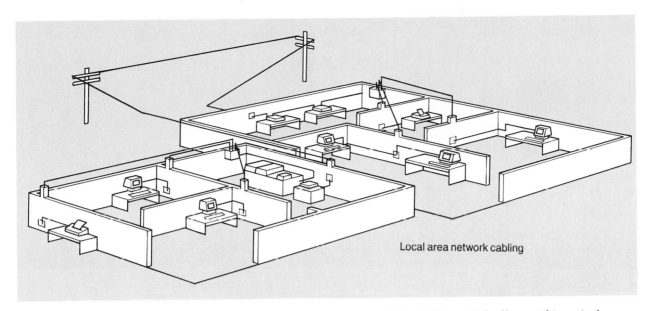

Local area network cabling

Figure 10-7. Local area network. An LAN may link offices within a single building, as here, or offices in several nearby buildings.

NETWORKS

A **network** is simply a telecommunications system that connects two or more computers and their peripheral devices. These networks are used to connect mainframes, minicomputers, and microcomputers in either a local area—in which case they are referred to as *local area networks,* or *LANs*—or a much larger area. LANs in particular have received a lot of attention in recent years as means of integrating microcomputers into computer information systems.

Networks and Geographical Dispersion

An organization the size of Atlantic-Pacific Bank will have several kinds of networks. On the one hand, you may find you need to communicate with another microcomputer down the hall in another office. On the other hand, the bank may wish to move money electronically around the globe through several time zones throughout the night in order to take advantage of the most favorable interest rates in different parts of the world.

The types of networks are as follows:

▶ **Local Area Networks:** Using copper wire or coaxial cable or fiber-optic cables, **local area networks (LANs)** are networks in which all the computers and terminals are located in the same offices or buildings—for instance, several buildings on a college campus. An example of an LAN is shown in Figure 10-7.

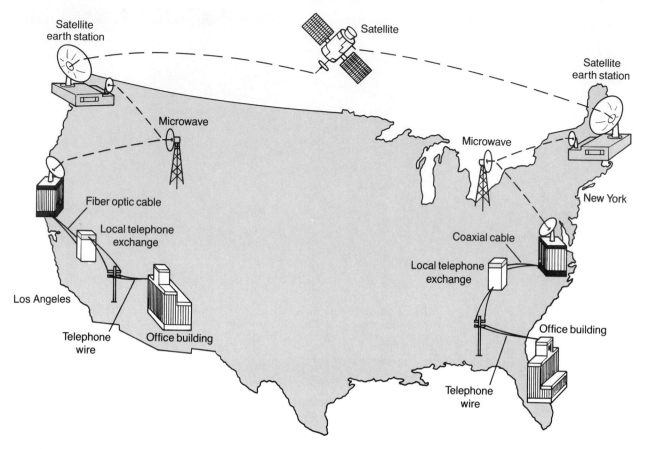

Figure 10-8.   Wide area network. Besides cable, WANs use microwave relays and satellites as means of communicating long distances within the same country. A WAN may also be linked to various organizations' LANs.

▶ **Metropolitan area networks:** Using microwave, optical fiber, copper wire, and perhaps **cellular radio** (mobile phones in cars), **metropolitan area networks (MANs)** are usually created by a local telephone company to serve customers in the same city.

▶ **Wide area networks:** Abbreviated **WANs, wide area networks** use microwave relays and satellites to reach users over long distances in the same country, as shown in Figure 10-8. Examples of such networks in the United States are Tymnet, Telenet, and Uninet.

▶ **International networks:** Reaching clients outside the country, an **international network** uses coaxial cables and/or satellites, as shown in Figure 10-9. Examples are Western Union and RCA.

Figure 10-9. International network. Networks connecting different countries necessarily use not only cable and microwave relays but also satellites. Sometimes satellites communicate directly with each other.

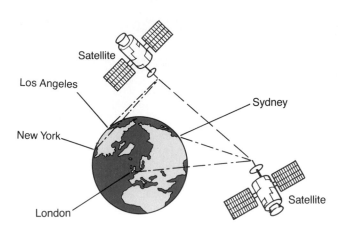

SATELLITE EARTH STATIONS

Almost a tenth of the way to the moon, over 20 domestic communications satellites transmit and receive voices, images, and data to and from the earth below. Satellites such as *Galaxy I, Westar IV,* and *Satcom III* make their home in the Clarke Belt, a narrow orbit 22,300 miles above the equator. . . .

What does this exotic space-age technology have to do with personal computers? Plenty. According to Link Resources Corporation of New York City, data transmission will grow from a current 19% of satellite usage to 40% by 1990. Many large corporations already take advantage of satellites for mainframe-to-mainframe links, but the major growth in satellite digital transmission will be driven by PCs. . . .

While telephone transmission costs are directly related to distance, the cost for satellite transmission is the same for 100 miles or 1000 miles. Geostationary space antennas can relay data across the continent in a fraction of a second (270 milliseconds in either direction). This point-to-multipoint approach to data communications enables many locations to be reached economically and quickly.

—Richard Lewis, *PC World*

Networks are now commonplace in many organizations, where data may be sent between micro and mainframe computers and similar hardware within the same building or cluster of buildings or country or different countries. The networks—particularly LANs—may take the form of what is known as a *star network*, with all stations connecting to a central controller, or a single-cable system, also known as a *bus LAN*, in which one line connects all stations.

Types of Networks

The most common networks are:

▶ Star network
▶ Ring network
▶ Bus network
▶ Hierarchical network

These are shown in Figure 10-10. The points in a network are called **nodes** and the lines joining them are called **arcs.**

Star Networks The **star network** is frequently used to connect one or more small computers or peripheral devices to a large host computer or CPU. Many organizations use the star network or a variation of it in a **time-sharing system,** in which several users are able to share a common central processor.

In a time-sharing setup, each terminal receives a fixed amount of the central CPU's time, called a **time slice.** If you are sitting at a terminal and cannot complete your task during the time slice, the

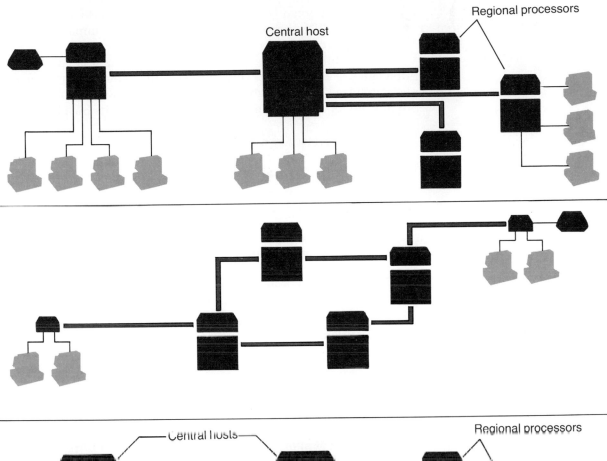

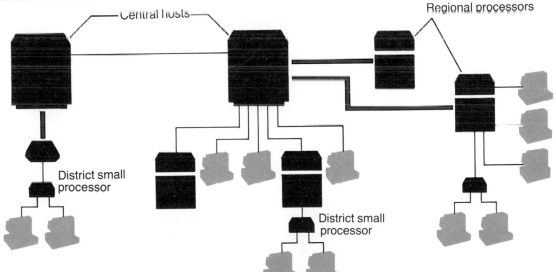

Figure 10-10.   Three types of networks. *Top:* Star network. *Middle:* Ring network. *Bottom:* Hierarchy.

computer will come back to you to allow you to do so. Actually, because the CPU operates so much faster than terminals, you will probably not even notice that the CPU is away.

By establishing time sharing, many people in a large organization can use a centralized computing facility. Time sharing can also be purchased from an outside service, which is an economical way to operate for a small company that cannot afford its own large computer.

The advantages of time sharing are:

▶ It allows economical allocation of an expensive resource, the CPU.

▶ It allows geographically dispersed users access to a large, powerful system.

The disadvantages are:

▶ Communication costs—particularly the cost of long-distance telephone lines—can be high for users in remote locations.

▶ Because the system is being shared with others, there is a possibility that data will not be secure.

The star network is frequently used in a LAN to connect several microcomputers to a central unit that works as a communications controller. If the user of one microcomputer wants to send a document or message to a user at another microcomputer, the message is routed through the central communications controller.

Another common use of the star network is as a LAN to connect several microcomputers to a mainframe computer that allows access to an organization's data base—oftentimes through what is known as a data base machine. A **data base machine** is a specialized computer that is connected to a second computer (CPU); their sole function is to manage the data base and store the DBMS program.

Access and control of star networks typically is maintained by a polling system. **Polling** means that the central computer, or communications controller, "polls" or asks each device in the network if it has a message to send and then allows each in turn to transmit data.

Ring Networks   The **ring network**—which, as Figure 10-10 shows, can be as simple as a circle of point-to-point connections of computers at dispersed locations, with no central host computer or communications controller—is appropriate for distributed data processing systems. A **distributed data processing system** is a decentralized computer system in which computers do their own processing in various locations but are connected to each other, usually via a LAN for computers that are geographically close or via telephone lines if they are far apart. This linkage allows the computers to share processing loads, programs, data, and other resources. Typically the computers are microcomputers or minicomputers.

The advantages of distributed data processing are:

▶ Processing requirements and demands are shared among several computers.

▶ People at local sites have independence and control over their own computer resources.

▶ A corporation may have decentralized control and organization.

The disadvantages are:

▶ There may be communications problems between CPUs, especially if they are made by different manufacturers.

▶ There may be problems in keeping data secure—that is, in keeping unauthorized people from seeing it.

▶ More skilled programmers and computer operators are required because there are more computer operations than in a time-sharing or centralized operation.

▶ Tighter organizational control is required of all computing facilities.

Access and control of ring networks is typically maintained by a "token-passing" system. IBM's Token-Ring network, for example, is thought by some observers to be a watershed event comparable to the development of the IBM PC itself, for the Token-Ring network is designed to link all types of computers together, including not only personal computers but also possibly minicomputers and mainframes. As Figure 10-11 indicates, a **token-passing network** resembles a merry-go-round: To deliver a message, you would hand your addressed note to a rider (the token) on the merry-go-round, who would drop it off at the appropriate place.

Bus Networks **Bus networks** are similar to ring networks except that the ends are not connected. All communications are carried on a common cable or bus and are available to each device on the cable. The advantages and disadvantages are similar to those for ring networks.

Access and control of bus networks are typically maintained by a method called **contention,** whereby if a line is unused, a terminal or device can transmit its message at will, but if two or more terminals initiate messages simultaneously, they must stop and transmit again at different intervals.

Hierarchical Networks As Figure 10-10 shows, the **hierarchical network** somewhat resembles the star network. It consists of several computers linked to a central host computer or CPU, but these other computers may also play host to smaller computers. For instance, the host at the top of the hierarchy may be a mainframe; the ones below it may be minicomputers. These computers may be used to

Figure 10-11. The Token-Ring network. The person sending the message waits for a free token to pass by on the ring, then changes the token to "busy" and adds data. The person receiving the message copies the data and then sends the token back to the sender. The sender sets the token free, making it available to carry another message.

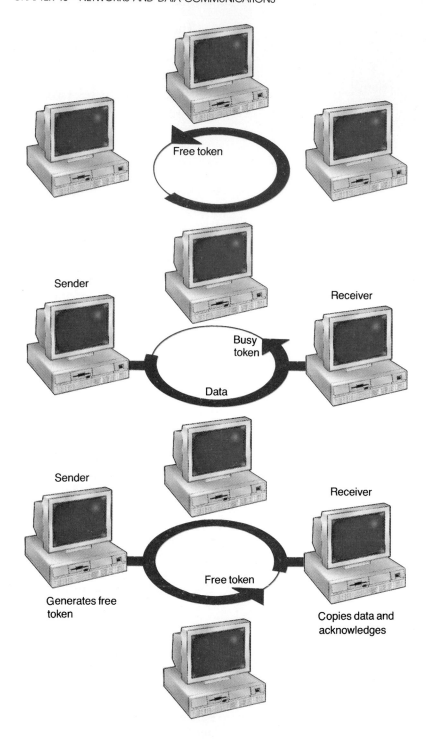

Free token

Sender

Receiver

Busy token

Data

Sender

Receiver

Free token

Generates free token

Copies data and acknowledges

Teleconferencing. Improved networking systems will permit better teleconferencing, such as the services offered by AT&T and Western Union.

gain access to large data bases and to assist lower-level computers (such as microcomputers and terminals) with sophisticated computations.

Installing a Network: Owning versus Renting

Atlantic-Pacific Bank is a big organization with many branches. Should it have its own network or rent parts of a network from the outside? You have three choices:

▶ A private network
▶ A vendor network
▶ A value-added network

Private Network Atlantic-Pacific could design and install its own network; this would be a **private network.** The advantages are:

▶ The network will custom-fit your organization's needs.
▶ Security of data and operations will be tighter—this is of particular importance for a bank—because no outside organization will have direct access to the network.

The disadvantages are:

▶ A private network may be more expensive.
▶ Your organization will have to assume total responsibility for the design, installation, and operation of the network—a task for which it may be difficult to find people since data communications is a rather specialized occupation.

Vendor Network If you decide not to have a private network, you could have a **vendor network,** in which an outside company furnishes all the hardware, software, and protocols—everything except the transmission line. The transmission line would be furnished by a **common carrier,** an organization such as AT&T or Western Union, which has been approved by the Federal Communications Commission and state regulatory agencies to offer a broad range of communications services to the public. There are also **specialized common carriers,** public networks that are more restricted in their services, such as MCI Communications Corporation, Southern Pacific Communications Corporation, and ITT World Communications.

One well-known vendor network is IBM's Systems Network Architecture, better known as SNA. Introduced in 1974 as a standard way of connecting IBM host computers to terminal networks, SNA has been enhanced over the years so that it now can support a wide variety of hosts and peripheral devices.

The advantages of using a vendor network are:

▶ Outside expertise is available to design, install, and operate the network, so you need not hire staff of your own.

▶ Security of data and operations can still be controlled because the network is not shared with other users.

Disadvantages are:

▶ Vendor networks are still more expensive than alternatives.

▶ You do not have complete control over the network.

Value-Added Network   Whereas the vendor in a vendor network provides everything but the transmission line itself, the vendor of a **value-added network (VAN)** leases communication lines from a common carrier and then enhances (improves the value of) these lines by adding improvements such as error detection and faster response time. A value-added network allows communications within your own organization as well as between user organizations. Examples of value-added networks are GTE Telenet and Tymnet, Inc., which receive data from customers over telephone lines.

The advantages of a value-added network are:

▶ It requires only a small initial investment.

▶ The responsibility for designing, installing, and operating the network remains outside your organization.

▶ Charges are based on usage—you pay only for the services you use.

▶ You can communicate with other users outside your organization.

The disadvantages are:

▶ You have no control over the network itself.

▶ Because you are sharing resources with other companies, security of your data and operations may be a concern.

ISDN: PLANETWIDE
COMMUNICATIONS

The initials **ISDN**—for **Integrated Services Digital Networks**—describe something that is not here yet but perhaps will be by the next decade. Its effects are awesome to contemplate. Telephone numbers, for instance, might be assigned for a lifetime, like Social Security numbers, so that wherever you lived you could always be reached by phone. Or wherever you were, you could press the telephone buttons B-U-R-G-E-R-K-I-N-G to reach the nearest Burger King.

ISDN reflects the hope of many people that as most major countries build digital networks for computer communications over the next few years—networks that will replace the analog telephone networks—they will be integrated with each other. Widespread use of narrowband ISDN is expected by 1990 and of broadband ISDN by 1995.

Clearly, ISDN would change the nature of both the communications and the computer industries. A telephone bought in the United States could also work in England. A computer could communicate with any other computer. A person could make a telephone call on the same line and at the same time as he or she was communicating with a computer. Information could be obtained from a distant computer as quickly as from one's own microcomputer.

SUMMARY

- **Data communications** refers to the way in which data is transmitted from one location to another; it includes anything that has the elements of sender, transmission line, message, and receiver, such as the different parts of a computer system in different locations. **Videotex** is a form of data communications that allows words and pictures to be sent and received on at-home video screens.

- **Telecommunications** is a form of data communications that uses electromagnetic signals or light energy over a distance (such as telephone, radio, and television signals).

- **Teleprocessing** combines telecommunications and data processing; it means data processing at a distance. A teleprocessing system consists of terminals connected to a central computer by communication lines. Telecommunication and teleprocessing systems are often in network form—an interconnected system of computers and/or peripheral devices at remote locations.

- A telecommunications system has three parts: (1) communications interface, (2) transmission, and (3) communications processing.

- **Communications interface** comprises the sending and receiving instruments, such as telegraph keys and telephone handsets. Because of the extensive telephone network already in place in this country, much computer communication is over telephone lines. The telephone uses an **analog signal**—an electronic signal that will represent a range of frequencies—for voice transmission. However, most input and output devices and most CPUs will send and receive only **digital signals,** which are the presence or absence of an electronic pulse.

- A **modem** (short for modulate/demodulate) is the device that converts digital signals to analog signals, and vice versa. **Modulation** is the process of converting from digital to analog signals, and **demodulation** converts analog signals to digital ones.

- A modem may be an acoustic coupler modem or a direct-connect modem. An **acoustic coupler** has a cradle of rubber cups that will accept a standard telephone handset; this kind of modem is slow at transmitting and receiving data. A **direct-connect modem** connects directly to a telephone line.

- For microcomputers, direct-connect modems are of two types: stand-alone and internal. The **stand-alone modem** stands apart from the computer and is connected by a cable to the computer's serial port. The **internal modem** is a plug-in circuit board or is built in at the factory. Both types have modular telephone jacks in their rear panels. One connects the modem to the telephone wall jack; the other connects the telephone.

- Data travels in two ways—serially and in parallel. With **serial data transmission,** bits flow in a continuous stream. With **parallel data transmission,** each bit making up a character flows through a separate line simultaneously. Serial transmission is the way most data is sent over telephone lines, and the plug-in board making up the serial connector in a microcomputer's modem is usually called a **serial port,** although it may also be called an **RS-232C connector** or an **asynchronous communications port.** Parallel transmission is not used for communications over telephone lines, although it is a standard method of sending data from a computer to a printer.

▶ The speed at which information is sent is expressed in **bits per second (bps).** The speeds used for personal computers are 300, 1,200, 2,400, 4,800, and 9,600 bps.

▶ Telecommunication **transmission,** the second part of a telecommunications system, is described by four characteristics: (1) direction of flow of data, (2) communication lines, or data roadways, (3) speed of data transmission, and (4) mode of transmission, or sequencing.

▶ The three directions, or modes of data flow are (1) simplex, (2) half-duplex, and (3) full-duplex. **Simplex transmission** allows data to travel in one direction only. Some terminals are send-only or receive-only. Simplex transmission is not frequently used in telecommunications systems today—generally only when the terminal or processor requires it. **Half-duplex transmission,** sometimes called "one way at a time transmission," is in both directions, but not simultaneously. This type of transmission, which is the most common kind of transmission operation, requires terminals or processors that can both send and receive messages, and the transmission lines must be able to operate in either direction. **Overhead** is the process of reversing direction of transmission, which requires a certain amount of **turnaround time. Full-duplex transmission,** sometimes called "two-way operation," works in both directions simultaneously. It is the fastest of the three forms of transmission, but it is not yet widely used because coordination is difficult and it requires special equipment.

▶ There are three major kinds of communications lines, or data roadways: (1) wire cable, (2) microwave, and (3) fiber optics. **Wire cable** is the oldest and most common transmission line and is a major part of the American telephone system. Wires are sometimes bundled together to form a single cable. A **coaxial cable** replaces multiple wires with a single core. **Microwave transmission** consists of high-frequency waves that travel in straight lines through the air rather than through wires; the waves are relayed via antennas placed about 25 to 35 miles apart. More than half the American telephone system is now made up of microwave technology. **Communications satellites** are also used as microwave relay stations. **INTELSAT** (*International Telecommunications Satellite Consortium*) has launched many of these satellites and accounts for most long-distance international communications. The United States representative to the consortium is **COMSAT** (*Communications Satellite Corporation*). **Fiber op-**

tics is a new communications technology that transmits data as pulses of light through tubes of glass half the diameter of a human hair. Fiber optics materials are lighter and less expensive than wire cables, more flexible than microwave and not limited to line-of-sight transmission, and faster and more reliable than the other communications materials. However, fiber optics are limited in the distance over which information may be transmitted.

▶ Because different messages require different numbers of bits, the speed of transmission of data is important for certain purposes. Each kind of communication line has a certain speed or capacity for transmitting information; this is called **bandwidth.**

▶ Some of the bandwidths are (1) **voiceband** (110–9600 bps), the bandwidth of the standard telephone line; (2) **medium band** (9,600–256,000 bps), the bandwidth of special leased lines frequently used to support high-speed terminals connected to CPUs; and (3) **broadband,** or **wideband** (256,000–1 million bps), which is the highest quality channel and is used to support CPU-to-CPU communications.

▶ Two factors determine how fast data can be transmitted: (1) the capabilities of the sending and receiving CPUs, since data cannot be transmitted faster than it can be produced or received; and (2) the kind of transmission line or medium, with telephone lines being the slowest, and microwaves, satellites, and fiber optics being the fastest.

▶ The mode of transmission, or sequencing, of data can be asynchronous (one character at a time) or synchronous (groups of characters at a time). In **asynchronous transmission,** 7- or 8-bit characters are sent or received one at a time, preceded by a "start" bit and followed by a "stop" bit. The data can be transmitted at any time that is convenient for the sender. The **protocol,** which is a set of rules for the exchange of information between sender and receiver, in asynchronous, is the start and stop bits that indicate to the receiver the arrival of data. In **synchronous transmission,** data is sent without start and stop bits, but the sender and the receiver must be synchronized by a clock, which means that the blocks of characters are sent and received in a timed sequence. Synchronous transmission requires more expensive equipment than asynchronous transmission, but the former transmits data faster than the latter.

▶ **Communications processors** (the third part of a telecommunications system) have circuitry similar to CPUs and memories, and they can be programmed.

However, their purpose is limited: to enhance data communications between two points. Communications processors fall into three broad categories, with some overlap: (1) message switchers, (2) multiplexers and concentrators, and (3) front-end processors.

▶ A **message switcher** is a processor that receives data messages from terminals, determines their destination, and routes them one at a time to the CPU. It distributes messages coming from the CPU to the appropriate terminal. Message switchers have the advantage of reducing long-distance transmission costs, because only one line is needed. These switchers are efficient, with low-speed terminals that are intermittently used at remote sites. Only one terminal at a time can communicate with the CPU.

▶ A **multiplexer** allows several terminals to use one line simultaneously to communicate with a CPU. It collects messages, puts them in order, and transmits them along a broadband channel. A **concentrator** is a multiplexer that can be programmed and that has increased processing capability and greater flexibility. Multiplexers and concentrators are frequently used at terminal sites that have large input and output requirements.

▶ A **front-end processor** is located at the site of the CPU or the host computer; it relieves the central computer of some of the communications tasks, leaving it free for processing applications programs. Communications processors are computers in themselves; they differ from data processors in their purpose.

▶ A **network** is a telecommunications system that connects two or more computers and their peripheral devices.

▶ **Local area networks (LANs)** use copper wire, coaxial cable, or optical fiber to connect all the computers and terminals located in the same offices or buildings.

▶ **Metropolitan area networks (MANs),** usually created by a local telephone company, use microwave, optical fiber, copper wire, and perhaps **cellular radio** (mobile radio phones) to serve customers in the same city.

▶ **Wide area networks (WANs)** use microwave relays and satellites to reach users over long distances in the same country.

▶ **International networks** use coaxial cables and/or satellites to reach clients outside a country.

▶ The most common networks are (1) star, (2) ring, (3) bus, and (4) hierarchical. The points in a network are called **nodes** and the lines joining them are called **arcs.**

▶ A **star network** consists of one or more small computers or peripheral devices connected to a large host computer or CPU. Star networks are often used in a **time-sharing system,** in which several users are able to share a common central processor by receiving a **time slice,** which is a fixed amount of CPU time alloted to the user's terminal. Time sharing can be established within a single organization or purchased from an outside service. Its advantages are (1) that it allows economical allocation of an expensive resource and (2) that it allows geographically dispersed users access to a large, powerful system. Its disadvantages are (1) that communications costs can be high for users in remote locations and (2) that data may not be secure.

▶ A common use of the star network is as a LAN to connect several microcomputers to a mainframe computer that allows access to an organization's data base. The mainframe is often a **data base machine,** a specialized computer connected to a second computer (CPU). Its function is to manage the data base and store the DBMS program.

▶ Access and control of star networks typically is maintained by a polling system. **Polling** means that the central computer, or communication controller, "polls" or asks each device in the network if it has a message to send and then allows each in turn to transmit data.

▶ A **ring network** is a **distributed data processing system,** which is a decentralized computer system in which connected computers do their own processing in various locations, usually via telephone lines. This linkage allows the computers, typically minicomputers, to share processing loads, programs, data, and other resources. Distributed data processing has several advantages: (1) Processing requirements and demands are shared among several computers. (2) People at local sites are independent and have control over their own computer resources. Its disadvantages include: (1) There may be communications problems between CPUs. (2) Data may not be secure. (3) More skilled programmers and computer operators are required because there are more computer operations than in time-sharing, or centralized, operation. (4) Tighter organizational control is required of all computing facilities.

▶ Access and control of ring networks is typically maintained by a "token-passing" system, which may link not only personal computers but also mini-computers and mainframes. A **token-passing network** resembles a merry-go-round; the message is given to a "rider" (the token) on the merry-go-round, which drops it off at the appropriate address.

▶ **Bus networks** are similar to ring networks except that the ends are not connected. All communications are carried on a common cable or bus and are available to each device on the cable. The advantages and disadvantages are similar to those for ring networks. Access and control of bus networks are typically maintained by **contention,** whereby if a line is unused, a terminal or device can transmit its message at will, but if two or more terminals initiate messages simultaneously, they must stop and transmit again at different intervals.

▶ **Hierarchical networks** resemble star networks. They consist of several computers linked to a central host computer or CPU, but these computers may also play host to smaller computers.

▶ A **private network** is a company's own network. Its advantages are (1) that it will custom-fit the organization's needs and (2) that the security of data and operations will be tight. Its disadvantages are (1) that it may be expensive and (2) that the organization will have to assume total responsibility for the design, installation, and operation of the network.

▶ In the case of a **vendor network,** an outside company furnishes all the hardware, software, and protocols, but not the transmission line, which is furnished by a **common carrier**—an organization approved by the Federal Communications Commission and state regulatory agencies to offer communications services to the public. There are also **specialized common carriers,** public networks that are more restricted in their services, such as MCI Communications Corporation, Southern Pacific Communications Corporation, and ITT World Communications. The advantages of a vendor network are (1) that outside expertise is available to design, install, and operate the network and (2) that the security of data and operations can still be controlled because the network is not shared with others. Its disadvantages are that (1) it is expensive and (2) that the user does not have complete control over the network.

▶ A **value-added network (VAN)** is like a vendor network; however, in this case the leased communications lines are enhanced by adding improvements such as error detection and faster response time. A value-added network also allows communications within an organization as well as between user organizations. Its advantages are as follows: (1) It requires only a small initial investment. (2) The responsibility for designing, installing, and operating the network remains with the outside service. (3) Charges are based on usage. (4) The user can communicate with other users outside the organization. Its disadvantages include: (1) The user has no control over the network. (2) Because the user is sharing resources with other companies, data and operations may not be secure.

▶ **Integrated Services Digital Networks (ISDN)** may be available soon. These computer communications networks will use digital technology to replace analog telephone networks. This technology will allow a computer to communicate with any other computer, allow a telephone bought in one country to work in any other country, and allow a person to make a phone call and use the same line at the same time to communicate with a computer; it will also change the nature of publishing and improve videotex systems. Planning is now in progress to make these systems compatible—even among countries.

KEY TERMS

Acoustic coupler, p. 323

Analog signal, p. 321

Arc, p. 335

Asynchronous communications port, p. 323

Asynchronous transmission, p. 329

Bandwidth, p. 328

Baud rates, p. 323

Bits per second (bps), p. 323

Broadband, p. 328

Bus network, p. 339

Cellular radio, p. 334

Coaxial cable, p. 327

Common carrier, p. 341

Communications satellite, p. 327

Communications interface, p. 321

Communications processor, p. 330

COMSAT, p. 327

Concentrator, p. 331

Contention, p. 339

REVIEW QUESTIONS

1. Name the three basic parts of any telecommunications system.
2. What is the function of a modem? Define digital and analog signals.
3. What is half-duplex transmission?
4. Describe the three major data roadways.
5. How is the speed of data transmission measured?
6. What is the difference between asynchronous and synchronous transmission?
7. Describe the operations of one type of communications processor.
8. What is a time-sharing network? A distributed data processing system?
9. Compare the advantages of a vendor network with the advantages of a private network.

CASE PROBLEMS

Case 10-1: Using the Present While Waiting for the Information Age

Despite the claims of the futurists, the Information Age has not arrived just yet. There are a great many bottlenecks, such as the old-fashioned telephone network now in existence, which has limited ability to handle information: Low-cost information can be transmitted to personal computers at only 120 characters per second, slightly faster than what most people comfortably read—whereas the IBM PC, for example, can receive 5 million characters per second. In addition, of course, there are a great many people who do not *have* personal computers—your great aunt, perhaps. The term "Information Age" is premature. This fact has some implications for electronic mail.

Electronic mail applies to any communications service that permits the transmission and storage of messages by electronic means. This includes the telex machine, widely used since World War I and operated by Western Union, which leases telex lines to subscribers. It also includes facsimile ("fax") machines, which transmit both text and photographic images. The future, however, lies with the computer-mailbox services, in which a personal computer is used to send a message over telephone lines to a central computer, which then transmits it to the recipient's personal computer.

At present, the situation in computer-mailbox services resembles the early days of the telephone. Both the sender and the recipient must subscribe to the same service, but until a service has lots of subscribers, people are not inclined to subscribe. MCI is one company that is trying to expand electronic mail.

With MCI Mail, the sender must have a personal computer (or telex, word processor, or electronic typewriter with a memory) linked to a telephone in order to send an electronic letter, but the letter is sent to a special high-speed laser printer at a regional center, which prints it out; the letter is then hand-delivered—at its fastest, about four hours—either through the U.S. mail or by courier service. This is an example of mixing the new technology with the old. For two years, Federal Express offered ZapMail, a service that was less demanding of the user and that allowed graphics and already-typed material to be transmitted. In this process, the sender's document was picked up by courier and taken to a Federal Express office, where it was "faxed"—sent by facsimile machine—to another Federal Express office, then delivered by courier to the recipient. However, Zap-Mail was discontinued because of many problems (light originals wouldn't reprint, facsimile machines broke down, telephone line disturbances interrupted transmission).

Your assignment: The Information Age may not have entirely arrived just yet, but the next few years will be pivotal and there will be major changes. The trick is to anticipate trends. Both MCI and Federal Express have tried to bridge the present and the future, not an easy undertaking. Look back over this chapter—and the preceding three chapters on hardware. Can you think of ways of using the present—present transportation, consumer habits, people's expectations, and so on—linking them with new communications technology, and applying them to certain kinds of enterprise?

Case 10-2: Avoiding Local Area Confusion in LANs

Local area networks (LANs) have been around since the mid-1970s, but there have been conflicts as to what technologies are best. The result is that the LAN market is characterized by "local area confusion." Some LANs are made by computer manufacturers that connect only their equipment, others work with a variety of equipment. Standards have begun to evolve, but manufacturers must still come together to agree on protocols, the coding and formats that permit computers to communicate with each other.

When considering whether to install an LAN you want to know how your business or office will actually change when it is implemented. Will current software work under the network? Are all printers available to all users via software control? Is there a mail facility for storing messages and sending them from one user to another? Can any user send jobs to another station if that station is not currently in use? What do employees have to learn?

Your assignment: Suppose you were the dean of a small technical college that is expanding onto a brand-new campus. You are to consult with the architect about the best kind of facilities, and you are to specify the kind of features you want in an LAN that will be wired into all the offices, dormitories, classrooms, and laboratories. What kind of requirements would you state?

PART 4

COMPUTER-BASED INFORMATION SYSTEMS

"Although we continue to think we live in an industrial society," writes futurist John Naisbitt, "we have in fact changed to an economy based on the creation and distribution of information."

This has tremendous significance for your career over the next 20 years. The amount of scientific and technical information now doubles every 5½ years, but with more powerful information systems and more scientists, the doubling could increase to 20 months, according to some estimates. And with mass-produced knowledge the driving force in our economy, during the last decade of this century computer skills may be needed in as many as three-quarters of all jobs. Indeed, a key question, says James Renier, the president of Honeywell Information Systems, is whether workers can learn to "relate the computer to their jobs on their own initiative," without having to turn constantly to a computer professional for help.

The five chapters that follow describe the kinds of computer-based information systems with which the successful manager and professional must learn to be familiar: from systems concerned with detailed record keeping to systems that assist in making decisions at the executive level. After a discussion of how systems analysis and design works, we describe three levels of systems: (1) *transaction processing information systems*, which help an organization keep track of its employee, material, facility, and money resources; (2) *management information systems*, which provide managers with structured reports; and (3) *decision support systems*, which help executives analyze and make decisions about complicated problems. We conclude with a discussion of *artificial intelligence and expert systems*, which promise to have tremendous impact on our ways of using information.

Chapter 11

SYSTEMS ANALYSIS:
PUTTING THINGS IN ORDER

The world's way of doing business moves on, even as many people are looking elsewhere.

Not long ago, *The New York Times* reported that—four years shy of its centennial—a venerable department store, Bugbee's of Putnam, Connecticut, had closed. Once an eastern Connecticut landmark, Bugbee's was more than a source of clothing, it was a vanished place of shared experiences and rituals. The death of Bugbee's, said the *Times*, symbolized for many people "the continuing fragmentation of communal life in small towns such as Putnam, towns once largely self-sufficient that have been transformed into satellites of larger cities." The times changed, in other words, and Bugbee's was unable to keep up with them.

Whatever the enterprise or career you are in, there are often better ways of working. The trick is to identify when changes are needed and what those changes should be. The case study on the opposite page shows a company that had a problem—a backlog, amounting, in some instances, to 64 years' worth of items in stock—that it resolved by finding a better system. In this chapter and the next, we describe a valuable tool for the manager's toolkit: a collection of techniques called systems analysis and design that you can use to identify and solve problems.

SYSTEMS ANALYSIS

AND DESIGN

WHAT IT IS,

WHY WE NEED IT

All businesses, small or large, have information systems—even Bugbee's department store when it first opened in 1888 as a store for "dry and fancy goods." An **information system** includes people, procedures, hardware, software, and data, all working together to produce accurate and timely information. Information must flow successfully into the organization from the outside and also flow successfully within the organization. Thus, an information system must tie together and coordinate the various departments (see Figure 11-1).

CASE STUDY: ELIMINATING A 64-YEAR SUPPLY

Closing the Valve on Inventory Mistakes

ROGERS, Ark.—Inventory accuracy and the percentage of customer orders filled on time have increased dramatically, while the dollar volume of aggregate finished goods and component inventory has plummeted since the Crane Co. implemented a new manufacturing [computer] system in its plant here.

Crane, a division of the Valves and Fittings Division of Crane USA, manufactures bronze, stainless steel and iron valves. Before Crane implemented the new software package, all of its manufacturing records were kept on cards and updated by hand. Workers pulling parts for a rush order sometimes forgot to account for them on the card file. And if a card was lost, the entire record was lost.

Mistakes caused huge inventory buildups at Crane. Often the purchasing department reordered an item simply because a vendor was giving a price break. "The inventory was unreal," Mirian Von Struble, purchasing manager, explained. "There was a 64-year supply on some things. And there were always missing items. We had no control."

In addition, she said, parts were not inspected as they were received from vendors. "We spent many hours just retooling parts so we could use them," said Bill Wells, machine shop general foreman.

In 1979 Crane USA approved a plan to implement a Material Requirements Planning II system at the plant here. . . .

Under the new procedures, products would no longer be built without an engineering bill of material and specific manufacturing standards. "We can now provide accurate bills of material that truly represent the way the product is supposed to be built," Joe Weber, engineering manager, maintained.

The parts stockroom was another department where new procedures were implemented. "Now, there's only one way to put the inventory in and one way to take it out," [software evaluator Robert] Holiman said.

The receiving department also made changes. Employees are now issued drawings of each part ordered, and parts that do not match specifications are quickly rejected. As a result, suppliers no longer send unsatisfactory parts, Holiman said.

Plant Manager Russell Dutton said the change has had a ripple effect on the rest of the company. "In the assembly department, there are always matched sets of parts when they begin assembling a product," he said.

And in purchasing, according to Von Struble, "We're able to respond to the needs of production much faster now."

Crane's inventory has shot up to 95% accuracy, and the percentage of customer orders filled on time has doubled. Holiman, who became materials manager for Crane when implementation was complete, said Crane reduced its aggregate finished goods and component inventory from $8.5 million to less than $5.1 million in two years.

—*Computerworld*

Figure 11-1. A centralized information system. This illustration, which appeared earlier in the book as Figure 2-11, shows that the four principal functional departments of a business organization draw on the same flow of information.

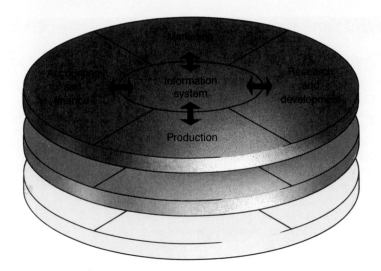

Systems analysis and design is the process of examining an organization's information system and improving it. Systems analysis and design is basically a problem-solving procedure, and the problems and solutions may or may not involve computers—that depends on the particular information needs of the specific organization being studied.

As we mentioned briefly in Chapter 2, systems analysis and design consists of five steps:

1. Identifying an organization's information needs and determining the feasibility of meeting those needs

2. Evaluating the effectiveness of the organization's present information system and specifying the new information requirements in detail

3. Formulating alternative information systems and recommending one system

4. Testing and implementing the new information system

5. Maintaining the new information system

Let us suppose that on your job at Atlantic-Pacific Bank one day you receive a phone call from Marlene Douglas, an executive you met on a plane while traveling. She tells you on the phone that she has recently been promoted to chief executive officer (CEO) of a stylish clothing manufacturer that calls itself Know-wear because it specializes in designing and manufacturing clothes for collegians and young professionals—people in "knowledge work." The company is bleeding, she says, the money going out faster than it is coming in. It earned no profits last year and is on a certain path to bankruptcy—unless she can turn it around. Despite a good reputation, it has lost touch with its market, the young knowledge professionals. Perhaps, she says, you might be willing to leave Atlantic-Pacific Bank and

join Know-wear. You might be of help, she says, because you seem closer to that market. Also, she is impressed with your background in computers. Your job would be to act as an assistant to the CEO, working on her pet projects. The company already has computers, Ms. Douglas explains, but your first assignment would be to determine how these machines might be used further to help Know-wear bail out of its difficulties.

Even on the first day of your new job you can appreciate the importance of good procedures for information flow within the company. Know-wear's Production department must set its clothing production schedules on the basis of orders and predicted sales provided by the Marketing department. And, obviously, the Production department needs to be informed if any current order is cancelled or if sales forecasts are revised.

But, like most companies, Know-wear must also continually react to changes in the outside business and political environment. The company's information systems must monitor and adapt to price cutting by competitors, the emergence of new synthetic fabric materials, government regulations, and many, many other events.

When Organizations Need Systems Analysis and Design

Organizations may go along for years using the same methods for gathering and handling information. What would make them want to do things differently?

Changes in information systems come about because of changes inside or outside of the organization itself. For example:

▶ **Organizational growth:** As an organization grows, so does its demand for timely information. A company with 100 employees, for example, has a much greater need for a computerized payroll system than does a company with only 10 employees.

▶ **Better, cheaper technology:** As computer hardware and software decrease in cost and increase in capabilities, an organization is better able to justify their acquisition.

▶ **Change in corporate structure:** The acquisition (taking over) of one company by another or merging of two companies can change a corporation's structure and hence the information system. For example, when two organizations merge, their respective information systems must also be merged, which usually requires modifications or even creation of a new system.

▶ **Change in government regulations:** A change in tax laws, for instance, can change the way a company has to handle payroll deductions.

▶ **New opportunities:** Companies may see new ways of making money that require changes in their information systems. For example, when banks saw it was good business to install 24-hour automatic teller machines, they had to change their deposit and withdrawal information systems.

There are other reasons why an organization, profit or nonprofit, might need to revise its information system. Many changes may affect only a few people, in which case a systems analysis and design may not be needed; end-users (like you) can perform the work themselves. However, other changes may be quite far-reaching in their effects on the people and information flow within the organization; this kind of situation requires a detailed, formal systems analysis and design and the help of a systems analyst.

Let's explore these two possibilities:

▶ Doing it yourself
▶ Working with a systems analyst

End-User–Developed Systems: Do It Yourself

Will you really have to get involved in doing your own systems analysis and design? We think it's best you be prepared. In many organizations, end-user computing has been growing at the rate of 50–70% a year.

There are many advantages to user-developed systems:

▶ The time taken to develop them is much shorter than it is when systems analysts are required to develop them, because the time priority is set by the user, not someone else.
▶ Misunderstandings are reduced because the users themselves are directly involved in analyzing and designing data.
▶ Quite often the cost is less.

As you might expect, however, there are some disadvantages—most of which can be summarized under the word *risks (see box, opposite page)*:

▶ Because end-users have not been trained in systems analysis and design, the quality of the systems they develop is usually not up to those created by professionals—namely, systems analysts.
▶ Frequently, users do not know the procedures, resources, and time requirements for developing systems.

Systems Analyst–Assisted Systems: Why Should You Be Involved?

If changes in a computerized information system are major, you are going to need the help of experts, most particularly that of a **systems analyst**—an information specialist with specific training in systems

THE RISKS OF USER-DEVELOPED APPLICATIONS

As more and more end-users have begun to take into their own hands the tasks previously performed only by systems analysts, there has also been an increase in certain kinds of problems. Professor Mary Sumner in the School of Business at Southern Illinois University, Edwardsville, writing in Data Management *(June 1986), points to nine risks.*

1. **Lack of quality assurance.** Data validation and testing, documentation, and controls for recovering lost data, for instance, are lacking.

2. **Dependency of others on user applications.** What happens when somebody developing an important system for a department suddenly leaves the company? Data processing professionals leave documentation that others can follow; nonspecialists often do not.

3. **Lack of data security.** Many users may have access to important, sensitive data.

4. **Tendency to accept output without validation.** What happens when data on user-generated reports do not agree with the same reports generated from production-level systems? Sometimes managers base their decisions on improperly prepared reports by users.

5. **Users unable to handle routine data processing procedures.** "In one organization," writes Sumner, "no one had anticipated the time it took to back-up data files, generate needed reports on a timely basis, and handle maintenance problems." Many chores simply did not get done.

6. **Failure to specify correct requirements.** "In one firm," according to Sumner, "a user failed to store information that was needed for year-end reporting. If a monthly transaction log had been kept, the problem would have been avoided."

7. **Mismatch between hardware and software.** Suppose users design a data base application on a microcomputer without anticipating file capacity requirements. This actually happened, says Sumner, and after six months "the data file had expanded to nearly 100,000 records and simple operations such as sorts were no longer feasible. As a result, the entire application had to be redesigned on a mainframe."

8. **Lack of cost justification.** Initial applications for microcomputers may be justified to management, but ongoing uses may be not questioned. Users may generate hundreds of "one-time-only" reports, but ultimately the time and costs of these reports have to be justified in business terms.

9. **Lack of management control over application development.** Without a design methodology or discipline imposed on users, says Sumner, users may not be "able to evaluate alternative design options or assess whether they should be developing a particular application at all."

analysis, design, and implementation. If a computer-based information system is being installed or changed, the systems analyst will most likely be assisted by programmers.

It is sometimes tempting to think that the "experts" understand your needs better than you do—especially if they seem to understand the mysteries of computers and data processing and you do not.

That is precisely why you should be involved.

After all, it is *you*, the user, who will have to live with the results of the new information system after the systems analyst and programmers have left. Moreover, it is highly likely that it will be you, the user, who initiates the request for systems analysis and design because you will be the one who has perceived that the present information system is not working as well as it should.

WHAT DOES A SYSTEMS ANALYST DO?

Experienced systems analysts are paid quite well—perhaps $50,000 a year or more. How do they get into this line of work and what do they actually do?

Most, of course, have technical training in computer information systems, usually having earned a college degree in computer science, management information systems, or business. They have also acquired a strong knowledge of hardware and software, from microcomputers through mainframes. Many have been programmers and know several programming languages, especially business-related ones such as COBOL.

When analyzing and designing a computer-related application, systems analysts work with managers and lower-level workers within a company in order to make sure the completed application will actually serve the users' needs.

It takes the combined efforts of user, systems analyst, and programmers to successfully develop a computer-based information system. The user is able to describe his or her needs and evaluate the worth of alternative information systems. The systems analyst works with the user and the programmers to analyze, design, and implement new information systems. The programmers do the technical work required.

But it is you the user who is key: The ultimate success of the information system depends more on your perceptions and capabilities than on anyone else's. To be successful in a career today, then, you need to understand the systems approach and the procedures for systems analysis and design.

Today's organizations can be very complex. You cannot expect (as, unfortunately, too many managers and administrators have) to simply bring in a computer system and have it be effective. An information specialist needs special tools with which to study an organization and decide how best to use a computer-based information system. The best known tool is the systems approach.

According to the **systems approach,** which is a general way of dealing with complex situations, a problem can be looked at as a system that can be broken down into subsystems. For example, an information system consists of the following five components: people, procedures, hardware, software, and data. Thus, if an information system is to be studied, each one of these components must be studied. The problem can be analyzed in smaller parts and then the parts can be brought back together to arrive at a solution. (The systems approach is derived from systems theory, which we discussed in the box in Chapter 2, pp. 26–28.)

INFORMATION AND THE SYSTEMS LIFE CYCLE

To develop a computer-based information system you must first have a careful analysis of the complex system of your organization. At Know-wear, the activities of each department must be carefully coordinated with those of every other department, or the company's goals of producing goods and getting profits will not be met. Advertising and sales promotions within Marketing must be coordinated with the manufacturing and inventory scheduling within Production. If Production must expand its manufacturing facilities as a result of Marketing's forecast of increased demand for a particular line of Know-wear clothes, then the Accounting and Finance department must be alerted so that it can borrow or otherwise obtain the funds for Production's expansion. Marketing's perception of future customer demands must be fed to Research and Development if that department is to have the time to plan and develop new products.

All this information swapping and movement need not be computer-based, and of course in the past it was not. People simply called or sent memos to each other. However, often the computer can do a lot of this more efficiently, thereby increasing productivity.

It is important to note, however, that not every currently manual method of handling information need be computerized. The objective of systems analysis and design is not to replace every manual information channel, but rather to identify which ones need improving and then to design better ways of providing information support. These new systems may or may not be computer-based.

We said that the *systems approach* is a general way of dealing with complex situations. *Systems analysis and design* is a generic term that refers to applying a systems approach to the development of an information system. Note that systems analysis and design is not supposed to just happen every now and then. It should be an ongoing activity, so that an organization's information systems are being continually reevaluated and modified. As one specific kind of approach—probably the most widely used—systems analysis and design uses a process called the **systems life cycle approach** (or *systems development cycle*), which, as Figure 11-2 shows, consists of five principal steps:

1. **System investigation**—in which information needs are identified and the feasibility of meeting those needs is determined. (The result of this step is the determination of the *need*.)
2. **System analysis**—in which the existing information flow is ana-

Figure 11-2.   The systems life cycle approach. The five steps of investigation, analysis, design, implementation, and maintenance, along with their feedback loops, make up the activity of systems analysis and design, which a business should apply to its information systems on an ongoing basis.

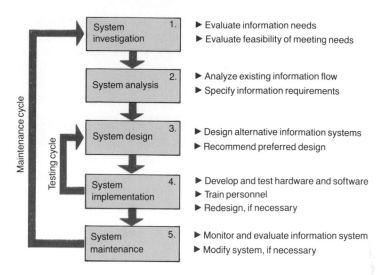

lyzed and new information requirements are specified in detail. (The result here is the determination of the *system requirements*.)

3. **System design**—in which alternative information systems are designed and a preferred design recommended. (The result here is the creation of *design specifications*.)

4. **System implementation**—in which new hardware and software are developed and tested, personnel are trained, and any necessary redesign accomplished. (The results produced here are *system specifications*.)

5. **System maintenance**—in which the information system is monitored and evaluated and, if necessary, modified. (The result here is to ensure that *the system meets the system requirements*.)

The first two steps are described in the rest of this chapter. The last three steps are described in the next chapter.

SYSTEM

INVESTIGATION

HOW IS IT

WORKING NOW?

In any organization there will probably be more projects proposed for systems analysis and design than can be undertaken. You discover this very quickly at Know-wear. As the first step in your assignment to determine if a computer system can help Know-wear, you spend your first few days on the job talking to people in the various departments about the Know-wear information processing system, which is a manual system. You are quickly inundated with complaints. The vice-president of Marketing thinks the sales reports come out so late that they are practically useless. The Production vice-president thinks the inventory control system is a mess. Ms. Douglas feels the accounts receivable system is not working—the money is not coming in fast enough from customers.

With so many problems obvious at the outset, you recommend to Ms. Douglas that Know-wear hire a systems analyst. At first she balks at spending money on another salary, but she agrees once you discuss what a systems analyst does and how much money could be saved with a properly designed information system. She puts you in charge of hiring the analyst and being the liaison between the analyst and Know-wear employees.

The first step after hiring the analyst is a **system investigation** of each proposed project in order to define the problem and evaluate the feasibility of solving it within an affordable budget and schedule. This means that someone or some collection of people must decide what proposed projects deserve further study, which ones are the most important, and what resources of money, people, and time may be required for each. The point now is not to come up with a detailed design for a new system. Rather, the point is to evaluate the need for and feasibility of a new or revised system. These findings will be described at the end of this stage in a formal written document called a *system study charter*.

The steps in a system investigation are:

▶ Define the problem.

▶ Propose two or three alternative information systems.

▶ Evaluate the feasibility of the alternative systems and recommend one alternative.

▶ Write a system study charter.

In many ways, system investigation is a miniversion of a complete system analysis and design. The purpose of this step, though, is just to get an idea of the scope of the problem and solution so that management can decide if they want to invest in continuing the project.

Defining the Problem

To discover the problem or problems in an information system, the current system must be examined. A brand-new information system will be useless if it does not address existing problems, but the true problems are often hidden below the complaint, "This job is driving me crazy!" Thus, a **system needs survey** should be conducted to determine the problems in information flow and the needs of information users. This investigation will be continued in more detail in the system analysis stage if management decides to continue the study. The system needs survey report must be specific, clear, and easily understood. It should specify *what* information is needed, *who* needs it, *where*, *when*, and *why*. It should also define the problem in the current system.

For large information systems, a systems analyst may be the one to conduct the system needs survey. If so, the user of the system should be involved; indeed, the user's contributions and support are essential to the project's success. Even with the best intentions in the world, there may be misunderstandings between users and systems analysts. Users may talk the language of their trade, and systems analysts may talk computer jargon. In addition, users frequently describe problems that are actually side effects or by-products of a larger problem. Know-wear's sales manager, for instance, says that inventories are so low for a certain line of clothing that she cannot fill customer orders quickly enough, when in fact the real problem is that sales cannot be predicted accurately enough to allow the Production department to schedule the assembly of sufficient clothing outfits.

Let us say that you and the systems analyst decide to look at Know-wear's problem in accounts receivable for your first system investigation. *Accounts receivable* is that arm of the Accounting and Finance department that sends out the bills (called *invoices*) to customers and keeps track of payments. At Know-wear, money is not coming in fast enough from customers—the customers here being the retail clothing stores in shopping malls and elsewhere that sell clothes directly to the public. The problem does not seem to be the stores' fault so much as a paperwork tie-up at Know-wear, but that is what you have to investigate. This is clearly not an investigation you could do by yourself as an end-user; accounts receivable is such an important and enormous part of the company's operations that it affects everyone. You are going to need the professional help of the systems analyst. Even so, it's important to realize that *all the following steps are the same whether they are done by an end-user alone or with the help of a systems analyst.*

The two of you start by looking at the present accounts receivable system at Know-wear. When you talk to the accounts receivable manager, he tells you that the department is going through a temporary busy period, but everything will be caught up soon. He does admit, however, that the monthly report on overdue accounts is usually late and out of date. Thus, if he calls stores to inquire about invoices that the report indicates have not been paid, he often finds the customers saying they already have paid. After several telephone calls back and forth, the Know-wear manager must apologize and admit that indeed invoices have been paid. The result is that he has only succeeded in creating ill will on the part of those customers toward Know-wear.

As you talk to other people in the Accounting and Finance department, you discover that morale is quite low. The accounting clerks feel overworked. You and the systems analyst notice stacks of paperwork piled up on desks with notes such as "To be processed," "To be filed," and "Miscellaneous." Managers in other departments complain that the reports they receive from Accounting and Finance are late and out of date.

After analyzing the current flow of information, you and the systems analyst agree that the accounts receivable system has serious problems, but you also suspect that these problems extend to the entire sales, order entry, and accounting system. This will require further investigation if the accounts receivable project gets the go-ahead for further analysis. You summarize your preliminary findings in parts 1 and 2 of the system study charter, shown in Figure 11-3.

Developing Alternative Solutions

Now that you have some idea of what the problems are, you can come up with some preliminary solutions. As we said earlier, the goal is not to design a completely new information system at this point but just to come up with a few possible plans so management—specifically, Ms. Douglas—will have some idea of the scope of the project. The alternative solutions suggested now are developed from the systems analyst's training and experience.

The Know-wear systems analyst proposes three possible solutions: (1) Hire more accounting clerks and further analyze the present manual system to design a more efficient manual system. (2) Introduce a computer-based accounts receivable system. (3) Introduce a computer-based information system that would encompass all sales, order entry, and accounting procedures. These proposals are presented in part 3 of the system study charter (Figure 11-3).

Evaluating Feasibility

Are the proposed solutions really feasible? The answer to this question has three parts:

▶ Economic
▶ Technical
▶ Operational

Let us consider these.

Economic Feasibility   What is the *net cost/benefit*? What is the *rate of return*?

Benefits include increased sales, reduced operating costs, better customer goodwill because of improved service, and better management decisions because of improved quality of information. *Costs* include money spent on the new system and possibly lost customer goodwill because of interruptions in normal operations when a new information system is being phased in. The **net/cost benefit** is the

Figure 11-3. The system study charter. This report summarizes the system investigation for the Know-wear accounts receivable project.

```
                    SYSTEM STUDY CHARTER

PROJECT: Accounts  Receivable, Know-wear, Inc.


1.   PRESENT INFORMATION SYSTEM

The present Know-wear accounts receivable department uses a
manual system. Personnel include one manager, one assistant
manager, six accounting clerks, and one secretary. The department
produces invoices upon notification that goods have been shipped
to customers. The department also keeps track of payments made on
invoices, producing several reports for use of managers (see next
section).


2.   SYSTEM NEEDS SURVEY

In discussions with accounting personnel and users of accounting
information, it was determined that the following reports are
needed:
```

What	Who	Where	When	Why
Report on customers with overdue accounts	Accounts receivable manager needs	Accounts receivable office	Monthly	To monitor the amounts customers owe the company
Report on date orders taken and date orders filled	Order entry manager needs	Order entry office	Monthly	To monitor the time lag between order entry and actual shipping
Report on goods shipped and billed for each customer	Marketing manager needs	Sales office	Weekly	To keep abreast of actual sales to customers

```
These reports are currently being generated, but managers
complain that the reports are usually late and out of date.  The
problem appears to be that the accounts receivable department is
not set up to handle the volume of work it has.  We suspect,
however, that the problem extends to the entire sales, order
entry, and accounting system.  Further investigation of these
problems will be required.


3.   PROPOSED ALTERNATIVE INFORMATION SYSTEMS

Objectives of the alternative information systems:

To produce invoices in a timely manner after goods have been
shipped; to keep accurate and up-to-date records of payments; to
produce reports for managers that are accurate, up-to-date, and
produced on time.

Alternative proposals:

     1.   Hire more accounting clerks and further analyze the
          present manual system to design a more efficient
          manual system.  (No matter what course of action is
          pursued, the accounts receivable department should be
          given temporary help right away so they can catch up
          on their backlog.)

     2.   Introduce a computer-based accounts receivable system.

     3.   Introduce a computer-based information system that
          would encompass all sales, order entry, and accounting
          procedures.
```

Figure 11-3, *continued.*

4.   FEASIBILITY

A.   Economic feasibility (Note: All costs are very rough
      estimates and are subject to change):

Costs:

	1991	1992	1993	1994
Tangible costs:				
System analyst's salary	$30,000	$32,000		
Programmer's salary	10,000	18,000	100,000	40,000
Additional systems support personnel				
Intangible costs:				
Potential lost customer goodwill during transition period				
Total expected costs:	$40,000	$50,000	$100,000	$40,000

Benefits:

	1991	1992	1993	1994
Tangible benefits:				
Reduction in clerical salaries by normal attrition (3 clerks at $13,000	0	0	$39,000	$39,000
Added profits from more sales and less lost sales due to improved customer service	0	20,000	50,000	50,000
Intangible benefits:				
Improved quality of decisions by use of more timely and relevant information	0	10,000	25,000	25,000
Total expected benefits:	0	$30,000	$114,000	$114,000

Cost/Benefit Analysis:

	1991	1992	1993	1994
Benefits:	0	$30,000	$114,000	$114,000
Costs:	40,000	65,000	100,000	40,000
Net, yearly	-$40,000	-$35,000	-$14,000	$74,000
Net, cumulative	-$40,000	-$75,000	-$61,000	$13,000

The improved system should recover all costs within two years
after being put into operation.

Net cost/benefit for 1993 = expected benefit - expected cost
                  ($30,000 + $114,000) - ($105,000 + $100,000)
                  = -$61,000

Net cost/benefit for 1994 = expected benefit - expected cost
                  $144,000 - ($205,000 + $40,000)
                  = $13,000   This number is positive so
                              is a good net cost/benefit

Figure 11-3,
continued.

B.   Technical feasibility:

The personnel, systems analysts and programmers needed to develop the system are currently on staff, so availability should not be a problem.

Hardware could be purchased or leased, with leasing the preferred alternative at the beginning until the system is deemed to be successful. Software may be easily purchased, but may have to be modified before it can be used in the system.

C.   Operational feasibility:

Initial observations of reactions to the proposed information system indicate users will not be resistant or indifferent. There are no government regulations that might impede the project, nor any specific customer requirements.

5.   POTENTIAL PROBLEMS

Cost: The final system cost could exceed the estimates presented here, owing to several potential problems. Final cost will probably be within plus or minus 10% of the estimate.

Time schedule: More time may be needed to develop and implement the new system. Time requirements are expected to be within plus or minus 10% of the projected schedule.

6.   SYSTEM DEVELOPMENT SCHEDULE

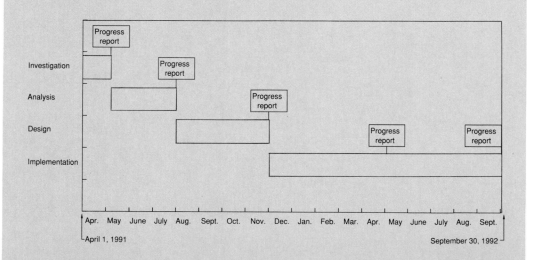

7.   RECOMMENDATION

My recommendation is to pursue the development of a new information system (proposal #3) because the problems in the order entry/accounts receivable process will probably increase, and the payoff from the new system should be rapid.

expected benefit minus the expected cost. The **rate of return** is the ratio between estimated benefits and estimated costs.

To compare proposed alternative systems, specific cost estimates must be made. In many cases this is difficult to do, especially when the costs and benefits are intangible, such as customer goodwill. This is where the systems analyst's experience is valuable.

Technical Feasibility What hardware, software, and people are required? Are they available? How reliable is the necessary hardware and software? The uncertainties in developing a computer-based information system can be reduced if the company or a similar company has already thoroughly tested hardware and software that can be easily purchased.

Operational Feasibility How acceptable will the proposed system be to users and management? If potential users are resistant or indifferent, the system may not be used. If higher management does not support the project, its chances of success are low. Are there any external constraints, such as government regulations or specific customer requirements? If either insiders or outsiders are constrained in some way, you have to weigh just how operational the system will be.

The feasibility report of the Know-wear systems analyst is presented in part 4 of the system study charter (Figure 11-3). For the sake of brevity, we present only the feasibility report for the third alternative proposal—a computer-based information system that would include all sales, order entry, and accounting procedures. The systems analyst concludes that this project is feasible on all three counts—economically, technically, and operationally.

The System Study Charter

The **system study charter** is the formal document that summarizes the first step in the systems life cycle—systems investigation. Along with system study charters for other projects, it will be used by management to decide which information system project to pursue.

The system study charter should include the following:

1. A brief description of the present information system, identifying the users and describing the information provided.
2. A summary of the system needs survey. This should describe the users' current and future information needs and inadequacies in the present system to meet those needs. This is where the problem is defined.
3. A summary of the proposed alternative information systems. This should include a short, clear, and precise statement of the objectives of the proposed systems.
4. A report on the feasibility of the proposed projects.

5. A statement of any potential problems. The systems analyst for Know-wear, for instance, points out that final cost estimates could exceed those presented here, as might the time for developing and implementing the system.

6. A development schedule, also known as a Gantt chart, for the proposed system. This should estimate the time for each phase and when equipment and people will be required. For the remaining four stages of the systems analysis and design of Know-wear's accounts receivable project, the systems analyst estimates that the entire project will take about a year and a half, should management approve it. The systems analyst has scheduled in a progress report at the end of each stage and an interim progress report during the final, implementation stage (see Figure 11-3, part 6).

7. Go/No go recommendations. These should include a recommendation to pursue or not pursue the project and a short statement justifying the recommendation. "My recommendation," writes the Know-wear systems analyst, "is to pursue the development of a new information system because the problems in the order entry/accounts receivable process will probably increase, and the payoff from the new system should be rapid."

The system investigation for Know-wear's accounts receivable project is summarized in the system study charter shown in Figure 11-3.

SYSTEM ANALYSIS

WHAT NEEDS TO

BE DONE?

Management, including the CEO, Ms. Douglas, examines the system study charters you and the systems analyst have prepared. You explain how a comprehensive computer-based information system could solve many of the problems plaguing various departments at Know-wear, and so Ms. Douglas gives the green light to proceed with the second stage of the project. This second stage, **system analysis,** is concerned with collecting and analyzing data about the present and future information needs of prospective users.

System analysis asks, "What needs to be done?" However, it is not concerned with *designing* a new or alternative information system—that comes in stage 3—only with making a detailed analysis of the existing system and developing the *requirements* for an improved information system, which are described in a system requirements report.

Structured system analysis has a top-down approach—this is consistent with the philosophy of structured programming. That is, the systems analyst examines the flow of information, starting with upper-level management and moving down through the organization's hierarchy.

There are three steps in the system analysis stage:

▶ Gathering data

▶ Analyzing the data

▶ Writing the system requirements report

You will see how these are developed as you watch the Know-wear systems analyst at work.

Gathering Data

You have already seen the gathering of some preliminary facts in stage 1. Now you need to add detail. Data gathering is primarily concerned with determining how the present information system operates. Although there are numerous sources of data, let us look at four of the most common:

▶ Written documents

▶ Interviews

▶ Questionnaires

▶ Observation

Written Documents   **Written documents** may consist of organization charts, flowcharts, and other written materials.

An **organization chart** is a drawing that indicates the positions, by title, and lines of authority within an organization (see Figure 11-4). Since they represent the formal lines of communication and flow of information, such charts are valuable in giving the systems analyst a top-down perspective. The organization chart for Know-wear, Inc., allows the analyst to view the people and departments that are affected by the present information system and that might be affected by changes in the system.

Flowcharts are also valuable to an analyst for describing the current information system. System flowcharts describe what input devices are used, what files have been created or are accessible, and what people receive written information. Program flowcharts (which we explained in Chapter 5) and HIPO (Hierarchy plus Input-Process-Output) charts may also be of value in showing the logic of the current information system. We will explain this in detail below.

Besides organization charts and flowcharts, a systems analyst should look at any other written documents relating to the system under study: reports, forms, procedures manuals, and so on.

Interviews   The analyst cannot work just from paper. Personal **interviews** *(see box, p. 371)* with key people in the organization can yield important data, for such people can often describe the actual flow as opposed to the intended flow of information. The analyst asks users of the current Know-wear accounts receivable system how well it is performing—that is, what information is and is not provided.

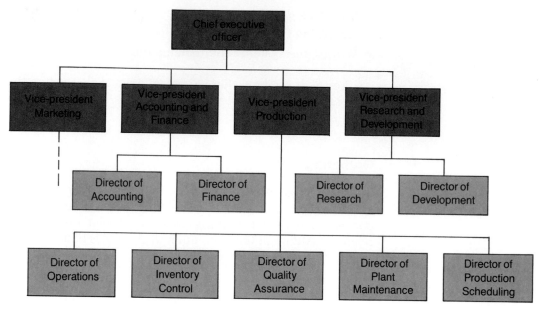

Figure 11-4.   An organization chart.
Charts like this one indicate the titles
of an organization's executives and
the lines of authority.

Questionnaires   Although personal interviews are generally more
effective, **questionnaires** are also frequently used because they cost
less and allow the analyst to obtain more responses in a short time.
An analyst may find out from questionnaires how frequently people
use the present information system, the time required to use it, and
special equipment and personnel requirements. Questionnaires
have drawbacks, however. Some people will not fill them out no
matter what the inducements. People are also wary of putting on
paper opinions for which they think they may be held accountable
later. And, of course, answers to questionnaires may be highly bi-
ased. As you may begin to suspect, system analysis can become a
political matter *(see box, p. 372)*.

Observation   **Observation** is always valuable, but it should not be
done secretly. Arrangements should be made with the work unit's
supervisor, and the analyst should let people know they are under
observation. Sometimes the analyst may actually join the people
being observed; this is known as participant observation. The point
of observation is to see how information flows from person to person, who interrelates with whom, and how information comes into
and leaves the group.

Analyzing the Data

If data gathering is to define what is being done, data analysis is to
determine why certain procedures are being used and look for better

TIPS FOR INTERVIEWING

The expression "Garbage in, garbage out" also applies in system analysis: The results of your analysis can be no better than the information that has gone into it. Information comes not only from paper but from interviews—and there are right ways and wrong ways of conducting an interview. The following are some tips:

▶ **Plan your questions beforehand.** You may vary from them during the interview, but you should not try to "wing it"—that is, go in unprepared. Do your homework, determining the questions for which you need answers, the people probably best able to answer them, and the *specific* questions that the *specific* individual being interviewed can address.

▶ **Establish proper rapport with the interviewee.** This means, above all, respect his or her time. Ask for an appointment, arranging your schedule to fit that of the person being interviewed. Dress and behave in a businesslike manner, avoiding office gossip and discussion of personal problems. Avoid technical jargon. Use your best small-talk abilities (without going on at length) to comment on the weather, the interviewee's office, and so on, in order to put the subject at ease. Do not go on the offensive so that the subject feels threatened; on the other hand, do not try to overdo it with flattery. Talk straight. Thank the subject for the interview and ask if you may contact him or her later to clarify any questions.

▶ **State the problem and focus the questions.** Identify yourself, state the purpose of the interview, and share the problem definition. Identify the managers who authorized the system analysis. Have your first question ready, or perhaps an open question, such as: "The office procedures manual states that copies of the customer order should go to other departments besides yours, but I'm not sure I understand which ones. Can you explain how this works?" Follow up with specific questions, focusing on particular details of concern. Concentrate not only on how things work but on why they work as they do.

▶ **Get the information.** You should listen carefully to the answers, observing the respondent's body movements and voice inflection to help you evaluate the responses. Take notes on key points, but do not record every word, since you must listen to the subject and be prepared to ask follow-up questions. Make a written summary of the interview as soon as possible, concentrating on the key issues. Share the summary with the respondent and allow him or her to correct mistakes or make adjustments. Do follow-up interviews, if necessary.

ways of doing them. Of the several tools used in this step, the nine most common are:

▶ System flowcharts
▶ Grid charts
▶ Decision tables
▶ Data flow diagrams
▶ Checklist
▶ Top-down analysis

THE POLITICS OF SYSTEM ANALYSIS

Good ideas and grand schemes always have to deal with a hard reality: They must be acceptable to the people who have to live with them. A systems analyst, therefore, must be adept at handling the politics within an organization. What do you do if you encounter—or, better, what do you do to avoid encountering—such problems as resistance, ignorance, and conflict with management?

Writer Charles Paddock, writing in the journal *SOS,* suggests what are known as *organizational development techniques*. To increase the chances of a system's being successfully adopted, he proposes "survey feedback, group diagnostic meetings, communication training, laboratory training, training sessions, role negotiation, and the organizational mirror technique." To bring this about, a system analysis project needs to be divided into two parts: social and technical. The social part is handled by a behavioral scientist who works "to improve interpersonal communication and human decision-making, facilitate conflict resolution, and increase trust and openness in organizations." The technical part—the matters being discussed throughout this chapter—can be handled by the systems experts.

Adding a behavioral scientist may reduce conflict with users, but it opens the possibility for some conflict between behavioral professionals and technical professionals. Thus, the behaviorist must be chosen with some care—preferably one whose personality will round out those of other members of the system analysis team.

▶ HIPO charts
▶ Prototyping
▶ Automated design tools

Here is how they work.

System Flowcharts   As we discussed in Chapter 4, *program flowcharts* are primarily used by programmers to write application programs; their purpose is to specify the details of a problem for ease in coding. **System flowcharts,** by contrast, focus on input and output operations, and thus are used to show information flow within a system. The standard input and output symbols and standard process symbols for system flowcharts are shown in Figure 11-5. Because they present an overview, system flowcharts are a valuable tool for systems analysis and design.

Grid Chart   A **grid chart,** also called an **input/output chart,** is often used in analysis to show the relationship between input and output documents. Figure 11-6, for example, shows the relationship between forms (input) and reports (output). A sales order is used to produce a sales report, a purchase order for an inventory report, and so on. Horizontal rows represent input documents (such as a purchase order); vertical rows represent the output documents. An "X" at the intersection of a row and column means that the input document is used to create the output document. Thus, if you look down

Figure 11-5. System flowchart symbols. *Top:* Input, output, and storage symbols. *Bottom:* Process symbols. These symbols are used by systems analysts rather than by programmers; their purpose is to represent information flow within a system.

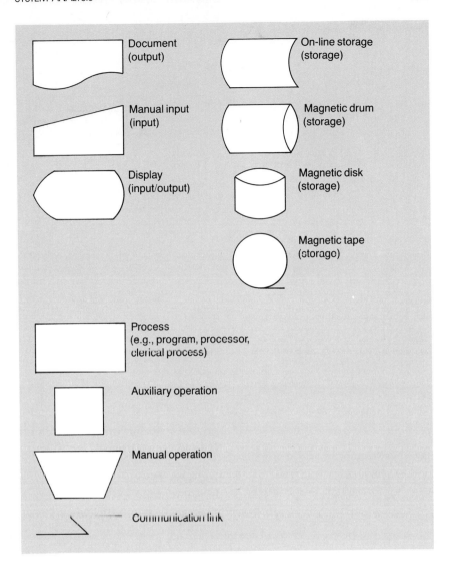

Document
(output)

On-line storage
(storage)

Manual input
(input)

Magnetic drum
(storage)

Display
(input/output)

Magnetic disk
(storage)

Magnetic tape
(storage)

Process
(e.g., program, processor, clerical process)

Auxiliary operation

Manual operation

Communication link

Figure 11-6. Grid chart. This chart indicates the relationship of input documents to output reports. For instance, time cards and paychecks are needed as the input to produce a payroll report.

Forms (input) / Reports (output)	Sales report	Inventory report	Payroll report	Financial report
Sales order	X			
Purchase order		X		
Time card			X	
Paycheck			X	
Check voucher				X

Figure 11-7.   Decision table.

Decision rules

Conditions	1	2	3	4	5	6	7	8
Best price	Y	N	Y	N	N	Y	N	N
Delayed delivery acceptable	Y	Y	N	N	N	Y	N	N
Previous quality acceptable	N	Y	Y	N	Y	N	Y	N

Actions	1	2	3	4	5	6	7	8
Buy	✓							
Perhaps buy		✓	✓			✓		
Do not buy				✓	✓		✓	✓

a column for an output document, the chart indicates all the input documents needed to produce it.

Decision Tables   Somewhat resembling the grid chart in format, a **decision table** (Figure 11-7) shows the decision rules that apply when certain conditions occur, and what action should take place as a result.

Data Flow Diagram   As the example in Figure 11-8 shows, a **data flow diagram** shows the flow of data and information and which data files are available.

Checklist   A **checklist** of questions is frequently used to ensure that the user and systems analyst address key issues when they are evaluating the present system. An example is shown in Figure 11-9.

Top-down Analysis Methodology   Known as a divide-and-conquer method of analysis, the **top-down analysis methodology** is used to first identify the top-level function of a complex system, then analyze it, and then break it down into secondary-level components, each of which may in turn be identified, analyzed, and subdivided.

The advantage of the top-down tool is, of course, that breaking the system down into smaller components makes it easier to deal with. The disadvantage is that actually doing it can be much more

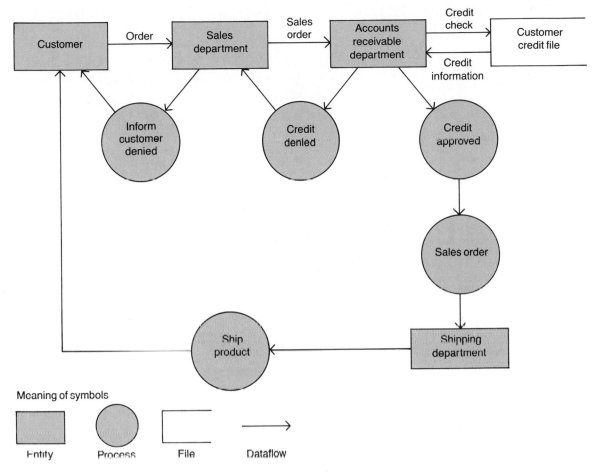

Figure 11-8.   Data flow diagram.

difficult than simply saying it should be done—the system may be quite complex.

HIPO Charts   HIPO—pronounced *high*-poh—stands for Hierarchy plus Input-Process-Output. Consisting of a package of diagrams that describes the structured program from general to particular, a **HIPO chart** is primarily a visual tool. A HIPO package consists of three separate diagrams, as represented in Figure 11-10, (p. 377):

▶ A **visual table of contents,** a graphical depiction of independent modules used in a structured program, with a short legend describing what some symbols (such as arrows) mean.
▶ An **overview chart,** which shows, from left to right, the inputs, processes, and outputs of a particular module in the visual table of contents. An overview chart is shown in Figure 11-11 (p. 378).

Figure 11-9.   Checklist. This is an example of a checklist of questions that systems analysts and users can use to address important issues in the analysis step. The questions listed here are fairly general but can be made specific to the particular project under analysis.

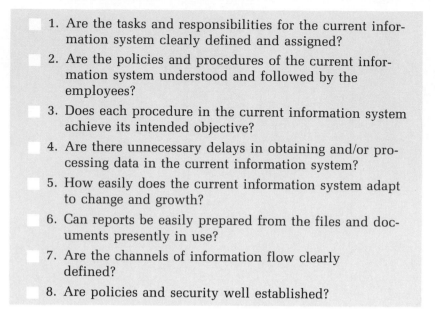

1. Are the tasks and responsibilities for the current information system clearly defined and assigned?

2. Are the policies and procedures of the current information system understood and followed by the employees?

3. Does each procedure in the current information system achieve its intended objective?

4. Are there unnecessary delays in obtaining and/or processing data in the current information system?

5. How easily does the current information system adapt to change and growth?

6. Can reports be easily prepared from the files and documents presently in use?

7. Are the channels of information flow clearly defined?

8. Are policies and security well established?

This chart, you will notice, is an elaboration of module 3.0 in Figure 11-10.

▶ A **detail diagram,** which looks like the overview chart in format but is used to represent a finer level of detail, presenting the particulars of the functions to be performed and the data items required.

Most programming problems using a HIPO chart use only the visual table of contents and the overview chart; only large programs use the third level, the detail diagram.

Prototyping   An increasingly common analytical tool, **prototyping** consists of building a prototype system—that is, a model of the actual system—which, to the user, will look much like the finished product. Just as auto manufacturers build the very first new car in order to test it before going into production and making many copies, so it makes sense to do prototyping in system analysis. Thus, for instance, the systems analyst would create an on-screen example of a possible menu or interactive display screen for users to try out, and then modify it as needed before the system is actually installed.

Clearly, the advantages of a prototype system are:

▶ It enables the user to physically sit down and use the system, finding glitches he or she might not have thought of without a working model.

▶ It makes the system more flexible to change, because users are apt to change their minds about what they want.

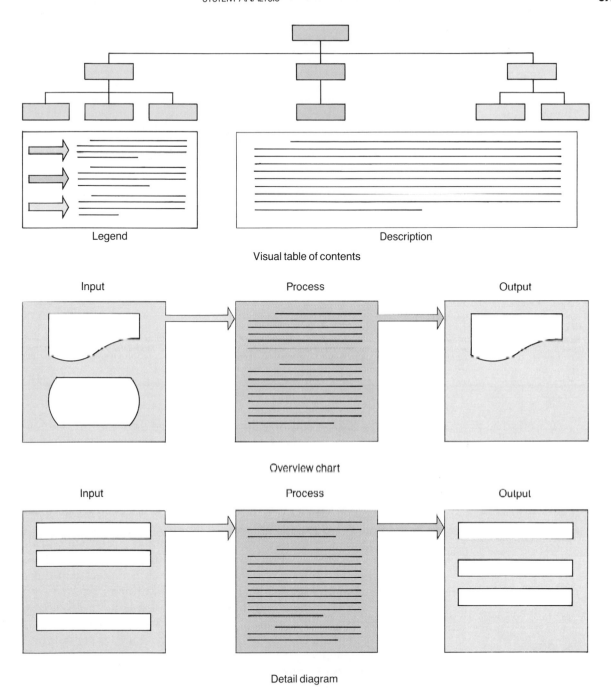

Visual table of contents

Figure 11-10. A HIPO package. Notice that this consists of three different kinds of diagrams: *top*, a visual table of contents; *middle*, an overview chart; *bottom*, a detail diagram.

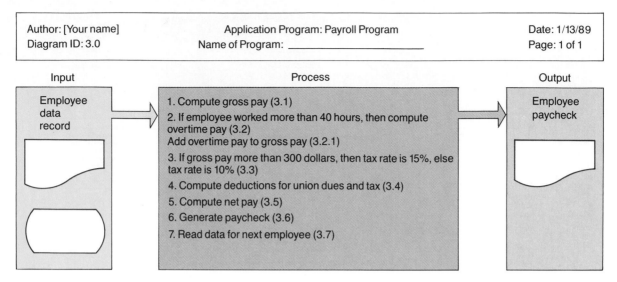

| Author: [Your name] | Application Program: Payroll Program | Date: 1/13/89 |
| Diagram ID: 3.0 | Name of Program: _____ | Page: 1 of 1 |

Input	Process	Output
Employee data record	1. Compute gross pay (3.1) 2. If employee worked more than 40 hours, then compute overtime pay (3.2) Add overtime pay to gross pay (3.2.1) 3. If gross pay more than 300 dollars, then tax rate is 15%, else tax rate is 10% (3.3) 4. Compute deductions for union dues and tax (3.4) 5. Compute net pay (3.5) 6. Generate paycheck (3.6) 7. Read data for next employee (3.7)	Employee paycheck

Figure 11-11.   Overview chart. This second-level chart in a HIPO package shows the details of a module presented in the visual table of contents in Figure 11-10.

The disadvantages, however, are:

▶ A prototype can be difficult to manage and control.

▶ A prototype is hard to use for large information systems.

Automated Design Tools   A sophisticated approach is to use **automated design tools,** which are software packages that follow certain criteria to evaluate hardware and software alternatives according to the processing requirements supplied by the systems analyst. These tools are sometimes referred to as **computer-aided software engineering (CASE) tools,** and they focus on improving the productivity of software development—especially when a project requires coordination among several analysts and programmers, each of whom is producing documentation that must be organized, cross-referenced, and digested.

To appreciate how helpful CASE tools are, imagine you have been assigned by Ms. Douglas—in an attempt to determine long-range fashion trends—to index 50 years of a particular clothing or fashion magazine (resembling, say, *Vogue* or *Gentlemen's Quarterly*). Even if you are given ten people to help you, and each of you works on five years' worth of magazines, if you are all using pencils and index cards, you know you are going to be sitting in libraries a long, long time. However, software is available that will identify key terms in articles researched by your ten people and automatically produce an organized, integrated index. CASE tools resemble this kind of software: They enable systems analysts and designers to inte-

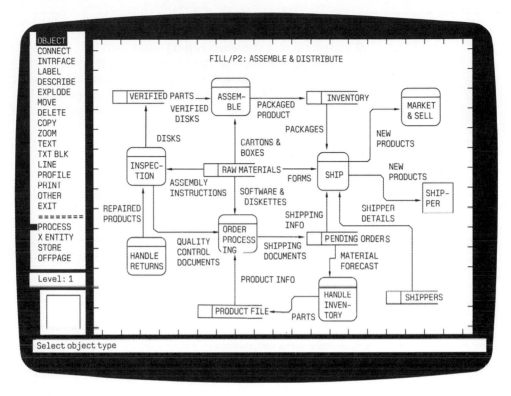

Figure 11-12. Excelerator. An example of a drawing screen for a data flow diagram, using this automated design tool.

grate and organize the documentation of several analysts and programmers working on different pieces of the same system. This automated ability greatly enhances the accuracy and consistency of design specifications and helps to speed up the analysis and design process.

An example of one automated design tool is the microcomputer software program known as Excelerator, which allows a systems analyst—using a graphics feature to diagram entire systems, from conceptual overviews down to individual data records—to design and document almost any software system. Excelerator uses a dictionary consisting of information about the system design that allows you to standardize names, cross-check the completeness of the design, and evaluate enhancements by producing reports from the data dictionary. It also supports structured design techniques, a top-down "explosion" feature that allows you to develop the system design in top-down approach, beginning with an overview of the system and progressing to finer levels of detail, then exploding the whole into different types of graphs and diagrams, using the graphics facility. Figure 11-12 shows an example of an Excelerator data flow diagram.

Now comes the time to tie together in a report—the system requirements report—the results of the system analysis stage.

The System Requirements Report

The **system requirements report** describes the findings of the system analysis. It ensures that users and the systems analyst agree on the details of the current system and on the need for a new or improved information system. Since the report is prepared for higher management, it should be written to ensure their continued interest and support.

The system requirements report has five sections:

▶ A statement of scope and objectives

▶ A description of the present information system

▶ An estimate of system requirements

▶ A revised system development schedule

▶ A request to management for authorization to proceed

Let us see what these look like, using the Know-wear project. The complete system requirements report for the Know-wear project is shown in Figure 11-13.

1. Scope and Objectives This is simply a detailed statement of the scope and objectives of the system analysis study. The CEO of Know-wear, you will recall, was concerned about the amount of paperwork involved in accounts receivable and the delays in money coming in. But, as you and the systems analyst have determined, there is more to it than that. As part 1 in Figure 11-13 shows, the objectives have broadened so that delays in money coming in from stores cannot be separated from concerns such as shipping time, meeting of promised delivery dates, quicker response time to customer inquiries, and reduced billing error rates. In other words, the project extends, as the system analyst writes, "from the point the customer order is obtained from the customer, to the shipment and invoice leaving for the customer, to the receipt of payment from the customer."

2. Description of Present Information System This second section of the system requirements report describes the current information flow, the procedures used, and any problems—and opportunities— that exist. Here is where some artwork helps, such as overview diagrams and HIPO diagrams.

Part 2 of the system requirements report for Know-wear includes six drawings (see Figure 11-13), all produced using the Excelerator CASE tool:

▶ *Overview of Present System:* A presentation graph showing an overview diagram of how the present sales and order system works, and indicating how people and materials move from place to place. (Accounts receivable cannot be separated from the sales process—late customer payments are often a reflection of sales order foul-ups.)

Figure 11-13. The system requirements report. This report draws together the conclusions of stage 2, system analysis, of the Know-wear project.

SYSTEM REQUIREMENTS REPORT

PROJECT: Accounts Receivable, Know-wear, Inc.

1. SCOPE AND OBJECTIVES

Scope:

The project extends from the point the customer order is obtained from the customer, to the shipment and invoice leaving for the customer, to the receipt of payment from the customer.

Objectives:

1. To reduce the average time between the receipt of the customer order and the shipping of the ordered products.

2. To reduce the average time for response to a customer inquiry concerning order status.

3. To reduce the billing error rate.

4. To improve cash flow by reducing the time before a customer pays for merchandise.

2. DESCRIPTION OF PRESENT INFORMATION SYSTEM

Overview diagram of present sales and order management system:

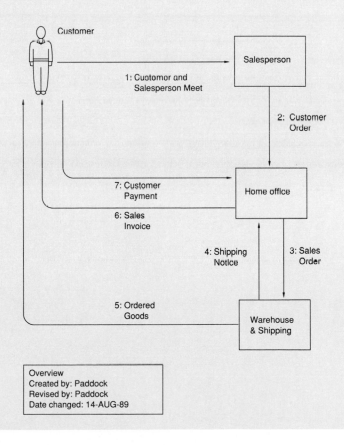

Figure 11-13, *continued.*

Figure 11-13, *continued.*

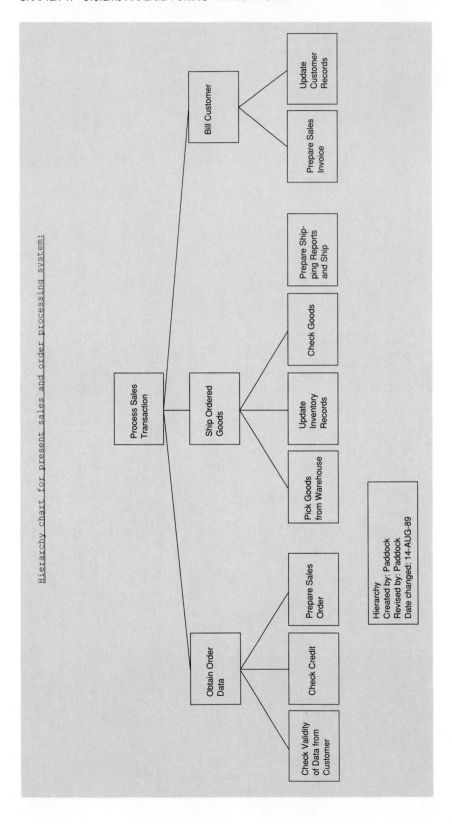

Hierarchy chart for present sales and order processing system:

Figure 11-13, *continued.*

Content diagram for present system:

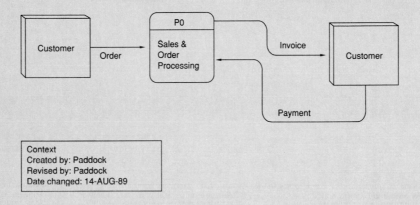

Overview of processes for present system:

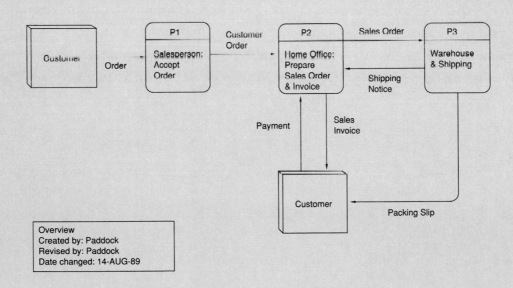

Figure 11-13,
continued.

Data flow diagram for process 2:

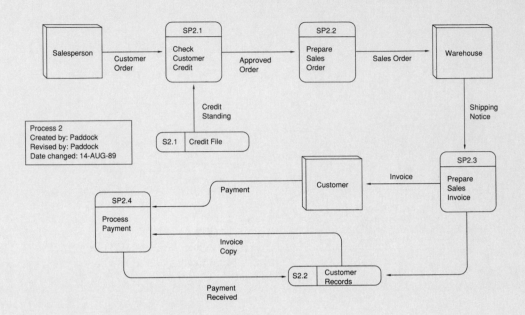

Data flow diagram of subprocesses for process 3:

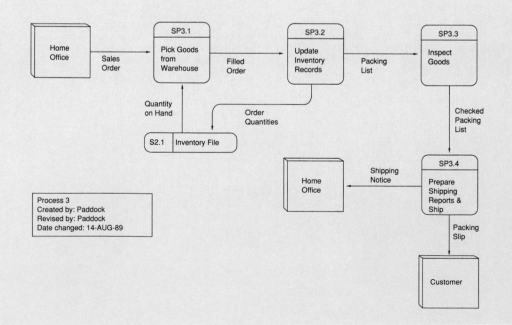

Figure 11-13, *continued.*

Users:

Billing Department, Accounts Receivable Department, Sales Order Department, Cash Receipts Department, Credit Department, Sales Office, Shipping Department.

Problems:

1. The past few years the rate of sales growth has been declining.

2. Net income has fallen from $57 million last year to $47 million this year. Another drop in net income is expected next year.

3. Cost of sales and operating costs have been rising faster than sales.

4. Average time required to fill a customer order has become long and many promised delivery dates are being missed.

Inadequacies of present system:

1. Using mail to process customer orders slows down the process and leads to delivery dates being missed.

2. Too few clerks are employed for the amount of paperwork that is being done. Overworked clerks make errors in processing customer orders and in preparing monthly statements.

3. Credit checks cause excessive delays in processing.

Information provided by present system:

1. Order entry function produces a customer invoice.

2. Accounts receivable function produces an account statement.

3. SYSTEM REQUIREMENTS

1. Capacity: Average of 700 customer orders daily, with a peak of 1,000.

2. Response time for telephone or in-person inquiries: one minute or less.

3. Accuracy: No more than one processing error per 1,000 transactions.

4. Delivery reliability: 98% of promised delivery dates are met.

Feasibility of changing current information system:

Based on expected costs and benefits, the system should pay off within two years of operation, so it should be economically feasible. It also should be technically feasible since the computer hardware and software should be available for use. As for operational feasibility, that can only be assured when the users show their acceptance of the system and management gives full support to the system development project.

Figure 11-13, *continued.*

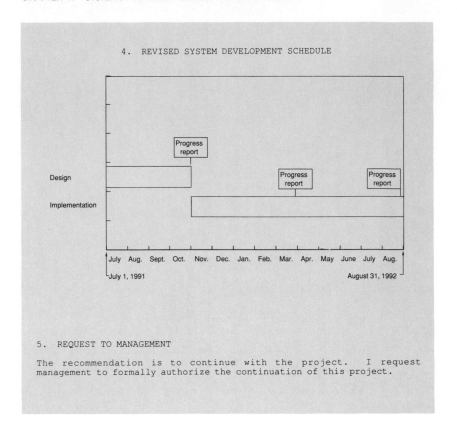

4. REVISED SYSTEM DEVELOPMENT SCHEDULE

5. REQUEST TO MANAGEMENT

The recommendation is to continue with the project. I request management to formally authorize the continuation of this project.

▶ *Hierarchy Chart for Present System*: A hierarchy diagram of the present sales and order processing system. The system is divided into three primary tasks: obtain order data, ship ordered goods, and bill customer.

▶ *Context Diagram for Present System*: A context data flow diagram of the present sales and order processing sytem, with the primary external entities that interact with it.

▶ *Overview of Processes for Present System*: An overview data flow diagram of the present sales and order processing system, showing three primary processes and the data that flows among them. The primary processes are labeled *P1*, *P2*, and *P3*.

▶ *Data Flow Diagram for Process 2*: A data flow diagram that explodes the processes detail of primary process *P2* from the overview data flow diagram. The four subprocesses are labeled *SP2.1*, *SP2.2*, *SP2.3*, and *SP1.4*. There are also two data stores required: *S2.1*, "Credit file," and *S2.2*, "Customer records file."

▶ *Data Flow Diagram of Subprocess for Process 3*: A data flow diagram that explodes the processing detail of primary process *P3* from the overview data flow diagram. The four subprocesses are labeled *SP3.1*, *SP3.2*, *SP3.3*, and *SP3.4*. The only required data store is *S3.1*, "Inventory file."

All subprocesses may be illustrated in further detail in their own data flow diagrams, although this is not done here. (For example, subprocess *SP2.1* might consist of the following sub-subprocesses: *SP2.1.1*, "Check credit history with Know-wear"; *SP2.1.2*, "Check with credit bureau"; and *SP2.1.3*, "Notify customer of credit decision.") Note that process *P1* of the overview data flow diagram is not exploded because it consists of only one subprocess—checking the validity of data from the customer.

Part 2 of the system requirements report also has some text that describes the following important facts (see Figure 11-13, part 2):

▶ Who the users of the present information system are: seven departments, from Billing to Shipping.

▶ What the problems of the present information system are: decline in sales growth and net income, rise in sales and operating costs and in the time required to fill customer orders.

▶ The inadequacies of the present system: use of mail to process customer orders, too few clerks to handle the paperwork of orders, delays in processing because of credit checks of customers.

▶ The information provided by the present system: invoices and account statements.

3. System Requirements This third section of the system requirements report is an estimate of the resources required. It also indicates what the systems analyst and users believe to be the feasibility of changing over from the present information system.

Figure 11-13, part 3, shows what you and the systems analyst have determined is necessary for a new Know-wear system. You want the system to be able to handle 700 customer orders a day from dress shops and clothing stores, with a capacity for 1,000. You also want the response time for telephone inquiries to be a minute or less. Processing must be accurate and promised delivery dates must be met. You conclude that such a system can become feasible within two years.

4. System Development Schedule This fourth part of the system requirements report is a tentative schedule for completing the project, as shown in Figure 11-13, part 4. Note that you and the systems analyst were able to complete the system analysis stage in a shorter amount of time than you anticipated in the development schedule in Figure 11-3 (part 6), in part because you built in enough time in your original estimate to allow for surprises and delays.

5. Request to Management This step includes the recommendation that the project be continued. This final step of the system analysis stage is a formal request by the systems analyst for authorization to continue with the project.

BACK TO THE
FUTURE

It is not comforting to know that something is wrong, but it *is* reassuring to discover exactly what it is. You have identified what is not working right and what needs to be done. Now you can go from the analytical to the creative, from the present to the future, and begin to design something that *will* work.

SUMMARY

▶ **Systems analysis and design** is the process of examining and improving an **information system.** It consists of five steps: (1) Identifying a company's business information needs and determining the feasibility of meeting them. (2) Evaluating the effectiveness of the present information system and specifying new requirements. (3) Formulating alternative information systems and recommending one. (4) Implementing and (5) maintaining the new system. Systems analysis and design requires close cooperation between computer specialists and the users of the new information system.

▶ Changes inside or outside a company may dictate changes in information systems: for example, organizational growth; better, cheaper technology; change in corporate structure; change in government regulations; new business opportunities.

▶ When changes may affect only a few people, a systems analysis and design may not be needed, and end-users can perform the work themelves. If changes are far-reaching within an organization, a systems analysis and design will be needed and will require the help of a systems analyst.

▶ The advantages of user-developed systems are (1) the time taken to develop them is often less than when the help of a systems analyst is needed, (2) misunderstandings are reduced because the users themselves analyze and design the data, and (3) often the cost is less. The disadvantages are (1) the quality of the systems developed is usually not as good as those designed by professionals and (2) often users do not know the procedures, resources, and time requirements for developing systems.

▶ A **systems analyst** is an information specialist with specific expertise in system analysis, design, and implementation. A systems analyst is assisted by programmers. The user, systems analyst, and programmers must combine efforts to develop a computer-based information system. The user describes his or her needs. The systems analyst works with

the user and the programmers to analyze, design, and implement new information systems. The programmers do the technical work required.

▶ Users are best equipped to deal with these specialists when they understand the **systems approach,** a general way of dealing with complex situations in which a problem can be looked at as a system that can be broken down into subsystems.

▶ Systems analysis is an ongoing activity; a company's information systems need continual reevaluation and updating. The evaluation process called the **systems life cycle approach** (or *systems development cycle*) consists of five steps: (1) *System investigation*—in which information needs are evaluated and the feasibility of meeting those needs determined. (2) *System analysis*—in which the existing information flow is analyzed and new information requirements are specified. (3) *System design*—in which alternative information systems are designed and a preferred design recommended. (4) *System implementation*—in which new hardware and software are developed and tested, personnel trained, and necessary redesign accomplished. (5) *System maintenance*—in which the information system is monitored and evaluated and, if necessary, modified.

▶ The first step in the systems life cycle is a **system investigation** of each proposed system design project to help management decide which projects are most important. The system investigation evaluates the need for and feasibility of a new or revised system, which are described in a formal written document. The steps in a system investigation are: (1) Define the problem. (2) Propose alternative information systems. (3) Evaluate the feasibility of the alternatives and recommend one. (4) Write a system study charter.

▶ A **system needs survey** defines the problem; it is a statement of the information needs and requirements of a proposed information system. The system needs survey report must be a specific, clear, and easily understood statement of *what* information is needed, *who* needs it, *where*, *when*, and *why*.

▶ The analyst then develops preliminary alternative solutions to give management an idea of the scope of the project.

▶ The question of the feasibility of any systems project has three parts: (1) *Economic:* What is the net cost/benefit? What is the rate of return? (2) *Technical:* What hardware, software, and people are required? (3) *Operational:* How acceptable will the proposed system be to users and management?

▶ Two common tools for measuring economic feasibility are net cost/benefit and rate of return. **Net cost/benefit** is the expected benefit (e.g., increased sales, reduced costs) minus the expected cost (e.g., money spent, disruptions suffered). **Rate of return** is the ratio of estimated revenues divided by the estimated costs.

▶ The **system study charter** is the formal document that summarizes the system investigation step in the systems life cycle. It should include the following: (1) A brief description of the present information system, identifying the users and describing the information provided. (2) A summary of the systems needs study, describing the user's current and future information needs and inadequacies in the present system. (3) A summary of the proposed alternative information systems, including a short, clear, precise statement of its objectives. (4) A feasibility report on the proposed projects. (5) A statement of any potential problems. (6) A development schedule for the proposed system, including estimated time, equipment, and people required. (7) Go/No go recommendations, including recommendations to pursue or not to pursue the project and a short statement of justifications.

▶ The second stage of an information systems project, **system analysis** is concerned with collecting and analyzing data about the present and future information needs of the users. System analysis does not concern the design of a new system, only a detailed analysis of the existing system and the development of requirements for an improved system. There are three steps: (1) Gathering data. (2) Analyzing the data. (3) Writing a system requirements report.

▶ Data gathering is primarily concerned with determining how the present system operates. The four most common sources of data are: (1) Written documents. (2) Interviews. (3) Questionnaires. (4) Observation.

▶ **Written documents** include organization charts, flowcharts, and other written material. An **organiza-**tion **chart** is a drawing that indicates the positions, by title, and lines of authority within an organization. They represent the formal lines of communication and information flow and give the systems analyst a top-down perspective. **Flowcharts** describe the current information system. System flowcharts describe the input devices used, the files created or accessible, and the people receiving written information. Program flowcharts or HIPO charts may show the logic of systems information.

▶ Personal **interviews** with key people in the organization will yield important data, for they often can describe the actual flow as opposed to the intended flow of information.

▶ **Questionnaires** are less effective than interviews, but are frequently used because they cost less and allow the analyst to obtain more responses in a short time. Questionnaires may reveal how frequently people use the present information system, the time required to use it, and special equipment and personnel requirements.

▶ **Observation,** which should be done openly, can show how information flows from person to person, who interrelates with whom, and how information comes into and leaves the group. Observation by an analyst who joins the group being observed is known as participant observation.

▶ The third stage in the development of an information systems project is to analyze the data to determine why certain procedures are being used and to look for better ways of doing them. The nine most common tools used in this step are (1) system flow charts, (2) grid charts, (3) decision tables, (4) data flow diagrams, (5) checklist, (6) top-down analysis, (7) HIPO charts, (8) prototyping, and (9) automated design tools.

▶ **System flowcharts** are used to represent information flow within a system by focusing upon input and output operations. Because they present a macro view or overview, system flowcharts are a valuable tool for systems analysis and design.

▶ A **grid chart,** also called an **input/output chart,** is used in analysis to show the relationship between input and output documents. Horizontal rows represent input documents; vertical rows represent the output documents. An "X" at the intersection of a row and column means that the input document is used to create the output document.

▶ **Decision tables** show what decision rules apply when certain conditions occur and what action should take place as a result.

▶ A **data flow diagram** shows the flow of data and information and which data files are available.

▶ A **checklist** of questions is used to ensure that the user and systems analyst address key issues when they are evaluating the present system.

▶ **Top-down analysis methodology** is used to first identify the top-level function of a complex system, then analyze it, and then break it down into secondary-level components, each of which in turn may be identified, analyzed, and subdivided.

▶ HIPO stands for *Hierarchy plus Input-Process-Output.* A **HIPO chart** is a visual tool consisting of a package of diagrams that describes the structured program from general to particular. A HIPO chart consists of three separate diagrams: (1) a **visual table of contents,** which graphically depicts the independent modules used in a structured program; (2) an **overview chart,** which shows the inputs, processes, and outputs of a particular module in the visual table of contents; and (3) a **detail diagram,** which looks like an overview chart but is used to show a finer level of detail, presenting the particulars of the functions to be performed and the data items required.

▶ **Prototyping** consists of building a prototype system—a model of the actual system that will look much like the finished product. The advantages of a prototype system are (1) it enables the user to try out the system and (2) makes the system more flexible to change. The disadvantages are that (1) a prototype can be difficult to manage and control and (2) a prototype is difficult to use for large information systems.

▶ **Automated design tools** are software packages that follow certain criteria to evaluate hardware and software alternatives according to the processing requirements supplied by the systems analyst. These tools are sometimes called **computer-aided software engineering (CASE) tools;** they focus on improving the productivity of software development, especially when the project requires coordination among several analysts and programmers. An example of an automated design tool is the microcomputer software program Excelerator, which allows a systems analyst to use a graphics feature to design and document a software system.

▶ The **system requirements report** describes the findings of the system analysis. It ensures that user and systems analyst agree on the details of the current system and on the need for a new information system. The system requirements report has five sections: (1) A detailed statement of scope and objectives. (2) A description of the present information system, including current information flow, procedures used, and any problems. Overview diagrams and HIPO diagrams are helpful here. (3) An estimate of system requirements—the resources required and the feasibility of changing over from the present information system. (4) A revised system development schedule. (5) A request to management for authorization to proceed.

KEY TERMS

REVIEW QUESTIONS

1. Describe two changes that might result in a company's needing to develop a new information system.

2. Why should you be involved in helping the experts set up a computerized information system at the company where you will work?

3. What is the viewpoint and the process of the systems approach?

4. What are the five steps of the systems life cycle?

5. What information should be included in a system study charter?

6. Describe one of the common methods of gathering data for system analysis.

7. What is a grid chart?

8. What is a data flow diagram?

CASE PROBLEMS

Case 11-1: Systems Analysis and College Registration

There are several pitfalls that can be the undoing of a systems analyst, points out Jerry FitzGerald and his co-authors in *Fundamentals of Systems Analysis.* Among them are:

▶ Improper definition of the problem by management, which is not redefined by the analyst.

▶ Excessive ambition by the analyst, which leads him or her to force a favorite solution to the problem.

▶ A problem solution that is "oriented more toward the technical peculiarities of a computer than to the objectives of the people who will use the system."

▶ Preoccupation with techniques or equipment rather than the objectives of the problem study.

Being alert to these pitfalls may also serve you well, whether you are using the techniques of systems analysis to deal with a problem or are engaging the services of a systems analyst.

Your assignment: Registering as a student for a new quarter or semester is often tedious, and at some colleges and universities it can be an anxious, exhausting experience, especially for a first-timer. Use the information you learned in this chapter to sketch the flow of steps involved in registering at your college, keeping the above pitfalls in mind. (You may make a separate flow diagram showing preregistration, if you wish.) Include the forms you must fill out, people you must see, and stations to which you must go. After you have done your system investigation and system analysis, try to think of a design for a new system. You probably want to approach this from the standpoint of how you personally can navigate the system better, but you may see ways in which the college could redesign the system to improve it.

Case 11-2: Writing a Request for an Interview

A well-kept secret of the computer age, says Charles J. McDonough, writing in the *Wall Street Journal,* is that for each element of computer processing, at least "two distinct segments of human activity are always needed: one before processing and one after. First, some employee has to do something very specific before the computer can do its thing; then when the computer finishes running that program, some employee must do something with the output." The result is that—the computer revolution notwithstanding—office employees are still spending most of their working time handling routine pieces of paper. Indeed, McDonough, the head of a Buffalo, New York, consulting firm, says that his company has found that "even the most highly computerized offices average four to five detail manual procedures to support each separate accomplishment by the computer." Expansion of computer activities may eliminate certain manual chores, but the paradox is that they require carefully coordinated adjustments in other clerical tasks and new staff instructions. The point is that, no matter how sophisticated office automation may be today, it still must run in conjunction with people. Thus, a systems analyst and the user liaison must be able to relate well to people—both in obtaining information from them and in getting their assistance in implementing a new system.

Your assignment: Suppose, in your role as user liaison at Know-wear, you received the following memorandum from the systems analyst, requesting an interview with the manager of the accounts receivable department. Edit the memo so that the systems analyst will have a better chance of cordial working relations.

Based on preliminary information, we find there seem to be an enormous number of errors originating in your work area. We have also received several customer complaints regarding mishandling of payments on their accounts. In addition, other Know-wear managers say reports from your department are seldom up to date, handicapping their decision-making abilities. For these reasons, the CEO has ordered a system investigation of your area.

Accordingly, will you please make yourself available for an interview in my office next week. I will need to know information such as the following: (a) How many employees report to you, how long have they worked for you, and what salaries do they make? (b) What are their job descriptions? (c) Why are they late recording customer payments? (d) Why has there been no attempt to computerize your department? (e) Which employees could be dispensed with if your department becomes automated? Justify your choices.

I have time available to see you on Thursday or Friday afternoon next week, and you can leave a message with my secretary as to which is convenient. The information you contribute will help me come up with a plan for improving the performance in your area.

Chapter 12

SYSTEMS DESIGN AND IMPLEMENTATION: THE NEW LOOK

Taking control—that is what system design is all about. A former eighth-grade science teacher, Fred Bramante, Jr.—whose small son coined the name for his first store, Daddy's Junky Music Store—decided the way to make money with his Salem, N.H., chain of six musical instrument stores was to get hold of inefficient inventory control, inept financial planning, and other matters that demanded maximum attention. "For example," reported *Inc.* magazine, "accessories such as straps and picks were falling through the cracks because they were so hard to track financially, even though they added up to a full 25% of sales."

To begin to remedy this situation, Bramante's marketing manager and financial head pieced together the data entry forms and flowcharts to see how information flowed, and interconnected every area of the business on a day-to-day operating business. That was the system analysis part.

They then went looking for a financial software system that would satisfy both the individual store managers' and the CEO's need for control. Reports *Inc.* (February 1987):

> Their idea was to turn off the old system and go right into the new without an overlapping backup, but they had lingering concerns about the potential mess that could be made by members of the staff who didn't trust computers. So in preparation, eight simple Apple IIe's had been brought into the stores to breed familiarity. "Apples ask dumb, cute questions that people feel comfortable with," explains [the marketing manager]. " 'Are you sure you want to do this?. . . You didn't put the disk in the disk drive, so I can't read the information. . . .' The Apples let people know a computer could help them. It was a perfect transition."

Taking control, then, means following the final three steps in systems analysis and design:

CASE STUDY: DESIGNING A NEW SYSTEM

Computer System to Offer Theater Facts and Tickets

A new, ultra-sophisticated information and ticket-buying system . . . could have the biggest effect on theatergoing habits since the advent of credit-card purchases more than 13 years ago.

The system, NYC/On Stage, promises to make decisions about attending New York City performances easier than ever, according to its creators.

Callers will be able to get up-to-the-minute details about the performing arts—from musicals on Broadway to new-wave dance in Soho lofts—and about ticket-buying options. The new system will be available 24 hours a day through an 800 number, and will provide access from anywhere in the country at no charge to the caller, said Henry Guettel, executive director of the Theater Development Fund, the non-profit support group for which it was designed. . . .

Mr. Guettel described NYC/On Stage as a tree on which the caller, using a phone with tone dialing, climbs—through a progression of queries and responses—to the final ticket purchase.

"Say you're out in Chillicothe and coming into New York on Wednesday," Mr. Guettel said. "You want to go to a Broadway musical Wednesday night and the ballet on Thursday. When the 800 number is dialed, a voice invites the caller to dial 1 for theater, 2 for music and dance, or 3 for children's entertainment.

"You press 1 and instantly hear, 'Press 1 for musicals or 2 for plays,'" Mr. Guettel said. The next step is choosing "Broadway," "Off Broadway" or "Off Off Broadway." Then the caller will hear a list of all the productions in that subgroup, each followed by a three-digit number.

Anyone pressing the three-digit number for "Groucho," for example, which comes up on the "Plays, Off Broadway" list, will be told where it is running, the performance schedule including any last-minute changes, and something about the show. The 30-second announcement will conclude with instructions on how to buy tickets. Most charge services will mail tickets ordered more than 10 days in advance of the performance. . . .

The system uses complex new technology that enables a telephone to draw from a central bank of information in much the same way a home computer interacts with a data base. The Voicetek Corporation, a computer company specializing in so-called audiotext technology, created computer hardware called a voice store and forward system that is the cornerstone of its business. The software—the actual NYC/On Stage program—was also developed by Voicetek. . . .

—Jeremy Gerard, *New York Times*

▶ Formulating alternative information systems and recommending one system

▶ Implementing the new information system

▶ Maintaining the new information system

An example of the help end-users receive from systems design involving a new computer system is described in the box above. Let us now consider the final three steps of the systems analysis and design process.

SYSTEM DESIGN

HOW SHOULD A

NEW SYSTEM WORK?

Ms. Douglas gives you and the systems analyst permission to proceed—to design a new information system. Now you are no longer looking at the present system, for **system design** focuses on creating and specifying a new information system to meet current and future needs. Thus, you need to restate the scope and objectives of the project somewhat from what you indicated in the system analysis stage. The system design scope and objectives are shown in part 1 of Figure 12-1; you might wish to compare them with the scope and objectives given back in part 1 of Figure 11-13.

There are three steps in the system design stage:

▶ Design of alternative systems.
▶ Selection of the best alternative.
▶ Preparation of a system design report.

Designing Alternative Systems

System design can be very simple, particularly for information systems that do not interact with other information systems within the organization. For most information systems, however, there are trade-offs between costs and efficiency, making system design a complex task. *Costs* are how much time and money will be required to create the system. *Efficiency* is concerned with how quickly and accurately the system can collect data, convert it to information, and distribute it to users. Usually, though not always, the most efficient system is the most expensive.

Still, a good way to begin system design is to simply ignore the costs and create the best information system imaginable. Although the result may be economically impractical, the approach has the effect of stimulating design inventiveness. Moreover, out of this exercise, affordable design alternatives probably will emerge.

Many of the tools used in structured programming and structured analysis, as discussed in Chapter 4, such as structured design review and walkthroughs, are used to specify the design alternatives. In addition, for each alternative design, the systems analyst should prepare detailed system flowcharts and HIPO charts to document the input, output, and processing requirements, along with clerical, security, and control procedures. Finally, a cost estimate is made for each alternative.

Part 2 of Figure 12-1 shows two alternative system designs developed by you and the systems analyst for a new information system that will reduce shipping time, speed up replies to customer inquiries, and reduce billing errors for Know-wear. The two alternatives are as follows:

Figure 12-1.   The system design report. This report summarizes the results of the Know-wear system design study.

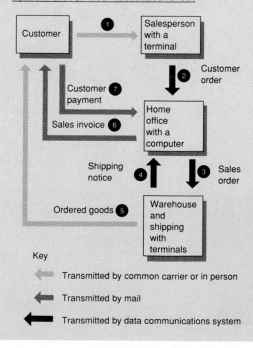

```
                        SYSTEM DESIGN REPORT

PROJECT: Accounts Receivable, Know-wear, Inc.


1.   SCOPE AND OBJECTIVES

Scope:

The project extends from the point the customer order is obtained
from the customer, to the shipment and invoice leaving for the
customer, to the receipt of payment from the customer.

Objectives:

     1.  To reduce  the average time between the receipt of the
         customer order and the shipping of the ordered products
         so at least 98% of promised delivery dates are met.

     2.  To reduce the average time for response to a customer
         inquiry concerning order status to less than one minute.

     3.  To reduce the billing error rate from one error per 50
         transactions to one error per 1000 transactions.

2.   ALTERNATIVE SYSTEM DESIGNS

Alternative #1:

Salespeople will be equipped with computer terminals and customer
orders will be transmitted to the home office computer via a data
communications system. Sales orders will be communicated to the
warehouse via a data communications system, which will also be used
to transmit shipping notices back to the home office. Ordered goods,
invoices, and customer payments will be transmitted by common carrier
or mail as before. Invoices will be generated by the home office
computer system, however, and customer payments will be entered into
the computer. Reports for managers will be generated by the computer
system. Customer service representatives will have on-line access to
up-to-date information on the status of customer orders.

System design for Alternative #1:
```

Figure 12-1, *continued.*

Alternative #2:

In this proposal, goods will be stored at the home office, not in a warehouse at a separate location. This eliminates the need for an expensive data communications connection between the home office and the warehouse.

System design for Alternative #2:

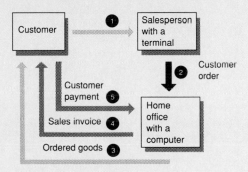

Key

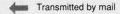 Transmitted by common carrier or in person

◀━ Transmitted by mail

◀━ Transmitted by data communications system

3.   ECONOMIC FEASIBILITY FOR TWO ALTERNATIVE DESIGNS:

One-time costs:

	#1	#2
System development costs	$ 34,800	$ 32,200
System hardware costs	402,000	327,000
System software costs	47,300	40,000
Total one-time costs:	$484,100	$399,200

Recurring costs:

	#1	#2
Information system maintenance	$25,000	$20,000
Data and information control	26,000	20,000
Information system administration	26,400	20,000
Total recurring costs:	$77,400	$60,000

Recurring benefits:

	#1	#2
Clerical cost savings	$116,000	$120,000
Savings from reduced errors	54,000	46,000
Added sales and other savings, resulting from better customer service	200,000	200,000
Total recurring benefits:	$370,000	$366,000

Figure 12-1, *continued.*

Cost/benefit analysis for Alternative #1:

	1991-1992	1993	1994
Benefits	0	$370,000	$370,000
Costs	$484,100	77,400	77,400
Net, yearly	-$484,100	$292,600	$292,600
Net, cumulative	-$484,100	-$191,500	$101,100

Net cost/benefit for 1993 = expected benefit - expected cost
$$\$370,000 - (\$484,100 + \$77,400)$$
$$= -\$191,500$$

Net cost/benefit for 1994 = expected benefit - expected cost
$$(\$370,000 + \$370,000) - (\$561,500 + \$77,400)$$
$$= \$101,100$$

Cost/benefit analysis for Alternative #2:

	1991-1992	1993	1994
Benefits	0	$366,000	$366,000
Costs	$399,200	60,000	60,000
Net, yearly	-$399,200	$306,000	$306,000
Net, cumulative	-$399,200	-$93,200	$212,800

Net cost/benefit for 1993 = expected benefit - expected cost
$$= \$366,000 - (\$399,200 + \$60,000)$$
$$= -\$93,200$$

Net cost/benefit for 1994 = expected benefit - expected cost
$$(\$366,000 + \$366,000) - (\$459,200 + \$60,000)$$
$$= \$212,800$$

4.   PROBABLE EFFECTS OF PROPOSED INFORMATION SYSTEM

The use of computer terminals rather than the mail to deliver customer orders to the home office may increase the chance of a clerical error. Clerks must be well-trained to accept these customer orders by computer.

The new software may need to be tailored to the company's specific applications, and problems may result from these alterations.

5.   RECOMMENDATION

I recommend that Alternative #2 be chosen since the overall cost of inplementation is less. However, the effect of the change from the procedure of using a warehouse in the present system to not using a warehouse in Alternative #2 should be taken into consideration before any change is made.

▶ **Alternative 1:** Salespeople equipped with computer terminals will transmit customer orders to the home office computer via a data communications system, which will also transmit sales orders to the warehouse and shipping notices from the warehouse back to the home office. Ordered goods, invoices, and customer payments will be transmitted by common carrier or mail, as before. Invoices will be generated by the home office computer system, and customer payments will be entered into the computer. Reports for managers will be generated by the computer system. Customer service representatives will have on-line access to up-to-date information on the status of customer orders.

▶ **Alternative 2:** In this proposal, goods will be stored at the home office, not in a warehouse in a separate location. This eliminates the need for an expensive data communications connection between home office and warehouse.

As a glance will show, the first alternative is clearly the more complex and thus the more expensive. Note that this alternative is also the same as the original method, except that parts of it involve a data communications system.

Selecting a Design

Sometimes the design of information systems is a direct evolutionary process that begins with the ideal information system, as conceived by the user and systems analyst, and is modified until a feasible system emerges. More often, however, alternative systems are developed, each with advantages and disadvantages in efficiency and cost, and management has to make a choice.

There are several factors to consider in choosing a design, some of the most important being:

▶ Compatibility
▶ Flexibility
▶ Security and control
▶ Economic feasibility

Compatibility Is the proposed information system going to fit well within the organization's overall information system? That is, will the part be compatible with the whole? The proposed information system must not only be compatible in hardware and software—that is, in the technical aspects. It must also be compatible with the people working with it; it must fit their needs and capabilities.

Flexibility Can the proposed system be modified or expanded? This is what is meant by flexibility. Of course, the system to be installed will be designed to meet future as well as present information needs, but any dynamic business must allow for changes beyond what can be anticipated at the design stage.

Security and Control   You will want the new information system to be easy to use and gain access to. Unfortunately, the easier it is for authorized people to get into it, the easier it may be for unauthorized people also. Thus, the system needs to be designed to control access and ensure security and yet not discourage use. We will have more to say about security in Chapter 17.

Economic Feasibility   To compare the economic feasibility of proposed systems, the systems analyst must prepare a detailed cost/benefit analysis. This means not only a careful evaluation of the costs of hardware, software, and intangibles but also an evaluation of the benefits. With your help, the systems analyst for Know-wear has worked up a careful cost/benefit analysis for the two proposed systems, as shown in part 3 of Figure 12-1.

The System Design Report

As at the end of the other stages, the end of the system design stage requires a report to document the findings. The purpose of the **system design report** is to give management enough background so they can decide upon the best alternative. The report will include the following information:

1. The scope and objectives of the design study, as we showed for Know-wear in part 1 of Figure 12-1.
2. Two alternative designs for the Know-wear project, as shown in part 2 of Figure 12-1. Any additional important details should be included in an appendix to the report or in another document.
3. An economic feasibility report, including costs and benefits, as shown in part 3 of Figure 12-1 for Know-wear.
4. Discussion of the probable effects of the proposed information systems on the organization. This includes not only the effects of incorporating new hardware and software but also the effects of a proposed system on humans. You and the systems analyst for the Know-wear project call attention to the possibility that use of computer terminals rather than mail to deliver orders to the home office may increase the possibility of clerical errors at first, since clerks must be trained to use the computers. These and other effects are outlined in part 4 of Figure 12-1.
5. The report should recommend one alternative, stating the assumptions and logic behind the recommendation. The report written by the systems analyst for Know-wear reflects the consensus of the two of you that the second alternative should be chosen because the implementation cost is less. However, the report ad-

vises management to consider the fact that a warehouse will not be used in that system whereas it is being used in the existing system (see Figure 12-1, part 5).

The complete system design report for the Know-wear project is shown in Figure 12-1.

SYSTEM
IMPLEMENTATION

HOW DO YOU
GET IT RUNNING?

Ms. Douglas signs off on Alternative 2. She asks the systems analyst to stay on to implement the project, and she asks you to stay in touch as the liaison for Know-wear.

Implementing a recommended design—**system implementation**—has five activities:

▶ Software development
▶ Hardware acquisition
▶ Personnel training
▶ Testing
▶ Conversion

These are shown in Figure 12-2 and described below. Note that **documentation**—the written detailed description of the systems analysis and design—is and has been an ongoing process throughout all stages.

Software Development

A computer-based information system, which, of course, is the type you are implementing here, requires application software or programs to operate. This software can be either developed or purchased (see box, p. 403). For larger projects, the systems analyst works with the user to determine whether to make or buy the required software. For smaller projects, the end-user makes this decision. In either case, if the software is to be created, the steps described in Chapter 4 for applications software development should be followed.

Software may be a combination of off-the-shelf software packages and of internally developed programs—that is, software developed within the company. For available software packages, the systems analyst must evaluate the software and see which is compatible with the information system being designed. For internally developed programs, each program is usually broken up into independent modules to be developed separately, often by different programmers; the modules are combined later, under the supervision of the systems analyst.

Figure 12-2. Implementation. Five activities are required to install an information system: software development, hardware acquisition, personnel training, testing, and conversion. Documentation is and has been an ongoing process.

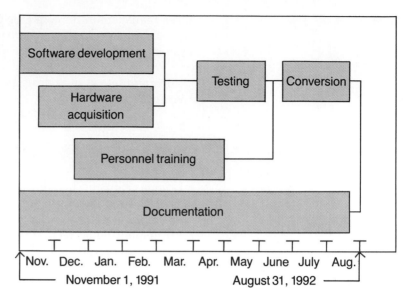

Hardware Acquisition

Some new information systems being implemented will not require additional hardware, which means that implementation is easier. However, additional equipment is often needed, and the systems analyst has the task of evaluating hardware alternatives and preparing the physical site for the new machines.

Some software packages will operate only on specific kinds of hardware, in which case the software development step will dictate the hardware acquisition. More frequently, software packages will operate on the equipment of different manufacturers, and so the systems analyst must request proposals from different makers and evaluate them. These proposals will often state the alternatives in costs and benefits between leasing equipment and outright purchase.

Before the new hardware arrives, the user and systems analyst must determine the site where it will be installed. Depending on equipment size and space available, preparing the site may or may not be a problem. Some systems, for example, may require more air conditioning or a greater power supply. The systems analyst's role is to determine the site requirements and to stay on top of the schedule for preparing the site.

Personnel Training

Two groups of people will need to be trained: (1) the technical personnel, who will develop, operate, and maintain the system, and (2) the system's users and their managers. Training is necessary so that people will understand their responsibility in making the system work.

SOFTWARE: MAKE IT OR BUY IT?

A lot of software is available for common business uses: accounting, payroll, scheduling, financial planning, and so on. All of these packages come with documentation, and some software manufacturers also provide people to train new users.

The advantages of such off-the-shelf software are:

▶ The cost is known at the outset. Moreover the costs are spread over several buyers, whereas the cost of in-house-developed software may have to be absorbed by one organization.

▶ It can be put into effect right away. Users need not wait for months (or even years) while their own in-house systems analysts and programmers go through the extensive design, coding, and testing phases.

▶ The buyer is usually dealing with a known product with past users and a reputation. By contrast, custom-developed software is an uncertain process: Not only is development time unknown—and can be affected by changes in technology—

but the whole application may have to be modified if it turns out that users don't like the software.

Nevertheless, there are disadvantages to off-the-shelf software:

▶ For some uses, no such software exists.
▶ Software developed for one purpose may not be satisfactory for another.

Some training can begin early, even before equipment is installed. Most early training is for the purpose of increasing the involvement of users in the new system in order to lessen the shock of adjustment and to nurture a good working relationship between users and technicians.

Once hardware and software are operating, training can be increased. Operating procedures must be clearly understood by both users and technicians.

Testing

With hardware and software in place and training started, you are now in a position to begin **testing**—testing not only equipment and programs but operating procedures also. This is when hostilities are apt to emerge, as you discover in the course of implementing Knowwear's new information system. The regular staff of clerks show their fear of being automated out of their jobs as they come face to face with the computer technicians. They begin to complain to you about the system changing their work patterns, breaking up their work groups, and causing them loss of status.

The systems analyst handles this all fairly adroitly, you think, letting employees offer suggestions for improving the system and asking them to provide data for testing. With Ms. Douglas's approval, you offer reassurance that no present worker will lose his or her job. You show how the technical staff will be able to make the users' lives easier, not harder.

During this shake-down phase, software, hardware, and procedures are each tested separately and then combined and tested together. The tests consist of feeding dummy or made-up data into the system, following it as it is converted to information, and evaluating the results. The systems analyst monitors this activity and makes (or has programmers make) whatever modifications are needed. Depending on the complexity of the information system involved, testing may take several months. Implementation for the Know-wear project, for example, takes ten months, although not all that time is taken up with testing.

Conversion

Conversion, which follows testing, is the process of changing over from the old information system to the new one. There are four common types of conversions:

▶ Direct
▶ Parallel
▶ Pilot
▶ Phased

Direct   The most risky type of conversion, the **direct conversion** consists of completely discontinuing the old way of doing things and immediately implementing the new one. This approach should be avoided unless the organization is willing to live without *any* information system should something go wrong with the new one—a distinct possibility with anything untried.

Parallel   In **parallel conversion,** the old and new information systems are operated side by side until the new one has shown its reliability and everyone has confidence in it. The old one is then discontinued. However, it is expensive to operate two systems simultaneously, and so the process should not be continued for long.

Pilot   Under **pilot conversion,** only a part of the organization tries out the new system—one plant may act as a test site, for instance. Before the new system is implemented throughout the organization,

The tasks of systems analysis and design. System
analysis begins with gathering data—in part by observation and interviews *(top left and right)*. System
design *(lower left)* is concerned with designing alternative systems, using detailed system flowcharts and
making cost estimates. In the system implementation
stage, two important tasks are hardware acquisition
and testing and personnel training.

it must prove itself at the test site. This approach is less risky than the direct method and less expensive than the parallel method, although a long installation period is often required in order to convert the whole company to the system.

Phased   In the **phased conversion,** a new information system is implemented over a period of time, gradually replacing the old. For example, order entry may be computerized first, then sales forecasting, and so on. Although this avoids the riskiness of some other approaches, it requires a long conversion time.

Ms. Douglas would clearly prefer the last method of conversion for Know-wear. The result would be that everyone—customers, staff, technicians, management—would have a chance to get used to the new system and there would be fewer disruptions and consequent loss of customer goodwill and employee morale. But Know-wear is in financial trouble, and it is important to get the company turned around soon. Ms. Douglas therefore elects the second riskiest option, the parallel conversion, with old and new systems operating side by side until everyone has confidence in the new one.

SYSTEM
MAINTENANCE
HOW DO YOU
TAKE CARE OF IT?

After implementation has been completed, you and the systems analyst go on to other projects. But, once installed, the information system does not just run along by itself, no matter how carefully the implementation stage was handled. All systems—and information systems in particular—are continually changing. As Know-wear grows, its information demands will change. The purpose of **system maintenance,** therefore, is to monitor and evaluate the current operation of the information system and to modify it when necessary.

Some modifications may become necessary because of sudden, unexpected problems, when quick evaluation and changes will be required. Some may be brought about because of less dramatic, gradual changes that may be harder to identify but whose long-term effect is to reduce the system's efficiency.

Many of the latter problems will be identified through periodic evaluations called **system audits** or **system reviews.** System audits—the first of which takes place immediately after the information system is successfully implemented—are examinations of the system by a systems analyst, who asks questions about the following:

▶ *Efficiency:* Does the system provide information to its users in an efficient and timely manner?

▶ *Reliability:* Are the hardware and software reliable and easy to use?

▶ *Training:* Is the training sufficient and effective?

▶ *Procedures:* Are the procedures for operating and using the system well documented and are they being followed?

▶ *Goals:* Are the original goals and objectives being met?

▶ *Recommendations:* Are there any recommendations or suggestions for improving the system?

BEDROCK FOR A

COMPUTER-BASED

INFORMATION

SYSTEM

Why, you might ask, is it necessary to be so *careful?* Is all this patient data gathering and analysis and weighing of alternatives really worthwhile—especially when a company must act quickly to save itself or to take advantage of rapidly changing market conditions?

Sometimes, of course, managers must act decisively and quickly, with no time to study alternatives—but the risks can be quite great. Moreover, as we have shown in the case of Know-wear, the systems analysis and design process is not used to study whether to introduce a new product or site a new plant. As we will see in the next three chapters, it is used to put in place a whole system of information gathering and processing that can enable a company to act far faster and with greater accuracy than it has before.

SUMMARY

▶ The stage following system analysis, **system design,** focuses on creating and specifying a new information system to meet current and future needs. The three steps in the system design stage are: (1) design of alternative systems, (2) selection of the best alternative, (3) preparation of a system design report.

▶ System design can be very simple or it can be a complex task involving trade-offs between costs and efficiency. Many of the tools used in structured programming and structured analysis, such as structured design review and walkthroughs, are used to specify the design alternatives. For each alternative design, the systems analyst prepares detailed system flowcharts and HIPO charts to document the output, input, and processing requirements, along with clerical, security, and control procedures. Finally, a cost estimate is made for each alternative.

▶ In choosing a design for an information system there are several factors to consider: (1) compatibility, (2) flexibility, (3) security and control, (4) economic feasibility.

▶ A **system design report** documents the findings at the end of the system design stage. The report includes: (1) the scope and objectives of the design study; (2) two or three alternative designs, with required resources for each; (3) an economic feasibility report, including costs and benefits; (4) discussion of the probable effects of the proposed information systems on the organization—including not only the effects of incorporating new hardware and software but also the effects of a proposed system on humans; (5) a recommended alternative, along with the assumptions and logic behind the recommendation.

▶ **System implementation** has five activities: (1) software development, (2) hardware acquisition, (3) personnel training, (4) testing, (5) conversion. **Documentation** continues throughout all stages.

▶ Computer-based information systems require computer programs to operate. Software may be a combination of internally developed programs and software packages.

▶ If additional equipment is needed to implement a system, the systems analyst has the task of evaluating hardware alternatives and preparing the physical site for the new machines.

▶ Two groups of personnel need to be trained: (1) the technical personnel who develop, operate, and maintain the system, and (2) the system's users and their managers. A significant part of training is making operating procedures clearly understood by these two groups. Training is necessary so that the people will understand their responsibility in making the system work.

▶ After the hardware and software are in place and training started, the new system is ready for **testing**—testing not only the equipment and programs but operating procedures also. During the testing phase, software, hardware, and procedures are each tested separately and then combined and tested together. The test consists of feeding dummy data into the system, following it as it is converted to information, and evaluating the results. The systems analyst monitors this activity and makes whatever modifications are needed. Testing can take several months.

▶ **Conversion,** which follows testing, is the process of changing over from the old information system to the new one. There are four common types of conversions: (1) direct, (2) parallel, (3) pilot, (4) phased.

▶ The most risky type of conversion, the **direct conversion** consists of completely discontinuing the old system and implementing the new one. This approach should be avoided unless the organization is willing to live without *any* information system should something go wrong with the new one.

▶ In **parallel conversion,** the old and new information systems are operated side by side until the new one has shown its reliability; the old one is then discontinued. Since it is expensive to operate two systems simultaneously, the process should not be continued for long.

▶ Under **pilot conversion,** only a part of the organization tries out the new system—for example, one plant acts as a test site before the new system is implemented throughout the organization. This approach is less risky than the direct method and less expensive than the parallel method, although a long installation period is often required to convert the whole company to the system.

▶ In the **phased conversion,** a new information system is implemented over a period of time, gradually replacing the old. Although this avoids the riskiness of some of the other approaches, it requires a long conversion time.

▶ The purpose of **system maintenance** is to monitor and evaluate the current operation of the information system and to modify it when necessary. Many problems are identified through periodic evaluations called **system audits** or **system reviews.** System audits are conducted by a systems analyst who examines the system and asks questions about: (1) *Efficiency:* Does the system provide information to its users in an efficient and timely manner? (2) *Reliability:* Are the hardware and software reliable and easy to use? (3) *Training:* Is the training sufficient and effective? (4) *Procedures:* Are the procedures for operating and using the system well documented, and are they being followed? (5) *Goals:* Are the original goals and objectives being met? (6) *Recommendations:* Are there any recommendations or suggestions for improving the system?

KEY TERMS

Conversion, p. 404

Direct conversion, p. 404

Documentation, p. 401

Parallel conversion, p. 404

Phased conversion, p. 406

Pilot conversion, p. 404

System audit, p. 406

System design, p. 395

System design report, p. 400

System implementation, p. 401

System maintenance, p. 406

System review, p. 406

Testing, p. 403

REVIEW QUESTIONS

1. What are the three steps in the system design stage?
2. What four factors should you consider in choosing a design?
3. Describe the various methods of conversion.
4. Outline the process of system implementation.
5. Describe system maintenance.

CASE PROBLEMS

Case 12-1: The Student Consulting Business

Three students from California Polytechnic State University, San Luis Obispo, were given a great deal of credit for helping Phyllis Gerrans's Fancy Frocks achieve success. In three years, reported the *New York Times*, the Santa Maria, Calif., dress manufacturing company grew from a three-person operation "with a fragile hope of survival" to a thriving enterprise with a staff of 48 plus five sales representatives around the country. Under a program sponsored by the U.S. Small Business Administration, the three business students were sent to counsel Gerrans—at no charge to her—in order to help her draw up an 18-month business plan, identify girls 16 to 21 who could serve as a clothing test market, scout potential competition, and put together financial projections.

Your assignment: If you are a business student, you might well be interested in volunteering for such a "management-assistance" program yourself, if your college runs one. Nearly 125,000 senior and graduate business majors from 530 colleges and universities are sent every year to counsel small-scale entrepreneurs. What you get is experience; what the entrepreneur gets is guidance on marketing objectives, financial analysis, and record-keeping methods, among other things. Whether or not such a program is offered at your school, choose a small enterprise you know something about (perhaps one run by another student) and use the techniques of systems analysis and design to determine how the business might be improved, particularly in regard to end-user microcomputer operations.

Case 12-2: Using Computers to Bring Changes to Basic Business Documents

Electronic data interchange, writes Paul B. Carroll in the *Wall Street Journal* (March 6, 1987), is beginning to pay off in paperless business transactions. As he puts it, "Electronic data interchange is simple in concept: Software translates documents into and then out of a generic form so that companies can perform transactions electronically, even though they use different documents, computers and software. Typically, the technology is used to cover only a dozen or so basic documents, such as purchase orders and bills (invoices). Still, results can be substantial even in such limited applications." As an example, Super Valu Stores began saving $5,000 or so a week because it no longer had to manually process invoices and other documents that used to arrive by mail or

over the phone, and so was able to save on staff that used to check purchase orders against inventory. A lot of such interest in EDI has come about because the software available to handle transactions has become more sophisticated and because the formats for purchase orders, invoices, and other basic documents have become "generic." Previously the formats varied widely among companies.

Your assignment: Only 1% to 2% of such routine transactions are executed through EDI, but one consultant feels, "This is the hottest thing since the telephone." If that's the case, see if you can analyze some system of financial transactions you are familiar with—your own personal finance system, the college bookstore's system, or whatever—and use the system design steps to devise an EDI system on paper.

Chapter 13

TRANSACTION PROCESSING INFORMATION SYSTEMS: KEEPING TRACK OF DETAILS

What is a business for? Perhaps, says Theodore Levitt, a Harvard Business School marketing professor quoted in the *Wall Street Journal*, it is not to make a profit; rather, it is "to create and keep a customer." To do that, he says, "you have to do all those things that will make people want to do business with you." A company, that is, should direct all its energies toward satisfying customers, and "the rest, given reasonable good sense, [will] take care of itself."

What managers need, says Levitt, is "marketing imagination," an understanding that people buy solutions to problems, not things. Customers need to be treated as valued assets. And because it takes so much effort to find customers in the first place, it is not reasonable to ignore them after the sale is made. Even customers that are behind on their payments deserve to be treated well—or certainly fairly, as the case study on the opposite page shows. And the treatment of customers begins not with top and middle managers but with the lowest level of managers and their employees. Customer relations begin with those prosaic activities of order entry, accounts receivable, and similar clerical tasks. It behooves us, therefore, to see if there are better ways of handling these chores. Here is the logical place to initiate a computer-based information system.

CASE STUDY: CUTTING DOWN ON BROKEN PROMISES

A Telephone Company Automates Its Billing Process

DALLAS—It tripled its customer base in just three years, but U.S. Telephone, Inc. found that its manual customer accounts collection process could not handle the work load.

"We have cycle billings, 20 cycles a month, and sometimes we didn't get an updated trial balance [a computation of money spent and owed] for six weeks," Chuck Giles, U.S. Telephone's vice-president of credit management, recalled. "We could ask a customer for payment, but we couldn't tell him the dollar amount of his most recent invoice."

U.S. Telephone was dissatisfied with its high delinquency rate of 75 to 80 days on the average for 10,000 customers. Even the best collectors managed just 1,800 accounts, with the average carrying 700. U.S. Telephone wanted to raise that average to 3,500.

"Our collectors posted cash and credits manually, then made telephone calls for collections. We were lucky to get a complete trial balance and an updated record every four weeks," Giles said.

Collectors spent 2½ hours each day posting cash and credits in the 75% manual system. Invoices dating back more than a year filled a 10-ft square room.

[Finally] the telecommunications firm installed an IBM 4300 processor with a new accounts receivable package and more than doubled the number of accounts that each collector handled, exceeding even its own goals.

The software it chose was the Accounts Receivable System from Management Science America, Inc. (MSA). . . .

"Today, most of our people are managing 4,000 accounts. Some have been managing more than 6,500," [director of customer information systems Lee] Daly noted. . . .

Delinquency is down from 33% to 16%, he added. The changeover has also allowed the company to improve its method of handling disputed bills. "Being a telephone company," Daly said, "we get calls now and then about bills. You know, 'I didn't

make this call to Fargo, N.D.' So we recently installed a change in the system that allows us to dispute one item rather than an entire invoice. If the invoice is for $1,000 and the item in question is for $50, the customer can pay the $950. . . ."

Giles noted that since the $50 disputed is set aside, the collectors can treat it as a promise to pay and not constantly review it. "They are only working with broken promises to pay, which saves a lot of time—particularly since they had been looking at all the accounts to determine who paid under the old system," Giles said.

Giles described U.S. Telephone's new accounts receivable package as "essentially paperless," with the collectors completely on-line, reading everything they need on terminal screens.

—Computerworld

THE TRANSACTION

PROCESSING

INFORMATION

SYSTEM, OR TPIS

KEEPING TRACK

OF RESOURCES

As we hinted in the introduction to this part of the book, the **transaction processing information system** is the basis for a computer-based information system, the foundation on which everything else is built. The purpose of the transaction processing information system—abbreviated **TPIS**—is to perform processing and produce documents that will help an organization keep track of its resources—materials, money, employees, and facilities. TPIS is also known as electronic data processing (EDP) and operational information systems (OIS).

The word *transaction* in a transaction processing information system refers to *clerical* transactions, the kind of tasks that clerks do, such as accounts payable, accounts receivable, and payroll. A TPIS takes in the data from such operations and stores them in computer-accessible form. This stored data forms the basis for the information systems we will discuss in Chapter 14—management information systems and decision support systems.

Fitting TPIS to the Organization

A TPIS must fit the structure of the departments within an organization. As we discussed earlier, and as shown in Figure 13-1, for a profit-oriented enterprise these departments or divisions encompass four functional areas:

▶ **Marketing:** This department is responsible for sales of the product—in the case of Know-wear, clothing. It is the customer's link to the organization.

▶ **Accounting and Finance:** This department keeps a monetary record of all activities in the organization. It allows people to make an assessment of the organization's well-being, with the help of financial statements and daily records.

▶ **Production:** Production is the organization's main line of activity. It consists of processing the resources that are input to the organization—materials, money, employees, and facilities—and turning out finished goods or services.

▶ **Research and Development:** Often abbreviated R & D, this department has the task of improving current products and creating future products to meet future customer needs.

Today many firms, including Know-wear, are organized with departments or divisions corresponding to these four functional areas. A TPIS carries on day-to-day activities, monitoring the inputs—the resources of employees, materials, facilities, and money—as they are processed into outputs of goods, services, and profits. The TPIS uses data files to keep track of what is happening. When organized in an integrated fashion, these data files constitute a data base.

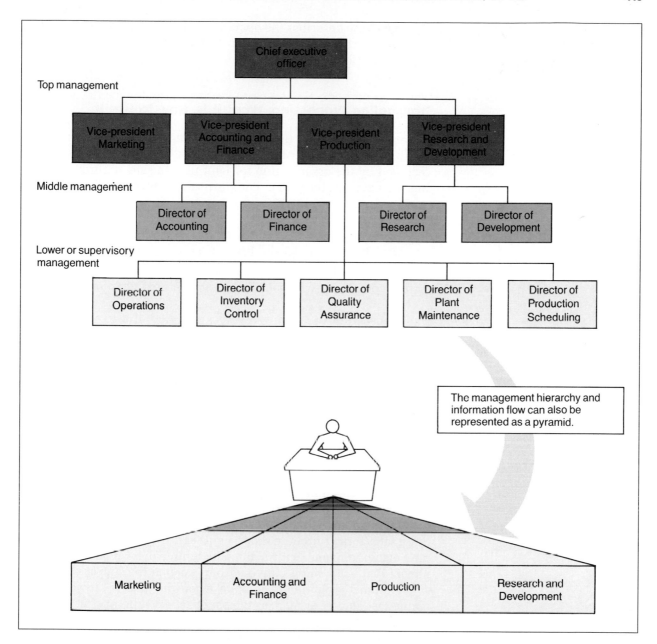

Figure 13-1.   The organization of an organization. This illustration shows the four functional areas of a business—Marketing, Accounting and Finance, Production, and Research and Development—organized into a management hierarchy. *Top:* The four functional areas are coordinated by a management hierarchy, with each area headed by a vice-president who reports to the CEO. *Bottom:* The management hierarchy can be represented another way, as a pyramid, with information flowing up and down the pyramid, from workers to top management and vice versa.

This data base describes the operations of the company and provides the basis for the other information systems in the organization, as we will see in Chapter 14.

Transaction Processing: What It Is, How to Use It

A **transaction** is any action or event dealing with the firm's clients or creditors or with the firm's own resources, anything that needs to be recorded by the organization for later use—a sale, a purchase, a firing, a customer complaint. The purposes of **transaction processing** are:

▶ To generate outputs, such as invoices, paychecks, and status reports, that will assist the firm in its operations.

▶ To create a data base to support companywide decision making and control, as we shall discuss in the next chapter.

Transaction processing involves four activities:

▶ Data entry
▶ Data processing
▶ Data storage
▶ Output generation

Let us see how these work.

Data Entry The purpose of **data entry** is to collect necessary data in a way that is cost-effective, error-free, timely, and convenient. Data entry can be done in two ways: manually and automatically.

Manual data entry is done by a clerk or keyboard operator reading a sales form, purchase order, or other document and converting it into machine-readable form, often by typing on a keyboard. The document that he or she is copying from is called the **source document.**

Automatic data entry is done when the data is already in machine-readable form, such as the bar codes on supermarket products, and can be input directly to the computer by an automatic device such as a bar code scanner or other point-of-sale (POS) terminal. The automatic method is, of course, faster and more accurate and convenient, and you can expect to see more such machines in use in the future—both because they make many fewer errors and because the cost of data entry operators is increasing and the cost of equipment is decreasing, as we discussed back in Chapter 6.

Data Processing Data entry and data processing may be coupled in three ways. The main differences are in how accurate these ways are; how up to the minute, or current, the data is; and how expensive the necessary technology is. The three possible combinations of data entry and data processing are:

▶ **Batch entry and batch processing:** Here a transaction is stored on a source document, such as a daily time sheet; later all transactions are collected and processed at one time (as one "batch"). This is the least expensive method and is appropriate for payroll, accounts payable, and customer billing. However, it is also the least accurate and least current method of processing.

▶ **Direct entry and batch processing:** Also known as on-line entry, direct data entry consists of storing a transaction immediately, but not processing it immediately. Often the data is stored on magnetic tape or disk. This arrangement is more current than batch entry plus batch processing. Typical applications include inventory control and retail sales, as when grocery sales are recorded on a POS terminal at a supermarket checkout counter; the terminal is connected to the store's computer, which records the transaction on magnetic tape. At the end of the day, sales are processed and inventory updated.

▶ **Direct entry and direct (immediate) processing:** Here a transaction is entered as it occurs and immediately processed. This method is as accurate as the preceding one but is even more current. However, the method has disadvantages: Equipment is expensive, one must have immediate access to the computer, and if the computer fails, the entire data entry operation must shut down. A typical application is the airline reservation systems of most major airlines.

Data Storage   As we discussed in Chapter 9, there are two systems for storing data: file management and data base management. In a *file management system*, files are created for specific applications. They are independent of other files. Thus, files may be created by the Marketing department that cannot be used by the Production department for its purposes. In a *data base management system*, files are created for multiple applications and are integrated. They can be logically organized in various ways and can be accessed by different users.

Originally, transaction processing systems were built to follow the four functional areas or departments of for-profit organizations and to support the applications of those departments. That is, they were file management systems. Now business organizations want their files to be used for broader purposes. Consequently, transaction processing must create data that can be stored in such a way that it can be accessed by many users; in other words, an organization must build a data base management system.

Output Generation   Besides storing data, transaction processing must also create data reports. There are two types of documents:

▶ Computer-generated documents such as payroll checks or customer invoices that can be produced more economically and reliably by computer than by hand.

▶ Reports of events, such as transaction listings of customers who have not paid their bills.

THE PARTS
OF A TPIS

Before the pattern cutters in Know-wear's Production department can go to work, the company must be assured it has money for materials and orders for finished goods. A transaction processing system is most commonly used in the Accounting and Finance department. Often its use here is the basis for the rest of a firm's information systems. At Know-wear, for instance, Ms. Douglas is so pleased at the new arrangements for the order entry and accounts receivable information system that she decides to further automate the handling of information within the organization. She asks you, in cooperation with a systems analyst and senior management, to be her liaison in further extending information systems to a TPIS at Know-wear.

An Accounting and Finance TPIS consists of seven elements:

▶ Payroll
▶ Order entry
▶ Accounts receivable
▶ Purchasing
▶ Accounts payable
▶ Fixed assets
▶ General ledger

As Figure 13-2 shows, it is through these elements that the TPIS monitors the flow of resources—materials, money, employees, and facilities—within the organization. Specifically:

▶ **Materials:** This resource is monitored in the *purchasing* and *order entry* sections of the Accounting and Finance department. The raw materials acquisition is tracked in purchasing, and the demand for finished product is recorded in order entry.

▶ **Money:** Money is recorded in the *accounts payable* and *accounts receivable* functions. The spending or paying out of money is recorded in accounts payable, and the income or receiving of money is recorded in accounts receivable.

▶ **Employees:** The people resources are recorded in *payroll*, which calculates employee salaries and wages and issues paychecks.

Figure 13-2.   The parts of a TPIS for the Accounting and Finance department. A TPIS tracks the resources that flow through an organization—materials, money, employees, and facilities—using five kinds of transaction processing: (1) vendor-oriented, (2) customer-oriented, (3) personnel-oriented, (4) facility-oriented, and (5) general ledger–oriented.

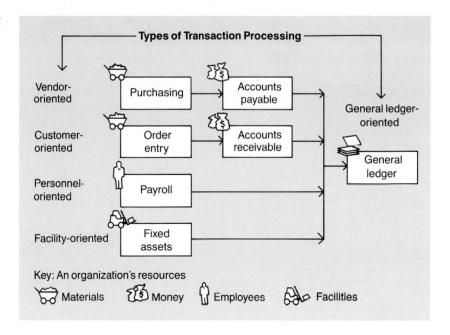

▶ **Facilities:** Facilities are recorded in *fixed assets*. Fixed assets consist of office equipment, factory equipment, and buildings.

All of these transactions are formally recorded in the *general ledger* of the Accounting and Finance department's TPIS.

As we have stated, a business is concerned essentially with taking in resources (input) and converting (processing) them into a final product or service (output) to sell. But the accounting procedures and paperwork required during the conversion or processing stage are not nearly this simple and straightforward. The TPIS required to keep track of transactions being processed is shown in Figure 13-2. Note that the seven elements can be arranged into five types of processing:

▶ Vendor-oriented processing, which includes purchasing and accounts payable

▶ Customer-oriented processing, which includes order entry and accounts receivable

▶ Personnel-oriented processing, which includes payroll

▶ Facility-oriented processing, which includes fixed assets

▶ General ledger–oriented processing.

We will take a look at these five types of transaction processing in the rest of this chapter.

VENDOR-ORIENTED PROCESSING

BUYING AND PAYING FOR SUPPLIES

Vendors, also known as suppliers, are those businesses outside the firm that supply it with raw materials, parts, or services to help the firm assemble or provide *its* products or services. Know-wear, for instance, deals with vendors of fabrics, thread, zippers, buttons, buckles, rivets, and other clothing-related materials. In addition, Know-wear deals with vendors of office supplies, computer equipment, janitorial services, and company cars, among other things.

Whenever an item in inventory runs low—the item can be anything from a carton of pencils to a warehouse full of denim—a request is sent to the Purchasing department, which in turn creates a **purchase order (PO),** a form that identifies the required materials and the vendor that will supply them. The original PO is sent to the vendor, while copies are distributed within the firm both to confirm that the order has been placed and to document the expected delivery date of the item or items ordered. These copies usually are sent to the originator of the purchase order request and to the firm's Shipping and Receiving department, as well as some others. The copy of the PO sent to the Shipping and Receiving department is called a **receiving report.**

Upon delivery to the firm's Shipping and Receiving department, the materials are checked against the original receiving report to make sure the correct materials have been delivered. The vendor may also deliver a bill along with the goods; this bill, along with a confirmation of the receipt of materials, is sent to the firm's Purchasing and Accounting departments. The Purchasing department notifies the originator of the request that the materials have arrived. The Accounting department records the acquisition of the materials and the bill for their delivery in the general ledger.

In **vendor-oriented processing,** the TPIS has two applications, as we saw in Figure 13-2—purchasing and accounts payable—which correspond to the two transactions involved in getting something from a vendor: ordering it and paying for it. Let us see how these work.

Purchasing

Purchasing is how the paperwork begins. Let us say that Know-wear's Production department is ordering materials for a certain line of outerwear clothing: parkas for the young executive's leisure time. The first transaction is the *request for materials,* which, as Figure 13-3 shows, requests in detail the specific materials and the amounts necessary. The request for materials is used to gain access to a data base, stored on magnetic disk, that contains the names, addresses, products, and past performances of all of Know-wear's vendors.

Vendor-oriented processing. Vendors are suppliers outside the firm who provide it with the materials or services that enable it to provide *its* product. When goods are delivered by the vendor to the firm's Shipping and Receiving department, the materials must be checked against a copy of the purchase order, called the receiving report. The Accounting department records the acquisition of the materials and the bill for their delivery in that part of the TPIS known as the general ledger.

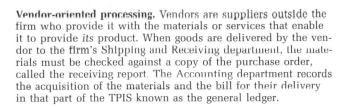

Once the best vendor in the data base is identified, the information is used to prepare the purchase order. The PO is then mailed to the vendor, the data base is updated to show this fact, and copies of the PO are circulated within the firm. Figure 13-3 shows how the purchase order and receiving report look for one of Know-wear's purchases.

Accounts Payable

The second kind of vendor-oriented transaction, **accounts payable** begins with the receipt of materials from the vendor. That is, materials delivered by the vendor usually are accompanied by an invoice (bill) for the costs. In the accounts payable application, the Accounting and Finance department accesses the data base of vendors and updates that data base by noting the receipt of materials, pertinent delivery information, and the invoice. The invoice is also used to update the general ledger, whose purpose we shall explain shortly. Periodically, all accounts payable are reviewed to decide which ones are due, and voucher checks are created and mailed as payment to the vendors; the general ledger is also updated. The scheme for this application is shown in Figure 13-4.

Figure 13-3. Vendor-oriented processing: Purchasing. *Top:* An input-processing-output diagram for purchasing. The input is a request for materials, which provides the description of materials to be purchased. Processing consists of checking the request for materials against the company's data base, which lists its vendors. The output is a purchase order and copies of the purchase order, including a receiving report. Additional output could be a printed general ledger report summarizing new entries. *Middle:* A purchase order from Know-wear for materials needed; this is sent to the vendor. *Bottom:* A receiving report, which is sent to Know-wear's Shipping and Receiving department; copies of the purchase order are also circulated to other departments within Know-wear.

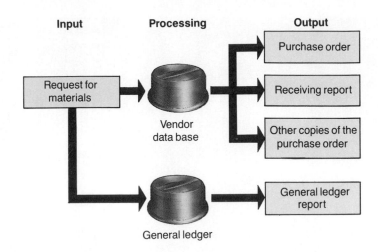

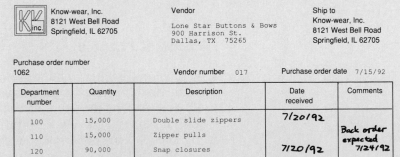

Figure 13-4 Vendor-oriented processing: Accounts payable. *Top:* The input consists of receipt of materials and an invoice from the vendor. Processing includes entering data into the vendor data base and updating the general ledger. The output consists of a voucher check for payment issued to the vendor. *Bottom:* Example of voucher check issued by Know-wear, Inc.

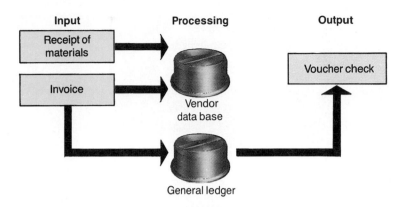

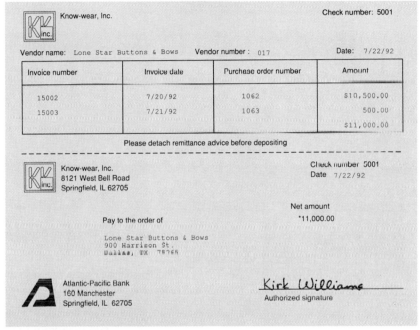

CUSTOMER-ORIENTED

PROCESSING

TAKING ORDERS

AND GETTING PAID

Vendor-oriented processing is concerned with acquiring and paying for raw materials. **Customer-oriented processing** focuses on what the firm is in business to do: sell finished products or services. That is, it is concerned with getting orders from customers for finished goods or services and with receiving payment for them.

From the standpoint of business information flow, customer-oriented processing has two activities: order entry and accounts receivable. Let us see how these work.

Order Entry

Remember, we are dealing with information from the standpoint of the Accounting and Finance department, not that of the Marketing department. Marketing is concerned with promoting and selling the

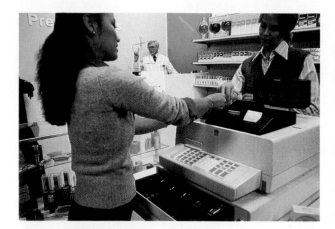

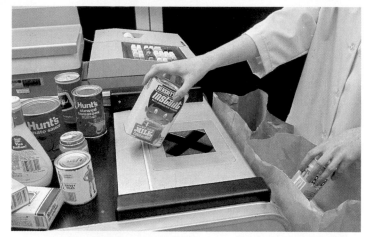

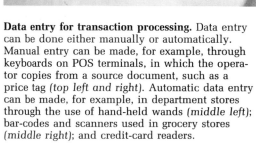

Data entry for transaction processing. Data entry can be done either manually or automatically. Manual entry can be made, for example, through keyboards on POS terminals, in which the operator copies from a source document, such as a price tag *(top left and right)*. Automatic data entry can be made, for example, in department stores through the use of hand-held wands *(middle left)*; bar-codes and scanners used in grocery stores *(middle right)*; and credit-card readers.

Figure 13-5. Customer-oriented processing: Order entry. *Top:* When a customer order is received and the product is shipped, a notice of shipment is sent to the customer. The customer data base is updated to reflect shipment, and the transaction is recorded in the general ledger data base. An invoice is also mailed to the customer. *Bottom:* Example of customer invoice issued by Know-wear, Inc., to Thriller Threads.

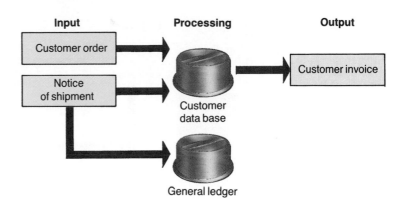

Order number	Order date	Shipping date	Shipping Instructions	Terms	Salesperson
56234	8/10/92	8/15/92	Via truck	2% discount/ 10 days Net/30 days	Mary Shields

Quantity ordered	Quantity shipped	Description	Price per unit	Amount
12	12	Parka, large	$35.00	$420.00
5	5	Trench coat, small	58.00	290.00

Know-wear, Inc.
8121 West Bell Road
Springfield, IL 62705

Sold to Thriller Threads 350 Townsend Seattle, WA 98103

Ship to Thriller Threads 350 Townsend Seattle, WA 98103

Invoice number 14111

Customer number 0025

Invoice date 8/15/92

Total $710.00

product; Accounting and Finance is concerned only with taking orders and collecting money. In this scheme, therefore, the first step is the request for a product by a customer—an order, whether by phone, mail, or personal visit. The customer order is the source document that makes up the input for the **order entry** application. It is used to create internal documents in the company that will result in shipment of the product ordered.

In the case of Know-wear, orders come in from salespeople via the mail (under the old way of doing things) or via the new data communications system. For instance, a purchase order is received from Thriller Threads, a clothing store catering to young professional people. The clothes order is filled from current inventory in the Know-wear warehouse and shipped to the customer by truck. A notice of shipment is mailed to the customer at the same time the product is sent. As Figure 13-5 shows, the customer data base is updated to reflect the shipment of the goods. In addition, the general

Figure 13-6.   Customer-oriented processing: Accounts receivable. *Top:* When customer payment is received, the customer data base and general ledger are updated. A customer statement of account or receipt is also mailed. *Bottom:* Example of statement of account issued by Know-wear to Thriller Threads.

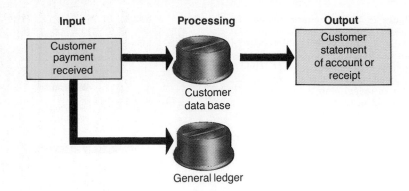

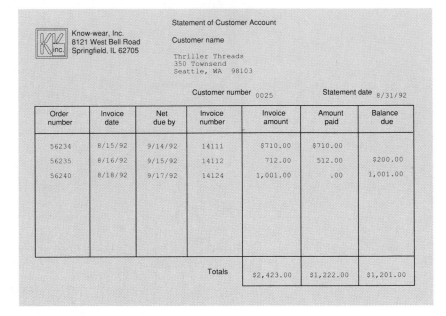

Order number	Invoice date	Net due by	Invoice number	Invoice amount	Amount paid	Balance due
56234	8/15/92	9/14/92	14111	$710.00	$710.00	
56235	8/16/92	9/15/92	14112	712.00	512.00	$200.00
56240	8/18/92	9/17/92	14124	1,001.00	.00	1,001.00
			Totals	$2,423.00	$1,222.00	$1,201.00

ledger is updated to reflect the increased balance due from the customer. Finally, a customer invoice is created and mailed to the customer.

Accounts Receivable

The second TPIS application for customer-oriented transaction processing, **accounts receivable** monitors money received from customers in payment for orders filled. As Figure 13-6 shows, when Know-wear receives payment from the customer, the customer data base is updated to reflect the change in status of the account. In addition, the general ledger data base is updated to reflect the change in the accounts receivable balance. Finally, the customer is sent a receipt or statement of account to show that payment was received. The customer data base is usually reviewed every month to see which customers are late in payment and to send revised statements of account.

PERSONNEL-ORIENTED PROCESSING

PAYING PEOPLE

We have shown how vendor-oriented and customer-oriented processing keep track of an organization's material and money resources. **Personnel-oriented processing** is concerned with monitoring a company's employee resources—in other words, with making sure workers and managers are paid the correct amount for the jobs they do and the hours they work, and with deducting from their earnings whatever needs to be withheld for taxes and the like.

At Know-wear, employees are paid every two weeks. Hourly workers are paid according to their wage rate and the number of hours worked; salaried workers are paid a fixed amount depending on their position. The Accounting and Finance department must calculate and make several deductions from the paycheck: federal, state, and local taxes; social security; union dues, if applicable; and insurance premiums. The company must calculate total pay and net pay and provide each employee with a paycheck along with an accounting of deductions. It must also keep records for tax and accounting purposes.

The TPIS supports personnel-oriented processing through the **payroll** application. The transaction starts, as Figure 13-7 indicates, with the employee time cards, which record the number of hours worked for wage employees and the days worked for salaried employees. Time cards are submitted every pay period—every two weeks at Know-wear—and are used to calculate the resulting payroll. The payroll TPIS application takes an employee's identification number (9002, in your case) and uses it to gain access to the payroll data base; the TPIS can then determine the employee's wage rate or salary, deductions, and other information necessary to calculate the paycheck. Both the payroll and the general ledger data bases are updated to reflect the latest payroll transactions. The output from the payroll application, of course, consists of paychecks, as shown in Figure 13-7.

FACILITY-ORIENTED PROCESSING

KEEPING TRACK OF THINGS

An organization's resources include not only materials, money, and employees, but also facilities—that is, things. **Facility-oriented processing** concerns monitoring the acquisition of facilities or **fixed assets** used by a firm—office equipment, such as word processors and photocopiers; production equipment, such as (for Know-wear) sewing machines and forklift trucks; and buildings.

As Figure 13-8 shows, the fixed asset application for a TPIS begins when a fixed asset, such as a building or piece of equipment, is purchased. This acquisition is recorded through a general ledger entry. The output is a **property inventory,** which describes the fixed assets and states who is responsible for them. The fixed assets de-

Figure 13-7. Personnel-oriented processing: The paycheck. *Top:* Time cards are the signal to update the payroll data base; the general ledger data base is updated at the same time. The output consists of paychecks. *Bottom:* Know-wear paycheck and paycheck stub, which lists deductions from gross pay.

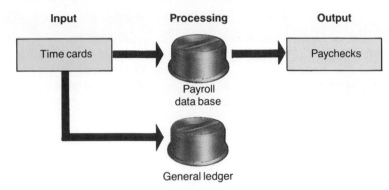

Input	Processing	Output
Time cards	Payroll data base	Paychecks
	General ledger	

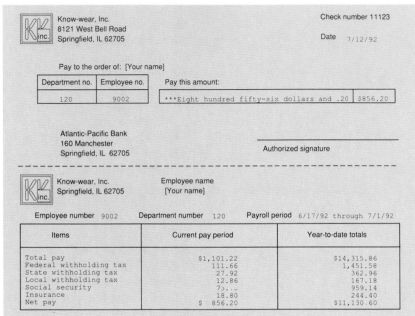

Know-wear, Inc.
8121 West Bell Road
Springfield, IL 62705

Check number 11123

Date   7/12/92

Pay to the order of: [Your name]

Department no.	Employee no.	Pay this amount:
120	9002	***Eight hundred fifty-six dollars and .20 $856.20

Atlantic-Pacific Bank
160 Manchester
Springfield, IL 62705

Authorized signature

Know-wear, Inc.
Springfield, IL 62705

Employee name
[Your name]

Employee number 9002   Department number   120   Payroll period 6/17/92 through 7/1/92

Items	Current pay period	Year-to-date totals
Total pay	$1,101.22	$14,315.86
Federal withholding tax	111.66	1,451.58
State withholding tax	27.92	362.96
Local withholding tax	12.86	167.18
Social security	73...	959.14
Insurance	18.80	244.40
Net pay	$ 856.20	$11,130.60

scribed in Figure 13-8 for Know-wear list some items (even including artificial plants) that belong to the Marketing department. For tax purposes, fixed assets are depreciated—that is, they diminish in value over time.

GENERAL LEDGER–
ORIENTED
PROCESSING THE
ONGOING RECORD

We have made many references to the general ledger throughout this chapter. What, exactly, *is* the **general ledger?** It is the data base designed to record all the financial transactions of the business. It consists of a series of entries or statements that are balanced against one another. For example, when Know-wear's Marketing department spends $100 cash on a fake ivy plant, which is a fixed asset (for what could be more fixed than an *artificial* plant?), the general ledger does the following:

Figure 13-8. Facility-oriented processing: Fixed assets. *Top:* Purchase of a fixed asset, such as a typewriter, building, or car, triggers an update of the general ledger data base. The output is a property inventory. *Bottom:* Property inventory of fixed assets that are the responsibility of Know-wear's Marketing department.

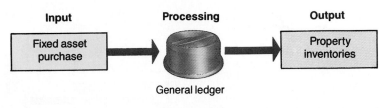

Input	Processing	Output
Fixed asset purchase	General ledger	Property inventories

Responsibility property inventory — Page 1

Know-wear, Inc.

Responsible department: Marketing   Department number   120   Date: 12/31/92

Property number	Description	Acquisition date	Original cost	Accumulated depreciation	Book value
01010	Typewriter	12/10/88	$550.00	$440.00	$110.00
01077	Artificial Plants	12/11/90	600.00	285.00	315.00
01098	Calculator	4/12/91	750.00	263.00	487.00
01123	Desk	10/15/91	1,002.00	543.00	459.00
02246	Cabinet	7/10/92	410.00	34.00	376.00
03111	Automobile	9/21/92	6,432.00	600.00	5,832.00
Totals			$9,744.00	$2,165.00	$7,579.00

Sylvia Williams
Signature Responsible Officer

▶ It **debits**—adds—$100 to the financial account known as "fixed assets."

▶ It **credits**—subtracts—$100 from the financial account known as "cash."

This is known as a **double entry bookkeeping system** because a single transaction creates a general ledger entry involving two or more financial accounts whose debit entries equal the credit entries. The entry would look as follows:

	Debit	Credit
Fixed assets	100	
Cash		100

To check for errors, the Accounting and Finance department periodically—perhaps once a month—runs what are called **trial balances;** that is, all the credits are totaled and all the debits are totaled, and if the two totals are not equal, then a mistake has been made.

As Figure 13-9 shows, the inputs for the trial balance processing consist of all the general ledger entries made in the previous six

Figure 13-9.   General ledger–oriented processing: Trial balance.
Top: All the TPIS applications described so far (plus some manual entries not discussed) have been input to the general ledger. *Bottom:* When credits and debits are totaled separately for a trial balance, they should come out the same, as shown here for an end-of-year statement for Know-wear.

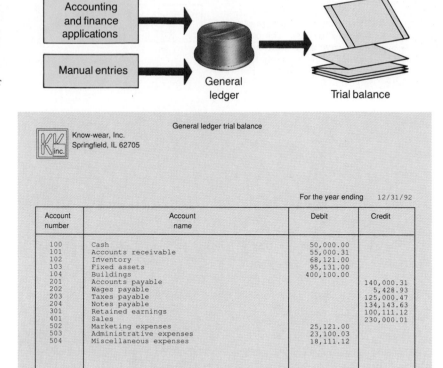

application areas—purchasing, accounts payable, order entry, accounts receivable, payroll, and fixed assets—plus others that may have been made that are not part of the TPIS. The processing consists of totaling the debits and credits, and the output is the trial balance. Figure 13-9 shows what a trial balance might look like for Know-wear at the end of the year. Notice that debits and credits balance—to the penny.

ONWARD TO
MIS AND DSS

A transaction processing system is the logical beginning for a computer-based information system, and is necessary if supervisory managers are to be able to exert operational control over the processes and people for which they are responsible. But what about the people *above* the supervisory level? Can middle managers and top executives take advantage of this business information? That is the topic of the next chapter.

SUMMARY

▶ The purpose of a **transaction processing information system (TPIS),** the lowest level of computer-based information system, is to perform processing and transmit messages to help an organization keep track of its resources—its materials, money, employees, and facilities. The word *transaction* refers to *clerical* transactions such as accounts payable, accounts receivable, and payroll.

▶ A TPIS fits the four functional departments of the business organization—Marketing, Accounting and Finance, Production, and Research and Development. **Marketing,** the department responsible for sales of the product, is the customer's link to the organization. **Accounting and Finance** records the organization's monetary activities, providing financial statements and daily records of the organization's well-being. **Production** is the department that processes the resources input to the organization—materials, money, employees, and facilities—into finished goods or services. **Research and Development,** often abbreviated R & D, creates new products to meet future customer needs and improve the firm's market share.

▶ A **transaction** is any action or event dealing with the firm's clients, creditors, or its own resources, anything that needs to be recorded for later use—a sale, a purchase, a firing, a customer complaint. **Transaction processing** is done to generate outputs that assist the firm in its operations and to create data bases to support companywide decision making and control. Transaction processing has four activities: (1) data entry, (2) data processing, (3) data storage, and (4) output generation.

▶ The purpose of **data entry** is to collect necessary data in a cost-effective, error-free, timely, and convenient way. Data entry can be either manual or automatic.

▶ Data entry and data processing may be coupled in three ways: (1) batch entry and batch processing, (2) direct entry and batch processing, and (3) direct entry and direct (immediate) processing.

▶ In the first way, *batch entry and batch processing,* individual transactions are stored on **source documents,** original documents (such as a daily time sheet) from data is copied. The source documents are collected and processed together at one time. The least expensive method, this is appropriate for payroll, accounts payable, and customer billing.

However, it is the least accurate and up-to-the-minute method of processing.

▶ In *direct entry and batch processing,* transactions are stored immediately by direct (also known as online) data entry, often on magnetic tape or disk, but processed later. Typical applications include inventory control and retail sales, such as grocery sales recorded on a POS terminal at the checkout counter and sent to the store's computer for storage on tape. At the end of the day, all sales are processed and inventory updated. This arrangement is more current than batch entry plus batch processing.

▶ In *direct entry and direct (immediate) processing,* a transaction is entered and processed immediately as it occurs. This method is as accurate as the preceding one and even more current. However, the equipment is expensive, the computer must be immediately accessible, and if it fails, the entire data entry operation must be shut down. Typical applications are in quality and inventory control.

▶ The two systems for storing data are file management and data base management. In a file management system, independent files are created for specific applications. In a data base management system, files are created for multiple applications. They can be organized in various ways and accessed by different users. Since business organizations now use their files for broader purposes, transaction processing must create data that can be stored in such a way that it is accessible to many users; in other words, businesses must build a data base management system.

▶ Transaction processing must create two types of data reports: (1) Computer-generated documents such as payroll checks or customer invoices that are more economical and reliable than manual documents. (2) Reports of events, such as transactions listings of customers who have not paid their bills.

▶ A TPIS consists of seven elements: (1) payroll, (2) order entry, (3) accounts receivable, (4) purchasing, (5) accounts payable, (6) fixed assets, and (7) general ledger. It is through these elements that the TPIS monitors the four types of resources within the organization: (1) *Materials:* This resource is monitored in the purchasing and order entry sections. Raw materials acquisition is tracked in the purchasing section, and the demand for finished products is recorded in the order entry section. (2) *Money:* This resource is recorded in the accounts payable and accounts receivable sections. Payments are recorded in the accounts payable, and income is recorded in accounts receivable. (3) *Employees:* The people resources are recorded in the payroll section, which calculates employee salaries and wages and issues paychecks. (4) *Facilities:* This resource is recorded in the fixed assets section. Transactions for all four resources are formally recorded in the general ledger section.

▶ The elements of a TPIS can be arranged into five types of processing: (1) vendor-oriented processing, which includes purchasing and accounts payable; (2) customer-oriented processing, which includes order entry and accounts receivable; (3) personnel-oriented processing, which includes payroll; (4) facility-oriented processing, which includes fixed assets; and (5) general ledger–oriented processing.

▶ In **vendor-oriented processing,** the TPIS has two applications, corresponding to the two transactions involved in getting something from a vendor: ordering it and paying for it. **Vendors** or suppliers are businesses that provide the firm with raw materials or services. The **purchasing** application begins when a department needs an item. The purchasing section creates a **purchase order (PO)** to send to the vendor that supplies the item. Copies of the PO, called **receiving reports,** are distributed within the firm to confirm that the order has been placed and to document the expected delivery date. **Accounts payable** begins when materials are received from the vendor. Upon delivery, the materials are checked against the original receiving report and the bill is sent, along with a confirmation of the receipt of materials, to the Purchasing and Accounting departments. Purchasing notifies the originator of the request that the materials have arrived. Accounting records both the receipt of the order and the bill in the general ledger.

▶ **Customer-oriented processing** concerns getting orders from customers for products or services and receiving payment for them. The two activities of customer-oriented processing are order entry and accounts receivable. The source document that makes up the input for the **order entry** application is the customer order. It is used to create internal documents in the company that result in shipment of the products ordered. **Accounts receivable** monitors payments received from the customers. It updates the customer data base to reflect the change in status of the account, updates the general ledger data base to show the change in the accounts receiv-

able balance, and produces a receipt or statement of account to send to the customer.

▶ **Personnel-oriented processing** concerns monitoring a company's employee resources. It makes sure employees are paid the right amount for their jobs and the hours they work and that the proper deductions are made. The TPIS supports personnel-oriented processing through the **payroll** application. An employee's identification number is used to access the payroll data base and determine the employee's wage or salary, deductions, and other information necessary to calculate the paycheck. Both the payroll and the general ledger data bases are updated to reflect the latest payroll transactions.

▶ **Facility-oriented processing** concerns monitoring the acquisition of facilities or **fixed assets** used by a firm—office equipment, production equipment, buildings, whatever the U.S. government allows to be depreciated or diminished in value for tax purposes. Acquisitions are recorded through a general ledger entry. The output is a **property inventory,** which describes the fixed assets and states who is responsible for them.

▶ The **general ledger** is a data base designed to record all of the financial transactions of the business. It is a series of entries that are balanced against one another. For example, when a company spends $100 for a fixed asset, the general ledger **debits**—adds—$100 to the financial account known as "fixed assets" and **credits**—subtracts—$100 from another account known as "cash." This is called a **double entry bookkeeping system** because a single transaction creates a general ledger entry involving two or more financial accounts whose debit entries equal the credit entries. To check for errors in the general ledger, the Accounting and Finance department periodically runs **trial balances**—all the credits are totaled and all the debits are totaled, and if the two totals are not equal, then a mistake has been made.

KEY TERMS

REVIEW QUESTIONS

1. Describe the purpose of the TPIS. What type of tasks does this system perform?
2. What are the four resources within an organization?
3. What are the four activities of transaction processing? Describe each.
4. Name the seven elements of a TPIS.
5. Describe vendor-oriented processing.
6. Describe customer-oriented processing. How is a customer order filled and billed?
7. How are paychecks generated by the TPIS?
8. What is the general ledger?

CASE PROBLEMS

Case 13-1: Treat the Customer Right

"**Y**ou can't do enough for customers," writes New Hampshire consultant Jack Falvey in the *Wall Street Journal.* "The rule is that you get paid for everything you do for customers." Technology, buildings, balance sheets, and the other elements that make up a business "must support the central theme of doing something for someone. When that someone no longer pays for what we do, we are out of business."

Falvey tells the story of a customer who, attracted by TV advertising, took some film to an air freight office to ship overnight to Chicago. It was important that the film arrive the next day, but "Absolutely, positively, in spite of many next-day phone calls, relay of numbers," and so on, the film did not get there. It was found two days later and returned.

Then the company proceeded to turn the customer into a customer for the competition. When he received an invoice for the cost of shipment both ways, the customer wrote explaining the air freight shipper's failure to perform and the resultant cost to his business and asked that the invoice be canceled. But, Falvey writes, "the customer was no longer a customer but an accounts receivable credit number." The credit department began sending multiple dunning notices and eventually hired an outside collection agency to harass him further.

Your assignment: Clearly, the air freight company should have apologized to the customer and given him a free next shipment, thus, says Falvey, "retaining the person who provides the income from which we run our business." On the principle that all parts of a company—delivery, service, credit people, and so on—are effectively sales representatives for that company, can you conceive of ways to design an order entry/accounts receivable system that will not have the unpleasant effects described here?

Case 13-2: Finding the Transactions for Trimming Travel Costs

Many companies have made a practice of taking a close look at how they can save travel dollars when they send their executives around the country. Air fares, for example, can range widely even between the same cities—as much as $600 difference, for example, between San Francisco and Chicago, depending on whether one goes direct or changes planes in Kansas City. Travel experts say that, with discount air fares, bulk hotel rates, and rental car contracts, a company can lower its travel costs by 15% to 40% a year. Before this can happen, however, a firm must have hard statistics to bargain with. Travel agents, hotels, and airlines will not negotiate unless they know what a company's usual travel patterns are.

Your assignment: Saving money starts with gathering data. Suppose you have been hired as a travel consultant to help trim travel costs for a company. You need to find out which cities the people in the company usually travel to and how many trips they make each year. Most of this information is on expense accounts, reports submitted by employees for their supervisors' approval and for reimbursement of expenses for travel, meals, and hotels. Some of the expenses are billed directly through the vendor-oriented processing part of the company's TPIS . You want to put these ongoing transactions on a computer. Can you determine how you might begin to do this, using the TPIS?

Chapter 14

MANAGEMENT INFORMATION SYSTEMS AND DECISION SUPPORT SYSTEMS: MAKING INFORMATION USEFUL TO MANAGERS

An organization's appetite for information seems insatiable. In part, as we have been suggesting throughout this book, this appetite is stimulated by the increased complexity and rate of change in today's environment—by the growth of business, for instance, in the international marketplace, which has increased the need of many businesses for more information.

How can an organization and its all-too-human employees handle the rising tide of information? One answer is to make better use of what is already pouring into it.

The transaction processing information system (TPIS) is a first step. Large organizations have been using successful computerized TPISs for the past several years to handle clerical tasks that previously were handled manually, such as preparing the payroll, writing purchase orders, and maintaining inventory. The next step, as the case study shows, is to find a way to make this system useful for "the people in the middle" and then at the top. This takes the form ultimately of decision support systems—computerized systems that help end users not only make decisions but also, finally, help an organization realize its strategic vision.

CASE STUDY: THE DECISION AID

Decision Support Systems: Management Finally Gets Its Hand on the Data

The easiest way to provide an overview of decision support systems is to give some examples of what they can do.

▶ A U.S. mining company was faced with a major capital budgeting decision. Should it develop a new copper mine in Africa? Assessing the potential payback of such a 20-year project required hundreds of assumptions about cost, price, and demand variables. To handle this task, the company developed a decision support system that could handle all the variables and the "what if" questions necessary to assess the project.

▶ With more than 100 operating units keeping separate financials [financial records] over different periods of time, a large multinational electronics company found it almost impossible to compile current financial data that reflected overall corporate performance. The company solved the problem with a decision support system that allowed it to produce a consolidated financial statement within hours of closing the books on worldwide operations.

▶ A large money-center bank wanted to develop its portfolio management business without significantly increasing its staff. The bank also wanted to assist its portfolio managers in evaluating a wide range of investment strategies for its clients, a very time-consuming task using traditional methods. The bank addressed both problems by implementing a decision support system that allowed bank personnel to evaluate the status of portfolios, investigate alternative investment strategies, and improve client presentations.

These examples illustrate the diverse applications of a decision support system, one of the most misunderstood terms of today's "information age."

Simply stated, a decision support system is a complex set of computer programs and equipment that allows end users—usually managers and professionals—to analyze, manipulate, format, and display data in different ways. The analysis and manipulation usually help in decision making, because the user can pull together data from different sources and view them in ways that may differ from the original formats. The system also makes it possible for the data to be printed out, or to be prepared in the form of charts or graphs.

—Carl Wolf and Jim Treleaven, *Management Technology*

THE BASICS OF A MANAGEMENT INFORMATION SYSTEM

After a TPIS is in place, the next step for the efficient handling of business information is to install a **management information system (MIS).** A TPIS is useful in handling standard clerical and accounting applications, but it is an awkward system for supporting management decision making. A management information system (MIS) is designed to assist managers in performing their work; it may be defined as a network of computer-based processing procedures that are integrated with manual and other procedures to provide timely, effective information to support managerial planning and control.

In order to fully understand MIS, let us describe three important concepts:

▶ The basic tasks of management
▶ Management information needs
▶ The desirable properties of an MIS

What Managers Do: The Classic Tasks of Management

Management is the process of transforming resources—materials, money, employees, facilities—into products or services. As we mentioned in Chapter 2, the primary activity of all managers is to make decisions in five areas: organizing, communicating, staffing, planning, and controlling. Let us describe these again.

▶ **Organizing:** Managers need to make decisions about **organizing** or coordinating people and resources, including what structures and procedures should be set up, what authority delegated, what system of responsibility and accountability arranged.

▶ **Communicating:** Managers must be able to **communicate** their requests and requirements to subordinates and superiors. As we have seen, this management task is now receiving a good deal of computerized assistance, in the form of word processing, electronic mail, and telecommunications.

▶ **Staffing:** Decisions about **staffing** are decisions about hiring workers and managers and training them to achieve the organization's goals.

These three management tasks are important, but the most crucial are the two that follow, planning and controlling. Without these, there would probably be chaos in the organization. Planning and controlling are the two management tasks that an MIS is specially designed to support.

▶ **Planning:** In **planning,** managers formulate short-range and long-range goals for the organization, including the policies, procedures, and standards necessary to achieve them. Planning is also concerned with identifying opportunities, problems, and alternative courses of action.

▶ **Controlling:** Managerial **control** is concerned with continually monitoring, with the help of performance measures, the organization's progress in reaching its goals. This means managers must keep track of resources, including employee performance, and make any necessary adjustments.

Better facts. An effective management information system should produce information that is accurate, timely, and complete yet concise. Spreadsheets and graphics can help summarize facts into more understandable form.

What Managers Need: Not Data but Information

In order to monitor the organization's resources and do efficient planning and controlling, managers need information not only about events in the outside environment—about competitors, political events, economic trends, and technological advances—but also about internal events. A large amount of information is brought into the organization through the TPIS and, in fact, this situation has led to the problem of information overload. Because the data from transaction processing is so extensive and so quickly retrievable electronically, many managers are overwhelmed with the amount of data. However, managers do not just need data; they need data that is analyzed and synthesized into useful form—in short, data that is turned into information. An MIS should be able to offer this kind of help.

An MIS: What Should It Do?

Not more facts but *better* facts are what a manager needs. What do we mean by "better"? An effective MIS should produce information that is *accurate, timely,* and *complete yet concise.* Let us describe what we mean:

▶ **Accuracy:** High accuracy—that is, completely error-free information—is usually expensive. For example, true accuracy might require that every time a clerk enters information into a data base, that information must be verified by another clerk. Obviously, this would double the data entry costs. Sometimes high accuracy is cost-justifiable, but often it is not. Ninety percent accuracy might be fine for the inventory of pencils in Know-wear's stockroom, but 90% accuracy is too low for billing of accounts receivable—Know-wear could be losing a tenth of their revenue!

▶ **Timeliness:** Given the rapid pace of business, what is considered information today may not be information tomorrow. Information, then, should be supplied quickly. A quality-control manager

on a production line of men's shirts cannot wait three days, for example, to discover that a defect is producing shirts with 40-inch sleeves and size 13 collars, or Know-wear may well find itself with 96,000 oddball shirts to dispose of somehow.

▶ **Completeness with conciseness:** A report is not useful if it is accurate and timely but incomplete. A manager needs *all* the facts. However, the trick is not to overwhelm managers with unnecessary and unwanted facts. Some managers may require more details than others; thus, one of the more difficult responsibilities of a systems analyst is to determine what is essential and what is nonessential information for a particular manager. The accountant at Know-wear who monitors customers who are late paying their bills needs information about all overdue customers, including their balances and due dates. The accountant does not need balances and due dates for all customers in accounts payable, however. These customers need to be given a reasonable amount of time (such as 30 days) to remit payment.

THE THREE PARTS OF

MIS MANAGMENT,

INFORMATION,

SYSTEM

Now that we have described the tasks of managers, their need for information, and the properties they need in a system providing them with information, let us see how a management information system works. As we stated at the outset, an MIS is a network of computer-based processing procedures integrated with manual and other procedures to provide timely, effective information to support managerial planning and control.

To more fully understand what an MIS is, let us examine its parts:

▶ Management
▶ Information
▶ Systems

The Management in an MIS

Figure 14-1 repeats the illustration we showed at the beginning of the last chapter. The four functional areas of Marketing, Accounting and Finance, Production, and Research and Development are each coordinated by a management hierarchy of lower managers and middle managers topped by a vice-president or division head who reports to the chief executive officer, the CEO. The result is an organization chart, as shown in the top part of Figure 14-1. Also as shown, within each division or functional area, information tends to flow vertically—from top to bottom and from bottom to top, from vice-

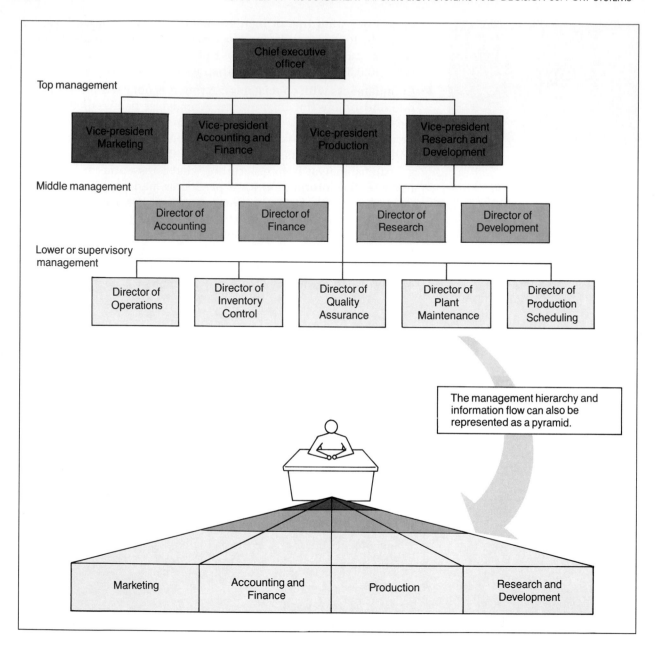

Figure 14-1.   Two perspectives of an organization—and the flow of information. *Top:* An organization can be viewed as being made up of four business functional areas—Marketing, Accounting and Finance, Production, and Research and Development. (This is considered a *vertical* perspective.) *Middle:* An organization may also be viewed as having three levels of management—top, middle, and lower. (This is considered a *horizontal* perspective.) *Bottom:* The flow of information may be *vertical* (up and down each functional area) or *horizontal* (between functional areas).

president down to middle and lower managers and vice versa. In addition, information may flow horizontally, such as between departments.

The responsibilities of the three levels of management are described in the following sections.

Top Management Top management includes only a few of the most powerful managers in the organization, the typical title being vice-president of one of the four business functions, such as shown in Figure 14-1. The primary responsibility of top management is *strategic planning*—establishing the overall direction of the company through long-range planning. Top managers have the task of establishing firm performance goals and coordinating the activities of the entire organization to achieve these goals. Their problems are totally unstructured and their activities vary greatly—for example, establishing financial goals for the firm, determining new markets and products, and evaluating potential mergers and acquisitions.

Clearly, the decisions of top managers will have the greatest effect on the organization, although the effect may not be felt for several years. In order to make such decisions, top managers need both external and internal information.

Middle managers. Such managers—regional sales managers, public relations managers, directors of employee relations, and the like—are concerned with tactical planning and control. This involves formulating budgets, doing production scheduling, monitoring sales performance, and other tasks that help implement the plans of top management.

Middle Managers There are many more middle managers than there are top managers, and their responsibilities are to do *tactical planning and control*—to implement the plans of top management and to monitor the firm's current operations. Typical titles for managers at this level are regional sales manager, public relations manager, training and development coordinator, and director of employee relations.

In establishing the means for achieving the overall strategic plan, middle managers perform fairly structured activities—formulating budgets, doing production scheduling, making short-term forecasts, and monitoring sales, production, and personnel performances. They rely more on internal information than external, and the effect of their decisions is felt much sooner than the effects of top management's decisions.

Lower or Supervisory Management By far the largest group, supervisory managers, are responsible for *operational control*—for implementing the plans of middle management and controlling day-to-day operations. Supervisory managers are first-line supervisors who directly oversee the actual operations of a business; they have titles such as local sales manager, accounts receivable manager, word processing supervisor, records supervisor, and group leader.

The activities of lower-level managers are structured, routine, and oriented toward the present—for example, meeting production and marketing schedules, maintaining inventory records, determining raw material requirements, controlling quality, and otherwise seeing to the achievement of well-defined short-term objectives. They rely on internal information.

What Kind of Information for MIS?

Each management level requires a unique kind of information to support decision making:

▶ Top managers need information that is highly summarized, future-oriented, and external as well as internal. This information is needed to support strategic planning. Information flow is primarily *horizontal across functional lines.*

▶ Middle managers need information that is summarized but contains enough detail to allow effective control. Such information has a past orientation to describe recent business activity. Information flow is *both horizontal and vertical.*

▶ Supervisory managers need information that is very current. This information is needed to control day-to-day business operations. Information is primarily *vertical along functional lines.*

These three management information needs are supported by separate, yet closely related, information systems:

▶ Top management has information needs that are supported primarily by decision support systems, as we describe in the second half of this chapter.

▶ Middle managers need management information systems, which are described first in this chapter.

▶ Supervisory managers need information on current operations. These managers are supported by transaction processing information systems, as we described in Chapter 13.

The Data Base Management System as Part of MIS

Management information systems evolved out of transaction processing information systems. The MISs were not intended to replace or to improve on the TPISs but rather to satisfy another information need altogether: to serve middle management. However, for an MIS to exist, a TPIS had to be in place in order to make computer-accessible data bases available.

Except by looking at the kind of managers the system serves, how can you tell the difference between a TPIS and an MIS? One way is this: A TPIS usually operates only within *one* functional area of the organization—Marketing, for instance, but not Production. The transaction processing that goes on in a TPIS produces data bases that are specialized for each functional area. An MIS, by contrast, frequently requires access to data from *more* than one functional area—for example, Marketing *and* Production.

Getting data from more than one data base requires some sophisticated software—specifically DBMS software. Let us show how this works.

As we mentioned in Chapter 9, programs were originally written for applications within a particular department or functional area. This was called a *file management system*: Marketing people would write programs for their data files and Production people would write for theirs. Unfortunately, this led to more and more separate data files, with frequent duplication of data about customers, employees, and products. The file management system not only led to high storage and maintenance costs—one transaction might require updates of several different files—but also, of course, restricted people from having access to each other's files.

Data base management systems were developed to resolve these problems. As mentioned, a data base management system (DBMS) consists of programs that act as an interface between data bases and users and that allow users easy access to data. A DBMS is particularly valuable to an MIS because middle managers must be able to cross departments in an organization in order to get data—Marketing people, for instance, must have access to data bases in Production or Research and Development. Figure 14-2 shows how the pyramidal arrangement of data bases that are used to support transaction processing—each department with its own data base—may be rethought in a DBMS arrangement so that a user can view all four data bases as a single large integrated organizational data base.

TYPICAL
MIS REPORTS

A great deal of a manager's job involves making reports to his or her supervisor. Even at the top of the pyramid, the CEO must make reports—to the stockholders or the board of directors.

Sometimes reports are given orally, at other times they are given in writing. However, if you are one of those people for whom speaking or writing is not easy, you will be pleased to learn that a great deal of this activity has been computerized. The reports we are concerned with here are those produced by computer-based business information systems.

As we saw in the last chapter, a TPIS produces reports of day-to-day operations—specific, detailed information that helps lower-level managers maintain close operational control. TPIS reports are not very helpful to middle managers, however. Since middle managers are more concerned with planning and controlling, they need information that is more summarized and that has a wider perspective than that offered by a TPIS. An MIS provides this. By giving managers access to all departmental data bases in the organization, an MIS can provide managers with reports summarizing the organization's performance, which can give them a basis for making organizational plans.

There are many kinds of MIS reports, some of which are specialized for certain industries. A pharmaceutical house, for instance, might have a report that carefully tracks the shelf life of certain types

Figure 14-2. Information flows and the management hierarchy. *Near right:* Information flows in different ways depending on the level of management: vertically for lower management, both horizontally and vertically for middle managers, and primarily horizontally for top managers. *Opposite page, left:* A transaction processing information system, at the lowest level of an organization, consists of four separate data bases corresponding to the four separate business departments. Information flow is primarily vertical along functional lines. *Right:* At the middle level, the four data bases may be thought of as being integrated into an organizational data base, which gives middle managers more flexibility in a management information system. Information flow is both horizontal and vertical.

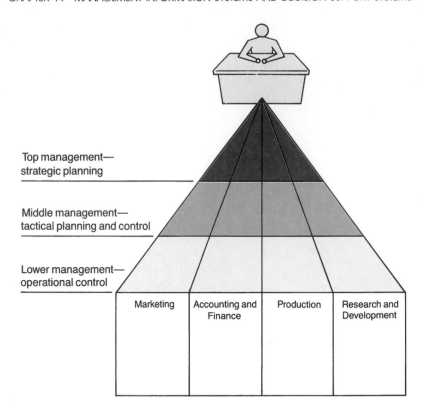

Top management—
strategic planning

Middle management—
tactical planning and control

Lower management—
operational control

Marketing	Accounting and Finance	Production	Research and Development

of drugs that deteriorate after a period of time. A shoe manufacturer, on the other hand, would have no need for such a program. However, both firms would most likely have MIS reports that summarize past due customer accounts.

The most significant attribute of MIS reports is that their format and their informational content is predetermined. There are three categories of MIS reports:

▶ Periodic
▶ Exception
▶ Demand

Every time one of these reports is to be generated, the MIS programs gain access to the organizational data base and calculate, summarize, and report the required information.

Let us see what these reports are and how they are used at Know-wear.

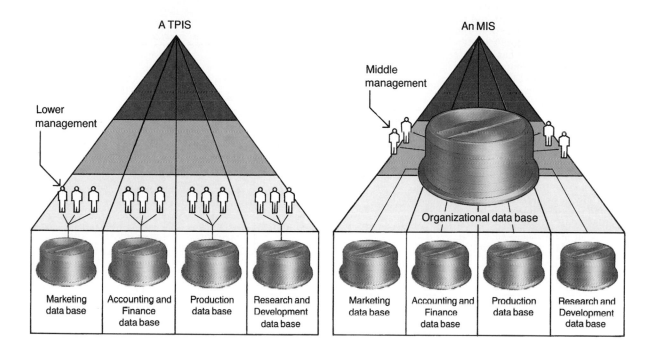

Periodic Reports

Periodic reports are reports generated at regular intervals—quarterly, monthly, or weekly. Examples of periodic reports include quarterly financial reports, monthly sales analyses, and weekly production reports. An example of a periodic report for Know-wear is a profitability report, as shown in Figure 14-3.

Two of the most common periodic reports are:

▶ The income statement
▶ The balance sheet

Both are used a great deal in business.

The Income Statement An **income statement** is a statement of the organization's financial performance—income (revenue), expenses, and the difference between them—for a given period of time. A

Figure 14-3.   A periodic report: The customer profitability report. This report, which is issued on a regular basis, does two things: (1) analyzes the profitability of customers and (2) evaluates a salesperson's performance. Note that Know-wear's profitability for the second customer has decreased substantially compared to sales a year earlier, and that the salesperson, John Foster, may be well advised to keep closer track of sales there. Foster's sales efforts show some positive results for the current month, but he is behind for the year to date. ("Net sales" means Foster's total sales minus any allowances made to him and minus any items he sold that were returned by the customer. "Gross margin" means sales revenue minus the cost of goods sold. "Margin percent of sales" describes how much—what percentage—each customer is contributing to the profitability of the firm.)

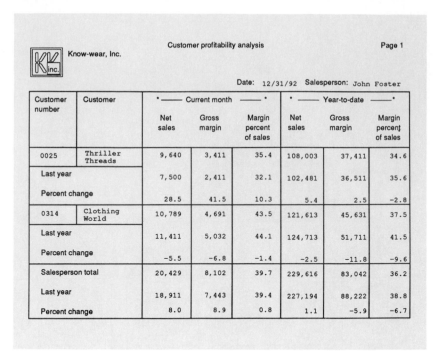

Customer number	Customer	* —— Current month —— *			* —— Year-to-date —— *		
		Net sales	Gross margin	Margin percent of sales	Net sales	Gross margin	Margin percent of sales
0025	Thriller Threads	9,640	3,411	35.4	108,003	37,411	34.6
Last year		7,500	2,411	32.1	102,481	36,511	35.6
Percent change		28.5	41.5	10.3	5.4	2.5	-2.8
0314	Clothing World	10,789	4,691	43.5	121,613	45,631	37.5
Last year		11,411	5,032	44.1	124,713	51,711	41.5
Percent change		-5.5	-6.8	-1.4	-2.5	-11.8	-9.6
Salesperson total		20,429	8,102	39.7	229,616	83,042	36.2
Last year		18,911	7,443	39.4	227,194	88,222	38.8
Percent change		8.0	8.9	0.8	1.1	-5.9	-6.7

Customer profitability analysis — Know-wear, Inc. — Page 1 — Date: 12/31/92   Salesperson: John Foster

yearly income statement, for example, would report all income generated by the firm through sales and other sources for the preceding 12 months, all expenses for that period, and the net income—that is, the difference between income and expenses.

An example of an income statement for Know-wear is shown in Figure 14-4.

The Balance Sheet   The income statement is for a fixed period of time. The **balance sheet** reports the *overall* financial condition of the firm on a specific date, listing assets, liabilities, and the owner's share (proprietor's equity) in the firm. As the bottom half of Figure 14-4 shows, total assets for Know-wear are equal to the sum of liabilities and proprietor's equity.

Exception Reports

Exception reports call attention to unusual situations. They are put out by the MIS when certain predefined conditions occur, such as when inventory levels drop dangerously low, production output is behind schedule, sales are low throughout an entire region, or the amount in accounts receivable is beyond an acceptable level.

An example of an exception report for Know-wear appears in Figure 14-5.

Figure 14-4. Periodic reports: The income statement and balance sheet. *Top:* Income statement for Know-wear. The top line expresses all the income generated for the year, all of it through sales revenue. The cost of goods sold, operating expenses, and taxes are then subtracted from sales revenue in order to arrive at the net income after taxes—the profit for the firm. Note that these are abbreviated figures: The net income is not really $1,117 but is expressed in thousands of dollars—that is, $1,117,000. *Bottom:* Balance sheet for Know-wear. This shows the financial status of the firm as of the date indicated. Assets consist of cash on hand, cash owed by customers (accounts receivable), and value of inventory or products on hand, equipment, and buildings. Liabilities are money owed to vendors (accounts payable), employees, tax collectors, and holders of long-term loans (notes payable). The owner's equity consists of total assets minus total liabilities; since it is also expressed in thousands, this is $3,311,000.

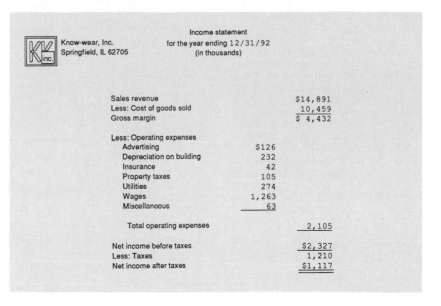

Know-wear, Inc.
Springfield, IL 62705

Income statement
for the year ending 12/31/92
(in thousands)

Sales revenue		$14,891
Less: Cost of goods sold		10,459
Gross margin		$ 4,432
Less: Operating expenses		
Advertising	$126	
Depreciation on building	232	
Insurance	42	
Property taxes	105	
Utilities	274	
Wages	1,263	
Miscellaneous	63	
Total operating expenses		2,105
Net income before taxes		$2,327
Less: Taxes		1,210
Net income after taxes		$1,117

Know-wear, Inc.
Springfield, IL 62705

Balance sheet
as of 12/31/92
(in thousands)

Assets			Liabilities		
Current assets:			Current liabilities:		
Cash	$1,978		Accounts payable	$2,198	
Accounts receivable	211		Wages payable	78	
Inventory	459		Taxes payable	1,215	
Total current assets		$2,648	Total current liabilities		$3,491
Fixed assets:			Long-term liabilities		
Equipment	$2,399		Notes payable	$3,677	
Buildings	5,432		Total long-term liabilities		$3,677
Total fixed assets		$7,831			
Total assets		$10,479	Total liabilities		$ 7,168
			Owner's equity		3,311
			Total liabilities and owner's equity		$10,479

Figure 14-5. Exception report: Aged receivables. An aged receivables report is produced by Know-wear's MIS whenever customers' accounts receivables have "aged" beyond a certain acceptable level—that is, when customers are late in payment. By monitoring the payment history of a customer, Know-wear may increase or decrease that customer's credit limit, the maximum amount that customer will be sold on account. The aged receivables report may also be produced as a periodic report.

Know-wear, Inc.

Exception Report Page 1

Aged accounts receivable

Date: 10/31/92

Customer number	Customer name	Credit limit	Current balance	* —— Days past due —— *				Total due
				1–30	21–60	61–90	Over 90	
0025	Thriller Threads	18,000	6,431	5,569				12,000
0131	Fashion-Go-Round	7,500	2,111			1,123	2,121	5,355
0311	Miracle Mile Stores	12,000	4,000					4,000
0314	Clothing World	14,500	7,123	969	458			8,550
Company total			19,665	6,538	458	1,123	2,121	29,905
Percent of total due			65.8	21.9	1.5	3.8	7.1	100.0

Demand Reports

A **demand report** is the opposite of a periodic report; as its name implies, it is prepared on an as-needed, nonscheduled basis—that is, "on demand." Examples of demand reports are revised sales forecasts, employee salary reviews, and current production performance reports.

Figure 14-6 shows two demand reports used at Know-wear. The national sales manager in the Marketing department, for example, may request a demand report called an "employee salary review" because competitiveness in recruiting salespeople means that newly hired employees must be paid more than older employees—but older employees must also be paid enough to keep them from being lured away to other companies (assuming they have earned a pay hike).

DECISION SUPPORT

WHY WE NEED IT

"We are drowning in information but starved for knowledge." This, says J. Daniel Couger, a professor of computer and management science at the University of Colorado, Colorado Springs, is the corollary to the proposition stated by futurist John Naisbitt—that our industrial society is becoming an information society.

"This level of information is clearly impossible to handle by present means," says Couger in *Computerworld*. "Uncontrolled and

Figure 14-6. Demand reports: Employee salary review and insurance evaluation. Two instances of demand reports—reports produced on demand by the MIS at the request of managers—at Know-wear. *Top:* The employee salary review shows that three of the four salespeople were doing acceptable or better jobs and so were given a raise in annual salary; Mike Davis was not performing well enough to deserve a raise. *Bottom:* An insurance evaluation demand report, which describes the value and insurance coverage for equipment in the Marketing department.

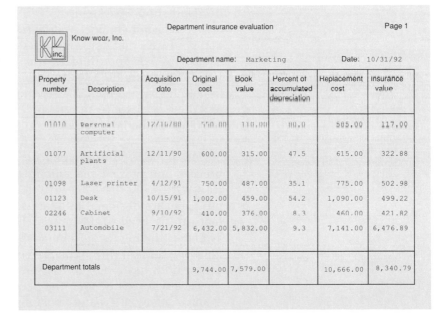

unorganized information is no longer a resource in an information society. Instead, it becomes the enemy of the information worker. . . . Information technology brings order to the chaos of information pollution and, therefore, gives value to data that would otherwise be useless."

The third stage of evolution in information technology—and the most valuable in coping with "information pollution"—is the decision support system (DSS). The lower-level systems of TPIS and MIS are helpful in dealing with the structured and predictable. But 80% of all managerial decision making is in response to the unpredictable. Most important decisions of the sort handled by a DSS are of the "what-if" variety.

"What if there is a strike?" a manager may want to know. "How would that affect inventory levels?" Or, "What if there is a downturn in the national economy? How would that affect sales?" The stuff of management is making decisions about unexpected problems, sudden opportunities, unique alternatives—situations that are unanticipated, rarely repeated, and needing quick analysis and resolution.

Moreover, because managers often feel they are drowning in a sea of data, what they need is not more data or more information but tools that will help them analyze and make decisions about the information they have. The answer is not TPIS and MIS but DSS—a decision support system.

A **decision support system (DSS)** is a set of computer programs and hardware that helps managers arrange information from various sources in new and different ways. Middle-level managers can use a DSS for analysis and research, but the system is principally intended to help high-level managers in their decision making. Thus, the system must be *flexible* and *interactive*—that is, the user must be able to obtain immediate access to data through an interactive computer terminal.

Most DSSs are designed for large computer systems that can process and store large amounts of data quickly and efficiently. However, the Lotus 1-2-3 integrated program and other spreadsheet programs are designed to operate on microcomputers and are tools that can be used to develop a DSS. More powerful DSSs are now available for microcomputers—for example, Interactive Financial Planning System (IFPS), marketed by Execucom Systems of Austin, Texas. IFPS has a version designed for mainframe use as well.

There are many potential benefits of DSS, such as the ability to examine many alternative business situations. But the system must be easy to learn and use. Thus, a well-designed DSS is expensive. The cost can be justified, however, if a wider pool of data will improve decision making or when timely access to information is critical.

We will take a detailed look at what constitutes a DSS. First, however, let us quickly review the distinctions among the three kinds of management systems:

VIEWS ON TPIS, MIS, AND DSS

Are There Really Differences Among Information Systems?

When we state in this book that TPISs are for supervisory managers, MISs for middle managers, and DSSs for top managers, we have used this division as a way of presenting basic concepts. In point of fact, however, the three systems overlap, and there is some dispute as to whether, for example, there are truly differences between MIS and DSS. Here is how Ralph H. Sprague, Jr. and Eric D. Carlson describe the controversy. Note that they use EDP (electronic data processing) for what we have been calling TPIS.

We seem to be on the verge of another "era" in the relentless advancement of computer-based information systems in organizations. Designated by the term *decision support systems* (DSS), these systems are receiving reactions ranging from "a major breakthrough" to "just another buzz word."

One view is that the natural evolutionary advancement of information technology and its use in the organizational context has led from electronic data processing (EDP) to management information systems (MIS) to the current DSS thrust. In this view, DSS pick up where MIS leave off. An alternative view portrays DSS as an important subset of what MIS have been and will continue to be. Still another view recognizes a type of system that has been developing for several years and "now we have a name for it." Meanwhile, the skeptics suspect that DSS is just another buzz word to justify the next round of visits from the vendors. . . .

A decision support system may be defined by its capabilities in several critical areas. . . .

▶ They tend to be aimed at the less well structured, underspecified problems that upper-level managers typically face.

▶ They attempt to combine the use of models or analytic techniques with traditional data access and retrieval functions.

▶ They specifically focus on features that make them easy to use by noncomputer people in an interactive mode.

▶ They emphasize flexibility and adaptability to accommodate changes in the environment and decision-making approach of the user. . . .

DSS represent not merely an evolutionary advancement of EDP and MIS, and certainly will not replace either. Nor are they merely a type of information system aimed exclusively at top management, where other information systems seem to have failed. Rather, DSS comprise a class of information system that draws on transaction processing [EDP] systems and interacts with the other parts of the overall information system to support the decision-making activities of managers and other knowledge workers in organizations. There are, however, some subtle but significant differences between DSS and traditional EDP or so-called MIS approaches. Moreover, these systems require a new combination of information systems technology to satisfy a set of heretofore unmet needs.

—Richard H. Sprague, Jr. and Eric D. Carlson, *Building Effective Decision Support Systems*

▶ **TPIS:** Focusing on data generated by the firm's transactions and operations, a TPIS is exemplified by the payroll system that processes employee time cards, produces employee paychecks, and records the appropriate journal accounting entries.

▶ **MIS:** Designed to provide management with structured reports, MIS is illustrated by quarterly labor analysis reports that summarize labor costs.

▶ **DSS:** Intended to support management decision making in the analysis of semistructured and unstructured problems, DSS is exemplified by information that helps managers quickly evaluate trends in salaries of employees within a particular job classification over the last five years. DSS, then, is a natural step in the evolution of information systems from TPIS and MIS.

THE THREE PARTS
OF DSS DECISION,
SUPPORT, SYSTEM

It has not always been possible to provide computerized support for decision making about unanticipated problems, but recent technological advances have changed all that. Microprocessors, telecommunications, large storage capacity, user-friendly software, and data base management systems have helped to extend the range of the ordinary manager's control over information.

To understand DSS and how it fits in with other information systems, let us examine each of its parts:

▶ Decision
▶ Support
▶ System

Decision: Making Things Happen

Nearly everyone in organizational life has to make decisions, but obviously the decisions are different the higher you go in the organization. As a Know-wear sales representative, for example, you will have to make different decisions than you will if you become the Vice-President of Marketing—whose types of decisions will be different from those of the Vice-President of Production.

Despite these differences, however, there are seven activities common to decision making. If you become a manager or administrator, whatever kind it is, you will probably perform the following tasks:

▶ **Searching:** The decision process typically begins with a *search* for available data—facts, figures, and reports.
▶ **Specifying:** The data uncovered may allow you to *specify* the problem more precisely, eliminating some alternatives and revealing new ones.
▶ **Computing:** The data may have to be manipulated in some way; that is, you may have to do some mathematical and statistical *computing.*
▶ **Assimilating:** After the computations, you *assimilate* or pull together the accumulated facts, reports, and summaries.

Decision making. The task of decision making has seven activities: searching for data, specifying the problem, computing data, assimilating facts *(top)*, drawing inferences, formulating a decision, and *(bottom)* communicating the decision to the people affected by it.

▶ **Drawing inferences:** After assimilating the facts, you draw conclusions or *inferences* from the data.

▶ **Deciding:** The assimilating and inference steps will allow you to *decide*—to formulate a decision.

▶ **Communicating:** Finally, you *communicate* the decision to the people who are affected in some way by the decision. These seven activities constitute the brain work of a manager. They describe how a manager spends his or her day.

Support: Getting Help with the Information Glut

"We've got information coming out of our ears!" is the cry of many managers. "What we need now is some way to make sense of it." What is needed, in other words, is some way to take hold of it so a manager can make decisions about it.

Because MIS reports are passive and predetermined, they are not as helpful in supporting managerial planning and decision making. Something active and flexible is needed, something that will support the seven decision-making tasks above.

A number of components of computer technology can assist in these tasks. For example:

▶ *Searching* for facts, figures, and reports can be enhanced by large data bases containing numeric and text data.

▶ *Specifying* and *computing* are helped by computational models, such as electronic spreadsheets or statistical packages.

▶ *Assimilating, drawing inferences,* and *deciding* are helped by computer graphics and word processing.

▶ *Communicating* is given a boost with telecommunications, such as teleconferencing with other managers about a problem.

Perhaps the need for decision support is best demonstrated by the increasing use of microcomputers in business organizations. With their increasingly easy-to-use software and good graphics, microcomputers give managers immediate, convenient access to data and analytical tools that help them with their decision making. And, although microcomputers are limited in their ability to store and manipulate large amounts of data or to process it quickly, when microcomputers are connected to mainframes these drawbacks disappear.

System: Elimination of the Limitations

Computers are limited in what they can do. So are people. When computers and people are put together in a system, however, their combined strengths are powerful. Computers offer speed, access, and computational power. People offer creativity, reasoning, and perspective. Paired in a DSS, they provide a system for increasing the effectiveness of management decisions.

A DSS, then, does not produce a product. Whereas a TPIS may produce a list of transactions and an MIS a report, a DSS does neither. Rather it is designed to produce a *service* that will affect the quality of management decisions.

THE MODEL WAY
OF DOING THINGS

To TPIS, MIS, and DSS let us add another set of initials—**MS.** It stands for **management science,** defined as the application of quantitative techniques or models to the analysis of management problems. Decision support systems are actually related to a combination of MIS and MS. MIS provides managers with structured reports; MS provides them with models. By models, we do not mean something you buy in a hobby store. **Models** are ideas, hypothetical notions that consist of technical recommendations and procedures for analyzing and solving complex management problems. Although management science by itself has had only limited effects on managerial decision making—the complexity of MS techniques has restricted their widespread use—it has shown the value of using models as a problem-solving tool.

There are three types of management science models, as follows:

▶ **Optimization: Optimization models** are used to identify the best— that is, optimal—solution in very specialized problems. The best known and widely used such model is *linear programming,* used in the oil industry for scheduling refinery operations, as well as in banking, transportation, and public utilities.

▶ **Heuristics:** A model that probably will be used more in the future, **heuristics** consist of a set of rules or guidelines that lead to a solution to a particular type of problem. For example, in the banking industry, guidelines are set up for loan officers to follow when authorizing loan applications; the applicant must meet certain criteria for income level, credit rating, and so on.

▶ **Simulation:** The MS models found to be most effective in business organizations, **simulation models** are used to represent complex problems by conceptualizing them and describing them mathematically. More flexible than other models and capable of analyzing a wider range of problems, simulation models are used to determine allocations of a firm's resources. For example, a model may consider external factors such as current economic conditions and internal factors such as available investment capital in order to arrive at a projected solution. Simulation is one of the most widely used tools of middle- and top-level managers for planning and decision making.

Models like these are used frequently in business to formulate strategies for making decisions.

AN IDEAL DSS

What would an ideal DSS look like? Let us say that Know-wear has had a growth surge. New offices have been opened around the United States and Canada, and the CEO, Ms. Douglas, finds that she needs help in making strategic decisions. It is time, she begins to see, for her and her vice-presidents to take advantage of a complete computer-based business information system—namely, to install a decision support system. Once again, Ms. Douglas taps you to help do the spadework of putting such a system in place.

In setting up a DSS, a company must consider three aspects:

▶ Which of two types of DSS to use—ad hoc or institutional
▶ The performance objectives
▶ The building blocks of the DSS—hardware, software, and decision makers

The Two Types of DSS

Decision support systems are of two types:

▶ Ad hoc
▶ Institutional

The **ad hoc DSSs**, also known as general DSSs, are designed to handle a wide variety of management decision problems and are especially suited to unexpected, nonrecurring management problems. The Generalized Planning System (GPLAN) is one example of an ad hoc DSS. It is used by businesspeople to support a wide variety of decisions ranging from inventory control to financial management.

Institutional DSSs are specialized and use terminology and analysis procedures established within certain areas, such as medicine or advertising. Because of their lack of flexibility, they are not able to support organizationwide decision making. Examples of institutional DSSs are MYCIN, which is used by physicians to help in diagnosing patient symptoms; IRIS, used in personnel and labor relations; and IMS, used for evaluating advertising strategies.

Financial planning languages (FPLs) evolved from high-level languages into institutional decision support systems and from there into ad hoc DSSs. Although they have a definite financial orientation, they have attained a great deal of flexibility and now are used in a variety of decision support roles, including mathematical, statisti-

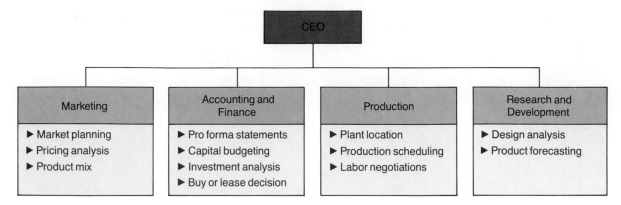

Figure 14-7.   The uses of FPLs. Common applications of Financial Planning Languages are shown for the four principal business areas.

cal, and forecasting procedures; sensitivity and "what-if" analyses; goal seeking and optimization; report generation and graphic displays. Figure 14-7 lists some common applications of FPLs in the four business areas of Marketing, Accounting and Finance, Production, and Research and Development.

The questions that FPLs are able to address are those "what-if" types of questions that arise so frequently in business: "What if fuel prices increase 20% next year?" "What if interest rates increase 2% next month?" "How sensitive is net income to changes in sales price? labor costs? interest rates?"

For instance, at Know-wear, the CEO learns that certain garment workers are considering going on strike. Management forms a negotiation team in preparation for the strike, but prior to the negotiations, the team is asked to evaluate how long the company could survive profitably on its inventories before being affected by the strike. Armed with this information, the team has a better grasp of its strategy by knowing how hard to negotiate with the union.

The DSS is used in the following manner. The team uses historical data to predict sales for the next three months. A model is chosen, a data base is accessed, and a prediction equation formulated. Based on this equation, "what-if" questions are asked—"What if inventory decreases by 80%? What would be the effect on sales?" With the results of this projection, the negotiation team informs management to build up inventories by a certain amount before the strike. From answers to related questions, the team informs the CEO how badly the strike could affect the company, depending on its length.

At Know-wear, the Marketing vice-president hears that the CEO is considering a DSS and suggests that the company acquire IMS—which, of course, would be useful for her in her advertising decisions but would not be useful to anyone else. The CEO refers the matter to a systems analyst and asks you to be the liaison in the matter.

The systems analyst disagrees with the Marketing vice-president's choice, believing that a more general or ad hoc DSS would better serve the organization. He suggests the use of an ad hoc system called IFPS—Interactive Financial Planning System. After a thorough systems analysis and design, Know-wear adopts IFPS.

Performance Objectives for a DSS

In general, the objectives of a DSS are to provide a flexible, powerful tool to support management decision making. More precisely, the objectives are:

▶ To support all management levels—top, middle, and supervisory—in all phases of decision making
▶ To analyze unexpected problems
▶ To integrate information flow and decision-making activities
▶ To be easy to use yet powerful and flexible

Let us look at these more carefully.

Management Levels   DSSs are designed to support the *planning* activities of middle- and upper-level managers as well as the *decision-making* activities of all managers in all phases of decision making. Thus, DSSs are used not only for data collection and analysis but also to support decision-making tasks: searching, specifying, computing, assimilating, drawing inferences, forming decisions, and communicating.

Unexpected Problems   Perhaps only 20% of the problems that managers encounter are standard and routine, and these can be effectively evaluated using MIS reports. However, as we mentioned earlier, 80% of all managerial decision making is in response to problems that are unexpected. Moreover, these problems usually require action in a very short period of time.

Information Flow and Decision-Making Activities   As we have mentioned, the flow of information within an organization is both vertical within a department (for example, between management levels in Marketing) and horizontal between departments (for example, between Marketing and Production vice-presidents). A DSS should enhance this flow, especially horizontally, at the higher management levels. Generally, the flow of information is in the form of reports that communicate decisions and coordinate problem-solving activities. This means the information must flow easily in and out of the organization's data base and that the DSS must be able to quickly update and have access to the data base.

Decision support systems. Two crucial pieces of hardware in a DSS are interactive graphic terminals, which permit managers to display charts and graphs *(top)* and window or split screens *(middle)*, and telecommunications equipment, which lets managers share data and reports with other managers *(left)*.

Ease of Use Users of a DSS are managers, not computer programmers; thus, one of the most crucial performance objectives of a DSS is that it be easy to use. If the DSS is not powerful, not flexible, and not easy to use, then it simply will not be used. Commands should be English-like—for example, BROWSE might allow a manager to examine the contents of a data base.

DSS Building Blocks: Hardware, Software, Decision Maker

Effective decision support systems have come about because of technological advances in hardware and software, and because managers have become more sophisticated about using management science techniques and computers to help them in making decisions. Let us, therefore, examine the three building blocks of a DSS:

▶ Hardware
▶ Software
▶ Decision maker

Hardware The DSS software is typically located in a mainframe computer to which are attached terminals used by the company's managers. Therefore, probably the two most crucial pieces of hardware in the system are interactive graphic terminals and telecommunications networks:

▶ **Interactive graphic terminals:** Graphics capabilities are essential because charts and graphs aid decision making ("a picture is worth a thousand words"). An interactive graphic display terminal allows the decision maker to have a natural, responsive interaction with the DSS software.
▶ **Telecommunications networks:** Such networks, which allow sophisticated time-sharing computer systems to be developed, allow managers to share data and reports with other managers, to quickly coordinate problem-solving activities, and to have access to far-flung data bases within the organization and to data bases outside the organization.

Software Four types of software are needed in a DSS:

▶ **Data base management system:** A DBMS extends the range of data that can be collected, retrieved, and analyzed. It allows a manager to interact with the firm's internal data bases as well as with external data bases. The internal data will have been recorded primarily through the activities of transaction processing. The external data will be obtainable from commercially available data bases.
▶ **Simulation and application languages:** These specialized languages allow decision makers to do model building—to develop

their own management science models and to purchase custom-made models. The models are contained within the data base as preprogrammed structures. The most common models are for financial statement simulations, risk analysis, and forecasting.

▶ **A DSS query language:** A query language that is understandable to managers is necessary if decision makers are to communicate easily with the DSS. The query language should use such commands as ADD, GRAPH, CHART, CALCULATE, SELECT, BROWSE, GET, and so on. Such commands perform basic arithmetic operations, create bar graphs and charts, calculate ratios, perform statistical operations, and numerous other activities.

▶ **DSS executive software:** This acts as an operating system in that it handles many of the operational duties for the DSS, sparing the user these chores. Executive software is essential for monitoring and coordinating DSS activities. One of the most important functions of the DSS executive software is the coordination and control of the other three types of software.

Decision Maker   A decision maker is the human element, of course—the manager at his or her desk, eyes on the terminal screen, fingers on the keyboard. Three roles can be distinguished in interacting with the DSS; these can be performed by the same person or by three different persons:

▶ **The model builder:** This is the person who conceptualizes and develops the model.

▶ **The model user:** This is the person who actually runs the model. He or she specifies the inputs and evaluates the alternatives.

▶ **The decision maker:** This is the person who analyzes the results of the model, makes any modifications, and comes to the final decision.

For the most effective interaction between human and machine and thus the most effective support of human decision making, one person should perform all three roles.

PUTTING IT ALL TOGETHER FOR THE VERY TOP: EIS

The highest executives in a firm typically do not have the expertise or the time to develop and to extensively use DSS models. These executives are the firm's top decision makers and need access to a wide variety of information—information available from TPIS, MIS, and DSS. A recent development has been the creation of very easy to learn and to use information systems to support these highest level executives. These systems are called Executive Information Systems.

DSS OUTPUT
GRAPHIC DISPLAY AND REPORTS

The output for a DSS is highly diverse and depends on what problem you are investigating. The output may be:

▶ In pictorial format, such as charts and graphs displayed on a graphic terminal

▶ In a report format, such as the expected sales of a product or production output of a factory

Know-wear, Inc.

Five-year financial plan
(in thousands)

Page 1

Date:12/31/93

Income statements for the year ending

	Actual 1993	Budget 1994	* ----------- 1995	1996	Projections 1997	----------- * 1998	1999
Sales	$17,600	$23,100	$28,600	$34,100	$39,000	$44,500	$50,000
Cost of goods sold	11,820	13,000	15,000	18,000	19,412	21,000	23,000
Gross margin	$ 5,780	$10,100	$13,600	$16,100	$19,588	$23,500	$27,000
Marketing expenses	$ 1,300	$ 1,900	$ 2,600	$ 3,800	$ 4,131	$ 4,900	$ 5,250
Administrative expenses	986	1,100	1,300	1,400	1,500	1,750	1,980
Miscellaneous expenses	371	480	560	640	700	790	810
Total expenses	$ 2,657	$ 3,480	$ 4,460	$ 5,840	$ 6,331	$ 7,440	$ 8,040
Net income before taxes	$ 3,123	$ 6,620	$ 9,140	$10,260	$13,257	$16,060	$18,960
Federal taxes	1,624	3,442	4,753	5,335	6,894	8,351	9,859
Net income after taxes	$ 1,499	$ 3,178	$ 4,387	$ 4,925	$ 6,363	$ 7,709	$ 9,101

Figure 14-8. Projected income statement. These are projected ("pro forma") financial statements of income for Know-wear for the years 1995–1999. The numbers were derived using a DSS.

Two common forms of output of DSSs are **pro forma**—which means "projected"—balance sheets and pro forma income statements, both of which predict the future financial position of the firm.

At Know-wear, the CEO has used the new DSS to develop a pro forma income statement (Figure 14-8) and a projected balance sheet (Figure 14-9).

Two common decision-making activities using these pro forma statements are:

▶ Performing **"what-if" analysis**—changing assumptions to see what might result. (We examined "what-if" analysis with spreadsheets in Chapter 3.)

▶ Performing **goal-seeking analysis**—stating a goal and the variables influencing it to see what is required to achieve that goal.

The Know-wear CEO and the Vice-President of Accounting and Finance had to make many forecasts and projections to develop the pro forma financial statements shown in Figures 14-8 and 14-9; however, these are simply projections and are not definite. The CEO wants to do some "what-if" analysis—change a few of the assump-

Know-wear, Inc.		Five-year financial plan (in thousands)					Page 1

Balance sheets as of year end							Date:12/31/93
	Actual 1993	Budget 1994	*----- 1995	----- 1996	Projections 1997	----- 1998	----- * 1999
Current assets:							
Cash	$ 2,100	$ 2,500	$ 2,600	$ 2,700	$ 2,900	$ 3,300	$ 3,700
Accounts receivable	2,800	3,000	3,200	3,600	4,200	4,700	4,900
Inventory	3,100	3,900	4,200	4,500	4,800	5,300	5,500
Total current assets	$ 8,000	$ 9,400	$10,000	$10,800	$11,900	$13,300	$14,100
Fixed assets:							
Equipment	$ 1,200	$ 2,000	$ 2,200	$ 2,300	$ 2,600	$ 2,700	$ 2,900
Buildings	1,200	1,600	1,900	1,998	2,103	2,211	2,314
Total fixed assets	$ 2,400	$ 3,600	$ 4,100	$ 4,298	$ 4,703	$ 4,911	$ 5,214
Total assets	$10,400	$13,000	$14,100	$15,098	$16,603	$18,211	$19,314
Current liabilities:							
Accounts payable	$ 2,400	$ 2,600	$ 2,900	$ 3,300	$ 3,700	$ 3,750	$ 3,950
Wages payable	84	96	102	108	141	148	156
Taxes payable	1,411	1,712	1,950	2,111	2,300	2,450	2,510
Total current liabilities	$ 3,895	$ 4,408	$ 4,952	$ 5,519	$ 6,141	$ 6,348	$ 6,616
Long-term liabilities:							
Notes payable	$ 3,400	$ 4,600	$ 4,511	$ 4,700	$ 5,000	$ 6,111	$ 6,211
Total long-term liabilities	$ 3,400	$ 4,600	$ 4,511	$ 4,700	$ 5,000	$ 6,111	$ 6,211
Total liabilities	$ 7,295	$ 9,008	$ 9,463	$10,219	$11,141	$12,459	$12,827
Owner's equity	3,105	3,992	4,637	4,879	5,462	5,752	6,487
Total liabilities & owner's equity	$10,400	$13,000	$14,100	$15,098	$16,603	$18,211	$19,314

Figure 14-9. Projected balance sheet. The projected balance sheet of Know-wear's assets, liabilities, and owner's equity covers the years 1995–1999.

tions and see what the results are. Ms. Douglas wonders, for example, what would be the effect on net income in the year 1997 if sales in that year increased by 10%; of course, expenses are sure to increase with sales. Costs of goods sold, for example, increase as more of Know-wear products are sold. Ms. Douglas estimates these increased costs, and the results are shown in Figure 14-10; projected sales increased from $39 million to $42.9 million while net income went from about $6.4 million to $6.8 million. (Note that in order to obtain higher sales, higher expenses must be projected, also.)

The CEO is also interested in goal seeking—setting net income at a certain value and determining what level of sales is needed to achieve that specific net income. This is shown in Figure 14-11; if the goal is a net income of $7.0 million in 1997 and a large increase in expenses is also assumed in that year, the DSS shows that sales of over $74 million are needed. Note that even if sales continue to increase along with expenses in the years 1998 and 1999, the company's net income will drop severely.

Know-wear, Inc.

Five-year financial plan
(in thousands)

Page 1

Date: 12/31/93

Income statements for the year ending

	Actual 1993	Budget 1994	1995	1996	Projections 1997	1998	1999
Sales	$17,600	$23,100	$28,600	$34,100	$42,900	$44,500	$50,000
Cost of goods sold	11,820	13,000	15,000	18,000	21,000	21,000	23,000
Gross margin	$ 5,780	$10,100	$13,600	$16,100	$21,900	$23,500	$27,000
Marketing expenses	$ 1,300	$ 1,900	$ 2,600	$ 3,800	$ 4,524	$ 4,900	$ 5,250
Administrative expenses	986	1,100	1,300	1,400	2,000	1,750	1,980
Miscellaneous expenses	371	480	560	640	1,208	790	810
Total expenses	$ 2,657	$ 3,480	$ 4,460	$ 5,840	$ 7,732	$ 7,440	$ 8,040
Net income before taxes	$ 3,123	$ 6,620	$ 9,140	$10,260	$14,168	$16,060	$18,960
Federal taxes	1,624	3,442	4,753	5,335	7,367	8,351	9,859
Net income after taxes	$ 1,499	$ 3,178	$ 4,387	$ 4,925	$ 6,801	$ 7,709	$ 9,101

Figure 14-10.   What-if analysis: Revised income statement. Using the DSS, Know-wear top management has changed the figures in the column for the year 1995 to reflect a 10% sales increase.

BEYOND DSS

So far in this book, we have written about computer-based information systems that aid or support decision making. Is it possible systems could be devised to *replace* human decision making? The answer is: They already have been.

Programmed decision systems (PDSs), which use operational data to produce decisions, are effective in situations that are so structured that decisions can be clearly defined without intervening judgment. Unlike DSSs, which support decision making, typical programmed decision systems make decisions that were once handled by human decision makers. Common uses of PDSs include loan and credit approval, inventory reordering, and IRS audit decisions. Such decisions have become so routine and defined that they now can be programmed by precisely stating decision rules that will dictate the decision for every combination of circumstances. These decision rules are incorporated into software so that certain operational input data will cause the appropriate action to be taken.

To demonstrate the different uses of TPIS, MIS, DSS, and now PDS, consider Know-wear's inventory of raw materials—in this

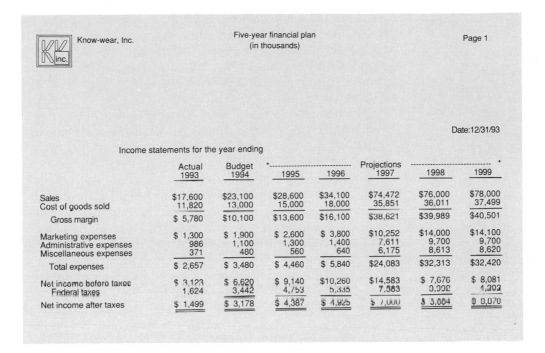

Know-wear, Inc.

Five-year financial plan
(in thousands)

Page 1

Date:12/31/93

Income statements for the year ending

	Actual 1993	Budget 1994	1995	1996	Projections 1997	1998	1999
Sales	$17,600	$23,100	$28,600	$34,100	$74,472	$76,000	$78,000
Cost of goods sold	11,820	13,000	15,000	18,000	35,851	36,011	37,499
Gross margin	$ 5,780	$10,100	$13,600	$16,100	$38,621	$39,989	$40,501
Marketing expenses	$ 1,300	$ 1,900	$ 2,600	$ 3,800	$10,252	$14,000	$14,100
Administrative expenses	986	1,100	1,300	1,400	7,611	9,700	9,700
Miscellaneous expenses	371	480	560	640	6,175	8,613	8,620
Total expenses	$ 2,657	$ 3,480	$ 4,460	$ 5,840	$24,083	$32,313	$32,420
Net income before taxes	$ 3,123	$ 6,620	$ 9,140	$10,260	$14,583	$ 7,676	$ 8,081
Federal taxes	1,624	3,442	4,753	5,335	7,583	3,992	4,202
Net income after taxes	$ 1,499	$ 3,178	$ 4,387	$ 4,925	$ 7,000	$ 3,684	$ 3,879

Figure 14-11. Goal-seeking analysis. Know-wear's CEO has set net income at $7.0 million in 1995 and assumed a large increase in expenses. The DSS shows that a sales of over $74 million are needed to achieve that goal. (Numbers in this figure are expressed in thousands: 74,472 means "$74,472,000.") Note that if expenses continue to increase in the years 1998 and 1999, net income will drop.

case, bolts of Irish tweed. The receipt and use of raw materials is recorded in an TPIS through transaction processing. A report summarizing the level of raw material inventory is produced by the MIS. An analysis of the length of time that the Irish tweed is held in inventory over a year's time is performed using a DSS. Finally, the automatic reordering of the cloth once its inventory has reached a certain specified level is accomplished by the PDS.

THE NEED FOR
STRATEGIC VISION

Where is a company going? This is the biggest "what-if" question of all. A company needs a strategic plan, and a decision support system is critical in helping explore the alternatives to achieving that plan, as we have suggested throughout this chapter.

But something more than a strategic plan is required. "We are restructuring from a society run by short-term considerations and rewards in favor of dealing with things in much longer time frames." This is another one of the so-called megatrends or "restructurings" identified by futurist John Naisbitt. This trend will also have an important effect on information systems, says the University of Colorado's Professor Couger. "Short-term approaches are turning to long-term," he states. "We must reconceptualize what business we are in, or conceptualize what business it would be useful for us to think we are in."

Strategic planning, says Couger, is worthless, unless there is strategic *vision*—a "clear image of what you want to achieve, which then organizes and instructs every step toward that goal." An example of an extraordinarily successful strategic vision, he points out, was that of the National Aeronautics and Space Administration in the 1960s: Put a man on the moon by the end of the decade. With that kind of vision, no one had to be told or reminded of where the organization was going. Compare that kind of organizing focus with the vague "We are going to be the world leader in space exploration."

In short, writes Couger, "In a constantly changing world, strategic planning is not enough; it becomes planning for its own sake. Strategic planning must be geared to a strategic vision with a clarity that remains in spite of the confusion natural to the first stages of change."

In a constantly changing world, perhaps the most exciting changes in ways of handling information are those in which machines themselves do the thinking. We turn now to artificial intelligence and expert systems.

SUMMARY

▶ Most organizations consist of four functional divisions: Marketing, Accounting and Finance, Production, and Research and Development. Within each division are three levels of management: lower (supervisory), middle, and top. For lower managers, information flows primarily vertically within each division. For middle management, information flows both vertically and horizontally between divisions. For top managers, information flows primarily horizontally.

▶ A **management information system (MIS),** which is designed to assist managers in the performance of their work, is a network of computer-based processing procedures that are integrated with manual and other procedures to provide timely, effective information to support managerial planning and control.

▶ Management is the process of transforming resources—materials, money, employees, facilities—into products or services. The primary task of managers is to make decisions in five areas: organizing,

communicating, staffing, planning, and controlling. Planning and controlling are the two management tasks that an MIS is specially designed to support.

▶ **Organizing** decisions include what structures and procedures should be set up, what authority delegated, what system of responsibility and accountability arranged.

▶ **Communicating** consists of transmitting requests and requirements to subordinates and superiors. Current computerized communicating assistance includes word processing, electronic mail, and telecommunications.

▶ **Staffing** consists of decisions about hiring and training employees to achieve the organization's goals.

▶ **Planning** is the formulation of short- and long-range goals for the organization—including policies, procedures, and standards necessary to achieve them. Planning is also concerned with identifying opportunities, problems, and alternative courses of action.

▶ **Controlling** is monitoring of the organization's progress toward its goals—keeping track of resources, including employee performance, and making necessary adjustments.

▶ An effective MIS produces information that is accurate, timely, and complete yet concise. *Accuracy*—completely error-free information—is usually expensive, but sometimes the cost is justified. *Timeliness*—quickly supplied information—is necessary to keep up with the rapid pace of business. *Complete but concise* information includes all relevant facts, not unnecessary and unwanted facts.

▶ A management information system consists of three parts: management, information, and systems.

▶ *Management* in an organization has three levels: top, middle, and supervisory (lower).

▶ Top management, which includes a few of the most powerful managers, has the primary responsibility of strategic planning—establishing the overall direction of the company through long-range planning. The problems of these managers are unstructured and their activities are varied, such as establishing new markets and products and evaluating potential mergers and acquisitions. To make decisions, top managers need both external and internal information.

▶ Middle managers, who are more numerous than top managers, are responsible for tactical planning and control—implementing the plans of top management and monitoring the firm's operations. They perform fairly structured activities—formulating budgets, doing production scheduling, making short-term forecasts, and monitoring sales, production, and personnel performance. Middle managers rely more on internal information than on external, and their decisions take effect much sooner than those of top managers.

▶ Supervisory or lower management, by far the largest group, is responsible for operational control—implementing the plans of middle management and controlling day-to-day operations. Their activities are structured, routine, and oriented toward the present—such as meeting production and marketing schedules, maintaining inventory records, determining raw material requirements, controlling quality, and monitoring the achievement of well-defined short-term objectives.

▶ Each management level requires a unique kind of information to support decision making. Top managers need information that is highly summarized, future-oriented, and external as well as internal. Middle managers need information that is summarized but contains enough detail to allow effective control; such information has a past orientation to describe recent business activity. Supervisory managers need information that is not summarized but is very current in order to control day-to-day business operations.

▶ These three management information needs are supported by three separate, yet related, information systems: top management by decision support systems (DSSs); middle management by management information systems (MISs); supervisory management by transaction processing information systems (TPISs).

▶ A data base management system (DBMS) is a set of programs that act as interface between data bases and users and that allow users easy access to data. A DBMS is valuable to an MIS because middle managers must be able to cross departments in an organization in order to get data.

▶ MIS reports have predetermined formats and informational content. The three categories of MIS reports are periodic, exception, and demand. Every time a report is to be generated, the MIS programs access the organizational data base and calculate, summarize, and report the required information.

▶ **Periodic reports** are reports generated at regular intervals—quarterly, monthly, or weekly—such as quarterly financial reports, monthly sales analyses, and weekly production reports.

▶ Two of the most common periodic reports are the income statement and the balance sheet. An **income statement** is a statement of the organization's financial performance—income, expenses, and the difference between them, or net income—for a given period of time. The **balance sheet** reports the *overall* financial condition of the firm, listing assets, liabilities, and the owner's share in the firm.

▶ **Exception reports** are put out by the MIS when certain predefined unusual conditions occur, such as when inventory levels drop dangerously low, production output is behind schedule, sales are low throughout an entire region, or the amount in accounts receivable is beyond an acceptable level.

▶ A **demand report** is the opposite of a periodic report; it is prepared on an as-needed, nonscheduled basis. Examples of demand reports are revised sales forecasts, employee salary reviews, and current production performance reports.

► A **decision support system (DSS)** is a set of computer programs and hardware intended primarily to help top managers arrange information from various sources in new and different ways. A DSS must be flexible and interactive—immediately accessible through an interactive terminal.

► The distinctions among the three kinds of management systems are: (1) A TPIS generates data from the firm's transactions and operations—such as a payroll system that processes employee time cards, produces employee paychecks, and records appropriate journal accounting entries. (2) An MIS provides structured reports for management—for example, quarterly labor analysis reports that summarize labor costs. (3) A DSS supports management decision making with an analysis of semistructured and unstructured problems—for example, trends in salaries within a particular job classification over the last five years.

► A DSS has three parts: decision, support, and system.

► The *decision* part includes seven activities: searching, specifying, computing, assimilating, drawing inferences, deciding, communicating. (1) Searching is for available facts, figures, and reports. (2) Specifying means defining the problem precisely, eliminating some alternatives and revealing new ones. (3) Computing is a mathematical and statistical manipulation of data. (4) Assimilating is pulling together accumulated facts, reports, and summaries. (5) Drawing inferences is arriving at conclusions from the data and computations. (6) Deciding is decision making based on the assimilated facts and inferences. (7) Communicating is conveying the decision to those people who are affected by it.

► The *support* aspect of the DSS helps managers make sense of the information glut by facilitating the seven decision tasks: (1) Searching is enhanced by large data bases containing numeric and text data. (2) Specifying and (3) computing are helped by computational models, such as electronic spreadsheets. (4) Assimilating, (5) drawing inferences, and (6) deciding are helped by computer graphics. (7) Communicating is assisted with word processing and telecommunications.

► The *system* part of a DSS combines the strengths of both people and computers: the speed, access, and computational power of computers and the creativity, reasoning, and perspective of people. Paired in a DSS, they increase the effectiveness of management decisions.

► **Management science (MS)** is the application of quantitative techniques or models to the analysis of management problems. **Models** are ideas, hypothethical notions that consist of technical recommendations and procedures for analyzing and solving complex management problems.

► The three types of MS models are: (1) **Optimization models,** used to identify the optimal (best) solution in very specialized problems. The best known such model is linear programming, used in the oil industry for scheduling refinery operations. (2) **Heuristics** is a set of rules for solving a particular type of problem—for example, authorizing loan applications. (3) **Simulation models** represent complex problems by conceptualizing them and describing them mathematically. Simulation models are used to determine allocations of a firm's resources, such as projecting a company's capital available for investment.

► In setting up a DSS, a company must consider three aspects: (1) which of two types of DSS to use, ad hoc or institutional; (2) the performance objectives; and (3) the building blocks of the DSS—hardware, software, and decision makers.

► The two *types of DSS* are: (1) **Ad hoc,** or general, **DSSs,** designed to handle a variety of management problems, especially those that are unexpected and nonrecurring; (2) **institutional DSSs,** specialized systems using terminology and analysis procedures established within certain areas, such as medicine or advertising.

► **Financial planning languages (FPLs)** evolved from high-level languages into institutional DSSs and from there into ad hoc DSSs. FPLs have a financial orientation but are flexible, and they now are used in a variety of decision support roles.

► The *performance objectives* of a DSS are: (1) To support all management levels—top, middle, supervisory—in all phases of decision making. DSSs support the planning activities of middle and upper management and the decision-making activities of all managers in all phases of decision making. (2) To analyze unexpected problems, which account for about 80% of all managerial decision making and which usually require action in a very short period of time. (3) To integrate information flow and decision-making activities, especially horizontally at the higher management levels; generally the information is in the form of reports communicating decisions and coordinating problem-solving activities and so must flow easily into and out of the organization's data base. (4) To be easy to use yet powerful and flexible—a crucial matter because DSS users are managers, not programmers.

▶ The three *building blocks* of a DSS are: (1) hardware, (2) software, and (3) the decision maker.

▶ The two most important pieces of *hardware* in a DSS are: (1) interactive graphic terminals, since graphics capabilities are essential to produce charts and graphs, and managers must have a natural, responsive interaction with the DSS software; and (2) telecommunications networks, which let managers share data and reports, quickly coordinate problem-solving activities, and have access to data bases within and outside the organization.

▶ Four types of *software* are needed in a DSS: (1) A data base management system (DBMS), which extends the range of data that can be collected, retrieved, and analyzed and which allows managers to interact with the firm's transaction data bases as well as with external data bases. (2) **Simulation and application languages,** which allow decision makers to do model building—to develop their own models and to purchase custom-made models. (3) A **DSS query language,** an easily understood language that is necessary in order for managers to communicate with the DSS. (4) **DSS executive software,** which acts as an operating system in that it handles many of the operational duties for the DSS and monitors and coordinates DSS activities.

▶ The *decision maker* is the human element, playing one or more of the three roles for interacting with the DSS: (1) the model builder, who conceptualizes and develops the model; (2) the model user, who actually runs it; and (3) the decision maker, who analyzes the results of the model, makes any modifications, and comes to the final decision.

▶ The output for a DSS depends on the problem under investigation. It may be in (1) pictorial format, such as charts or graphs on a graphic terminal, or (2) report format, such as expected sales or output.

▶ Two common forms of DSS output are pro forma balance sheets and pro forma income statements. **Pro forma** means "projected." Pro forma statements are used for performing (1) **what-if analysis**—that is, changing assumptions to see what might result, and (2) **goal-seeking analysis**—that is, stating a goal and the variables influencing it to see what is required to achieve that goal.

▶ **Programmed decision systems (PDSs)** use operational data to produce decisions in structured situations with clearly defined judgment criteria. Unlike DSSs, which support decision making, PDSs re-place human decision making.

KEY TERMS

Ad hoc DSS, p. 453
Balance sheet, p. 444
Communicating, p. 435
Controlling, p. 436
Decision support system (DSS), p. 448
Demand report, p. 446
DSS executive software, p. 457
DSS query language, p. 457
Exception report, p. 444
Financial planning language (FPL), p. 453
Goal-seeking analysis, p. 458
Heuristics, p. 452
Income statement, p. 443
Institutional DSS, p. 453
Management information system (MIS), p. 435
Management science (MS), p. 452
Model, p. 452
Optimization model, p. 452
Organizing, p. 435
Periodic report, p. 443
Planning, p. 436
Pro forma, p. 458
Programmed decision system (PDS), p. 460
Simulation model, p. 452
Simulation and application languages, p. 456
Staffing, p. 435
What-if analysis, p. 458

REVIEW QUESTIONS

1. What do managers do? Describe the classic tasks of management.
2. To aid managers in decision making, the MIS needs to produce information with what three attributes?
3. Describe the three levels of management. What type of information is needed at each level?
4. Compare the MIS to the TPIS. How are they alike and how do they differ?

5. Name and describe the three categories of MIS reports.

6. Describe the income statement and balance sheet.

7. Describe a DSS. What types of situations and decisions does it support that an MIS would not?

8. What are the seven activities common to decision making? How are these activities supported by the DSS?

9. What is a model? Name the three types of models.

10. Describe the two types of DSS.

11. Describe the four types of software needed in a DSS.

CASE PROBLEMS

Case 14-1: Using MIS for Marketing— Building a Mailing List

Mailing lists can be the sales and marketing lifeblood of a business, an effective way of targeting advertising that is less a "shotgun" approach, as ads in newspapers and on television often are. While one probably would not advertise hamburgers or breakfast cereals via direct mail, this channel can be successful in reaching customers for specialty or specialized products. *Inc.* magazine reported, for instance, on the efforts of the new owner of the London Wine Co. in Brookline, Massachusetts, when he took over the family business and decided he wanted to increase sales 50% to $1.5 million in only one year. Since the store had limited shelf and floor space and almost no parking, he realized that more business could not come from increasing foot traffic into the store. By obtaining a direct-mail management program designed to run on a personal computer, however, London Wine was able "to track each response and tailor its mailing to the tastes and needs of the individual recipients."

Your assignment: One secret of a successful direct-mail computer program is its ability to compile very detailed records on customers, so that you can select customers with specific characteristics and then shape the advertising accordingly. Suppose you were instructed to develop a sophisticated mailing list for Know-wear, based on its present customer list of retail clothing stores and chains. What kind of information could be provided by the MIS that would be helpful for this purpose?

Case 14-2: DSS for Sales and Merchandising

In Chicago, retail giant Sears, Roebuck "is constantly searching to learn who its customers are, what they like, what they are like, what they are avoiding, how they are changing," reported *Time* magazine. "Through one of the largest systems of IBM computers outside the U.S. Government, the company keeps track of what is being bought and where." The head of the Merchandising Group each morning calls up on his terminal a display that can tell him the dollar volume of all Sears stores the previous day. "He can also look at sales figures by region, specific store or product line." In Rocky Mount, North Carolina, Boddie-Noell Enterprises, Inc., which operates 208 Hardee's fast-food restaurants, has an information system that is tied to each restaurant's own computer and each cash register. As an article in *Inc.* describes it, "Number of transactions, nonfood sales, net sales, paid insurance, total cash, promotion, eat in, eat out, drive through, cash short, tax—every action of the [restaurant] unit's life is chronicled in glowing green." In Visalia, California, considered a microcosm of the West Coast's "Middle America," scanners in a super-market checkout stand note every brand, package size, and price, and record the information in a computer file on a customer's family's buying habits. Detailed information on the family's purchases is sent to Chicago, where, along with information on other families, it is studied by marketing experts. (All families have volunteered for the project.) The data is used by many consumer product companies, including General Foods, General Mills, and Procter & Gamble, to measure how new-product sales compare to those of competitors and to analyze consumer buying trends.

Your assignment: These examples show how some of the biggest names in American business use computer-based information systems to make major decisions about merchandising. Let us suppose you are the owner of a muffler shop or of a fabric and yardage store and are considering expanding into a chain of stores. You thus have some sales and merchandising experience to go by, but you clearly have a number of strategic what-if and goal-seeking questions to ask. What kinds of questions would they be and what kinds of information variables might you have to manipulate?

Chapter 15

ARTIFICIAL INTELLIGENCE AND EXPERT SYSTEMS: WISDOM IN A MACHINE

In every corner of every large enterprise, there are people who have vital knowledge—machine operators, engineers, managers of all kinds who, because of their experience or their talent, are the most skillful at solving particular problems. What happens when these people are under the weather, ill, or temperamental or when they run off to take another job? Shouldn't their abilities be available on a wider basis?

Here we are entering into something wholly new—the matter of cloning a person's mind so that not just one but maybe one thousand people can have similar abilities. We are talking, in other words, about duplicating intelligence itself.

The human mind can perform marvelous feats of memory and decision making that scientists still don't quite know how to duplicate. But that doesn't mean they aren't trying—and trying very hard. The name given to the field of study concerned with creating machines that emulate human intellectual activity is *artificial intelligence,* or *AI.* A practical and exciting offshoot of this field—one you will find increasingly important in your career—is the development of *expert systems,* software that attempts to put the knowledge of experts to use in diagnosis and decision making.

CASE STUDY: FROM HUMAN EXPERTS TO EXPERT SYSTEM

How Accounting Firm Put Expertise into Its Computers

Some of the biggest hassles in developing "expert systems" go beyond microchips and software glitches—to the experts themselves. The systems, still in their infancy, seek to boil down years of acquired knowledge held by experts and cram it into a program that can guide even the raw beginner.

But experts often can't describe just how much they know, how they keep track of it or how they know when to use which data. "Actually capturing the expertise of these people—that's one of the biggest problems," says Prof. William F. Messier Jr., who works on an expert system in the accounting field at the University of Florida.

The Big Eight [one of the top eight] accounting firm Coopers & Lybrand resorted to unusual efforts to clear that hurdle. The firm's new ExperTAX program is now going out to its 96 U.S. offices for internal use and will play a role in planning under the [1986] tax law. It draws on 40 top partners to create what may be the most advanced system yet applied to accounting.

ExperTAX cost more than $1 million and over 7,000 hours to develop and works on an IBM Personal Computer AT. It uses a Q&A format to run a maze of 2,000 rules and outline a client's best tax options. The goal is to get senior expertise out to 10,000 clients served mostly by junior auditors. It replaces the old method of questionnaires up to 200 pages long, which senior tax experts had to wade through to pinpoint the best approach themselves.

When the project began, programmers found that simply interviewing tax partners to record their best tips didn't work. "These are, if you will, the senior prima donnas of knowledge in tax planning," says partner David Shpilberg, who oversaw the development effort.

The partners didn't know where to start and weren't comfortable with vague questions. They doubted their wisdom could be reduced to software and felt clients were too varied for advice to apply across the board. "The first sessions didn't take us anywhere. We'd go on for hours and not learn a thing," Mr. Shpilberg says. So he tried an experiment with two video cameras, a trio of tax experts, a rookie accountant—and a blue velvet curtain. The aim: to mimic a computer by having the trio act as the expert system, the curtain act as the computer screen and the rookie act as the user.

One end of a long table was covered with thousands of pages from a recent audit; at the other end was the tax trio. The curtain was hung across the middle. The rookie sat on the documents side and conducted an audit using only the reams of paper and words of advice that came through the "screen."

While cameras recorded their approach, the partners began guiding the rookie through the old questionnaire and asking things that, it turned out, had been buried deep in the form or weren't listed at all. These became some of the first queries used in ExperTAX. Was the client on a cash or accrual basis? In services or manufacturing? Did it want to mimimize or maximize taxes?

Six more sessions followed with experts in other areas of tax law, leading to a software prototype. Each partner then spent a total of 54 hours working with it, adding questions and new data. The result: an "intelligent" system that lists questions with multiple-choice answers, asks new ones based on the response and demands details if a user's answer is insufficient.

Cooper & Lybrand's Mr. Shpilberg says the system won't replace accountants; it aims at enhancing the advice people provide rather than merely automating a process. "Twenty years from now our computers will be auditing our clients' computers. Unless we have more creative ability to enhance decision-making, our service runs the risk of just becoming a straight commodity," he says.

ARTIFICIAL

INTELLIGENCE

WHAT IT IS,

WHAT IT ISN'T

One of the greatest problems in artificial intelligence is defining "intelligence." If intelligence is the ability to reason—to adapt, solve structured problems, find answers to mathematical equations—then computers may be considered intelligent. But this intelligence refers to the computer's *processing* capability—which is certainly not the same as human intelligence.

Silicon Life Versus Carbon Life

Artificial intelligence may be thought of as "silicon life," whereas human intelligence may be thought of as "carbon life." The differences, say writers Richard Morley and William Taylor, writing in *Digital Design,* are as follows:

> Humans have the ability to acquire large amounts of information through sensors. Brains come equipped with apparently infinite memory. Humans seldom need to search through that memory because memories are just there when needed. However, while the memory capacity is there, the compute power is not. Determining the cube root of 351 without a calculator might take a little time. Finding the cube root of 27 is much simpler because the answer, 3, is more easily remembered. Instead of compute power, humans have memory and reasoning ability, which are much more useful in real life.

For our purposes, **artificial intelligence** is the expansion of the capabilities of computers to include the ability to reason, to learn, to strive for self-improvement, and to simulate human sensory capabilities. People in the field of artificial intelligence—computer scientists, linguists, and psychologists all working together—examine the ways a computer can solve unstructured problems, as people do, and attempt to develop computers that can think, hear, talk, move, even feel. Their goal in developing AI is not to replace people but to make people more productive

Software, Hardware, or Firmware?

The CEO at Know-wear has begun hearing about AI and expert systems and asks you to look into it. Like most newcomers to the subject, you may wonder whether AI is hardware or software. Actually, it is a bit of both—with a difference. Traditional computers emphasize numbers and have been designed to maximize processing efficiency rather than memory capabilities—AI computers have been designed to do the reverse: have *more memory* and *less processing*

COMPARISON OF COMPUTING POWER

Pocket calculator	-10^3
Slug	-10^6
Bee	-10^9
Today's computers	-10^9
Today's gap	
Proposed computers	-10^{11}
Human vision	-10^{12}
Human/chimps	-10^{13}
Sperm whale	-10^{14}

This compute power comparison indicates relative compute power. The measurement is very rough but, in general, the more memory the better and the faster the better. A mosquito or bee seems to process about the same amount of information as today's large-scale computers. Before hardware technology approaches human/chimp technology in compute power, it must improve by a factor of 10^4. While the hardware may be available by the year 2000, the software for emulating intelligence may not. The comparison between computer technology and biological technology should not be taken too literally. Bees are not computers. They do not work in the same way and comparing them may be invalid.

—Richard E. Morley and William A. Taylor, *Digital Design*

power. Frequently, these machines are called **LISP machines** because, as we discuss later in the chapter, LISP is the programming language often used in artificial intelligence applications. Like traditional computers, LISP machines have on-off, one-zero logic, but they have additional *firmware*—chips with read-only memories—specially designed to support AI applications.

AI is also a type of programming—thus it is also a software approach to problems. However, AI programming is much more complex than traditional programming, which concentrates on numeric information. AI knowledge contains nonnumeric information, such as A = SD or (as Morley and Taylor put it), "Plant corn when oak leaves are the size of mouse ears." Thus, AI deals with symbols and facts and implements complex algorithms.

Now that we have explained what AI is not, let us consider what it is—the three major divisions.

The Three Divisions of AI

Artificial intelligence includes three distinct but related areas:

▶ Natural language processing
▶ Robotics
▶ Expert systems

Natural Language Processing What is the communications medium that is exclusive to people—and to people everywhere in the world? We call it "natural language." For years, linguists have been working to understand this language—originally trying to teach it to chimpanzees, first through the use of hand signals (the sign language used for deaf people), then through experiments in communicating with computers. **Natural language processing** is concerned with programs that allow the computer to read, speak, or understand languages as people use them every day.

The major problem with natural language processing is that the words we use have many different meanings. By the 1960s, only 80% accuracy in natural language processing had been achieved. Since then, things have improved markedly. You can appreciate how far we have come if you've ever seen that television commercial of a woman dictating something like, "Ms. Wright was right in turning to the right to write . . . ." Behind her an IBM Personal Computer receiving the dictation is writing out the spoken words correctly.

Robotics In Chapter 6, we described *robotics* as the study of the design, construction, and use of robots. Within the scope of AI, robotics is principally concerned with devising the software that allows robots to have perception systems for vision, speech, and touch. Already there are "no-hands" assembly lines, such as the one

FLASHBACK

AI from A to Z: A Modern History

The beginnings of artificial intelligence and computer science are essentially the same: Both began near the end of World War II as part of the Allied war effort. Both the British and the Americans worked on the problems simultaneously, trying to develop electronic machines that could be guided by a stored program to carry out complex numerical computations, such as might be required to compute weapons projectories.

The British research was led by Alan Turing, who argued that a *general-purpose* computing machine, not just a numbers processor, could have many different and far-reaching uses. As a result of his prewar formal logic research, he believed that the instructions to the machine should be based on what are known as *logical operators*, such as AND, OR, and NOT. His idea was for a machine that could handle both mathematical calculations and symbolic material—instructions in ordinary everyday language.

The U.S. contingent had a more practical purpose, at least for the times. The matter of symbolic language was too difficult to be handled under the circumstances, they felt, and instead they focused on developing electronic machines for handling only numeric instructions based on arithmetic operators, such as $+$, $-$, and $>$. If this approach was more limiting than Turing's, it was also more do-able.

The British soon reached the same pragmatic conclusion, and the result was some very fast processors—actually calculators—of numerical data. Researchers on subsequent machines focused more on the speed of calculations than on internal storage capability (primary storage). Thus, from this fork in the road, computers have evolved that have been long on processing efficiency and short on memory.

Alan Turing

Since the end of the war, research into artificial intelligence has gone through three periods of development, which some observers classify as the Classical Period, the Romantic Period, and the Modern Period.

The Classical Period: 1940s to 1960s

During this period, the focus was on truly science fiction–type research: how to make machine intelligence that was equal to, or even better than, human intelligence. Researchers were taking a wide-ranging perspective, asking questions such as: How can we create general problem-solving procedures? How can we develop inference capabilities? Using chess, checkers, and puzzles, the researchers explored such techniques as:

▶ *Exhaustive search*, in which programs calculated and looked at every possible outcome at any point in time

▶ *Guided evaluation*, in which the program selected paths to search first that appeared most promising

The problem with these lines of inquiry was that the number of alternatives to search was so great that practical problems were unsolvable. Researchers also worked on theorem proving—developing techniques that would allow generalizations or conclusions about some activity based on what was known—but here, too, there was but limited success. The main problem was simple: More computing power was required.

During this period, AI researchers migrated from a number of academic disciplines: computer science, of course, but also psychology and linguistics. Researchers from these areas continued to migrate to AI through the following phases as well, although gradually their work became more specialized.

The Romantic Period: 1960s to 1970s

The overriding objective of this period was to create a machine that would *understand*. The focus, therefore, became natural language processing, computer vision, and robotics. Instead of addressing general problem-solving techniques, researchers concentrated on *knowledge representation*—how to encode or represent information in a way that the machine could understand. This proved to be a very difficult objective.

If the work in this period was still the stuff of science fiction, it was, nevertheless, more practical than before, for people were beginning to realize that the key element to AI lay in knowledge—and specific rather than global knowledge. Although few practical successes had occurred, by the end of the 1970s several large corporations in the United States had formed AI research teams.

The aims of the Romantic Period were indeed romantic, for the objective of allowing computers to "understand" knowledge on a global scale was not reached. Despite all the basic accomplishments in knowledge representation, natural language processing, computer vision, and robotics, the machines still could not recognize analogies and learn from experience—which remains the sticking point today.

The Modern Period: 1970s to the Present

As researchers turned from general problem solving to more specific and pragmatic applications, they also began a period of self-evaluation and self-criticism. Although corporations continued to form AI groups, researchers began to realize that their ability to develop workable systems and practical results was too slow and too costly. Many such groups were dissolved, although some have since been re-formed.

Knowledge representation is still recognized as an essential component of all AI; however, researchers now focus more on specific and deep knowledge than on generalized knowledge. The objectives have moved away from mirroring humans to helping humans. Most particularly, AI has evolved in the direction of expert systems, at least in commercial ventures, a direction that has been faulted because too many unsubstantiated claims have been made.

Figure 15-1. No hands. Multiple-exposure photography captures the motion of an advanced IBM robotic system during a printer component assembly operation at IBM's Austin, Texas, factory. IBM uses a variety of robotic systems throughout the company to perform a variety of manufacturing tasks.

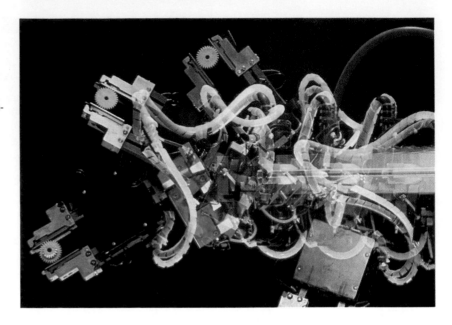

CREATING A ROBOT THAT CAN SEE WITH HUMAN PRECISION

Few people realize how remarkable it is that our eyes adapt swiftly from, say, a darkened movie house to going out into bright sunlight. The difference in light can change by a factor of a million, and the coloring of the light is also different.

No camera ever made can adjust automatically to the changing color of the ambient light. That fact is where much of the research converges among biologists, psychologists, and physicists. First we want to find out more fully how the human eye works, then we want to see if we can adapt the principles to robots.

—Stanford University psychology researcher Brian Wandell

built by IBM to assemble its PC Convertible computer (see Figure 15-1), in which industrial robots snap memory boards into place. In plants that assemble circuit boards, vision systems check to see that all parts fit precisely.

In these instances, however, viewing conditions, lighting, and other matters are fixed. Researchers are working on more complicated systems in the hope of creating robots that can ''see'' and find their way around factories without having to run on tracks.

Expert Systems   As we mentioned, **expert systems** consist of computer-based information systems that have been developed by processing and distilling the knowledge of an expert or many experts in a particular field. The expert systems themselves then become expert consultants to users. However, such systems can apply the experience without bias, telling us on demand what assumptions are being made and what their line of reasoning is—and they can do so without becoming tired and cranky and without trying to bluff us with their opinions; indeed, they can tell us the limit of their knowledge and estimate the uncertainty of their conclusions.

Where do expert systems fit into the computer-based information systems—TPIS, MIS, and DSS—that we described in the last two chapters? Whereas those are *general* information systems, expert systems are specific *approaches* or tools for solving specific problems, such as loan approval.

Because of the importance that expert systems are beginning to take on in business and the professions, it is worth taking a deeper look at this discipline. We shall do so in the next three sections.

EXPERT SYSTEMS

THE VARIETIES

OF KNOWLEDGE

What are the practical things that expert systems can do? Some examples, reported by William Bulkeley in the *Wall Street Journal* (December 5, 1986):

▶ One program developed for IBM mainframe data bases is written in COBOL, the widely used business language, which makes it easier to "embed" expertise in existing commercial programs. For example, because humans have trouble keeping track of constant price changes, "a computerized pricing expert could alert an order clerk about featured deals or say when a customer is nearing eligibility for volume discounts."

▶ The Balsams Resort in the White Mountains of New Hampshire installed an expert system that improves reservation clerks' performance in giving customers the types of rooms they want, avoiding the one-night gaps common at resorts and thereby increasing occupancy by six to 10 rooms a night.

▶ A bookstore customer can use a touch-screen to tell the system the type of book he or she wants, then the screen displays authors' names and asks the customer to touch the names he or she likes. Based on the response, the system suggests some other titles by other writers.

To fully understand this area, consider the classic definition by Stanford University's Edward Feigenbaum, a leading researcher in expert systems. An *expert system*, he says, may be defined as

> an intelligent computer program that uses knowledge and inference procedures to solve problems that are difficult enough to require significant human expertise for their solution. Knowledge necessary to perform at such a level, plus the inference procedures used, can be thought of as a model of the expertise of the best practitioners of the field.
>
> The knowledge of an expert system consists of facts and heuristics. The "facts" constitute a body of information that is widely shared, publicly available, and generally agreed upon by experts in a field. The "heuristics" are mostly private, little-discussed rules of good judgment (rules of plausible reasoning, rules of good guessing) that characterize expert-level decision making in the field. The performance level of an expert system is primarily a function of the size and the quality of a knowledge base it possesses.

An expert system has three parts:

▶ People
▶ Subsystems
▶ Major components

Examples of Various Expert Systems

For Computer Science Graduate Students

*G*CA helps graduate students plan their computer science curriculum. The system gathers information about a student's academic history and interest and then acts as a faculty adviser by suggesting a schedule of courses for the student. GCA's expertise includes departmental and university regulations regarding graduate degree programs, course descriptions, and sequences of courses frequently taken by computer science students. The knowledge in GCA is organized as four interacting subsystems under the direction of a manager program. These subsystems determine 1) the number of courses the student should take, 2) the courses the student is permitted to take, 3) the best courses to take, and 4) the best schedule for the student.

For Nontechnical Users of Information on Data Bases

IR-NLI provides nontechnical users with a natural language interface to the information retrieval services offered by on-line data bases. The system acts as a front end to several available data bases and decides which will be the most appropriate for an-

swering the user's requests. IR-NLI combines the expertise of a professional intermediary for on-line searching with the capability for understanding natural language and carrying out a dialogue with the user.

For Investment Portfolio Managers

FOLIO helps portfolio managers determine client investment goals and select portfolios that best meet those goals. The system determines the client's need during an interview and then recommends percentages of each fund that provide an optimum fit to the client's goals. FOLIO recognizes a small number of classes of securities (e.g., dividend-oriented, lower-risk stocks and commodity-sensitive, higher-risk stocks) and maintains aggregate knowledge about the properties (e.g., rate of return) of the securities in each class.

For Tax Lawyers

TAXMAN assists in the investigation of legal reasoning and legal argumentation using the domain of corporate law. The system provides a framework for rep-

The People Involved

The people involved in expert systems are of three kinds: so-called knowledge engineers, subject-area experts, and users.

Knowledge Engineers Those who actually build expert systems are called **knowledge engineers** and the work they do is called **knowledge engineering.** A knowledge engineer is more than a systems analyst. He or she is a computer specialist, often an outside consultant, and the person who concentrates on duplicating in an information system the behavior of a specific expert—whether geologist, physician, or locomotive mechanic—in order to solve a narrowly defined problem. The job of the knowledge engineer is to "debrief" or extensively interview a recognized expert or experts and codify that ex-

resenting legal concepts and a transformation methodology for recognizing the relationships among those concepts. Transformations from the case under scrutiny to related cases create a basis for analyzing the legal reasoning and argumentation.

For Computer Salespeople

XSEL helps a salesperson select components for a [DEC] VAX 11/780 computer system and assists in designing a floor layout for them. XSEL selects a central processing unit, primary memory, software, and peripheral devices, such as terminals and disk drives, and then passes it to XCON [another expert system] to be expanded and configured. XSEL contains domain knowledge about the relations between components and the various applications a customer might have about how to lead a user through a selection process.

For Geologists

PROSPECTOR acts as a consultant to aid exploration geologists in their search for ore deposits. Given field data about a geological region it estimates the likelihood of finding particular types of mineral deposits there. The system can assess the potential for finding a variety of deposits, including massive sulfide, carbonate lead/zinc, porphyry copper, nickel sulfide, standstone uranium, and porphyry molybdenum deposits. Its expertise is based on 1) geological rules which form models of ore deposits, and 2) a taxonomy of rocks and minerals.

For Telephone Switching Engineers

COMPASS analyzes telephone switching systems maintenance messages for GTE's No. 2 EAX Switch and suggests maintenance actions to perform. The system examines maintenance messages describing error situations that occurred during the telephone call-processing operation of the switch. It then identifies groups of messages likely caused by a common fault, determines the possible specific faults in the switch, and suggests maintenance actions to verify and remedy the faults. The system embodies the expertise of a top switch expert and integrates knowledge about individual switch structure, switch faults, maintenance messages, and possible maintenance actions.

—Donald A. Waterman, *A Guide to Expert Systems*

pert's knowledge into rules, which are represented symbolically and then transferred to a computer program—the expert system—that mimics the expert's problem-solving strategies.

Subject-Area Experts The experts are the people who have specialized knowledge—perhaps based in part on education, but often based on years of experience, the kind that, for a senior person, can translate into good intuitions and hunches about how to solve a problem. One of the first systems, for instance, used the advice of an old-timer at General Electric to help test for malfunctions in diesel locomotives.

Users The users are, of course, the people who will actually use the expert system to help them with their decision making. Users may be

EXPERT SYSTEMS AND MICROCOMPUTERS

In the spring of 1987, a new magazine was launched entitled *PC AI: The Artificial Intelligence Journal for Personal Computing*. Does this mean that AI programs, including expert systems and natural languages, have moved from large computer systems to relatively small, desktop computers? The answer is: We are proceeding rapidly in that direction.

At present, two kinds of expert system products are available for microcomputers:

▶ Expert system application packages
▶ Software tools for developing expert systems

The *application packages* are a small but growing part of the market. ELIZA, for instance, is a classic program developed by Joseph Weizenbaum of MIT back in 1964. It fools people into thinking a computer acts out the part of a psychologist. Another package, available from DecisionWare, is RightWriter, which helps writers who have created their documents with a standard word processor then analyze the results for grammar, punctuation, consistency, style, and usage. RightWriter marks errors in the document and inserts comments directly into the text.

More plentiful for microcomputers at this time are *development tools* for expert systems. Such tools are languages such as LISP, PROLOG, Smalltalk, and OPS, or what are known as expert system *shells*— special kinds of software that allow one to custom-tailor particular kinds of expert systems, using particular IF-THEN rules. Insight I, introduced in 1984, was one of the first expert system shells developed for microcomputers. Another shell is EXSYS, which can be used to develop knowledge bases for expert systems.

experts themselves, but in theory, at least, anyone can use an expert system—once such systems become popular. The earliest are apt to be in accounting and manufacturing, but more will become available.

The Subsystems

The process of, on the one hand, extracting knowledge from an expert and, on the other hand, imparting that knowledge to a user is helped along by two supporting computerized subsystems.

The **knowledge acquisition subsystem** consists of programs that help the knowledge engineer and the expert define, specify, and codify the expert's problem-solving ability. The subsystem also allows the two to more easily update and insert new knowledge into the system and to delete outdated and incorrect knowledge.

The **explanation subsystem** enables users to query the expert system as to why it has chosen to ask certain questions or how it has reached certain conclusions.

Both these systems should be expressed in natural language, so that people can communicate with the expert system in the most natural and comfortable way.

Figure 15-2. How an expert system works. The three principal components are the knowledge base, the inference engine, and the working memory.

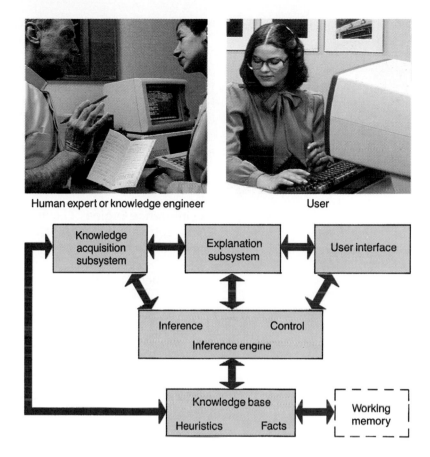

The Major Components

The three major components of an expert system are:

▶ The knowledge base
▶ The inference engine
▶ Working memory

These are shown in Figure 15-2.

The Knowledge Base   The knowledge base, of course, is the heart of the system, and its creation is the main enterprise of the knowledge engineer. The **knowledge base** is the translation of knowledge from human experts into rules and strategies. As we quoted from Feigenbaum, such knowledge is of two types:

▶ **Facts:** Also known as "deep knowledge," **facts** are based on generalized learning from school and books that is well known and widely accepted by experts in a field.

▶ **Heuristics:** Known as "surface knowledge," **heuristics** consist of "rules of thumb," private knowledge attained through experience.

Unlike a data base, which consists of static relationships between fields, records, and files, a knowledge base is dynamic and ever-changing, as reflects the advice of human experts.

The knowledge engineer encodes facts and relationships, using a variety of approaches. By far the most widely used approach is the use of **rules,** which express knowledge in an IF-THEN format—for example, "IF the distance is over five miles, THEN drive your car."

The Inference Engine   The **inference engine,** which is actually a part of the software, has two primary tasks—inference and control, as shown in Figure 15-2.

▶ **Inference:** Here the inference engine employs reasoning to examine existing facts and rules, adds new facts if it finds them consistent with present information and rules, and draws conclusions.

▶ **Control:** This is the process of controlling the search of the knowledge base—a time-consuming process if the knowledge base is large and complex.

Working Memory   The **working memory** refers to the size of the memory in the hardware. In large, complex knowledge bases, a large internal memory—primary storage as opposed to secondary storage—is essential if a search of the knowledge base is to be done in a timely way.

Knowledge-Based Systems versus Expert Systems

Although the terms are frequently used interchangeably, there is a growing trend toward giving *knowledge-based systems* and *expert systems* different definitions. The short distinction is that knowledge-based systems contain simply a collection of factual information, whereas an expert system contains the facts *and* the expert's problem-solving techniques; however, let us elaborate on this.

Knowledge-based systems are generally smaller than expert systems. They are not really based on what you might consider to be the knowledge of an expert. Their knowledge consists of widely accepted rules and facts—which makes such systems helpful for defining and outlining structured procedural activities. An example of a knowledge-based system might be one that allows bank tellers to screen and approve certain types of car loans. Certainly such a system extends the traditional job of teller, but the knowledge that goes into such a system is hardly based on someone's deep-seated experience and expertise; rather it is based on what someone had learned over a few months of being trained in this area.

Expert systems, by contrast, are generally larger and they are modeled on true human expertise. Both deep and surface knowledge are contained within the knowledge base, and heuristics are extensively used. Finally, expert systems are used by experts themselves—to confirm their own judgments. An example of an expert system is one called AUDITOR, which "helps a professional auditor evaluate a client's potential for defaulting on a loan. The system uses information about the client's payment history, economic status, credit standing, and other knowledge to determine whether money should be held in reserve to cover a client's loan default."

APPLYING

EXPERT SYSTEMS

Why do you suppose so many people, including those at Knowwear, are excited about the concept of expert systems?

Imagine having your own personal consultant—based on your favorite and most knowledgeable university professor—available anytime you wanted. Or imagine being a military jet pilot—and having an AI copilot based on the most decorated aviator. Your advisor would never tire of answering your questions, become indignant at your tone, or hold you accountable in any way.

Categories of Expert System Applications

Expert systems may be applied to a wide variety of problems—perhaps an infinite variety. However, a good way to understand the usefulness of such systems is to look at the ten categories of expert system applications shown in Table 15-1. Let us describe these.

Interpretation Consider a medical warning system that monitors a patient's critical signs, such as blood pressure. The data coming into such a system is called **sensor data**—data that comes from the system itself rather than from human interaction. Common forms of sensor data are X ray, audible sounds, and vision. Expert systems that use sensor data for input fall into the *interpretation* category. If any one measurement (such as blood pressure) or combination of measurements reaches a certain critical level, then the expert system will take automatic action or will send an alarm signal to a human expert (such as a nurse). The expert system interprets the data and makes inferences based on that data.

Prediction The national weather service forecasts—predicts—the weather based on data about atmospheric conditions. This is an example of the *prediction* kind of expert system, which makes predictions based on given situations or data. Often, the expert system used

Table 15-1. Generic Categories of Expert System Applications

Category	Problem Addressed
Interpretation	Inferring situation descriptions from sensor data
Prediction	Inferring likely consequences of given situations
Diagnosis	Inferring system malfunctions from observables
Design	Configuring objects under constraints
Planning	Designing actions
Monitoring	Comparing observations to expected outcomes
Debugging	Prescribing remedies for malfunctions
Repair	Executing plans to administer prescribed remedies
Instruction	Diagnosing, debugging, and repairing student behavior
Control	Governing overall system behavior

Source: Donald A. Waterman, *A Guide to Expert Systems* (Reading, Mass.: Addison-Wesley, 1986), p. 33. Adapted from *Building Expert Systems*.

for prediction interacts with simulation models to help the latter infer likely outcomes given certain conditions. So far, few prediction systems have been developed. Examples of those that have are systems that estimate global oil demand based on current world political and geographical conditions or those of national intelligence services that predict where armed conflict will next occur.

Diagnosis   Perhaps the best-known example of a diagnosis expert system is the MYCIN system for diagnosing bacterial infections in hospital patients (see Figure 15-3). The *diagnosis* expert system uses a variety of inputs such as situation descriptions, behavior characteristics, or knowledge about operations in order to diagnose—infer or locate—certain problems. Common areas of application include not only medicine but also engineering and computer systems.

Design   *Design* expert systems, which are used in microelectronics, create or configure a system to meet certain criteria, based on certain performance objectives. One well-known such system is Digital Equipment Corporation's XCON, used to configure the company's VAX computer systems. Many of Digital Equipment Corporation's customers have unique requirements, and this expert system allows the company to quickly and efficiently configure customized VAX systems for them.

Planning   Similar in objective to a design system, *planning* systems specify an entire course of action based on target objectives and time requirements. Widely used in the military (as in air strike plans to meet specified objectives over several days' time), as well as in chemistry and electronics, the planning expert system also could be made to apply in business. For example, at Know-wear, it might be developed in planning the introduction of a new product, such as a line of raincoats, to achieve a certain percentage of market share over a three-year period.

Monitoring An example of a monitoring system is the expert system called REACTOR, which monitors instrument readings in a nuclear reactor, looking for signs of an accident. A *monitoring* system typically deals with time; it accepts physical measurements— temperature, voltage, pressure, and the like—and compares them to previously defined values. If the data reaches a certain value, the system may automatically take corrective action (such as shut down parts of a nuclear reactor).

Debugging *Debugging* expert systems find problems or malfunctions and suggest remedies. Examples are systems that choose a repair procedure to fix a fault in a diesel locomotive and those that tune a computer system to correct a performance problem.

Repair Very few repair expert systems actually exist. Unlike diagnosis, planning, or debugging systems, *repair* systems actually physically repair equipment, such as a mass spectrometer or other electrical equipment. In the future, a robot may be used to perform the actual repairs.

Instruction Teaching electronics students to troubleshoot electrical circuits or explaining to medical students how to select antimicrobial therapy are two examples of instruction systems. *Instruction* systems develop a model of what the student knows and then correct deficiencies in the model. Their objective is to teach students specialized skills by extending their current ones. This kind of expert system has been receiving more and more attention recently.

Control Controlling the treatment of patients in a hospital's intensive care unit or managing the manufacturing and distribution of computer systems are two examples of the control category of expert system. The *control* system combines other categories—indeed, any of the foregoing nine categories—into a broader kind of expert system.

BUILDING EXPERT
SYSTEMS

What are the steps in developing an expert system? Without going into great detail, the areas to consider are:

▶ AI programming languages
▶ Knowledge engineering tools

Figure 15-3. **MYCIN.** One of the first expert systems, MYCIN was developed to aid physicians during the crucial 24–48 hours when much decision making about patients is imprecise because not all the relevant information is in hand. The program's record for correct diagnoses and treatments for meningitis and bacteremia has equaled the performance of human experts. The physician holds an interactive dialogue with MYCIN about a particular patient. Questions from MYCIN are preceded by *1)*, *2)*, and so on; the answers keyed in by the physician are preceded by **. If the user types *WHY*, a program is triggered that leads the physician through the line of reasoning that produced MYCIN's diagnosis.

```
         NAME                    AGE         SEX          RACE
1) **    JOHN DOE                34          MALE            CAUCASIAN

2) ARE THERE ANY POSITIVE CULTURES OBTAINED FROM JOHN DOE?
** NO

3) ARE THERE ANY PENDING CULTURES OF JOHN DOE?
** YES

        SITE          DATE            STAIN         :METHOD OF
                      COLLECTED       EXAMINED?     :COLLECTION
                                                    :URINE, SPUTUM ONLY]

    4) **CSF          30 JAN 77       YES
            STAIN OF SMEAR MORPH
            (TYPE NONE IF NO ORGANISM WAS SEEN ON THE SMEAR)
        5) ** NONE
        [NO OTHER PENDING CULTURES.]

[CONSIDERING ORGANISMS (OTHER THAN THOSE ISOLATED FROM CULTURES) WHICH MIGHT BE
PRESENT. . .]

13) HAS JOHN DOE RECENTLY HAD SYMPTOMS OF PERSISTENT HEADACHE OR OTHER ABNORMAL
NEUROLOGIC SYMPTOMS (DIZZINESS, LETHARGY, ETC.)?
**YES

(14) HAS JOHN DOE RECENTLY HAD OBJECTIVE EVIDENCE OF ABNORMAL NEUROLOGIC SIGNS
    (NUCHAL RIGIDITY, COMA, SEIZURES, ETC.) DOCUMENTED BY PHYSICIAN,
    OBSERVATION, OR EXAMINATION?
**YES

THE CSF CULTURES WILL BE CONSIDERED TO BE ASSOCIATED WITH MENINGITIS
(15) PLEASE GIVE THE DATE ON WHICH CLINICAL EVIDENCE (SYMPTOMS, SIGNS, OR
    LABORATORY TESTS) OF MENINGITIS FIRST APPEARED.

PLEASE ENTER CSF FINDINGS IN THE FOLLOWING TABLE.

        CSF           PERCENT     PROTEIN     CSF         PERIPHERAL
        WBC           PMM                     GLUCOSE     GLUCOSE
(23) **100            99          280         5           UNKNOWN

(34) IS MENINGITIS A HOSPITAL-ACQUIRED INFECTION?
**WHY?
```

[2.0] THIS WILL AID IN DETERMINING THE ORGANISMS (OTHER THAN THOSE SEEN ON CULTURES
       OR SMEARS) WHICH MIGHT BE CAUSING THE INFECTION. IT HAS ALREADY BEEN
       ESTABLISHED THAT
       [2.1] THE INFECTION WHICH REQUIRES THERAPY IS MENINGITIS, AND
       [2.2] ORGANISMS WERE NOT SEEN ON THE STAIN OF THE PENDING CSF CULTURE, AND
       [2.3] THE TYPE OF THE INFECTION IS BACTERIAL, AND
       [2.4] NEUROSURGERY IS NOT ONE OF THE RELEVANT ITEMS FROM THE HISTORY OF
              JOHN DOE, AND
       [2.5] THE AGE OF JOHN DOE IS GREATER THAN 10 DAYS
       THEREFORE, IF
       [2.6] THE INFECTION WAS ACQUIRED WHILE THE PATIENT WAS HOSPITALIZED THEN
              THERE IS EVIDENCE THAT THE ORGANISMS (OTHER THAN THOSE SEEN ON
              CULTURES OR SMEARS) WHICH MIGHT BE CAUSING THE INFECTION ARE E. COLI
              (75) STAPHYLOCOCCUS-COAG-POS (3) PSEUDOMONAS-AERUGINOSA (3)
              KLEBSIELLA PNEUMONIAE (5)

(BACK TO QUESTION 34...)
** YES

       MY THERAPY RECOMMENDATIONS WILL BE DESIGNED TO TREAT FOR ORGANISMS THAT
EITHER ARE VERY LIKELY OR, ALTHOUGH LESS LIKELY, WOULD HAVE A SIGNIFICANT EFFECT ON
THERAPY SELECTION IF THEY WERE PRESENT. IT IS IMPORTANT TO COVER FOR THE FOLLOWING
PROBABLE INFECTION(S) AND ASSOCIATED ORGANISM(S).

INFECTION-1 IS MENINGITIS

  + <ITEM-1> E. COLI (FROM CLINICAL EVIDENCE ONLY)
  + <ITEM-2> PSEUDOMONAS-AERUGINOSA (FROM CLINICAL EVIDENCE ONLY)
  + <ITEM-3> KLEBSIELLA-PNEUMONIAE (FROM CLINICAL EVIDENCE ONLY)
  + <ITEM-4> DIPLOCOCCUS-PNEUMONIAE (FROM CLINICAL EVIDENCE ONLY)

40) DOES JOHN DOE HAVE A CLINICALLY SIGNIFICANT ALLERGIC REACTION TO ANY
ANTIMICROBIAL AGENT?
** NO
[CONSIDERING AMPICILLIN-AND-GENTAMICIN FOR USE AGAINST INFECTION-1...]
41) DO YOU HAVE REASON TO SUSPECT THAT JOHN DOE MAY HAVE IMPAIRED RENAL FUNCTION?
** NO

42) JOHN DOE'S WEIGHT IN KILOGRAMS (OR <NUMBER> POUNDS)
** 70
[REC-1] MY PREFERRED THERAPY RECOMMENDATION IS AS FOLLOWS:
    IN ORDER TO COVER FOR ITEMS <1 2 3 4 >
          GIVE THE FOLLOWING IN COMBINATION:
          (1) AMPICILLIN
          DOSE: 3.5 G (28.0 ML) Q4H IV [CALCULATED ON BASIS OF 50 MG/KG]

          (2) GENTAMICIN
          DOSE: 119 MG (3.0 ML, 80 MG/2 ML AMPULE) Q8H IV (CALCULATED OF BASIS OF 1.7
          MG/KG) PLUS CONSIDER GIVING 5 MG Q24H INTRATHECAL
          COMMENTS: MONITOR SERUM CONCENTRATIONS

          SINCE HIGH CONCENTRATIONS OF PENICILLINS CAN INACTIVATE AMINOGLYCOSIDES, DO
          NOT MIX THESE TWO ANTIBIOTICS IN THE SAME IV BOTTLE.

AI Programming Languages

As we saw earlier in the book, programming languages have been devised for specific needs, and all have their advantages and limitations. So also with the languages developed for artificial intelligence. By far the most popular are LISP, used extensively in the United States, and PROLOG, the standard in Europe and Japan.

LISP   Short for *LISt* Processor, **LISP** is the oldest and still regarded as the most widely used symbolic language in the United States. LISP was developed in the 1950s at about the same time that FORTRAN was developed, but because it required such enormous memory capacity—on the order of 1 million bytes of internal storage—it fell behind FORTRAN in favor because the technology simply was not available in those early days to produce computers with that much memory at reasonable costs. Still, LISP is more than just a programming language; it is an entire programming environment, a set of extensive functions that greatly facilitates the development of expert system programs—especially by providing support for the AI problem-solving techniques just described.

PROLOG   Based on work done in Edinburgh in the 1970s and implemented in France in 1977, **PROLOG**—short for *PRO*gramming language for *LOG*ic—is the AI language of Europe and also the language of choice for Japan's so-called fifth-generation computers. PROLOG is a higher-level language than LISP, and some computer scientists claim that PROLOG in fact is based on LISP. Both LISP and PROLOG have produced descendants—indeed, entire families, including such languages as POPLOG, INTERLISP, and POP.

Knowledge Engineering Tools

LISP and PROLOG are used to develop particular expert systems and knowledge-based systems, each with its own inference engine, knowledge base, and other components. Once this initial hard work has been done, however, some shortcuts can be taken. That is, after an expert system (such as MYCIN) has been developed, enterprising types may see a similar problem that could be solved using similar inference and components—but without the same knowledge base. They will therefore remove the knowledge base and market the remaining **shell**—the expert system skeleton—to be applied to other problems. An example is **EMYCIN,** the first knowledge engineering tool, which was derived from MYCIN. An advantage of many shell systems is that they run on microcomputers, which makes training of ordinary users much more feasible.

Knowledge engineering tools help us develop expert systems and knowledge-based systems more rapidly because they incorporate particular aspects of knowledge engineering—specifically

---

THE SHELL GAME: CHEAPER WAY TO EXPERT SYSTEMS

Most [companies] are buying the prefabricated expert system skeletons, or shells, being offered by a bevy of new, small high-tech firms. Using a shell, a company can build a simple but useful expert system, including the cost of training a programmer, for less than $100,000. Since shell systems run on personal computers, the entry price on them is low, and the market is soaring. . . .

Recognizing the market potential of low-cost shells, many expert system suppliers have been turning away from the custom-made approach. . . .

One major corporate user of shells is du Pont, which estimates that it has 150 expert systems in place performing such tasks as selecting the right kind of rubber for customers, diagnosing equipment failures and scheduling machines on the factory floor. To make the use of the technology as cost-effective as possible, the company's strategy has been to buy easy-to-use shells and train its own nontechnical employees to produce expert systems from them.

—Fred V. Guteri, *Dun's Business Month*

strategies for representation, inference, and control, as well as problem-solving techniques. Nowadays, when such new systems are developed, only very highly trained programmers start with LISP, PROLOG, or similar sophisticated AI languages; most developers start with knowledge engineering tools, which, with their built-in problem-solving techniques, are much easier for people to use, although less flexible than AI languages.

Besides EMYCIN, among the knowledge engineering tools that have been developed are:

▶ **TIMM.** An abbreviation for *The Intelligent Machine Model*, **TIMM** was also introduced in 1983. It is an example-oriented knowledge acquisition system, focusing on cases that represent good examples according to the human expert.

▶ **M.1.** Introduced in 1984 and available for use on the IBM Personal Computer, **M.1** is intended for consultative types of problems.

▶ **S.1.** Also introduced in 1984, **S.1** is designed to solve diagnosis and prescription problems.

Some knowledge engineering tools are only for mainframes and minicomputers, but some are also useful on microcomputers.

It should be clear that building an expert system is not something you can do without a lot of help. Just as a systems analyst has been helpful to you at Know-wear in the past, to build an expert system you would need the involvement of a knowledge engineer and some people in the apparel industry who are recognized experts in whatever area you might want to establish an expert system for. Let us see how to proceed.

THE STEPS IN
DEVELOPING AN
EXPERT SYSTEM

Devising an expert system requires the help of experts, but developing a small—or knowledge-based—system can be accomplished by a manager rather than a knowledge engineer. Indeed, it is much like the task of doing systems analysis and design without the help of a systems analyst, as we described earlier in the book. This means that developing a knowledge-based system can be applied to isolated, small situations handled by end-users—people like you.

However, large systems that are needed for large results require a team of knowledge engineers and generally a year or more to develop. As Figure 15-4 shows, the development consists of six phases:

1. Select the appropriate problem
2. Develop a prototype system
3. Develop a complete system
4. Evaluate the system

Figure 15-4. How an expert system is developed.

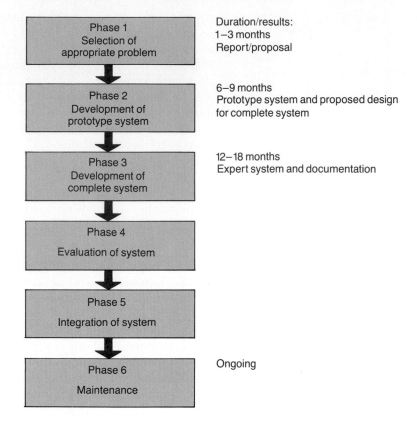

5. Integrate the system
6. Maintain the system

1. Select the Appropriate Problem

If you are a manager developing your own knowledge-based system, you don't want to waste your time, so selecting the right problem is important. If you are a top manager trying to determine whether to develop an expert system, this first phase is also critical because undertakings like this are quite expensive. The economic justification for automating a particular kind of expertise must be carefully considered; there must be no false starts, no solving of the wrong problem, no concentrating on problems for which an expert system does not give enough payback. In this phase you need to do the following:

▶ **Identify the problem.** The best cases deal with knowledge that is scarce and that would benefit by wider distribution. A question to ask: Exactly what kind of advice will the system make available and to whom?

▶ **Find an expert.** "The expert you want is the one the company would least like to give you," says one knowledge engineer. "It's the person the company can least afford to do without." The knowledge engineer will help the expert structure his or her knowledge and identify and formalize the important concepts and rules used to solve problems.

▶ **Determine the approach.** What knowledge engineering tools should be used? If none can be used, what AI language—LISP, PROLOG, or other—will be required for programming?

▶ **Analyze the costs and benefits.** Are the costs of the expert's time, the knowledge engineer's time, and the hardware and software feasible? Will the benefits of a completed expert system include reduced costs, increased productivity, enhanced or new products and services?

▶ **Prepare a development plan.** If there are no hitches so far, the final step is to prepare a development plan stating the reason for the system, steps to take, costs expected, and results targeted.

2. Develop a Prototype System

A **prototype system** is a small-scale model of an expert system. It is designed to test the knowledge engineer's ideas—or the manager's ideas, if a knowledge-based system is being developed—about the potential of a larger model. This phase includes the following activities:

▶ **Learn about the domain and task.** You learn everything about the problem from books and reports and teach the expert how to formulate his or her judgments and expertise in terms of heuristics and inference strategies, "thinking out loud" about solving certain tasks.

▶ **Specify performance criteria.** This step consists of fine-tuning the criteria developed in the first phase so that they can be used to judge the performance of the expert system.

▶ **Select an expert system building tool.** This is probably the most important step in this phase.

▶ **Develop an initial implementation.** This step establishes that the selected tool, with its representation of the expert's knowledge and strategy for drawing inferences, is adequate.

▶ **Test the implementation with case studies.** Using the prototype, the knowledge engineer and expert test other cases and modify the prototype.

▶ **Develop a detailed design.** The outcome here is a design document that includes an estimate of the number of rules to be included, a more precise statement of performance criteria, and a detailed schedule and budget for the entire development.

3. Develop a Complete System

Now the prototype can be expanded to a complete system, in accordance with the following activities:

▶ **Implement the core structure.** Here the knowledge engineer and the expert fine-tune the knowledge representation scheme and the inference procedures, perhaps even redoing the prototype.

▶ **Expand the knowledge base.** This is the main task of this phase—to create more rules for handling more subtle aspects of the problem.

▶ **Tailor the user interface.** We have not mentioned the user in a while. Now is the time to again consider what kinds of phrasing and explanations should be used that will be comfortable for the persons who will be using the expert system. Graphic presentations are particularly helpful. Both the words and graphics chosen are important in making the final result acceptable to the users.

▶ **Monitor the system's performance.** At this point, the knowledge engineer begins to take a lesser role in the development, and begins to monitor the project rather than actively participate in it. In turn, the expert, with all the insight and experience gained during the development process, can now start to take control—we might say ownership—of the system.

4. Evaluate the System

Once the knowledge engineer and expert believe the system is complete, it can be tested against the performance criteria specified during prototyping. Other experts will also be invited to try the system and to try it using other cases.

5. Integrate the System

Until now the expert system has probably been off in a room of its own. Now is the time to integrate it into the organization's workplace and provide training for prospective users:

▶ **Arrange technology transfer.** Users, systems personnel, and experts are trained in how to use and maintain the system. Once experts are convinced of the value of expert systems, they tend to welcome them. The most critical aspect is to help them realize that it will relieve them of onerous tasks rather than replace them in their jobs.

▶ **Interface the system with other elements.** An expert system may need to acquire information from other data bases or hardware or need to generate information that should be included in outside data bases.

EXPERT SYSTEMS VERSUS EXPERT DECISION SUPPORT SYSTEMS

We know, from Chapter 14, what a *decision support system* is—a set of computer programs and hardware that helps managers arrange information from various sources in new and different ways. In particular, a DSS can help middle-level managers do analysis and research and help high-level managers in making decisions. A DSS is a *general* information system.

We also know, from the present chapter, what an *expert system* is—a computer-based information system developed by processing the knowledge of an expert in such a way that this expertise is made available to others. An expert system is a *specific approach* or tool for solving a specific problem (such as approving a loan).

Now, what happens when these two are combined into an *expert decision support system*? We have the best of both: a tool for helping decision makers by recommending specific actions. The EDSS has expertise, not in a narrow, specific area, but wide-ranging expertise—the kind that can be applied to a variety of different problems. The EDSS will lead the user through certain procedures in order to help him or her analyze problems and make decisions.

6. Maintain the System

Maintenance of the system, particularly its knowledge base, is an ongoing process. A major characteristic of expert systems is that they are open-ended: Their knowledge bases allow the addition of new information or the modification of existing information. Thus, expert systems have much more flexibility than systems developed using traditional programming languages.

THE FUTURE OF AI AND EXPERT SYSTEMS

Some of the most interesting developments in AI are yet to come. A hot topic at present is **neural networks,** computers patterned after the complex interconnections among nerve cells in the brain (*see box*).

Does the new world of AI and expert systems seem like one we want to live in? This is a serious question. Eminent computer scientist Joseph Weizenbaum, in *Computer Power and Human Reason*, actually argues that much research on artificial intelligence should be discontinued—that our society will be unable to absorb the ethical, psychological, and social shocks of widespread AI. If future computers become capable of intelligent behavior, will people become overly dependent on them? Will AI systems become so complex that people will no longer understand their decisions and ac-

NEURAL-NET COMPUTERS

Computers That Can Learn

Nobody really knows how natural computers—the human brain—really work. Nevertheless, scientists are beginning to try to mimic on silicon chips the way information is handled by the brain. These new devices are known as neural-net computers.

Conventional computer circuits are linked in a series, with each transistor connected to only two or three other switches, so that signals are processed step by step. This is known as the "von Neumann architecture," after computer genius John von Neumann, who formulated the design in the 1940s. Memory and processor are separated, with a communications link connecting them—which means the processor must spend time waiting for data to be sent to and from it. This arrangement is fine for balancing financial records, performing mathematics, or playing chess, but it simply does not offer enough possibilities for doing tasks that nearly all humans can do, such as recognize speech.

Neural nets, on the other hand, consist of transistors hooked up to many, many other switches, so that a signal will fan out across the whole network, and all the transistors will process it in parallel. This avoids the "von Neumann bottleneck." As a result,

developers say, computers can synthesize knowledge from data they have not dealt with before. For example, after being trained to recognize a human face from a few angles, a neural-net computer can recognize it from an unfamiliar angle—a form of learning known as "pattern matching." Pattern matching is also important in recognizing speech. Language, for instance, is full of exceptions—the "a" sound may be long in "save," "gave," and "Dave" but it is short in "have."

The key to neural networks is that a great deal of processing can be going on simultaneously—something not possible with most supercomputers. As an article in *Business Week* (June 2, 1986), states, describing a neural-net computer developed by TRW near San Diego, Calif.: "Suppose, for example, that you wanted to find the one person on earth whose height and weight comes closest to your own. A conventional supercomputer would take about seven minutes to slog through the statistics for 5 billion people, one by one. But with TRW's neural network, the answer would pop out in roughly 75 thousandths of a second."

tions, thereby losing control of human destiny? One may scoff at these as being matters of science fiction, but then we must point out that a lot that was once fiction has now, as it were, become science. Consider: Would you rather have a computerized surgeon—a machine—operating on your brain or a human surgeon with access to a machine to give him or her assistance in the operation?

The problem is that it is not realistic to believe that we can stop further explorations and developments in AI even if we wanted to. Thus, we will no doubt begin to see expert consultants in fields such as medicine, law, financial planning, business management, process control, and crisis management. The combination of humans and machines in decision making will not simply produce better human decisions; together they will develop *synergy*, achieving together what each is incapable of achieving alone.

SUMMARY

▶ The name given to the field of study concerned with creating machines that emulate human intellectual activity is *artificial intelligence* or *AI*. A practical offshoot are *expert systems*, software that attempts to put the knowledge of experts to use in diagnosis and decision making.

▶ **Artificial intelligence** is the expansion of the capabilities of computers to include the ability to reason, to learn, to strive for self-improvement, and to simulate human sensory capabilities. The goal of researchers working in the AI field is not to replace people but to make them more productive.

▶ AI is both hardware and software—with a difference. Unlike traditional computers, which emphasize numbers and have been designed to maximize processing efficiency rather than extensive memory capabilities, AI computers have *more memory* but *less processing power*—that is, they have been designed to do the reverse. AI is also a type of programming—thus it is also a software approach to problems.

▶ Frequently, AI computers are called **LISP machines,** because LISP is the programming language often used in artificial intelligence applications. LISP machines have additional *firmware*—chips with read-only memories—specially designed to support AI applications.

▶ AI programming is much more complex than traditional programming; AI knowledge contains nonnumeric information, such as A = SD. Thus, AI deals with symbols and facts and implements complex algorithms.

▶ Artificial intelligence includes three distinct but related areas: (1) natural language processing, (2) robotics, and (3) expert systems.

▶ **Natural language processing** is concerned with programs that allow the computer to read, speak, or understand languages as people use them every day.

▶ Robotics is the study of the design, construction, and use of robots. Within the scope of AI, robotics is principally concerned with devising the software that allows robots to have perception systems for vision, speech, and touch.

▶ **Expert systems**—expert consultants to users— consist of computer-based information systems that have been developed by processing and distilling the knowledge of an expert or many experts in a particular field.

▶ Expert systems are specific *approaches* or tools for solving specific problems, such as loan approval. An expert system is an intelligent computer program that uses knowledge and inference procedures to solve problems that are difficult enough to require significant human expertise for their solution.

▶ An expert system has three parts: (1) people, (2) subsystems, and (3) major components.

▶ The people involved in expert systems are of three kinds: (1) knowledge engineers, (2) subject-area experts, and (3) users.

▶ **Knowledge engineers** actually build expert systems, and the work they do is called **knowledge engineering.** The knowledge engineer concentrates on duplicating in an information system the behavior of a specific expert (such as a geologist) in solving a narrowly defined problem. The knowledge engineer extensively interviews a recognized expert or experts and codifies that expert's knowledge into rules, which are represented symbolically and then transferred to a computer program—the expert system—that mimics the expert's problem-solving strategies.

▶ Subject-area experts are the people who have specialized knowledge—based on education and experience—that can translate into good intuitions and hunches about how to solve a problem.

▶ Users—who may be experts themselves—are the people who will actually use the expert system to help them with their decision making.

▶ The process of extracting knowledge from an expert and imparting that knowledge to a user is helped along by two supporting computerized subsystems: (1) the knowledge acquisition subsystem, and (2) the explanation subsystem. Both these systems should be expressed in natural language for ease of use.

▶ The **knowledge acquisition subsystem** consists of programs to help the knowledge engineer and the expert define, specify, and codify the expert's problem-solving ability. The subsystem also allows the two to more easily update and insert new knowledge into the system and to delete outdated and incorrect knowledge.

▶ The **explanation subsystem** enables users to query the expert system as to why it has chosen to ask certain questions or how it has reached certain conclusions.

▶ The three major components of an expert system are: (1) the knowledge base, (2) the inference engine, and (3) the working memory.

▶ The **knowledge base,** the heart of the system, translates the human experts' knowledge into rules and strategies. Such knowledge is of two types: (1) **Facts,** or "deep knowledge," is based on generalized learning from school and books that is well known and widely accepted by experts in a field. (2) **Heuristics,** or "surface knowledge," consists of "rules of thumb," private knowledge attained through experience.

▶ A knowledge base is dynamic and ever-changing, as reflects the advice of human experts.

▶ The most widely used approach to encoding facts and relationships is the use of **rules,** which express knowledge in an IF-THEN format.

▶ The **inference engine,** a part of the software, has two primary tasks: (1) inference, by which it employs reasoning to examine existing facts and rules, adds new facts if it finds them consistent with present information and rules, and draws conclusions; and (2) control, which is the process of controlling the search of the knowledge base.

▶ The **working memory** refers to the size of the memory in the hardware. In large, complex knowledge bases, a large primary storage is essential if a search of the knowledge base is to be done in a timely way.

▶ **Knowledge-based systems** are generally smaller than expert systems. Their knowledge consists of widely accepted rules and facts—which makes such systems helpful for defining and outlining structured procedural activities.

▶ Expert systems, by contrast, are generally larger and they are modeled on true human expertise. Both deep and surface knowledge are contained within the knowledge base, and heuristics are extensively used. Expert systems are used by experts themselves—to confirm their own judgments.

▶ There are ten categories of expert system applications: (1) interpretation, (2) prediction, (3) diagnosis, (4) design, (5) planning, (6) monitoring, (7) debugging, (8) repair, (9) instruction, and (10) control.

▶ The expert system *interprets* data automatically and makes inferences based on that data. The data may be **sensor data**—data that comes from the system itself, as in a medical monitoring system, rather than from human interaction.

▶ The expert system makes *predictions* based on given situation or data, as in weather forecasting.

▶ The *diagnosis* expert system uses a variety of inputs to diagnose—infer or locate—certain problems. Common areas of application are medicine, engineering, and computer systems.

▶ *Design* expert systems, which are used in microelectronics, create or configure a system to meet certain criteria, based on certain performance objectives.

▶ *Planning* systems specify an entire course of action based on target objectives and time requirements. It is widely used in the military as well as in chemistry and electronics.

▶ A *monitoring* system typically deals with time; it accepts physical measurements and compares them to previously defined values. If the data reaches a certain value, the system may automatically take corrective action (such as shut down parts of a nuclear reactor).

▶ *Debugging* expert systems find problems or malfunctions and suggest remedies. Examples are systems that choose a repair procedure to fix a fault in a diesel locomotive.

▶ *Repair* systems actually physically repair equipment, such as electrical equipment.

▶ *Instruction* systems develop a model of what the student knows and then correct deficiencies in the model. Their objective is to teach students specialized skills, such as electronics, by extending their current ones.

▶ The *control* system combines any of the other categories into a broader kind of expert system that, for example, controls the treatment of patients in a hospital's intensive care unit.

▶ Two areas to consider in building an expert system are (1) AI programming languages and (2) knowledge engineering tools.

▶ Of the programming languages devised for artificial intelligence, the most popular are LISP and PROLOG.

▶ **LISP** (*LISt* Processor) is the oldest and probably the most widely used symbolic language in the United States. It is an entire programming environment, a set of extensive functions that greatly facilitates the development of expert system programs—especially by providing support for AI problem-solving techniques.

▶ **PROLOG** (*PRO*gramming language for *LOG*ic) is the AI language of Europe and of Japan's so-called fifth-generation computers. It is a higher-level language than LISP.

▶ After an expert system has been developed (such as MYCIN), enterprising types may see a similar problem that could be solved using similar inference and components—but without the same knowledge base. They will therefore remove the knowledge base and market the remaining **shell**—the expert system skeleton—to be applied to other problems. An example is **EMYCIN,** the first knowledge engineering tool, which was derived from MYCIN.

▶ **Knowledge engineering tools** help us develop expert systems and knowledge-based systems more rapidly because they incorporate particular aspects of knowledge engineering—specifically strategies for representation, inference, and control, as well as problem-solving techniques. Nowadays, most new system developers start with knowledge engineering tools, which, with their built-in problem-solving techniques, are much easier for people to use, although less flexible than AI languages.

▶ Besides EMYCIN, among the knowledge engineering tools that have been developed are: (1) **TIMM** (The Intelligent Machine Model), an example-oriented knowledge acquisition system, focusing on cases that represent good examples according to the human expert; (2) **M.1.,** available for use on the IBM Personal Computer and intended for consultative types of problems; and (3) **S.1.,** designed to solve diagnosis and prescription problems.

▶ There are six steps in developing a large expert system: (1) select the appropriate problem, (2) develop a prototype system, (3) develop a complete system, (4) evaluate the system, (5) integrate the system, and (6) maintain the system.

▶ In step 1, selecting the appropriate problem, one must perform the following tasks: (1) identify the problem; (2) find the expert; (3) determine the approach, such as what knowledge engineering tools to use; (4) analyze the costs and benefits; and (5) prepare a development plan.

▶ A **prototype system** is a small-scale model of an expert system. In step 2, developing a prototype system, one must perform the following: (1) learn about the domain and the task; (2) specify performance criteria; (3) select an expert system building tool; (4) develop an initial implementation; (5) test the implementation with case studies; and (6) develop a detailed design.

▶ In step 3, developing a complete expert system, there are four activities: (1) implement the core structure, (2) expand the knowledge base; (3) tailor the user interface; and (4) monitor the system's performance.

▶ In step 4, evaluating the system's performance, the system is tested against the performance criteria specified during prototyping.

▶ In step 5, integrating the system, the following tasks are accomplished: (1) technology transfer is arranged, with users and others being trained in how to use the system, and (2) the system is interfaced with other data bases or hardware to make it perform better.

▶ In step 6, maintaining the system, new or modified information is added to the knowledge bases.

▶ Some of the most interesting developments in AI are yet to come. A hot topic at present is **neural networks,** computers patterned after the complex interconnections among nerve cells in the brain.

KEY TERMS

REVIEW QUESTIONS

1. Define *artificial intelligence.* Define *expert systems.*
2. Briefly distinguish among the three major divisions of AI: natural language processing, robotics, and expert systems.
3. Describe the activities of the three types of people involved in an expert system—knowledge engineers, subject-area human experts, and users.
4. Describe the two computerized subsystems: the knowledge acquisition subsystem and the explanation subsystem.
5. Explain the three major components of an expert system: the the knowledge base, the inference engine, and the working memory.
6. Distinguish between knowledge-based systems and expert systems.
7. What are some of the ten classes of applications of expert systems?
8. Describe the six steps in developing a large expert system.

CASE PROBLEMS

Case 15-1: Expert Systems and "Magnetic Surface Rights"

In 1986, Paperback Software International, a Berkeley, Calif., company that distributes software packages comparable to, but substantially less costly than, market leaders, unveiled a program called VP-Expert, priced at only $99.95. The software had some enhancements such as a data base and ability to work with Lotus 1-2-3 and dBase III formatted files. The prototype VP-Expert is an expert system that recommends which wine to drink with which meal. The data base contains 600 wines, and the system will make the selection according to five main courses (fish, beef, fowl, etc.). Users can change the main courses or add to the wine list.

Your assignment: The company also planned to introduce a wine guide with a data base of over 600 wines, and users would be able to choose wines based on 20 different main courses. The information was based on the knowledge of a leading wine critic whom Paperback Software International had signed for "the magnetic surface rights for his books." Although such a "computerized wine guide" is certainly not essential, the concept may suggest a commercial idea by which you could create an expert system. Think of other how-to books, directories, guide books, and compilations. Imagine one that you could obtain "magnetic surface rights" for—that is, the rights to extract or reproduce their contents on magnetic disk for computer use—and turn into some enterprise. Think of a data base that people could tap into for expert answers to their questions.

Case 15-2: Artificial Intelligence and Artificial Emotions

Consider these experiments in the artificial intelligence laboratory at the University of California, Los Angeles. The AI program Daydreamer can make computational assumptions that correspond to anger, sadness, and other feelings (it defines "happiness" as the mental state that accompanies goal achievement, "joy" if the goal is extremely important), and through a "scenario generator" produce a sequence of actions necessary to achieve a goal. It is even able to have conflicting emotions simultaneously, and can learn from experience by "daydreaming" about different outcomes of events. Another AI program, Edison, is supposed to invent new gadgets, an attempt to demystify the act of creativity. OpEd reads and answers questions about newspaper editorials; its ultimate aim is to write rebuttals to editorials.

Your assignment: The preceding were reported in an article in *Omni* magazine by Kathleen McAuliffe, who observes: "There's something deeply unsettling about all this. For one thing, do we really want silicon minds [computers] bogged down with sappy emotions? And for another, do we need the competition? Computers that can feel and invent and maybe even question the intelligence of their creators are downright threatening to our own humanity." You should be mindful that although computers have defeated expert chess players, they have never yet beaten a chess grand master; thus, there may well be limits to how far the UCLA projects can be carried. Still, they cause us to face the basic issue of human *consciousness.* Write a page of notes describing your concerns and also what some of the benefits of this kind of "artificial emotion" might be.

PART 5

THE REWARDS AND RISKS OF THE INFORMATION AGE

The value of information is, like beauty, in the eye of the beholder or user. Data that is meaningless to one person may be pure gold to another. Regardless, information is one of the most valuable assets today—both to you personally and to organizations generally.

However, the problem with information is not the lack of it, as we have seen. The problem is to make better use of the information that is usually already there. The need is for increased *productivity*—making better use of people's time. Although it is difficult to measure the productivity improvements of managers and professionals, it is among this group that the greatest gains are possible.

Clearly, the computer offers one of the best opportunities here—for improving both personal productivity, as in the use of word processing and spreadsheets, and corporate productivity, as in providing access to the data generated by a TPIS, MIS, or DSS. It is important to recognize the computer for what it is. It is an exceptionally powerful tool for today and an indispensable tool for tomorrow. However, though it is an incredibly fast and accurate device, it has no intelligence. Humans are what give it intelligence.

In the next three chapters, we will describe both the rewards and the dangers of the information revolution. First we will describe the evolution in information systems. Then we will examine information security. Finally, we will consider what computers and information will be in the future—and what they will mean for your career.

Chapter 16

MANAGING INFORMATION RESOURCES: MORE INTEGRATION, MORE EASE, MORE POWER

How well do managers make decisions? Consider some typical decision flaws, as compiled by the Center for Decision Research in Chicago. According to *Newsweek* (August 17, 1987), researchers found the following kinds of mistakes:

▶ **Poor framing:** Decision makers allow a decision to be "framed" by the context or language in which it is presented, rather than exploring it from every perspective. For example, American car makers were slow to recognize the inroads made by Japanese and German cars because they viewed their market through the frame of how they competed with other U.S. automakers.

▶ **Availability bias:** Decision makers rely on the most available evidence—because it's handy—even if it contradicts other trends.

▶ **Strategic anchoring:** The fact that a certain dollar figure is mentioned may "anchor" a financial discussion in a certain range— for example, the pricing of a product—even if the actual value should be a lot higher or lower.

▶ **Association bias:** Decision makers select a course of action because they associate it with some past successful action—even if the present problem does not resemble the past one.

There are lessons to be learned from these mistakes. For example, some Japanese companies, using techniques based on framing, have learned to view complaining customers not as irritants but as valuable informants about their products. In the same way, we may also try to suspend our biases in order to more effectively use technology.

There are all kinds of myths and misconceptions about technology. As Lowell Steele, a veteran of 29 years at General Electric, once pointed out, many managers think the "best possible" technology should be obtained, expect most innovative efforts to be successful, put greater reliance on the development of new technology than on extensions of what is currently available, and trust that companies are indeed competent to make use of technical advances. Such misconceptions can have long-term consequences.

Yet if new technology—in particular, information technology—offers the risk of vulnerability, it also offers the opportunity for a competitive edge, as the box on the next page shows.

> ## USING INFORMATION FOR COMPETITIVE ADVANTAGE

"Information technology," says a report produced by the Arthur Andersen management consulting firm, "is transforming not only products and processes but also the nature of competition itself." Indeed, there is now a term for this, *information for competitive advantage* (IFCA), "a strategic planning process [that] can help executives shape their competitive environment by effectively exploiting information technology." By making best use of new information technology, companies can provide new ways of influencing buyers and suppliers, differentiating their products, and controlling competitors and competing products.

How can a company do this? F. Warren McFarlan, writing in the *Harvard Business Review*, says a company should adopt information technology for competitive advantage only if it can answer "yes" to the following five questions:

► **Can information technology keep your competitors away from your customers?** McFarlan points out that customers do not want devices from different vendors on their premises, nor do they want to go to the trouble of learning complex software all over again after they have already learned another package. Thus, if a financial services company installs or sells its customers an attractive financial product that depends on sophisticated software, competitors will find it difficult to catch up—particularly if the original company keeps on improving the product and software, making itself a moving target.

► **Will the information technology make it difficult for customers to switch to competitors?** "Are there ways to encourage customers to rely increasingly on the supplier's electronic support," asks McFarlan, "building it into their operations so that increased operational dependence and normal human inertia make switching to a competitor unattractive?" An example, he points out, is electronic home banking. When a customer has learned to use the system and coded all the creditors for that system, he or she will find it inconvenient to change banks.

► **Can the technology change the basis of competition?** Some competition is based on costs, and information technology may help

CASE STUDY: INFORMATION OF VALUE

Information Technology Changes the Way You Compete

▶ To solve customer service problems, a major distributor installs an on-line network to its key customers so they can directly enter orders into its computer. The computer's main purpose is to cut order-entry costs and to provide more flexibility to customers in the time and process of order submission. The system yields a larger competitive advantage, adding value for customers and a substantial rise in their sales. The resulting sharp increase in the company's market share forces a primary competitor into a corporate reorganization and a massive systems development effort to contain the damage, but these corrective actions have gained only partial success.

▶ A regional airline testifies before the U.S. Congress that it has been badly hurt by the reservation system of a national carrier. It claims that the larger airline, through access to the reservation levels on every one of the smaller line's flights, can pinpoint all mutually competitive routes where the regional is performing well and take competitive pricing and service action. Since the regional airline lacks access to the bigger carrier's data, it allegedly is at a decided competitive disadvantage.

▶ A large aerospace company has required major suppliers to acquire CAD (computer-aided design) equipment to link directly to its CAD installation. It claims this has dramatically reduced total cost and time of design changes, parts acquisition, and inventory, making it more competitive.

These examples are not unusual. With great speed, the sharp reduction in the cost of information systems (IS) technology (i.e., computers, remote devices, and telecommunications) has allowed computer systems to move from applications for back-office support to those offering significant competitive advantage. Particularly outstanding are systems that link customer and supplier. Though such links offer an opportunity for a competitive edge, they also bring a risk of strategic vulnerability. In the case of the aerospace manufacturer, operating procedures have shown much improvement, but this has been at the cost of vastly greater dependence, since it is now much harder for the manufacturer to change suppliers.

In many cases, the new technology has opened up a singular, one-time opportunity for a company to redeploy its assets and rethink its strategy. The technology has given the organization the potential for forging sharp new tools that can produce lasting gains in market share.

—F. Warren McFarlan, *Harvard Business Review*

to lower costs. Other competition is based on product differentiation, but "dramatic cost reduction can significantly alter the old ground rules of competition," McFarlan says. An example, he says, is the situation of airlines that are able to get their on-line reservations systems into travel agencies. By positioning their flight recommendations on the CRT screen, the airlines can influence the travel agent's purchase recommendations.

▶ **Can information technology change the balance of power in supplier relationships?** Interorganizational systems can redistribute power between buyer and supplier. A furniture retailer was linked to order entry systems of different sofa suppliers, and the one with the lowest price got the order. The retailer also, said McFarlan, continually monitored the suppliers' finished-goods inventories, factory scheduling, and commitments against the schedule to make sure inventory would be available to meet unexpected demands by the retailer, which gave the retailer considerable control over the supplier.

▶ **Can information technology generate new products?** Information systems technology, says McFarlan, "can lead to products that are of higher quality, that can be delivered faster, or that are cheaper. Similarly, at little extra cost, existing products can be tailored to customers' needs."

These are the challenges that may well confront you in the future.

PAST AS PROLOGUE

WHERE ARE WE

HEADING?

Sometimes it is difficult to see the forest for the trees. Let us, therefore, briefly review where we have been in order to have a clearer idea of where we are going.

Toward Integration and Ease of Use

In the last twelve chapters, we have examined software, hardware, and systems separately. Let us now reexamine them and see how they are evolving and how they fit together into an information processing system.

Software All the advances in computers would be of limited value without software to instruct the computers on the operations to be performed. Historically, businesses developed their own software, mainly to run large computers and transaction processing information systems. Recently, however, the trend has been toward purchasing integrated packages, both for microcomputers and for mainframes. As we have seen, integrated software packages combine word processing, spreadsheets, data base management, graphics, and communications programs. Such packages are capable of creating a data base of information, maintaining it, and retrieving information from it.

For both users and programmers, structured programming concepts have greatly improved the efficiency of the programming process. Also, applications languages are being developed that are very high level and much more user-friendly, which will benefit nontechnical users. The evolution in software is toward integrated software packages and higher-level user-friendly languages. The key words are *integration* and *ease of use.*

Probably most dramatic, however, is the increasing use of research in artificial intelligence. We may expect to see expert systems not only in specific applications, as in knowledge-based systems, but also in large-scale applications in the three levels of information systems: TPIS, MIS, and DSS.

Hardware   Technology is the driving force of the information revolution, and this technology is centered on improvements in hardware. Here are some of the recent developments:

▶ **Input devices:** These are now designed to eliminate data entry steps by allowing direct data entry from source documents, thereby reducing human errors and removing the need for batch data entry. A particularly fascinating development is the refinement of voice input.

▶ **Output devices:** These are becoming more varied, more reliable, and faster. High-quality output devices are readily affordable for low-cost computer systems. Graphics terminals and laser printers have greatly extended the capability of presenting output, enabling sophisticated desktop publishing, graphics presentations, and the like.

▶ **CPUs:** Integrated circuits are less expensive, faster, and more reliable. The famous Intel "386" chip has opened the door to microcomputers with CPUs that exceed the power that only mainframes had a few years ago. The processors of tomorrow promise to be even more powerful, particularly with new developments in parallel processing.

▶ **Secondary storage devices:** Optical disks and other devices allow more information to be stored and retrieved than would have been thought possible a few years ago, which means that large data bases can now be created and maintained relatively easily.

▶ **Data communications:** The communication links that allow the integration and common sharing of various information resources are constantly improving. Micros and mainframes now work constantly together, and many offices have multiuser systems for micros.

▶ **Microcomputers:** One of the most dramatic hardware advances, the microcomputer, when combined with communication links, can give users a wide variety of powers, from solving individual problems locally to calling up information from large centralized data bases. The microcomputer is a tool that enhances personal productivity, whereas the mainframe or minicomputer is a corporate tool.

As with software, the evolution in hardware has been toward integration of equipment, use of communications systems, and the development of ever more user-friendly capabilities. Especially important is the capability to integrate microcomputers into an organization's total computer information system through data communications links.

Systems As we have seen, within large organizations, computer applications can be categorized into three areas: transaction processing information systems (TPISs); management information systems (MISs); and decision support systems (DSSs). TPISs focus on record keeping and clerical operations. MISs focus on management reports. DSSs focus on supporting decision-making and planning activities. Although each system is separate and performs a distinct function within the organization, all require and use a common data base of corporate information.

The revolution in information systems is in the development of DSSs and the use of common data bases inside and outside the organization. The result is, once again, toward integrating information and making it user-friendly. The key to this integration has been the recent development of powerful yet easy to use data base management systems that allow TPIS, MIS, and DSS systems to efficiently share common data. In particular, the OS/2 operating system permits windowing, multiuser use, and multiprocessing, and allows better integration between system software. As mentioned, we will probably also see further integration of expert systems and AI into TPIS, MIS, and DSS.

The Tripod of Information Processing

Software, hardware, and systems describe the architecture or tools used in information processing, but they do not describe the *activity* of information processing. What is it, in fact, that users actually *do* when they process information?

As Figure 16-1 shows, there are three components of information processing:

▶ Word processing
▶ Data processing
▶ Data base processing

Figure 16-1. Tripod. These three activities of information processing are tied together by telecommunications.

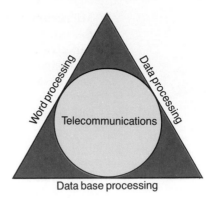

Telecommunications

Word processing

Data processing

Data base processing

These three components form the legs of a "tripod" of information processing that are connected by a common element: telecommunications. Let us review these activities.

Word Processing Because one hears the phrase "data processing" so often, it is tempting to think that this is what computers do for the most part. Actually, 90% of all symbols processed by a company are *words*. Ninety percent of all information is recorded by characters, not numbers. Thus, word processing—by which we mean any creation, storage, and retrieval of textual data or information—is truly a most significant use of computers.

Data Processing There is a great deal of difference between word processing and data processing. Data processing operates on data according to a logical set of instructions (the program) and requires human interaction only for monitoring. Word processing, on the other hand, is concerned with words, sentences, and paragraphs, and human interaction is constantly required to interpret and manipulate the text; logical definitions and instructions will not suffice. When compared to word processing tasks, data processing tasks seem to have had more importance attached to them. The reasons may lie in the fact that "data processing" had its origins in military and space projects, whereas "word processing" evolved out of clerical and secretarial work. But, as we have shown, word processing is no longer just for secretaries. Managers and professionals of all types use both data and word processing, but particularly the latter. They spend much more time creating and retrieving text—written reports, management directives, sales data—than analyzing pure numeric data.

Data Base Processing Data base systems capable of storing both numeric and text data are the foundation of any information processing system. Data processing and word processing provide the data that make up a data base. If you are a sales manager, for instance, you will want to be able to pull sales figures (numeric data) and long-

Telecommunications. Telephone and data communications technology—represented by Chicago's Sears Tower antennas—provides the means for networks, which in turn lead to new business activities such as home banking.

range sales promotions (text data) from a data base. Originally, computer files were organized like the paper records files that preceded them, but when it was discovered that this arrangement only led to increased volumes of files and inefficient computer use, data base management systems were developed to make optimal use of computers and their storage devices. Nearly all data base systems currently operate principally on numeric data. However, text management systems are being rapidly developed, and integrated records in the form of data, text, image, and voice are a certainty in the future.

Telecommunications The importance of telecommunications to information processing cannot be overstated. It is what integrates the three activities of information processing: word processing, data processing, and data base processing. As we have been demonstrating, it allows users at various locations to have access to common information as well as to each other.

In Search of Synergism

The significance of telecommunications can truly be expressed in the word **synergism:** The total effect of the activities of information processing is greater than the sum of the effects taken independently. In other words, one technology not only allows another technology to develop but also expands its capability and influence.

The synergistic effect is seen in networks, which allow users to gain access to data on computers, text on word processors, images on microfilm, and voice on the network itself. The telecommunications permitted by the network is the underlying technology of the automated office. It is what permits electronic mail, voice messaging, teleconferencing, data base access, and so on.

All these marvels are possible today. The question is: Just how advanced are most organizations in this scheme of things? We turn, therefore, from this review of past concepts to a consideration of the present.

WHERE IS
INFORMATION
PROCESSING TODAY?

If you have any contact with present business organizations, it may seem to you we are describing some pretty idealized concepts. How many executives are in fact using teleconferencing, executive workstations, and the like?

An organization with a full-blown integrated, user-friendly information processing system does not develop overnight, of course. It is achieved in stages. This evolutionary process is shown in Table 16-1. In general, progressive computer-using organizations have followed four stages of evolution, according to scholar Richard Nolan (in *Data Base*, Fall, 1975):

▶ Initiation
▶ Contagion
▶ Control
▶ Integration

As the table shows, these stages have roughly paralleled developments of the last four decades and have gone from little user involvement to more user involvement, from loose planning and control of information to tighter planning and control. However, some firms today—those that have just purchased their first computers—will be just beginning, in the initiation stage. Most firms are in either the second or third stage. Only the most advanced are in the last.

Let us see what happens in these four stages.

Table 16-1 Stages in the Evolution of Information Processing Systems.
The four stages in the history of this evolution also correspond to the four stages a company goes through when implementing a computer-based information system.

Characteristic	I Initiation	II Contagion	III Control	IV Integration
Time	1950s	1960s	1970s	1980s
Applications	TPIS	TPIS	MIS	DSS
User involvement and awareness	None	Superficially enthusiastic	Accountable with limited control	Accountable and controllable
Planning and control of information processing department (computer resources)	Loose budget, minimal controls	Internal planning and control	Formalized control and planning	Long-range planning and improved control

Stage 1: Initiation

In the **initiation** stage, an organization has purchased its first computer, and there is a great deal of excitement. There are high expectations—usually too high—that must be brought into line.

Applications programs are purchased or developed that focus on elementary transaction processing for accounting and clerical operations. Because the company's interest is in replacing manual procedures, there is usually some employee concern and even unrest.

Access to the computer and involvement by users is generally carefully controlled and in fact typically discouraged. Computer technical support people are hired—which generally proves upsetting to the existing salary scale for noncomputer technical personnel, since computer support people command higher salaries. The computer department—which later will probably come to be known as the information processing department—has very free reign and loose managerial budget control.

Stage 2: Contagion

In the **contagion** stage, computer applications become infectious. Although the focus is still on transaction processing, computer applications spread into areas other than accounting. The full range of

Computerization and displacement. In the contagion stage in the evolution of an information system, some employees—such as certain garment or automobile workers—may be displaced from their jobs by automation. Often they are transferred to other jobs or simply not replaced when they quit or retire.

transaction processing information system (TPIS) technology is brought in to support accounting and other selected applications

Many manual operations are computerized, resulting in the loss of some jobs. Some employees are displaced, usually through transfers to other activities, or jobs are simply not filled when people leave. Although users' expectations are not as high as they were during the initiation stage, there is still a great deal of enthusiasm. Upper management is now better able to control operations in the computer department, and some formal internal planning and control begins to emerge.

Stage 3: Control

Once a TPIS has been developed and is operating well, the next step in the evolution of information processing is the development of an MIS, a management information system to **control** operations. At this stage, management has a better tool to control corporate resources. User involvement also increases greatly; there is a high degree of interaction between the computer department and the various other functional business areas, at least at the managerial level. Information processing is freed from "the computer room," which is no longer considered a mysterious cave.

Users are now held more accountable for the computer resources that they request and require, and this necessitates more careful planning and control of the computer department. In fact, control of the department begins to increase significantly. Systems analysts begin to be quite active. Requests for services for systems analysis and design exceed capabilities, and backlogs result. This in turn forces more accountability from the computer department—which probably by now has been upgraded to the information processing department.

Stage 4: Integration

In the final stage, **integration,** the organization builds on the previous TPIS and MIS to develop more fully integrated information systems. This is the stage at which decision support systems (DSSs) emerge.

Networks that were introduced in the previous stage are now heavily used and effectively integrate hardware, software, and systems. Users have easy access to the information system and interact with it on a regular basis. Correspondingly, they are also held accountable for the system's use.

The information processing system becomes much more of a user-oriented system, with the computer department—now information systems department—allocating much of its resources toward maintaining existing programs and data bases. The management of the department becomes more actively involved with long-range planning and developing improved methods of controlling their operations.

Telecommunications systems allow convenient access to people and information located at various remote sites, with external as well as internal data bases. The computer is used much more effectively as a tool for decision making by managers.

> **WANT AD**

THE NEED FOR

MANAGEMENT

Only a few companies are yet into the integration stage. Indeed, even for firms in this stage, the pace of evolution toward highly integrated systems is rather slow.

Why have so few companies achieved what is technologically feasible and so clearly beneficial to their operations? It is certainly not because of hardware limitations. Advances in hardware have outpaced applications. Software *could* be a reason for holding back, but, as we have seen, the activity and pace of software development has been accelerating. Systems could also be a limitation. However, TPIS and MIS are well-developed concepts; only DSS still needs some refining, although the pace of development here is accelerating also.

Wanted: Forward-looking managers. The biggest reason for the slow progression toward integrated information processing systems is a lack of management support for and understanding of high technology along with a lack of managers with capabilities in this area.

The *real* reason for the slow progression toward integrated information processing systems can be expressed in one word: management. There is a lack of management support for and understanding of high technology, and a lack of managers with capabilities in this area.

Although information is crucial to every manager's operations—indeed, crucial to everyone within the organization—no one is really managing information in most companies. Rather, everyone assumes that "information is everybody's business"—which means, paradoxically, it is really *nobody's* business. There is a strong need for managerial expertise to control and plan for information processing. The technology needs to be managed by people who look on it not as an end but as a means—as a tool for improving the organization's performance and productivity.

What kind of people would make such managers? (Would *you* make such a manager?) Data processing people would seem to be the most natural for this position, since they know the technology and are usually good at applying it. However, their business knowledge is often limited.

The situation stems from the fact that the philosophy of most organizations has been to isolate the technical people, taking them out of the mainstream of business operations so they can concentrate on developing and implementing computer technology—which means, of course, that they become more involved with technology than with business.

The need, then, is for information managers who possess managerial and business skills as well as technical knowledge. Actually the problem is twofold:

▶ There is a need to establish managerial positions within the organization—managerial positions with real clout—with responsibility for information processing.
▶ There is a need to find individuals with the correct combination of technical and managerial skills to fill these positions.
▶ To address these needs, a new concept has recently emerged—that of information resource management.

INFORMATION RESOURCE MANAGEMENT

Information resource management recognizes that information systems technology does change the way you do business and the way you compete. It realizes that computer resources have shifted from closed shop DP departments to open, user-oriented organizations. It recognizes that there is a real need for businesspeople to understand how to use information.

Information resource management (IRM) is the concept that information should be viewed as a corporate resource and managed accordingly. This means that computer hardware, software, systems, and personnel require careful management in order to benefit the entire organization and that fragmented and overlapping information functions should be combined and placed under the control of a senior information executive, a *vice-president* or *director of information management* or *chief information officer.* Let us see what this person does and how he or she affects end-users.

The Vice-President of Information Management

What would be the job description of a **vice-president of information management** or **chief information officer (CIO)?** He or she would have at least four responsibilities:

▶ Coordinate and give direction to the managers of data base systems, systems analysis and design activities, management science applications, telecommunications, and office systems. The supervisors or middle managers in charge of these tasks are shown in Figure 16-2.
▶ Help other people in the company cope with change in technology, information needs, and health concerns. **Ergonomics,** the study of human factors related to computing, is discussed in the box on page 516.

WHAT DOES A CIO DO?

Blazing Trails in the Electronic Information Wilderness

Ross Watson, the chief information officer of Hercules Inc., got a call for help recently from the product managers of the company's carpet-yarn group. They weren't happy about carpet-fiber sales—information gleaned mostly from talks with customers and salesmen at carpet shows.

Mr. Watson's corporate staff group, which includes six in-house trainers who teach people to use computers as information tools, got the product people to define clearly just what type of market information they wanted. Then they taught them how to find it. They showed them how to do fast searches of online external data bases with their personal computers, drawing on the wealth of private and government reports—market and export-import data that are constantly being updated.

As a result of learning this new use of their PCs, Mr. Watson says, the product managers today are managing their business better and getting more reliable information. Managers in other companies, too, are getting such help to solve all sorts of information problems. The need for fast access to external information, as distinguished from computerized internal company data like payroll and customer accounts, is making CIOs and other information-center professionals increasingly important in the strategic management of businesses.

The firms that do the best job of spotting outside trends and changes gain an important competitive advantage. That's because changes are occurring so fast that a product manager can be derailed—or propelled to success—by anything from a new superchip development in Santa Clara, Calif., to a switch in Pentagon policy, from a new merger in the works to new legislative action or a new development in the capital markets. Managers can get quick access to all such information by tying their personal computers to external data bases.

Reginald Ellis of Imperial Chemical Industries is an example of one new type of manager overseeing this kind of electronic research today. He is "online coordinator" world-wide for ICI, where nearly everyone has a desktop PC capable of tapping into outside data bases. His department trains people to do their own online searching. In rare cases where a department may require no more than a single search in a quarter, or for those few who "wouldn't touch a terminal with a barge pole," he will do searches for them.

Of course, electronic research will never replace all the traditional modes of getting information critical to business decisions—such as a telephone call, a visit to a technical library or a conversation with a learned colleague. And "you can't carry your terminal on the train," as one ICI manager points out. Also, searching efficiently online depends a lot on the skill of the individual doing the research.

But the value of online searching is proved by the increasing activity in this field. Companies like General Electric and Minnesota Mining and Manufacturing, as well as data base providers, are training managers in this relatively new use of PCs. GE has a market information center that trains managers all over the company who want to do online research. The center uses more than a dozen online services for strategic account planning and profiling customers and competitors.

At Exxon Co. in Houston, making effective use of information-system technology is a fundamental business strategy. Individual productivity is improved most when end-users themselves are given access to external and internal data bases, Exxon found. Departments dealing with operations and staff functions are increasing their direct use of data bases for such things as industry and market analysis, and to check government legislation, litigation and economic indicators. . . .

Whether information managers operate as a service to their "internal" customers or train people to do hands-on searching for information, their role is clearly becoming more important. People are moving into information-management positions not just from the data-processing ranks; they often have backgrounds in planning and other professional skills. The new, model information manager is beginning to manage information resources just as the financial officer marshals financial resources, concentrating on getting the pulse of what's happening outside the company and managing this information for competitive advantage.

—Jack W. Simpson, *Wall Street Journal*

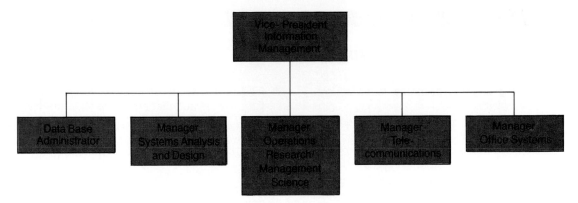

Figure 16-2. The tasks of the vice-president of information management.
The supervisors reporting to the vice-president of information management
are shown in this chart.

▶ Keep up with changes in technology. However, the vice-president of information management is a generalist—the details of new technology are left to the specialists.

▶ Keep information secure and private files private. This issue will be discussed further in Chapter 17.

Organization: The Need for Clout

It is not enough just to *have* a vice-president of information management. That person must have clout within the organization.

Clout does not come from having brains or energy or strong personality. It comes from having power within the organization. Power comes from position. The lack of a high organizational position for a vice-president of information management has been identified by many observers as being one of the major obstacles to the rapid evolution of integrated information processing.

In many firms, the information processing department reports directly to the vice-president of Accounting and Finance, a logical outgrowth of the time when information processing consisted mainly of TPIS and clerical and accounting operations. However, this kind of reporting limits the perspective and capabilities of the information processing system.

In other firms, the information processing department reports to *all* the functional vice-presidents—not just Accounting and Finance, but Marketing, Production, and Research and Development as well. This scheme, however, has the drawbacks of a servant trying to serve too many masters.

Companies that have adopted an IRM orientation as a philosophical position have elevated the director of information management to the vice-presidential level, putting that person on an equal footing with other vice-presidents, with the same access to the presi-

ERGONOMICS AND COMPUTERS

Tips for Using Display Terminals with Comfort

Perhaps 15 million workers in the United States operate display terminals every day: office workers, secretaries, accountants, reporters, and so on. Many complain the machines produce eyestrain, blurring vision, sore shoulders, stiff necks, and feelings of irritability and stress. Some have also expressed concerns about the long-range effects of low-level radiation, and others have worried about the possibility of pregnant display terminal operators having miscarriages or giving birth to babies with birth defects. A study by the National Institute for Occupational Safety and Health (NIOSH) found no evidence of these latter hazards, although the way the study was conducted means the results are still inconclusive.

Such concerns have contributed to *ergonomics,* the study of human factors related to computing. "Ergonomics" has become a buzz word in the advertising of computer-related equipment, because business customers are vitally interested in purchasing equipment that will increase the productivity of the people using it. Secretarial chairs in particular have been redesigned to reflect the curves of the human body.

NIOSH and others have made several recommendations on such matters as heights of keyboards and positioning of display terminal screens. Here are some tips for using a display terminal comfortably:

▶ Adjust your chair so that your feet are flat on the floor, legs clearing the underside of the worktable, and thighs parallel to the floor. Use a footrest, if necessary. The chair should provide back support.

▶ Rest your forearms so that they are parallel to the floor. Keyboards that are detachable are best.

▶ Put material you are copying on a stand as close to the screen as possible, so you will not have to swivel your head back and forth very much.

▶ Raise the display terminal screen high enough so that you can see without tipping your head up or down. (If you wear bifocal glasses, you can get special display terminal glasses with a larger reading area.)

▶ Position the display terminal screen vertically, not tipped up, to avoid glare from bright overhead lights or windows. Use an adjustable, shaded copy lamp, if possible; keep overhead lighting as low as possible; and draw blinds to minimize glare. Glare-reducing screens are available for the face of the computer.

▶ Focus the screen for brightness, contrast, and flicker control. Green on black or amber on black are the best display terminal screen color combinations; white on black is legible, but may have more flicker than green displays.

▶ Take frequent vision breaks. Every 10 minutes look up and focus in the far distance. (A mirror on the wall will enable you to focus on a far object, if you work in a small, enclosed space.) Every hour and a half or two hours, get up and move about and stretch. Some experts believe operators should not use computers for more than four or five hours a day.

Computer-related stress, it has been found, is not as apt to occur among managers, who generally find

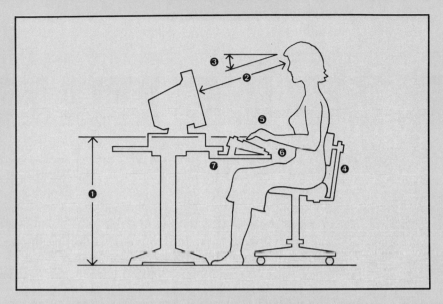

Workstation design. In its publication *Potential Health Hazards of Video Display Terminals*, the National Institute for Occupational Safety and Health makes the following recommendations: ① The European recommendation for the height of the home row keys is 28¼ to 29½ inches. The U.S. military standard is 29¼ to 31 inches. ② The viewing distance should be between 17¼ and 19¾ inches, with a maximum of 27½ inches. ③ Generally, the center of the screen should be at a position between 10 and 20 degrees below the horizontal plane at the operator's eye height. One researcher recommends that the top of the screen be below eye height, another that the top line of the display be 10 to 15 degrees below the horizontal, with no portion of the screen at an angle greater than 40 degrees below the horizontal. ④ One researcher recommends that the angle between the upper and lower arms be between 80 and 120 degrees. ⑤ The angle of the wrist should be no greater than 10 degrees. ⑥ The keyboard should be at or below elbow height. ⑦ Don't forget enough room for your legs—feet should be flat on the floor and thighs parallel to the floor.

computers enhance their jobs by reducing tedium and giving them more information. However, many clerical workers have found that display terminals can make their jobs more tedious and stressful. The stress often comes about because the computer can keep count of the operator's keystrokes and thus constantly evaluates the operator's productivity—even when he or she is having some off days. Some clerical operators feel overmonitored by their supervisors.

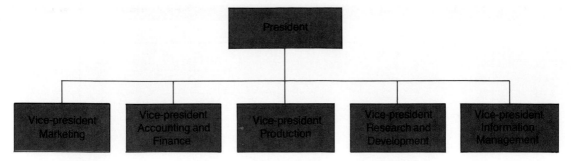

Figure 16-3. The new organization chart. The vice-president of information processing has been elevated to the same level as the vice-presidents responsible for the four other principal business functions.

dent of the company as that of other vice-presidents (see Figure 16-3). From this position, the company's information processing system can evolve in an integrating fashion, under the direction of a manager with organizational clout and broad perspective.

ONWARD IS IRM

"BIG BROTHER"?

If IRM is so good, why haven't more firms adopted it? The signs are that the vast majority will in the near future. Those that do not are simply not ready to accept the intangible nature of information; they have difficulty acknowledging that it should be treated as a resource like any other corporate resource. However, one interesting reason why there may be some reluctance is that, to many people, IRM sounds like a dictatorial "Big Brother" watching. In management, information means power: The more you know, the more secure your position. Other managers mistakenly fear that a director of information management might have the potential to limit, control, and select the information available to others in the organization—and thereby limit their power.

Security and privacy are responsibilities of the director of information management but should be major concerns of everyone who deals with computers—including you. We turn to these issues in the next chapter.

SUMMARY

▶ A company should adopt information technology as a strategic resource if it can answer yes to the following five questions: (1) Can information technology keep your competitors away from your customers? (2) Will the information technology make it difficult for customers to switch to competitors? (3) Can the technology change the basis of competition? (4) Can the technology change the balance of power in supplier relationships? (5) Can information technology generate new products?

▶ Software is what makes the advances in computers valuable. Historically, businesses developed their own software, mainly to run large computers and operational information systems. Recently, businesses have been purchasing integrated packages, for both microcomputers and mainframes. The evolution in software is toward integrated packages and higher-level user-friendly languages. The key words are *integration* and *ease of use.*

▶ Technological improvements in hardware are central to the information revolution: (1) Input devices now are designed to allow direct entry from source documents, thereby reducing human error and removing the need for batch data entry. (2) Output devices are becoming more varied, more reliable, and faster. High-quality output devices such as graphics terminals and printers are readily affordable for low-cost computer systems. (3) CPUs have integrated circuits that are less expensive, faster, and more reliable; today's microcomputers have CPUs that surpass those of mainframes only a few years ago. (4) Secondary storage devices allow storage and retrieval of more information than imaginable a few years ago; large data bases now can be created and maintained relatively easily. (5) Data communications, which allow the integration and common sharing of various information resources, are constantly improving. (6) Microcomputers, a dramatic advance, can be combined with data communications to give users a wide variety of powers, from solving individual problems locally to calling up information from large centralized data bases.

▶ Computer applications systems can be categorized into three areas: (1) Transaction processing information systems (TPISs) focus on record keeping and clerical operations. (2) Management information systems (MISs) focus on management reports. (3) Decision support systems (DSSs) focus on supporting decision-making and planning activities. Each separate system performs a distinct function, but all use a common data base of corporate information. The revolution in information systems is in the development of DSSs and the use of common data bases inside and outside the organization.

▶ The three activities of processing information are: (1) word processing, (2) data processing, (3) data base processing. This "tripod" of information processing is connected by a common element: telecommunications.

▶ Word processing—the creation, storage, and retrieval of textual data or information—is by far the most significant use of computers, accounting for 90% of all symbols processed by a company.

▶ Data processing—work with numerical data—operates according to a logical set of instructions, or program, with little human interaction; it makes up the remaining 10% of a company's activity.

▶ Data base processing—the storing of both numeric and text data—is the foundation of any information processing system. Computer files organized like the paper files that preceded them led to increased file volume and inefficient computer use, so data base management systems were developed to make optimal use of computers and their storage devices. Nearly all data base systems currently operate on numeric data, but text management systems and records in the form of data, text, image, and voice are a certainty in the near future.

▶ Telecommunications is what integrates word processing, data processing, and data base processing. It allows users at various locations to have access to common information as well as to each other.

▶ **Synergism** expresses the significance of telecommunications; it means: The total effect of information processing activities is greater than the sum of the effects taken independently. One technology not only allows another technology to develop but also expands its capability and influence.

▶ An organization with a full-blown integrated, user-friendly information processing system develops in stages, generally: (1) initiation, (2) contagion, (3) control, and (4) integration.

▶ In stage 1, **initiation,** an organization purchases its first computer and purchases or develops applications programs for elementary transaction processing of accounting and clerical operations. This stage is characterized by high expectations (usually too high), some employee concern or even unrest, controlled access to the computer, hiring of computer technical support people, and loose managerial budget control of the computer department.

▶ In stage 2, **contagion,** computer applications spread into other areas besides accounting. The full range of TPIS technology is brought in to support accounting and other applications. Many previously manual operations are replaced, some employees are displaced, and although expectations are more realistic, enthusiasm is still high. Upper management has better control of operations in the computer department, and some formal internal planning and control begin to emerge.

▶ Stage 3, **control,** occurs with the development of an MIS to control operations after the TPISs have been developed. Management now has a better tool to control corporate resources. User involvement with the computer department increases, especially at the managerial level. Users are held more accountable for the computer resources they use, necessitating more planning and control of the computer department. Systems analysts become quite active, requests for services for systems analysis and design exceed capabilities, and backlogs result. This forces more accountability from the computer department—which by now may be called the information processing department.

▶ In stage 4, **integration,** the organization builds on the TPIS and MIS to develop more fully integrated information systems such as DSSs. Networks integrating hardware, software, and systems are heavily used; users have regular access to and interaction with the information system and are accountable for its use; managers use the computer more effectively for decision-making support. The computer department allocates much of its resources toward maintaining existing programs and data bases, and department management is more actively involved in long-range planning and control of their operations. Through telecommunications, remote hardware is integrated with both internal and external data bases.

▶ **Information resource management (IRM)** is the concept that information should be viewed and managed as a corporate resource. Computer hardware, software, systems, and personnel require careful management in order to benefit the entire organization; fragmented and overlapping information functions should be combined under the control of a

senior information executive, a vice-president of information management.

▶ The **vice-president of information management,** or **chief information officer (CIO)** has four major responsibilities: (1) Coordinate and direct managers of data base systems, systems analysis and design activities, management science applications, telecommunications, and office systems. (2) Help other people in the company cope with change in technology, information needs, and health concerns, including **ergonomics**—the study of human factors related to computing. (3) Keep up with changes in technology. (4) Keep information secure and private.

KEY TERMS

Chief information officer (CIO), p. 513

Contagion, p. 509

Control, p. 510

Ergonomics, p. 513

Information resource management (IRM), p. 513

Initiation, p. 509

Integration, p. 511

Synergism, p. 508

Vice-president of information management, p. 513

REVIEW QUESTIONS

1. Describe some of the recent developments in software. In hardware. In systems.

2. What three activities make up the "tripod" of information processing?

3. What is the synergistic effect of telecommunications on information processing?

4. Describe the developing information processing system in an organization as it passes through the four stages of evolution.

5. What is the real reason for the slow progression toward integrated information systems in most companies today?

6. Define information resource management.

7. What are the four basic duties of the vice-president of information management?

CASE PROBLEMS

Case 16-1: The Interrupt-Driven Day

A phrase that describes the environment of many office workers is the "interrupt-driven day." One writer, C.W. Miramker in the *San Francisco Examiner,* characterizes such people thus: "Teeming with ideas and eager to tackle them, these people are incessantly pestered by phone calls, meetings, conferences, loquacious co-workers, visitors and more phone calls." The result, unfortunately, is that they have trouble getting work done because they cannot get time to think. Of course, this may be just a characteristic way people do things. That is, they get started on one project, then get interrupted, and then have to spend time on another project.

However the "interrupt-driven day" is viewed, some enterprising spirits see some new technological ways of coping with it. One is through the use of the portable computer, which allows people to be productive whenever and wherever they can get time. The other is through "windowing" or the "desktop environment," software that allows one to be involved with several applications programs—spreadsheets, word processing, data base, and so on—at the same time through overlapping windows on the monitor.

Most windowing software allows the user to "zoom in" on one window and hide the others. Often a mouse is used to move the cursor, rather than a series of keystrokes. What is important here is the ease of use with which one may interchange programs—something that has not been possible with microcomputers in the past.

Your assignment: Manpower Inc., one of the world's largest providers of temporary typists and stenographers, has operated since 1948 by testing people looking for part-time work and then placing them in jobs. A few years ago, in an effort to become the dominant supplier of operators for word processors, it started a program to train temporaries to use these machines. Suppose you were an executive in a temporary help firm like Manpower. You would probably have a high interrupt-driven day, as calls came in for temporary help (from different industries with different seasonal and personnel needs); as training programs were instituted; and as people called on you for new estimates, budgets, planning memos, and other demands. How would you use the tools described in this chapter to handle your workload and extend the services your firm has to offer?

Case 16-2: Synergism and the Reading Computer

Earlier in the book we mentioned data entry devices that can digitize and store all sorts of text and graphic material. An example of this is a device developed by Kurzweil Computer Products of Cambridge, Massachusetts, which has the ability to recognize letters and numbers in a great variety of typefaces, a task conventional computers cannot do. The machine is finding use among institutions that need large banks of computerized texts. A Boston publisher, for instance, uses the Kurzweil scanner to record the contents of books that it reprints in large-type editions for the visually impaired. The Nexus news information network uses it to scan newspapers and magazines. The federal government is using it to read documents printed in Russian and other languages.

Your assignment: In this chapter, we mentioned the concept of synergism—how one technology not only allows another technology to develop but also expands its capability and influence. Suppose you were able to acquire the Kurzweil scanner and link it with a large data base and telecommunications capability. Do you see how these might be used in some new form of enterprise? Think of the present kinds of information that now exist in typewritten or printed form: patent records, legal cases, political speeches, training manuals, geological data, medical histories, recipes, and so on.

Chapter 17

PRIVACY, SECURITY, AND ETHICS: KEEPING INFORMATION SAFE

"The only truly secure computer system," it has been pointed out, "is one that is shut down."

The remark came in the wake of the discovery in mid-1984 that a subscriber's **password**—the secret words or numbers that must be keyed in before the system will operate—to a major credit bureau had been stolen, making it possible (though it did not happen) for unauthorized people to cash in on other people's good credit. The credit bureau was TRW Information Services, based in Anaheim, California, with information on the credit histories of over 90 million people—a computerized data base and communications service second in size only to that of the Internal Revenue Service.

In another famous invasion, a group of West German computer hobbyists in 1987 broke into an international computer network—known as the Space Physics Analysis Network (SPAN)—of the National Aeronautics and Space Administration located in Germany and for three months roamed freely through 135 computers.

What did the thief or thieves, whoever they were, do once inside these systems? Interestingly, no theft or fraud was found, but the **hackers**—the term started out to mean "computer enthusiasts" but now seems to mean people with more malicious intent who invade other people's files and data bases—did not keep the passwords to themselves; they posted them on "electronic bulletin boards" available to microcomputer hobbyists with telephone connections. Still, in the TRW case the possibility for credit card fraud existed: Even if the hacker could not change a file, he or she could use someone else's credit card account number to charge up bills. The SPAN case illustrates another problem: The network was deliberately designed to be reasonably accessible because it was intended for the use of authorized researchers on NASA projects and so contained no sensitive information. Thus, security was sacrificed for ease of use.

Both these stories illustrate just how vulnerable the computer industry remains to breaches in security. They also show why organizations have such intense interest in security, including, as the box on the next page describes, fields such as **biometrics**—the measurement and use of individual characteristics such as fingerprints as unique identifiers.

CASE STUDY: WHAT PRICE SECURITY?

Senses of Security

The security industry has come a long way from night watchmen and frothing guard dogs.

Now, computerized card readers seal off buildings, and fingerprint-scanners scrutinize parents picking up children at day-care centers. Some machines even identify people by their eyes or voice patterns.

Businesses and government agencies are quickly turning to "electronic access-control" devices, largely because traditional security systems are often costly and less reliable. . . . "The development of access systems based on computers has probably been the single most important driving force in the industry," says Joseph Freeman, a Newtown, Conn., security consultant.

Non-security applications of access systems, however, might have a bigger impact on the workplace. These machines can be used as time clocks for payroll and can keep track of workers' visits to the company cafeteria—an Orwellian feature that has already triggered debate among security experts.

Electronic access cards have emerged as the most popular high-tech security method: a computer-linked device "reads" an identification card that is typically placed into a slot or waved in front of a sensor. The computer then releases the door lock and records the time.

The card systems are also attractive because electronic access devices are less expensive than security guards. Nynex Corp. saves $1 million annually because of the card-access devices it installed in 50 New York buildings, says Albert Larsen, a maintenance manager with the regional telephone concern. The buildings are also safer, especially for employees working night shifts, Mr. Larsen contends.

Meanwhile, more exotic identification systems are emerging. Called "biometric" devices, these machines identify people by fingerprints, voices or

even the retina of the eye. Fingerprint readers, for instance, scan the print as a person places a finger into a boxlike device; it matches the finger's lines and crevices with data previously logged in the computerized unit.

A wide range of businesses use the machine, although fingerprint scanners are primarily targeted toward users who require more stringent security. La Reserve, a pricey White Plains, N.Y., hotel, installed a fingerprint scanner in its wine cellar because thieves walked away with more than $3,000 worth of wine each year. And in Omaha, Neb., a day-care center uses a fingerprint reader to identify people authorized to pick up children, says Randy Fowler, president of Identix Inc., a Palo Alto, Calif., maker of such products.

Sales of biometric systems are expected to expand rapidly—more than sixfold to $95 million at the end of the decade . . . . But there are drawbacks. "It's possible to control-access a door for $1,000," says Mr. Freeman. "Biometrics costs (at least) five times that." Moreover, some systems aren't always reliable. Voice recognition devices, for instance, might not work if a person has a bad cold, Mr. Freeman says.

PRIVACY AND SECURITY WHERE PERSONAL AND BUSINESS CONCERNS MEET

Credit checking has become a big business. As one writer put it, "someone peeks at someone's credit history about a million times a day." Most such peeks are done by the some 2,000 credit bureaus around the country, which gather data on people's bill-paying practices from banks, merchants, and other creditors. Most of these credit bureaus are tied to the massive data bases of five major firms (of which TRW is one of the largest), which have records on more than 150 million individuals.

Although there is no going back on the trend toward large credit data bases, the integrity of such data bases depends on two important issues: privacy and security. **Privacy** is primarily a personal concern; it is the assurance to individuals that personal information will be used properly, is accurate, and is protected against improper access. Credit reports such as TRW's include both credit and personal history, including payment records, delinquencies, marital status, employment history, credit card numbers, and credit account limits.

Security is primarily an organizational concern; it is a system of safeguards designed to protect a computer system and data from deliberate or accidental damage or access by unauthorized persons. Security is thus concerned with preserving hardware, software, and information against fire, sabotage, and espionage, as well as various kinds of thefts—thefts of computer time, of programs, of data, and of passwords. The penetration of the NASA global network represents a problem in security.

Let us explore the issues of privacy and security in more detail.

PRIVACY HOW MUCH DO WE HAVE LEFT?

No doubt a great deal of your life is already in a number of computer files and data banks. And there is nothing wrong with that so long as it is kept in the limited form for which it was intended. Employers, physicians, and financial aid officers need to know different things about you; they do not need to know everything. Moreover, there are few of us who get through life without having some embarrassments, relationships, medical matters, and so on that we would just as soon not share with others. We have the legal right to keep such matters to ourselves.

Data Banks: Reaching Beyond the Manila Folder

Keeping personal information private has always been a concern, of course. Back in 1983, Harvard Law School professor Arthur Miller complained that "The manila folder just doesn't travel as far as the

Government data banks. The U.S. census is a necessary foundation of American democracy. However, a concern of democratic governments is that information be kept private and not be used for unauthorized surveillance of citizens.

computer entry.'' Miller was referring to government surveillance by computers, in which information about citizens is now more widely disseminated than it was during times when information was kept mainly in filing cabinets. About 85 federal data bases contain some 288 million records on 114 million people. The largest collection of records is in the Treasury Department, which includes the Internal Revenue Service. Of course, state and local governments have their own files, based on taxes, voter and car registrations, and so on.

Do government organizations snoop into private records and communications? Apparently they do. A 1985 study by the Office of Technology Assessment for Congress found that a quarter of 142 federal departments responding to their survey indicated they ''used or planned to use electronic communications-crashing techniques, including intercepting electronic mail, picking off satellite transmissions, tapping into cellular radio frequencies, and monitoring computer usage'' of individual and corporate communications. Those departments included the Drug Enforcement Administration, the FBI, the U.S. Customs Service, the IRS, and the Criminal Division of the Justice Department—but did *not* include (because the information is classified) the CIA, the National Security Agency, and the Defense Intelligence Agency, which may well do their own electronic eavesdropping.

Of equal concern is the extent to which government agencies exchange data. Fifteen federal agencies trade data on individuals, and the number of computer matches have tripled from 1980 to 1984, with more than 2 billion records being exchanged during that period, according to the Office of Technology Assessment; state and local matches have grown even more rapidly. Such matches started in an attempt to catch welfare and tax cheaters and defaulters on student loans, and to keep federal employees from receiving excess benefits. The intentions may be noble, but the problem is that errors may appear—and quite often have—that then are moved around to different agency files.

The concern about the way information is treated may be extended to nongovernmental institutions as well. As *New York Times* reporter David Burnham put it, one question about computers is concern about "their use by political groups, private companies and law-enforcement agencies to compile dossiers on virtually anyone by taking bits of information from such sources as telephone directories, drivers licenses, vehicle registrations, voter registration lists, land ownership records, and birth, marriage and death certificates." The worry is that these dossiers are used for purposes far different from those for which the information was originally volunteered. For example, the *Times* reported that a major clothing company that was looking for small women was able to obtain, for advertising purposes, a list of 63 million licensed drivers to find names and addresses of women under 5 feet 3 inches and less than 120 pounds who were between 21 and 40 years old. In a reverse development—a government agency using business sources—the Internal Revenue Service, in a move to locate tax cheaters, experimented with obtaining lists of high-income households from a commercial marketing company to see if those names also appeared on official federal tax rolls.

It is quite likely that a lot of information about you will get into data bases because you volunteer it—for instance, giving your job history to a computerized employment service. This will become particularly true as computers are used for more and more purposes. While this has some dangers, more worrisome is the kind of data that might be collected about you without your knowledge—from point-of-sale terminals, from teleshopping linked to a home computer, from electronic banking. Indeed, this is a downside risk of the automated office. A Yale University sociologist reports that some major American corporations "collect detailed and apparently trivial data to detect the flow of communication in their organizations," according to the *New York Times*. "Using computers, they gather data such as which executives receive copies of internal memorandums, eat lunch together or converse on the internal telephone system."

Privacy and the Law

"The right to be let alone is the most comprehensive of rights and the right most valued by civilized men," wrote U.S. Supreme Court Justice Louis Brandeis in 1928. Can this right still be protected? Critics say that computer technology includes some methods of information use that currently outstrip the ethical and legal standards for their use. Even so, there are some privacy laws, as follows:

A TEST TO SEE HOW DATA MOVES AROUND: MISSPELL YOUR NAME

All you have to do to see how data moves around is subscribe to a magazine or contribute to a worthwhile cause. Sure enough, your mailbox soon becomes stuffed with solicitations to subscribe to other magazines and contribute to other charities. Indeed, it makes an interesting test if you misspell your name slightly or use it in an unusual way (perhaps dropping the first name and using only the middle name, for instance), then watch how unsolicited mail comes to you in that form. But this experiment can also show you how erroneous information can be entered into computer files and widely circulated—a fact that should give one pause when considering how misinformation about you in government or credit files can go uncorrected for years.

▶ **Fair Credit Reporting Act:** Passed into law in 1970, this law gives you the right to gain access to records kept about you by credit bureaus—and to challenge the records if you think they are inaccurate. This is important because some believe that the credit reporting business has a poor reputation for maintaining accuracy in its information. TRW Inc., the firm referred to earlier, is said to estimate that a third of the one million people who each year demand to see their records challenge the information they see.

▶ **Freedom of Information Act:** Also passed in 1970, this law gives ordinary people the right to have access to data gathered about them by federal agencies. Sometimes a lawsuit may be required, and it often takes a great deal of time to obtain the information. In addition, an individual may find that the photocopies of his or her file have been heavily censored—information blacked out—in the interests of "national security" or some such.

▶ **Federal Privacy Act:** This law was passed in 1974 in the wake of the Watergate abuses, in which federal agencies were used to try to "get" Nixon Administration political enemies. This law prohibits secret personal files, stipulates that individuals must be allowed to know what is stored in files about them and how such information is used, and extends the restrictions not only to government agencies but also to private contractors dealing with the government. Organizations may not launch "fishing expeditions" to collect data about individuals; they must justify the effort.

Note that most of these laws were written before the technological explosions of the 1970s that produced electronic mail systems, corporate data communications networks, and cellular telephones—none of which are protected by privacy laws. One 1987 piece of legislation introduced in the U.S. Senate was modeled after approaches used by Sweden, West Germany, and France, which regulate the use of government data bases and some private ones.

Keeping information private is of vital concern. Part of keeping it private is keeping it secure. Let us examine this aspect next.

COMPUTER CRIME, PIRACY, AND INDUSTRIAL ESPIONAGE

As Figure 17-1 shows, there are a number of ways by which computer security may be compromised and a number of people in a position to do the compromising. For our purposes, security covers the following multitude of sins and possible problems:

▶ Computer crime—use of computers to steal money, goods, information, or computer time

▶ Piracy—stealing or unauthorized copying of programs or software

▶ Industrial espionage—stealing of computer industry trade secrets

Let us examine each of these.

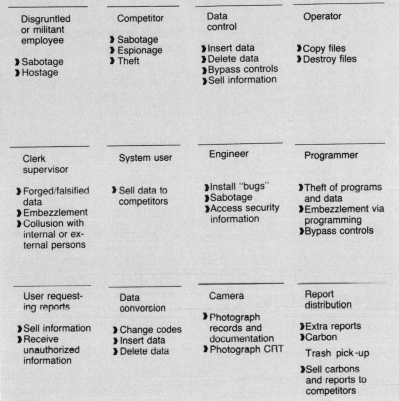

Disgruntled or militant employee	Competitor	Data control	Operator
❯ Sabotage ❯ Hostage	❯ Sabotage ❯ Espionage ❯ Theft	❯ Insert data ❯ Delete data ❯ Bypass controls ❯ Sell information	❯ Copy files ❯ Destroy files

Clerk supervisor	System user	Engineer	Programmer
❯ Forged/falsified data ❯ Embezzlement ❯ Collusion with internal or external persons	❯ Sell data to competitors	❯ Install "bugs" ❯ Sabotage ❯ Access security information	❯ Theft of programs and data ❯ Embezzlement via programming ❯ Bypass controls

User requesting reports	Data conversion	Camera	Report distribution
❯ Sell information ❯ Receive unauthorized information	❯ Change codes ❯ Insert data ❯ Delete data	❯ Photograph records and documentation ❯ Photograph CRT	❯ Extra reports ❯ Carbon Trash pick-up ❯ Sell carbons and reports to competitors

Figure 17-1. Computer vulnerabilities. The number of people with access to corporate files and the number of ways of getting at sensitive data are extensive. A company's director of information security must take into account all these possibilities.

Computer Crime

Computer crime is big business and becoming bigger. In a recent year, the American Bar Association found in a survey of 283 business and governmental institutions that *half* had been struck by incidents of computer crime in the preceding year. The crimes included unauthorized use of business computers for personal purposes, theft of tangible and intangible assets, and destruction of data. Indeed, one expert estimates that computer crime is a $100 million to $5 billion a year industry, although no one really knows the magnitude of the problem.

What are the various types of computer crime? Some of them are as follows:

▶ **Theft of computer time:** This happens frequently, and may range from the trivial—people using their employers' computers to type term papers or figure their bowling averages—to the serious, as in the case of two programmers convicted of stealing $244,000 worth of their employer's computer time to rescore music for a private business they were operating on the side.

▶ **Manipulation of computer programs or data:** This can range from changing one's grades in the college's computer files to, as happened with IBM's worldwide electronic-message network, people planting "computer viruses" that can cripple enormous computer systems. Some of the tricks of data manipulation are the **Trojan Horse,** in which a programmer adds instructions to someone else's program that allow it to work normally but also to do additional illegal things, and **data diddling,** in which data is modified before it goes into a computer file. In one instance, a 16-year-old hacker inserted dirty words into a company's computerized sales lists; the company suspended business until the system was (literally) cleaned up. In another case, someone programmed harmful instructions that launched a so-called computer virus that destroyed 40% of a hospital's patient records.

▶ **Theft of data:** This category includes the crimes of hackers who use microcomputers to break into large data banks and data bases, as in the TRW and NASA cases mentioned earlier. It also includes embezzlements; in one famous case, a former computer consultant for Security Pacific Bank in Los Angeles obtained an electronic funds transfer code and arranged to divert $10 million to a Swiss bank account. One trick of embezzlers, called the **salami method,** is to take only a few cents ("slices") from many bank accounts, so that the small sums will not be missed but the aggregate will be quite large.

The list of crimes using computers is nearly endless. As an example, let us look at the potential security problems for an agency that sells tickets to various musical, theatrical, and sporting events through record and department stores and other outlets. What can prevent dishonest employees from reserving tickets in fraudulent names, then selling them or "scalping" them at reduced rates? What is to prevent disgruntled employees from sabotaging or erasing ticket reservations for events that are months away—and that will not show up until long after the employees have left? What is to prevent hacker types who might work in the ticket outlets from breaking into the agency's system through their home computers? Such are the concerns with which a business must now deal.

Piracy

Piracy is illegal copying of software. At the level at which you will probably first encounter it, if you have not done so already, a floppy disk of a commercially developed program is bought at a microcomputer store; the diskette is then duplicated onto a blank diskette (using a microcomputer) for use by others—games for friends, word processing software for fellow students, electronic spreadsheet programs for business colleagues, or whatever. Duplicated disks may be given to friends or, worse yet, sold for a profit. Many software manufacturers have tried to build in software protection codes to prevent duplication, but there are many computer hobbyists around who enjoy cracking the codes and there is even software available that can break codes.

SHAREWARE VERSUS PUBLIC-DOMAIN SOFTWARE

"**S**hareware" is not the same as "public-domain software." A software program in the public domain is available for free. Generally, it's a program the author wrote for himself, found useful and is willing to share. . . .

"Shareware" falls between public-domain, or free, software and the decidedly private domain of big-ticket software houses such as Microsoft. As with the public-domain programs, shareware programs are initially distributed for free—through user groups, or, more often, through telephone bulletin-board systems like CompuServe. But if the user finds the program valuable, he is honor-bound to pay for it—either paying the author's suggested price or whatever price the buyer considers fair.

Shareware prices are low—ranging from $5 to $50 for the most part—and some of the stuff is junk. But many of these programs are markedly better than the high-priced alternatives in the private domain.

—T.R. Reid and Michael Schrage, *Washington Post*

Industrial espionage. Pharmaceutical companies are particularly vulnerable to industrial espionage—theft or misappropriation of trade secrets—because of the technical nature of their secrets.

Piracy also describes the activity whereby programmers steal programs from companies they work for. Although programmers might feel the programs "belong" to them because they developed them, the law states that programs belong to the employer. The U.S. Supreme Court has also ruled that software can be patented. The **Copyright Act of 1976** states that flowcharts, source code, and object code are copyrightable.

An interesting response to piracy is the idea of **shareware,** which operates on a kind of honor system. Shareware is software that is yours for the asking plus payment of a nominal fee for the disk (such as $5). If you like the software—word processor, spreadsheet, utility, game, or whatever—you can send the author some money for it, which may entitle you to updates and other information. But nothing *requires* you to send a fee. Shareware works for new software authors and outsiders for one reason: The cost of marketing software for commercial publishers by the usual means of advertising and promotion is tremendous. By offering their programs as shareware, new authors can get exposure and still derive some income—without having to spend much money themselves. An example of successful shareware is the word processing program PC-Write.

Industrial Espionage

Industrial espionage—the misappropriation of company trade secrets, either by theft or by more subtle means—has always been a problem in the business world. Aerospace, electronics, pharmaceutical, and cosmetic companies are particularly vulnerable because of the technical nature of their secrets.

There are perfectly legitimate ways to gather business intelligence; IBM, for instance, has an elaborate system that relies on detailed reports from its sales force as well as published sources to scout the competition. However, it is quite a step from this to photographing a competitor's factory layout or breaking into another company's data bases. As a company becomes more vested in technology, it must become more watchful of industrial espionage.

In a famous case, IBM security people helped the FBI in 1982 arrest two employees of Japanese computer maker Hitachi, Ltd., who were trying to obtain IBM trade secrets. The company and its employees later pleaded guilty in federal court to conspiring to transport stolen IBM property out of the United States and were fined several thousand dollars.

ETHICS IN
COMPUTING

What are computer criminals like? Interestingly, they are people you would probably find it easy to socialize with. They are often young, likely to be regarded as ideal employees, usually occupy positions of trust in their organizations, and have had no previous law-breaking experience. They do not see themselves as stealing but as simply "borrowing." They see the crimes not as crimes but as challenges, all the more so because they are clean and nonviolent acts and because quite often the crimes are reasonably easy to accomplish.

By "computer criminals," we are referring to the white collar rogues mentioned previously. However, what if you do a friend a favor and make a copy on a blank diskette of a microcomputer game that he or she has admired? This may seem like a nice thing to do—except that you have broken the law. Although you are permitted to make a copy for your own back-up purposes, in case the original is damaged, making duplicate diskettes for other uses is a federal offense, a violation of the U.S. Copyright Code. Yet bootleg copying is so widespread that it is believed there may be as many as ten illegal copies for every legitimate program sold.

"Just one copy can't hurt," people argue, but the copies add up, and the effects are reflected in the prices manufacturers feel they have to charge for their software. They may also be felt in the reluctance of such manufacturers to develop new software packages. Copiers may try to argue that "everyone does it" (so their individual illegal acts of copying will barely be felt or will only make them "even" with everyone else). They may also find it unlikely that they will be prosecuted, and indeed most software manufacturers find costly legal fees make court cases impractical.

The real point, however, is that copying software is simply unethical. A lot of effort by programmers and others went into developing the disk, and the developers deserve to be paid for their efforts. Not doing so is like your spending weeks writing a term paper, only to have someone else photocopy it and turn it in for a grade.

For some years, computer professional societies, such as the Data Processing Management Association and the Association for Computing Machinery, have had approved codes of ethics and standards of conduct for their members.

SECURITY CONTROLS

As we indicated earlier in the book, the trend is toward making computers easier to use and information easier to obtain. How, then, does a company keep unauthorized people from getting into its computer system?

There are a number of measures, which are described in the following sections.

Passes and Passwords

Authorized employees may need to have some sort of pass, such as a badge or a card, which they may show to company security guards in order to enter a computer room. Or the card may be a magnetized type, like the ones used to gain access to an automatic teller machine. This will at least keep unauthorized people away from the computer room. As we mentioned at the beginning of this chapter, the field of biometrics is now being pursued as a way of creating unique identification systems.

In addition, every computer system should require special passwords for access. Passwords should not be obvious—a group of Los Angeles teenagers once penetrated part of a bank's computer system just by trying a few logical passwords. It is advisable to have passwords of at least six characters; this length mathematically increases the odds against guessing. Moreover, passwords should be changed randomly and frequently, especially if a great deal of money is at stake.

Technical Controls

As Figure 17-2 shows, security **dial-back devices** can eliminate the problems of access by hackers and former employees. This may come to be a standard technical solution in future computer systems.

Encryption devices are another possibility. Data sent over telecommunications lines is encrypted or scrambled—put into code that can only be decoded by an authorized person. The American National Standards Institute has endorsed the **Data Encryption Stan-**

MICRO HEADACHES

Personal Computer Security Is Corporate Nightmare

Personal computers are getting to be a nightmare for corporate security officers.

"[Microcomputers] are being distributed throughout organizations without any plan," said John Omara, executive director of the Computer Security Institute in Northborough, Mass. "Professional security officers have been faced with almost insurmountable problems."

Horror stories abound. Local computer cops mention the executive at a medium-sized San Francisco firm who kept the company's accounts receivable files on floppy disks, which he left strewn around his desk. He quickly halted that practice when he came to work one day and found the disks stolen.

The culprit, assumed to be a company employee, never was caught. It took weeks to reconstruct the data, making it difficult for the company to collect its bills during that time. Fortunately, it appears the thief just wanted some blank disks rather than the vital data they contained. . . .

Chevron Corp. terminated and prosecuted one of its employees after discovering that he had been selling the company's software to outsiders. . . .

The value of the data processed and stored—everything from accounts receivable to confidential customer lists—on these [company microcomputers] is almost infinite. The loss of some of the most crucial data—for even a few days—could drive some companies out of business. . . .

Carl Jackson, the past president of the Information Systems Security Association, estimates that outsiders are responsible for just 3% to 5% of all security problems. Dishonest or disgruntled insiders are involved in about 10% of all reported incidents, while physical threats such as fires, food spills or electrical surges cause 20%. The largest category, some 65% of all problems, covers human errors and accidents.

"Even a telephone can cause problems," said Cheryl Helsing, who was director of information security for six years at Bank of America. . . . "The phone has a magnetic coil, so when it rings you could lose some of your data if it's too near your floppy disk."

She recalls the time a secretary for a local company spent three months transferring data from paper files into the computer without once making a backup copy. One day she came to work and discovered that every single file had been erased.

"They give these microcomputers to employees, give them a quick course in something like word processing and never tell them the important security things like protecting and backing up data," said Wayne Cerow, a computer crime investigator in Phoenix. "I go into offices at night and find important floppy disks all over the desktops."

Computerization of work causes another difficult problem: lack of control and accountability. In the old days of manual work, for example, three people might have to participate in the writing of a $10,000 check.

"Now it's all done by one person on the computer and that leads to all sorts of possibilities for fraud," said Charles Wood, an independent computer security consultant in San Francisco. "And often there is no audit trail to tell you what happened, which to me is shocking."

The computer consultants have a plethora of tools for protecting corporate microcomputer hardware and software. Yet they say the most important technique involves training employees to be responsible for the security of corporate data.

That includes learning not to share passwords used to gain entry to computer programs, creating duplicates of essential data, avoiding careless errors that can destroy data stored on magnetic disks and locking up disk files at night.

—John Eckhouse, *San Francisco Chronicle*

Figure 17-2. Dial-back system. This system prevents unauthorized outsiders from breaking into a company's information system using microcomputers and phone lines. One such system works as follows: ① A person dials up the computer, using a touch-tone phone. ② The computer acknowledges the call, asks for a password, which the person gives. The computer then disconnects. ③ The computer checks its files to see if the password matches an authorized phone number, then calls the number back. Only then is the person able to get on-line with the system. ④ If the call came from an unauthorized number, the computer dials the authorized location and warns the user that there has been an attempt to use that password.

dard **(DES),** a standardized code which, though it can be broken, most companies use because the method of interception by outsiders is expensive. Few companies are using any encryption packages, however.

Some software has built-in access restrictions, so that users are limited to only certain parts of the program. Or the software may have a user profile—information about regular users, such as job, budget number, access privileges, supervisor, and even loss-causing potential—that can be checked if there is a problem. Such software may also provide an **audit trail**—a means by which auditors can see if someone has had access to the data and, if so, to what parts.

Data encryption. Protection of messages during transmission between locations may be accomplished by data encryption devices which transform messages into unintelligible form at the point of transmission, then translate them into intelligible form again at their destination.

Management Controls

There are a number of straightforward steps by which managers can try to ensure computer security:

▶ **Screen applicants:** Employers should verify résumés and check recommendations when hiring.

▶ **Separate employee functions:** A programmer should not also be allowed to be a computer operator, since this would put him or her in the position of being able to run as well as write unauthorized programs. Separating functions is not always possible in smaller companies, however.

▶ **Keep a log system:** A log should be kept of all transactions involving access to data within the company.

▶ **Train employees:** Both employees and executives need to have a clear understanding of standards, and should be required to sign statements on computer use. Employees must be made to realize that information belongs to the company and otherwise educated about pitfalls and penalties.

▶ **Provide grievance channels:** The company's general counsel or an internal auditor or even a corporate ombudsman—a grievance counselor—is a good person to listen to employee complaints outside the normal supervisor-reporting channels. This can diminish employee resentments that can translate into computer crime or other security lapses.

Disaster. The destruction of data processing programs and files can be even more harmful to a company than the destruction of physical goods. The earthquake damage to this supermarket is serious enough, but it has been calculated that an average-sized distributing company would go out of business in only 3½ days if it lost all its data processing facilities. Companies must thus take steps to guard against destruction of their information processing by natural disasters, terrorism, and sabotage.

Law Enforcement Controls

About one-third of the states have enacted their own computer crime laws, but for years there have been attempts to get legislation passed at the federal level. Law enforcement efforts have also dragged behind, handicapped by a lack of definition for "property" and "value" as they relate to computerized information. Oftentimes prosecutors have been reluctant to prosecute hackers or other computer thieves because company security has been slipshod or naïve.

All of the above may reduce the possibility of unauthorized access to a company's important data and equipment. However, the worst *can* happen, of course—particularly that resulting from natural disasters. What if essential data *is* destroyed?

COMPUTER DISASTERS

"Today, money is just a blip on a transistor," says one banker. "Without power, we're paralyzed." Indeed, for some banks, even a brief loss of electrical power could mean the loss of hours of transactions. A severe dislocation such as an earthquake, flood, or concentrated act of terrorism or sabotage could shut down a bank for a few hours and have an immediate impact on state and even national economies, since banks cannot survive more than a few days of confused accounting.

According to a study by the Graduate School of Business at the University of Minnesota, without data processing centers, banks could survive a maximum of 2 days, distribution companies 3½ days, and manufacturing companies about 5 days. Some companies, say security specialists, give more attention to the security of their parking garage than to their computer systems and files. But, as the above numbers show, it is crucial that companies take steps to make their information assets secure from fires, floods, earthquakes, and sabotage, as well as from hackers, dishonest insiders, and disgruntled former employees.

DISASTER PREVENTION PLANNING AND RECOVERY

Disaster recovery will not "just happen"; it has to be planned for. A **disaster recovery plan** is a plan for rapid resumption of essential data processing operations that were interrupted by destruction or major damage. In anticipation of damage from disasters such as hurricane, tornado, flood, fire, or earthquake or damage from civil disorder, a disaster recovery plan specifies the following:

▶ **Who does what:** Employees are given specific assignments. Some are members of a disaster recovery team. A system of alerting employees during a disaster is set up.

▶ **What equipment is needed:** The plan specifies what hardware is needed and from where it can be borrowed or leased in event of emergency.

▶ **What programs have priority:** This is a critical decision. A bank might decide it has to put processing of customer checks before anything else.

▶ **What facilities and supplies are needed:** The plan must designate temporary buildings, air conditioning for large computers, and so on, that will be required in case of a disaster. The plan must also indicate what forms and paperwork will keep the work flow moving during the recovery period.

▶ **How input and output should be handled:** The disaster recovery plan must specify how input data should be gathered and how processed information should be distributed during the recovery time.

At first you might think that the biggest loss might be of an institution's expensive hardware—all that input and output equipment, computers, and telecommunications gear. Equipment is insurable, however, and can be replaced. What is more important is the loss of processing *time*; as mentioned, a bank could go out of business in two days if it lost its data processing capability. More significant than that, however, is the loss of processing *data*. How would an institution the size of an insurance company reconstruct its files if they were destroyed?

The trick is to continue to do business while the telephone lines are still down and the broken glass is still being swept up. To this end, companies have devised two ways of continuing operations in the event their own offices are wrecked:

▶ Use of disaster recovery centers.

▶ Mutual aid pacts

Disaster recovery centers consist of alternative computer setups that go unused except during emergencies. A typical arrangement would have computer, disk drives, communications network, and guaranteed power. A disaster recovery center may be either a **hot site,** which is a fully equipped center, with security, fire protection, telecommunications, and so on, or a **cold site,** which is simply an empty shell with power, water, and air conditioning in which a company may install its own equipment.

A disaster recovery center may be supported by a consortium of companies, since the centers go unused except during emergencies. However, companies may also join forces in mutual aid pacts. That is, they agree to lend each other computer time and facilities should one of their members be hit by disaster. For instance, in the Washington, D.C., area, a number of banks formed Bancon as a nonprofit organization to assist each other in processing checks—one bank alone processes half a million checks a day—in the event of an emergency. Members have agreed to share check MICR (magnetic-ink character recognition) encoding equipment during certain hours if a member suffers a setback, and the processing would then be done by an outside service bureau.

Whatever disaster recovery plan is adopted, a company should have a storage area away from its main computer facility in which to house back-up copies of hardware inventory, program listings, master and transaction files, and program and operating systems documentation, as well as the disaster plan manual.

THE BIRTH OF
AN INDUSTRY

In the 1950s and early sixties, when companies began to install mainframe computers, security of computerized information was not much of an issue. As one DP old hand from those days said, "There was only one group of people who knew how to diddle with a computer—our group. Now, with a number of micro and personal computers and large numbers of people becoming computer literate, there's a much broader understanding of use and how to get into corporate records."

As we contemplate the problems of security, it is clear that we are witnessing the birth of a new industry: protection of information. This is not like just any other industry, however, for there are many important legal and moral issues that must be resolved. How these are handled today will determine a great deal about how we live tomorrow.

Tomorrow—that is the subject of the next and final chapter.

SUMMARY

▶ **Privacy** is primarily a personal concern; it is the assurance to individuals that personal information will be used properly and protected against improper access. **Security** is primarily a business concern; it is a system of safeguards designed to protect a computer system and data from deliberate or accidental damage or access by unauthorized persons.

▶ Concern has been growing about possible invasion of privacy by computer misuse. Computer technology may include methods of information use that outstrip the current ethical and legal standards for their use. Even so, there are some privacy laws: (1) The **Fair Credit Reporting Act,** passed in 1970, gives individuals the right to gain access to records kept about them by credit bureaus—and to challenge the records that may be inaccurate. (2) The **Freedom of Information Act,** also passed in 1970, gives ordinary people the right to have access to data about them gathered by federal agencies. This sometimes requires a lawsuit, may be time-consuming, and may result in heavily censored photocopies. (3) The **Federal Privacy Act,** passed in 1974, prohibits secret personal files, stipulates that individuals must be allowed to know the content and use of files about them, and extends the restrictions beyond government agencies to include private contractors dealing with the government. Government organizations may not launch "fishing expeditions" to collect data about individuals; they must justify the effort.

▶ Three problems that might compromise computer security are: (1) Computer crime—use of computers to steal money, goods, information, or computer time. (2) Piracy—stealing or unauthorized copying of programs or software. (3) Industrial espionage—stealing of computer industry trade secrets.

▶ *Computer crime* includes various activities; among them are the following: (1) Theft of computer time ranges from the trivial—people using their employers' computers for games or personal use—to the serious, such as people using their employers' computers to operate their own businesses. (2) Manipulation of computer programs or data ranges from changing grades in college computer files to altering important instructions in a business system for personal gain. Two tricks of data manipulation are the **Trojan Horse,** which is adding instructions to someone else's program so it works normally but also does additional illegal things, and **data diddling,** in which data is modified before it goes into a computer file. (3) Theft of data includes using microcomputers to break into large data banks and data bases. It also includes embezzlement; one trick, called the **salami method,** is to take from many accounts only a few cents ("slices") that will not be missed but that will add up to quite a large sum.

▶ **Piracy** is illegal copying of software. It includes the copying of commercially developed software by private individuals, who give or sell copies to their friends. Many manufacturers build in software protection codes to prevent duplication, but these codes can be cracked. Piracy also describes the activity of programmers who steal programs they write for their employers. Programs legally belong to the employers of the programmers who develop them.

▶ The U.S. Supreme Court has ruled that software can be patented. The **Copyright Act of 1976** states that flowcharts, source code, and object code are copyrightable.

▶ **Shareware** is software such as word processors, spreadsheets, and the like, that people may purchase for a very small fee (for example, $5). If they like it, they can send the author more money for it, which entitles the buyers to updates and other information.

▶ **Industrial espionage** is the misappropriation of company trade secrets, either by theft or by more subtle means. Legitimate ways for a business to gather intelligence include getting reports from its sales force as well as from published sources about the competition. However, photographing a competitor's factory layout or breaking into another company's data bases is espionage.

▶ Copying of software is unfortunately widespread, but it is unethical because software writers are cheated out of the rewards they deserve for their work. Moreover, software manufacturers are forced to charge higher prices for the products they do sell.

▶ Passes and passwords are two security measures to prevent unauthorized computer access. A pass, such as a badge or a card, perhaps with magnetized coding, may be required of authorized employers by computer room security guards. The new field of **biometrics**—the measurement and use of individual characteristics such as fingerprints as unique identifiers—may provide new forms of identification systems. Every computer system also should require special **passwords**—secret words or numbers that must be keyed into the system before it will operate. Passwords should not be obvious, should be at least six characters long, and should be changed randomly and frequently.

▶ Technical controls can improve security against unauthorized system entry: (1) Security **dial-back devices,** which call back the caller, assuming the correct password has been submitted, and connect him or her to the computer, may eliminate the problems of access by former employees and by hackers. **Hackers** used to mean "computer enthusiasts" but now seems to apply to people who invade other people's files and data bases. (2) Encryption devices scramble or encode data sent over telecommunications lines so it can be decoded only by an authorized person. The **Data Encryption Standard (DES),** endorsed by the American National Standards Institute, is one such code. (3) Some software has built-in access restrictions to limit users to certain parts of a program. (4) Software may have a user profile—information about regular users, such as job, budget number and access privileges, which can be checked if there is a problem. (5) Such software can also provide an **audit trail**—a means by which auditors can see who has had access to what parts of the data.

▶ The following management controls can help to ensure computer security: (1) Screen applicants by verifying resumes and checking recommendations before hiring. (2) Separate employee functions so programmers are not also computer operators, able to run as well as write unauthorized programs. (3) Keep a log system of all transactions involving access to data within the company. (4) Train employees so they have a clear understanding of standards; require them to sign statements on computer use, acknowledging that information belongs to the company. (5) Provide grievance channels, such as a grievance counselor or internal auditor, for employee complaints in order to diminish resentment that might translate into computer crime or other security lapses.

▶ Law enforcement controls of computer crime have lagged behind; about one-third of the states have enacted computer crime laws, but so far no legislation has been passed at the federal level. Law enforcement efforts are handicapped by lack of definition of "property" and "value" relating to computerized information, and prosecutors are reluctant to prosecute when company security has been slipshod or naive.

▶ Data processing facilities are not immune to being hit by disasters. And even a brief loss of electrical power to a bank, for example, could mean loss of hours of transactions; a severe dislocation such as an earthquake, flood, act of terrorism, or sabotage could shut down a bank for a few hours with immediate impact on state and even national economies.

▶ A **disaster recovery plan** is a plan for rapid resumption of essential data processing operations that have been interrupted by destruction or major damage. It specifies the following: (1) Who does what—employees are assigned specific activities and a system is set up to alert employees during a disaster; (2) what equipment is needed—what hardware and where it can be borrowed or leased in an emergency; (3) what programs have priority when disrupted processing operations are being resumed; (4) what facilities, such as temporary buildings, and what supplies, such as forms, will be needed during the recovery period; (5) how input and output should be handled—how data should be gathered and how output should be distributed during recovery.

▶ A **disaster recovery center** is an alternative computer setup that is used only during emergencies. Typically, it would have a computer, disk drives, communications network, and guaranteed power. A **hot site** is a fully equipped center; a **cold site** is simply an empty shell with power, water, and air conditioning in which a company installs its own equipment. A disaster recovery center may be supported by a consortium of companies, or the companies may join in mutual aid pacts to lend each other computer time and facilities if one of their members is hit by disaster.

KEY TERMS

Audit trail, p. 535

Biometrics, p. 523

Cold site, p. 539

Copyright Act of 1976, p. 531

Data diddling, p. 530

Data Encryption Standard (DES), p. 533

Dial-back device, p. 533

Disaster recovery center, p. 539

Disaster recovery plan, p. 538

Fair Credit Reporting Act, p. 528

Federal Privacy Act, p. 528

Freedom of Information Act, p. 528

Hacker, p. 523

Hot site, p. 539

Industrial espionage, p. 531

Password, p. 523

Piracy, p. 530

Privacy, p. 525

Salami method, p. 530

Security, p. 525

Shareware, p. 531

Trojan Horse, p. 530

REVIEW QUESTIONS

1. How does the theft of passwords from TRW involve the problems of privacy and security?

2. What are some of the concerns about the possible misuse of computers dealing with personal information?

3. Describe one of the recent privacy laws.

4. What are the three areas of concern for computer security?

5. What is a possible computer crime? What steps could be taken to prevent it?

6. What can be gained by the use of passes and passwords?

7. Describe the steps by which managers can ensure computer security.

8. What is a hot site? What is a cold site?

CASE PROBLEMS

Case 17-1: Can You Make Money from Murphy's Law?

One of the interesting things about the computer industry is the number of third-party companies that have sprung up to serve particular needs that did not exist before. For instance, when Laurence Murphy was a vice-president of Brinks, Inc., the armored-car company, he failed in 1981 to convince the company that the time was right to enter the information security marketplace so he and another man joined forces to establish the Vault Co. of Atlanta. What makes the Vault different from other data storage and disaster recovery facilities, according to Murphy in an article in *ComputerWorld*, is that it is not just a warehouse but provides total physical and environmental security. The data library, which can store up to 100,000 computer tapes at $1 a month each, is watched over by closed-circuit television monitors and bonded security guards behind bulletproof glass. States the article: "Only a trained data librarian utilizing a comput-

erized tape retrieval system has access to the tapes stored in the library, which is both temperature and humidity controlled and equipped with a Halon fire-protection system. Clients must undergo a signature-matching process to verify their authority to take delivery of tapes." Now about 200 U.S. companies take in revenues of about $50 million a year providing so-called off-site computer data storage.

Your assignment: Long ago, another Murphy offered his famous Murphy's Law—"If anything can go wrong, it will." Look back over this chapter and, playing devil's advocate, think of the things that someone could do that are illegal and that might beat the system—ways of stealing data, selling pirated software, and so on—or ways in which a data processing system could be compromised or destroyed—that is, Murphy's Law in operation. (If you can think of a "scam," probably others have, too.) Now think of some solutions to these security holes. You may have the basis for starting up a new enterprise.

Case 17-2: Hiring by Computer—and the Privacy Issue

Will "pounding the pavement" and classified advertising become obsolete employment techniques? Perhaps so, if the growth in computerized employer–employee matchmaking services continues. According to press reports, computerized employment agencies "have helped fill thousands of jobs for engineering, data processing, marketing, finance and other professionals." Using telecommunications, employers connect with the employment service's data base and specify requirements such as skills, salary, and education. Within seconds, the computer provides them with people matching those characteristics. Employers can conduct a search of several states or narrow it to a single zip code, if they do not want to pay employee relocation costs. Some services also do part of the job interviewing process,

prescreening job applicants by asking them 80 to 100 multiple-choice questions. The advantage of computerized recruitment services to job hunters is that they give them the opportunity to apply for thousands of jobs all over the country. The services believe this method will be the primary source of recruitment in the coming years.

Your assignment: This whole topic is worth your serious consideration if computerized recruitment services become as important in the employment process as some people believe they will. Think about the issues: How do you feel about being interviewed by questionnaire instead of face to face? Résumés are often written to emphasize certain types of experience, depending on the job, but how would you deal with this aspect if you can put into a data base only one résumé? What privacy guarantees would you want to be assured of?

Chapter 18

THE FUTURE: INFORMATION— THE MAIN RESOURCE

The computer as tool—that is the idea we have stressed repeatedly throughout this book. Although we might like to think otherwise, human beings "are only occasionally productive, only occasionally goal-oriented," as humanist William Chace points out. "Much of the time humans day-dream, waste time, spin their wheels and, in general, prove inefficient and prodigal of their abilities. . . . Not so with computers." This does not mean computers are better than us. Rather, they are the tools that make us better—more productive, more efficient, more quickly able to achieve our goals. Indeed, as the case study on page 546 makes clear, the computer is responsible for a new spirit of enterprise.

THE COMPUTER AS CAREER TOOL

How will the computer figure in your career as we rapidly approach the end of the century? Let us consider this next.

The Outlook in High-Technology Jobs

Many students are considering a high-technology career—in electronics, computers, engineering, and the like—on the theory that these industries will be a major new source of jobs. Certainly there will continue to be great demands for people in these fields, particularly for those in electrical engineering and computer science.

But there are some important things to note about high technology:

▶ Even high-tech industries don't employ a great many high-tech jobs. U.S. Department of Labor studies show that only 15% of all jobs in electronics firms and 25% in computer and data processing firms are technologically oriented. Indeed, only 6% of all new

Career growth area. Accounting is an area that is expected to provide many jobs in the future—and accounting is relying more and more on computer technology.

jobs will be in high-tech areas, and no high-tech occupations are among the 18 top categories in job growth.

▶ High-tech jobs tend to be polarized, with highly skilled, highly paid jobs at one end and low-skilled, low-paid jobs at the other end. Computer programmers—a reasonably well-paying occupation that requires a college degree—will increase 70% between 1986 and the year 2000 (335,000 jobs). On the other hand, data processing equipment repair jobs (56,000 jobs), which don't pay as well and don't require a college degree, will increase 81%.

▶ There is a great deal of flux and change in high-tech jobs. One three-year study of such jobs in California found that for every three high-tech jobs created each year in the state, one was lost, owing to intense competition that resulted in mergers, movement of assembly-line jobs overseas, and so on.

High technology has been compared to potatoes: Potato farming employs few people and is unlikely to employ a great many more in the next decade or so. Yet there are hundreds of thousands of more people making a living off making and selling French-fried and baked potatoes. Technology seems to operate the same way. "There are not going to be a lot of jobs in technology per se," states one economist, "but there will be a lot of high-technology jobs." In other words, the growth of jobs in the future will occur more in industries that arise to make use of the technology rather than to create it.

Jobs That Use Technology

It is the intelligent use of technology or innovation, concludes MIT researcher David Birch, that generates employment. Innovation is the use of technology to create new or replacement goods or processes.

CASE STUDY: ENTREPRENEURS MAKE COMPUTING MORE INTUITIVE

User Friendlier

With the advent of the desktop personal computer, ease-of-use has emerged as the critical element needed to open computing to the masses, and entrepreneurs are flooding the marketplace with all kinds of hardware gadgets and software tricks to make these machines, if not more human, then at least less intimidating.

Today, innovative companies are bringing out products to liberate the computer user from the tyranny of the keyboard. Hard-to-remember written codes are evolving into familiar graphic symbols. Computerese is becoming less arcane, and computing is becoming more *intuitive.*

At advanced research centers, computer scientists are testing the "user-interface" concepts of the future. Massachusetts Institute of Technology's architecture machine group developed a system that simulates visually on a wall-sized screen the act of walking down a hall, opening a file cabinet, and pulling out documents. Its computer is controlled with hand motions detected by wrist-mounted sensors. Much university research today explores artificial intelligence (AI) techniques that could let a computer interpret speech or body gestures. "The real problem of the

future is to build a computer with common sense," observes MIT professor Marvin Minsky, a pioneering AI theorist. "You want a system to make a guess why you did something, and act accordingly."

Devices already on the market are making it easier to interact with personal computers:

▶ San Diego engineer Dennis Kuzara builds an inexpensive "light pen" that can locate or draw electronic images directly on a computer screen. He heads Design Technology, the manufacturing end of the business. His wife, Sherry, runs Inkwell Systems, the software and marketing arm.

▶ Pierlugi Zappacosta is president of . . . Logitech Inc., a Redwood City, Calif., maker of a mouse, the

Where will the new jobs be? If trends continue, nearly 75% of all new jobs in the future will come from service-producing industries, according to the Bureau of Labor Statistics. Indeed, service jobs are already outpacing manufacturing or goods-producing industries. Service jobs, which are usually more interesting and rewarding than factory jobs, include retail shops, airlines, fast-food chains, public utilities, and a host of other occupations.

A quarter of the expected employment by 1995—31 million jobs—will be in an area the Bureau of Labor Statistics calls "miscellaneous services." This category is expected to provide one of every three new jobs in the decade ahead. Miscellaneous services include not only recreation, hotels, and medical care, but also business services: consultants, personnel services, public relations, security systems, computer and data processing services, among other occupations. Employment in business services is expected to reach about

little rolling box championed by Apple Computer for control of its Macintosh.

▶ In Woburn, Mass., Jim Logan runs Microtouch Systems Inc., a . . . manufacturer of a video monitor that lets a user run a computer by just touching commands on the screen surface.

▶ In Fremont, Calif., Ron Stephens is president of Votan, a . . . firm whose product lets users control an IBM PC with voice commands.

▶ Founder Keith Plant's Speech Plus of Mountain View, Calif., is involved in speech synthesis. Computers that talk make it easier for production-line workers to understand data. . . .

New technologies let people do a lot more than merely point and talk to their video screens. The same devices making computers easier to use are simultaneously unleashing the power of computers for people who never had much use for them. From its conventional role as a calculation machine, the computer is evolving into a tool of creativity.

Some psychologists say the human brain parcels its thinking into two regions. The left hemisphere of the brain deals with logic, step-by-step analysis, and verbal thinking; the right side is the seat of intuition, metaphorical thinking, and visual comparison.

The thought processes of chess masters and mathematicians are linked with the left side of the brain; those of artists and musicians with the right. By virtue of the electronic logic etched into their circuits, computers have been excellent tools for "left-brain thinkers." Most computing tasks such as word processing and financial modeling are typical left-brain functions. But the very qualities that make computers so good at logic make them intimidating to people who are not mathematically inclined. In their efforts to make computing easier—through the use of intuitive devices like touch screens, mice, and light pens—engineers have made the machines more responsive to the right side of the brain. Now, entrepreneurs are responding with products tailored to intuitive thinkers.

"We've talked about our product as a computer for the right side of the brain," acknowledges Chris Berg, marketing manager of Mindset Corp. of Sunnyvale, Calif., which has developed an IBM-compatible personal computer with the ability to process complex color graphic images at high speeds. It can be controlled with a mouse or touch tablet. "Intuition is not plodding. It's spontaneous, erratic. Speed is very important," Berg explains.

—Sabin Russell, *Venture*

6.2 million by 1995. Another category, "miscellaneous professional services," includes lawyers, engineers, accountants, and architects, and is expected to provide 3 million jobs by 1995.

As we have been suggesting throughout this book, all these kinds of white-collar, managerial, or professional occupations will be making great use of computers in the future. The question is: How much computer training is necessary?

No High-Tech Skills Needed?

The computer is a high-tech tool, to be sure. But high-tech skills are not necessarily required to use it. In this sense, our experience does not follow the experience of industrial workers earlier in this century, when industrial machinery made many unskilled jobs semiskilled. Although, as we have seen, computerization has been introduced into millions of office jobs with the help of packaged software—word processing, spreadsheets, data base, and so on—one can learn to use a microcomputer without having to learn programming, for instance. Perhaps, as we suggested earlier, computer skills will be needed in up to three-quarters of all jobs by the end of this decade, but it does not follow that high-tech skills will be required to use the computer as a tool. Many service sector jobs may call for a level of computer expertise that can be acquired in only a week or two of practical instruction. In other words, learning to use computers will be like learning to drive a car.

The Threat of Automation

Perhaps, you think, it all sounds too easy. After all, you *have* heard about the threat of automation replacing workers. Indeed, automation gives rise to some serious concerns. In France, for instance, medical students have been advised to consider going into specialties that depend heavily on manual dexterity, such as obstetrics and surgery, rather than into other medical specialties that depend more on intellectual judgment and that may therefore be vulnerable to displacement by computers. In Japan, where the robot revolution has rolled through industry, labor resistance to further factory automation has developed—this in a country in which many large firms once adopted a lifetime employment guarantee for workers. And in the United States, some middle managers find themselves in the difficult situation of implementing factory automation systems that will eliminate their present jobs.

There is no doubt that computer automation will change the workplace. The Bureau of Labor Statistics predicts that by 1995 the number of jobs will change, with jobs in mining, private households, and farming staying even or declining; many other jobs growing only slightly; and jobs in trade and services showing the biggest increases.

Computers, robots, and other forms of high-tech automation will have complex effects. Some jobs, of course, *are* being eliminated. Others are being made more complicated and some are becoming more compartmentalized. But there are ways of dealing with the jobs issue. Any future manager needs to realize that enhancements in productivity brought about by automation can be wiped out by a work force resisting machine encroachments or by back-stabbing competition for remaining jobs. It is better to retain the talent and expertise that reside in the organization's employees by retraining them for computer-related jobs and describing to them the job opportunities that will become available to them once automation is in place.

Automation, then, is a manageable social problem, if we want to take hold of it. But we must look to see if there are other problems that may not be solvable.

Training. Many companies are finding out that the way to handle a work force threatened by layoffs from automation is, in fact, not to lay off people but instead retrain them, thus retaining existing talent. The people here analyze advantages of computers for other departments of the company and train personnel in basic concepts.

SHOULD WE REALLY
TRUST COMPUTERS?

Remember HAL, the computer in the movie *2001, A Space Odyssey*, that ran amok and killed all but one man on its spaceship? HAL almost seemed to symbolize an earlier generation's worst fears as to what computers could become—independent thinking, apparently friendly, but also insane and homicidal. As late as 1983, a Louis Harris public opinion poll found that there was still a great deal of fear among Americans about computers. For instance, 63% said "yes" in answer to the question, "Do you believe it is possible that computerized information will be taken over by the federal government and combined with electronic surveillance of individuals to control the population under a totalitarian state?"

What kinds of concerns *should* we have about computers? There are at least three areas over which we should cast a cautious eye:

▶ Health and stress
▶ "Computer error"
▶ Changes in quality of life

Health and Stress

Could computers be hazardous to your health? Take, for a moment, the locations where computers are made, such as California's "Silicon Valley," Santa Clara County, about 30 miles south of San Francisco. There are no smokestacks in Silicon Valley, and the plants that produce computers look like college campuses. Indeed, computer makers have enjoyed the reputation of being a "clean" industry. Yet in recent years there have been lawsuits by manufacturing workers who say their health has been damaged by toxic chemicals used in making microprocessors, air quality officials have discovered that semiconductor firms release several tons of smog-producing gases into the atmosphere every day, and local cities have found that their underground water supplies have been tainted by toxic chemicals from chip-producing firms. Computer makers, however, argue that their industry is still one of the cleanest around, and this may well be true compared to traditional heavy industries such as steel and automaking.

As we saw in the box on page 516 in Chapter 16, some people have raised concerns that computers—particularly display terminal screens—may be hazardous to users. Although there is no evidence that there is any risk to pregnant women or that low-level radiation levels are hazardous, there are legitimate concerns that operators may suffer from eye and back strain and stress. As we mentioned in Chapter 17, however, these have little to do with computer technology and much to do with improper adjustment and location of equipment and, most especially, unrealistic productivity demands made of clerical workers. Health and stress have become labor issues among office workers, only 10% of whom are unionized. These concerns may well increase as the number of workers using display terminals increases.

"Computer Error"

The expression "computer error" is often used to blame on a machine what are really human errors. However, computer-related failures do occur and can have a number of causes, as follows:

▶ **Faulty equipment:** This is what people often want us to believe is the cause when they say there is a computer error or the computer is "down." Usually, semiconductor manufacturers put chips through extremely rigorous tests so that failure is rare, although there was a good deal of furor a few years ago when it was discovered that National Semiconductor had supplied the military with chips that were not satisfactorily tested. But if chips are relatively reliable, other computer-related equipment can sometimes go awry: Air conditioning systems break down, printers quit, antiquated switching plants in the public telephone system fail, and

Silicon Valley. Cradle of the Computer Revolution, this area of hills and red rooftops in which so many computers are made lies in Santa Clara County, 30 miles south of San Francisco.

so on. Sometimes such malfunctioning equipment produces spectacular results: In June 1980, a faulty integrated circuit in a communications multiplexor wrongly signaled the North American Air Defense Command that a wave of Russian missiles was headed toward the North American continent. The mistake was detected, but not before Strategic Air Command bomber crews had been sent aloft.

▶ **Interrupted power supply and electronic "hash":** Power fluctuations and "noise"—static or electromagnetic pollution—are serious enemies of computers. A 25% voltage drop for even a tenth of a second can shut down many computers. Indeed, a great deal of time is spent trying to recover data lost from an electrical problem. Obviously, in the computerized future we will be highly dependent on electric power, and with continual growth in demand for electricity, some people worry that we will exhaust available supplies in a few years. In addition, a rise in electronic "hash" or "noise" is producing an epidemic of static that disrupts communications equipment and destroys data. Many firms have been forced to install expensive screens to shield computer hardware.

Backup. Stores like those in the Ralph's supermarket chain are paired with sister stores, so that if the controller for the checkout system fails in one store, the controller in the other store can take over.

▶ **Design flaws:** Often hardware and software manufacturers simply do not allow for the mistakes users might make on their equipment. For instance, microcomputer software is usually made without so-called audit trail reports, which indicate who was the last person to use the software and what changes he or she made— features that are usually included with mainframe software. Experts say that today's microcomputer hardware and software offer inadequate back-up facilities, so that it is easier to lose data.

▶ **Programmer errors:** Programmers have several opportunities to discover and fix program errors, but some may go undetected— particularly if the programmers are working under pressure to meet deadlines.

▶ **Data entry errors:** This is not a "computer error" but human error, and it is the most common source of mistakes. If you have ever been victimized by a computer billing foul-up, this is probably the cause of it—as it was for the Salt Lake City woman who was mistakenly credited with $161 billion in her Sears Roebuck charge account.

While a great deal of activity can still be done manually in the event of computer failure, albeit with difficulty, there are some situations in which activity ceases until the power comes back on. Until recently in some telephone areas, for instance, directory-assistance operators could not give telephone customers information because their directories exist only in computer form.

Banks, airlines, and retail stores usually have various back-up systems in case a mainframe computer should fail. If there is a power outage, there are emergency generators and batteries. If a mainframe computer goes down, there is often an alternative computer. In New York, Citibank has two main computers, each serving different regions but each capable of handling the entire system in an emergency. In Phoenix, when the reservations computer for Best Western's 2800 hotels goes out, the system can be switched onto a computer used for accounting and other back-office business. In Los Angeles, each store in the Ralph's supermarket chain is paired with another store, so that if the controller for the checkout scanning system goes out at one store, the sister store can take over. Reliability has been improved in many industries by use of **fault-tolerant computers**—mini- and mainframe computers such as those made by Tandem. These computers are built with two CPUs performing the same program. Under normal circumstances, the output from only one CPU is used. However, if one of the two CPUs fails, the other one is used to produce output.

Changes in Quality of Life

Computers will change the quality of life. During the 1950s when television was a novelty in American living rooms, critics speculated that television would produce a nation of unimaginative zombies. Likewise with computers—some scholars speculate they can even reduce curiosity and imagination because computers formalize the way we think. For the society as a whole, they may further the gap between first-class and second-class citizens: The former may be those with insider knowledge, access to data banks, credit cards, and so on; the outsiders will be the poor and unemployed and those living in the illegal "underground" cash-and-barter economy that the computer cannot penetrate.

These are some of the downside issues of the automated future facing us. However, there is a plethora of new, exciting challenges ahead. Let us turn to them.

HIGH-TECH AIDS
FOR THE FUTURE

"If you really want your people to innovate, buy a science fiction book, take the cover off and tell them it's history." The advice came from Atari, Inc., founder Nolan Bushnell to a conference of information industry representatives. "The future is not totally dependent on innovation. Most of the ideas are out there. Just read science fiction; most of the things they write about are going to come true."

Bushnell was talking partly tongue in cheek, but certainly a lot of the hardware and software around today *do* seem like science fiction come true. What are some of the innovations of the future that will affect how we live and work? Let us look at some possibilities.

Primary Storage

In a 1945 *Atlantic Monthly* article, Vannevar Bush, inventor of analog computers at MIT, took a look at things he thought would happen in the next 20 years. One of them was the invention of a gadget called a "Memex," which was a desk-size information machine that would have the capacity of about 10,000 books—the size of a small-town library—which people would be able to have in their homes. By the end of the present decade, it is now speculated, a processor with a cubic meter of space will be able to contain all the information in the Library of Congress.

Already we can foresee the changes that may come about because of 32-bit microcomputers—"supermicros." For less than $5,000, one of these machines will provide the computing power that previously could only be had from a $900,000 mainframe. Moreover, whereas today many chips are made from a 3- or 6-inch silicon wafer, in the future it may be possible to make chips that fill entire wafers and that can be joined to others as building blocks to make "chip machines." From these could be produced "component institutions"—component schools, component libraries, even "offices on a wafer."

In addition, the very basis of computer technology will no doubt change, with computers that process data not as electrical signals but as pulses of light—optic computers that will run hundreds or thousands of times faster than today's big supercomputers. Further, as we mentioned in Chapter 7, researchers are proposing biochips, which, using recombinant-DNA genetic engineering techniques, would permit computers to be grown as biological molecules. Perhaps in the future computers will be based on carbon rather than silicon.

Storage Technology

The floppy disk will probably begin to go the way of the punched card as more and more microcomputers begin using hard disk as secondary storage devices. Microcomputer storage devices will also continue to shrink in size, with more microfloppy disks and micro-Winchester hard disks that will hold millions of bytes of information.

As we mentioned in Chapter 8, we are also seeing a trend toward optical storage devices.

Printers

Future generations of copiers may be so good at duplication that the U.S. Treasury Department has been for the last few years looking into what will have to be done to make paper money less vulnerable to

Fiber optics. Loops of a hair-thin glass fiber, illuminated by laser light, represent the transmission medium of fiber optics, which will geatly increase the flexibility of telecommunications. A cable with such fibers can carry more than 40,000 voice channels.

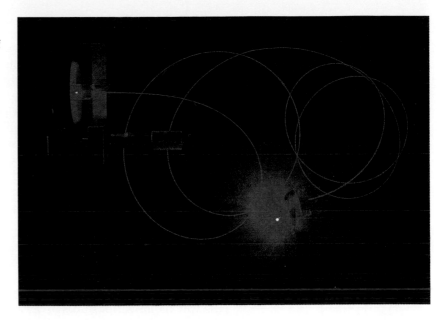

easy counterfeiting on a photocopying machine. Printers will also doubtless have better quality. Low-cost ink-jet printers and laser printers with outstanding graphics capabilities are already available and are bound to get even better.

Graphics Capabilities

About 30% of all software packages now sold are graphics applications, and sales are expected to continue to grow for the next five years as more managers become their own graphic artists. More microcomputer manufacturers are also building graphics capabilities into their products so that computers can generate some sort of chart.

In addition, new high-resolution video screens are being developed that will show finely developed detail.

Networking

Networking and data communications may well turn out to be more important than any of the above technologies, with the functions of this technology being extended worldwide.

Fiber optics, cheaper modems, and more frequencies providing more communication channels will probably greatly increase the extent and flexibility of telecommunications. In addition, we will certainly see an expansion in cellular telephone services using networks of radio towers interspersed in "cells" throughout a city to expand the use of portable and mobile phones.

Artificial Intelligence

If the developments above are revolutionary, **artificial intelligence (AI)** promises to be superrevolutionary. "AI will change civilization in a profound way," states Nils J. Nilsson, director of the AI center at SRI International. "It will change the way we work, the way we learn, and even the way we think about ourselves."

As we have seen, artificial intelligence—the field of study that explores how computers can be used for tasks requiring the human characteristics of intelligence, imagination, and intuition in order to perform specific tasks—is already here, and its subspecialty of knowledge engineering has yielded two applied fruits: **expert systems** and **knowledge-based systems.**

New Directions in Expert Systems

It seems almost generally accepted that expert systems will change the way organizations operate by altering the way people think about solving problems. Will expert systems solve our productivity problems, help individuals operate nuclear reactors and other complex equipment, enable managers to focus on more difficult tasks? Such are the expectations. Yet the hoopla presently being generated over commercial expert systems may well give AI a black eye if the advertised claims fail to deliver.

Before breakthroughs can occur, there must be further results in four areas, as follows.

Knowledge Representation   Today's expert systems, according to Patrick Winston of MIT, are "idiot savant—their knowledge is very thin." The present rule-based approach to solving problems, he points out, must be extended. Two possible problem-solving strategies are (1) classification, in which an expert relates a single situation to a larger group of cases, and (2) hypothesis building, in which hypotheses are formulated to explain the known information and then each hypothesis is evaluated further.

Problem Solving   Closely related to knowledge representation and sometimes called *precompiled problem solving*, this approach begins with a broad plan of attack, then refines the solution strategy along the way according to the peculiarities of the solution.

Connectionist Systems   If tomorrow's expert systems come to truly rival the authority of human experts, it will probably be because they won't run on the single-processor computers of today. As we mentioned earlier about the "von Neumann bottleneck," parallel processing allows problems to be handled by division of labor: So-called **connectionist systems,** or communication networks, will allow separate parts of a problem to be worked on simultaneously, and important results—not processing steps, but intermediate conclusions or nonconclusions—will be shared.

Marvin Minsky, one of the founding fathers of AI, is exploring a concept he calls the **Society of Mind system,** a theoretical attempt to construct a general intelligence not constrained to a particular problem domain. In this scheme, each processor represents a different expert, and all processors are connected with each other and coordinated by a "black box" that does not know how each works.

Natural Language Processors   It is widely accepted that for AI to truly achieve results it must be able to communicate with people in the language they can easily understand—English, in our case. Although scientists are delving deeply into the ability of machines to understand spoken and written input, the problem is much more difficult than many original researchers thought.

AI and Beyond

What should anyone contemplating a career in management, administration, or the professions watch for? The first wave will be small knowledge systems, many of them operating on microcomputers, such as complete law expert systems. For this first wave to take place, however, you and other managers and professionals must learn to use knowledge engineering techniques. This will probably start to come about when small knowledge engineering building tools are developed that have good natural language interfaces to support quick and easy development of prototype systems.

The second wave promises to have the most dramatic effect: true expert systems that resemble true human experts. These AI systems, called **Knowledge Information Processing Systems (KIPSs),** will combine the problem-solving ability of a computer's decision models with the know-how of experts, and will be available as part of intelligent workstations.

Clearly, these developments will radically change the structure and organization of today's data processing and information processing departments, and the power on an ordinary executive or professional's desk will be truly astonishing.

HELLO TO THE
INFORMATION AGE

Computers give us many choices. Still, the choices are only those that can be put there by human beings. When computers sometimes seem awesome to contemplate, we would do well to consider humanist William Chace's observation:

> The computer is, when all is said and done, a tool, no more than a tool, and it is our tool. We will use it after

craftsmen have made it available to us. So it was once with the hammer, cannon and the knife; so once it was with the automobile, the radio and the airplane. Originally objects of awe, curiosity, and even terror—we have exerted our full authority over them all.

So now it is with the digital computer. We will, certainly in the 21st century, claim it as one more man-made instrument that we have controlled and demystified.

SUMMARY

▶ The future job market in the high-tech field seems less secure than commonly thought: Only 6% of new jobs created between now and 1995 will be for high-technology workers. High-tech jobs tend to be polarized, with highly skilled, highly paid jobs at one end and low-skilled, low-paid jobs at the other. The high-tech job market also fluctuates widely, with mergers, relocations, and so on, eliminating some jobs as others are created.

▶ Employment opportunities for the future will be in the service-producing fields such as retail, airlines, and public utilities. One in three jobs created in the next decade will be in "miscellaneous services," including business services, recreation, hotels, and medical care.

▶ Computer skills may be required in up to three-quarters of all jobs by the end of the decade, but these skills need not be high-tech. The computer expertise required for many service-sector jobs probably can be learned in a week or two of practical instruction.

▶ There is no doubt that computer automation will change the workplace. By the end of the decade, 15% of today's manufacturing jobs will have disappeared, owing to automation and robotization. Many argue, however, that the automated machines will create more jobs than they eliminate.

▶ To deal with the jobs issues, managers must realize that enhancements in productivity can be wiped out by a work force resisting machine encroachments or by back-stabbing competition for remaining jobs. It is better to retain the talent and expertise of employees by retraining them for computer-related jobs and describing to them the job opportunities that will become available after automation.

▶ Today most Americans trust computers, but three areas should be examined: (1) health and stress, (2) "computer error," and (3) changes in the quality of life.

▶ *Health and stress* have not been thought a problem in the computer industry. Yet there have been lawsuits by manufacturing workers charging that toxic chemicals used in making microprocessors have damaged their health; air quality officials have discovered that semiconductor firms release smog-producing gases; and cities have discovered water supplies tainted by toxic chemicals from nearby chip-producing firms.

▶ Questions of health and stress have also been raised by computer users. Some have worried about the effect of radiation on pregnant women from display terminals, but the level of radiation is deemed not harmful according to present government standards. Visual and postural problems usually have to do with the positioning of display terminals and users. Stress has less to do with computer technology than with working conditions involving computers and unrealistic expectations by management for productivity by clerical workers.

▶ *"Computer error"* is often used to blame on a machine what are really human errors. However, computer-related failures do occur and can have a number of causes: (1) Faulty equipment; (2) interrupted power supply, power fluctuations, and "noise"—static or electromagnetic polution (a 25% voltage drop for even a tenth of a second can shut down many computers; a rise in electronic "hash" or "noise" is producing an epidemic of static that disrupts communications equipment and destroys data); (3) equipment design flaws; (4) programmer errors; (5) data entry errors. Computer reliability has been improved in many industries by use of **fault-tolerant computers.**

▶ *Changes in quality of life* may be a downside risk of an automated future. Some scholars speculate that computers may reduce curiosity and imagination because they formalize the way we think. For the society as a whole, computers may widen the gap between first- and second-class citizens: The former may have access to data banks, credit cards, and so on; the latter may be the poor and unemployed.

▶ Some of the technological innovations we may expect in the future include improvements in primary storage, storage technology, printers, graphics capabilities, and networking. (1) Primary storage capacity may be increased dramatically by chips that fill entire wafers and that can be joined together as "chip machines" that could be used to produce "component institutions" such as an office-on-a-wafer. Biochips, using recombinant-DNA genetic engineering, may permit computers to be grown as molecules. (2) Hard disk may replace floppy disks as the most popular storage device for microcomputers; floppy disks themselves will continue to shrink in size. There will probably be a trend toward optical storage. (3) Future printers will have outstanding graphics capabilities. (4) Microcomputer manufacturers are building graphics capabilities into their products, and graphics software will continue to gain in popularity. Affordable high-resolution video screens are being developed. (5) Networking and data communications will be enhanced by fiber optics, cheaper modems, more frequencies to provide more communication channels, and cellular telephone systems to expand use of portable and mobile phones.

▶ **Artificial intelligence (AI)**—the field of study that explores how computers can be used to perform specific tasks that require the human characteristics of intelligence, imagination, and intuition—is already here, and its subspecialty of knowledge engineering has yielded two applications: (1) **expert systems** and (2) **knowledge-based systems.**

▶ Before expert systems can truly solve business problems, there must be further results in four areas. (1) The present rule-based approach must be extended, using the strategies of classification—in which an expert relates a single situation to a larger group of cases—and hypothesis building—in which hypotheses are formulated to explain information. (2) Precompiled problem solving must be developed; this approach begins with a broad plan of attack, then refines the solution strategy. (3) **Connectionist systems,** or communications networks, will allow separate parts of a problem to be worked on simultaneously. Related is the **Society of Mind system,** which attempts to construct a general intelligence

not constrained to a particular problem domain. (4) AI must be able to communicate with people in the language they can easily understand; that is, there must be natural language processors.

▶ Future managers and professionals should watch for two developments: (1) the availability of small knowledge systems, many operating on microcomputers, and (2) the appearance of true expert systems, called **Knowledge Information Processing Systems (KIPSs),** which will combine the problem-solving ability of a computer's decision models with the know-how of human experts.

KEY TERMS

Artificial intelligence (AI), p. 556

Connectionist system, p. 556

Expert systems, p. 556

Fault-tolerant computer, p. 553

Knowledge-based systems, p. 556

Knowledge Information Processing System (KIPS), p. 557

Society of Mind system, p. 557

REVIEW QUESTIONS

1. How much training will be required to fill the majority of computer-related jobs in the near future?

2. What field is going to offer the greatest number of new jobs in the near future?

3. What are the three areas of computer technology over which we should cast a critical eye?

4. Take one of these areas and describe the dangers therein.

5. What is a possible solution to the question of job loss due to automation?

6. Describe one of the positive future possibilities of computer technology.

7. What four developments must occur before there are further significant breakthroughs in expert systems?

8. What two new "waves" should future managers and professionals watch for in knowledge systems?

CASE PROBLEMS

Case 18-1: New Management Ideas

A great number of things are going on that will affect the way managers will have to manage in the future. Consider the following reports:

▶ A three-year study of the American workplace finds that American workers want to do high-quality work, but this desire is seriously undermined by management practices. The Public Agenda Foundation of New York found that many workers report that lack of stress, convenient location, and good fringe benefits make their jobs more satisfying, but what makes them work harder are potential for advancement, a chance to develop abilities, and a challenging job.

▶ The coauthor of *In Search of Excellence,* told a conference that managers are out of touch with their employees and customers because they are not paying attention to quality needs, to the people on the production line. Thomas Peters said it is essential to instill a sense of trust within a company. "If you insist on treating the people in your organization like children, do not be surprised when they respond that way."

▶ Futurist Alvin Toffler (author of *The Third Wave*) says that people of the industrial society now be-ginning to fade were comfortable with uniformity, liked to be like their next-door neighbors, accepted permanence, and were guided by their employer. People in the new society protest routine, want to feel they are doing something valuable, are diverse, improvise, mistrust experts and authority, have multiple bosses, and set themselves in motion.

▶ Yale economics professor Jennifer Roback says that a number of fast-track professional women in their 30s who have become new mothers find they want more time off to spend with their children and more flexible working hours than their employers are accustomed to offering. Because many companies have difficulties accommodating these desires, Roback says the answer lies in self-employment, that such women should start their own firms and become entrepreneurs.

Your assignment: If you become a manager during the next several years, you may be dealing with a different kind of employee than the employee of the past, including many who will not want to work under normal hours or office conditions. How can you use the new technology discussed in this book to give such employees the kind of independence they may want yet still be able to ensure productivity?

Case 18-2: How Computers Can Shape Government History

A fascinating look at how technology changes our perceptions and ways of doing business was reported in the *New York Times*. Government administrators are worried that several computer technologies will have an adverse effect on the collection and storage of government documents such as drafts of speeches and preliminary memorandums outlining policy options. These early drafts are not only of value to historians but also to new government agency heads wanting to know the reasoning behind a predecessor's decision and to federal judges trying to weigh the issues in lawsuits involving government files.

Here are some of the ways information technology can hamper systematic collection of such records.

▶ Paper, once used, cannot be reused, so it almost automatically gets stored. However, floppy disks used in microcomputers are expensive, and so there is pressure to erase old data and reuse the disks.

▶ The information stored on disks is frequently not properly labeled.

▶ Information stored on computer tapes cannot be guaranteed for more than 20 years, because the electronic signal deteriorates.

▶ Information is recorded on a form such as a kind of microfilm that becomes obsolete and the machines used to make the information available are dropped from the government inventory.

Your assignment: Clearly, some policies for handling such information are needed. Suppose you were an information consultant to the Government Services Administration, the government's warehouse and supply agency; the National Bureau of Standards; and the U.S. Congress. What kind of procedures would you suggest for preserving documents? Suppose you were making recommendations to a large insurance company, whose interest in preserving records is no less critical. Would your recommendations be any different?

HISTORY OF THE INFORMATION AGE

Nothing can be fully understood without context, and history is context. The history of the Information Age is told in this appendix; however, in order to set the scene for the present, let us begin with the recent past—with a description of the developments in technology of the last 40 years that enabled the computer to be created.

The Challenge of the Chip

The principal driving force of the Information Revolution is a device no thicker than your thumbnail and half its size—the *microchip* or *integrated circuit*. Ordinary consumers probably first became aware of the impact of these chips during the 1970s when pocket calculators began to appear. More dramatic are the chips now found in home or personal computers, which consume less than one watt of power yet have the computational ability of a 1946-era room-size computer requiring 140,000 watts of power, enough electricity to run a small power station. Today, machines ranging from cardiac pacemakers to communications satellites are familiar applications of microchip technology. And, of course, so are the new business machines of interest to us: computers, telecommunications equipment, and so on.

The Vacuum Tube

The power of the computer is intimately linked to the size of the electronic device within it that controls the flow of electric current. The earliest electronic device was the vacuum tube (Figure A-1), an electronic tube about the size of a light bulb. In one of the earliest computers, the 1946 ENIAC, 18,000 vacuum tubes were required—and all had to operate simultaneously. One critic objected that because "the average life of a vacuum tube is 3,000 hours, a tube failure would occur every 15 minutes. Since it would average more than 15 minutes to find the bad tube, no useful work could ever be done." Nevertheless, the ENIAC was able to complete ten months' worth of calculations in one day.

Figure A-1.   Three generations of technology.
Vacuum tubes *(top left)* gave way to transistors
and then to integrated circuits or chips *(bottom
right)*. The relative sizes of the three forms of
technology are shown at top right.

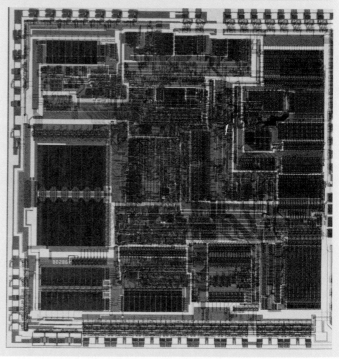

The Transistor

In 1959, the vacuum tube was succeeded by the transistor (Figure A-1), a type of electrical circuitry several times smaller than the vacuum tube. Invented by three Bell Laboratories scientists—John Bardeen, Walter Brattain, and William Shockley, who later shared a Nobel prize for their efforts—transistors also had other advantages in that they needed no warm-up time, consumed less energy, and were faster and more reliable.

The Integrated Circuit

Beginning in 1965, the transistor began to be replaced by the integrated circuit (Figure A-1), which was much smaller. Indeed, an integrated circuit less than one-eighth inch square now may contain hundreds of components and replace an entire circuit board of transistors. This further miniaturization set the stage for "democratizing" computers. No longer were computers the exclusive property of business, university, and government organizations. The real revolution was about to begin: computers for everybody.

Integrated circuits are made with one of the earth's most abundant materials, a nonmetallic substance called silicon, found in common beach sand and in practically all rocks and clay. The element has given rise to the name "Silicon Valley" for California's Santa Clara County, an hour's drive south of San Francisco and originally the principal site of the electronics industry making what came to be known as the **silicon chip,** another name for integrated circuit. Silicon is used because it is a **semiconductor**—that is, a crystalline substance that will conduct electric current when it is "doped" with chemical impurities. A cylinder of silicon is sliced into wafers, each about 3 inches in diameter, and each wafer is etched repeatedly with patterns of electrical circuitry, then divided into several hundred small chips. A chip 1 centimeter square is so powerful it can hold 10,000 words—the length of a daily newspaper. Integrated circuits have proved to be extremely reliable, because semiconductor firms give them rigid work/not work tests. Mass production has also made them inexpensive to manufacture, and their compactness has made them inexpensive to operate because of reduced travel time for the electricity and hence low power use.

The Microprocessor

In 1969, an Intel Corporation design team headed by Ted Hoff developed the microprocessor. In this development, the integrated circuits evolved from specialized chips designed for computer memory and logic into general-purpose processors on a chip, or microprocessors. It is these devices that are found in the variety of products we see today, from microwave ovens to personal computers.

Figure A-2. Charles Babbage.

What about the future? Futurists speculate about entire wafers being used for superpowerful chips, about an office-on-a-chip, about biochips and superconductors. We describe some of these fascinating possibilities in the text of the book. Now, however, let us turn from a description of the technology to an account of the people behind the developments of the Information Age.

The Beginning: Babbage, Lady Byron, and the Brass and Pewter Computer

The abacus—beads strung on wires—has been used in the Orient for 5,000 years to do calculations, and a French mathematician named Blaise Pascal developed a cigar-box-sized mechanical adding machine in 1642. However, the computer itself—the basis for office automation and the Information Revolution—was conceived in Victorian England over 160 years ago.

The tale of Charles Babbage, called "the father of the computer," is one of genius, obsession, and disappointment. Born in England in 1791, Babbage (Figure A-2) was a man of inherited wealth who be-

Figure A-3. A model of the difference engine.

Figure A-4. **The analytical engine.** This model was built by Babbage's son.

came a well-known mathematician and inventor. As a young man, he conceived the notion that logarithmic tables, which at that time were laboriously computed by hand, might be more accurately calculated by machinery. In 1822, he assembled the basic scheme for a machine that would calculate the successive differences in polynomial equations and presented the idea as a paper to the Royal Astronomical Society, which awarded the paper its gold medal. Encouraged by this success, Babbage then undertook the building of a demonstration model of what he called a difference engine (Figure A-3), using a grant from the English government.

In a workshop on the Babbage estate, craftsmen began manufacturing rods, ratchets, wheels, and gears, which were then assembled into a giant machine. However, it was soon discovered that the smallest irregularities were enough to throw the tons of brass and pewter parts into fits of grinding and shaking, bringing the steam-driven machine to a halt. The state of the art of Victorian technology failed to support Babbage's vision. As the machine became increasingly expensive, the government withdrew its financial support.

Undaunted, Babbage conceived of another mechanical marvel called the analytical engine (Figure A-4), which he hoped could do not just one kind of calculation but a variety of tasks. The analytical engine was the first machine to possess the five key concepts of modern computers: (1) an input device, (2) a processor, or number calculator; (3) a control unit to direct the task to be performed and the sequence of calculations; (4) a storage place or memory, to hold information waiting to be processed; and (5) an output device.

Figure A-5. Augusta Ada Byron.

The government considered this project hopeless also, but Babbage attracted support from an unexpected quarter, the poet Lord Byron's daughter, the beautiful Augusta Ada Byron (Figure A-5), who later became the Countess of Lovelace. If Babbage was the "father of the computer," Lady Lovelace was the "first programmer." A woman not only of leisure but also of intellectual accomplishments, including that of mathematician, Lady Lovelace was 27 when she came to Babbage's work, and over the next 10 years she helped develop the instructions for doing computations on the analytical engine. Her notes, "Observations on Mr. Babbage's Analytical Engine," contain thoughts not only on the machine but also on the nature of mechanical intelligence. ("The Analytical Engine has no pretensions whatever to originate anything. It can do whatever we know how to order it to perform. It can follow analysis; but it has no power of anticipating any analytical relations or truths." In other words, a computer by itself cannot be considered creative.)

Lady Lovelace died of cancer at age 36. Babbage continued to persevere on his machines, without completing either one. Ironically, late in life he saw another engineer complete a simpler model of the difference engine. He died in 1871 at age 80, suffering the disappointment of having an idea ahead of its time, an idea that the technology of his era could not fulfill.

Figure A-6. Herman Hollerith and his tabulating machine. This electrical tabulator and sorter was used to process punched cards.

Hollerith and the Punched-Card Revolution

Technology often advances by the adoption of ideas from unlikely quarters. The analytical engine of Charles Babbage, for instance, used a concept theoretically devised by Frenchman Joseph Jacquard for weaving textiles. Jacquard, noting the repetitious nature of the task required of weavers working on looms, devised a stiff card with a series of holes punched in it. The card blocked certain threads from entering the loom and let other threads go on to complete the weave. Babbage realized that the punched-card system could also be used to control the order of calculations in the analytical engine, and he incorporated the device in his machine. The Babbage/Jacquard idea, kept alive in Lady Ada Byron's notes, finally found utility in the United States in the 1890 census.

America in the late 19th century burgeoned with a growing population of new immigrants from Europe, so large a mass yearning to breathe free that as a consequence the census of 1880 required $7\frac{1}{2}$ years to tabulate, since all counting had to be done by hand. Realizing that it faced the danger of not completing a census before having to do the next one (the U.S. Congress requires a census of the country's population every ten years), the Census Bureau held a competition to find a new method of counting.

Many ideas were submitted, but three were chosen as final contenders: William Hunt's system of colored cards, Charles Pidgin's system of color-coded tokens, and Herman Hollerith's electronic tabulation machine (Figure A-6). A final test, involving a count of the population of St. Louis, Missouri, however, yielded the following results: Hunt's system—55 hours; Pidgin's system—44 hours; Hollerith's machine—$5\frac{1}{2}$ hours. The Census Bureau, accordingly, adopted the Hollerith electric tabulator, and as a result, an official count of the 1890 population (62,622,250) was announced only six weeks after the census was taken.

Like the Jacquard cards, Hollerith's punched cards involved stiff paper with holes punched in specific places, representing data to be processed. In the machine, rods passing through the holes completed an electrical circuit, causing a counter to advance one unit. The difference between Babbage's and Hollerith's machines, however, was crucial: Babbage's was mechanical and physically incapable of operating with precision; Hollerith's was *electrical*.

Hollerith realized that there was a commercial need for the rapid tabulation of figures and statistics, and in 1896 he left the Census Bureau to found the Tabulating Machine Company. The company was successful in selling services to railroads and other clients, including the government of czarist Russia. In 1924, the successor to this company merged with two others to form the International Business Machines Corporation, known today as that giant of the computer industry, IBM.

From Electromechanical to Electronic Computers: Aiken to ENIAC

For over 30 years, Thomas J. Watson, Sr., one of the supersalesmen of the 20th century, ran International Business Machines Corp. (IBM) with an autocratic hand. As a result, the company that emerged as a successor to Herman Hollerith's Tabulating Machine Company was highly successful at selling mechanical calculators to business.

It was only natural, then, that a young Harvard associate professor of mathematics, Howard H. Aiken, after reading Charles Babbage and Ada Byron's notes and conceiving of a modern equivalent of Babbage's analytical engine, should approach Watson for research funds (Figures A-7 and A-8). The cranky head of IBM, after hearing a pitch for the commercial possibilities, thereupon gave Aiken a million dollars. As a result, the Harvard Mark I was born.

Nothing like the Mark I had ever been built before. Eight feet high and 55 feet long, made of streamlined steel and glass (Figure A-9), it emitted a sound that one person said was "like listening to a roomful of old ladies knitting away with steel needles." Whereas Babbage's original machine had been mechanical, the Mark I was electromechanical, using electromagnetic relays (not vacuum tubes) in combination with mechanical counters. Unveiled in 1944, the Mark I had enormous publicity value for IBM, but it was never really

Figure A-7. Howard Aiken. The inventor of the Mark I is shown at left.

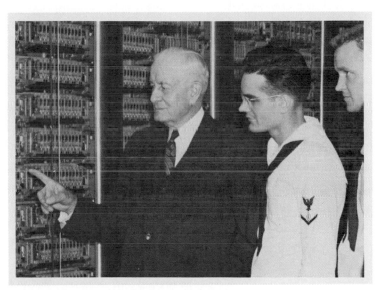

Figure A-8.   Thomas J. Watson, Sr. The "Old Man" of IBM, he gave Aiken the funds with which to develop the Mark I.

Figure A-9. The Mark I. This magnificent-looking and—for the times—streamlined machine was the first electromechanical computer. It may be seen in the Smithsonian in Washington, D.C.

efficient. The invention of a truly *electronic* computer came from other quarters.

Who is the true inventor of the electronic computer? In 1974, a federal court determined, as a result of patent litigation, that Dr. John V. Atanasoff was the originator of the ideas required to make an electronic digital computer actually work. However, some computer historians dispute this court decision, attributing that designation to Dr. John Mauchly. The background is as follows.

In the late 1930s, Atanasoff (Figure A-10), a professor of physics at what is now Iowa State University, spent time trying to build an electronic calculating device to help his students solve complicated mathematical problems. One night, while sitting in an Illinois roadside tavern, after having driven 189 miles to clear his thoughts, the idea came to him for linking the computer memory and associated logic. With the help of a graduate student, Clifford Berry, and using vacuum tubes, he built the first digital computer that worked electronically. The computer was called the ABC, for "Atanasoff-Berry Computer" (Figure A-11).

During the years of 1940–41, Atanasoff met with Mauchly, who was then a professor with the Moore School of Electrical Engineering at the University of Pennsylvania. Mauchly had been interested in building his own computer, and there is a good deal of dispute as to how many of Atanasoff and Berry's ideas he might have utilized. In any case, in 1942 Mauchly and his assistant, J. Presper Eckert, were asked by American military officials to build a machine that would rapidly calculate trajectories for artillery and missiles. The machine they proposed, which would cut the time needed to produce trajectories from 15 minutes to 30 seconds, would employ 18,000 vacuum tubes—and all of them would have to operate simultaneously.

This machine, called ENIAC—for *Electronic Numerical Integrator and Calculator*—was worked on 24 hours a day for 30 months

Figure A-10. John V. Atanasoff. As a young man, he and Clifford Berry developed the components of the first electronic digital computer.

Figure A-11. The ABC. The Atanasoff-Berry Computer.

Figure A-12. The ENIAC. Coinventors J. Presper Eckert Jr. *(left)* and John W. Mauchly *(center)* are shown with the first fully working electronic computer. The ENIAC occupied 1,500 square feet of space.

and was finally turned on in February 1946, too late to aid in the war effort. A massive machine that filled an entire room (Figure A-12), it was able to multiply a pair of numbers in about 3 milliseconds, which made it 300 times faster than any other machine.

There were a number of drawbacks to ENIAC—including serious cooling problems because of the heat generated by all the tubes and, more importantly, ridiculously small storage capacity. Worst of all, the system was quite inflexible. Each time a program was changed, the machine had to be rewired. This last obstacle was overcome by the Hungarian-born mathematical genius Dr. John von Neumann (Figure A-13).

The holder of degrees in chemistry and physics, a great storyteller, and a man with total recall, von Neumann was a member of the Institute for Advanced Study in Princeton, New Jersey. One day in 1945, while waiting for a train in Aberdeen, Maryland, a member of the ENIAC development team, Herman Goldstine, ran into von Neumann, who was then involved in the top-secret work of designing atomic weapons. Since both persons had security clearances, they were able to discuss each other's work, and von Neumann began to realize that the difficulties he was having in the time-consuming checking of his advanced equations could be solved by the high speeds of ENIAC. As a result of that chance meeting, von Neumann joined the ENIAC team as a special consultant.

When the Army requested a more powerful computer than ENIAC, von Neumann responded by proposing the EDVAC (for Electronic Discrete Variable Automatic Computer), which would utilize the stored program concept. That is, instead of people having to rewire the machine to go to a different program, the machine would, in less than a second, "read" instructions from computer storage for

Figure A-13. John von Neumann. The Hungarian-born mathematical genius who helped originate the stored program concept.

switching to a new program. Von Neumann also proposed that the computer use the binary numbering system (the ENIAC worked on the decimal system), to take advantage of the two-state conditions of electronics ("on" and "off" to correspond to 1 and 0).

Mauchly and Eckert and others at the Moore School of Engineering set out to build the EDVAC, but the first computer using the stored program concept was actually the EDSAC, built in 1949 at Cambridge University in England. One reason that EDVAC was delayed was that Eckert and Mauchly founded their own company in 1946 to build what would ultimately be called the UNIVAC computer.

From UNIVAC to PC

It is hard to believe now that people used to refer to a computer as a "Univac," but this is the name by which it probably first came to public attention. UNIVAC was the name that Presper Eckert and John Mauchly gave to their *Universal Automatic Computer*, on which they began work in 1946, fresh from their work on ENIAC. In 1949, Remington Rand acquired the company, and the first UNIVAC became operational at the Census Bureau in 1951.

However, it was in the next year, a presidential election year, that the public really came to know the term UNIVAC. During vote counting the night of the 1952 election, UNIVAC surprised CBS network executives by predicting—after analyzing only 5% of the vote counted—that Eisenhower would defeat Stevenson for President (Figure A-14). Of course, since then, computers have been used extensively by television networks to predict election outcomes.

Figure A-14. The UNIVAC. J. Presper Eckert points out to newsman Walter Cronkite a printout from UNIVAC during the 1952 presidential election.

UNIVAC was also the first computer used for data processing and record keeping by a business organization—it was installed by General Electric in Louisville, Kentucky, in 1954. Also in that year, IBM's 650 mainframe computer was first installed, an upgrade of the company's punched-card machines. Because businesspeople were already used to punched-card data processing, the IBM 650 was readily accepted by the business community, thus giving IBM a substantial foot in the door to the computer market, an advantage it still enjoys today.

We have described the movement of computers from vacuum tubes (1951) to transistors (1959) to integrated circuits (1965). By 1960, a number of companies had entered the computer market, among them Control Data Corporation (CDC), National Cash Register (NCR), and General Electric.

In 1964, after reportedly spending a spectacular $5 billion, IBM announced an entire new line of computers called the System/360 (Figure A-15), so-called because they covered "360 degrees" of a circle. That is, the System/360 came in several models and sizes, with about 40 different kinds of input and output and secondary storage devices, all compatible so that customers could put together systems tailor-made to their needs and budgets. Despite the tremendous disruption for users, the System/360 was a resounding success and repaid IBM's investment many times over.

But in the 1960s and 1970s, competitors to IBM saw holes they could fill. Large mainframe computers began to be supplemented by minicomputers, such as those made by Digital Equipment Corporation (DEC), Data General Corporation, and Hewlett-Packard. Cray, formed by Seymour Cray, began developing the supercomputer. A former IBM employee named Gene Amdahl marketed his Amdahl 470V/6, which was one and one-half times faster than a comparable IBM computer, yet cost less and occupied only a third the space.

Figure A-15. The IBM System/360.
This $5 billion system helped IBM control 70% of the market for mainframe computers.

Besides General Electric, RCA also tried to penetrate the mainframe computer market, but later withdrew. Of the original mainframe makers, the survivors today are IBM, NCR, UniSys (Sperry-Univac and Burroughs reconstituted), and Honeywell—and IBM has the majority of the mainframe market.

In the 1970s, the volatile computer industry was thrown into an uproar when the microprocessor was invented, pointing the way to the relatively inexpensive microcomputer. Led by the famous Apple II, invented by Steve Jobs and Steve Wozniak at Apple Computer, then by other products from Tandy-Radio Shack, Commodore, Atari, and Texas Instruments, the microcomputer market has been the battleground of over 150 different computer manufacturers—among them those two industrial giants, IBM and AT&T.

IBM introduced its IBM PC (for Personal Computer) in the summer of 1981, and immediately zoomed to the top in microcomputer sales—not surprising, considering IBM's long-term presence in the computer industry and its strength as a marketing-oriented organization. The IBM PC led to several enormous industries, among them IBM-compatible hardware and "clones," popular software such as that produced by Lotus and Software Publishing, and telecommunications entities such as local area networks and on-line-retrieval bulletin boards.

American Telephone & Telegraph, on the other hand, which used to be thought of as "Ma Bell" or "the Phone Company," was forced by the U.S. government to divest itself of 22 local Bell operating companies (regrouped into seven regional holding companies) and to allow competition from other long-distance telephone services, such as MCI and GTE's Sprint, and Allnet Communications. In return, the government permitted AT&T to enter the computer market. The question in many observers' minds, however, was whether AT&T could relinquish the habits of a monopoly and become an aggressive marketing force in a highly competitive business. The announcement of AT&T's personal computer, the PC6300 (produced by the Italian office equipment maker Olivetti) in June 1984 was the company's opening gun. The strategy has been to approach office automation from the company's historic base in communications, so that AT&T products can be linked together for both computing and communicating.

In 1987, in an attempt to cut into sales of "IBM-compatible" microcomputers—computers made by companies other than IBM (such as Compaq) that nevertheless run IBM-type software and equipment—International Business Machines announced its line of Personal System/2 computers, most of which significantly improved on speed and memory capacity.

According to *Business Week* (April 17, 1987), the top 15 office equipment and computer manufacturers, ranked in terms of their market value for the year 1986, were the following: IBM, Digital Equipment, Hewlett-Packard, Xerox, NCR, UniSys, Tandy, Apple Computer, Cray Research, Automatic Data Processing, Pitney-Bowes, Tandem Computers, Honeywell, Wang Laboratories, and Amdahl.

Appendix B

STRUCTURED PROGRAMMING IN BASIC
An Introduction

THE PRELIMINARIES

What Is a Program?

Consider the many ways people communicate ideas. We speak to one another to voice our thoughts. We write to make thoughts last and we read to learn something new. We use symbols to represent ideas and make them real. A piece of paper with green print represents far greater wealth than the paper's actual value, but its meaning is clearly understood. These symbols are abstractions of what is real; they are all tools that give substance to ideas.

A computer program is just another of these tools. By arranging a series of instructions in a carefully planned manner, you can direct a computer to a specific action. Instructions are just text formulated by the programmer and input to a computer. When the text, converted to machine-readable form, is run, the program allows the computer to accept information, process it, and produce results as instructed.

Programming in BASIC is one way you can formulate computer instructions. The BASIC language includes a set of specific statements that you use with proper syntax and ordering to produce a program. A typical BASIC program (shown in Figure B-1) instructs the computer to accept a temperature in degrees Fahrenheit. It then converts the number to Celsius and prints it.

Communicating with the Computer

A BASIC program is a block of text, and it can be read as such. However, you must take some steps before the computer can use the program. First you type the program into the computer, and then you review what you have typed, save the program, change it, or run it. Several commands, called system commands, make all of these things possible. System commands are typically one-word commands that you key in, then press the ENTER or RETURN key.

Program Entry Mode. System commands are often different on different computers, but they accomplish the same functions. To start, the computer must be in some form of program entry mode. This

```
100 REM FAHRENHEIT TO CELSIUS -- T. COURY
110 REM
120 REM THIS PROGRAM WILL ACCEPT A NUMBER THAT IS THE TEMPERATURE
130 REM IN DEGREES FAHRENHEIT AND WILL CONVERT AND PRINT
140 REM IT IN CELSIUS
150 REM
160 REM OUTPUT: C = DEGREES CONVERTED TO CELSIUS
170 REM INPUT: F = DEGREES INPUT IN FAHRENHEIT
180 REM PROCESS: THE CONVERSION FORMULA IS
190 REM          C = ( 5 / 9) * (F - 32)
200 REM
210 REM
220 PRINT "ENTER TEMPERATURE IN DEGREES FAHRENHEIT."
230 INPUT F
240 LET C = (5 / 9) * (F - 32)
250 PRINT F; "DEGREES FAHRENHEIT IS"; C; "DEGREES CELSIUS'
9999 END

RUN

ENTER TEMPERATURE IN DEGREES FAHRENHEIT.
? 32
32 DEGREES FAHRENHEIT IS O DEGREES CELSIUS.

RUN

ENTER TEMPERATURE IN DEGREES FAHRENHEIT.
? 98.6
98.6 DEGREES FAHRENHEIT IS 37 DEGREES CELSIUS.
```

Figure B-1 A program in BASIC.

establishes a user work area that will accept a program that is typed into the computer. Some editing may also be available and minimally consists of deleting the last character typed and replacing an entire line. Check the documentation for your system, or ask an instructor for more details on how to do this.

Let's enter a simple BASIC program. You do not have to understand how the program works to do this. When past the program entry mode, type in the following program just as presented; end each line by pressing the RETURN or ENTER key:

```
100 REM A SAMPLE PROGRAM TO TYPE IN
110 REM
120 PRINT "WHAT IS YOUR NAME"
130 INPUT N$
140 PRINT "HELLO "; N$
9999 END
```

The program is now stored in the user work area, which is a part of the computer's memory. If one of the lines you entered is not identical to the corresponding line above, retype the line. The computer matches the lines you type by the numbers that start them; in the case of duplicate numbers, it saves the latest version you typed in.

LIST. The computer can print the program you entered as it currently exists in the work area using the system command LIST. Simply enter:

```
LIST
```

and you will see the program that you typed in.

RUN. Simply entering a program does not make it perform. The RUN command tells the computer to execute the statements of the program contained in the work area. Enter:

```
RUN
```

The computer should print:

```
RUN

WHAT IS YOUR NAME
?
```

The question mark indicates that the computer needs an entry from you. Answer the question "WHAT IS YOUR NAME" by typing in your name followed by the RETURN or ENTER key. The program will finish running and the system will wait for your next command as shown below:

```
WHAT IS YUR NAME
? TOM
HELLO TOM
```

SAVE. At a later date you may want to have the computer say "HELLO" again, but you will probably not want to retype the program, so you will need to store it on a secondary storage medium—usually a disk. Since the user work area is only temporary storage, what you entered will disappear when you end your current session.

The SAVE command will transfer the program from the user work area to secondary storage where you can recall it sometime in the future. The SAVE command varies considerably from system to system but usually has a form similar to the following:

```
SAVE "filename"
```

where "filename" is the name of the file under which you want to store the program. Consult your system's reference manual for the specifics and then try saving your program.

Other System Commands.   Many other system commands help programmers develop a good working program. Look for them in the reference manual for your particular computer installation. They are often very system-dependent, for example:

▶ Preparing the user work area for new program entry.

```
NEW
CLEAR
```

▶ Recalling a file from secondary storage and placing it in the user work area.

```
LOAD "filename"
OLD filename
```

▶ Listing the files currently stored on the secondary storage device.

```
FILES
DIR
```

▶ Removing from secondary storage files that are no longer needed.

```
KILL "filename"
DELETE filename
```

▶ Renaming a file currently on secondary storage.

```
NAME "old filename" AS "new filename"
RENAME old filename new filename
```

▶ Editing a file using a system editor.

```
EDIT filename
```

THE BASICS

You have seen a few BASIC programs and know how to enter and run them on a computer, so what's next? It is time to write them! BASIC programs include several elements whose arrangement must follow specific rules. Knowing where to place the numbers, spaces, commas, statements, and other components of a program is the science of BASIC programming, and this science is our focus. But programming is also an art, and this art involves combining the compo-

ASIDE: How to Read a Syntax Description

Throughout this appendix when you see a BASIC statement presented, a syntax description will generally follow. Its purpose is to help explain the statement and to present a framework for using it. Just glance at the definitions now and refer to them when needed.

Syntax Description Elements and Definitions

[ ]	The brackets indicate that whatever is contained within them is optional.
	Three periods indicate that whatever immediately precedes them may be repeated a number of times.
CAPITALIZED	Words that are completely capitalized are BASIC statements, i.e., GOTO, INPUT, LET, PRINT
condition	This is replaced by a valid condition as described under the IF statement, i.e., A < B
constant	This is replaced by a valid constant, i.e., 1, 34, "JOE"
expression *expn1* *expn2* oto.	These are replaced by a numeric or string expression, variable, or constant, depending on the context, ie., A/2, C, B * (4 * A), A$, LEN(A$)
line number	This is replaced by a valid number that introduces a BASIC statement.
line number *line number1* *line number2*	Each is replaced by the line number for a BASIC statement that is to be branched to.
variable	This is replaced by a valid variable name, i.e., A, C, A$, B$

nents in an effective and logical fashion. You will learn the art as well as the science of programming in the pages that follow.

Some BASIC Programming Considerations

Line Numbers. A BASIC program generally executes sequentially, each statement in line number order. These line numbers start each statement; they act as a label for the entire line.

Legal line numbers are usually numbers between 1 and 99999, but the maximum number differs from system to system. Commonly,

BASIC programmers number programs in increments of 10 starting at 100. This allows a neat and easily readable program. It's also easy to maintain because you can insert a new statement between existing statements by starting it with a line number that fits numerically between the two existing line numbers. For example, we could add to our "HELLO" program by typing the following line:

```
145 PRINT "HOW ARE YOU TODAY?"
```

After executing a LIST command the modified program would appear as:

```
100 REM A SAMPLE PROGRAM TO TYPE IN
110 REM
120 PRINT "WHAT IS YOUR NAME?"
130 INPUT N$
140 PRINT "HELLO ", N$
145 PRINT "HOW ARE YOU TODAY?"
9999 END
```

If you type a new line with the same number as one that exists, the new line will replace the old line.

Spacing.   Spacing, while unimportant to many computers, matters to programmers. Only spaces that will appear in the output are critical since the computer will not insert spaces; it interprets all print commands literally. Use spaces as much as possible to improve readability since any statement line that does not contain spaces is difficulttoread!

DO

Show spaces that are part of a literal string.
```
200 PRINT "HELLO JOE"
              ^
```

Space between the line number and the rest of the statement.
```
130 INPUT N$
   ^
```

Space between components of the statement line.
```
140 PRINT "HELLO"; N$
         ^        ^
```

Space between values and operators of an expression (more on this later).
```
500 LET Y = (3 * X) / (X – 5)
       ^ ^   ^ ^   ^ ^   ^^
```

DO NOT

Insert spaces between the digits of a line number.
```
1 00 REM A SAMPLE PROGRAM TO TYPE IN
 ^
```

Insert spaces between statement words.

130 IN PUT N$

^

Insert spaces between the digits of a number in an expression. (Do not insert commas either.)

500 LET X = Y + 1 000

^

The End of the Program.   You tell the computer that it's reached the end of a program with the—you guessed it—END statement. It is the last statement in any program and occurs only once. END does not necessarily show where program execution ends; it shows where the computer stops interpreting the program. Always use the highest possible line number for the END statement to ensure that it will be the last line of the program. The number 9999 represents the highest line number in our examples so this line will contain each program's END statement.

Stopping Execution.   Very often, execution shouldn't stop at the last line of a program. If a program contains data, or a subroutine or function, execution should stop before the END statement. Put a STOP at the proper place in a program to terminate execution at the appropriate time; you can use STOP as often as needed. This statement's value will become clearer to you later.

Program Remarks.   Documenting a program will help you with not only its development but also its maintenance. The REM statement lets you put remarks within a program. REM tells the computer to ignore the line when it executes the program. The examples presented here make generous use of remarks as program documentation. REM documentation also makes it easier for others to read and understand your program, but too many remarks can become annoying and obscure the actual statements, of course.

Variables

BASIC programming involves storing, generating, and manipulating information, and variables help make all this work possible. Variables allow data to be stored and retrieved from a computer's memory; the variable acts as a label for the data and both points to where it is stored and describes the type of information it contains. One way to visualize this is shown in Figure B-2. The file folder represents a part of the computer's memory, and the label represents the variable. The label can identify the correct folder for storing or retrieving files, and it can also indicate the type of file to be stored. Similarly, a variable identifies the correct memory location for storing or retrieving data, and it too identifies the type of data stored in the memory location.

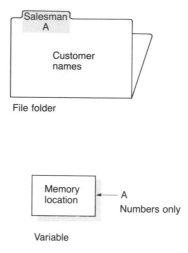

Figure B-2 A file folder and a variable.

Variable Types. The two most common variable types are numeric and alphanumeric variables. We subdivide the numeric type into integer or real variables, and the two types may be subdivided further still. For our purposes we will define both integers and real numbers as numeric, and any variable that will be used to store a number for computations belongs to the numeric type. The alphanumeric variable, also called a string or character variable, can store any sequence of characters but cannot be used for computations.

When programming, there is a big difference between numbers and characters. If you want to store a person's name in a character variable, you would represent the name as "JOE." The letters J - O - E are stored without the quotation marks (or the dashes and spaces) since the quotes only tell the computer that the characters contained within them are to be interpreted literally. These three letters, called a literal string, would be stored in an alphanumeric variable.

You could also use an alphanumeric variable to store Joe's street address. If his address is 16050 you could store the string "16050" in an alphanumeric variable. The number 16050, shown without the quotes, can only be stored in a numeric variable. You can add 1 to 16050 but you cannot do arithmetic operations with the string "16050". In other words, 16050 represents the number sixteen thousand and fifty, while "16050" represents five characters which just happen to be numbers.

Naming Variables. To create a variable name you choose some combination of characters that the program will use to represent the memory location where the variable's information is to be stored. In previous examples, we used F, C, and N$ as variable names. F in line 230 of Figure A-1 stores the number representing the temperature in degrees Fahrenheit. This numeric variable is used in line 240's computation. N$ in line 130 of the "HELLO" program, an alphanumeric variable, will store the user-entered name; the print instructions follow in line 140. You cannot use an alphanumeric variable for computations even if you enter numbers.

The rules for naming variables vary from system to system, but most systems allow numeric names to have one letter (optionally followed by one digit), and alphanumeric names have one letter and an optional digit. You must end an alphanumeric variable's name with a dollar sign ($). For example, A, B, Z, A1, and B9 are legal numeric variables and A$, B$, Z$, A1$, and B9$ are legal alphanumeric variables.

Many versions of BASIC allow longer variable names (six, eight, 30, or more characters) and some allow special characters (such as the period or underline). If this is the case, use names that describe the data the variable will contain: e.g., CUSTOMER.NAME$, CUS-TOMER.ADDRESS$, and ITEM$ for alphanumeric variable names, and PRICE, TOTAL, and GRAND.TOTAL for numeric variable names. If you can use only one or two characters, it is still good practice to think carefully when you select a name. Can you imagine the confusion if the program in Example A-1 used C for degrees Fahrenheit and F for degrees Celsius?

Assigning Values to Variables

There are various ways to assign values to variables. A numeric variable can receive a constant value directly, or it can receive the result of a computation. The program can also use a variable as a counter, either within a loop or as a part of the program control. You can assign a literal string to alphanumeric variables. Though they cannot be used for arithmetic computations, these alphanumeric strings have string manipulation statements and functions.

Assignment Using the LET Statement.　The LET statement assigns values to all types of variables. Look at Figure B-3 briefly and then continue reading. Each type of assignment will be discussed in greater detail as we continue.

```
100 LET A = 3
200 LET B = A
300 LET C = (5 / 9) * (F - 32)
400 LET K = K + 1
500 LET A$ = "LITERAL STRING"
600 LET N$ = "JOE"
700 LET B$ = A$
```

The LET is optional on many systems, so:

```
400 K = K + 1
```

is equivalent to line 400 above.

Figure B-3 Some typical LET statements.

```
100 REM EBIT CALCULATION -- T. COURY
110 REM
120 REM THIS PROGRAM WILL CALCULATE EARNINGS BEFORE
130 REM INTEREST AND TAXES BASED ON FIXED COST,
140 REM VARIABLE COST, AND SALES.
150 REM
160 REM OUTPUT: E = EBIT CALCULATED
170 REM INPUT:  F = FIXED COST IN DOLLARS
180 REM          V = VARIABLE COST AS A FRACTION OF TOTAL SALES
190 REM          Q = NUMBER OF UNITS SOLD
200 REM          P = UNIT PRICE
210 REM PROCESS:  EBIT IS CALCULATED BY THE FOLLOWING FORMULA,
220 REM          EBIT = TOTAL SALES - VARIABLE COSTS - FIXED COSTS
230 REM
240 REM OTHER VARIABLES:
250 REM          S = TOTAL SALES
260 REM          V2 = VARIABLE COST IN DOLLARS
270 REM
280 REM
290 PRINT "CALCULATION OF EBIT"
300 PRINT
310 PRINT "ENTER FIXED COST IN DOLLARS ";
320 INPUT F
330 PRINT "ENTER VARIABLE COST AS A FRACTION OF SALES (IE. .7) ";
340 INPUT V
350 PRINT "ENTER QUANTITY SOLD ";
360 INPUT Q
370 PRINT "ENTER UNIT PRICE ";
380 INPUT P
390 PRINT
400 LET S = Q * P
410 LET V2 = S * V
420 LET E = S - V2 - F
430 PRINT "EARNINGS BEFORE INTEREST AND TAXES >> $"; E
9999 END

RUN

CALCULATION OF EBIT

ENTER FIXED COST IN DOLLARS ? 50000
ENTER VARIABLE COST AS A FRACTION OF SALES (IE. .7) ? .6
ENTER QUANTITY SOLD ? 10436
ENTER UNIT PRICE ? 20

EARNINGS BEFORE INTEREST AND TAXES >> $ 33487.99
```

Figure B-10 The EBIT program and execution.

Now let's review the program. Look at Figure B-10, a listing and sample run for the EBIT problem. The program starts with a series of remarks to explain what is to be done. These may be more extensive than this small program required, but they provide a good example. Lines 290 to 390 issue prompts and accept input from the user. Lines 300 and 390 (PRINT statements) are used only to skip a line in the output. Since the statement includes no expressions, nothing but a blank line will print. The other PRINT statements in this range—used with INPUT statements—issue prompts so the user knows what number is needed. The semicolon that ends each PRINT statement causes the user entry to appear on the same line as the prompt. Once all the data has been entered, the values are calculated in lines 400 to 420, and the answer is finally output in line 430.

Now that your program is complete, you can calculate EBIT whenever you need to. Another useful calculation would be the break-even sales amount. Let's now write a program to perform this calculation.

Break-even Analysis. The break-even sales level occurs when EBIT equals zero. The equation may be algebraically simplified to:

Break-even sales = Fixed cost/(1 − Variable cost fraction)

The sales level is the output, fixed cost and variable cost fraction are the inputs, and the processing is described by the above equation. The program is actually simpler than the previous one, and its flowchart is almost identical. Figure B-11 shows a listing and sample run.

```
100 REM BREAK-EVEN ANALYSIS -- T. COURY
110 REM
120 REM THIS PROGRAM WILL FIND THE BREAK-EVEN
130 REM SALES LEVEL BASED ON FIXED COST AND
140 REM VARIABLE COST.
150 REM
160 REM OUTPUT: S = BREAK-EVEN SALES
170 REM INPUT:  F = FIXED COST IN DOLLARS
180 REM         V = VARIABLE COST AS A FRACTION OF SALES
190 REM PROCESS: THE BREAK-EVEN EQUATION IS FOUND BY ALGEBRAICALLY
200 REM          SOLVING THE EBIT EQUATION FOR SALES AT EBIT = 0.
210 REM          THE EQUATION IS:
220 REM          BREAK-EVEN SALES = FIXED COST / 1 - VARIABLE
                 FRACTION
230 REM
240 REM
```

Figure B-11, *continued.*

Figure B-11 The break-even program.

```
250 PRINT "BREAK-EVEN ANALYSIS"
260 PRINT
270 PRINT "ENTER FIXED COST IN DOLLARS ";
280 INPUT F
290 PRINT "ENTER VARIABLE COST AS A FRACTION OF SALES (IE. .7) ";
300 INPUT V
310 PRINT
320 LET S = F / (1 - V)
330 PRINT "BREAK-EVEN SALES LEVEL >> $"; S
9999 END

RUN

BREAK-EVEN ANALYSIS

ENTER FIXED COST IN DOLLARS ? 50000
ENTER VARIABLE COST AS A FRACTION OF SALES (IE. .7) ? .6

BREAK-EVEN SALES LEVEL >> $ 125000
```

Branching—Moving from Place to Place

The EBIT problem was solved easily with only a few INPUT statements, some calculations, and the output statement, but as problems become more complex, so do the solutions. Branching within a program can perform these difficult tasks, and can make some seemingly impossible programs simple. In BASIC, a program normally executes sequentially from line to line, but branching allows a variation to the sequential execution.

Branching can occur in one of several ways. A program may execute a few lines, then skip to another line and continue there. It may execute only certain lines depending on a condition, or it may repeatedly execute lines a specific number of times. Each common type of branching has an application that suits it best.

The GOTO Statement. The GOTO statement creates an unconditional branch. The format for this statement is:

line number GOTO *line number*

When a GOTO occurs in a program, execution continues at the *line number* specified in the statement. Any lines between the GOTO statement and the *line number* are skipped and are not executed. As a caution, be sure that the *line number* you meant to branch to exists! Figure B-12 shows the GOTO statement.

```
100 REM START OF A PROGRAM
110 REM
120
130    part of a
140       program
150
160 GOTO 200
170 these
180    lines are
190       skipped
200 execution continues here
```

Figure B-12 The GOTO statement.

The GOTO statement usually works in tandem with some other type of branching statement, and we will be covering these shortly. GOTO is the easiest to use, and its applications will be presented with the statements usually associated with it.

The IF Statement. The IF statement allows conditional branching based on the comparison of two expressions. The format for this statement is:

line number IF *condition* THEN *line number*

When an IF statement occurs, the condition is evaluated and, if true, execution will continue at *line number*. The *condition* is the comparison of the two expressions, and it has the following format:

expression1 conditional operator *expression2*

where the conditional operator is one of the following symbols:

Symbol	Meaning	Symbol	Meaning
=	equal to	<>	not equal to
>	greater than	>=	greater than or equal to
<	less than	<=	less than or equal to

Also, *expression1* and *expression2* must both be of the same type, either both numeric or both alphanumeric. The expressions may be constants, variables, or equations, and they are evaluated before their values are compared. This may seem somewhat complicated at first, but don't give up. Figure B-13 illustrates several examples of the IF statement.

Comparing a numeric variable and a constant:

```
200 IF N = 1 THEN 500
210 IF N > 1 THEN 500
220 IF N <> 1 THEN 500
```

Comparing two numeric variables:

```
230 IF N = M THEN 500
240 IF N < M THEN 500
```

Comparing an equation and a constant:

```
250 IF (N + M) / 2 <= 50 THEN 500
```

Comparing an alphanumeric variable and a constant:

```
260 IF A$ = "END" THEN 500
270 IF N$ < "L" THEN 500
```

Comparing two alphanumeric variables:

```
280 IF A$ = N$ THEN 500
290 IF A$ < N$ THEN 500
```

Figure B-13 IF statement examples.

Lines 200 to 220 of Figure A-13 illustrate the comparison of a numeric variable with a constant. These types of statements typically control execution based on a value that has been calculated or entered for N. Lines 230 to 240 are similar, but these compare the results of two calculations. Line 250 illustrates the comparison of an equation and a constant. This might be found in a program used for calculating grades. If M and N were test scores, then line 250 would cause a branch to line 500 if the average of the scores were less than or equal to 50.

Figure B-13 also shows the comparison of alphanumeric expressions. As a programmer you have to remember how a computer evaluates these comparisons to avoid errors in programming. Line 260 compares the value of A$ with the string "END", and branching occurs if they are equal. This will be true only if "END" is contained in A$, and false if not. Computers are very particular about equality, of course; "END" is not equal to " END" or "E N D", which contain spaces.

For comparisons other than equality, the alphanumeric expressions are ordered alphabetically. For example, "AAA" is less than "BBB," and "JOE" is less than "JOHN." The only time this rule cannot be used is when a nonalphabetic character is a part of the comparison. In this case you must understand how the computer represents all characters in order to know what sequence will be used for evaluation. For now, we will use only alphabetic characters in any alphanumeric expression.

Line 270 compares the variable N$ with the constant "L". If N$ contains "A", "DEANNA", or "KZZZZ" then the condition is true and execution transfers to line 500. If it contains "L", "MOTHER", or "THERESA", it is false and execution does not transfer.

The final two lines of the example compare the contents of two variables, not a variable and a constant. Transfer will occur in line 280 only if the content of A$ is identical to the content of N$, and in line 290 if the content of A$ is less than the content of N$.

Additional IF Statement Forms. A few additional forms of the IF statement are available with many of the more recent versions of BASIC. An ELSE option may be available, allowing the following additional format:

line number IF *condition* THEN *line number1* ELSE *line number2*

This option allows branching to *line number1* if the *condition* is true, and to *line number2* if the *condition* is false. For example, in the following statement:

```
100 IF N = 1 THEN 500 ELSE 600
```

if N = 1 is true then the program will branch to line 500 and execution will continue there. If it is false, execution will continue at line 600. Also note that any lines between 100 and 500 would not be executed unless branched to by a different statement.

If the ELSE option is not available in a particular version of BASIC, you can still use a GOTO statement in the line following the IF/THEN statement to create the same type of control. For example, the following two statements:

```
100 IF N = 1 THEN 500
110 GOTO 600
```

will function just as the IF-THEN-ELSE statement in line 100 of the previous example. To ensure compatibility with most versions of BASIC, we will use the latter method in the examples presented.

Another option often available with the IF statement is direct statement execution rather than transfer to a line number. The new forms for both the IF-THEN and the IF-THEN-ELSE are:

line number IF *condition* THEN statement
line number IF *condition* THEN *statement* ELSE *statement*

and examples of these are:

```
100 IF A = B THEN PRINT "A EQUALS B"
100 IF A = B THEN PRINT "A EQUALS B" ELSE PRINT "A DOES NOT EQUAL B"
```

This IF statement is convenient if only one statement is to be executed contingent upon the evaluation of the condition. Sometimes multiple statements or segments of a program that are functionally related must be controlled by a condition, and one of the structured branching techniques fits this niche.

Structured Branching.   In structured programming, it is common to use the IF statement to form one of the four logical patterns that are illustrated in Figure B-14. The patterns are not a required part of the BASIC language, but they help you to produce a structure for accurate and consistent program development. The GOTO statement with the IF helps to produce the patterns, and the combination of the two will add structure to an otherwise unstructured language.

The techniques presented and the examples in which they are used are by no means the only way to write programs, and they are often not the shortest and most efficient method of programming. These patterns will help you to maintain a modular and structured program for logical and accurate development, which saves you a great deal of time and effort in the long term.

The first pattern is the IF-THEN structure. If the condition is true, then execute one or more statements; otherwise continue normal execution. In other words, a series of statements is associated with the condition. These statements will be executed only if the condition is true; if it is not true, they will be ignored.

In Figure B-14 the condition of Pattern 1 is actually tested in line 160. If the condition (A less than B) is true, then the statements of lines 190 to 210 will be executed, and the program will continue at line 230. If false, they will be ignored, and execution will then immediately continue at line 230. The GOTO statement at line 170, used with the IF statement, allows this transfer of control. When the condition is false, the GOTO forces a branch around the statements of lines 190 to 210, and execution continues at line 230. The GOTO won't execute if the condition is true.

The remarks shown in the structure are not a required part of the BASIC language, but you should always include them because they add clarity. Remarks associate the proper statements with the conditions and make the programmer's intent more obvious to anyone else who reads the program. The statements within the structure itself, such as those in lines 190 to 210, are indented to further clarify the associations. Following these guidelines will make you a structured programmer and save you time and effort by helping you avoid errors.

The second pattern has two parts and is called an IF-THEN-ELSE structure. If the condition is true, then one or more statements execute. This is similar to the previous pattern, but if the condition is false, then another set of statements is performed. The branch will

Pattern 1: The IF-THEN Structure
```
100 REM
110 REM
120
130    part of a
140            program
150
160 IF A < B THEN 180
170 GOTO 220
180 REM IF A < B THEN BEGIN
190            statement
200            statement
210            statement
220 REM END IF A < B
230 program continues here
```

Pattern 2: The IF-THEN-ELSE Structure
```
240 REM
250 REM
260
270    part of a
280            program
290
300 IF A < B THEN 320
310 GOTO 370
320 REM IF A < B THEN BEGIN
330            statement
340            statement
350            statement
360    GOTO 410
370 REM ELSE
380            statement
390            statement
400            statement
410 REM END IF A < B
420 program continues here
```

Pattern 3: The WHILE Structure
```
430 REM
440 REM
450
460    part of a
470            program
480
490 IF A < B THEN 510
500 GOTO 560

510 REM WHILE A < B THEN BEGIN
520            statement
530            statement
540            statement
550        GOTO 490
560 REM END WHILE A < B
570 program continues here
```

Pattern 4: The UNTIL Structure
```
580 REM
590 REM
600
610    part of a
620            program
630
640 REM REPEAT
650            statement
660            statement
670            statement
680 REM UNTIL A < B
690 IF A < B THEN 710
700 GOTO 640
710 program continues here
```
Note: The condition A < B is an example.
Any condition may be used.

Figure B-14 IF statement structures.

return to the main program stream only after one set of statements or the other executes. In this case, picture two sets of instructions associated with the condition. One set executes if the condition is true and the other if it is false. Unlike the first pattern, part of the structure will always execute; then the branch returns.

In Pattern 2 of Figure B-14, lines 330 to 350 are the statements that execute when the condition is true, and lines 380 to 400 execute when the condition is false. When true, the IF will force transfer to line 320 as the statement of line 300 indicates. After lines 330 to 350 execute, the GOTO of line 360 branches to continue program execution at line 420. You must do this to bypass the statements associated with the ELSE portion of this structure. When the condition of the IF statement in line 300 is false, the GOTO of line 310 will force transfer to line 370. The statements associated with the ELSE will then execute and the program will continue.

The third pattern is the WHILE structure; WHILE will execute a block of statements as long as (while) a condition is true. This is illustrated in lines 430 to 570 of Figure B-14. The statements of lines 520 to 550 execute as long as A is less than B. The condition is tested in line 490 and if it's true the statements that follow it will execute. Line 550 then transfers control back to line 490 where the condition is checked once again. This will continue until A is no longer less than B, and the GOTO of line 500 will then force transfer to line 570, where the program continues. It should be noted that one of the statements within the structure must change the value of either A or B to allow the condition to become false. If not, the condition of A less than B will never change, and you will have created an infinite loop, a troublesome and embarrassing programming error.

The final pattern is the UNTIL structure, which you can consider as the opposite of the WHILE structure. UNTIL allows execution of a block of statements until a condition is met. UNTIL also differs from the WHILE structure in that it does not check the condition until after the statements have been executed, whereas the WHILE checks it before execution. This means that in an UNTIL structure, the associated statements will always be executed at least once; they may not be executed at all in the WHILE structure if the condition is false at the initial trial. These structures are called pretest (WHILE) or posttest (UNTIL) conditional looping structures. The differences account for many subtle programming errors.

Lines 650 to 670 of Figure B-14 contain the statements of the UNTIL structure, and as you can see, they execute before line 690 checks the condition. If A is less than B, then the program continues at line 710. If A is not less than B, then the GOTO of line 700 forces transfer back to line 640, and the statements of the UNTIL execute again. The caution regarding an infinite loop applies here. Somewhere within the body of the structure the condition must change to allow transfer to line 710 and program continuation.

As a final note concerning all four patterns, each of the statements within the structures may actually represent another structure. An IF structure may be contained within another IF, a WHILE within a WHILE, an IF within a WHILE, or any other combination that you may require. Nesting of structures occurs frequently in well-designed programs, and if the patterns established are followed, the programs will remain clear and accurate.

Financial Analysis Revisited.   We have already written two simple financial analysis programs, EBIT Calculation and Break-Even Analysis. With the new programming techniques just presented, a more

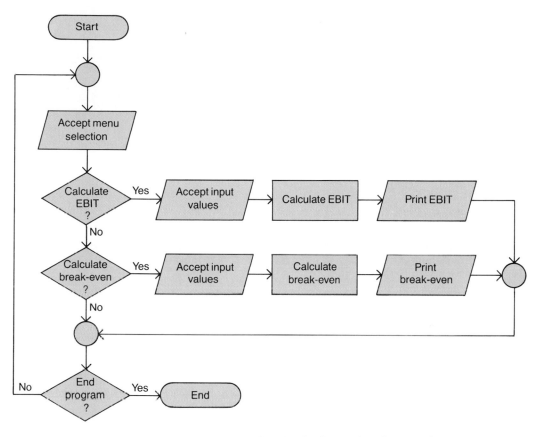

Figure B-15 Flowchart for the financial analysis program.

useful single program could combine the calculations of the previous two. The new program will present a menu with three possible selections, one for each of the two previous analyses and one to end the program. Based on the user's choice, the program will request proper inputs and it will then calculate and display the results.

The flowchart of Figure B-15 illustrates the logic needed for this program. The first process will print the menu and accept the selection. Selections 1, 2, and 3 correspond to calculate EBIT, calculate break-even sales, and end program, respectively. Once the selection has been entered, the program must evaluate it and perform the necessary functions. This process repeats until the user chooses a 3, which signals the end of the program.

The program listed in Figure B-16 uses three of the structures described in the previous section. Almost the entire program is contained within the UNTIL structure starting in line 330 with the REPEAT comment. The menu prints and the choice is accepted in lines 340 to 410. An IF-THEN-ELSE structure occurs next, with the condition $C = 1$. If true, the program accepts data for the EBIT calculation and calculates the output (lines 450 to 600). If false, the ELSE portion of the statement will execute, and it contains an IF-THEN

```
100 REM FINANCIAL ANALYSIS 1 -- T. COURY
110 REM
120 REM THIS PROGRAM WILL FIND EITHER EBIT OR BREAK-EVEN
130 REM SALES LEVEL DEPENDING ON A MENU SELECTION.
140 REM
150 REM OUTPUT: E = EBIT CALCULATED
160 REM     OR  S = BREAK-EVEN SALES
170 REM INPUT:  F = FIXED COST IN DOLLARS
180 REM         V = VARIABLE COST AS A FRACTION OF TOTAL SALES
190 REM         Q = QUANTITY OF UNITS SOLD
200 REM         P = UNIT PRICE
210 REM PROCESS: EBIT IS CALCULATED BY:
220 REM          EBIT = TOTAL SALES - VARIABLE COSTS - FIXED COSTS
230 REM            BREAK-EVEN SALES IS CALCULATED BY:
240 REM          BREAK-EVEN SALES = FIXED COST / (1 - VARIABLE FRACTION)
250 REM
260 REM OTHER VARIABLES:
270 REM          S = TOTAL SALES IN EBIT ONLY
280 REM          V2 = VARIABLE COST IN DOLLARS IN EBIT ONLY
290 REM          C = MENU CHOICE
300 REM
310 REM
320 REM ***************    PROGRAM BEGINS    ***************
330 REM REPEAT
340     PRINT
350     PRINT "1. CALCULATE EBIT"
360     PRINT "2. CALCULATE BREAK-EVEN SALES"
370     PRINT "3. END PROGRAM"
380     PRINT
390     PRINT "ENTER THE NUMBER OF YOUR CHOICE ==> ";
400     INPUT C
410     PRINT
420     IF C = 1 THEN 440
430     GOTO 620
440     REM IF C = 1 THEN BEGIN
450         REM **********    CALCULATE EBIT    **********
460         PRINT "CALCULATION OF EBIT"
470         PRINT
480         PRINT "ENTER FIXED COST IN DOLLARS ";
490         INPUT F
500         PRINT "ENTER VARIABLE COST AS A FRACTION OF SALES (IE. .7) ";
510         INPUT V
520         PRINT "ENTER QUANTITY SOLD ";
530         INPUT Q
540         PRINT "ENTER UNIT PRICE ";
550         INPUT P
560         PRINT
```

Figure B-16 The financial analysis program.

```
570         LET S = Q * P
580         LET V2 = S * V
590         LET E = S - V2 - F
600         PRINT "EARNINGS BEFORE INTEREST AND TAXES >> $"; E
610         GOTO 770
620     REM ELSE
630         IF C = 2 THEN 650
640         GOTO 760
650         REM IF C = 2 THEN BEGIN
660             REM *****   CALCULATE BREAK-EVEN    *****
670             PRINT "BREAK-EVEN ANALYSIS"
680             PRINT
690             PRINT "ENTER FIXED COST IN DOLLARS ";
700             INPUT F
710             PRINT "ENTER VARIABLE COST AS A FRACTION OF SALES (IE. .7) ";
720             INPUT V
730             PRINT
740             LET S = F / (1 - V)
750             PRINT "BREAK-EVEN SALES LEVEL >> $"; S
760         REM END IF C = 2
770         REM END IF C = 1
780 REM UNTIL C = 3
790 IF C = 3 THEN 810
800 GOTO 330
810 PRINT
820 PRINT "PROGRAM COMPLETE..."
9999 END

RUN

1. CALCULATE EBIT
2. CALCULATE BREAK-EVEN SALES
3. END PROGRAM

ENTER THE NUMBER OF YOUR CHOICE ==> ? 1

CALCULATION OF EBIT

ENTER FIXED COST IN DOLLARS ? 50000
ENTER VARIABLE COST AS A FRACTION OF SALES (IE. .7) ? .6
ENTER QUANTITY SOLD ? 10436
ENTER UNIT PRICE ? 20

EARNINGS BEFORE INTEREST AND TAXES >> $ 33487.99

1. CALCULATE EBIT
2. CALCULATE BREAK-EVEN SALES
3. END PROGRAM

ENTER THE NUMBER OF YOUR CHOICE ==> ? 2
```

Figure B-16, *continued.*

```
BREAK-EVEN ANALYSIS

ENTER FIXED COST IN DOLLARS ? 50000
ENTER VARIABLE COST AS A FRACTION OF SALES (IE. .7) ? .6

BREAK-EVEN SALES LEVEL >> $ 125000

1. CALCULATE EBIT
2. CALCULATE BREAK-EVEN SALES
3. END PROGRAM

ENTER THE NUMBER OF YOUR CHOICE ==> ? 4

1. CALCULATE EBIT
2. CALCULATE BREAK-EVEN SALES
3. END PROGRAM

ENTER THE NUMBER OF YOUR CHOICE ==> ? 3

PROGRAM COMPLETE...
```

structure with the condition C = 2. If this condition is true, then break-even sales will be calculated in lines 660 to 750, and if false, both IF structures end. At this point, the UNTIL condition is checked (C = 3); the program will end if the condition proves true and it will repeat otherwise. If the user enters a number other than 1, 2, or 3, the UNTIL will ignore the entry and repeat to allow a new prompt. Your programs should always include techniques to ensure that the program will process only valid entries and ignore those that are invalid. Verify all data entry to prevent unexpected results!

This program demonstrates the use of nested structures and the advantage of the UNTIL structure's posttest in some situations. The UNTIL contains an IF-THEN-ELSE, which contains an IF-THEN. One condition is checked in the first IF, and the second is checked only if the first is false. The UNTIL will then repeat the checking as long as its condition is not met. The posttest allows you to enter the choice before any checking is done. If a WHILE structure were used in its place, the user's choice of an entry would have to occur both before the structure is entered and within the structure itself, since the condition cannot be checked until a choice is entered. To avoid this "priming" problem, use the UNTIL structure. With a WHILE, the condition would change from UNTIL C = 3 to WHILE C <> 3.

The FOR/NEXT Looping Structure. Another popular structure is the FOR-NEXT loop, used when a series of statements is to be executed a specific number of times. Unlike the WHILE or UNTIL structures, the FOR-NEXT loop does not have a condition, and it does have a specific syntax that is part of the BASIC language. The first part of the syntax initiates the loop and is:

line number FOR *variable* = *expn1* TO *expn2* [STEP *expn3*]

The second part of the syntax designates the end of the loop, and the statements between the two parts are those that are executed repeatedly. The syntax description for this part is:

line number NEXT *variable*

The *variable* and all expressions (*expn1*, *expn2*, *expn3*) are numeric, and *variable* is the same in both the FOR and the NEXT statements of the structure.

When the computer encounters the FOR statement during program execution, *variable* is assigned the value of *expn1*. Execution then continues with the statements following the FOR. When the computer reaches the NEXT statement, the program branches back to the FOR statement of the loop. The value of *expn3* is added to *variable* and the execution once again proceeds with the statements in the body of the loop. This looping continues until *expn3* is added to *variable* and *variable* becomes greater than *expn2* if *expn3* is positive, or less than *expn2* if *expn3* is negative. At this point execution continues with the statement directly following the NEXT with the associated *variable*. As indicated in the syntax structure, STEP *expn3* is optional. If it is omitted, *expn3* is assumed to be a +1, and this is added to *variable* during each iteration of the loop.

There are a few more facts that you need to know about the FOR-NEXT structure, but since quite a bit has been presented already, let us discuss a few examples to help clarify its use. Study Figure B-17 briefly and continue reading. Each of the examples will be discussed as we proceed.

The first example of Figure B-17 illustrates a simple loop that will print the numbers from 1 to 10 with each on a separate line. The structure starts with the FOR of line 100. When this executes, the variable K will be assigned the value of 1, and execution will then continue with the PRINT of line 110. A 1 is printed and the NEXT forces transfer back to line 100. Since STEP has been omitted, it has an assumed value of +1, and this is now added to K giving it a value of 2. The cycle continues with the PRINT, the NEXT and the transfer back to the FOR with 1 being added to K each time. Now assume we are at line 120 and K has the value of 10. Transfer occurs to the FOR in line 100, but since K already has the value of 10, the loop does not execute again; execution now transfers to the line directly following the NEXT of line 120 since the NEXT indicates the end of the looping structure. The last value for K printed within the loop was a 10.

A simple loop to count from 1 to 10:

```
100 FOR K = 1 TO 10
110 PRINT K
120 NEXT K
```

This is the same as:

```
130 FOR K = 1 TO 10 STEP 1
140 PRINT K
150 NEXT K
```

A loop containing a variable as the initial value:

```
160 FOR I = J TO 100
170 PRINT I
180 NEXT I
```

A loop containing a variable as the initial and terminal value:

```
190 FOR I = J TO K
200 PRINT I
210 NEXT I
```

A loop that will count by fives:

```
220 FOR K = 1 TO 20 STEP 5
230 PRINT K
240 NEXT K
```

A loop that will count backward:

```
250 FOR K = 10 TO 1 STEP -1
260 PRINT K
270 NEXT K
```

A loop that contains an equation:

```
280 FOR J = 1 TO 100 -K
290 PRINT J
300 NEXT J
```

Figure B-17 The FOR-NEXT loop.

The value of K after the FOR-NEXT structure has completed differs from system to system. In some computers the value will be 10 and in some 11. You can test this by running the short program of Figure A-18. (Some versions of BASIC do not actually add the value of the STEP expression to the variable unless the loop is to be executed again. Instead, the sum of the STEP expression and the variable is compared with the terminal value, and stored in the variable only if the condition requires another iteration of the loop.)

```
100 FOR K = 1 TO 10
110 PRINT K
120 NEXT K
130 PRINT "THE LOOP HAS ENDED. THE VALUE OF K IS "; K
```

Figure B-18 Is it 10 or 11?

Look once again at the examples of Figure A-17. The loop illustrated in lines 130 to 150 is identical to the one preceding it. As previously mentioned, if STEP is omitted it is assumed to be STEP 1. The third example (lines 160 to 180) uses a variable as the initial value assigned to I. By changing its assignment before the loop is executed, you can use the value of J to determine the initial value of the counting. If J is 50, then the loop will count from 50 to 100. If J is greater than 100, then the loop will not execute at all. Lines 190 to 210 present a similar example, but both the initial value and terminal value are variables and determined by a previous assignment.

Write a short program that will accept J and K as input and then execute the loop of lines 190 to 210. This will allow you to try different values and observe the results. The best way to learn BASIC is to experiment with it!

The example of lines 220 to 240 in Figure B-17 illustrates the use of the STEP option to allow increments other than 1. In this example, the variable K will begin with 1 and be raised by increments of 5 with each iteration. The next value for K will be 6 (1 + 5), followed by 11, and ending with 16. Did you notice that 20 is never actually reached? This happens because the STEP value is added to the variable, and the loop terminates when the sum is greater than the terminal value. In this case, 16 + 5 is greater than 20, so the loop ends.

If the STEP is negative, the objective of the loop is to count backward, as illustrated in lines 250 to 270. K is initialized (begins) with 10 and will count down to 1, where the loop ends.

The final example illustrates the use of a short equation as one of the expressions. An equation may replace any of the expressions, and this use is common in applications such as sorting, which we will discuss later.

An Application of the FOR-NEXT. We have already discussed a program to solve EBIT. Let's add another dimension to the program to make it even more useful. When trying to predict EBIT for sales that have not occurred, you don't know the actual quantity sold. You can usually determine a range of possible quantities, but this range will

```
100 REM EBIT CALCULATION WITH A VARIABLE QUANTITY -- T. COURY
110 REM
120 REM THIS PROGRAM WILL CALCULATE AN EBIT TABLE
130 REM BASED ON FIXED COST, VARIABLE COST, AND
140 REM A SALES LEVEL WITH A VARIABLE QUANTITY.
150 REM
160 REM OUTPUT: Q = QUANTITY INDEX
170 REM         S = TOTAL SALES
180 REM         F + V2 = TOTAL COST
190 REM         E = EBIT
200 REM INPUT:  F = FIXED COST IN DOLLARS
210 REM         V = VARIABLE COST AS A FRACTION OF TOTAL SALES
220 REM         Q1 = MINIMUM QUANTITY TO BE SOLD
230 REM         Q2 = MAXIMUM QUANTITY TO BE SOLD
240 REM         I = QUANTITY INCREMENT
250 REM         P = UNIT PRICE
260 REM PROCESS:  EBIT IS CALCULATED BY THE FOLLOWING FORMULA,
270 REM         EBIT  = TOTAL SALES - VARIABLE COSTS - FIXED COSTS
280 REM
290 REM OTHER VARIABLES:
300 REM         V2 = VARIABLE COST IN DOLLARS
310 REM
320 REM
330 PRINT "CALCULATION OF EBIT TABLE BASED ON VARIABLE QUANTITY"
340 PRINT
350 PRINT "ENTER FIXED COST IN DOLLARS ";
360 INPUT F
370 PRINT "ENTER VARIABLE COST AS A FRACTION OF SALES (IE. .7) ";
380 INPUT V
390 PRINT "ENTER MINIMUM QUANTITY TO BE SOLD ";
400 INPUT Q1
410 PRINT "ENTER MAXIMUM QUANTITY TO BE SOLD ";
420 INPUT Q2
430 PRINT "ENTER QUANTITY INCREMENT ";
440 INPUT I
450 PRINT "ENTER UNIT PRICE ";
460 INPUT P
470 PRINT
480 PRINT " POSSIBLE", "  TOTAL", "  TOTAL"
490 PRINT " QUANTITY", "  SALES", " COST", "  EBIT"
500 PRINT "----------", "----------", "----------", "----------"
510 FOR Q = Q1 TO Q2 STEP I
520     LET S = Q * P
530     LET V2 = S * V
540     LET E = S - V2 - F
550     PRINT Q, S, F + V2, E
```

Figure B-19 EBIT with variable quantity.

```
560 NEXT Q
9999 END

RUN

CALCULATION OF EBIT TABLE BASED ON VARIABLE QUANTITY

ENTER FIXED COST IN DOLLARS ? 50000
ENTER VARIABLE COST AS A FRACTION OF SALES (IE. .7) ? .6
ENTER MINIMUM QUANTITY TO BE SOLD ? 5000
ENTER MAXIMUM QUANTITY TO BE SOLD ? 15000
ENTER QUANTITY INCREMENT ? 500
ENTER UNIT PRICE ? 20
   POSSIBLE       TOTAL          TOTAL
   QUANTITY       SALES          COST          EBIT
  -----------   ----------    ----------    ----------

   5000          100000        110000        -10000
   5500          110000        116000        -6000
   6000          120000        122000        -2000
   6500          130000        128000         2000
   7000          140000        134000         6000
   7500          150000        140000         10000
   8000          160000        146000         14000
                               *
                               *
                               *
   14000         280000        218000         62000
   14500         290000        224000         66000
   15000         300000        230000         70000
```

also have a range of EBIT values associated with it. We should modify the original EBIT program to allow it to print a table that represents an entire range of values for quantity sold. Total sales and total cost also change with quantity and these too may be added to the table. Figure B-19 illustrates this program and a sample run.

This program works like the original EBIT program. Instead of a specific quantity, a minimum, maximum, and incremental quantity are entered. This allows the FOR-NEXT structure of lines 510 to 560 to generate a table. Go over the function of all of the statements in the program until you understand them all, including the quantities in the FOR statement and in the calculation of line 520. Did you observe the print formatting using the comma? More elegant methods of formatting are available, but this method works easily and simply.

This program could be added as choice 3 to the financial analysis program of Figure B-16, with the end as program choice 4. As new types of calculations are developed and choices added, the financial analysis program could develop into a very useful tool.

Branching and Nesting with the FOR-NEXT. Any type of branching structure including another FOR-NEXT can fit within the body of a FOR-NEXT structure, but you have to observe certain rules. First, an IF statement cannot branch into the structure between the FOR and the NEXT. For example, the following is not legal:

Illegal

```
100 IF A < B THEN 120
110 FOR K = 1 TO 10
120 PRINT K
130 NEXT K
```

A FOR-NEXT structure may only be entered by first executing the FOR statement. It is, however, permissible to exit a structure using an IF statement. An example of this is:

Legal

```
100 FOR K = 1 TO 10
110 IF K = 5 THEN 130
120 NEXT K
130 PRINT K
```

Though the example is legal, it makes no sense, but there are applications which require this kind of branch; one such application is presented in Figure B-20.

It is also possible to branch within the FOR-NEXT structure, or even to the NEXT statement itself, as long as the FOR has already been executed. When an IF statement forces branching from within a loop to the FOR statement, the FOR will initiate the loop once again. Consider the following example:

An infinite loop

```
100 FOR K = 1 TO 10
110 IF K = 5 THEN 100
120 NEXT K
```

Look at the example above. When K is assigned the value of 5, the IF in line 110 will force a transfer back to line 100 and the loop will start from 1 again—another example of the infamous infinite loop! An example that may be of use is:

Skip the 5

```
100 FOR K = 1 TO 10
110 IF K = 5 THEN 130
120 PRINT K
130 NEXT K
```

In this example the loop will print the numbers from 1 to 4 and 6 to 10. The IF in line 110 will prevent a 5 from being printed. Branching to the NEXT simply causes another iteration of the loop if its condition permits.

```
100 REM CALCULATE SQUARE ROOT -- T. COURY
110 REM
120 REM THIS PROGRAM WILL CALCULATE THE SQUARE ROOT
130 REM OF A POSITIVE REAL NUMBER USING NEWTON'S METHOD.
140 REM
150 REM OUTPUT: S = SQUARE ROOT OF NUMBER ENTERED
160 REM INPUT:  N = REAL NUMBER ENTERED
170 REM PROCESS: THE SQUARE ROOT IS CALCULATED USING ONLY THE
180 REM             FOUR BASIC ARITHMETIC FUNCTIONS AND NEWTON'S
190 REM             FORMULA, WHICH IS:
200 REM             NEW X = OLD X - (OLD X * OLD X - I) / (2 * OLD X)
210 REM             A MAXIMUM OF 100 ITERATIONS WILL BE ALLOWED.
220 REM             K IS USED AS A LOOP COUNTER VARIABLE.
230 REM             X IS USED AS A TEMPORARY VARIABLE.
240 REM             THE FIRST GUESS WILL BE N / 2.
250 REM
260 REM NOTE: THIS IS A NUMERIC METHOD AND IS SIMILAR TO MANY
270 REM          COMPUTATION METHODS USED IN CALCULATORS AND COMPUTERS.
280 REM
290 REM
300 PRINT "THIS WILL FIND THE SQUARE ROOT OF"
310 PRINT "A REAL NUMBER GREATER THAN ZERO."
320 PRINT
330 PRINT "ENTER THE NUMBER ";
340 INPUT N
350 IF N <= 0 THEN 300
360 LET X = N / 2
370 FOR K = 1 TO 100
380 LET S = X - (X * X - N) / (2 * X)
390 IF S = X THEN 420
400 LET X = S
410 NEXT K
420 PRINT "THE SQUARE ROOT OF"; N; "IS"; S
9999 END

RUN

THIS WILL FIND THE SQUARE ROOT OF
A REAL NUMBER GREATER THAN ZERO.

ENTER THE NUMBER ? 144
THE SQUARE ROOT OF 144 IS 12

RUN

THIS WILL FIND THE SQUARE ROOT OF
A REAL NUMBER GREATER THAN ZERO.

ENTER THE NUMBER ? 2
THE SQUARE ROOT OF 2 IS 1.414214
```

Figure B-20 The square root program.

As mentioned previously, FOR-NEXT structures may be nested. The number of nested structures is limited by various systems, but most support the nesting of at least a few FOR-NEXT structures. When these are nested, be sure not to cross the loops. In other words a FOR-NEXT structure must be completely contained within the loop of another FOR-NEXT structure, for example:

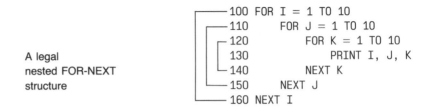

A legal
nested FOR-NEXT
structure

```
100 FOR I = 1 TO 10
110    FOR J = 1 TO 10
120       FOR K = 1 TO 10
130          PRINT I, J, K
140       NEXT K
150    NEXT J
160 NEXT I
```

This, however, is an illegal nested FOR-NEXT structure:

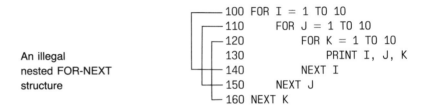

An illegal
nested FOR-NEXT
structure

```
100 FOR I = 1 TO 10
110    FOR J = 1 TO 10
120       FOR K = 1 TO 10
130          PRINT I, J, K
140       NEXT I
150    NEXT J
160 NEXT K
```

Now you know all there is to know about the FOR-NEXT loop!

The Final Revision to the EBIT Program. Yes, it's the same program again, but wait until you see what we do with it this time! Let's add another variation to the execution. In addition to a variable quantity, a variable price would increase the program's usefulness in certain situations. The program should now include a range of quantities for each value in a range of prices. This new program could evaluate a pricing policy in relation to an uncertain sales quantity. A table would be printed and could be used for the evaluation.

Since the table is likely to be large, and a display terminal may be used for output, it would be desirable to pause when printing output if the display is full. Otherwise the values would keep printing and could not be evaluated properly. This situation is easily resolved using the structure programming techniques previously presented.

Figure B-21 shows the logic for the program. The program uses two nested FOR-NEXT structures and an IF-THEN-ELSE structure to control the output. The calculations for EBIT remain the same but occur more frequently.

Figure B-22 shows the listing and demonstrates several interesting features. The constant L2, initialized in line 400, represents the number of lines that are contained on a display page. The program uses number of lines as a constant rather than just a value so that it may be changed easily to be used with various display sizes. By

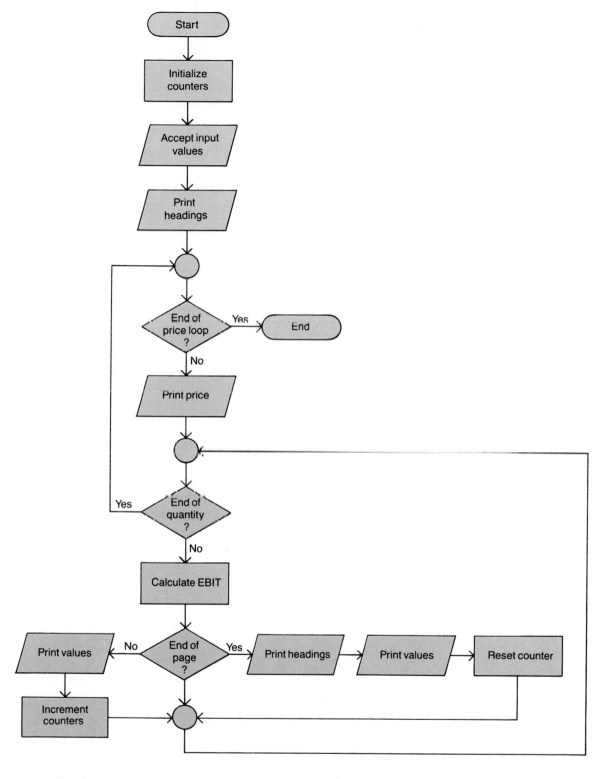

Figure B-21 Flowchart for EBIT with two variations.

```
100 REM EBIT CALCULATION WITH A VARIABLE PRICE & QUANTITY -- T. COURY
110 REM
120 REM THIS PROGRAM WILL CALCULATE AN EBIT TABLE
130 REM BASED ON FIXED COST, VARIABLE COST, AND A SALES
140 REM LEVEL WITH A VARIABLE PRICE & QUANTITY.
150 REM
160 REM OUTPUT: P = CURRENT PRICE
170 REM         Q = QUANTITY INDEX
180 REM         S = TOTAL SALES
190 REM         F + V2 = TOTAL COST
200 REM         E = EBIT
210 REM INPUT:  F = FIXED COST IN DOLLARS
220 REM         V = VARIABLE COST AS A FRACTION OF TOTAL SALES
230 REM         Q1 = MINIMUM QUANTITY TO BE SOLD
240 REM         Q2 = MAXIMUM QUANTITY TO BE SOLD
250 REM         I1 = QUANTITY INCREMENT
260 REM         P1 = MINIMUM PRICE SET
270 REM         P2 = MAXIMUM PRICE SET
280 REM         I2 = PRICE INCREMENT
290 REM PROCESS: EBIT IS CALCULATED BY THE FOLLOWING FORMULA.
300 REM         EBIT = TOTAL SALES - VARIABLE COSTS - FIXED COSTS
310 REM
320 REM OTHER VARIABLES:
330 REM         V2 = VARIABLE COST IN DOLLARS
340 REM         L1 = CURRENT LINE COUNTER
350 REM         L2 = NUMBER OF LINES PER PAGE
360 REM
370 REM
380 REM INITIALIZE COUNTERS AND CONSTANTS
390 LET L1 = 6
400 LET L2 = 24
410 PRINT "CALCULATION OF EBIT TABLE BASED ON VARIABLE PRICE & QUANTITY"
420 PRINT
430 PRINT "ENTER FIXED COST IN DOLLARS ";
440 INPUT F
450 PRINT "ENTER VARIABLE COST AS A FRACTION OF SALES (IE. .7) ";
460 INPUT V
470 PRINT "ENTER MINIMUM QUANTITY TO BE SOLD ";
480 INPUT Q1
490 PRINT "ENTER MAXIMUM QUANTITY TO BE SOLD ";
500 INPUT Q2
510 PRINT "ENTER QUANTITY INCREMENT ";
520 INPUT I1
530 PRINT "ENTER MINIMUM UNIT PRICE ";
540 INPUT P1
550 PRINT "ENTER MAXIMUM UNIT PRICE ";
560 INPUT P2
```

Figure B-22 EBIT with two variations.

```
570 PRINT "ENTER PRICE INCREMENT ";
580 INPUT I2
590 PRINT
600 PRINT "  UNIT", " POSSIBLE", "   TOTAL", "   TOTAL",
610 PRINT "  PRICE", " QUANTITY", "  SALES", "   COST", "   EBIT"
620 PRINT "----------", "----------", "----------", "----------", "----------"
630 FOR P = P1 TO P2 STEP I2
640     PRINT P;
650     FOR Q =Q1 TO Q2 STEP I1
660         LET S = Q * P
670         LFT V2 = S * V
680         LET E = S - V2 - F
690         IF L1 = L2 THEN 710
700         GOTO 820
710         REM IF L1 = L2 THEN BEGIN
720             PRINT
730             PRINT "HIT ENTER TO CONTINUE ";
740             INPUT Z$
750             PRINT "  UNTT", " POSSIBLE", "   TOTAL", "   TOTAL"
760             PRINT "  PRICE", "QUANTITY", "  SALES", "   COST", "   EBIT"
770             PRINT "----------", "----------", "----------", "----------", "----------"
780             PRINT P;
790             PRINT , Q, S, F, + V2, E
800             LET LQ = 6
810             GOTO 850
820         REM FLSE
830             PRINT , Q, S, F, + V2, E
040             LET L1 = L1 + 1
850         REM END IF L1 = L2
860     NEXT Q
870 NEXT P
9999 END

RUN

CALCULATION OF EBIT TABLE BASED ON VARIABLE PRICE & QUANTITY

ENTER FIXED COST IN DOLLARS ? 50000
ENTER VARIADLE COST AS A FRACTION OF SALES (IE. .7) . .6
ENTER MINIMUM QUANTITY TO BE SOLD ? 5000
ENTER MAXIMUM QUANTITY TO BE SOLD ? 15000
ENTER QUANTITY INCREMENT ? 1000
ENTER MINIMUM UNIT PRICE ? 15
ENTER MAXIMUM UNIT PRICE ? 25
ENTER PRICE INCREMENT ? 5
```

Figure B-22, *continued.*

UNIT PRICE	POSSIBLE QUANTITY	TOTAL SALES	TOTAL COST	EBIT
15	5000	75000	95000	-20000
	6000	90000	104000	-14000
	7000	105000	113000	-8000.004
	*			
	*			
	*			
	15000	225000	185000	40000
20	5000	100000	110000	-1000
	*			
	*			
	*			
	11000	220000	182000	38000

HIT ENTER TO CONTINUE ?

UNIT PRICE	POSSIBLE QUANTITY	TOTAL SALES	TOTAL COST	EBIT
20	12000	240000	194000	46000
	13000	260000	206000	54000
	14000	280000	218000	62000
	15000	300000	230000	70000
25	5000	125000	125000	0
	*			
	*			
	*			
	15000	375000	275000	100000

simply changing this assignment, the program will alter the number of lines displayed before a pause occurs. This type of tool will allow easy maintenance of your programs.

Minimum, maximum, and increment values are entered for both quantity and price, and these values then appear as the expressions in two FOR-NEXT loops. The quantity loop is contained within the price loop to allow the entire range of quantities to be printed for each price. We made this choice because it has the most likely applications.

After all the required input has been accepted and the initial heading printed, the price loop begins (line 630). A new price prints each time it changes (line 640). Note the semicolon ending the line to suppress line feed. The quantity loop starts in line 650, followed by the EBIT calculations. Before the results print, the program determines if it needs a pause. This is tested in line 690, and it pauses if the number of lines that have been printed equals the number of lines on the display. If this is true, then the statements in lines 720 to 810 execute, and if false, lines 830 to 840 execute. After one of the two blocks of statements completes execution, the program continues with another iteration of the quantity loop. It ends when Q1 is equal to Q2. You then encounter the NEXT P of line 870, and the price loop executes once again. This assigns a new price, and the quantity loop starts again from its initial value. The entire process continues until the price loop is complete, and the program finally ends.

Adding special features between pages of information is called a page break—a common programming feature. This occurs with displays and when it is desirable to print headings on separate pages of a printout. Notice the assignment in lines 390 and 800. This initializes the line counter for the page break. It is assigned a 6 since that number of lines is accounted for by the three lines of the heading, the two lines of the pause prompt, and the one line of the values (called a detail line) to be printed.

Now that this program is complete, why not add this to the financial analysis package we have been building? You would then have a program with five selections and much variety. At this point, the EBIT problem has probably been solved in more ways than one would care to think about.

SUGGESTED PROGRAMMING CHALLENGES

1. You have some friends who love junk food but are concerned about gaining weight. They want you to help prevent them from consuming more Calories than they use—an easy task since the only foods they consume are Big Whop McBurgers at 500 Calories each, slices of pizza at 200 Calories, and milkshakes at 300 Calories. Also, each of your friends will jog as long as needed to burn any Calories in excess of their normal daily allowance. Assume that this allowance is 2000 Calories for women and 3000 Calories for men, and that a person burns six Calories for every minute of jogging time.

   Write a program to accept the sex of your friend and the quantity of each of the above foods he or she consumed. Calculate the total Calorie intake and the appropriate allowance. The program should then determine whether the intake is greater or less than the allowance and display the number of minutes the person should jog to keep from gaining weight, or it should display the message, "YOU MAY KEEP ON EATING!"

2. A program is needed to help assess common stock transactions. Write a program to accept the price per share for which some stock was purchased, the number of shares purchased, the selling price per share, the time in months that the stock was owned, and the commission rate the broker charged as a percent of the transaction amount.

   The program should then calculate and display the total commission paid. Assume that total commission is the commission rate times the sum of the total purchase amount and the total selling amount. It should also display the amount of profit or loss and the percentage rate of the profit or loss on an annualized basis.

3. Assume you are an agent who helps organize giant oil shipments. Typically you try to find buyers for contracts that call for delivery of between 100,000 and 500,000 barrels of oil per day, and you generally receive a commission of between $0.0025 and $0.05 per barrel. A contract is usually labeled by terms such as $6 \times 3 \times 1$, which means that the selling

price per barrel may be adjusted every six months, that the contract is subject to renewal every three months, and that the maximum length is one year. You receive your commission at a prenegotiated amount per barrel for the number of barrels actually delivered.

Write a program to accept the commission rate per barrel, the number of barrels per day that is expressed in the contract, the renewal period, and the maximum length of the contract. Then calculate and display the amount of the commission and the cumulative amount for each period until the end of the contract.

4. Write a program to determine what equal payment is needed, compounded at some interest rate, to provide a required future sum (this is commonly referred to as the sinking fund problem). For example, assume you have a $10,000 loan that is due in five years. What equal, annual amount should be deposited in a savings account that pays 8% interest in order to pay the loan when it becomes due? The formula for solving this problem is:

> Payment per period = Amount needed / Annuity compound factor where annuity compound factor (ACF) for period, n, at a k percent interest rate (ACF k,n) is

$$\text{ACF } k,n = (1 + k)^{n-1} + (1 + k)^{n-2} + \cdots + (1 + k)^{1} + 1$$

For example, the ACF for the above problem would be

$$\text{ACF.08,5} = 1.08^4 + 1.08^3 + 1.08^2 + 1.08 + 1 = 5.867$$

and the annual deposit for each of five years should then be

> Payment per period = $10,000 / 5.867 = $1704.45

Your program should accept the amount needed, the number of periods, and the interest rate received per period. It should then calculate the annuity compound factor and the payment required per period with the latter being displayed.

5. The factorial function has many applications in mathematics and statistics. If n is some positive integer, then n *factorial* (commonly seen as n!) is defined as the product of all integers between 1 and n. For example, 4! would be computed as

$$1 \times 2 \times 3 \times 4 = 24$$

Also, by definition, 0! is equal to 1.

Write a program to accept a positive integer and display its factorial.

6. There is a unique sequence of integers known as the Fibonacci sequence, which is

$$0, 1, 1, 2, 3, 5, 8, 13, 21, \cdots$$

Each integer of the sequence is the sum of the previous two integers, and the first two elements are 0 and 1.

Write a program to accept an element position and give the corresponding Fibonacci number. For example, if a 7 were accepted, the number 8 would be displayed since it is the seventh Fibonacci number.

THE NEXT STEP

Now that we've reviewed the basics of BASIC programming, it's time for the next step. There are several more features of the language that will boost your power in developing better and more useful programs. These include methods for using tables, for storing data within the program itself, for using subroutines, and for processing a case structure. We'll cover each of these tools.

Arrays

Table Storage with Arrays. We have seen how BASIC uses variables to store and access information, but in order to take full advantage of a computer's processing power, you need to store related informa-

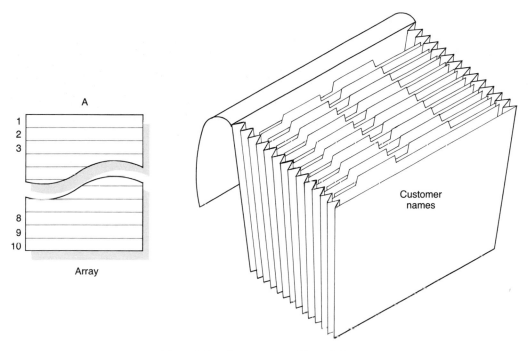

Figure B-23 The accordion file and the array.

tion in an array. If a variable is analogous to a file folder, then an array is analogous to an accordion file. As illustrated in Figure B-23, the array name is the label on the file, and—like the file—the array has a different slot for each of several elements. Actually, an array is a subscripted variable, with each subscript representing another storage position.

Single-dimension array variables appear as:

$$A\$(5), \ B\$(2), \ T(10), \ P3(5)$$

These are simply variables that have been defined as arrays; they are variable names followed by a number in parentheses. Each position within the array has a number (called its index), and the numbers start at one and end with the maximum number of storage positions (the array's dimension). An array is often called a table since the number that serves as an index can be used to find the element to which it refers.

The DIM statement sets the dimensions of an array. Rather than using a syntax description, we'll use the following example to describe the DIM statement:

$$100 \ DIM \ A\$(10), \ T2(20)$$

Used to define the size of an array, the DIM line belongs near the beginning of a BASIC program. This is necessary because an array must be defined in most versions of BASIC before you can use it. In other words, an element of any array may not be assigned a value before the DIM statement has defined the array. In addition to declaring that an array exists, the DIM statement also indicates the total number of elements that you can put in the array. In the example, A$(10) defines the A$ array with enough storage for ten elements; you address each element by using the variables A$(1) to A$(10).

Once the array has been defined, you treat each array variable just as any other variable. A$(1) or A$(5) may be used just as B$ or C$ would be. An array can, however, be much more desirable in some applications. The numbers that act as an index to the variable can be replaced by an expression—that is, another variable or even an equation. Consider the following example:

```
100 DIM A$(10)
110 PRINT "ENTER 10 NAMES."
120 FOR K = 1 TO 10
130 INPUT A$(K)
140 NEXT K
150 PRINT "THE NAMES YOU ENTERED WERE:"
160 FOR K = 1 TO 10
170 PRINT A$(K)
180 NEXT K
9999 END
```

The example simply accepts ten names from a user, places them into the A$ array, and prints them back. Imagine trying to write this short program without using an array! It would require ten separate variables, ten INPUT statements, and ten PRINT statements, just to accept and print the names, and the FOR-NEXT loops could not be used.

Using FOR-NEXT loops is common with array processing because the variable of the loop acts as an index for the array elements. Let us now consider a variation of the previous program that demonstrates the use of an array and FOR-NEXT loops. In addition to accepting and printing ten names as demonstrated, we will now write a program that will accept them, sort them alphabetically, and then print them.

Figure B-24 includes the program and a sample run. The array sort in lines 340 to 450 uses a bubble sort, so-called because as the loops are executed, the names that should alphabetically appear first in the array "bubble" to the top. The two loops needed for this sort are nested one within the other. The outer loop—the K loop—starts at 1 and ends at 9, which is one less than the number of elements in the array. As each iteration of the K loop completes, one more element has been sorted. The J loop indexes the comparisons, allowing two successive elements to be compared during each of its iterations. Did you notice that each time the K loop executes, the J loop's terminal value decreases by one? This is because each time the J loop completes, the last element it indexes ends up in its proper place.

```
100 REM NAME SORT -- T. COURY
110 REM
120 REM THIS PROGRAM WILL ACCEPT 10 NAMES, SORT THEM
130 REM AND PRINT THEM IN ALPHABETICAL ORDER.
140 REM
150 REM OUTPUT: N$() = THE ARRAY CONTAINING THE SORTED NAMES
160 REM INPUT:  N$() = THE ARRAY THAT WILL CONTAIN THE NAMES
170 REM PROCESS:  A BUBBLE SORT WILL BE USED TO ALPHABETIZE
180 REM              THE NAMES.
190 REM
200 REM OTHER VARIABLES:
210 REM          K  = A LOOP COUNTER
220 REM          J  = A LOOP COUNTER
230 REM          T$ = TEMPORARY NAME STORAGE
240 REM
250 REM
260 REM DIMENSION ARRAY
270 DIM N$(10)
280 REM ACCEPT INPUT
290 PRINT "ENTER 10 NAMES:"
300 FOR K = 1 TO 10
310     PRINT "ENTER NAME NUMBER "; K; " ";
320     INPUT N$(K)
330 NEXT K
340 REM SORT NAMES
350 FOR K = 1 TO 9
360     FOR J = 1 TO 10 - K
370         IF N$(J) > N$(J + 1) THEN 390
380         GOTO 430
390         REM IF N$(J) > N$(J + 1) THEN BEGIN
400             LET T$ = N$(J)
410             LET N$(J) = N$(J + 1)
420             LET N$(J + 1) = T$
430         REM END IF N$(J) > N$(J + 1)
440     NEXT J
450 NEXT K
460 REM PRINT NAMES
470 PRINT
480 PRINT "THE SORTED NAMES ARE:"
490 FOR K = 1 TO 10
500 PRINT , N$(K)
510 NEXT K
9999 END

RUN

ENTER 10 NAMES:
ENTER NAME NUMBER 1 ? ZACHARY
```

Figure B-24, continued.

Figure B-24 The sort program.

```
ENTER NAME NUMBER 2 ? ANTHONY
ENTER NAME NUMBER 3 ? DEANNA
ENTER NAME NUMBER 4 ? ROBERT
ENTER NAME NUMBER 5 ? TERI
ENTER NAME NUMBER 6 ? JOHN
ENTER NAME NUMBER 7 ? BETH
ENTER NAME NUMBER 8 ? TRACI
ENTER NAME NUMBER 9 ? FRANCES
ENTER NAME NUMBER 10 ? MARY
THE SORTED NAMES ARE:
              ANTHONY
              BETH
              DEANNA
              FRANCES
              JOHN
              MARY
              ROBERT
              TERI
              TRACI
              ZACHARY
```

The actual sorting occurs in lines 370 to 430. The IF statement compares the two successive elements currently being indexed by the J loop. If the predecessor is greater than the successor, then the items are switched; otherwise they are not. This repeats until all the needed elements have been compared.

Let's examine the bubble sort in Figure B-25. When the loops start with K and J equal to 1, the first comparison is made between items 1 and 2, which contain the names Zachary and Anthony. Since Zachary is "greater" than Anthony (alphabetically speaking), their positions are exchanged. The J loop moves to the next item, and the process continues until Zachary is in the tenth position. At this point the J loop ends, and the K loop continues with its next iteration. The J loop starts again from 1, but since its terminal value is dependent upon the current value of K, it will execute one less time than it did previously. This makes sense since Zachary is correctly in the last position, and we don't need a comparison for this position.

Two-Dimensional Arrays. Up to this point we have been working with single-dimension arrays, but BASIC also uses two-dimensional arrays. These are often called matrices (singular: matrix). Using the DIM statement to define a matrix:

Unsorted names	After first iteration K = 1, J = 1	After second iteration K = 1, J = 2
1 ZACHARY	1 ANTHONY ←	1 ANTHONY
2 ANTHONY	2 ZACHARY ←	2 DEANNA ←
3 DEANNA	3 DEANNA	3 ZACHARY ←
4 ROBERT	4 ROBERT	4 ROBERT
5 TERI	5 TERI	5 TERI
6 JOHN	6 JOHN	6 JOHN
7 BETH	7 BETH	7 BETH
8 TRACI	8 TRACI	8 TRACI
9 FRANCES	9 FRANCES	9 FRANCES
10 MARY	10 MARY	10 MARY

After last iteration K = 1, J = 9	After fourth iteration K = 2, J = 4	After fifth iteration K = 2, J = 5
1 ANTHONY	1 ANTHONY	1 ANTHONY
2 DEANNA	2 DEANNA	2 DEANNA
3 ROBERT	3 ROBERT	3 ROBERT
4 TERI	4 JOHN ←	4 JOHN
5 JOHN	5 TERI ←	5 BETH ←
6 BETH	6 BETH	6 TERI ←
7 TRACI	7 TRACI	7 TRACI
8 FRANCES	8 FRANCES	8 FRANCES
9 MARY ←	9 MARY	9 MARY
10 ZACHARY ←	10 ZACHARY	10 ZACHARY

Note: Positions are switched for all values of J when K is 1, but when K becomes 2, switching occurs only for J values of 4, 5, 7, and 8, and TRACI ends up in the ninth position. Try it by hand and it will become clear.

Figure B-25 What is a bubble sort?

```
100 DIM A$(10,10), B$(4,10), S(3,6)
```

The matrix has a row and a column, with the first number in the parentheses representing the maximum number of rows and the second the maximum number of columns. If C$ is defined as C$(5,5), then this matrix may contain a total of 25 items, and each could be referenced by indexing the two numbers of the array variable.

Figure B-26 shows a matrix. To access the first row and first column of the C$ array, use the variable C$(1,1). Each pair of numbers shown in the matrix refers to that position in the two-dimensional array variable C$.

Just as in the single-dimension array, the index number can be a numeric expression. The following example demonstrates how 25 numbers would be entered into a matrix:

Row \ Column	1	2	3	4	5
1	1,1	1,2	1,3	1,4	1,5
2	2,1	2,2	2,3	2,4	2,5
3	3,1	3,2	3,3	3,4	3,5
4	4,1	4,2	4,3	4,4	4,5
5	5,1	5,2	5,3	5,4	5,5

Figure B-26 The matrix.

```
100 DIM C(5,5)
110 FOR I = 1 TO 5
120 FOR J = 1 TO 5
130 PRINT "ENTER NUMBER "; I; ","; J; " ";
140 INPUT C(I,J)
150 NEXT J
160 NEXT I
```

An example of this type may be used if a program is to perform matrix arithmetic. Matrices are not as useful as single-dimension arrays for business processing.

As a final note concerning one- and two-dimensional arrays: the variable name that you use in a DIM statement is not the same as the name of the nonarray variable. Even though C(5,5) was defined in line 100 above, your program could also include a numeric variable named C. Since the C *array* always appears as C(num,num), the computer can't confuse it with the C *variable,* so you can use both in the same program.

Storing Data Within a Program

The READ and DATA Statements. In business programming, you generally use the READ and DATA statements to store information that you will use within a table. For example, if you write a program to calculate the depreciation of a fixed asset, you could store the standard depreciation values in the program and read them into a table for reference when needed. These statements often appear in place of file processing. Using READ-DATA to simulate reading from a file works well enough when you are new to BASIC, but it is not realistic for genuine applications.

Using the READ-DATA statements to access information is easy. The READ statement works as the INPUT statement does, but instead of accepting a user entry, the system retrieves information from the DATA statement. The syntax of the READ statement is:

line number READ *variable* [,*variable*] . . .

The syntax of the DATA statement is:

line number DATA *constant* [,*constant*] . . .

These would commonly appear in a program as:

```
100 READ N1$, N2$, A
110 PRINT N1$, N2$, A
            *
            *
            *
600 DATA "BRIAN", "JEWELL", 24
610 END
```

When the program is run, the READ statement will assign "BRIAN" to N1$, "JEWELL" to N2$, and the number 24 to A. These would then be printed in line 110.

Notice that the DATA statement is near the end of the program. Actually, you can place this statement anywhere since it does not affect program execution, but placing all the DATA statements at the end keeps the executable portion of the program readable. Make sure that you have enough data within the DATA statement for all the variables.

The READ statement may appear more than once—and usually does. When another READ executes, it takes the next item of data from the DATA statement. Picture a pointer that indicates the last data item that was retrieved by a READ statement. This pointer does not reset with a new READ; instead, it continues retrieving data where it left off. You're always allowed to have more than enough data but you can't have too little. Consider the following example:

```
100 READ  N1$, N2$, A
110 PRINT N1$, N2$, A
120 READ  N1$, N2$, A
130 PRINT N1$, N2$, A
            *
            *
            *
600 DATA "BRIAN", "JEWELL", 24, "JOHN", "STANOVICH", 31
610 DATA "JOHN", "SROKA", 30, "JOE", "BLOW", 31
9999 END
```

As before, the first READ will retrieve BRIAN, JEWELL, and 24, and these will be printed by line 110. The second READ will then retrieve JOHN, STANOVICH, and 31, and these will be printed by line 130. If another READ existed, it would continue with the next DATA statement and so on.

We haven't mentioned it until now, but the data types within the READ and DATA statements must match. An error will occur if an alphanumeric constant is read into a numeric variable or, in some

```
100 REM ACCELERATED DEPRECIATION CALCULATOR -- T. COURY
110 REM
120 REM THIS PROGRAM WILL CALCULATE AN ACCELERATED
130 REM DEPRECIATION TABLE BASE ON THE ACRS RECOVERY
140 REM TABLE FOR AN ASSET OF 1985.
150 REM
160 REM OUTPUT: D = DEPRECIATION AMOUNT FOR THE YEAR
170 REM INPUT:  O = ORIGINAL BASIS
180 REM         C = CLASS LIFE IN YEARS
190 REM PROCESS:  THE DEPRECIATION FOR EACH YEAR IS CALCULATED BY:
200 REM         DEPRECIATION = ACRS VALUE X BASIS
210 REM
220 REM OTHER VARIABLES:
230 REM         T1(3) = THREE-YEAR TABLE
240 REM         T2(5) = FIVE-YEAR TABLE
250 REM         T3(10) = TEN-YEAR TABLE
260 REM         I = INDEX
270 REM         Q$ = RECEIVE ANSWER TO REDO QUESTION
280 REM
290 REM
300 REM DIMENSION ARRAYS
310 DIM T1(3), T2(5), T3(10)
320 REM INITIALIZE THREE-YEAR TABLE
330 FOR I = 1 TO 3
340     READ T1(I)
350 NEXT I
360 REM INITIALIZE FIVE-YEAR TABLE
370 FOR I = 1 TO 5
380     READ T2(I)
390 NEXT I
400 REM INITIALIZE TEN-YEAR TABLE
410 FOR I = 1 TO 10
```

Figure B-27 The depreciation calculation program.

cases, if a number that is not within quotes is read into a string variable. Remember to maintain proper ordering in both the variables of the READ and the constants of the DATA to ensure matched assignments.

Observing these BASIC program examples will help you to develop a clear understanding of the applications. Figure B-27 presents a program that uses table processing with arrays and READ-DATA statements. The data contained within the program are the recovery percentages used for calculating accelerated depreciation using the *Accelerated Cost Recovery System* standard. The program will accept the original basis for an investment along with its class life, and it will calculate and display each year's depreciation allowance.

```
420     READ T3(I)
430 NEXT I
440 REM ACCEPT INPUT
450 PRINT "ENTER ORIGINAL BASIS ";
460 INPUT O
470 PRINT "ENTER CLASS LIFE IN YEARS (3, 5, OR, 10) ";
480 INPUT C
490 PRINT
500 PRINT "    YEAR", "DEPRECIATION"
510 PRINT "-----------", "------------"
520 REM CALCULATE DEPRECIATION
530 IF C = 3 THEN 550
540 GOTO 610
550 REM IF C = 3 THEN BEGIN
560     FOR I = 1 TO 3
570         D = T1(I) * O
580         PRINT I, D
590     NEXT I
600     GOTO 830
610 REM ELSE
620     IF C = 5 THEN 640
630     GOTO 700
640     REM IF C = 5 THEN BEGIN
650         FOR I = 1 TO 5
660             D = T2(I) * O
670             PRINT I, D
680         NEXT I
690         GOTO 820
700     REM ELSE
710         IF C = 10 THEN 730
720         GOTO 790
730         REM IF C = 10 THEN BEGIN
740             FOR I = 1 TO 10
750                 D = T3(I) * O
760                 PRINT I, D
770             NEXT I
780             GOTO 810
790         REM ELSE
800             GOTO 470
810         REM END IF C = 10
820     REM END IF C = 5
830 REM END IF C = 3
840 PRINT
850 PRINT "DO YOU WANT ANOTHER CALCULATION (Y OR N) ";
860 INPUT Q$
870 IF Q$ = "Y" THEN 440
880 PRINT
890 PRINT "PROGRAM COMPLETE..."
```

Figure B-27, *continued.*

```
900 DATA .29, .47, .24
910 DATA .18, .33, .25, .16, .08
920 DATA .09, .19, .16, .14, .12
930 DATA .10, .08, .06, .04, .02
9999 END

RUN

ENTER ORIGINAL BASIS ? 20000
ENTER CLASS LIFE IN YEARS (3, 5, OR, 10) ? 3

     YEAR        DEPRECIATION
------------ ------------
    1           5800
    2           9400
    3           4800

DO YOU WANT ANOTHER CALCULATION (Y OR N) ? Y
ENTER ORIGINAL BASIS ? 20000
ENTER CLASS LIFE IN YEARS (3, 5, OR, 10) ? 5

     YEAR        DEPRECIATION
------------ ------------
    1           3600
    2           6600
    3           5000
    4           3200
    5           1600

DO YOU WANT ANOTHER CALCULATION (Y OR N) ? Y
ENTER ORIGINAL BASIS ? 20000
ENTER CLASS LIFE IN YEARS (3, 5, OR, 10) ? 10

     YEAR        DEPRECIATION
------------ ------------
    1           1800
    2           3800
    3           3200
    4           2800
    5           2400
    6           2000
    7           1600
    8           1200
    9           800
    10          400

DO YOU WANT ANOTHER CALCULATION (Y OR N) ? N

PROGRAM COMPLETE...
```

The program initializes three tables in lines 320 to 430 by reading the data from the DATA statements of lines 900 to 930. The index to each of the tables represents the corresponding year of the depreciation percentage contained within the table. That's why the three-year table contains three elements, the five-year contains five elements, and so on. Once you've determined the proper class with the nested IF's of lines 530 to 820, each year's depreciation is calculated with the corresponding FOR-NEXT loop performing the table indexing. Finally, you see the value printed.

Using RESTORE with READ-DATA. Remember the data pointer mentioned earlier? The RESTORE statement resets that pointer. This statement has the following very short syntax:

line number RESTORE

When a RESTORE executes, the READ statement that follows it will start reading from the first constant of the first DATA statement just as it would on an initial READ. Consider a slight modification to an example used above:

```
100 READ  N1$, N2$, A
110 PRINT N1$, N2$, A
120 READ  N1$, N2$, A
130 PRINT N1$, N2$, A
140 RESTORE
150 READ  N1$, N2$, A
160 PRINT N1$, N2$, A
           *
           *
           *
600 DATA "BRIAN", "JEWELL", 24, "JOHN", "STANOVICH", 31
610 DATA "JOHN", "SROKA", 30, "JOE", "BLUW", 31
9999 END
```

After execution of the RESTORE of line 140, the data pointer resets to "BRIAN", and the READ of line 150 will retrieve this name along with "JEWELL" and 24. With no RESTORE at 140, the READ of 150 would assign "JOHN", "SROKA", and 30 to its variables.

The RESTORE is most commonly used in an application that requires multiple use of the same constants in a DATA statement, for example, a process that uses the READ-DATA combination to do a table search rather than reading the data into an array.

Subroutines in BASIC

GOSUB and RETURN. A subroutine in BASIC gives you another way of branching, with the added advantage of an unconditional return. The GOSUB and RETURN statements create this type of subroutine branching. The syntax for the GOSUB is:

line number GOSUB *line number*

and the RETURN:

line number RETURN

The GOSUB works much like the GOTO, but isn't used in the same situations. The *line number* referenced by GOSUB is actually the start of a group of statements that end with a RETURN. When BASIC sees a GOSUB, execution transfers to *line number* and the program proceeds from that point until it encounters a RETURN. The RETURN then forces transfer back to the line immediately following the GOSUB statement that initiated the branch.

Consider the following example:

```
100 REM A PROGRAM TO SQUARE A NUMBER
110 INPUT N
120 GOSUB 150
130 PRINT S
140 STOP
150 REM START OF THE SUBROUTINE
160 LET S = N * N
170 RETURN
9999 END
```

This shows the use of both a subroutine and the STOP statement introduced earlier. The GOSUB of line 120 forces transfer to the subroutine of line 150. The value of S is calculated and the RETURN statement branches back to the PRINT of line 130.

Be careful when you use subroutines. An error will occur if a RETURN executes without a GOSUB. This would happen without the STOP in the example. Recall that the STOP terminates the program at that point. Also, if a GOTO is used to branch to the subroutine, an error would occur since the RETURN is not matched by a calling GOSUB. A subroutine may be called within another subroutine, but various systems limit the level of nesting. A few levels are generally safe as is a well-structured program.

A Case Structure

The ON . . . GOTO Statement. A case structure selects an alternative based on some determination value. In BASIC, the ON . . . GOTO statement does the work and the determination value is contained within a numeric expression. The syntax for this statement is:

line number ON *expression* GOTO *line number* [,*line number*] . . .

The statement will force branching to one of the *line numbers* within it, and *expression* determines to which *line number* control branches. For example, if the value of *expression* were 3, then the GOTO would transfer to the third *line number* in the list. Make sure that you account for all possible values of *expression* in the ON . . . GOTO statement. That is, there should be enough *line numbers* to match the maximum value for *expression*, and *expression* should never be less than one or have a noninteger value. Also—as you may have guessed—*expression* is always numeric.

One of the most common uses for the ON . . . GOTO statement is in processing a menu selection (this may be used in place of the nested IF's in the financial analysis program). The following example illustrates this concept:

```
100 REM MENU PROCESSING USING A CASE STRUCTURE
110 PRINT "ENTER YOUR CHOICE (1, 2, OR 3) ";
120 INPUT C
130 IF C < 1 THEN 110
140 IF C > 3 THEN 110
150 ON C GOTO 160, 200, 300
160 REM PROCESS C = 1
                  *
                  *
                  *
200 REM PROCESS C = 2
                  *
                  *
                  *
300 REM PROCESS C = 3
                  *
                  *
                  *
9999 END
```

As the example illustrates, you will branch to line 160, 200, or 300 based on the value input for C—a 1, 2, or 3, respectively. Also, the IF statements ensure that a valid entry was accepted. And finally, ON . . . GOTO statements need comments for each section that will be branched to. This enhances a program's clarity and helps to keep it structured.

A Little Bit of Everything in a Payroll Program

Now that you have the bulk of what you need to produce useful BASIC programs, it is time to put what you've learned to use once again. A payroll program is a good application for this purpose, and it also introduces some concepts that will be beneficial in your future software development.

The next program contains many familiar components, as well as some that may not be so familiar. File processing is simulated using the READ-DATA statements. The program starts by reading a line of data that could represent what is known as a record in a sequential file. The record contains the employee's name, department, hourly wage, and the number of hours worked in the week.

Required outputs:

> Name, department, overtime pay per employee, total hours per employee, total pay per employee, total company regular pay, total company overtime pay

Data inputs:

> Name, department, pay rate, hours worked

User inputs:

> Menu selection

Process:

1. Print headings.

2. While not end of data:
   Calculate overtime and regular pay for each employee.
   (Overtime pays time and one-half.)
   Print the output.
   Store the items in arrays.
   Read the next data line.
3. Print the "Total" line.
4. Print the menu and accept choice:
   If the choice is "Print Payroll Sorted by Name" then:
       Sort arrays by name.
       Print the output.
   If the choice is "Print Payroll Sorted by Department" then:
       Sort arrays by department.
       Print the output with department first.
   If the choice is "End Program" then:
       Print message.
       End program.

Hints:

> Place an "END" mark in the data and read until it is found.
> Count the number of items that were read.
> Use a separate array for each item to be stored.
> Dimension the arrays to a number larger than the anticipated number of employee data records.
> Perform a sort only if the array is not in the required order.
> Remember to exchange the items of all arrays when required during the sort.

Good luck!

Figure B-28 The payroll program challenge.

```
100 REM PAYROLL WITH SORTED OUTPUT -- T. COURY
110 REM
120 REM THIS PROGRAM USES THE READ-DATA STATEMENT TO SIMULATE
130 REM READING PAYROLL RECORDS.  IT THEN CALCULATES THE PAYROLL
140 REM AND ALLOWS SORTED OUTPUT BASED ON A MENU SELECTION.
150 REM
160 REM OUTPUT: N$ = EMPLOYEE NAME
170 REM         D$ = DEPARTMENT
180 REM         H  = NUMBER OF HOURS WORKED
190 REM         D  = AMOUNT OF OVERTIME PAY
200 REM         P  = AMOUNT OF TOTAL PAY
210 REM         T1 = OVERTIME PAY FOR ALL EMPLOYEES
220 REM         T2 = TOTAL PAY FOR ALL EMPLOYEES
230 REM INPUT FROM DATA:
240 REM         N$ = EMPLOYEE NAME
250 REM         D$ = DEPARTMENT
260 REM         R  = PAY RATE
270 REM         H  = NUMBER OF HOURS WORKED
280 REM INPUT FROM USER:
290 REM         C  = MENU CHOICE
300 REM PROCESS:  OVERTIME IS CALCULATED BY: 1.5 X (H - 40) X R
310 REM           REGULAR PAY IS: HOURS (= 40) X R
320 REM           TOTAL PAY IS: REGULAR PAY + OVERTIME (IF ANY)
330 REM           ITEMS ARE SORTED USING A BUBBLE SORT.
340 REM
```

Figure B-29, continued.

Figure B-29 The payroll program.

Each simulated record is processed to calculate the wages earned, and certain data are then stored in arrays for later use. This procedure continues until all of the employees' records have been processed, and the entire payroll is stored.

You want to display the results of the payroll calculations as they are produced, but you also want to present sorted payroll listings. Based on a menu selection, you choose to list the payroll either in alphabetical order by name, or in order by department. (You need array storage to give you this output option.) The program will end when the final menu item is selected.

Figure B-28 presents a summary of what you need to produce the payroll program. As a programming challenge, use this summary to write the program.

You will need some creative thinking to write the payroll program, based on the topics we have covered. Most of what is shown in Figure B-29 is familiar, but there are a few things that need to be discussed.

```
350 REM OTHER VARIABLES:
360 REM         N  = EMPLOYEE COUNTER
370 REM         S$ = SORT ORDER FLAG
380 REM         I  = LOOP COUNTER
390 REM         J  = LOOP COUNTER
400 REM         T3 = TEMPORARY STORAGE
410 REM         T$ = TEMPORARY STORAGE
420 REM         N$() = ARRAY OF NAMES
430 REM         D$() = ARRAY OF DEPARTMENTS
440 REM         H()  = ARRAY OF HOURS
450 REM         D()  = ARRAY OF OVERTIME
460 REM         P()  = ARRAY OF PAY
470 REM
480 REM
490 REM DIMENSION ARRAYS
500 DIM N$(20), D$(20), H(20), O(20), P(20)
510 REM INITIALIZE ACCUMULATORS AND FLAG
520 LET N = 0
530 LET T1 = 0
540 LET T2 = 0
550 LET S$ = "NOT SORTED"
560 REM ***************    START OF MAIN ROUTINE    ***************
570 REM
580 PRINT "                          PAYROLL REPORT"
590 PRINT
600 PRINT , ,"   TOTAL", " OVERTIME", "   TOTAL"
610 PRINT "   NAME", "DEPARTMENT", "  HOURS", "    PAY", "   PAY"
620 PRINT "----------", "----------", "----------", "----------", "----------"
630 READ N$,  D$, R, H
640 IF N$ <> "END" THEN 660
650 GOTO 880
660 REM WHILE N$ <> "END" BEGIN
670     LET N = N + 1
680     IF H > 40 THEN 700
690     GOTO 750
700     REM IF H > 40 THEN BEGIN
710         LET O = 1.5 * (H - 40) * R
720         LET T1 = T1 + O
730         LET P = 40 * R + O
740         GOTO 780
750     REM ELSE
760         LET O = 0
770         LET P = H * R
780     REM END  IF H > 40
790     LET T2 = T2 + P
800     PRINT N$, D$, H, O, P
810     LET N$(N) = N$
820     LET D$(N) = D$
```

```
830     LET H(N) = H
840     LET O(N) = D
850     LET P(N) = P
860     READ N$, D$, R,  H
870   GOTO 640
880 REM END WHILE N$ <> "END"
890 PRINT
900 PRINT "TOTAL OVERTIME PAID FOR ENTIRE PAYROLL = "; T1
910 PRINT
920 PRINT "                        TOTAL PAYROLL AMOUNT = "; T2
930 REM PROCESS THE MENU ITEMS
940 PRINT
950 PRINT "1.  PRINT PAYROLL SORTED BY NAME."
960 PRINT "2.  PRINT PAYROLL SORTED BY DEPARMENT."
970 PRINT "3.  END PROGRAM"
980 PRINT
990 PRINT "ENTER NUMBER OF YOUR CHOICE (1, 2, OR 3) ";
1000 INPUT C
1010 IF C < 1 THEN 990
1020 IF C > 3 THEN 990
1030 ON C GOTO 1040, 1070, 1100
1040 REM CASE: C = 1 BEGIN
1050     GOSUB 1160
1060     GOTO 830
1070 REM CASE: C = 2 BEGIN
1080     GOSUB 1660
1090     GOTO 930
1100 REM CASE: C = 3 BEGIN
1110     PRINT
1120     PRINT "PROGRAM COMPLETE..."
1130     STOP
1140 REM***************    END OF MAIN ROUTINE    ***************
1150 REM
1160 REM SUBROUTINE TO PRINT PAYROLL SORTED BY NAME
1170 PRINT
1180 PRINT "PAYROLL SORTED BY NAME:"
1190 PRINT
1200 IF S$ <> "NAME" THEN 1220
1210 GOTO 1520
1220 REM IF S$ <> "NAME" THEN BEGIN
1230    FOR I = 1 TO N - 1
1240       FOR J = 1 TO N - I
1250          IF N$(J) > N$(J + 1) THEN 1270
1260          GOTO 1480
1270          REM IF N$(J) > N$(J + 1) THEN BEGIN
1280                REM EXCHANGE NAMES
1290             LET T$ = N$(J)
1300             LET N$(J) = N$(J + 1)
```

Figure B-29, continued.

```
1310              LET N$(J + 1) = T$
1320                  REM EXCHANGE DEPARTMENTS
1330              LET T$ = D$(J)
1340              LET D$(J) = D$(J + 1)
1350              LET D$(J + 1) = T$
1360                  REM EXCHANGE HOURS WORKED
1370              LET T3 = H(J)
1380              LET H(J) = H(J + 1)
1390              LET H(J + 1) = T3
1400                  REM EXCHANGE OVERTIME PAY
1410              LET T3 = O(J)
1420              LET D(J) = O(J + 1)
1430              LET O(J + 1) = T3
1440                  REM EXCHANGE TOTAL PAY
1450              LET T3 = P(J)
1460              LET P(J) = P(J + 1)
1470              LET P(J + 1) = T3
1480          REM END IF N$(J) > N$(J + 1)
1490      NEXT J
1500    NEXT I
1510    LET S$ = "NAME"
1520 REM END IF S$ <> "NAME"
1530 PRINT , ,"   TOTAL", " OVERTIME", "   TOTAL"
1540 PRINT "   NAME", "DEPARTMENT", "   HOURS", "    PAY", "     PAY"
1550 PRINT "----------", "----------", "----------", "----------", "----------"
1560 FOR I = 1 TO N
1570    PRINT N$(I), D$(I), H(I), P(I)
1580 NEXT I
1590 PRINT
1600 PRINT "TOTAL OVERTIME PAID FOR ENTIRE PAYROLL = "; T1
1610 PRINT
1620 PRINT "                    TOTAL PAYROLL AMOUNT = "; T2
1630 RETURN
1640 REM ***************   END OF SORT BY NAME    ***************
1650 REM
1660 REM SUBROUTINE TO PRINT PAYROLL SORTED BY DEPARTMENT
1670 PRINT
1680 PRINT "PAYROLL SORTED BY DEPARTMENT:"
1690 PRINT
1700 IF S$ <> "DEPT" THEN 1720
1710 GOTO 2020
1720 REM IF S$ <> "DEPT" THEN BEGIN
1730    FOR I = 1 TO N - 1
1740        FOR J = 1 TO N - I
1750            IF D$(J) > D$(J + 1) THEN 1770
1760            GOTO 1980
1770            REM IF D$(J) > D$(J + 1) THEN BEGIN
1780                REM EXCHANGE DEPARTMENTS
1790                LET T$ = D$(J)
```

```
1800              LET D$(J) = D$(J + 1)
1810              LET D$(J + 1) = T$
1820                 REM EXCHANGE NAMES
1830              LET T$ = N$(J)
1840              LET N$(J) = N$(J + 1)
1850              LET N$(J + 1) = T$
1860                 REM EXCHANGE HOURS WORKED
1870              LET T3 = H(J)
1880              LET H(J) = H(J + 1)
1890              LET H(J + 1) = T3
1900                 REM EXCHANGE OVERTIME PAY
1910              LET T3 = O(J)
1920              LET O(J) = O(J + 1)
1930              LET O(J + 1) = T3
1940                 REM EXCHANGE TOTAL PAY
1950              LET T3 = P(J)
1960              LET P(J) = P(J + 1)
1970              LET P(J + 1) = T3
1980           REM END IF D$(J) > D$(J + 1)
1990        NEXT J
2000    NEXT I
2010    LET S$ = "DEPT"
2020 REM END IF S$ <> "DEPT"
2030 PRINT , ,"   TOTAL", " OVERTIME", "   TOTAL"
2040 PRINT "DEPARTMENT", "   NAME", "  HOURS", "    PAY", "    PAY"
2050 PRINT "----------", "----------", "----------", "----------", "----------"
2060 FOR I = 1 TO N
2070    PRINT D$(I), N$(I), H(I), O(I), P(I)
2080 NEXT I
2090 PRINT
2100 PRINT "TOTAL OVERTIME PAID FOR ENTIRE PAYROLL = "; T1
2110 PRINT
2120 PRINT "                   TOTAL PAYROLL AMOUNT = "; T2
2130 RETURN
2140 REM **************    END OF SORT BY DEPARTMENT    **************
2150 REM
2160 REM PAYROLL DATA
2170 REM
2180 DATA "ZACHARY", "MARKETING", 7.25, 44
2190 DATA "ANTHONY", "FINANCE", 10.50, 40
2200 DATA "DEANNA", "MARKETING", 9.25, 35
2210 DATA "ROBERT", "MARKETING", 8.75, 40
2220 DATA "TERI", "FINANCE", 10.50, 50
2230 DATA "JOHN", "FINANCE", 10.00, 40
2240 DATA "BETH", "PRODUCTION", 7.75, 30
2250 DATA "TRACI", "PRODUCTION", 7.00, 45
2260 DATA "FRANCES", "MARKETING", 7.50, 48
2270 DATA "MARY", "PRODUCTION", 7.25, 40
```

Figure B-29, continued.

```
2280 DATA "END", "ZZZZZ", O, O
9999 END

RUN

              PAYROLL REPORT

                    TOTAL    OVERTIME      TOTAL
     NAME    DEPARTMENT    HOURS       PAY         PAY
  ----------  ----------  ----------  ----------  ----------
   ZACHARY    MARKETING      44        43.5        333.5
   ANTHONY    FINANCE        40         0          420
   DEANNA     MARKETING      35         0          323.75
   ROBERT     MARKETING      40         0          350
   TERI       FINANCE        50        157.5       577.5
   JOHN       FINANCE        40         0          400
   BETH       PRODUCTION     30         0          232.5
   TRACI      PRODUCTION     45        52.5        332.5
   FRANCES    MARKETING      48        90          390
   MARY       PRODUCTION     40         0          290

TOTAL OVERTIME PAID FOR ENTIRE PAYROLL = 343.5
            TOTAL PAYROLL AMOUNT = 3649.75


1. PRINT PAYROLL SORTED BY NAME.
2. PRINT PAYROLL SORTED BY DEPARTMENT.
3. END PROGRAM

ENTER NUMBER OF YOUR CHOICE (1, 2, OR 3) ? 1

PAYROLL SORTED BY NAME:

                    TOTAL    OVERTIME      TOTAL
     NAME    DEPARTMENT    HOURS       PAY         PAY
  ----------  ----------  ----------  ----------  ----------
   ANTHONY    FINANCE        40         0          420
   BETH       PRODUCTION     30         0          232.5
   DEANNA     MARKETING      35         0          323.75
   FRANCES    MARKETING      48        90          390
   JOHN       FINANCE        40         0          400
   MARY       PRODUCTION     40         0          290
   ROBERT     MARKETING      40         0          350
   TERI       FINANCE        50        157.5       577.5
   TRACI      PRODUCTION     45        52.5        332.5
   ZACHARY    MARKETING      44        43.5        333.5

TOTAL OVERTIME PAID FOR ENTIRE PAYROLL = 343.5
            TOTAL PAYROLL AMOUNT = 3649.75
```

```
1. PRINT PAYROLL SORTED BY NAME.
2. PRINT PAYROLL SORTED BY DEPARTMENT.
3. END PROGRAM

ENTER NUMBER OF YOUR CHOICE (1, 2, OR 3) ? 2

PAYROLL SORTED BY DEPARTMENT:
```

DEPARTMENT	NAME	TOTAL HOURS	OVERTIME PAY	TOTAL PAY
FINANCE	ANTHONY	40	0	420
FINANCE	JOHN	40	0	400
FINANCE	TERI	50	157.5	577.5
MARKETING	DEANNA	35	0	323.75
MARKETING	FRANCES	48	90	390
MARKETING	ROBERT	40	0	350
MARKETING	ZACHARY	44	43.5	333.5
PRODUCTION	BETH	30	0	232.5
PRODUCTION	MARY	40	0	290
PRODUCTION	TRACI	45	52.5	332.5

```
TOTAL OVERTIME PAID FOR ENTIRE PAYROLL = 343.5
              TOTAL PAYROLL AMOUNT = 3649.75

1. PRINT PAYROLL SORTED BY NAME.
2. PRINT PAYROLL SORTED BY DEPARTMENT.
3. END PROGRAM

ENTER NUMBER OF YOUR CHOICE (1, 2, OR 3) ? 3

PROGRAM COMPLETE...
```

When dealing with a record-processing situation, you need some method to detect the end of the records. In the payroll program the literal string "END" was placed as the last data name in line 2280, and records are read using a WHILE loop until the computer reaches this item. You check for "END" in line 640. A counter—the variable N—keeps track of the number of names being read from the DATA statements. You need a WHILE loop, rather than an UNTIL loop, to prevent an error from occurring if no records existed, because encountering a file without records is a possibility in genuine record processing. A "priming" READ for the WHILE condition exists in line 630.

The calculations and IF-THEN-ELSE structure of lines 680 to 780 promote the program's clarity, as do the calculations and assignments of lines 790 to 850. The WHILE loop ends with another READ and the process continues until the "END" string occurs.

The menu items are processed using the ON . . . GOTO statement and the case structure it produces. Two GOSUB's do the requested sorting and printing, and the program ends directly.

In the subroutines, a flag is checked (lines 1220 and 1700) before the array sorts. If the flag indicates that the last sort to occur is the current one, the array is printed just as it is. If another sort is needed, then the sort criteria are used for the comparison (lines 1250 and 1750). When an exchange is needed, an item in one of the arrays exchanges with one in the second array, and they maintain their association (lines 1280 to 1470, and 1780 to 1970). Finally, you print the array.

If you're not sure about how something works or why it is needed, go ahead and play with it! Add, change, or eliminate statements; the results will be very educational.

SUGGESTED PROGRAMMING CHALLENGES

1. Write a program to read and sort the following unordered numbers into an array of 20 elements. Your program should then ask the user to enter a number from 1 to 50, and it should search the array and display the position where the number was found. It should also indicate if the number is not in the list.

        DATA 4, 2, 19, 5, 20, 1, 35, 42, 46, 29
        DATA 34, 23, 50, 21, 11, 44, 47, 32, 39, 26

2. Write a program to help your friend, Kay the DJ, keep track of playing times for her albums. The data below contains names of albums and the playing times for each. Your program should read this data into two arrays and produce output that contains two lists. One list shows the albums in alphabetical order with the corresponding times, and the other list shows the albums in order from shortest to longest time. It should also display—separately—the shortest album, the longest album, and the average time for all the albums.

        DATA "TRESPASS – GENESIS", 43
        DATA "BORN IN THE U.S.A. –
          BRUCE SPRINGSTEEN", 46
        DATA "WINELIGHT –
          GROVER WASHINGTON JR.", 39
        DATA "ARC OF A DIVER –
          STEVE WINWOOD", 40

        DATA "THE BEST OF GILBERT
          & SULLIVAN", 54
        DATA "SHANGO – SANTANA", 46
        DATA "WHAT'S NEW –
          LINDA RONSTADT", 37
        DATA "FAMILY – HUBERT LAWS", 41

3. A program is needed to maintain the inventory for a restaurant's fine wine cellar. The data below contains the names of a few of the wines with the corresponding bin numbers, quantity on hand, and cost per bottle. Develop a program that reads this data into several arrays, displays the information for the wines, and processes each of the following menu selections.

        1. REMOVE WINE FROM THE CELLAR
        2. ADD WINE TO THE CELLAR
        3. INDICATE NEEDED ORDERS
        4. END THE PROGRAM

Menu items 1 and 2 should allow selection and adjustment of the appropriate array elements. For item 3, an order is needed if the quantity on hand for one of the items is less than or equal to 3. All wine is ordered by the case (12 bottles). When item 3 is selected, the information for each of the wines that needs to be ordered should be displayed along with the cost for each order, and the total cost for all cases ordered. The program should end only after item 4 has been selected.

    DATA "CHATEAU LAFITE-ROTHSCHILD",
        1, 3, 99
    DATA "CHATEAU MARGAUX", 2, 5, 95
    DATA "CHATEAU HAUT-BRION", 3, 7, 90
    DATA "CHATEAU LATOUR", 4, 2, 93
    DATA "CHATEAU MOUTON ROTHSCHILD",
        5, 1, 91
    DATA "CHATEAU TALBOT", 6, 9, 60

4. Four of your close friends—Chris, Jimmy, John, and Martina—are avid tennis players whom you have been observing for some time. You have noticed definite trends in their games and have devised a rating system that will help determine who will win various matches in different situations. The system assigns points to the type of court surface, the outcome of an immediately previous match, and the opponent. Add the points associated with each of the criteria, and the player with the greatest number of points will be predicted winner. The data is as follows:

	Surface		Last Match		This Opponent			
Player	Clay	Grass	Won	Lost	Chris	Jimmy	John	Martina
Chris	6	5	7	3	—	5	3	7
Jimmy	9	7	8	5	9	—	5	8
John	9	8	9	6	9	6	—	9
Martina	6	6	7	6	8	6	3	—

For example, if Jimmy and John are going to have a match on grass and both won their last matches, Jimmy would be given a rating of 7 + 8 + 5 = 20, and John would be given a rating of 8 + 9 + 6 = 23. John would then be predicted as the winner.

Write a program to accept the players of a match, the court type, and the outcome of the last match for each of the players. The program should then predict a winner. There are situations where a tie may occur and no winner can be predicted.

Structured Programming and Modularization

While being introduced to the art and science of computer programming using the BASIC language, we have emphasized the importance of structured programming. Programs that are well structured are easier to understand, debug, maintain, and modify.

When you ask computer programmers what they mean by the term "structured programming," you get a variety of responses. So while a definition may be difficult to come by, a list of characteristics of what would be considered a well structured program can be developed. The list is sure to include the following characteristics:

1. The use of comments embedded within the program that
    a. identify the author of the program
    b. describe the purpose of the program
    c. describe the intended use of the variables
    d. describe the function of a block of program statements
    e. locate major sections of the program. (e.g. the main program, subroutines, functions, data statements.)

2. The use of the three fundamental control structures.
   a. Sequence: executing statements in the order in which they appear in the program.
   b. Selection: executing one block of statements as opposed to doing nothing, or as opposed to executing one of any number of other blocks of statements depending on the outcome of a condition.
   c. Repetition: Repeating a block of statements depending on the outcome of a condition.

3. The use of indentation to identify the blocks of statements that are part of a control structure.

4. The use of vertical spacing to separate blocks of statements that perform specific tasks.

5. The use of self-documenting code, i.e. descriptive variable names, function names, etc.

6. The use of subroutines and functions to modularize the program. This allows the main program to be free of details that obscure the purpose of the program. By deferring such details to subroutines and functions, the main program can be used to control the order in which the major subtasks of the program must be performed in order to accomplish the purpose of the program.

The first five characteristics were adhered to in each of the examples presented thus far. Recall that the second two control structures (selection and repetition) were constructed using the conditional branch statement and the FOR loop (Fig. B-14 and B-17).

As noted earlier, some versions of BASIC include enhancements that make it easier to write well structured programs.

We are going to make use of one such version of BASIC* and rewrite the programs listed below. These revised programs have been written in a *modular* fashion, and are presented at the end of this appendix. So you can compare the revised programs to the original versions, the page numbers of the *original* versions are listed below with the program titles.

1. Financial analysis program   (Fig. B-16, pp 604–606)
2. EBIT with variable quantity   (Fig. B-19, pp 610–611)
3. EBIT with two variations   (Fig. B-22, pp 616–618)
4. The sort program   (Fig. B-24, pp 623–624)
5. The depreciation calculation program   (Fig. B-27, pp 628–630)
6. The payroll program   (Fig. B-29, pp 635–641)

As you compare the revised programs to the original versions, you should note the following changes:

*IBM PC BASIC Version A2.10

1. The WHILE loop is included as a statement supported by BASIC rather than constructed from the conditional and unconditional branch statements.

2. The END statement can be placed at the end of the main program and before the subroutines. As a result, the program will halt execution when it encounters the END statement rather than continue on into the statements of the subroutines.

3. Variable names can include more than two alphanumeric characters. (Also notice the use of the period.)

4. The single quote is used for the same purpose as the REM statement. This allows for a cleaner appearance. The REM is still used to mark major sections of the program.

5. A greater emphasis on a modular approach. The main programs are short and show the order in which the major subtasks of the program are to be executed. The details of the subtasks are included in the subroutine. Some subroutines are complex enough that they in turn call other subroutines to perform certain subtasks.

6. Subroutines are used to reduce the amount of duplicate code. There are examples in which the same subroutine is called from different places within the program.

The revised versions of the programs are functionally equivalent to the earlier versions. So a sample run of each one will not be included since it would be identical to the sample runs of the earlier versions.

THE FINAL STEP

The final step to becoming a proficient BASIC programmer is learning the many additional language statements and functions that are both a standard part of BASIC and unique to the system that you will use. The final step also involves the more difficult task of refining the art of programming itself. Learning the additional language techniques requires little more than some added study, but refining the art is probably best accomplished by practice and experience.

The remaining sections of this appendix present some typical features that you will find in one form or another in most versions of BASIC. These statements tend to be less standard than those we have presented, but this section will act as an overview to what is available.

Formatted Printing

The PRINT USING Statement. The PRINT USING statement will format the output of variables, allowing a programmer to define such things as the number of decimal places and insertion of commas in numeric variables, and the positioning of characters in alphanumeric variables. Two of the more common formats for the PRINT USING statement are:

line number PRINT USING *string expn; expression*
[; *expression*] . . .

and:

line number PRINT USING *line number, expression*
[, *expression*] . . .

In the first form of the statement the *string expn* is an alphanumeric variable or literal string containing a group of characters that will allow the formatting. Those characters are contained in the line numbered *line number* in the second form. The characters differ from system to system, but the pound sign (#) is generally used for number formatting. Some simple examples are:

Form One: PRINT USING "###.##"; 498.45690
Will Print: 498.46
Form Two: 100 PRINT USING 110, 498.45690
          110:###.##
          (The colon is required in this format.)
Will Print: 498.46

This statement has many additional features, and with a bit of practice you'll be using it to enhance the appearance of your program output.

The TAB Function. Another enhancement to print formatting is the TAB function, used with the normal PRINT statement. Like the comma, it acts as a tab key, with the advantage of variable tabbing. For example:

```
100 PRINT TAB(10); "THIS STARTS IN COLUMN 10"
```

The "T" of "THIS" will print in column 10 as indicated by the TAB function. The function may be used more than once in a PRINT statement, with different values for the column position.

Functions in BASIC

Arithmetic Functions. BASIC includes several arithmetic functions that you can incorporate into a program. These functions work like one of the function keys on a pocket calculator. Based on the value you enter into a function, you get different results. A function typically appears as:

```
100 LET S = SQR(X)
```

Function	Returns
ABS(X)	The absolute value of X
ATN(X)	The arctangent (in radians) of
COS(X)	The cosine of X where X is in radians
EXP(X)	The value of a raised to the X power
FIX(X)	The value of X with any fractional portion truncated
INT(X)	The greatest integer in X
LOG(X)	The base e log of X
RND(X)	A random number between 0 and 1
SIN(X)	The sine of X where X is in radians
SQR(X)	The square root of X
TAN(X)	The tangent of X where X is in radians

Figure B-30 BASIC arithmetic functions.

The SQR function will return the square root of the value contained in X. Figure B-30 summarizes several of the more common arithmetic functions.

String Functions. String functions selectively retrieve the characters contained in an alphanumeric variable, or they generate character strings based on values that direct the function. These functions tend to differ from system to system, so any that are presented here may not have the same form or function in a particular version of BASIC. Figure B-31 summarizes some of the string functions that may be available on your system.

User-Defined Functions. If one of the available standard BASIC functions fails to supply what you need for an application, then you may define your own, using the DEF FN statement. The syntax for defining functions is:

line number DEF FN*variable*(arg [,arg] . . .) = *expression*

Variable is the name of the function and may be numeric or alphanumeric. The *expression* returns a result based on the *arg* values assigned, and the *expression type must match that of the variable.*

The following example illustrates the use of the DEF FN statement to find a quadratic root (although this will not find complex roots):

```
100 DEF FNQ(A, B, C) = (-B + SQR(B^2 - 4 * A * C)) / (2 * A)
110 PRINT "ENTER COEFFICIENTS A, B, C, ";
120 INPUT A, B, C
130 PRINT "THE ROOT = "; FNQ(A, B, C)
9999 END
```

Function	Returns
ASC(A$), ASCII(A$)	The ASCII value of the first character in A$
CHR$(N)	The character with the ASCII code N
INSTR(N,A$,B$)	The position of the first occurrence of B$ in A$ starting with the Nth character of A$
LEN(A$)	The length of A$
LEFT$(A$,N), LEFT(A$,N)	The leftmost N characters of A$
MID$(A$,N,M), MID(A$,N,M)	The M characters of A$ starting with the Nth character
RIGHT$(A$,N), RIGHT(A$,N)	The rightmost N characters of A$, or the rightmost characters of A$ starting from the Nth position
SPACE$(N)	A string of N spaces
STRING$(N,M) STRING$(N,A$)	A string of N characters with the ASCII value of M or the first character in A$
VAL(A$)	The numeric value of A$ when A$ contains all numeric characters

Note: Functions defined twice indicate two commonly implemented versions that are system dependent.

Figure B-31 BASIC string functions.

The DEF FN statement is also useful for many types of string manipulations. You can define functions to justify numbers that are stored as strings, or words that need to be of a uniform size. When you're using a video display for output, you can control the print position (cursor position) with certain sequences of characters. This is also easily handled in a user-defined function.

Functions, like so many of the topics we've discussed, differ from system to system. Some versions of BASIC support multiple line functions which allow the development of program modules that may be executed with a function call. You can also vary the location of a function in a program. Some versions require you to define a function before you use it, and some do not. The specific type of user-defined function that your system supports would be documented in a user's manual.

Using functions can save you time and increase the modularity and clarity of your BASIC programs.

File Processing

Any programming language would be of limited use if it did not include some method for storing data external to a program. File processing describes a method for reading, processing, and writing data that is stored on some secondary storage medium. If we had used a file in the previous payroll program instead of the READ-DATA combination, the information could be added to or changed as well as read. This isn't possible when the data is stored within the program. If another program could use the same data for a different process, this would create a link between the two. In the payroll example, one program could store the employee information on a file, and the second program could then create the payroll information. Commonly called batch processing, this uses a sequential file structure. That is, the records of the file are read one after another in the order they occur.

BASIC provides a modified INPUT and PRINT statement to allow sequential file processing; they need some means of identifying the associated file and other related information. Additional statements allow what is referred to as Random I/O, Record I/O, or Direct I/O processing. This is a method of reading the records of a file in a selective or random order, and not necessarily in the order they were stored.

Many other statements and techniques associated with file processing will help you as you develop applications for business. Once you're proficient in their use, you will have all the tools you need to be a master BASIC programmer.

SUGGESTED PROGRAMMING CHALLENGES

1. The executive decision maker—Create this simple program by loading an alphanumeric array with a group of phrases and randomly displaying one of those phrases when a user presses the RETURN key. The idea is that a question would be considered and the random phrase would answer the question. If you use an array with ten elements, the following statement would create a random index for one of those phrases on most systems.

   ```
   LET I = INT(RND(X) * 10) + 1
   ```

2. Write a program to accept a letter and a phrase and display the number of occurrences of the letter in the phrase. For example

   ```
   ENTER A LETTER > E
   ENTER A PHRASE > ? COMPUTERS ARE FUN

   THERE ARE 2 E'S IN THE PHRASE.
   ```

3. Write a program to accept two dates (month, day, year), and display the number of days between those dates. Remember to account for leap years.

4. Write a program to accept a date in numeric form (00/12/00), convert the month to a word, and display it formally (September 12, 1986).

5. This is a challenge—Create a Vegas-style Blackjack program. The program could keep a deck of cards in DATA statements and shuffle by randomly filling an array. You deal the cards by reading the array. The program should also maintain a bank to allow for betting. The program becomes more exciting if you allow the computer to play the game.

6. This is very challenging—the eight queens problem. This problem is frequently encountered in the study of data structures. The challenge is to write a program that will indicate how to place eight queens on a chess board with none of them in check against another. Good Luck!

REVISED AND
MODULARIZED
PROGRAMS

```
100 REM FINANCIAL ANALYSIS 1 -- T. COURY
110 '
120 '    THIS PROGRAM WILL FIND EITHER EBIT OR BREAK-EVEN
130 '    SALES LEVEL DEPENDING ON A MENU SELECTION.
140 '
150 '    OUTPUT:  EBIT          = EARNINGS BEFORE INTEREST AND TAXES
160 '             BE.SALES      = BREAK-EVEN SALES
170 '    INPUT:   FIX.COST      = FIXED COST IN DOLLARS
180 '             VAR.PCT       = PERCENTAGE USED TO DETERMINE VARIABLE COST
190 '             QTY.SOLD      = QUANTITY OF UNITS SOLD
200 '             UN.PRICE      = UNIT PRICE
210 '    PROCESS: EBIT IS CALCULATED BY:
220 '               EBIT = TOT.SALES - VAR.COST - FIX.COST
230 '             BREAK-EVEN SALES IS CALCULATED BY:
240 '               BE.SALES = FIX.COST / (1 - VAR.PCT)
250 '    OTHER VARIABLES:
260 '             TOT.SALES     = TOTAL SALES
270 '             VAR.COST      = VARIABLE COST IN DOLLARS
280 '             MENU.SEL      = MENU SELECTION
290 '
300 '
310 '
320 REM *********************     PROGRAM BEGINS     *******************
325 '
330     GOSUB 1100                      ' DISPLAY MENU; INPUT SELECTION
340     WHILE MENU.SEL <> 3
350       IF MENU.SEL = 1 THEN GOSUB 1300  ' CALCULATE EBIT
360       IF MENU.SEL = 2 THEN GOSUB 1500  ' CALCULATE BREAK-EVEN SALES
370       GOSUB 1100                    ' DISPLAY MENU; INPUT SELECTION
380     WEND
390     PRINT
400     PRINT "PROGRAM COMPLETE ..."
410     END
420 '
1000 REM *******************     SUBROUTINES     ***********************
1010 '
1100 REM DISPLAY MENU AND OBTAIN USER'S MENU SELECTION.
1110 '
1120     PRINT
1130     PRINT "1. CALCULATE EBIT"
```

Figure B-32 The financial analysis program modularized.

```
1140      PRINT "2. CALCULATE BREAK-EVEN SALES"
1150      PRINT "3. END PROGRAM"
1160      PRINT
1170      INPUT "ENTER THE NUMBER OF YOUR CHOICE ==>"; MENU.SEL
1180      PRINT
1190      RETURN
1200  '
1300 REM CALCULATE EBIT
1310  '
1320      PRINT "CALCULATION OF EBIT"
1330      PRINT
1340      INPUT "ENTER FIXED COST IN DOLLARS "; FIX.COST
1350      PRINT "ENTER VARIABLE COST AS A FRACTION OF SALES (I.E.  .7) ";
1360      INPUT VAR.PCT
1370      INPUT "ENTER QUANTITY SOLD "; QTY.SOLD
1380      INPUT "ENTER UNIT PRICE "; UN.PRICE
1390      PRINT
1400      '
1410      LET TOT.SALES = QTY.SOLD * UN.PRICE
1420      LET VAR.COST  = TOT.SALES * VAR.PCT
1430      LET EBIT      = TOT.SALES - VAR.COST - FIX.COST
1440      '
1450      PRINT "EARNINGS BEFORE INTEREST AND TAXES >> $"; EBIT
1460      RETURN
1470  '
1500 REM CALCULATE BREAK-EVEN SALES
1510  '
1520      PRINT "BREAK EVEN ANALYSIS"
1530      PRINT
1540      INPUT "ENTER FIXED COST IN DOLLARS "; FIX.COST
1550      PRINT "ENTER VARIABLE COST AS A FRACTION OF SALES (I.E.  .7) ";
1560      INPUT VAR.PCT
1570      PRINT
1580      '
1590      LET BE.SALES = FIX.COST / (1 - VAR.PCT)
1600      '
1610      PRINT "BREAK-EVEN SALES LEVEL >> $"; BE.SALES
1620      RETURN
1630 '
```

```
100 REM EBIT CALCULATION WITH A VARIABLE QUANTITY -- T. COURY
110 '
120 '    THIS PROGRAM WILL CALCULATE AN EBIT TABLE
130 '    BASED ON FIXED COST, VARIABLE COST, AND
140 '    A SALES LEVEL WITH A VARIABLE QUANTITY.
150 '
160 '    OUTPUT:  QTY.IDX       = QUANTITY INDEX
170 '             TOT.SALES     = TOTAL SALES
180 '             EBIT          = EARNINGS BEFORE INTEREST AND TAXES
190 '    INPUT:   FIX.COST      = FIXED COST IN DOLLARS
200 '             VAR.PCT       = PERCENTAGE USED TO DETERMINE VARIABLE COST
210 '             MIN.QTY       = MINIMUM QUANTITY TO BE SOLD
220 '             MAX.QTY       = MAXIMUM QUANTITY TO BE SOLD
230 '             QTY.INCR      = QUANTITY INCREMENT
240 '             UN.PRICE      = UNIT PRICE
250 '    PROCESS: EBIT IS CALCULATED BY THE FOLLOWING FORMULA,
260 '             EBIT = TOT.SALES - VAR.COST - FIX.COST
270 '
280 '    OTHER VARIABLES:
290 '             VAR.COST      = VARIABLE COST IN DOLLARS
300 '
310 '
320 REM ***********************    PROGRAM BEGINS    *********************
330 '
340     GOSUB 1100              ' INPUT PARAMETERS FOR EBIT TABLE
350     GOSUB 1300              ' DISPLAY EBIT TABLE
360     END
370 '
```

Figure B-33 EBIT with variable quantity modularized.

```
1000 REM *********************    SUBROUTINES    *********************
1010 '
1100 REM INPUT THE PARAMETERS NEEDED TO CONSTRUCT THE EBIT TABLE.
1110 '
1120     PRINT "CALCULATION OF EBIT TABLE BASED ON VARIABLE QUANTITY"
1130     PRINT
1140     INPUT "ENTER FIXED COST IN DOLLARS "; FIX.COST
1150     PRINT "ENTER VARIABLE COST AS A FRACTION OF SALES (I.E.  .7) ";
1160     INPUT VAR.PCT
1170     INPUT "ENTER MINIMUM QUANTITY TO BE SOLD "; MIN.QTY
1180     INPUT "ENTER MAXIMUM QUANTITY TO BE SOLD "; MAX.QTY
1190     INPUT "ENTER QUANTITY INCREMENT "; QTY.INCR
1200     INPUT "ENTER UNIT PRICE "; UN.PRICE
1210     PRINT
1220     RETURN
1230 '
1300 REM DISPLAY EBIT TABLE
1310 '
1320     PRINT " POSSIBLE", "   TOTAL", "   TOTAL"
1330     PRINT " QUANTITY", "   SALES", "   COST", "   EBIT"
1340     PRINT "----------", "----------", "-----------", "------------"
1350     '
1360     FOR QTY.IDX = MIN.QTY TO MAX.QTY STEP QTY.INCR
1370        LET TOT.SALES = QTY.IDX * UN.PRICE
1380        LET VAR.COST  = TOT.SALES * VAR.PCT
1390        LET EBIT      = TOT.SALES - VAR.COST - FIX.COST
1400        PRINT QTY.IDX, TOT.SALES, FIX.COST + VAR.COST, EBIT
1410     NEXT QTY.IDX
1420     RETURN
1430 '
```

```
100 REM EBIT CALCULATION WITH A VARIABLE PRICE & QUANTITY -- T. COURY
110 '
120 '    THIS PROGRAM WILL CALCULATE AN EBIT TABLE
130 '    BASED ON FIXED COST, VARIABLE COST, AND A SALES
140 '    LEVEL WITH A VARIABLE PRICE & QUANTITY.
150 '
160 '    OUTPUT:  UN.PRICE      = UNIT PRICE
170              QTY.IDX       = QUANTITY INDEX
180 '            TOT.SALES     = TOTAL SALES
190 '            EBIT          = EARNINGS BEFORE INTEREST AND TAXES
200 '    INPUT:   FIX.COST      = FIXED COST IN DOLLARS
210 '             VAR.PCT       = PERCENTAGE USED TO DETERMINE VARIABLE COST
220 '             MIN.QTY       = MINIMUM QUANTITY TO BE SOLD
230 '             MAX.QTY       = MAXIMUM QUANTITY TO BE SOLD
240 '             QTY.INCR      = QUANTITY INCREMENT
250 '             MIN.PRICE     = MINIMUM PRICE SET
260 '             MAX.PRICE     = MAXIMUM PRICE SET
270 '             PRICE.INCR    = PRICE INCREMENT
280 '    PROCESS: EBIT IS CALCULATED BY THE FOLLOWING FORMULA,
290 '                 EBIT = TOT.SALES - VAR.COST - FIX.COST
300 '
310 '    OTHER VARIABLES:
320 '             VAR.COST      = VARIABLE COST IN DOLLARS
330 '             CUR.LINE      = CURRENT LINE COUNTER
340 '             MAX.LINES     = NUMBER OF LINES PER PAGE
350 '             CONTINUE$     = ALLOWS USER TO CONTINUE TO NEXT TABLE SECTION
360 '
```

Figure B-34 EBIT with two variations modularized.

```
500 REM **********************     PROGRAM BEGINS    **********************
510 '
520 '    GOSUB 1800              ' INITIALIZE COUNTERS AND CONSTANTS
530 '    GOSUB 1100              ' INPUT PARAMETERS FOR EBIT TABLE
540      GOSUB 1300              ' DISPLAY EBIT TABLE
550      END
560 '
1000 REM **********************     SUBROUTINES    **********************
1010 '
1100 REM INPUT THE PARAMETERS NEEDED TO CONSTRUCT THE EBIT TABLE.
1110 '
1120      PRINT "CALCULATION OF EBIT TABLE BASED ON VARIABLE PRICE & QUANTITY"
1130      PRINT
1140      INPUT "ENTER FIXED COST IN DOLLARS "; FIX.COST
1150      PRINT "ENTER VARIABLE COST AS A FRACTION OF SALES (I.E.  .7) ";
1160      INPUT VAR.PCT
1170      INPUT "ENTER MINIMUM QUANTITY TO BE SOLD "; MIN.QTY
1180      INPUT "ENTER MAXIMUM QUANTITY TO BE SOLD "; MAX.QTY
1190      INPUT "ENTER QUANTITY INCREMENT "; QTY.INCR
1200      INPUT "ENTER MINIMUM UNIT PRICE "; MIN.UNPRICE
1210      INPUT "ENTER MAXIMUM UNIT PRICE "; MAX.UNPRICE
1220      INPUT "ENTER PRICE INCREMENT "; PRICE.INCR
1230      PRINT
1240      RETURN
1250 '
```

```
300 REM DISPLAY EBIT TABLE
310 '
320     GOSUB 1700                                      ' DISPLAY TABLE HEADER
330     FOR UN.PRICE = MIN.UNPRICE TO MAX.UNPRICE STEP PRICE.INCR
340        PRINT UN.PRICE;
350        FOR QTY.IDX = MIN.QTY TO MAX.QTY STEP QTY.INCR
360            LET TOT.SALES = QTY.IDX * UN.PRICE
370            LET VAR.COST  = TOT.SALES * VAR.PCT
380            LET EBIT      = TOT.SALES - VAR.COST - FIX.COST
390            IF CUR.LINE = MAX.LINES THEN 1400 ELSE 1470
400            'THEN
410               PRINT
420               INPUT "HIT ENTER TO CONTINUE "; CONTINUE$
430               GOSUB 1700                            ' DISPLAY TABLE HEADER
440               PRINT UN.PRICE;
450               LET CUR.LINE = 6
460               GOTO 1490
470            'ELSE
480               LET CUR.LINE = CUR.LINE + 1
490            'ENDIF
500            PRINT , QTY.IDX, TOT.SALES, FIX.COST + VAR.COST, EBIT
510        NEXT QTY.IDX
520     NEXT UN.PRICE
530     RETURN
540 '
700 REM DISPLAY EBIT TABLE HEADER
710 '
720     PRINT
730     PRINT "   UNIT", " POSSIBLE", "   TOTAL", "   TOTAL"
740     PRINT "   PRICE", " QUANTITY", "   SALES", "   COST", "    EBIT"
750     PRINT "----------", "----------", "----------", "----------", "----------"
760     RETURN
770 '
800 REM INITIALIZE COUNTERS AND CONSTANTS
810 '
820     CUR.LINE  =  6
830     MAX.LINES = 24
840     RETURN
850 '


100 REM NAME SORT -- T. COURY
110 '
120 '    THIS PROGRAM WILL ACCEPT 10 NAMES, SORT THEM
130 '    AND PRINT THEM IN ALPHABETICAL ORDER.
140 '
150 '    OUTPUT:   NAMES$()   = THE ARRAY CONTAINING THE SORTED NAMES
160 '    INPUT:    NAMES$()   = THE ARRAY THAT WILL CONTAIN THE NAMES
```

Figure B-35 The sort program modularized.

```
170 '    PROCESS:   A BUBBLE SORT WILL BE USED TO ALPHABETIZE
180 '               THE NAMES.
190 '
200 '    OTHER VARIABLES:
210 '             J              = A LOOP COUNTER
220 '             K              = A LOOP COUNTER
230 '             TMP$           = TEMPORARY NAME STORAGE
240 '
500 REM ***********************   PROGRAM BEGINS    *********************
510 '
520     DIM NAMES$(10)
530     GOSUB 1100                 ' INPUT NAMES AND STORE IN NAMES$()
540     GOSUB 1300                 ' SORT LIST OF NAMES INTO ALPHABETICAL ORDER
550     GOSUB 1500                 ' DISPLAY THE LIST OF NAMES
560     END
570 '
1000 REM ***********************    SUBROUTINES    ***********************
1010 '
1100 REM INPUT LIST OF NAMES AND STORE THEM IN NAMES$()
1110 '
1120     PRINT
1130     PRINT "ENTER 10 NAMES:"
1140     FOR K = 1 TO 10
1150        PRINT "ENTER NAME NUMBER "; K; " ";
1160        INPUT NAMES$(K)
1170     NEXT K
1180     RETURN
1190 '
1300 REM SORT THE LIST OF NAMES INTO ALPHABETICAL ORDER USING THE BUBBLE SORT
1310 '
1320     FOR K = 1 TO 9
1330        FOR J = 1 TO 10 - K
1340           IF NAMES#(J) > NAMES$(J + 1) THEN 1350 ELSE 1390
1350           'THEN
1360              LET TMP$ = NAMES$(J)                 ' SWAP THE
1370              LET NAMES$(J) = NAMES$(J + 1)        ' TWO
1380              LET NAMES$(J + 1) = TMP$             ' NAMES
1390           'ENDIF
1400        NEXT J
1410     NEXT K
1420     RETURN
1430 '
1500 REM DISPLAY THE NAMES IN NAME$()
1510 '
1520     PRINT
1530     PRINT "THE SORTED NAMES ARE:"
1540     FOR K = 1 TO 10
1550        PRINT , NAMES$(K)
1560     NEXT K
1570     RETURN
1580 '
```

```
100 REM ACCELERATED DEPRECIATION CALCULATOR -- T. COURY
110 '
120 '     THIS PROGRAM WILL CALCULATE AN ACCELERATED
130 '     DEPRECIATION TABLE BASE ON THE ACRS RECOVERY
140 '     TABLE FOR AN ASSET OF 1985.
150 '
160 '     OUTPUT:    DEPR.AMT       = DEPRECIATION AMOUNT FOR THE YEAR
170 '     INPUT:     ORIG.BASIS     = ORIGINAL BASIS
180 '                CLASS.LIFE     = CLASS LIFE IN YEARS
190 '     PROCESS:   THE DEPRECIATION FOR EACH YEAR IS CALCULATED BY:
200 '                    DEPR.AMT = ACRS VALUE * ORIG.BASIS
210 '
220 '     OTHER VARIABLES:
230 '                TABLE.3YR()    = THREE-YEAR TABLE
240 '                TABLE.5YR()    = FIVE-YEAR TABLE
250 '                TABLE.10YR()   = TEN-YEAR TABLE
260 '                INDEX          = INDEX
270 '                RESPONSE$      = RECEIVE USER RESPONSE TO REDO QUESTION
280 '
500 REM *********************    PROGRAM BEGINS    *********************
510 '
520 '    DIM TABLE.3YR(3), TABLE.5YR(5), TABLE.10YR(10)
530 '    GOSUB 1100                      ' INITIALIZE TABLE OF ACRS VALUES
540      RESPONSE$ = "Y"
550      WHILE RESPONSE$ = "Y"
560         GOSUB 1300                   ' INPUT ORIGINAL BASIS AND CLASS LIFE
570         GOSUB 1500                   ' PRODUCE DEPRECIATION TABLE
580         INPUT "DO YOU WANT ANOTHER CALCULATION (Y OR N) "; RESPONSE$
590      WEND
600      PRINT
610      PRINT "PROGRAM COMPLETE ..."
620      END
630 '
1000 REM *********************     SUBROUTINES     *********************
1010 '
1100 REM INITIALIZE THE TABLES OF ACRS VALUES
1110 '
1120      FOR INDEX = 1 TO 3
1130         READ TABLE.3YR(INDEX)
1140      NEXT INDEX
1150      DATA 0.29, 0.47, 0.24
1160      '
1170      FOR INDEX = 1 TO 5
1180         READ TABLE.5YR(INDEX)
1190      NEXT INDEX
1200      DATA 0.18, 0.33, 0.25, 0.16, 0.08
1210      '
1230      FOR INDEX = 1 TO 10
```

Figure B-36 The depreciation calculation program modularized.

```
1240      READ TABLE.1OYR(INDEX)
1250    NEXT INDEX
1260    DATA 0.09, 0.19, 0.16, 0.14, 0.12
1270    DATA 0.10, 0.08, 0.06, 0.04, 0.02
1280    RETURN
1290 '
1300 REM INPUT THE ORIGINAL BASIS AND CLASS LIFE
1310 '
1320    PRINT
1330    INPUT "ENTER ORIGINAL BASIS "; ORIG.BASIS
1340    INPUT "ENTER CLASS LIFE IN YEARS (3, 5, OR, 10) "; CLASS.LIFE
1350    PRINT
1360    RETURN
1370 '
1500 REM PRODUCE DEPRECIATION TABLE
1510 '
1520    PRINT "   YEAR",  "DEPRECIATION"
1530    PRINT "------------",  "------------"
1540    IF CLASS.LIFE =  3 THEN GOSUB 1700         ' USE THREE-YEAR TABLE
1550    IF CLASS.LIFE =  5 THEN GOSUB 1800         ' USE FIVE-YEAR TABLE
1560    IF CLASS.LIFE = 10 THEN GOSUB 1900         ' USE TEN-YEAR TABLE
1570    PRINT
1580    RETURN
1590 '
1700 REM CALCULATE DEPRECIATION USING THE THREE-YEAR TABLE
1710 '
1720    FOR INDEX = 1 TO 3
1730       DEPR.AMT - TABLE.3YR(INDEX) * ORIG.BASIS
1740       PRINT INDEX, DEPR.AMT
1750    NEXT INDEX
1760    RETURN
1770 '
1800 REM CALCULATE DEPRECIATION USING THE FIVE-YEAR TABLE
1810 '
1820    FOR INDEX = 1 TO 5
1830       DEPR.AMT = TABLE.5YR(INDEX) * ORIG.BASIS
1840       PRINT INDEX, DEPR.AMT
1850    NEXT INDEX
1860    RETURN
1870 '
1900 REM CALCULATE DEPRECIATION USING THE TEN-YEAR TABLE
1910 '
1920    FOR INDEX = 1 TO 10
1930       DEPR.AMT = TABLE.1OYR(INDEX) * ORIG.BASIS
1940       PRINT INDEX, DEPR.AMT
1950    NEXT INDEX
1960    RETURN
1970 '
```

```
100 REM PAYROLL WITH SORTED OUTPUT -- T. COURY
110 '
120 '    THIS PROGRAM USES THE READ-DATA STATEMENT TO SIMULATE
130 '    READING PAYROLL RECORDS.  IT THEN CALCULATES THE PAYROLL
140 '    AND ALLOWS SORTED OUTPUT BASED ON A MENU SELECTION.
150 '
160 '    OUTPUT:    EMP.NAME$          = EMPLOYEE NAME
170 '               DEPT$              = DEPARTMENT
180 '               HOURS              = NUMBER OF HOURS WORKED
190 '               OVERTIME           = AMOUNT OF OVERTIME PAY
200 '               TOT.PAY            = AMOUNT OF TOTAL PAY
210 '               TOT.OVT            = OVERTIME PAY FOR ALL EMPLOYEES
220 '               TOT.GROSS          = TOTAL PAY FOR ALL EMPLOYEES
230 '    INPUT FROM DATA:
240 '               EMP.NAME$          = EMPLOYEE NAME
250 '               DEPT$              = DEPARTMENT
260 '               PAY.RATE           = PAY RATE
270 '               HOURS              = NUMBER OF HOURS WORKED
280 '    INPUT FROM USER:
290 '               MENU.SELECT        = MENU SELECTION
300 '    PROCESS:   OVERTIME IS CALCULATED BY : 1.5 * (HOURS - 40) * PAY.RATE
310 '               REGULAR PAY IS:           HOURS (<= 40) * PAY.RATE
320 '               TOTAL PAY IS:             REGULAR PAY + OVERTIME (IF ANY)
330 '               ITEMS ARE SORTED USING A BUBBLE SORT.
340 '
350 '    OTHER VARIABLES:
360 '               EMP.CTR            = EMPLOYEE COUNTER
370 '               SORT.STATUS$       = SORT ORDER FLAG
380 '               I                  = LOOP COUNTER
390 '               J                  = LOOP COUNTER
400 '               TMP                = TEMPORARY STORAGE
410 '               TMP$               = TEMPORARY STORAGE
420 '               NAMES$()           = ARRAY OF NAMES
430 '               DEPTS$()           = ARRAY OF DEPARTMENTS
440 '               HRS()              = ARRAY OF HOURS
450 '               OVTIME()           = ARRAY OF OVERTIME
460 '               GR.PAY()           = ARRAY OF PAY
470 '
500 REM *********************    PROGRAM BEGINS    *********************
510 '
520     DIM NAMES$(20), DEPTS$(20), HRS(20), OVTIME(20), GR.PAY(20)
530     GOSUB 1100                    ' INITIALIZE ACCUMULATORS AND FLAG
540     GOSUB 1300                    ' STORE EMPLOYEE PAY INFO IN ARRAYS
550     GOSUB 1600                    ' DISPLAY PAYROLL REPORT
560     GOSUB 1800                    ' DISPLAY MENU AND MAKE SELECTION
570     WHILE MENU.SELECT <> 3
580        IF (MENU.SELECT >= 1) AND (MENU.SELECT <= 2) THEN 590 ELSE 620
```

Figure B-37 The payroll program modularized.

```
590        'THEN
600           ON MENU.SELECT GOSUB 2000, 2400
610        'ENDIF
620        GOSUB 1800                    ' DISPLAY MENU AND MAKE SELECTION
630     WEND
640     PRINT
650     PRINT "PROGRAM COMPLETE ..."
660     END
670 '
1000 REM ***********************   SUBROUTINES   ***********************
1010 '
1100 REM INITIALIZE ACCUMULATORS AND FLAG
1110 '
1120     EMP.CTR = 0
1130     TOT.OVT = 0
1140     TOT.GROSS = 0
1150     SORT.STATUS$ = "NOT SORTED"
1160     RETURN
1170 '
1300 REM FILL ARRAYS WITH EMPLOYEE PAYROLL INFORMATION
1310 '
1320     READ EMP.NAME$, DEPT$, PAY.RATE, HOURS
1330     WHILE EMP.NAME$ <> "END"
1340        LET EMP.CTR = EMP.CTR + 1
1350        IF HOURS > 40 THEN 1360 ELSE 1410
1360        'THEN
1370           LET OVERTIME = 1.5 * (HOURS - 40) * PAY.RATE
1380           LET TOT.OVT  = TOT.OVT + OVERTIME
1390           LET TOT.PAY  = (40 * PAY.RATE) + OVERTIME
1400           GOTO 1440
1410        'ELSE
1420           LET OVERTIME = 0
1430           LET TOT.PAY = HOURS * PAY.RATE
1440        'ENDIF
1445        LET TOT.GROSS = TOT.GROSS + TOT.PAY
1450        '
1460        'TRANSFER EMPLOYEE RECORD TO ARRAYS
1470        LET NAMES$(EMP.CTR) = EMP.NAME$
1480        LET DEPTS$(EMP.CTR) = DEPT$
1490        LET HRS(EMP.CTR) = HOURS
1500        LET OVTIME(EMP.CTR) = OVERTIME
1510        LET GR.PAY(EMP.CTR) = TOT.PAY
1520        '
1530        READ EMP.NAME$, DEPT$, PAY.RATE, HOURS
1540     WEND
1550     RETURN
1560 '
```

Figure B-37, *continued.*

```
1600 REM DISPLAY PAYROLL REPORT
1610 '
1620     IF SORT.STATUS$ = "NOT SORTED" THEN 1630 ELSE 1650
1630     'THEN
1640        PRINT "                            PAYROLL REPORT"
1650     'ENDIF
1660     PRINT
1670     PRINT , , "   TOTAL", " OVERTIME", "   TOTAL"
1680     PRINT "   NAME", "DEPARTMENT", "   HOURS", "    PAY", "    PAY"
1690     PRINT "----------", "----------", "----------", "----------", "----------"
1700     FOR I = 1 TO EMP.CTR
1710        PRINT NAMES$(I), DEPTS$(I), HRS(I), OVTIME(I), GR.PAY(I)
1720     NEXT I
1730     PRINT
1740     PRINT "TOTAL OVERTIME PAID FOR ENTIRE PAYROLL = "; TOT.OVT
1750     PRINT
1760     PRINT "                  TOTAL PAYROLL AMOUNT = "; TOT.GROSS
1770     PRINT
1780     RETURN
1790 '
1800 REM DISPLAY MENU AND MAKE SELECTION
1810 '
1820     PRINT
1830     PRINT "1.  PRINT PAYROLL SORTED BY NAME."
1840     PRINT "2.  PRINT PAYROLL SORTED BY DEPARTMENT."
1850     PRINT "3.  END PROGRAM"
1860     PRINT
1870     INPUT "ENTER NUMBER OF YOUR CHOICE (1, 2, OR 3) "; MENU.SELECT
1880     PRINT
1890     RETURN
1900 '
2000 REM PRINT PAYROLL SORTED BY NAME
2010 '
2020     PRINT
2030     PRINT "PAYROLL SORTED BY NAME:"
2040     PRINT
2050     IF SORT.STATUS$ <> "NAME" THEN GOSUB 2200  ' SORT ARRAYS BY NAME
2060     GOSUB 1600                                 ' DISPLAY PAYROLL SORTED BY NAME
2070     PRINT
2080     RETURN
2090 '
2200 REM SORT ARRAYS BY NAME
2210 '
2220     FOR I = 1 TO EMP.CTR - 1
2230        FOR J = 1 TO EMP.CTR - I
2240           IF NAMES$(J) > NAMES$(J + 1) THEN GOSUB 2900   ' SWAP TWO RECORDS
2250        NEXT J
2260     NEXT I
```

```
2270      LET SORT.STATUS$ = "NAME"
2280      RETURN
2290 '
2400 REM PRINT PAYROLL SORTED BY DEPARTMENT
2410 '
2420      PRINT
2430      PRINT "PAYROLL SORTED BY DEPARTMENT:"
2440      PRINT
2450      IF SORT.STATUS$ <> "DEPT" THEN GOSUB 2600   ' SORT ARRAYS BY DEPARTMENT
2460      GOSUB 2700                                  ' DISPLAY PAYROLL SORTED BY DEPARTMENT
2470      PRINT
2480 RETURN
2490 '
2600 REM SORT ARRAYS BY DEPARTMENT
2610 '
2620      FOR I = 1 TO EMP.CTR - 1
2630         FOR J = 1 TO EMP.CTR - I
2640            IF DEPTS$(J) > DEPTS$(J + 1) THEN GOSUB 2900   ' SWAP TWO RECORDS
2650         NEXT J
2660      NEXT I
2670      LET SORT.STATUS$ = "DEPT"
2680      RETURN
2690 '
2700 REM DISPLAY PAYROLL SORTED BY DEPARTMENT
2710 '
2720      PRINT
2730      PRINT , ,"   TOTAL", " OVERTIME", "   TOTAL"
2740      PRINT "DEPARTMENT", "   NAME", "  HOURS", "    PAY", "    PAY"
2750      PRINT "----------", "----------", "----------", "----------", "----------"
2760      '
2780      FOR I = 1 TO EMP.CTR
2790         PRINT DEPTS$(I), NAMES$(I), HRS(I), OVTIME(I), GR.PAY(I)
2800      NEXT I
2810      PRINT
2820      PRINT "TOTAL OVERTIME PAID FOR ENTIRE PAYROLL = "; TOT.OVT
2830      PRINT
2840      PRINT "                    TOTAL PAYROLL AMOUNT = "; TOT.GROSS
2850      PRINT
2860      RETURN
2870 '
2900 REM SWAP THE JTH AND (J + 1)TH ENTRIES IN EACH OF THE ARRAYS CONTAINING A
2910 '    FIELD OF THE PAYROLL RECORD.
2920 '
2930      LET TMP$ = NAMES$(J)
2940      LET NAMES$(J) = NAMES$(J + 1)
2950      LET NAMES$(J + 1) = TMP$
2960      '
2970      LET TMP$ = DEPTS$(J)
```

Figure B-37, *continued.*

```
2980     LET DEPTS$(J) = DEPTS$(J + 1)
2990     LET DEPTS$(J + 1) = TMP$
3000     '
3010     LET TMP = HRS(J)
3020     LET HRS(J) = HRS(J + 1)
3030     LET HRS(J + 1) = TMP
3040     '
3050     LET TMP = OVTIME(J)
3060     LET OVTIME(J) = OVTIME(J + 1)
3070     LET OVTIME(J + 1) = TMP
3080     '
3090     LET TMP = GR.PAY(J)
3100     LET GR.PAY(J) = GR.PAY(J + 1)
3110     LET GR.PAY(J + 1) = TMP
3120     RETURN
3130 '
9000 REM ***********************    DATA SECTION    *************************
9010 '
9020     DATA "ZACHARY",  "MARKETING",   7.25, 44
9030     DATA "ANTHONY",  "FINANCE",    10.50, 40
9040     DATA "DEANNA",   "MARKETING",   9.25, 35
9050     DATA "ROBERT",   "MARKETING",   8.75, 40
9060     DATA "TERI",     "FINANCE",    10.50, 50
9070     DATA "JOHN",     "FINANCE",    10.00, 40
9080     DATA "BETH",     "PRODUCTION",  7.75, 30
9090     DATA "TRACI",    "PRODUCTION",  7.00, 45
9100     DATA "FRANCES",  "MARKETING",   7.50, 48
9110     DATA "MARY",     "PRODUCTION",  7.25, 40
9120     DATA "END",      "ZZZZZ",       0.00,  0
9130 '
```

TEXT/ILLUSTRATION CREDITS AND ACKNOWLEDGMENTS

xxxi Data from T.S. Sande, INDUSTRIAL ARCHEOLOGY (New York: Viking-Penguin Books, 1978, p. 48.)

2,17 "Who Needs the Office of the Future,"? HARVARD BUSINESS REVIEW, 11/12/82. Reprinted by permission of the HARVARD BUSINESS REVIEW. Excerpts from "Who Needs the Office of the Future?" by Harvey L. Poppel (November December 1982). Copyright © 1982 by the President and Fellows of Harvard College; all rights reserved.

3 Excerpt from P. Dworkin, "Hard Times for a Law Firm That Went Big on Advertising," *San Francisco Chronicle*, 8/6/82, pp. 6–7. Copyright © 1982 San Francisco Chronicle. Reprinted by permission.

5 Excerpt from "Systems On-line Timekeeping Aids Law Firm's Billing," COMPUTERWORLD, 5/7/84, p. 38. © 1984 CW Communications/Inc.

23 John Reifuss, "Two Architects Deliver Computer-Designed Post Offices," *The Commercial Appeal*, Memphis, TN. 9/84. Reprinted by permission of The Commercial Appeal.

41 "What Can a Supercomputer do?" from "Even Mathematicians Can Get Carried Away," by James Gleick, of March 8, 1987. Copyright 1987 by The New York Times Company. Reprinted by permission.

54 Excerpt from S. Norman Feingold, "Emerging Careers: Occupations for Post-Industrial Society," THE FUTURIST, 2/84, pp. 9–10. By permission of THE FUTURIST and Dr. S. Norman Feingold. 1984.

74 "The Tyranny of the Old-Fashioned Spreadsheet," from Robert A. Mamis, "Unlocking Management Creativity," INC., 6/83, p. 103. Reprinted with permission of INC. Copyright © 1983 by Inc. Publishing Corporation, 38 Commercial Wharf, Boston, MA 02110.

106 From Steven Olson, "The Sage of Software," SCIENCE84, 1/2/84, pp. 75–76. Reprinted by permission of SCIENCE84 magazine, © 1984 American Association for the Advancement of Science.

136–37 Excerpt from Susan Lammers, PROGRAMMERS AT WORK. Reprinted by permission of Microsoft Press. © 1986 by Microsoft Press.

152 From Niklaus Werth "Knowing What the Tool Should Achieve," from "History and Goals of Modula-2," BYTE, 8/84, pp. 150–51. Reprinted by permission.

157 Excerpted from John C. Dvorak, "Programmers' Problem—Their Artistic Souls," *San Francisco Sunday Examiner & Chronicle*, 4/20/86, p. D-3. © 1986 San Francisco Examiner. Reprinted by permission.

163 "Categories and Examples of Development Tools," from THE JAMES MARTIN PRODUCTIVITY SERIES. By permission of High Productivity Software, Inc., Marblehead, MA.

173 "The Talking Machine: The Communications Idea of the Future is at Work Right Now," from William Poole, "The Talking Machine," IMAGE, 7/27/86, p. 4. William Poole: "The Talking Machine: The Communications Idea of the Future Is At Work Right Now." Reprinted by permission of William Poole, San Francisco.

203 "Desktop Publishing: Do It Yourself," from Eric Pfeiffer, "The Desktop Dream," IMAGE, 10/26/86, p. 9. Eric W. Pfeiffer, San Francisco.

219 "Computer Power"—For Some Users, One Computer Just Isn't Enough," by Preston Gralla. PC WEEK, November 3, 1987, p. s/15. Reprinted from PC WEEK, November 3, 1987. Copyright © 1987 Ziff Communications Company.

221 Excerpt from Roger von Oech, A KICK IN THE SEAT OF THE PANTS. New York: Harper & Row, 1986, p. 59.

245 "The Advantages of OS/2," from "The Elusive Art of Multi-Tasking," by Erik Sandborg Diment, of April 12, 1987. Copyright 1987 by the New York Times Company. Reprinted by permission.

236–37 "Avoiding the 'von Neuman bottleneck' with Parallel Processing," from Tom Alexander, "Reinventing the Computer," FORTUNE, 3/5/84, pp. 86, 88. © 1984 Time Inc. All rights reserved.

254 "The Light Touch: Storage and the Company Disk," from Jerry Pournelle, "Computing at Chaos Manor: Jerry's Best of 1985 Awards," BYTE, 4/1/86, pp. 288, 290.

272 "The Uses of Optical Disk: Locating the 'Night Stalker,'" from Edward S. Rothchild, "An Eye on Optical Disks," DATAMATION, March 1, 1986, p. 73.

We are indebted to the many people and organizations who contributed photographs to this book. The page numbers and contributors are listed below.

286 © 1988 Peter Menzel.

287 © 1985 Joel Gordon.

293 F9-3 Courtesy of International Business Machines Corporation.

294 F9-4 Courtesy of AT&T.

311 Courtesy of Multi-Tech Systems, Inc.

320 Photo Courtesy of Hewlett-Packard Company.

321 © 1986 Joel Gordon.

322 F10-1 *Lower left*, Hayes Microcomputer Products; *lower right*. Bloodstock Research.

326 F10-3 *Top left*, AT&T Bell Labs; *top right*, US Sprint.

341 Four by Five.

353 Crane USA.

355 British Information Services.

358 Photograph Courtesy of Hewlett-Packard Company.

371 © 1987 Lawrence Migdale

394 *Left to right*, Tony Anendola, Barbara Oliver, Laurence Ballard/ Ken Friedman.

395 PhotoEdit/Robert Brenner.

403 Wang Laboratories.

405 *Top left*, Photograph Courtesy of Hewlett-Packard Company; *top right and middle left*, © 1987 Lawrence Migdale; *middle right*, Dan McCoy/Rainbow; *bottom*, Photograph Courtesy of Hewlett-Packard Company.

411 Courtesy of International Business Machines Corporation.

414 PhotoEdit/Robert Brenner.

419 *Top left*, Photo Courtesy of Hewlett-Packard Company; *top right*, Bart Barlow.

422 *Top left and right*, Courtesy of International Business Machines Corporation; *middle left*, Photo Courtesy of NCR Corporation; *middle right*, Sperry Corporation; *bottom*, Courtesy of International Business Machines Corporation.

434 Satour.

436 *Top*, Texas Instruments; *bottom*, Photo Courtesy of Hewlett-Packard Company.

437 Courtesy of International Business Machines Corporation.

439 © 1987 Lawrence Migdale.

451 Photographs Courtesy of Hewlett-Packard Company.

456 *Top*, Courtesy of AT&T; *middle*, Courtesy of International Business Machines Corporation; *bottom*, Photograph Courtesy of Hewlett-Packard Company.

471 New York Convention and Visitors Bureau.

472 The Computer Museum, Boston.

474 F15-1 Courtesy of International Business Machines Corporation.

479 F15-2 *Top left*, © 1987 Lawrence Migdale; *top right*, Photograph Courtesy of Hewlett-Packard Company.

502 American Airlines.

507 *Left*, Courtesy of Apple Computer, Inc.; *right*, Sears Roebuck.

510 *Left*, PhotoEdit/Mark Richards; *right*, Ford Motor Co.

512 Photograph Courtesy of Hewlett-Packard Company.

526 Bureau of the Census.

529 F17-1 David Aronson/Stock

Boston.

531 Perkin Elmer.

535 F17-2 Photograph Courtesy of Hewlett-Packard Company.

536 Courtesy of Racal-Milgo.

537 Copyright National Geographic Society.

545 Dan McCoy/Rainbow.

546 © 1987 Ed Kashi.

549 Courtesy of International Business Machines Corporation.

551 San Jose Convention and Visitors Bureau.

552 Ralph's Grocery Co.

555 AT&T Bell Labs.

564 A-1 *Top left*, Smithsonian Institution; *top right*, AT&T Bell Labs; *bottom*, Reprinted by permission of Intel Corporation, 1988.

566 A-2 The Bettman Archive.

567 A-3 Courtesy of International Business Machines Corporation; A-4 Historical Picture Service.

568 A-5 British Crown Copyright— reproduced with permission of the Controller of Her Britannic Majesty's Stationery Office.

569 A-6 The Bettmann Archive.

571–72 A-7, A-8, A-9 Courtesy of Cruft Photo Lab, Harvard University/Paul Donaldson.

573 A-10 Wide World; A-11 Photo Courtesy of Iowa State University.

574 A-12 The Bettmann Archive.

575 A-13 Institute for Advanced Study.

577 A-15 Courtesy of International Business Machines Corporation.

Note: Italicized page numbers refer to figures and/or tables.

Access arm: Device in a disk drive unit that moves a read/write head over a particular track. 266–67, *268*

Access time: Time between when the computer requests data from a secondary storage device and when the data transfer is complete. 269

Accounting and Finance: Department in an organization that maintains a financial record of all activities. 25, 28, 30, 43, 359, 362–63, 412
customer-oriented processing and 421–24
information processing department and 515
management and 437–39
transaction processing information system and 416–17, *417*

Accounts payable: Money owed, spent, or paid by or owed to an organization. 419
vendor-oriented processing and 419, 421

Accounts receivable: Income or money received by or owed to an organization. 424, *424*

Accumulator: Register in the ALU that holds accumulated data. 233

Acoustic coupler: Cradle that allows a modem to accept a standard telephone handset. *322*, 323

Activenture 254

Ada: Programming language developed under the sponsorship of the Department of Defense and named for Lady Ada Augusta Byron. 135, *141*, 143, 156, 169

Address register: Register located in the controller that holds the address of a location containing data called for by an instruction. 233

Ad Hoc DSS: Decision support system designed to handle management decision problems that are unexpected or nonrecurring. 453

Aetna Life and Casualty Insurance Company 327
After Dark 310
Aiken, Howard H. 570, *571*
Aldus Corporation *60*
ALGOL 151–52
ALGOrithmic Language. *See* ALGOL
Allnet Communications 578
Alphanumeric terminal: Terminal that displays alphanumeric output. 193
Alphanumeric variable 586
Alterable: Refers to an alterable optical disk that is expected to be available soon. 273
ALU. *See* Arithmetic/logic unit
Amdahl, Gene 576
Amdahl Corporation 578
Amdahl 470V/6 576
American List Corporation 318
American National Standards Institute (ANSI) 148–50, 215, 533
American Satellite Company 327
American Standard Code for Information Interchange (ASCII): Eight-bit code used in data communications, most microcomputers, and some large computers. *227*, 228, *261*
American Telephone & Telegraph 244–45, 319, 327, 341, 577–78
Americom system 327
Analog biochip 235
Analog signal: Electronic signal that will represent a range of frequencies. 321–23
Analytical engine 567–68, *567*
Analytical graphics: Graphics that help the user analyze compiled data. 90, *90*
ANSI. *See* American National Standards Institute
ANSI-COBOL: Version of COBOL standardized by the American National Standards Institute. 148
APL 151
Apple Access II 91
Apple Computer 6–8, 151, 547, 577–78

Apple II 218
Apple IIe 180
Apple Lisa 547
Apple Macintosh 63–64, 96, 180, 218, 265, 547
AppleWorks *60*, 94
Application generator: Software system with a number of modules that is preprogrammed for various functions, so the user can simply state which function is needed for a specific application. 160–62
Application language: Specialized language that allows decision makers to do model building—to develop their own management science models and to purchase custom-made models. 456–57
Applications integrator program 98
Applications program: Program designed to perform specific data processing and computational tasks. 105
Applications software: Applications program. 105
development of 98–99
personal computer 158–60
Applications software development: Process of creating software. 105–9
first task of *110*
A Programming Language. *See* APL
Arc: Line joining points in a network. 335
Arithmetic computation, BASIC 589, *589*
Arithmetic functions, BASIC 646–48, *647*
Arithmetic/logic unit (ALU): Electronic circuitry that controls all arithmetic and logical operations. 38, 220–21
Arithmetic operation: One of the four standard math operations—addition, subtraction, multiplication, and division. 38, 221
Aron, Joel 106

print. The number of bands on the drum equals the number of characters the printer is able to print on one line. One entire revolution of the drum is required to print each line. 198–200, *199*
DSS executive software 457
DSS query language 457
Dutton, Russell 353
Dvorak, August 215

Early Bird satellite 327
EBCDIC 226–28, *227*, 261
EBIT program 592–95, *593–94*, *610–11*, *614–19*, *615–18*, *652–55*
Eckert, J. Presper 572, 575
Edison 497
EDSAC 575
EDVAC 574–75
Eisenhower, Dwight David 575
Electroluminescent (EL) panel: Flat panel display that glows when electrically charged. 195
Electronic access card 524
Electronic data processing (EDP) 412
Electronic data processing system: Computer-based means of capturing transactions so that they can be reproduced when necessary. 44–45
Electronic Desk 94
Electronic Discrete Variable Automatic Computer. *See* EDVAC
Electronic filing: The technically enhanced storage and retrieval of data or information. 13–14
Electronic funds transfer 181
Electronic mail: The sending, storing, and delivery of messages electronically. 16–18, 348
Electronic mailbox: The storage of a message in a centralized computer "post office," which users check periodically. 18
Electronic mail/message system (EMMS): The use of electronic means to send, store, and deliver messages. 16
Electronic Numerical Integrator and Calculator. *See* ENIAC
Electronic publishing 63, 202–3
Electronic spreadsheet: A computerized spreadsheet that consists of a worksheet area made up of column headings across the top and row headings down the left-hand side. The place where a particular column and row intersect is called a cell, and its position, designated by the coordinates of column letter and row number, is referred to as the cell address. Electronic spreadsheets allow users working with numbers to easily recalculate

the results as different variables are changed. 13, 59, 72–82
cash flow management and 104
Electrostatic printer: Printer that operates by depositing invisible charges on the paper's surface in the shape of characters. 200
ELIZA 478
Ellis, Reginald 514
E-Mail 336
Employment, computerized 543
EMYCIN: The first knowledge engineering tool. 486–87
ENABLE 94
Encryption. *See* Data encryption
END statement 585
End-user: The user of a computer system—particularly a microcomputer. 4
support of 62
End-user applications development 128–29
ENIAC 136, 560, 572–74, *571*
Entrepreneurship 546–47
EPROM. *See* Erasable, programmable read-only memory
Erasable: Refers to an erasable optical disk that is expected to be available soon. 273
Erasable, programmable read-only memory (EPROM): Erasable PROM firmware. 233
Erase head: Electromagnet that erases data on magnetic disks. 259
Ergonomics: The study of human factors related to computing. 516–17
Ethics, computing and 532–33
Even parity 228–29
Excel 72
Excelerator 379, *379*
Exception report: Report put out by the MIS that calls attention to unusual situations, such as when production output is behind schedule. 442, 444, *445*
Execucom Systems 448
ExperTAX 469
Expert decision support system: Expert system technology that assists decision makers by recommending specific actions. 46, 491
Expert systems: Computer programs that essentially copy the knowledge of human experts in a particular field. 46, 208, 469, 474–92, 556
applications of 481–83, *482*
components of 479–80
decision support systems and 491
development of 478, 483–91, *488*
examples of 476–77
function of *479*
future and 491–92, 556–57
knowledge-based systems and 480–81

microcomputer and 478
personnel involved in 476–77
subsystems of 478
Explanation subsystem: Subsystem of an expert system that enables users to query the expert system as to why it has chosen to ask certain questions or how it has reached certain conclusions. 478
EXSYS 478
Extended Binary Coded Decimal Interchange Code. *See* EBCDIC
External data base: Enormous data base that exists outside one's own organization but that sells or makes available its contents to many users. 311–12
External storage: Secondary storage. 32, 38, 253–71
Exxon Co. 514

Facility-oriented processing: Monitoring of the acquisition of facilities or fixed assets used by a firm. 425–26
fixed assets in 425–26, *427*
Facsimile machine 18
Fact: Knowledge in a knowledge base that is based on generalized learning from school and books and is well known and widely accepted by experts in a field. 479
Fairchild Industries 327
Fair Credit Reporting Act (1970) 528
Falvey, Jack 432
Fancy Frocks 409
Fault-tolerant computer: Minicomputer or mainframe computer built with two CPUs performing the same program. If one of the CPUs fails, the other is used to produce output. 553
Federal Communications Commission 341
Federal Express 348
Federal Privacy Act (1974) 528
Feedback: Communication back to a system. 24–26
Feigenbaum, Edward 475
Feingold, S. Norman 54
Fiber optics: New communications technology that transmits data as pulses of light through tubes of glass half the diameter of a human hair. 325–28, *326*, 555
transmission speed of 328
Field: One or more characters that contain an item of data. 260, 289
Fifth-generation language: Natural language that is designed to make the connections humans have with computers more humanlike and to enable the computer to remember and improve upon earlier information—that is, simulate learning. 162–64

File: A collection of related records. 65, 260

File management 83–88

File management system 415, 441

Filename: The name under which a filed is stored. 70

File organization 273–79
  direct 276–77
  index sequential 277–79, *278*
  sequential 274–76 *275*

File processing 287–88
  BASIC and 648–49

Filing system
  data input for *85*
  data sorting in *86, 87*

Financial planning language (FPL): Decision support system used for mathematical, statistical, and forecasting procedures. 160, 453–54

Firmware: Read-only memories. 232

First-generation language: Machine language. 140

Fitzgerald, Jerry 391

Fixed assets: Office equipment, factory equipment, and buildings. 425–26, *427*

Flatbed plotter: Plotter that holds the paper still and allows a pen or pens of different colors, controlled by a computer, to move about on the surface to produce hard-copy drawings. 203–4, *204*

Flat panel display: Alphanumeric or graphics terminal that uses a liquid crystal display or electroluminescent substance that glows when electrically charged to project images on the screen. 195–96, *196*

Flexible disk: An oxide-coated disk of flexible plastic that is used with microcomputers for the storage of data. Flexible disks require a floppy disk drive to translate data on the disk into electronic impulses. *36, 37, 39,* 263–65, *264,* 284

Flexible disk drive: Microcomputer device used to translate data on flexible disks into electronic impulses, which are sent to the CPU. *36, 37, 39*

Flexible manufacturing system (FSM): Robots used on factory assembly lines to perform tasks previously performed by human beings. 206

Floppy: Flexible disk. *36, 37, 39,* 263–65, *264,* 284

Floppy disk: Flexible disk. *36, 37, 39,* 263–65, *264,* 284

Flowchart: Used for designing programs. Flowcharts graphically present the logic needed to solve a programming problem. 116, 144, 369

FOLIO 476

Food service industry, transaction processing in 284

Ford Motor Company 14

Form letter generator 71

Formula: Instructions for calculations in an electronic spreadsheet. They create relationships between numbers in particular cells. 77–79, *77, 78*

FORmula TRANslator. *See* FORTRAN

FOR/NEXT loop 606–14, *608*

FORTRAN 120, 135, 141–43, 148, 150–52, 486
  program in *153*

Fourth-generation language: Problem-oriented language designed to allow end-users to solve specific problems or develop specific applications. 158–62

Fourth-generation software 129

Fowler, Randy 524

Framework 68, 94, 158

Frankston, Robert 73, 136

Freedom of Information Act (1970) 528

Freeman, Joseph 524

Frisch, Dudek and Slattery Ltd. 5

Front-end processor: Processor located at the site of the CPU or host computer that relieves the central computer of some of the tasks of communications. 242, 332

Full-duplex transmission: Data transmission that works in both directions simultaneously. 324–25, *325*

Fylstra, Dan 73

Galaxy I 328

Gates, William 244

GCA 476

General Electric 500, 514, 576–77

Generalized Planning System (GPLAN) 453

General ledger: Data base designed to record all the financial transactions of a business. 426–28
  trial balance in *428*

General register: Register that has varied uses, such as for arithmetic and addressing. 233

Generic operating system: Operating system, such as UNIX, that works with more than one manufacturer's computer system. 243

Gerran, Phyllis 409

Gigabyte: One billion bytes. 224

GIGO: "Garbage in, garbage out," which means that the quality of the output of a computer system is no better than the quality of the input. 173

Giles, Chuck 411

Gill, Stephen 173

Global data base: Completely decentralized data base. 309

Goal-seeking analysis: Analysis that states a goal and the variables influencing it to see what is required to achieve that goal. 458–59, *461*

Goldstine, Herman 574

Goldwyn, Sam 196

GOSUB statement 631–32

GOTO statement 123, 596–97

Graphics: Visual representations of numerical data. 13, 89–91
  decision support system and 456
  future and 555
  levels of complexity in 194, *194*

Graphics terminal: Terminal that can display both alphanumeric and graphic data, such as charts and maps. 193–95

Graph in the Box 245

Grid chart: Chart used in analysis to show the relationship between input and output documents. 372–74, *373*

GTE Sprint 578

GTE Telenet 342

Hacker: Person, often with malicious intent, who invades other people's files and data bases. 523

Half-duplex transmission: Two-way data transmission that occurs one way at a time. 324, *325*

Hard copy: Paper output. 178

Hard-copy terminal: A keyboard with a printer attached. 179

Hard disk: Rigid oxide-coated metal disk with a magnetized surface that stores data as electronic impulses. 33–38, 284

Hard disk drive 36, 39, 266

Hardee's 467

Hardware: The machinery in a computer system—keyboard, video screen, CPU, and so on. 31
  decision support system and 456
  system implementation and 402

Harvard Total Project Manager 96

Hawken, Paul 216

Head crash: Occurs when a piece of dust, for example, sticks to the read/write head and scratches the disk, ruining the disk and destroying the data. 267

Head switching: Activation of a particular read/write head over a particular track and surface. 269

Health, computer and 550

Help option: In word processing, a help option assists the user who does not know what to do next. 71

Helsing, Cheryl 534

Physical record *301*

Physical structure: In a data base, the location of stored records on storage devices. 300

Pidgin, Charles 569–70

Pie chart 90, *90*

Pilot conversion: In converting from an old information system to a new one, only a part of the organization tries out the new system. The new system must prove itself at the test site before it is implemented throughout the organization. 404–6

Piracy: Illegal copying of software. 528, 530–31

Pitney-Bowes 578

PL/1: A procedure-oriented language with a modular structure in which a module can stand alone as a program or become part of a more complex program. 135, 141, 142, 150–51, 169

Planning: Management function that attempts to get the organization from its present position to a better one. It requires setting objectives and developing strategies and policies for achieving them. 30, 436
  expert systems and 482–83
  tactical 439

Plant, Keith 547

Plotter: A printerlike device that produces charts, maps, and drawings in two or three dimensions. 91, 203–4

Pointer: A number or other field in a record that points out—identifies—the storage location of another record that is logically related, then links it and other pointed-to records so that they form a list or chain through the data base. 301, *303*

Point-of-sale (POS) terminal: The new evolution in cash registers, a POS terminal consists of a keyboard for entering data, a CRT screen or digital display area for displaying dollar amounts, and a printer for printing out the list of items and prices for the customer. 185–86, *186*, 414

Polling: In a star network, the central computer, or communications controller, "polls" or asks each device in the network if it has a message to send and then allows each in turn to transmit data. 338

POP 486

POPLOG 486

Prediction, expert systems and 481–82

Presentation graphics: Graphics designed to help the user

communicate a message to other people. 90–91, *90*

Primary storage: Memory within the computer that holds data and instructions for processing. 32, 38, 221–23, 255–56, 554

Primary storage unit: Unit holding data for processing, instructions for processing, and processed data waiting to be output. 221

Printer: Output device that produces printed documents under the control of the computer program. 38–40, *39*, 196–203
  future and 554–55
  mechanisms of *199*

PRINT statement 590–91, *591*

PRINT USING statement 645–46

Privacy: The assurance to individuals that personal information is used properly and protected against improper access. 525
  law and 527–28

Private network: A company's own network. 341

Problem-oriented language: Language designed to solve specific problems. It is intended primarily to help nonprogrammers gain access to a data bank. 158–62

Procedural language: General-purpose programming language such as BASIC, COBOL, FORTRAN, and Pascal that express the logic, or procedure, of a problem. They are flexible and can solve a variety of problems. 142–58

Processing: The conversion of input data into information. 32, *34–35*, 37–38
  business 25
  program analysis and 112

Processing-oriented program: Operating system program designed to simplify processing operations and reduce the time and cost of program preparation. 239, *239*, 242–43

Processing rights: Specify who is allowed to enter data into a data base and in what format, and who has access to that data. 296

Processor: Part of a system that operates on the inputs to transform them into something. 24, 32
  communications 330–32
  systems theory 26

Production: The department that processes the resources input to the organization—materials, money, employees, and facilities—into finished goods and services. 25, 28, 30, 43, 360, 412
  information processing department

and 515
  management and 437–39

Production data base: Common operational data base. 308, *309*

Production run: The execution of object code. 141

Productivity
  computer and 55
  information and 499

Profitability report 443, *444*

Pro forma: Term meaning projected. Pro forma statements are used for performing what-if and goal-seeking analysis. 458

Program: A set of step-by-step instructions directing the computer to perform specific tasks. 31, 105

Program analysis: Analysis of a program's objectives, outputs, inputs, processing procedures, and feasibility. 109–14

Program design: The second step of the programming process in which a solution to the problem is designed. 114–20

Program development cycle: Program life cycle. 107

Program flowchart: Flowchart presenting the detailed sequence of steps needed to solve the problem. 116, *117*, 369
  symbols used in *118*

Program life cycle: The six steps of the programming process—define the problem; design a solution; write the program; test the program; document the program; and maintain the program. 107

Programmable read-only memory (PROM): Firmware that can be programmed only once, then the contents cannot be altered. PROMs operate faster than typical high-level language programs. 233

Programmed decisions system (PDS): System that uses operational data to produce decisions in structured situations with clearly defined judgment criteria. 460–61

Programming error 106

Programming language: A set of rules that provides a way of instructing a computer to perform certain operations. 134–35
  assembly 138–39
  high-level 139–42
  machine 135–38
  natural 162–64
  problem-oriented 158–62
  procedural 142–58

PROgramming language for LOGic. *See* PROLOG

Programming Language One. *See* PL/1

Programming life cycle *108*

WordPerfect
CORPORATION
School Software Direct Order Form

Qualifying teachers, as well as college, university, and other post-secondary students, can now purchase Word-Perfect Corporation (WPCORP) software directly from WPCORP at a reduced price. To qualify, a participant must be teaching or currently enrolled as a full-time student, and must agree in writing not to resell or transfer any package purchased under this program.

If you satisfy these qualifying conditions and would like to purchase software directly from WPCORP under the School Software Program, complete the following six steps and sign at the bottom of the form.

Step 1. From the list below, select the appropriate software for your computer (please note that each student is limited to *one* package of WordPerfect) and mark an "x" in the corresponding blank(s).

	Product	Disk Size	Computer	Price*
___	WordPerfect 4.2	5¼″	(IBM PC/XT/AT/Compatibles)	$125.00
___	WordPerfect 4.2	3½″	(IBM PC/XT/AT/Compatibles)	125.00
___	WordPerfect 1.1	5¼″	(Apple IIe/IIc)	59.00
___	WordPerfect 1.1	3½″	(Apple IIe/IIc)	59.00
___	WordPerfect 1.1	3½″	(Apple IIGS)	59.00
___	PlanPerfect 3.0	5¼″	(IBM PC/XT/AT/Compatibles)	99.00
___	PlanPerfect 3.0	3½″	(IBM PC/XT/AT/Compatibles)	99.00
___	WordPerfect Library	5¼″	(IBM PC/XT/AT/Compatibles)	59.00
___	WordPerfect Library	3½″	(IBM PC/XT/AT/Compatibles)	59.00
___	WordPerfect Executive	5¼″	(IBM PC/XT/AT/Compatibles)	79.00
___	WordPerfect Executive	3½″	(IBM PC/XT/AT/Compatibles)	79.00

Step 2. Make a photocopy of your current Student ID or Faculty card *and* a photocopy of some well-known form of identification displaying your social security number, such as your Driver License or Social Security Card. (WPCORP will hold this information strictly confidential and use it only to guard against duplicate purchases.) Your school ID must show current enrollment. If it does not show a date, you must send verification of current enrollment. If you have serious reservations about providing a social security number, call Educational Development at (801) 227-7131 to establish clearance to purchase any of the above software products at these special prices.

Step 3. Enter your social security number: __ __ __ — __ __ — __ __ __ __

Step 4. Enclose payment for the total cost of the package(s) ordered with personal check, money order, Visa, or MasterCard.

Account # _____

Expiration Date _____ ☐ VISA ☐ MasterCard

(Make check or money order payable to WordPerfect Corporation.)

Step 5. List your shipping address: 🜨 THE BENJAMIN/CUMMINGS PUBLISHING COMPANY. INC.

Ship To _____

_____

_____

Phone _____

Step 6. Enclose this signed and completed form, the photocopies of your identification cards, and your signed check or money order (or Visa or MasterCard account number and expiration date) in an envelope and mail to School Software Program, WordPerfect Corporation, 288 West Center Street, Orem, UT 84057.

The information provided herein is correct and accurate, and I will abide by the restricting conditions outlined by WPCORP in this document. I understand that at its sole discretion, WPCORP may refuse any order for any reason.

Signature _____ Date _____

*Utah residents add 6.25% sales tax.